1948

1948

A History of the First Arab-Israeli War

Benny Morris

YALE UNIVERSITY PRESS • NEW HAVEN AND LONDON

"David," by Marie Syrkin, reproduced by kind permission of
David Bodansky

Designed by Nancy Ovedovitz and set in Galliard Old Style by
The Composing Room of Michigan. Printed in the United States
of America.

Library of Congress Cataloging-in-Publication Data

Morris, Benny, 1948–
1948 : a history of the first Arab-Israeli war / Benny Morris.
p.   cm.
Includes bibliographical references and index.
ISBN 978-0-300-12696-9 (clothbound : alk. paper)
1. Israel-Arab War, 1948–1949.   2. Palestine—History, Military—20th
century.   3. Palestine—Politics and government—1917–1948.
4. Palestine—History—1917–1948.   5. Haganah (Organization)—
History—20th century.   6. Israel—History, Military—20th century.
7. Israel—Politics and government—1948–1967.   8. Israel—
History—1948–1967.   9. Israel—Foreign relations—Arab countries.
10. Arab countries—Foreign relations—Israel.   I. Title.
DS126.9.M67 2008
956.04'2—dc22   2007027380

A catalogue record for this book is available from the British Library.

The paper in this book meets the guidelines for permanence and
durability of the Committee on Production Guidelines for Book
Longevity of the Council on Library Resources.

10   9   8   7   6   5   4   3   2

For Eliya, Stav, Ayala, and Zohar

DAVID
Marie Syrkin

Suppose, this time, Goliath should not fail;
Suppose, this time, the sling should not avail
On the Judean plain where once for all
Mankind the pebble struck, suppose the tale
Should have a different end: the shepherd yield,
The triumph pass to iron arm and thigh,
The wonder vanish from the blooming field,
The mailed hulk stand, and the sweet singer lie.

Suppose, but then what grace will go unsung,
What temple wall unbuilt, what garden bare;
What ploughshare broken and what harp unstrung!
Defeat will compass every heart aware
How black the ramparts of a world wherein
The psalm is stilled, and David does not win.

Contents

Illustrations follow page 272

Acknowledgments

I thank my blood brother, Professor Beni Kedar, for reading the manuscript and for suggesting corrections and additions. I also thank Dr. Hillel Cohen for going through Palestine's Arabic newspapers from 1947 to 1948 for me and enlightening me on their contents.

I thank the University of Maryland, and especially Professor Haim Lapin of the history department and Jewish studies program, for providing me with a yearlong fellowship that enabled me to complete much of this book in College Park during 2005–2006.

Over the years, I have consulted my friend and colleague Yoav Gelber about this or that aspect of 1948, and he has always been generous with his time and knowledge.

I extend my thanks to Georges Borchardt for steering this work through the shoals of the publishing world to the safe and proven shores of New Haven and, at Yale University Press, to Jonathan Brent for taking me aboard and to Annelise Finegan for chaperoning the work through the production process. Working with them was a rare pleasure, as was working with Laura Jones Dooley, who brought great skill and experience to the editing.

Great thanks go also to Roni Bluestein-Livnon for her industry and care in making the maps; the fruit of her labor was crucial to the book.

Abbreviations

AAC	Anglo-American Committee
AHC	Arab Higher Committee
AHE	Arab Higher Executive
AHF	Arab Higher Front
ALA	Arab Liberation (or Salvation) Army
APC	armored personnel carrier
BGA	David Ben-Gurion Archive
CIGS	Chief of the Imperial General Staff (Britain)
CO	Colonial Office (Britain)
DFPI	Documents on the Foreign Policy of Israel
DMZ	Demilitarized Zone
DP	displaced person
FO	Foreign Office (Britain)
FM	Foreign Ministry (Israel)
FRUS	*Foreign Relations of the United States*
HA	Haganah Archive
HGS	Haganah General Staff
HHA	Hashomer Hatza'ir Archive
HIS	Haganah Intelligence Service
HIS-AD	Haganah Intelligence Service—Arab Department
HMG	His Majesty's Government
IAF	Israel Air Force

IDF	Israel Defense Forces
IDF-GS	Israel Defense Forces—General Staff
IDF-IS	Israel Defense Forces—Intelligence Service
IDFA	Israel Defense Forces Archive
ISA	Israel State Archive
IZL	*irgun zvai leumi* (National Military Organization, "Irgun")
JA	Jewish Agency
JAE	Jewish Agency Executive
J&EM	Jerusalem and East Mission
JI	Jabotinsky Institute
KMA	Kibbutz Meuhad Archive
KMA-ACP	Kibbutz Meuhad Archive—Aharon Cisling Papers
LA	Labor Archive
LHI	*lohamei herut yisrael* (Freedom Fighters of Israel, "Stern Gang")
MAC	Mixed Armistice Commission
NC	National Committee
OC	officer in command (sometimes rendered CO, commanding officer)
PCC	Palestine Conciliation Commission
PIAT	Projector, Infantry, Anti-Tank
PLO	Palestine Liberation Organization
POW	Prisoner of War
PRO	Public Record Office
RG	Record Group
SAMECA	St. Antony's College Middle East Centre Archive
SAMECA CP	St. Antony's College Middle East Centre Archive Cunningham Papers
SIME	Special Intelligence Middle East
STH	*sefer toldot hahaganah* (History of the Haganah)
TJFF	Trans-Jordan Frontier Force
UN	United Nations
UNGA	United Nations General Assembly
UNRWA	United Nations Relief and Works Agency for Palestine Refugees in the Near East
UNSCOP	United Nations Special Committee on Palestine
USNA	United States National Archive
WO	War Office (Britain)

List of Maps

1948

I

Staking Claims: The Historical Background

The War of 1948 was the almost inevitable result of more than half a century of Arab-Jewish friction and conflict that began with the arrival in Eretz Yisrael (the Land of Israel), or Palestine, of the first Jewish immigrants from Eastern Europe in the early 1880s. These "Zionists" (Zion, one of Jerusalem's hills, was, by extension, a biblical name for Jerusalem and, by further extension, a name for the Land of Israel) were driven both by the age-old messianic dream, embedded in Judaism's daily prayers, of reestablishing a Jewish state in the ancient homeland and by European anti-Semitism, which erupted in a wave of pogroms in the czarist empire. The nineteenth-century surge in national consciousness, aspiration, and development in Italy and Germany, Poland, Russia, and the territories of the multinational Austro-Hungarian Empire provided an intellectual backdrop, inspiration, and guide to Zionism's founders.

The Jewish people was born in the Land of Israel, which it ruled, on and off, for thirteen centuries, between 1200 BCE and the second century CE. The Romans, who conquered and reconquered the land and suppressed successive Jewish revolts in the first and second centuries CE, renamed the land Palaestina (derived from the country's southern coastal area, named Pleshet, in Hebrew, or Philistia, in Latin, after its second millennium BCE inhabitants, the Philistines) in an effort to separate the Jews, many of whom they exiled, from their land. Among the Gentiles, the name Palestine stuck.

By the early nineteenth century, after centuries of Byzantine rule and successive Persian, Arab, Crusader, Arab, and Ottoman conquests, Palestine was an impoverished backwater. But it had religious cachet for the three monotheistic faiths: it was the divinely "promised land" of the biblical "chosen people," the Jews; Jesus was born, preached, and died there; and the Muslim prophet Muhammad, according to an early interpretation of a line in the Qur'an, had begun his nighttime journey to heaven from Jerusalem, though the land was conquered for Islam only by his mid-seventh-century successors. Jews and Christians and, later, some Muslims, especially those living in Palestine, designated the country "the Holy Land."

But neither before the twelfth-century defeat of the Crusaders at the hands of the Muslim general Saladin nor after it was Palestine administered or recognized as a distinct and separate province by any of its Muslim rulers. The Ottoman Empire, which controlled the area from the early sixteenth century, divided Palestine into two or three subdistricts (sanjaks) that were ruled from the provincial capital of Damascus. From the 1860s, the southern half of Palestine, from a line just north of Jaffa and Jerusalem southward, was constituted as an independent sanjak (or mutasaraflik) and ruled from Istanbul, while the northern parts of the country, the sanjaks of Nablus and Acre, were ruled from the provincial capitals of Damascus and, from the 1880s, Beirut.

In 1881, Palestine had about 450,000 Arabs—about 90 percent Muslim, the rest Christian—and twenty-five thousand Jews. Most of the Jews, almost all of whom were ultra-Orthodox, non-nationalist, and poor, lived in Jerusalem, the country's main town (population thirty thousand). About 80 percent of the Arabs lived in seven to eight hundred agricultural villages, the rest in about a dozen small towns, including Gaza, Hebron, Nablus, Tiberias, Jaffa, Haifa, and Acre. Many rural inhabitants, especially in the lowlands, were tenant farmers, their lands owned—in a semifeudal relationship—by wealthy urban landowners, or effendis.

The first wave of Zionist immigrants—the First ʿAliya (literally, ascent)— brought to Palestine's shores between 1882 and 1903 some thirty thousand Jewish settlers. Their aim was to establish a gradually expanding core of productive Jewish towns and agricultural settlements that would ultimately result in a Jewish majority and the establishment of an independent, sovereign Jewish state in all of Palestine (defined usually as the ten-thousand-square-mile area lying between the Mediterranean Sea and the Jordan River but occasionally—in line with the Bible and subsequent Jewish conquests in the second century BCE—as also encompassing the north-south mountain ridge just east of the river, the biblical lands of Golan, Gilead, Moab, and Edom).

The Zionists planned to purchase land either piecemeal, *dunam* (a fourth of an acre) after dunam, or outright in bulk from the Ottoman sultan, who was always strapped for cash. But the sultan, who regarded Palestine, like all his territories, as sacred Islamic soil and whose vast empire was under increasing nationalist assault in the Balkans and European imperialist threat elsewhere, declined to part with the land. So the Zionists generally maintained discretion about their objective. In private correspondence, however, the settlers were often forthcoming: "The ultimate goal . . . is, in time, to take over the Land of Israel and to restore to the Jews the political independence they have been deprived of for these two thousand years. . . . The Jews will yet arise and, arms in hand (if need be), declare that they are the masters of their ancient homeland."[1] The nineteenth-century poet Naftali Hertz Imber, who later penned the lyrics for what was to become Israel's national anthem, "Hatikva" (the hope), wrote:

> If you long to inherit the land of your birth,
> Buckle on the sword and take up the bow,
> And go in the footsteps of your fathers.
> With weeping and tearful pleadings
> Zion will not be won.
> With sword and bow—hark ye!
> Jerusalem will be rebuilt.[2]

Of course, the integrity of the Ottoman imperial domain was not the only obstacle to Jewish statehood. There were also the native inhabitants, the Arabs. Often, the Zionists depicted Palestine as a "land without a people" awaiting the arrival of the "people without a land," in the British philo-Zionist Lord Shaftesbury's phrase from July 1853.[3] But once there, the settlers could not avoid noticing the majority native population. It was from them, as two of the first settlers put it, that "we shall . . . take away the country . . . through stratagems[,] without drawing upon us their hostility before we become the strong and populous ones."[4]

By "stratagems," of course, they meant purchase; buying land occasionally required "stratagems" since the Ottoman authorities were generally ill disposed toward Jewish land acquisition. But the purchase of Palestine proceeded at a snail's pace. And it was not mainly a problem of an effendi reluctance to sell. Most of the world's Jews were non-Zionists, and most, simply, were poor, especially in the Zionist movement's Eastern European heartland. And the rich, concentrated in Central and Western Europe, by and large refused to help. So, gathering a ruble here and a ruble there, the initially uncoordinated Zionist associations—Hovevei Zion, or Lovers of Zion— bought the odd tract of land for settlement and then sent out small groups of individuals or families to fulfill the dream.

The bulk of the settlers, of both the first and second waves of immigration (the Second 'Aliya was from 1904 to 1914), planted roots in the lowlands of

Palestine—in the Coastal Plain, the upper Jordan Valley (from the southern end of the Sea of Galilee to the northern tip of the Galilee Panhandle), and the Jezreel Valley connecting them. These were the less crowded areas of Palestine, often swamp-infested and vulnerable to bedouin depredation, and owned largely by effendis. (The peasants of the hilly Judean, Samarian, and Galilean heartland tended to own their lands and were rarely willing to sell.) But the gradual Jewish population of these lowlands in fact competed with and trumped the natural expansion into them, ongoing since the early nineteenth century, of spillover Arabs from the relatively thickly inhabited hill country. In hindsight, what was effectively a demographic-geographic contest for the lowlands, between 1881 and 1947, was won by the Zionist movement and gave the Zionists the territorial base for statehood.

The new settlers, beset by an unwonted and difficult climate, unfamiliar diseases, and brigandage, viewed the native inhabitants as, at best, unwanted interlopers from Arabia and, at worst, as rivals for mastery of the land and potential enemies. But they had to be appeased at least temporarily, given their numerical superiority and their kinship with the Muslim Ottoman rulers. Like most European colonists in the third world, the settlers saw the locals as devious and untrustworthy and, at the same time, as simple, dirty, and lazy. Most did not bother to learn Arabic, and some mistreated their Arab workers, as the famous Russian Jewish essayist Ahad Ha'am reported after a visit in February–May 1891.[5] The natives, in turn, regarded the foreign influx as inexplicable and the settlers as strange, foolish, infidel, and vaguely minatory.

Initially, the Zionist settlement enterprise was haphazard and disorganized. But in the mid-1890s, at last, an organizer—and prophet—arose. He was an unlikely savior. Theodor Herzl was born in Budapest in the Austro-Hungarian Empire in 1860 to an assimilated, German-speaking Jewish family. He was a doctor of law but quickly changed professions and became a successful journalist, feuilletonist, and playwright. The coffee shops, theaters, and salons of Vienna were his milieu. Herzl knew no Hebrew, Yiddish, Russian, or Polish and had no contact with the poor masses of Eastern Europe. The pogroms and the anti-Semitic discrimination in the czar's empire may have niggled at his conscience. But the eruption of the Dreyfus Affair in France in 1894 converted Herzl to Zionism. He was then the Paris correspondent of the *Neue Freie Presse,* a liberal Viennese daily. Alfred Dreyfus was an (assimilated) Jewish army captain on the French General Staff when he was wrongly convicted of spying for Germany and sent to Devil's Island. A number of French intellectuals protested and were shouted down as unpatriotic. Rightwing crowds flooded the streets of Paris shouting, "Down with the Jews!" Herzl was shocked—and quickly persuaded that popular anti-Semitism was not restricted to the backward czarist empire but was the patrimony of the entire Gentile world, including its refined French core, the heartland of liberalism, socialism, and democracy. Herzl reached a dismal conclusion: There was no hope and no future for the Jews in Europe; it could not and would not assimilate them. And in the large, multiethnic Continental empires, Jews would eventually face the hostility of the various minorities bent on self-determination. Ultimately, the Jews of Europe faced destruction. The solution was a separate, independent Jewish state to be established after a mass migration of Jews out of Europe.

Herzl dashed off a political manifesto, *The Jews' State* (1896), and spent his remaining years organizing the "Zionist" movement. He unsuccessfully canvassed Europe's potentates, including Sultan Abdulhamid II of Turkey, to grant the Jews a state. But the sultan, unwilling to relinquish any part of his steadily diminishing empire, rebuffed Herzl, a master bluffer, who had promised the Ottomans billions (which he did not have and probably could not have raised). And although some of Europe's leaders, notably Kaiser Wilhelm II of Germany, were interested in getting rid of their Jews, none was enthusiastic enough to challenge Ottoman rule in Palestine or to vouchsafe any of their own imperial domains for a Jewish purpose. Herzl was equally unsuccessful with Europe's Jewish financial barons. The Rothschilds and their ilk were wary of the wild-eyed prophet or of seeming to engage in an activity that smelled of dual loyalty. Herzl died (possibly of syphilis) in 1904, a broken man at the head of a poor, unsuccessful movement.

But Herzl's was a success story. He had generated enough noise to place the Jewish problem, and his preferred "Zionist" solution, on the international agenda and to hammer together the rudiments of a world-embracing Zionist organization. In Basel, in 1897, the First Zionist Congress, organized by Herzl, had resolved to establish a "publicly and legally secured home [*Heimstätte*]" for the Jewish people in Palestine. The delegates had avoided the words *state* and *sovereignty* for fear of alarming or antagonizing Gentiles, including the sultan, or Jewish magnates. But that was what the Zionists intended.

However, of course, Palestine was part of the Ottoman Empire—which was hostile to Zionism both because it was a Jewish enterprise (Islam had little respect for or empathy with the Jews, who were "sons of apes and pigs," in the Qur'an's unfelicitous phrase) and because it promised to reduce still further the sultan's domain—and it was inhabited. For most of Palestine's impoverished, illiterate inhabitants at the end of the nineteenth century, "nationalism" was an alien, meaningless concept. They identified themselves simultaneously as subjects of the (multinational) Ottoman Empire and as part of the (multinational) community of Islam; as Arabs, in terms of geography, culture, and language; as inhabitants of this or that region and village of a vaguely defined Palestine; and as members of this or that clan or family. There was no Arab national movement and not even a hint, in 1881, of a separate Palestinian Arab nationalism.

But European ideas had begun to penetrate the Levant, via commerce, tourists, missionaries, and books and newspapers. Nationalism began to touch the minds of a thin crust of the better educated and rich in Damascus, Beirut, and Baghdad. And Palestine's notable families, collectively known as the *a'yan*, from whom sprang the country's doctors and lawyers and municipal and religious leaders, were not completely immune. Perhaps the first expressions of their dawning Arab national consciousness are to be found in their, at first hesitant, later vociferous, appeals to Istanbul, from 1891 on, to halt the Zionist influx. They warned that Zionist immigration and settlement threatened to undermine the country's "Arab" character and perhaps, ultimately, to displace its inhabitants. "The Jews are taking all the lands out of the hands of the Muslims, taking all the commerce into their hands and bringing arms into the country," complained a group of Jerusalem notables. They called on the sultan to halt Jewish immigration and to bar Jewish land purchases.[6] Indeed, by 1899 the mufti of Jerusalem, Taher al-Husseini (the father of Muhammad Haj Amin al-Husseini, the future leader of the Palestinian national movement), was proposing that all Jews who had settled in the country after 1891 be harassed into leaving or expelled.[7]

These petitioners sensed that the initial trickle of settlers was but the thin edge of the wedge and would be followed by masses of European Jews who, backed by the Jews' reputed legendary wealth, would Judaize the country. They were vaguely aware of the anti-Semitism that was propelling the Jews to Palestine (indeed, some of them shared the prejudice). But they saw no reason why they should host Europe's expellees or pay any price for the plight of Europe's Jews. And they failed to acknowledge the Jews' historic ties to the land, denying these Russian-speaking, strangely appareled immigrants any innate rights or just claims.

In this sense, Yusuf Dia al-Khalidi, Jerusalem's mayor, was highly unusual. In a letter to Zadok Kahn, the chief rabbi of France, he wrote that the Zionist idea was, in theory, "natural, fine and just. . . . Who can challenge the rights of the Jews to Palestine? Good lord, historically it is really your country." But in practice, he was as opposed to Zionism as the rest of the Palestine notables. The land was already inhabited, and Zionist immigration would spark resistance; Palestine could be reclaimed only by the sword. Better that the Jews reestablish themselves elsewhere. "In the name of God, let Palestine be left in peace," he wrote in March 1899.[8] Kahn passed on al-Khalidi's letter to Herzl, who replied on 19 March. Herzl reassured al-Khalidi that the

Zionists, with their vast wealth, expertise, and initiative, would bring benefit to all of Palestine's inhabitants, Arab and Jew. The Jews, he averred, were not "warlike," and there was no reason to fear their influx.[9]

But al-Khalidi and his fellow notables were not persuaded. Indeed, in 1905 an exiled anti-Semitic Lebanese Arab nationalist, Negib 'Azoury, voiced what was probably on the minds of Palestine's politically conscious notables when he wrote that the Jews were bent on reconstituting their ancient state in the whole territory stretching from Mount Hermon to the Arabian Desert in the south and the Suez Canal in the west. The Jews, he added, were destined to clash, in a fight to the finish, with the emergent Arab national movement.[10]

However, Istanbul, while periodically issuing restrictive orders, never effectively clamped down on Jewish immigration, land purchases, and settlement. The Turks no doubt were misled by the apparent negligibility of the ongoing enterprise. But there was, too, Ottoman inefficiency and venality; almost everyone in the administration had a price. Bribes were routinely paid for entry permits and their extension, land deals, building rights. Slowly, the Zionists planted roots. Although the overwhelming majority of Jewish emigrants from Eastern Europe made tracks for North America and the British dominions—well over two million of them by 1914—a hard, resolute cadre reached Palestine, bought land, and settled. By 1914, there were some four dozen settlements (including the bare beginnings of Tel Aviv, in the windswept dunes north of Jaffa, and the first kibbutz, Degania, in the marshes just south of the Sea of Galilee, both founded in 1909) and sixty thousand to eighty-five thousand Jews, about two-thirds of them vigorous, idealistic Zionists, in Palestine.

The Zionists encountered little Arab violence in the first two and a half decades of settlement. The Arabs lacked political, nationalist awareness and were thoroughly disorganized. The Turks ruled the land and, though generally sympathetic toward their coreligionists, often backed the settlers in disputes over land or settlement. Intercession by local Western and Russian consuls with Ottoman administrators and by ambassadors in Istanbul also benefited the settlers.

But there were occasional acts of violence. Until 1908–1909, they were mostly of a "criminal" nature or appeared to be routine feuds between neighbors. An Arab with a knife, bent on robbery, would waylay a settler on an isolated footpath, as happened to David Ben-Gurion in August 1909 near Sejera in the Lower Galilee (Ben-Gurion emerged with a wound in the arm and a deep-seated suspicion of "the Arabs");[11] or a group of Arabs would harass a Jewish couple strolling along the beachfront, as happened in Jaffa in March 1908 (the attack triggered a wider Jewish-Arab melee in the town center); or settlers and their Arab neighbors would quarrel over farming rights and land usage in newly acquired tracts, as happened in Petah Tikva (Melabbes) in 1886, in Rehovot in 1892 and 1893, and in Gedera (Qatra) in 1887–1888. Despite an acknowledgment of Arab resentment or antagonism, the settlers and Zionist spokesmen were wont to dismiss such "brawls" as "common" among Arabs, "between one tribe and another, or one village and another."[12]

But in 1909–1914 the violence increased and took on a clearer "nationalist" flavor. During those six years, Arabs killed twelve Jewish settlement guards—the preeminent symbols of the Zionist endeavor—and Jewish officials increasingly spoke of Arab nationalist ferment and opposition. Already in 1907 Yitzhak Epstein, a Zionist educator, had published an article, "The Hidden Question," in which he acknowledged the emergence of a national conflict between Zionism and the Arabs. "We have forgotten one small matter," he berated the Zionist leadership. "There is in our beloved land an entire nation, which has occupied it for hundreds of years and has never thought to leave it. . . . We are making a great psychological error with regard to a great, assertive and jealous people . . . we forget that the nation that lives in [Palestine] today has a sensitive heart and a loving soul. The Arab, like every man, is tied to his native land with strong bonds." Zionism, he warned, would have to face, and solve, the "Arab Question," and he urged the settlers to get to know the Arabs, their culture, and their language to facilitate dialogue.[13]

In 1910–1911 Arabs in the north tried to resist the Zionist purchase of and settlement in a large tract of land in the Jezreel Valley. Ironically, the opposition focused on the tenant farmer village of Fula, built on and around the ruins of La Fève, a Crusader fortress Saladin had conquered in 1187. Henceforward, Arab spokesmen were regularly to identify the Zionists as the "new Crusaders." Arab notables sent off a stream of appeals to Istanbul, shots were traded, and an Arab and a settlement guard were killed. But nothing availed. The authorities upheld the purchase, Fula was evacuated, and within months, a Jewish settlement, Merhavia, took root on the site.

Arab anti-Zionist rhetoric flourished. The Zionists were now regularly charged with aiming to "kill, pillage, and violate Muslim women and girls"; explicitly anti-Semitic images were mobilized. The blind Muslim cleric and politician Sheikh Suleiman al-Taji al-Faruqi in November 1913 published a poem in the recently founded Arabic newspaper *Falastin,* declaring:

> Jews, sons of clinking gold, stop your deceit;
> We shall not be cheated into bartering away our country!
> . . . The Jews, the weakest of all peoples and the least of them,

Are haggling with us for our land;
How can we slumber on?[14]

The outbreak of World War I, pitting Britain and its allies, chiefly France, Russia, and later the United States, against Germany and the Austro-Hungarian and Ottoman empires, temporarily halted Arab-Zionist violence. But the war was to refashion the Middle East and significantly advance both the Zionist cause and Arab nationalist aspirations.

From the first, Palestine was on the front line. It served as the Ottoman army's base for two unsuccessful cross-Sinai offensives against British-ruled Egypt, in 1915 and 1916, and was in turn invaded by à British army from Egypt. Throughout, under Ottoman martial law, both Arab and Jewish inhabitants had been subjected to systematic confiscations, principally of agricultural produce and farm animals, and repression by the Turkish soldiery, worried by possible pro-Allied "nationalist" subversion behind the lines. In October–December 1917 the invading British army, under General Edmund Allenby, conquered the southern half of the country, including Jerusalem. The following September, after smashing the Turkish lines north of Jaffa, the British took Samaria and Galilee and then pushed on to Damascus and Aleppo, forcing a Turkish surrender and the dissolution of the Ottoman Empire. The British had been assisted, from summer 1916, in a minor way, by a well-remunerated revolt of Arab tribes in Hijaz, led by the Hashemite family; their camel-borne army drove northward through Transjordan in parallel with Allenby's northward advance through Palestine. Britain had promised the Hashemites sovereignty over the Arab-populated areas of the expiring Ottoman Empire.

But Palestine was ambiguously omitted from the future Arab domain (in the letter of 24 October 1915 from Henry McMahon, Britain's high commissioner in Egypt, to the Hashemite sharif of Mecca, Hussein ibn 'Ali). Instead, it was alternatively vouchsafed for future Anglo-French condominium (in the secret Sykes-Picot Agreement of 3 January 1916) and, more vaguely, as a Jewish "national home" (in the Balfour Declaration of 2 November 1917). That one-sentence declaration by the British foreign secretary, Arthur James Balfour—"His Majesty's Government view with favour the establishment in Palestine of a national home for the Jewish People and will use their best endeavours to facilitate the achievement of this object, it being clearly understood that nothing shall be done which may prejudice the civil and religious rights of existing non-Jewish communities in Palestine or the rights and political status enjoyed by Jews in any other country"—was to be seen by the Zionist movement, which had vigorously lobbied for it, as a historic breakthrough and a basis for its future sovereignty over Palestine. And indeed, the

British, including Balfour, and despite the avoidance of the word *state,* regarded the embodied promise as necessarily leading to self-determination. "My personal hope is that the Jews will make good in Palestine and eventually found a Jewish State. It is up to them now; we have given them their opportunity," Balfour was to say three months later.[15] The Arabs, who greeted the declaration with "bewilderment and dismay," came to regard it as a (negative) milestone, an act of betrayal.[16] Thereafter, no matter what the British did to the contrary, the Arab world was to regard London as the protector and facilitator of Zionism.

The British had been driven by Zionist lobbying, spearheaded by the able, charming Chaim Weizmann, a Russian Jewish chemist who had made Britain his home. But Weizmann had been preaching to the converted to the extent that many in the imperial cabinet, including Prime Minister David Lloyd George and Balfour himself, had long been philo-Zionists, for Protestant religious and humanitarian reasons. To be sure, there had also been imperial concerns: a British-created Jewish state might help guard the eastern approaches to that vital waterway, the Suez Canal, only recently imperiled by the Turks. And empowering the Jews in Palestine might reap rewards among the Jews of the United States and Russia, whose goodwill the British wanted, against the backdrop of World War I, either to acquire or sustain.

Without doubt, the British had ignored the will of Palestine's Arab inhabitants. But imperial powers at the time generally took no note of the wishes of third world peoples. And there were specific extenuating circumstances—the Arabs of Palestine, like the majority of those outside Palestine, had supported and were still supporting the (Muslim) Ottoman Empire in its war against the (Christian) Allied powers; and there was, at the time, no Palestinian Arab national movement nor any separate Palestinian Arab national consciousness. Indeed, "Arab" national awareness, with concomitant political aspirations, was barely in its infancy among the elites in the neighboring Arab centers of Beirut, Damascus, and Baghdad. Moreover, the primary agents of Arab independence during the war, the Hashemite leaders of the desert revolt, appeared not to be averse to Jewish rule over Palestine. When Weizmann met Faisal, Hussein ibn ʿAli's son and the commander of the Hashemite army, in a wadi in southern Transjordan in June 1918, the two men got on famously—and Faisal, interested in Zionist support for Hashemite ambitions, endorsed Zionist colonization of Palestine.

When the dust had settled, Faisal was installed by the British as ruler in Syria while his brother, ʿAbdullah, was given a separate emirate in Transjordan. In March 1920 Faisal declared himself "King of Syria and Palestine." But in July 1920, partly in response, the French, already masters of Beirut, invaded Syria and conquered Damascus, ejecting Faisal. The British then reinstalled Faisal as king of Iraq, which he and his offspring were to rule for almost forty years.

France emerged from the world war with League of Nations mandates over Lebanon and Syria while the British held sway directly over Mandated Palestine and Iraq and indirectly over Egypt and Transjordan. The grand Hashemite vision of one giant, powerful Arab state had dissipated into a handful of smaller, separate semi-independent or mandated Arab territories, at least temporarily under Western imperial boots. But the imperial powers were only partly to blame for this fracturing of the Arab world; so, too, were the Hashemite princelings and the separate local Arab nationalist groupings, in Damascus, Baghdad, Beirut, and Cairo. Each sought power and independence in his own turf; none wished to be ruled from the remote, medieval village of Mecca by the would-be, unifying tribal chieftain, Hussein ibn ʿAli.

The imperial carve-up left British-ruled Palestine cut off from its former provincial capitals, Damascus and Beirut, now under French control, and the Palestinian elite quickly understood that their future would be separate from that of Syria and Lebanon. Thus, 1920 was to prove crucial in the emergence of a separate Palestinian Arab national movement and a decisive moment in the evolving Zionist-Arab conflict. The events in Damascus had released Arab nationalist passions that were indirectly and directly to lead to the first major Arab-Jewish clashes in Palestine.

These broke out in March–April that year. In the Galilee Panhandle, a gray no-man's-land between the French and British areas of control, a band of Arab marauders—driven by either anti-French or anti-Zionist sentiments —in the first week of March assaulted the Jewish settlement of Tel Hai. The assault led to the Zionist evacuation of the area, to which the settlers returned only in October, after Britain and France had agreed that the Panhandle would be part of the Palestine Mandate. But this was a sideshow. More ominous was the outbreak, on 4 April, in the midst of the Muslim Nabi Musa (the Prophet Moses) festivities, of pogrom-like Arab rioting in Jerusalem's Old City. A Muslim religious procession, the marchers wielding knives and clubs, erupted in anti-Jewish violence; shouts of "Idbah al-Yahud" (Slaughter the Jews) and "Muhammad's faith was born with the sword" filled the air. At the end of three days, six Jews lay dead, with about two hundred injured and a handful raped. The British authorities had reacted lackadaisically and ineptly, drawing from the Jews the accusation that they had behaved like Russian policemen during pogroms. The Zionist leadership, prodded by veterans of Hashomer, the Zionist self-defense/guards association founded a dozen years before, and the Jewish battalions that had fought with the British army in World War I, reacted by establishing an underground "national" or ethnic militia, the Haganah Organization (Irgun

Hahaganah, Hebrew for defense organization), known simply as the Ha-ganah.

The 1920 outbreak was only the first in a series of bouts of violence—1921, 1929, 1936–1939—that grew progressively more lethal and more extensive. The spread of national consciousness during the 1920s and 1930s clearly paralleled, and probably drew sustenance from, the dramatic increase in literacy among Palestine's Arabs, one of the fruits of the enlightened British Mandate administration. Increased prosperity, triggering hopes of further betterment, relative political freedom, and the gradual emergence of an urban middle class also tended to radicalize the population. This burgeoning national consciousness periodically expressed itself in anti-Zionist violence.

But violence did not emerge only from "modern" nationalist passions; it also drew on powerful religious wellsprings. Nothing, it seemed, could mobilize the Palestinian Arab masses for action more readily than Muslim religious rhetoric and symbols. It was no coincidence that the April 1920 outbreak was triggered by religious festivities or that the far larger outbreak of 1929, in which about 130 Jews were murdered (including sixty-six ultra-Orthodox, non-Zionist yeshiva students massacred by their neighbors in Hebron) was prompted by accusations that the Jews intended to take over the Haram al-Sharif (the noble sanctuary, the Temple Mount), destroy its two sacred mosques, and rebuild the Solomonic temple at the site. And it was indicative that the emerging leader of the Palestinian Arab national movement, Muhammad Haj Amin al-Husseini, who was to dominate Palestinian politics until mid-1948, was a (Muslim) cleric (an unusual phenomenon in third world nationalist movements). Al-Husseini and others consciously deployed religious rhetoric and symbols to mobilize the masses for anti-Zionist and, later, anti-British violence.

But, of course, the chief recruiting agent for Palestinian Arab nationalism was Zionism itself. Above all, the fear of and antagonism toward the Zionist enterprise fueled national awareness and passions in the salons, coffee shops, and streets of Jerusalem, Jaffa, and Haifa.

Yet Palestinian Arab society was acutely fragmented, and British Mandatory rule aggravated this divisiveness. Palestine's Arabs exhibited little "national" solidarity, neither in 1920 nor in 1947. In the years between, few Palestinians proved eager, or even willing, to sacrifice life or purse for the national cause.

A major fault line ran between the Muslim majority and the generally more prosperous, better-educated Christians, who were concentrated in the large towns. The British authorities favored the Christians with contracts, permits, and jobs, further alienating the majority. Through the Mandate, and especially in such crisis periods as the Arab Revolt of 1936–1939 and 1947–1948, Muslims suspected Christians of collaborating with the "enemy" and secretly hoping for continued (Christian) British rule or even Zionist victory. These suspicions were expressed in slogans, popular during the revolt, such as "After Saturday, Sunday"—that is, that the Muslims would take care of the Christians after they had "sorted out" the Jews. This probably further alienated the Christians from Muslim political aspirations, though many, to be sure, kept up nationalist appearances. "The Christians [of Jaffa] had participated in the 1936–1937 disturbances under duress and out of fear of the Muslims. The Christians' hearts now and generally are not with the rioting," reported the Haganah Intelligence Service (HIS).[17] A Haganah list from the mid-1940s of Arabs with a "tendency to cooperation with the Jews" included "many . . . Christians" but few Muslims.[18]

Loyalties in Palestinian society continued, down to 1948, to run principally along family, clan, and regional lines. Envy and antagonism often divided families and clans within villages and, even more often, village from neighboring village (frequently there were age-old blood feuds and land disputes). And the inhabitants of one town often cared little for those of other towns; commercial rivalry habitually underpinned such hostility. Another, major fault line divided the sedentary rural population from neighboring bedouin tribes; the bedouins, of whom there were almost a hundred thousand in the late 1940s, were traditionally seen as a threat to village crops and herds.

Vaguer but still real fissures also separated townspeople from villagers, who tended to be less educated and less politically conscious and, within towns, between notable families and the mass of commoners.

Through the Mandate years the aʿyan themselves were badly split. The leading Jerusalem notable families—the Khatibs, Khalidis, Husseinis, Nashashibis, Nusseibehs, and Budeiris—had been vying for positions of leadership, with their attendant prestige, economic benefit, and social and political power, through the Ottoman centuries. In the 1920s these rivalries were reinforced by nationalist political considerations connected to the relations with the new Mandate authority and the challenge of Zionism. At the start of the Mandate, the Husseinis emerged as the country's most powerful urban clan. Musa Kazim al-Husseini, the mayor of Jerusalem, served as chairman of the Palestine Arab Executive, the national movement's leadership body until 1934, and Haj Amin al-Husseini was appointed by the British as Jerusalem's grand mufti (1921) and head of the country's Supreme Muslim Council (1922), subsequently emerging as the head of the Arab Higher Committee (AHC) and the leader of the Palestinian Arab national movement.

An Opposition (*mu'aridun*) emerged, rallying around another of the notable Jerusalem families, the Nashashibis. Through the 1920s and 1930s (and, more subtly, during the 1940s), the Opposition struggled against Husseini dominance, occasionally backing this or that British measure or proposal and assisting the Mandate government, covertly or overtly, and even occasionally receiving material support from the Jewish Agency for Palestine, the emergent "government" of the Yishuv, the Jewish community in Palestine. Each clan was supported by other notable clans and elements of the rural and urban masses (often a function of each clan's economic interests and holdings). For form's sake, the vying coalitions of clans set up "political parties." But in reality, what characterized Arab Palestine during the Mandate was a feudal "two-party" system with the Husseinis pitted against the Opposition. It was a struggle for power and its benefits, not an ideological clash, though the Husseinis, almost from the start, painted their opponents as collaborators with British rule and soft on Zionism. The Nashashibis, though also ultimately desirous of political independence for Palestine under Arab rule, appeared to be more "moderate" than the Husseinis, whom the British and Zionists branded as "extremists."

Throughout the Mandate, the leading Arab families, including Husseinis and Opposition figures, sold land to the Zionists, despite their nationalist professions. Jewish landholding increased between 1920 and 1947 from about 456,000 dunams to about 1.4 million dunams. The main brake on Jewish land purchases, at least during the 1920s and 1930s, was lack of funds, not any Arab indisposition to sell.[19] Moreover, hundreds of Arabs collaborated with the Zionist intelligence agencies.[20]

The bouts of violence of 1920, 1921, and 1929 were a prelude to the far wider, protracted eruption of 1936–1939, the (Palestine) Arab Revolt. Again, Zionist immigration and settlement—and the prospect of the Judaization of the country and possibly genuine fears of ultimate displacement—underlay the outbreak. But this time the threat was palpable: the resurgence of anti-Semitism in Central and Eastern Europe had washed up on Palestine's shores an unprecedented wave of Jewish immigration. The country's Jewish population more than doubled in less than a decade, rising from 175,000 in 1931 to 460,000 in 1939; 1935 alone had seen the arrival of 62,000 legal immigrants. A far smaller number of illegals also trickled each year into the country. In less than a decade, the Arab proportion of the population had declined from 82 percent to under 70 percent. "What Arab cannot do his math and understand that immigration at the rate of 60,000 a year means a Jewish state in all of Palestine?" Ben-Gurion, chairman of the Jewish Agency Executive (JAE), wrote to Moshe Shertok (Sharett), director of the agency's Political Department, in 1937.[21] (Throughout the Mandate period, there was also limited legal Arab immigration to Palestine from neighboring countries, prompted by the Mandate's relative prosperity, as well as an indeterminate amount of illegal immigration, often seasonal, linked to this or that harvest. For example, according to HIS, 525 Arabs arrived legally from neighboring countries in 1944, 829 in 1945, and almost three thousand in 1946, most of the latter Christian Arabs recruited to serve in the Palestine police.)[22]

The Zionist leaders intermittently attempted to reach a compromise with the Arabs. But none proved possible. The Palestinian Arabs consistently sought to halt Zionist immigration and demanded "all of Palestine"; the Zionists as consistently insisted on continued immigration and Jewish statehood. Ben-Gurion argued that the Jewish influx would better the condition of the Arabs as well as the Jews. Musa al-ʿAlami, a leading Palestinian moderate and assistant Mandate attorney general, countered: "I would prefer that the country remain impoverished and barren for another hundred years, until we ourselves are able to develop it on our own."[23] And Arab nationalists outside Palestine were no more amenable to an accommodation. At a meeting in 1936 between JA representatives (Eliahu Elath, Dov Hos, David Hacohen, and Yosef Nahmani) and leaders of the Syrian National Bloc (Shukri al-Quwwatli, Faiz Bey al-Khouri, and Lutfi Bey al-Haffar), al-Quwwatli countered, "What is the use of economic well-being if we are not masters in our own home," after Hos made the conventional arguments.[24]

Both communities increased in power and size during the beneficent years of the Mandate. But the Jews fared far better than the Arabs. They received enormous contributions and investments from Western Jewry and large British government loans; the Arabs benefited from little foreign investment or loans. Jewish numbers had grown under the Ottomans from some twenty-five thousand to sixty to eighty-five thousand between 1881 and 1914. By the end of 1947, they had reached 630,000. The Arab increase had been less dramatic—from 450,000 (1881) to 650,000 (1918) to 1.3 million (1948).

Economically, Palestinian Arab fortunes had steadily improved—but the Jews' had soared. The net domestic product of the Palestine Arab community in 1922 had been 6.6 million pounds sterling; in 1947 it was 32.3 million. During the same period, the Yishuv's had rocketed from 1.7 million pounds sterling to 38.5 million. The net product of the Jewish community in the manufacturing sector had jumped from 491,000 pounds sterling in 1922 to 31 million in 1947 (the Palestinian Arab equivalent was 539,000 pounds sterling to 6.7 million in 1945).[25]

In most other fields, the Yishuv had also advanced by leaps and bounds. Perhaps most significantly, the Jews managed to forge internal, democratic governing institutions, which in 1947–1948 converted more or less smoothly into the agencies of the new State of Israel. The Jewish Agency for Palestine served as the Yishuv's government, its Executive (the JAE), from 1929 until 1948, functioning as a cabinet. A number of bodies, such as the Jewish National Fund, the Histadrut Agricultural Center, and the agency's Settlement Department, promoted land reclamation and settlement activity. The Yishuv established a "national" health care system, the Histadrut's Sick Fund, and educational systems catering to its constituent communities (secular, socialist, Orthodox, ultra-Orthodox). In 1925—with a population of about 150,000—the Jews established their first university, the Hebrew University of Jerusalem. By comparison, Palestine's Arabs established universities (in the West Bank and Gaza Strip) only in the 1970s (ironically, while under Israeli military occupation).

From 1920, the Yishuv had a "national" militia, the Haganah, which in mid-1948 became the army of the new state, the Israel Defense Forces (IDF). To run its institutions, the Yishuv efficiently taxed itself. By contrast, the Arabs relied for their institutions, such as the Supreme Muslim Council, and their services on British government funding.

Starting in April 1936, armed Arab bands, based in the villages and the urban casbahs, began to attack Jewish traffic and passersby. At the same time, the Palestinians reorganized politically, setting up National Committees (NCs) in each town and the Arab Higher Committee to oversee their struggle nationally. Both the AHC and the NCs initially represented the various political factions. The AHC declared an open-ended general strike and demanded British withdrawal and Palestinian independence under Arab rule. At the least, the rebels hoped to bludgeon the British into curbing the growth of the Zionist enterprise and Jewish immigration.

The revolt enjoyed popular support throughout the Arab Middle East. Even before its outbreak, the Arab world had been smoldering with the idea of a *jihad* (holy war) against the Yishuv. The speaker of the Iraqi parliament, Sa'id al-Haj Thabit, on a visit to Palestine in March 1936, repeatedly called for such a jihad.[26]

But the revolt was somewhat lackadaisical: initially, few Palestinians actually participated in hostilities, and they were disorganized and poorly led and equipped. By October they had managed to kill only twenty-eight Britons and eighty Jews (at a cost of some two hundred Arab dead). The British and the Yishuv reacted with restraint, though London began to curtail Jewish immigration. After five months of struggle, the Palestinians were exhausted and the sterling-earning citrus harvest season was kicking in. The British were happy to call it quits and covertly helped Haj Amin al-Husseini suspend the rebellion. London then dispatched to Palestine yet another committee of

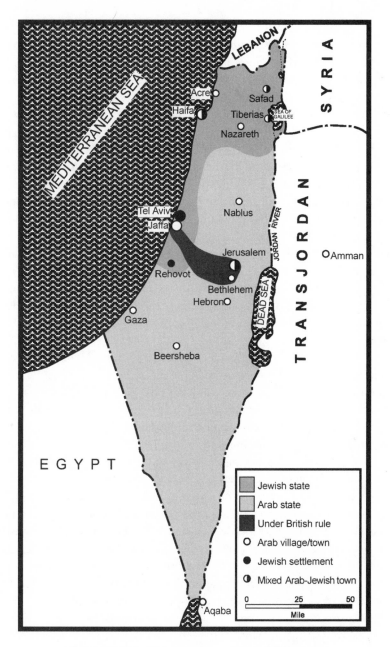

The Peel Commission partition proposal, July 1937

inquiry, this time a royal commission, headed by Lord Peel. On 7 July 1937 the commission published a 404-page report. It exhaustively traced the history of the conflict and present realities and concluded both that the Mandate was unworkable and that the Jews and the Arabs could not live under one political roof. The commissioners recommended partition, with the Jews getting 20 percent (the Galilee and much of the Coastal Plain) on which to establish a state, and the Arabs getting more than 70 percent (Samaria, much of Judea, and the Negev), which should eventually be fused with Transjordan to create an enlarged Hashemite state under Emir ʿAbdullah. Something less than 10 percent of the country, including Jerusalem and Bethlehem, with their holy sites, and a strip of territory connecting the capital to the Mediterranean at Jaffa, should be retained by the British. The commission further recommended that the bulk of the three hundred thousand Arabs who lived in the territory earmarked for Jewish sovereignty should be transferred, voluntarily or under compulsion, to the Arab part of Palestine or out of the country altogether. The commission "balanced" this by recommending that the 1,250 Jews living in areas earmarked for Arab sovereignty be moved to the Jewish area—deeming the proposed transaction "an exchange of population."

In their testimony before the commission, the Zionist mainstream representatives had laid claim to the whole of the Land of Israel—the traditional Zionist platform. But in private conversations, Weizmann and others indicated a readiness for compromise based on partition as well as, quite probably, suggesting the "transfer" solution to the demographic problem posed by the prospective large Arab minority in the Jewish area. Zionism's leaders, from Herzl through Menahem Ussishkin and Arthur Ruppin, had periodically proposed—in private letters and diaries—transfer as the requisite solution to the "Arab problem." But transfer had never been adopted by the movement or any of the main Zionist parties (including the right-wing Revisionists) as part of a platform or official policy. Once the Peel Commission had given the idea its imprimatur, however, the floodgates were opened. Ben-Gurion, Weizmann, Shertok, and others—a virtual consensus—went on record in support of transfer at meetings of the JAE at the Twentieth Zionist Congress (in August 1937, in Zurich) and in other forums.

To be sure, these advocates realized and usually acknowledged that the idea was impractical and unrealistic—the British could not be expected to carry out transfer, and the Yishuv, even if willing, was powerless—and transfer was never adopted as official Zionist policy. Yet through the late 1930s and early and mid-1940s Zionist leaders continued in private to espouse the idea. For example, Weizmann in late January 1941 told Ivan Maiskii, the Soviet ambassador to London: "If half a million Arabs could be transferred, two million Jews could be put in their place. . . . Weizmann said that . . . they would be transferring the Arabs only into Iraq and Transjordan."[27] Interestingly, senior British officials and Arab leaders, including Emir ʿAbdullah and Nuri Saʿid, Iraq's premier politician (the same Nuri Saʿid who in July 1939 called for the destruction of Zionism), shared this view.[28] All understood that for a partition settlement to work and last, the emergent Jewish state would have to be ridded of its large and potentially or actively hostile Arab minority. As ʿAbdullah's prime minister, Ibrahim Pasha Hashim, put it in 1946: "The only just and permanent solution lay in absolute partition with an exchange of populations; to leave Jews in an Arab state or Arabs in a Jewish state would lead inevitably to further trouble between the two peoples."[29] ʿAbdullah, according to Britain's representative in Amman, Alec Kirkbride, concurred.[30]

The Peel recommendations enshrined the principles of partition and a "two-state" solution as the international community's preferred path to a settlement of the conflict and were adopted by the mainstream of the Zionist movement (the minority right-wing Revisionists dissented). But the Husseini-led Palestinian leadership, and the Arab states in its wake, rejected both the explicit recommendations and the principle: all of Palestine was and must be ours, they said. They also, of course, abhorred the transfer recommendation.

Responding to the Peel proposals, which Whitehall immediately endorsed, the Husseinis renewed the rebellion in late September 1937. The Opposition, which initially approved the recommendations and then recanted, sought to extend the truce, but vilified as traitors, they were effectively cowed and silenced by a Husseini campaign of terrorism.

The second and last stage of the rebellion, lasting until late spring–summer 1939, was far bloodier than the first. The Arab rural bands renewed their attacks and were active in the towns as well. The Revisionist movement's military arm, the Irgun Zvai Leumi (IZL, the National Military Organization, or simply Irgun), which had been formed by activist breakaways from the Haganah, subjected the Arab towns to an unnerving campaign of retaliatory terrorism, with special Haganah units adding to the bloodshed through selective reprisals. More important, the British now took off the gloves. In October 1937 they outlawed the AHC and the NCs and arrested many of their members. Haj Amin al-Husseini himself fled into exile, where he remained—alternating mainly between Beirut and Cairo—until his death in 1974. After the rebellion peaked in summer 1938 (the rebels briefly occupied the Old City of Jerusalem and Beersheba) and after being temporarily freed by the Munich Agreement from the specter of war in Europe, the British went on the offensive, clamping down hard. Between October 1938 and April 1939

British units pushed into the casbahs and the rebel strongholds in the hill country and virtually annihilated the bands after coercing much of the rural population into collaboration. Dozens of houses were demolished, crops were destroyed, rebels and their accomplices were hanged, and thousands were jailed. In suppressing the rebellion, the British fenced and mined Palestine's northern borders and secured towns and crossroads around the country with reinforced concrete police and army posts, called Tegart forts (which were to figure large in the battles of 1948 and mostly exist to this day, serving as Israeli and Palestinian Authority police stations). In identifying the rebels' infrastructure, the British were assisted by the Haganah Intelligence Service, organized toward the end of the rebellion, and by newly created Opposition-aligned, anti-Husseini "peace bands," that denied the rebels entry into dozens of villages. There was no formally announced end to the rebellion, but hostilities tapered off in spring and summer 1939, with the surviving rebels fleeing to Lebanon and Syria.

Yet the rebellion, coming as it did as Britain faced a worldwide three-front war against Japan, Italy, and Germany, almost succeeded—not militarily but politically. From the September 1938 Munich crisis onward, Britain came to view its Palestine policy almost exclusively through the prism of its needs and interests in the forthcoming global struggle. Simply put, London sought to appease the Arabs to assure quiet in the Middle East, which sat astride Britain's lines of communication to southern Asia and the Far East. In May 1939 Whitehall issued a new white paper. It promised Palestine's inhabitants statehood and independence within ten years; severely curtailed Jewish immigration, limiting it to fifteen thousand entry certificates per year for five years, with all further Jewish immigration conditional on Arab approval (thus assuring an overwhelming Arab majority when independence came); and significantly limited Jewish land purchase. In sum, this amounted to a complete reversal both of the Balfour Declaration policy and its much-modified translation, the Peel Commission recommendations: Palestine was to remain Arab, and there would be no Jewish state. The Yishuv denounced the white paper as "illegal" and "appeasement" and mounted huge protest demonstrations; the IZL initiated sporadic attacks on British installations.

The Palestinian street was overjoyed. But al-Husseini—as was the Palestinians' wont—managed to pluck defeat from the jaws of victory. Instead of welcoming the British move, which Winston Churchill denounced as a cowardly "surrender to Arab violence," al-Husseini and his colleagues rejected the white paper. They flatly demanded full cessation of Jewish immigration, immediate British withdrawal, and immediate independence.

In the brief months before world war broke out, nothing changed. The

Arab Revolt thus ended in unmitigated defeat for the Palestinians. Somewhere between three thousand and six thousand of their political and military activists had been killed, with many thousands more either driven into exile or jailed; the leadership of the Palestine Arab national movement was decimated, exiled, or jailed; and a deep chasm, characterized by blood feuds, divided the society's elite families. Indeed, much of the elite was so disillusioned or frightened by what had happened that it permanently renounced political activity. The Palestinians had also suffered serious economic harm, through both the general strike and British repression. They had prematurely expended their military power against the wrong enemy and had been dealt a mortal blow in advance of the battle with the real enemy, Zionism. The damage to their war effort in 1947–1948 was incalculable.

The triangular conflict in Palestine was put on hold for the duration of World War II. The British made it clear to the Yishuv that they would not countenance renewed troubles, and the Jews took heed. They shelved the struggle against the white paper, and tens of thousands of young Jews volunteered for service in the British army. Even the IZL sent volunteers to aid British military operations. The Zionist movement closed ranks in support of the Allies in the war against the Nazis. Palestine, awash with British troops, served as a giant rear base and workshop for the Eighth Army, which engaged the Italians and Germans in North Africa.

The Palestinians, reeling from the suppression of their rebellion and largely unsympathetic to Western liberal, democratic values, grimly hoped for an Axis victory. In this, they were at one with most of the Arab world. The Palestinians, Khalil al-Sakakini, a Christian Jerusalem educator, jotted down in his diary, "rejoiced [as did 'the whole Arab world'] when the British bastion at Tobruk fell [in 1941] to the Germans."[31] One of the first public opinion polls in Palestine, conducted by al-Sakakini's son, Sari Sakakini, on behalf of the American consulate in Jerusalem, in February 1941 found that 88 percent of the Palestinian Arabs favored Germany and only 9 percent Britain.[32] The exiled al-Husseini himself helped raise a brief anti-British revolt in Baghdad in spring 1941 and then fled to Berlin, where he served the Nazi regime for four years by broadcasting anti-British, jihadist propaganda to the Middle East and recruiting Bosnian Muslims for the Wehrmacht. He was deeply anti-Semitic. He later explained the Holocaust as owing to the Jews' sabotage of the German war effort in World War I[33] and the millennia of Gentile anti-Semitism as due to the Jews' "character": "One of the most prominent facets of the Jewish character is their exaggerated conceit and selfishness, rooted in their belief that they are the chosen people of God. There is no limit to their covetousness and they prevent others from enjoying the Good. . . . They have no pity and are known for their hatred, rivalry and hardness, as Allah described them in the Qur'an."[34]

But World War II was a crucible from which both the Jewish and Arab national movements would emerge strengthened and largely triumphant. The war's vast weakening of British (and French) power and the concomitant rise in national consciousness and ideologies in the third world resulted almost immediately in the liberation from imperial rule of vast domains, stretching from Indonesia through India to the Arab Middle East. At war's end, Transjordan (later Jordan), Syria, and Lebanon became independent, and other Arab territories—including Egypt and Iraq—enjoyed a loosening of the imperial grip.

For the Jews, the world war meant, above all, the Holocaust. But while destroying Zionism's main potential pool of manpower, Eastern European Jewry, the Holocaust also reenergized the movement as a powerful vehicle of the victimized and stateless, who now enjoyed the international community's sympathy. In a larger sense, history was repeating itself, to the benefit of Zionism. As the pogroms in Russia in the 1880s had launched modern Zionism, so the largest pogrom of them all propelled the movement, almost instantly, into statehood. And much as World War I had issued in the first important statement of support for a Jewish "national home," the Balfour Declaration, so the aftermath of World War II resulted in that decisive international warrant, the United Nations Partition Resolution of 29 November 1947, which would underpin the emergence of the State of Israel.

In effect, the white paper policy remained in force through the war, even though Churchill—a pro-Zionist—had taken over the premiership in London in May 1940. In October 1941 he had written: "If Britain and the United States emerge victorious from the war, the creation of a great Jewish state in Palestine inhabitated [sic] by millions of Jews will be one of the leading features of the Peace Conference discussions."[35] But during the war, there was, in fact, little Churchill could do, apart from winning the war quickly enough to save at least some of Europe's Jews. A secret cabinet committee he had set up in 1943 had recommended, as he had sought, a switch in British policy in favor of partition, but it was never acted upon. And although Churchill was continuously peeved by the Arabs' pro-Axis behavior, he knew full well that Britain needed a quiescent Middle East in the rear of its fighting formations and could not afford to rile them over Palestine. As Colonial Secretary Malcolm MacDonald put it, "If there was trouble in Palestine . . . there would be repercussions in Transjordania, Iraq, Saudi Arabia, and Egypt and even echoes of that trouble in India."[36] But Churchill did authorize the establishment of both the Palmah, a guerrilla strike force of Haganah members to be used if the Germans conquered Palestine, and the Jewish Brigade, a large formation composed mainly of volunteers from the Yishuv that fought with the British army in Italy. The veterans of both were to stand the Yishuv in good stead in the 1948 War.

In the first months of World War II, Zionist organizations stepped up efforts to save European Jews from the impending massacre—and to strengthen the Yishuv by bringing them to Palestine—through an illegal immigration operation run mainly by the newly created Institute for Illegal Immigration (*hamossad le'aliya bilti ligalit*), a secret arm of the Haganah. The British countered with a Royal Navy cordon that intercepted the rickety steamers, and many were stopped and their passengers reshipped to detention camps in Mauritius and, later, Cyprus. But by mid-1941 both Zionist and British efforts had become largely irrelevant: the Germans had overrun Europe and closed its ports while changing their policy toward the Jews from one of encouraging emigration to initiating mass murder. Few Jews reached Palestine from Europe during 1941–1945.

Nonetheless, the war significantly speeded up the march toward Jewish statehood. In January 1942, Chaim Weizmann, in an article in *Foreign Affairs*, explicitly demanded the establishment of a Jewish "state" in all of Palestine.[37] And in May, an Extraordinary Zionist Conference, attended by most leaders of American Zionism, a number of exiled European Zionist leaders, and three members, including Ben-Gurion, of the JAE from Jerusalem, formalized this demand by voting to support what became known as the Biltmore Program (drafted by Meyer Weisgal, a Weizmann aide). Meeting at the Biltmore Hotel, New York, the delegates called for "the Land of Israel to be established as a Jewish Commonwealth integrated in the structure of the new [postwar] democratic world."[38] By "commonwealth" they meant state. This was to remain Zionist policy down to the end of 1947.

Palestine remained under British control, and the 1939 white paper continued to guide Whitehall's policies. But during the two and a half years between the end of World War II and the start of the first Arab-Israeli war, developments on the ground—in Washington, Palestine, and Europe—were to prove more important than the character and mindset of Whitehall's mandarins or their calculations and declarations. In the United States, the Jews decisively won the battle for the hearts and minds of the American people and its leaders, due to the impact of the Holocaust and effective Zionist propaganda. The existence of the five-million-strong Jewish community proved extremely important. The Jews, themselves energized and united by the Holocaust, were well organized and wealthy and were traditionally big donors to political campaigns. They also tended to vote in high numbers, were concentrated in such key electoral states as New York and California, and were, by tradition, Democrats. It was Zionism's luck that Democrats controlled the White House and Congress during the war and postwar years.

Perhaps the surprising thing is that, despite Jewish clout, the administration of President Franklin D. Roosevelt had managed during the 1930s and the first years of the war to desist from anything but insignificant expressions of sympathy for Zionism. Roosevelt avoided a forthright commitment to Jewish statehood. The plight of European Jewry may have weighed heavily on the side of Zionism; but American global interests, as they emerged in the war against Germany, Italy, and Japan and as perceived by most senior officials in the relevant departments (State, Defense), militated in the other direction. The officials worried about the continued supply of oil, American bases, and open lines of communication as well as, from the war's end, countering Soviet influence and power. The continued goodwill or, at least, neutrality of the Arab world remained a major American interest. In May 1943 Roosevelt assured King ʿAbdul ʿAziz Ibn Saʿud of Saudi Arabia that both Arabs and Jews would be heard before the powers decided on the contours of the postwar settlement in Palestine.

But the last months of the war saw a dramatic, gradual shift in American policy. In March 1944 the White House, under pressure from various departments, may have persuaded Congress to withdraw a joint resolution calling on Britain to rescind the white paper and supporting a Jewish state. But Roosevelt assured the Jews that "full justice will be done [after the war] to those who seek a Jewish national home, for which our Government and the American People have always had the deepest sympathy and today more than ever in view of the tragic plight of hundreds of thousands of homeless Jewish refugees."[39] During the second half of 1944, both the Republicans and Democrats included in their election platforms pro-Zionist provisions, with the Republican presidential contender, Governor Thomas Dewey, declaring support for the establishment of a "Jewish . . . commonwealth" in Palestine. At Yalta, in February 1945, Roosevelt, in conversation with Joseph Stalin, described himself as "a Zionist" (to which the Soviet dictator rejoined, "me too," but then added that Jews were "middlemen, profiteers, and parasites").[40] Though the following month Roosevelt assured Ibn Saʿud that he would support "no action . . . that would prove hostile to the Arab people,"[41] the growingly Zionist orientation of American public opinion, fueled by the revelation of the full horror of the Holocaust, proved inexorable. Roosevelt's sudden death in April clinched the Zionist victory in Washington, with the more sympathetic vice president, Harry Truman, taking over the White House.

Truman was not the committed philo-Semite or Zionist Arab propagandists and Zionist politicians later made out. In 1944, Truman had pointedly declined to support his party's pro-Zionist platform. And he reportedly told his cabinet in July 1946 that he had "no use for them [the Jews] and didn't care what happened to them."[42] Without doubt, he was often annoyed and even angered by the perpetual Zionist importunings, blandishments, cajolery, and pressure to which he was subjected during 1945–1948. And once converted to supporting partition, he was pessimistic about the outcome: "I fear very much that the Jews are like all underdogs. When they get on top they are just as intolerant and cruel as the people were to them when they were underneath."[43]

But in August 1945, in Potsdam, Truman came out in principle in support of resettling the Holocaust survivors, the Jewish displaced persons (DPs), in Palestine (in response to which Arab League secretary-general ʿAbd al-Rahman ʿAzzam declared that this could touch off a new war between Christianity and Islam, as had the medieval Crusades.[44] ʿAzzam had long been tagged by the British as "intransigent." Back in 1939, he had told Weizmann that "there was nothing for it but a fight to the death against the Jews.")[45] Truman pointedly asked the British prime minister to lift the restrictions on Jewish immigration to Palestine.[46] Soon, this had crystallized into open support for the immediate resettlement in Palestine of "100,000" DPs.

For Palestine's Arabs, the war years passed without significant change. True, their financial assets grew substantially because of Allied spending and investment.[47] But militarily and politically, things remained much the same. Few—perhaps five or six thousand—signed up with the Allied armed forces or otherwise gained military experience; there was no increment in local military force or organization. And the political (and military) leadership that had been shattered in 1938–1939 remained either in exile, neutered, or hors de combat. But by mid-1943, it had become increasingly clear to Palestinian and outside Arab leaders that the Allies would win and that, whatever their true feelings, the Arabs had better at least edge toward, if not jump outright onto, the bandwagon. To gain anything from the Allied victory in the postwar settlement, Palestine's Arabs would need to have a recognized leadership and an organization capable of managing the coming struggle and reaping its possible rewards. During 1943 the former heads of Palestine's Istiqlal Party—ʿAwni ʿAbd al-Hadi, Rashid Haj Ibrahim, and Ahmad Hilmi Pasha—launched an effort to reunite the Palestinian nationalist movement. In August, Ahmad Hilmi began to reorganize the Arab National Fund, designed to counter Jewish land purchasing, and in November, the fifteenth conference of the Palestinian Arab chambers of commerce met in Jerusalem and set

in motion a process to elect new Palestinian national representation. The Is-
tiqlalists' platform called for the rigid implementation of the provisions of
the 1939 white paper.[48]

Because of Husseini opposition, matters hung fire. But not to be outdone,
the Husseinis also began to reorganize. True, their main leaders were in exile—Haj Amin in Berlin, serving the Nazis, and Jamal Husseini, interned in
Southern Rhodesia. But the remaining local leadership, spearheaded by Emile
Ghury, a Greek Orthodox journalist, in April 1944 formally relaunched the
Palestine Arab Party, whose central demands were immediate Palestinian
Arab independence, the cessation of Jewish immigration, and "the dissolution of the Jewish National Home." By September, the Husseinis were once
again the most active and powerful political faction in Arab Palestine.[49] Returning to the fray, the Palestinians, led by the Husseinis, on Balfour Declaration day, 2 November, launched nationwide protests.

The "repoliticization" of Palestine's Arabs at war's end coincided with the
British-supported drive for pan-Arab unity, which had captivated the political
imagination of the Middle East since before World War I. During 25 September–7 October 1944, delegates from seven Arab countries met in Alexandria and founded "a League . . . of Independent Arab States," henceforward known as the Arab League. On 22 March 1945, these states formally
signed a pact in Cairo. A secretariat was set up in the Egyptian capital, with
the Egyptian ʿAbd al-Rahman ʿAzzam as secretary-general.[50]

The Palestinians had sent Musa al-ʿAlami to the gathering in Alexandria.
He was designated first an "observer," then a "delegate," the Palestinian
Arab community thus enjoying, at least theoretically, an equal footing with
existing or emergent Arab states.

At the end of the conference, the delegates issued the Alexandria Protocol.
A section was devoted to the issue of Palestine. The Arab states resolved that
"Palestine constitutes an important part of the Arab world and that the
rights of the [Palestine] Arabs cannot be touched without prejudice to peace
and stability in the Arab world." The League endorsed the demand for a
stoppage of Jewish immigration, the cessation of land sales, and "independence for Palestine." In light of the international circumstances—almost
universal horror over the Holocaust and growing American pressure to resettle the remnants of European Jewry in Palestine—the Arab states declared
that they were "second to none in regretting the woes which have been
inflicted on the Jews of Europe by European dictatorial states. But the question of these Jews should not be confused with Zionism, for there can be
no greater injustice and aggression than solving the problem of the Jews of
Europe by another injustice, that is, by inflicting injustice on the Palestine
Arabs."[51]

To add cogency to their demands for a voice in the expected postwar settlement, four of the states—Egypt, Syria, Lebanon, and Saudi Arabia—in early 1945 declared war on the Axis, thus assuring membership in the nascent United Nations Organization, the heir to the interwar League of Nations.

The establishment of the Arab League at once strengthened the Palestinian cause and weakened the voice of Palestinian nationalism. On one hand, the Arab states collectively weighed in behind Palestinian Arab demands. But at the same time, the pact gave the member states the right to select who would represent the Palestinian Arabs in their councils, so long as Palestine was not independent. Coupled with the continued factional deadlock within Arab Palestine, this assured, in the words of one historian, that "the initiative in Palestine Arab politics thus passed to the heads of the Arab states" and "major political decisions on the organization of Arab resistance to Zionism were thereafter taken not at Jerusalem but at Cairo."[52]

And indeed, it was to be at the initiative of the Arab League that in November 1945 the AHC was reestablished as the supreme executive body of the Palestine Arab community. Months of haggling between the factions had failed to produce agreement. A twelve-member AHC was appointed, with five Husseini representatives, two independents, and five other members, including Gharib Nashashibi, representing the other (now resurrected) pre-1939 parties.[53] But the return to the Middle East of the mufti's cousin, Jamal Husseini, and renewed Husseini-Opposition quarreling precipitated the disbandment, in March 1946, of the reestablished AHC. The Opposition set up its own organization, the Arab Higher Front, and Jamal reconstituted an AHC manned only by Husseini family members and affiliates. In June, to break the stalemate, the Arab League foreign ministers intervened and, nominally replacing both the AHF and the new AHC, imposed upon the Palestinians a new leadership body, the Arab Higher Executive (AHE), with Haj Amin al-Husseini as (absent) chairman and Jamal Husseini as vice-chairman. The Husseinis were now firmly back in the saddle, this time with the imprimatur of the Arab League. Haj Amin now returned to the Middle East from his temporary refuge in France and began directing Palestinian Arab affairs from Cairo. In January 1947, the nine-member AHE was renamed the AHC.[54] The Palestinian Arabs appeared once more to have a relatively unified, if not particularly representative, leadership.

THE YISHUV RISES

But viewed against this political shadowboxing, developments in the Zionist camp proved to be far more significant. If the outbreak of the world war had put an almost immediate brake on Jewish resistance to the white paper, its approaching end opened the floodgates. No longer was there need to close ranks in the fight against the Nazis; the Third Reich was finished. Moreover, Europe was awash with hundreds of thousands of Holocaust survivors, desperate to rebuild their lives away from the killing fields and, if it was up to the Zionists, to resettle in Palestine. But Britain—meaning the cabinet in London, the Royal Navy in the Mediterranean, and the security forces in Palestine—stood between the DP camps and the Promised Land. On 27 September 1945 the Zionist leadership proclaimed that the blockade was "tantamount to a death sentence upon . . . those liberated Jews . . . still languishing in . . . Germany."[55] A revolt that had been postponed for six years was now about to break out.

Already in May 1943 Field Marshal Harold Alexander, commander of Britain's forces in the Middle East, had warned London that there was a "probability" of an anti-British revolt by the Yishuv at war's end: "[The] Jews mean business and are armed and trained."[56] A year earlier, in mid-1942, SIME (Secret Intelligence Middle East), the Middle Eastern arm of Britain's Secret Intelligence Service, MI6, had estimated, fairly accurately, that the Haganah had thirty thousand members, with arms for 50–70 percent of them. The IZL could field another thousand trained men, with several thousand supporters.[57]

The Yishuv had not wasted the war years. More than twenty-six thousand of its men and women had joined the British army and acquired a measure of military training;[58] arms had been stolen or illegally purchased, and Haganah numbers had increased. Most significantly, in May–June 1941 the Haganah—with British assistance, as mentioned earlier—had established a small, permanent strike force, the Palmah (an abbreviation of *plugot mahatz,* or shock companies), headed by Yitzhak Sadeh, the veteran Red Army soldier and Haganah commando leader. The Yishuv leadership regarded the Palmah as both an instantly available crack force to fend off Arab attacks and as a commando unit to be used against the Nazis should the Afrika Korps conquer Palestine.

As it turned out, the Germans failed to break through the Allied defenses in Egypt. Nonetheless, the Palmah saw some action. In June 1941, it provided forty scouts and sappers who accompanied the Allied units that invaded Vichy-controlled Lebanon and Syria. (It was at Eskandelion [Iskenderun], in southern Lebanon, that, leading one reconnaissance squad, Moshe Dayan lost his eye to a Vichy sniper). And during 1943–1945, the Palmah provided the British with some two dozen saboteurs and radio operators who were parachuted into Nazi-occupied Europe to link up with partisan units and threatened Jewish communities.

From 1942, the Palmah constituted a small, standing army, its platoons dispersed among several dozen kibbutzim and two or three towns. The recruits put in a fortnight each month working in the fields (to cover their upkeep) and devoted the rest of their time to training. By war's end, the Palmah had grown to some two thousand men and women.

But another group first disturbed the calm in Palestine. Already in the war's first months, British installations were periodically attacked by the LHI (Lohamei Herut Yisrael or Freedom Fighters of Israel, dubbed "the Stern Gang" by the British). The organization was established in 1939–1941 by several dozen breakaway IZL members who opposed the truce with the British. The LHI—led initially by Avraham ("Yair") Stern—continued to view the British, not the Germans, as the Jewish people's main enemy; it was the British who were preventing Jews from escaping Europe, reaching Palestine, and attaining independence.

At the end of 1940, the LHI tried to establish an "alliance" with Nazi Germany for the "common" struggle against Britain. An operative named Naftali Lubinczik was sent to Beirut, where he made contact with Otto Werner von Hentig, a German Foreign Ministry official and intelligence officer, and explicitly offered "military, political and intelligence" cooperation. But Berlin was uninterested. Lubinczik returned to Palestine, where the British jailed him. But Stern was not easily deterred. At the end of 1941, some months after the beginning of the Holocaust, with the Afrika Korps at the gates of Egypt, Stern tried again. He dispatched one of his deputies, Natan Friedman-Yelin, to make contact with German officials in Turkey, with instructions to propose that Germany allow out hundreds of thousands of Balkan Jews. What he was to offer the Nazis in return is not clear. In any event, he got only as far as Aleppo, where Allied police picked him up.[59]

Nor did the LHI's campaign in 1940–1943 in Palestine amount to much. The LHI's minute size, Haganah and IZL tip-offs, and effective British clampdowns saw to that. LHI operations were limited almost completely to thefts of weaponry (sometimes from Jewish caches rather than British military stockpiles) and bank robberies. In one payroll heist, in January 1942, LHI gunmen shot dead two Histadrut officials.

But starting in 1944, the British faced a far more serious challenge. On 1 February, several days after Menachem Begin, a leader of the Revisionist movement in Poland and an ex-Polish army soldier, took over command of the organization, the IZL announced the resumption of the armed struggle. The war in Europe was near its end, and Britain was still barring the door to Palestine. The IZL, like the LHI and some senior mainstream Zionist leaders, felt that the Arabs were insignificant: the main battle for Jewish statehood would have to be fought against the British. During February, IZL squads blew up government immigration and income tax offices; in March, they attacked a series of police buildings. On 17 May, IZL squads raided the British radio station in Ramallah and, on 22 August, attacked the British police headquarters in Tel Aviv–Jaffa. On 27 September, the organization attacked police stations in Beit Dajan, Qalqilya, Haifa, and Qatra. On 8 August, the LHI tried to assassinate the high commissioner in Palestine, Harold MacMichael.[60]

The mainstream Zionist leadership and press roundly condemned the dissidents' attacks. The Irgun members were labeled "misguided terrorists," "young fanatics crazed by the sufferings of their people into believing that destruction will bring healing."[61] Under Zionist mainstream pressure, the LHI suspended its attacks in November 1944, after its members assassinated the British minister of state in the Middle East, Lord Moyne, in Cairo. But the IZL defied the JAE and continued its attacks. The Haganah declared an "open hunting season" (in Zionist historiography, the "Saison") against the IZL, and Haganah intelligence and Palmah teams systematically assaulted and incarcerated IZL members, confiscated their weapons caches, and occasionally handed them or their names and addresses to the British. The Saison lasted from November 1944 to March 1945.[62]

But the changed international situation and growing activist rumblings within the Haganah eventually issued in a radical change of tack. The end of the war in Europe triggered the reopening of the struggle against the white paper by mainstream Zionism. In June, a Jewish Agency memorandum demanded that Britain allow a hundred thousand immigrants into Palestine immediately;[63] the DPs could not be allowed open-endedly to languish in Europe "among the graveyards of the millions of their slaughtered brethren," Ben-Gurion declared.[64]

Churchill wondered whether Britain could cast off the burden of Palestine: "I do not think we should take the responsibility upon ourselves of managing this very difficult place while the Americans sit back and criticize," he wrote on 6 July. "I am not aware of the slightest advantage which has ever accrued to Great Britain from this painful and thankless task. Somebody else should have their turn now."[65] But Churchill never got the chance. In the general elections that month he was swept from office and a Labour government, headed by Clement Attlee, took over. Ernest Bevin, no friend of Zionism, became foreign secretary. In August Bevin proposed that immigration to Palestine be limited to fifteen hundred per month. Weizmann and Ben-Gurion demurred, and so, within weeks, would Truman.

Truman had sent Earl G. Harrison, the US representative on the Intergovernmental Committee on Refugees, to visit the European DP camps, many of them run and financed by the American occupation authorities.

Harrison found that the DPs wanted to immigrate to Palestine and recommended that Britain immediately issue one hundred thousand additional entry certificates. Truman forwarded the recommendation to Attlee with an in-principle endorsement. In mid-October 1945, ignoring a British request for discretion, Truman publicly supported the "100,000" recommendation. London was furious.

This diplomatic drama played out against the background of increasing anti-British violence in Palestine. The IZL and LHI, who had continued to attack police stations, telephone poles, and banks, were joined in early October by the Haganah, nonplussed by the result of the British elections and Labour's abandonment (or betrayal) of the Zionist cause (the year before, the Labour Party Executive had even advocated the transfer of Arabs out of the prospective Jewish state). The three armed groups negotiated a formal accord, known as the Hebrew Rebellion Movement (*tnu'at hameri ha'ivri*), and on the night of 9–10 October several Palmah squads raided the British detention camp at 'Atlit and freed 208 incarcerated illegal immigrants.[66] What followed was even more dramatic: on the night of 1 November Palmah sappers blew up railway tracks at 153 points around Palestine and, a few days later, destroyed a patrol vessel and two British coast guard stations, at Giv'at Olga and Sayidna 'Ali. The British reacted by raiding a handful of kibbutzim, which were suspected of housing illegal immigrants, and panicky troops killed nine civilians and wounded sixty-three. Anti-British emotions crested. Bombings of British installations continued through the winter and spring, culminating in the spectacular simultaneous destruction by Palmah sappers, on the night of 17 June 1946, of eleven bridges connecting Palestine to Transjordan, Syria, Lebanon, and Egypt.

Meanwhile, the Haganah renewed its illegal immigration campaign. Boats were intercepted by the Royal Navy and their passengers interned. But others got through. Between August 1945 and 14 May 1948, some 70,700 illegals landed on Palestine's shores. The Zionist leadership understandably used the plight of the DPs to further Zionist goals, even occasionally risking and sacrificing lives to further the movement's ends.[67] As the leaders understood, Britain's dilemma was stark: to stick to its guns and flatly reject Truman's "100,000" proposal would jeopardize the cornerstone of British foreign policy, the Anglo-American alliance—at a time when American goodwill was vital on a broad front of political, military, and economic issues (containing Soviet expansionism, keeping the British pound afloat, and so on). But to allow the hundred thousand into Palestine would enrage the Arab world and invite renewed rebellion in Palestine and, possibly, general turbulence in the Middle East. A foretaste was provided on 2 November 1945, when Arab mobs rioted across the Middle East and North Africa, burning Jewish shops, homes, and synagogues in Alexandria, and slaughtering about a hundred Jews in British-governed Tripolitania (Libya).[68]

Whitehall chose the path of least resistance—the establishment of yet another committee of inquiry, this time jointly with the Americans. At the very least it would buy a few months; and perhaps it would result in mobilizing Washington to share costs and/or responsibility. The British wanted the committee to focus on the DPs, with "Palestine" to be omitted from the terms of reference. Washington objected. The appointment of the Anglo-American Committee (AAC) was announced on 13 November. The threat of an Anglo-American rupture was averted, and the Haganah briefly suspended its attacks to enable the inquiry to go forward in an atmosphere of relative calm.

The twelve-man committee was instructed "to examine political, economic and social conditions in Palestine as they bear upon the problem of Jewish immigration and settlement therein" and "to examine the position of the Jews in those countries in Europe where they have been victims of Nazi and Fascist persecution, [to assess how they might be reintegrated in those countries,] . . . and to make estimates of those who wish or will be impelled by their conditions to migrate to Palestine or other countries outside Europe."[69]

The AAC—the "twelve apostles," as they were dubbed—was chaired by a British judge, Sir John Singleton, and included the American Quaker Frank Aydelotte, director of the Institute for Advanced Study at Princeton, James McDonald, former League of Nations high commissioner for Refugees from Germany, Pulitzer Prize—winner Frank W. Buxton, a former editor of the *Boston Herald,* and lawyer Bartley Crum; and British Labour Party MP and assistant editor of the *New Statesman and Nation* Richard H. S. Crossman; Conservative Party MP Reginald E. Manningham-Buller; and Labour's Lord Robert C. Morrison.

In launching the committee, Bevin preempted its recommendations by publicly setting out Britain's short- and long-term goals. He hoped that the committee would propose relieving Britain of the Mandate and replacing it with an international "trusteeship." After a time, an independent, Arab-majority state would be established. He warned the Jews not to push their way to "the head of the queue," lest they trigger an anti-Semitic reaction. Meanwhile, Britain would curb Jewish immigration, imposing a ceiling of fifteen hundred entry certificates a month. The Jewish Agency denounced Bevin's "prejudging" the committee's findings.[70]

During February and March 1946 the committee studied the situation of the DPs in Europe, toured the Middle East, and heard out Arab and Zionist representatives and British officials. Some outside observers, such as the philo-Zionist South African prime minister Jan Smuts and Dr. Walter C. Lowdermilk, an expert on agricultural development, were also consulted.

The Palestinians' "Arab Office," headed by Musa al-ʿAlami, cautioned the AAC against regarding "Jewish colonization in Palestine and Arab resistance to it in terms of white colonization of America and Australia and the resistance of the Red Indians and Aborigenes." Nor would Zionist-engendered prosperity persuade the Arabs to shelve their opposition to a movement that was bent on their dispossession.[71] The Jewish Agency presented a report that emphasized Arab (and specifically Palestinian Arab) backwardness and Zionism's role as a bearer of enlightenment and progress. The agency offered reams of statistics and graphs to demonstrate Zionist beneficence. Of particular effect was the month the committee members spent touring DP camps, especially in Poland. Jewish Agency agents, working behind the scenes, made sure that the committee met and heard only Jews propounding the Zionist solution. The committee found that the displaced Jews in Poland lived in an "atmosphere of terror," with "pogroms . . . an everyday occurrence." (Indeed, some fifteen hundred Jews were slaughtered by anti-Semitic Poles in the year following the end of World War II.) The committee members were persuaded of the need for wholesale immigration of the DPs to Palestine.

Before reaching Palestine, the members visited Arab capitals. At Riyadh, King Ibn Saʿud told them: "The Jews are our enemies everywhere. Wherever they are found, they intrigue and work against us. . . . We drove the Romans out of Palestine. . . . How, after all this sacrifice, would a merchant [that is, Jew] come and take Palestine out of our hands for money?" Ibn Saʿud then presented each member with a golden dagger and an Arabian robe and headdress and showed off his harem. He offered to find Judge Singleton a spouse.[72]

In the hearings in Palestine, the Jewish leaders again offered statistics and graphs and argued that the Arabs already had a number of states; the Palestinian Arabs did not need a separate state of their own. Ben-Gurion banned all but mainstream Zionist spokesmen from appearing before the AAC (though, defying the leadership, Hebrew University president Yehuda Leib Magnes also testified, advocating a binational solution). The Arabs preferred to impress the AAC with "a sumptuous luncheon at Katy Antonius's or a ceremonial visit to a large estate rather than any systematic marshalling of facts and figures to make a convincing presentation."[73]

But perhaps more important than the formal testimony were the committee's tours around the country. The contrary realities of Zionist and Arab existence left an abiding impression. After visiting Kibbutz Mishmar Haʿemek, at the western edge of the Jezreel Valley, Crossman wrote: "I've never met a nicer community anywhere." By contrast, two hundred yards down the road, he later reported, was "the stenchiest Arab village I have ever seen," where Crossman was treated to tea "on the [earthen] floor of a filthy hovel."[74]

And Aydelotte later wrote: "I left Washington pretty strongly anti-Zionist. . . . But when you see at first hand what these Jews have done in Palestine . . . the greatest creative effort in the modern world. The Arabs are not equal to anything like it and would destroy all that the Jews have done. . . . This we must not let them do."[75] Buxton was later to compare the Haganah to the American revolutionary army, "a rabble in arms in the fine sense."[76]

The AAC's report was released simultaneously in Washington and London on 1 May. It represented, roughly, a compromise between the views of its two component blocks, the American and British. The committee accepted that most of the DPs wished to settle in Palestine and recommended that "100,000" entry permits be issued "as rapidly as conditions will permit." The committee sympathized with the propensity of each side to regard Palestine as its homeland and rejected partition. For the short and medium term, the AAC recommended that the British Mandate be converted into, or continued under the guise of, a United Nations trusteeship. Later, Palestine should be granted independence within a unitary or binational framework. The AAC's recommendations were unanimous.

But the AAC had done nothing to heal the basic Anglo-American rift. Truman once again endorsed the passage of a hundred thousand DPs to Palestine and approved the scrapping of the white paper's land sale provisions, which the AAC had deemed discriminatory; Attlee ruled out mass immigration until the Yishuv was disarmed (which he knew was a nonstarter).

The Jewish Agency endorsed the report's immigration recommendation but rejected all the rest. The Arabs rejected everything. They demanded immediate independence for an Arab-ruled Palestine, not "binationalism," whatever that might mean, and called for an immediate cessation of immigration. One Foreign Office cable, in the wake of the report, spoke of Arab hatred of the Jews as being greater than that of the Nazis. The AHC—in a letter from Jamal Husseini to Attlee—issued an "ultimatum" and threatened "jihad." In a follow-up interview with British high commissioner Sir Alan Cunningham, Husseini declared his willingness "to die" for the cause. When Cunningham responded that this didn't really trouble him and that what worried him was the welfare of "the ordinary Arab population," Husseini rejoined that "they were prepared to die too."[77]

The publication of the report triggered violent demonstrations in Baghdad and Palestine; in Beirut, the US Information Center was set on fire. At least one Baghdad newspaper called for jihad: "The Arabs must proclaim a crusade [that is, holy war] to save the Holy Land from [the] western gang which understands only the language of force." Another called on the Arabs to "annihilate all European Jews in Palestine."[78] The AAC report was officially condemned by the Arab League Council meeting at Bludan, Syria, on 8–10 June 1946.

The publication of the report led to a resumption of Jewish attacks on British targets culminating in the Palmah's Night of the Bridges. On 29 June the British responded with Operation Agatha, dubbed in Zionist historiography Black Sabbath, designed to cripple the Haganah. For two weeks the security forces scoured Jewish towns and rural settlements for men and arms, even occupying the Jewish Agency building in Jerusalem (which, in fact, contained a Haganah headquarters), and arrested four JAE members, including Shertok. But HIS had obtained advanced warning, and most Haganah commanders escaped the dragnet. The operation only marginally affected Haganah capabilities.

But politically, while further damaging Britain's image in the United States, the operation persuaded the JAE (meeting in Paris in early August 1946) to abandon the path of military confrontation.[79] However, Black Sabbath also provoked vengefulness, with the IZL, ironically, taking up the cudgel for its sometime enemy, the Haganah. With faulty coordination with the Haganah, IZL sappers on 22 July placed a number of bomb-laden milk containers in the basement of the King David Hotel in Jerusalem, which served as a British military and administrative headquarters. The resulting explosion, which brought down one of the hotel's wings, was the single biggest terrorist outrage in the organization's history. The IZL subsequently claimed that it had given the British ample warning but that they had failed to evacuate the building; the British maintained that no adequate warning had been given. Ninety-one British, Arab, and Jewish officers and officials died.

In response, the commander of the British forces in Palestine, Lieutenant General Sir Evelyn Barker, issued a nonfraternization order in which he accused all of Palestine's Jews of complicity in the outrage. British personnel were barred from frequenting Jewish homes or businesses or to have "any social intercourse with any Jew," in order to punish "the Jews in a way the race dislikes as much as any, by striking at their pockets." Barker was subsequently rebuked by Attlee but was not removed from command.[80]

The upshot of the violence and of the Anglo-American discussions about the AAC report in summer 1946 was the Morrison-Grady, or Provincial Autonomy, Plan, Britain's last effort to devise a compromise. The plan left defense, foreign affairs, and most economic matters in British—or "International Trusteeship"—hands while, subdivided into four "cantons," Jews and

Arabs were offered a measure of local autonomy (responsibility for municipal affairs, agriculture, education, and so on). The plan also provided for the immediate transfer to Palestine of one hundred thousand DPs and eventual independence for Palestine as a unitary (or binational) state. In September, the British convened a conference in London, attended by British officials and representatives of the Arab states, to discuss the plan. But nothing came of it. The Zionists, who did not attend, insisted on "Jewish statehood," and the Arabs demanded "immediate Arab independence." The American response was equally unequivocal: on 4 October 1946, Truman formally rejected Morrison-Grady, hesitantly endorsed partition and Jewish statehood (a solution, he said, that "would command the support of public opinion in the United States"),[81] and called for an immediate start to "substantial" immigration. Truman's statement was in large measure prompted by the upcoming midterm American elections. Attlee was bowled over: he complained that Truman "did not wait to acquaint [himself] with the reasons" for the plan.[82] Meanwhile, the Haganah pressed on with its illegal immigration campaign.

On 27 January 1947, the British took one last shot at resolving the crisis. They reconvened the London conference, this time with the AHC represented. But the Zionists continued to boycott the talks, and the United States declined to send an observer. The Arabs continued to refuse anything short of complete, immediate independence, and the Jews, anything less than Jewish statehood in all or part of Palestine.

With no acceptable military solution to the Jewish guerrilla-terrorist and illegal immigration campaigns, and with no political solution to the Zionist-Arab impasse, Britain had reached the end of the road.

2

The United Nations Steps In:
UNSCOP and the Partition Resolution

On 14 February 1947, the British cabinet decided to wash its hands of Palestine and dump the problem in the lap of the United Nations. Ernest Bevin was later to say: "The Arabs, like the Jews, [had] refused to accept any of the compromise proposals which HMG had put before both parties."[1] The military chiefs of staff were unhappy with the decision; it would open the door to Soviet penetration and subvert the morale of the troops in Palestine. But Clement Attlee and Bevin had already decided, in principle, in a tête-à-tête on 27 December 1946, that in the new, postwar circumstances, Britain could give up Palestine and Egypt (as well as Greece),[2] and the cabinet stood firm: Britain had made what it saw as a series of reasonable offers and no one was interested. And the United States, far from expressing a willingness to shoulder or share responsibility, was continuously subverting Britain's efforts.

"We have decided that we are unable to accept the scheme put forward either by the Arabs or by the Jews, or to impose ourselves a solution of our own. . . . The only course now open to us is to submit the problem to the judgment of the United Nations," Bevin told the House of Commons on 18 February 1947, adding that Britain would not recommend to the United Nations "any particular solution."[3] The international community would have to take up the burden and chart a settlement. During the London conference, the Arabs had not been averse to the problem going before the United Nations, where they anticipated a favorable outcome. Conversely, the Zionist delegates had been wary. This may have affected Bevin's decision.

Historians have since argued about Britain's reasons. Some have suggested that Bevin and the cabinet had not been entirely straightforward: by threatening the two sides with the prospect of the unknown and the unpredictable, Britain's intention had been to force the Jews and/or the Arabs to accept the latest set of Whitehall proposals or to agree to a continuation of the Mandate. Certainly David Ben-Gurion, then and later, believed that the move was a ploy designed to prolong British rule: Bevin would hand the United Nations an insoluble problem; the United Nations would flounder and fail, and Britain would be reempowered to stay on, on its own terms, without UN or US interference.[4]

Other historians (myself included) have taken the British decision at its face value: Bevin and his colleagues had truly had enough of Palestine; passing the ball to the United Nations was their only recourse. In the aftermath of world war, Britain was too weak and too poor to soldier on. IZL and LHI veterans and their political successors have since claimed that it was mainly their terrorist campaigns that ultimately persuaded Bevin and the British public to abandon Palestine. Others have pointed to the large-scale Haganah operations of 1945–1946 (the railway line and bridge demolitions) as being decisive: these portended an eventual full-scale British-Haganah clash that Whitehall was unwilling to contemplate. Also, the struggle against the Haganah's illegal immigration campaign was a headache of major proportions. Most historians agree about the importance of the growing Anglo-American rift, the DPs, and the pressure from Washington in the British government's decision-making: given the Cold War context and Britain's financial insolvency, Whitehall could ill afford to alienate Washington over a highly emotional issue that, when all was said and done, was not a vital interest.

The British decision of February 1947 was firmed up over the following months by bloody events on the ground, in Palestine, in the Mediterranean, and in Britain itself; Jewish provocations and British reprisals spiraled almost out of control. British efforts to block and punish Jewish terrorism and illegal immigration took on new, bloody dimensions—though, it must be added, British officials and troops by and large displayed restraint and humanity in face of Jewish excesses.[5] By the end of 1947, with evacuation only months away, Britain appeared no longer capable of properly governing Palestine and had lost the will to continue. The violence of the IZL and LHI underlined the moderate Zionists' argumentation in Washington and London that, in the absence of a solution—that is, a Jewish state—Jewish desperation would approach boiling point.

Without doubt, Britain's decision to withdraw heightened the terrorists' expectations; they sensed that the enemy was on the run. The British had almost a hundred thousand troops in Palestine, almost five times as many as had been used to crush the Arab Revolt of 1936–1939 (a tribute, perhaps, to the greater efficiency and lethality of the Jewish terrorists). Against the backdrop of the Holocaust and the scrutiny in Washington and the world press of every British action, there were strict limits to what Attlee and Bevin could allow themselves in pursuit of effective counterterrorism.

On 1 March 1947, IZL gunmen killed more than twenty British servicemen, twelve of them in a grenade attack on the British Officers Club in Tel Aviv. On 31 March the LHI sabotaged the Haifa oil refinery; the fire took three weeks to put out. And on 4 May, IZL gunmen penetrated the British prison in Acre: two dozen IZL members were set free (as, unintentionally, were some two hundred Arab prisoners), but nine of the attackers were killed and eight were captured. The captured men were tried, and on 8 July death sentences were confirmed against three of them.

In a repeat of the "whipping" cycle (when the IZL had flogged a British officer after the British had flogged several IZL men), on 12 July the IZL abducted two British sergeants and threatened to hang them if the British hanged the IZL men. The British—despite a widespread dragnet and Haganah help—failed to locate the sergeants and went ahead with the hangings, on 29 July. The IZL hanged the sergeants the next day—and boobytrapped their bodies. A British captain was injured when they were cut down.[6] "The bestialities practiced by the Nazis themselves could go no further," commented the *Times* of London.[7] The "hanging of the two young sergeants struck a deadly blow against British patience and pride," Arthur Creech Jones, Britain's colonial secretary, was to comment thirteen years later.[8] But bestiality was by no means a monopoly of the Jewish terrorists. On the evening of 30 July, responding to the hangings, British troops and police in Tel Aviv went on the rampage, destroying Jewish shops and beating up passersby. In one area, the berserk security men sprayed Jewish pedestrians and coffee shops with gunfire, killing five and injuring ten. High Commissioner Sir Alan Cunningham, in a cable to London, explained what had happened—in the process highlighting the sorry state of his force's morale: "Most of them are young . . . they have had to work in an atmosphere of constant danger and increasing tension, fraught with insult, vilification and treachery; and it can be understood that the culminating horror of the murder of their comrades . . . in every circumstance of planned brutality, should have excited them to a pitch of fury which momentarily blinded them to the dictates of principle, reason and humanity alike."[9]

Nor was this all. In London, Manchester, Liverpool, Newcastle, Gateshead, and Holyhead there were anti-Semitic demonstrations; Jewish shop- and synagogue windows were smashed.

In Palestine, several policemen were fired—though no criminal proceed- ings were ever instituted against anyone. In Parliament, in special session on 12 August, there was an all-party consensus to quit Palestine, quickly; "no British interest" was served by soldiering on, said Churchill.

On 2 April the British had asked the UN secretary-general to convene a special session of the General Assembly, which duly met in New York on 28 April–9 May. The General Assembly resolved to set up the United Nations Special Committee on Palestine (UNSCOP) to recommend a solution to the Palestine conundrum.

The Arab delegations opposed UNSCOP's appointment and sought, in- stead, a full-scale General Assembly debate and decision on immediate indepen- dence for an Arab-dominated "united democratic . . . Palestinian state."[10] They were handily defeated, the majority of the fifty-five UN members pre- ferring to leave debate and decision until after the committee had examined the problem. The Arabs then tried to restrict the committee's terms of refer- ence to Palestine and Palestinian independence. The Zionists, for their part, sought to include the problem of Europe's Jewish DPs—of whom there were more than four hundred thousand.[11] Again, the Arabs lost.

The final terms, hammered out in the General Assembly's First (Political) Committee, authorized UNSCOP to recommend a solution on the basis of an investigation in the country and "anywhere" else it saw fit, an allusion to the DP camps. Holland, Sweden, Czechoslovakia, Yugoslavia, Canada, Aus- tralia, India, Iran, Peru, Guatemala, and Uruguay were asked to send repre- sentatives. UNSCOP included no Zionist, Arab, or Great Power members.

Zionist officials were not enamored with this composition, given the membership of three Muslim, or partly Muslim, states (Iran, India, and Yu- goslavia) and two Dominions (Canada and Australia) that, it was feared, would automatically defer to London.

The Arabs were not overly concerned about the ultimate upshot in the General Assembly. With five member states and a handful of reflexive Islamic and third world supporters, they expected an easy victory. They came to the assembly cocky and disorganized and remained so until the bitter end. They failed to appreciate the significance of Soviet deputy foreign minister Andrei Gromyko's General Assembly speech of 14 May 1947, a speech that stunned almost all Western and Zionist observers (though almost no one understood its full purport). Hitherto, Soviet policy on Palestine had been anti-British and pro-Arab. Now, while criticizing the British, Gromyko spoke of "the Jewish people['s] . . . exceptional [and 'indescribable'] sorrow and suffering" during the Holocaust and of the survivors' suffering as DPs across Europe since then; asserted the Jews' right to self-determination; and suggested that if a unitary state proved impracticable, then Palestine should be partitioned into Jewish and Arab states.[12] Moscow had announced a pro-Zionist tack—and sent UNSCOP off to the Middle East with a clear message.

What led to this unheralded Soviet volte-face remains uncertain. Anti-British considerations probably predominated; in all likelihood, Moscow was intent on causing a rift between London and Washington. But the Soviets, at some level, to judge from Gromyko's speech, which devoted a full three paragraphs to Jewish suffering, were also moved by the horrors of the Holocaust and by a sense of camaraderie with fellow sufferers at Nazi hands.

Sensitivity to Jewish suffering also appears to have played a part in the pro-Zionist leanings of a number of UNSCOP members, including Paul Mohn, the committee's Swedish deputy chairman, Justice Ivan Rand, the chief Canadian member, Jorge García Granados, the Guatemalan ambassador to the United States and United Nations, and Enrique Rodríguez Fabregat, the Uruguayan former minister of education. But other members, including those representing India (Judge Sir ʿAbdur Rahman), Iran (Nasrollah Entezam, former minister of foreign affairs), Australia, and Holland, came to the committee with pro-Arab or at least pro-British outlooks.[13] In general, foreign observers noted the relatively uneven quality of UNSCOP's composition and the members' relative unpreparedness for their mission, in terms of prior experience in similar positions, language skills, and knowledge about the Middle East. The brilliant American academic and diplomat Ralph Bunche, a member of UNSCOP's secretariat, privately remarked that this was "just about the worst group I have ever had to work with. If they do a good job it will be a real miracle."[14]

With the Swedish judge Emil Sandstrom—religious, "sly as a fox,"[15] "dry and colorless"[16]—in the chair, UNSCOP began work in New York on 26 May and spent five summer weeks in Palestine. In private, the British tended to dismiss as unimportant the work and prospective recommendations of the committee; they trusted that, when the committee's work was done, the General Assembly would see its way independently and wisely,[17] and they took care not to try overtly to influence its decisions. The Zionists, by contrast, fully appreciated the committee's significance and made every effort to persuade the committee to see the light.[18] The Jewish Agency attached to UNSCOP as liaison three capable officials—Aubrey (Abba) Eban, later Israel's legendary foreign minister; David Horowitz, later governor of the Bank of Israel; and Spanish-speaking Moshe Toff (Tov), the head of the

Latin American Division in the Jewish Agency Political Department. The Zionists and the British surrounded the committee with spies and bugging devices to monitor its internal deliberations.

The AHC announced its intention to boycott UNSCOP and failed completely to prepare for its visit. Palestine's Arabs greeted UNSCOP with a one-day general strike. The AHC charged that UNSCOP was "pro-Zionist" and accompanied the committee's deliberations with uncompromising radio broadcasts ("all of Palestine must be Arab"). Opposition figures were warned that they would pay with their lives if they spoke to UNSCOP.

The committee first toured the country, visiting towns and villages. As had happened with the AAC, the face-to-face encounters in the settlements and villages were persuasive. The members were warmly welcomed by their Jewish hosts, often with flowers and cheering crowds, and the Jewish Agency made sure that they met with settlers who spoke their languages (Swedish, Spanish, Persian, and so on). The Arabs, in contrast, displayed sourness, suspicion, or aggressiveness. Everywhere the Arabs refused to answer the committee's questions: in a school in Beersheba, the teachers continued with their lessons when UNSCOP entered the classrooms, and the pupils were instructed not to look at the visitors; in the Galilee village of Rama, the inhabitants evacuated the village, and UNSCOP was "greeted only by a delegation of children who . . . cursed them."[19] The committee was impressed by the cleanliness and development in the Jewish areas and, conversely, by the dirt and backwardness of the Arab villages and towns. They were particularly horrified at the (common) sight of child labor and exploitation in Arab factories and workshops.[20] By contrast, the Jewish settlements struck the committee as "European, modern, dynamic . . . a state in the making";[21] the Jews palpably were making the desert bloom.[22] As the Persian member, Entezam, was overheard (by a Persian-speaking HIS agent) telling his deputy: "What asses these Arabs are. The country is so beautiful and, if it were given to the Jews, it could be developed and turned into Europe."[23] UNSCOP's members may have felt that the Zionists often indulged in overkill, but the message proved effective.

After the tours in the countryside came oral testimony (accompanied by a veritable flood of written depositions, thirty-two tons of material in all).[24] The Zionist spokesmen first set out the case for a Jewish state in all of Palestine, then in private conversations agreed to accede to a partition, in which part of the country would be earmarked for Jewish statehood while the rest would be united with Jordan under Hashemite rule.[25] Ben-Gurion said that separating the Jews and the Arabs would lead to "fertile cooperation between the two states."[26] Throughout, he vilified British rule and policy and had only bad words for the Palestinian Arab national movement. Chaim

Weizmann from the first played the "good cop," focusing on past Jewish suffering, present Zionist moderation, and the future benefits of Zionism for all the Middle East. He posited partition, with the Jews receiving the Galilee, the Coastal Plain, and the Negev. He seems to have been instrumental in persuading UNSCOP to support this solution.[27]

Sandstrom and his aides secretly met with the commanders of the Haganah and IZL. The Haganah men—Yisrael Galili, Yigael Yadin, Yosef Avidar, and Ehud Avriel—appeared to Sandstrom self-assured, capable, and resolute. They grossly exaggerated the Haganah's strength ("90,000" members) and asserted that it would be able to repel any Arab attack, including by the Arab states. Sandstrom met separately with Menachem Begin. Begin predicted that were it come to war, the Arabs would be soundly defeated. He rejected partition, arguing that "one is not allowed to make commerce with a motherland"—but said that he would not fight the majority if that is what it accepted. Sandstrom came away from these meetings and, more generally, his sojourn in Palestine with a certainty that the Yishuv would beat the Arabs and emerge from a war with most of Palestine under its control.[28]

Without doubt, UNSCOP's members were heavily influenced by two affairs that occurred during their watch—the mutual British-IZL hangings and the Exodus Affair. The hangings underlined the unviability of the Mandate and the barbarism to which the two sides were being driven by the situation.[29]

The Exodus Affair had an even greater impact. Since August 1946, the British had been sending captured illegal immigrants to detention camps in Cyprus. But soon there was no room left in the island's camps, which held some twelve thousand prisoners. During summer 1947, the British tightened the screws. Clandestinely, Britain's MI6 unleashed a campaign of sabotage against the Haganah's ships in European ports: the *Vrisi* was sunk in Genoa harbor on 11 July; the *Pan Crescent,* another immigrant ship, was damaged and grounded near Venice on the night of 30–31 August.[30]

Overtly, Whitehall resolved to send captured illegal immigrants back to Europe. On 12 July, the converted American ferry *President Warfield,* renamed by the Mossad Le'aliya Bet *Exodus from Europe—1947,* set sail for Palestine from Sète, in southern France, with forty-five hundred DPs aboard. The Haganah-Mossad command dispatched the *Exodus* in mid-July for technical and operational reasons, not out of a political desire to splice the journey with the work of UNSCOP. But the Zionist leaders were not unaware of the political benefits that might accrue from such a coincidence.[31] And certainly they were quick to exploit the affair politically once the *Exodus* reached Palestine waters.

Shadowed across the Mediterranean by the Royal Navy, on 18 July the *Ex-*

odus was intercepted and boarded by Royal Marines some 19 miles off Palestine, opposite Gaza. In contrast with past policy, the Haganah decided, in advance, to resist, with an eye to highlighting Jewish weakness and suffering and British brutality.[32] The boarding was opposed, and a "battle" raged through the night. The British, occasionally using live fire, gradually overcame the defenders, who brandished clubs, metal bars, screws and bolts, bottles, and tomatoes. Three passengers were killed and twenty-eight seriously wounded,[33] and the point—illustrating the desperate plight of the DPs and linking their fate to that of Palestine—was convincingly articulated. As if to help Zionist propaganda, the British towed the stricken vessel to Haifa and transferred almost all the passengers to three ships, which then departed for France.

But the French refused to cooperate. *L'Humanité* described the three boats containing the *Exodus* transportees as "a floating Auschwitz." Most of the passengers refused to disembark, and the French refused to accept passengers offloaded by force. The British, maneuvered into a corner of their own making, set sail for Hamburg, where the army on 8 September forcibly disembarked the passengers and shipped them to hastily prepared camps. Jews, this time escorted by British troops, had been returned to the land of their annihilators. The ordeal of the *Exodus* seemed to symbolize contemporary Jewish history and British insensitivity. Nothing could have done more to promote the Zionist cause. The affair, and the British acts of sabotage in Mediterranean harbors, as well as behind-the-scenes British diplomatic pressures, had a negative effect on Mossad Le'aliya Bet operations. But the Zionists had engineered a major propaganda coup.

The disembarkation in Haifa of the *Exodus* passengers, including dozens of injured, took place with Judge Sandstrom and the Yugoslav UNSCOP member, Vladimir Simitch, looking on, a bevy of journalists in tow. They had been "invited" to the port by Jewish Agency Political Department director Moshe Shertok.[34] Sandstrom and Simitch spent two hours on the pier and spoke with passengers, and came away shaken. The Yugoslav was quoted as saying: "It is the best possible evidence we have."[35]

The following day the two men recounted what they had seen to other committee members, and together, all of them heard the testimony of an American cleric, Stanley Grauel, who had disembarked from the *Exodus*.[36] The affair had also indirectly cast light on the IZL's motives in hanging the British sergeants.

Despite the boycott of UNSCOP, the Arab cause did not go unrepresented. Committee members privately met, through Bunche or British mediation, several Arab officials and intellectuals. The most important conversation apparently took place at a festive dinner, on 16 July, on the eve of the committee's departure from Palestine. Sandstrom and two aides spoke at length with Hussein al-Khalidi, a member of the AHC and mayor of Jerusalem. Al-Khalidi argued that the Jews had always been a minority and had no "historic rights" in Palestine and that the Arabs should not have to suffer because of Hitler and the DPs in Europe. The Jews, he said, had always enjoyed a pleasant life in Arab lands—until they demanded a sovereign state. Al-Khalidi rejected both partition and a binational state and called for a democratic unitary state with an Arab majority.[37]

Sandstrom also met several intellectuals at the Government Arab College in Jerusalem. Ahmed Khalidi, the college head (and Hussein al-Khalidi's brother), complained that the Jewish education system in Palestine was "chauvinistic." Musa Nasser, headmaster of the Bir Zeit secondary school, advocated a unitary state, in which the Arabs would remain a majority and Jewish immigration would be severely curtailed; perhaps the Jews would eventually receive "autonomous pockets."[38] The committee also received a string of memoranda from Palestinian Arab advocates (including, apparently, from Musa al-ʿAlami and Cecil Hourani).[39]

The AHC boycott in one way worked in the Palestinians' favor: it enabled the Indian member, ʿAbdur Rahman—who privately complained that the boycott was having "a disastrous effect on his colleagues"—to persuade the committee to hear outside Arab leaders.[40] On 21 July UNSCOP traveled to Lebanon, meeting Prime Minister Riad al-Sulh. The following day they met Foreign Minister Hamid Faranjieh. Echoing the Arab League consensus, the Lebanese leaders called for an end to Jewish immigration and the establishment in Palestine of an independent, democratic Arab government. The Zionists, they charged, had territorial ambitions beyond Palestine, encompassing Jordan, Syria, and Lebanon.

On 23 July, at Sofar, the Arab representatives completed their testimony before UNSCOP. Faranjieh, speaking for the Arab League, said that Jews "illegally" in Palestine would be expelled and that the future of many of those "legally" in the country but without Palestine citizenship would need to be resolved "by the future Arab government." UNSCOP tried to get other Arab representatives to soften or elucidate this answer but got nowhere—which led Mohn to conclude in his memoirs that "there is nothing more extreme than meeting all the representatives of the Arab world in one group . . . when each one tries to show that he is more extreme than the other."[41] The Iraqi foreign minister, Muhammad Fadel Jamali, compared the Zionists to the Nazis. On the other hand, in private meetings outside Sofar, leading Maronite figures, including the patriarch, Antoine Pierre Arida, and former Lebanese president Emile Eddé, told UNSCOP that Lebanon's Christians supported partition and the establishment of a Jewish state. The

Maronite archbishop of Beirut, Ignatius Mubarak, even disputed the Arab claims to Palestine and Lebanon.[42]

From Lebanon, half the UNSCOP team, including Sandstrom, Simitch, Entezam, and Bunche, flew to Amman for a series of "unofficial" meetings. King 'Abdullah was less than forthright: he spoke ambiguously and carefully of the "difficulty" the Arabs would have in accepting a Jewish state in any part of Palestine. But he did not completely rule out partition. The DPs, the Jordanians argued in a twelve-page memorandum, could be settled outside Palestine. Jordanian prime minister Samir Rifa'i said that the Jews of Palestine would enjoy full minority rights and all would receive citizenship.[43] Privately, 'Abdullah was "enthusiastic" about partition but hinted that the Arab parts of Palestine should be joined to Transjordan.[44] But the Jewish Agency was disappointed with 'Abdullah's statement; its officials had expected full-throated support for partition.

UNSCOP then flew to Geneva. Sandstrom pressed for a visit to the DP camps. A heated debate within UNSCOP was resolved by a vote of six to four in favor of visiting the camps, which all understood augured a pro-Zionist tilt on the core issue.

On 8 August an UNSCOP subcommittee began a weeklong visit to DP camps in the American and British zones of control in Germany and Austria. "That night I was in hell," recalled Fabregat, after a visit to the Rothschild Hospital in Vienna, which treated four thousand hungry, mostly tubercular, patients. At the DP camp at Hahne, a mile from Bergen-Belsen, "one hundred per cent" of the Jewish DPs wanted to immigrate to Israel, reported John Hood, the Australian member. This was what all the members on the tour heard from the mostly randomly chosen DPs; and this was what some of the Western officers, including General Lucius Clay, the military governor of the American Zone in Germany, also told them.[45]

Back in Geneva, UNSCOP hammered out its report.[46] Its work was accompanied by continuous Arab, Zionist, and British pressures as well as espionage. The Lebanese politician Camille Chamoun, the Arab League liaison to the committee, submitted a memorandum warning that any solution not acceptable to the Palestinian Arabs would result in catastrophe;[47] Musa al-'Alami lobbied vigorously with Donald MacGillivray, the British liaison officer to UNSCOP.[48] The British, for their part, submitted a last-minute memorandum that, by suggesting that partition was a possible option and outlining ways partition could be fashioned, unwittingly appear to have helped consolidate the (eventual) pro-partition majority.[49]

The most vigorous lobbyists were the Zionists, who bombarded UNSCOP with memoranda and wined and dined its members.[50] They recruited Crossman, who had become a fervent pro-Zionist during his days with the AAC, to come to Geneva and "work" on the committee. He argued for partition, with a Jewish state consisting of the Galilee, the Coastal Plain, and the Negev.[51] Another Zionist asset in Geneva was the Palestinian Opposition figure ʿOmar Dajani (codenamed by HIS "the Orphan"), whose father had been murdered by the Husseinis in 1938. He advocated a Jewish-Transjordanian partition.[52]

From the start of the deliberations in Geneva, there was unanimity in UN-SCOP about the need to terminate the Mandate. As for the rest, there was dissension. But by the end of August, a clear majority emerged in favor of partition into two states, one Jewish, the other Palestinian Arab—or as Sandstrom defined it, "Partition with Economic Union," with an international trusteeship for the Jerusalem-Bethlehem area, where Christendom's holy sites, as well as Judaism's and Islam's, were concentrated. The demarcation of the borders, left until the last days of the deliberations, was largely the work of Mohn, the Swedish deputy member, who was relatively expert in the demography and geography of Palestine.[53] The guiding principle was demographic—that the Jewish state should include as few Arabs as possible and the Arab state as few Jews. But Mohn and his colleagues also accounted for the concrete needs of the two states-to-be, including contiguity and immigrant absorptive capacity (the latter with respect to the Jewish state). Little attention was paid to physical features and natural contours, such as hills and streams, in defining the borders. Mohn spent a great deal of time persuading UNSCOP that all of the Negev should be Jewish.

Mohn's map, accepted by the UNSCOP majority on 30 August, was based on dividing Palestine into seven parts—one part (Jerusalem-Bethlehem) under international control, and six roughly triangular areas to constitute the Jewish and Arab states (with three triangles each). Each threesome was to be contiguous, with two overlapping "kissing" or "kiss" points (near Afula and near Gedera), where the Jewish and Arab triangles would meet (with bridges or tunnels providing the continuity). The kiss points were to be under international supervision. The Jews were to get 62 percent of Palestine (most of it desert), consisting of the Negev (including Beersheba), the Coastal Plain from just north of Haifa down to Rehovot (including Tel Aviv and the Arab town of Jaffa), and eastern Galilee (including largely Arab Safad and the mixed town of Tiberias), and the Arabs about 35 percent of the country, consisting of Judea (including Hebron), Samaria (including Nablus and Jenin), and central and western Galilee (including the Arab towns of Acre and Nazareth and the Jewish town of Nahariya). The members signed the report and map just before midnight, 31 August. In the antechamber in the Palace of the Nations stood Eban, Horowitz, and MacGillivray; no Arabs were present. An UNSCOP member darted out of the committee room and said: "Oh, here are the expectant fathers," then darted back in. Then, at midnight, UNSCOP filed out. "Fabregat approached and embraced me," recalled Horowitz. "'It's the greatest moment in my life,' he [Fabregat] said with tears in his eyes."[54] Sandstrom commented a few days later: "Seldom have so many had so much trouble for so little a country."[55]

The report described UNSCOP's work, the elements of the Zionist-Arab conflict and the contending claims, and surveyed previous proposals (including the Peel Commission report). There followed UNSCOP's unanimous recommendations, the recommendations of the seven-member UNSCOP majority, and the recommendations of the three-member minority. (Hood, the Australian representative, while leaning toward the Zionist case, abstained—probably in deference to the wishes of his government.)[56]

The chief unanimous recommendations were the termination of the Mandate at the earliest possible time and the granting of independence to Palestine. The majority—the representatives of Sweden, Holland, Canada, Uruguay, Guatemala, Peru, and Czechoslovakia—proposed partition, with an enclave (a *corpus separatum*) under international control consisting of Jerusalem and Bethlehem. The Jewish and Arab states were to be bound in economic "union"—were to function as one economic entity—and the British would continue to administer the country for two years, during which 150,000 Jews would be allowed into the Jewish-designated areas in monthly quotas. During the first year of independence the inhabitants of each state desiring to move to its neighbor would be free to do so. As it stood, the Jewish state, according to UNSCOP, was to have half a million Jews and 416,000 Arabs, along with some ninety thousand bedouins who were not counted as permanent residents.[57] The corpus separatum of Jerusalem-Bethlehem was to have a population of two hundred thousand, half Jewish and half Arab. The Arab state was to have some seven hundred thousand Arabs and eight thousand Jews. The proposed arrangement was described as the "most realistic and practical" possible.

The UNSCOP minority proposal, penned by the Yugoslav, Iranian, and Indian representatives, was for Palestine to be given independence as a "federal state," with locally governed, separate Jewish and Arab autonomous areas (which they confusingly called "states"). Its frills removed, the proposal charted the establishment of a unitary state under Arab domination, to be established after a three-year transitional period. Jewish immigration was to be allowed only to the two Jewish areas (limited to the Coastal Plain and part of the northern Negev)—and, overall, was to be curtailed by the federal authorities in a manner that always left the Arabs with a countrywide majority.[58]

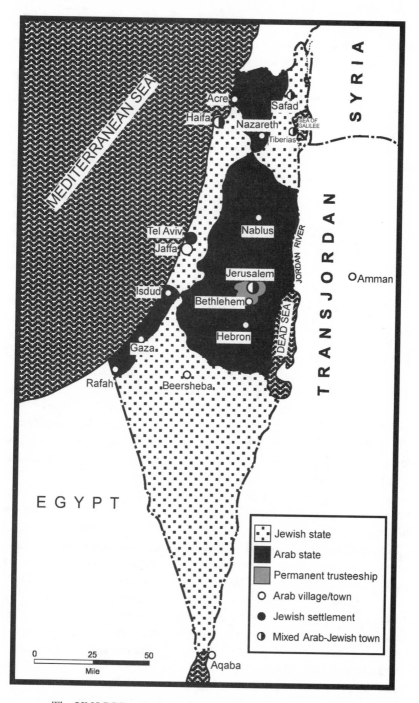

The UNSCOP majority partition proposal, 1 September 1947

The UNSCOP majority arrived at their recommendations mainly because they could see no better alternative.[59] The Zionists saw things more positively. They regarded the majority recommendations as a "giant achievement" or, in Ben-Gurion's words, "the beginning, indeed more than the beginning, of [our] salvation."[60]

The Arab reaction was just as predictable: "The blood will flow like rivers in the Middle East," promised Jamal Husseini. Haj Amin al-Husseini went one better: he denounced also the minority report, which, in his view, legitimized the Jewish foothold in Palestine, a "partition in disguise," as he put it. The Arab states, too, expressed dismay and negativity concerning the majority recommendations; "No Arab Government," Lebanese prime minister Riad al-Sulh told a British diplomat, "would dare to accept recommendations of U.N.S.C.O.P. Public opinion was now highly incensed and the Government[s] were forced to take some action . . . or be swept away."[61] According to Musa al-ʿAlami, the Arab population of Palestine would rise up against both the majority and minority reports. In the case of the majority report, the rising would "command universal support"; as to the minority report, "the rising might still be fairly successful."[62] ʿAzzam, the Arab League secretary-general, reacted both passionately and analytically: "[To the Arab peoples] you are not an [existing] fact—you [the Jews] are a temporary phenomenon. Centuries ago, the crusaders established themselves in our midst against our will, and in 200 years we ejected them. . . . Up to the very last moment, and beyond, they [the Arabs] will fight to prevent you from establishing your State. In no circumstances will they agree to it." But ʿAzzam added that, in the past, the Arabs had "once had Spain, and then we lost Spain, and we have become accustomed to not having Spain. . . . Whether at any point we shall become accustomed to not have a part of Palestine, I cannot say. The chances are against it, since 400,000 of our brethren will be unwilling citizens of your State. They will never recognize it, and they will never make peace."[63]

But UNSCOP had delivered its judgment. What could or would the Arab states do? While blustering, they generally acknowledged their military weakness. ʿAdil Arslan, one of Syrian president Shukri al-Quwwatli's advisers, later minister of defense, jotted down in his diary: "Poor Palestine, no matter what I say about defending it my heart remains a seething volcano because I cannot convince anyone of importance in my country or in the rest of the Arab countries that it needs anything more than words. . . . Because we have a small and ill-equipped army, we cannot stand up to the Zionist forces if they should suddenly decide to launch a strike at Damascus."[64]

British diplomats were surprised by the absence of mass demonstrations in the Arab world.[65] The British saw the majority report as grossly unfair to the

Arabs (Alexander Cadogan, the UK's representative to the United Nations, commented: "The majority plan is so manifestly unjust to the Arabs that it is difficult to see how we could reconcile it with our conscience").[66] Yet the official response was born of realpolitik, not moral qualms: the cabinet resolved, in a secret decision on 20 September, to quit Palestine completely; but the British would not enforce or shepherd partition. As Creech Jones, the colonial secretary, predicted, Palestine would be overtaken by "a state of chaos."[67] In other words, either the United Nations would set up the machinery for resolving the conflict and an orderly transfer of power or the Arabs and the Jews would settle the problem on their own, by force of arms. In either case, it was no longer Britain's responsibility.

THE GENERAL ASSEMBLY PARTITION
RESOLUTION, 29 NOVEMBER 1947

On 26 September Creech Jones announced at the UN General Assembly, sitting as the Ad Hoc Committee on Palestine, that Britain planned "an early withdrawal." Over the next two months, on the basis of the UNSCOP recommendations, three specially appointed subcommittees of the Ad Hoc Committee hammered out the terms of the resolution to be submitted to the General Assembly.[68]

All sides mounted intensive lobbying campaigns. The atmosphere was overheated: "The whole of New York," of course, was "mad," "so vast, so dirty, so crushing to the individual," one Jewish Agency emissary reported.[69] More to the point, for Walter Eytan, who had "studied the map of the United Nations very, very thoroughly"[70] and now orchestrated the Zionist contacts at Lake Success (where the General Assembly was meeting), were the activities of the hostile British delegation, "held to be the ablest of all the delegations" in the international body.[71] Moreover, Eytan was concerned about his own staff of Jewish Agency Political Department "diplomats" and the attached American Zionist officials—who, he said, were motivated by a "hunt after *kavod* [glory, honor], ambitions, considerations of prestige, etc.—all playing the major part in people's lives and minds. The number of *tocheslecker* [ass-lickers] surrounding Weizmann at present makes me sick."[72] Nonetheless, the Zionists efficiently deployed their manpower, assigning an official with the appropriate language and diplomatic skills to "work" on each UN delegation: Eliahu (Elias) Sasson, the Aleppo-born Arabist, making contacts with the Syrians, the Yemenis, and the Iraqis; Moshe Toff (Tov), working with the Colombians, Ecuadorians, and Mexicans; the Russian-born Eliahu Epstein handling the Soviets; and the South African–born Michael Comay dealing with the South Africans, New Zealanders, and

Australians.[73] But there were ruffled feathers among officials assigned minor countries, such as "Luxemburg, Ethiopia and Liberia. . . . [They were] too foolish to realize that each of these countries has exactly as much of a vote as others with more important-sounding names."[74]

The Zionists suffered from violent mood swings. In late September it was "pessimism."[75] A fortnight later, they were buoyed by the American reiteration (on 11 October) of support for the majority recommendations, despite a last-ditch struggle against partition by the State Department. The Soviet Union followed suit two days later. "We are not dissatisfied with the results achieved [so far]," reported Eytan, but he realistically cautioned: "I realize that there is many a slip twixt the cup and the lip, and we shall not start cheering until the whistle blows."[76] On 13 November Britain announced that it would withdraw all its troops from Palestine by 1 August 1948.

It was Subcommittee One that translated the UNSCOP majority recommendations into the proposals that were approved by the General Assembly, as Resolution 181, on 29 November 1947. The prospective minorities in each state posed a major problem. The Zionists feared that the Arab minority would prefer, rather than move to the Arab state, to accept the citizenship of the Jewish state. And "we are interested in less Arabs who will be citizens of the Jewish state," said Golda Myerson (Meir), acting head of the Jewish Agency Political Department. Yitzhak Gruenbaum, a member of the Jewish Agency Executive and head of its Labor Department, thought that Arabs who remained in the Jewish state but were citizens of the Arab state would constitute "a permanent irredenta." Ben-Gurion thought that the Arabs remaining in the Jewish state, whether citizens of the Arab or Jewish state, would constitute an irredenta—and in the event of war, they would become a "Fifth Column." If they are citizens of the Arab state, argued Ben-Gurion, "[we] would be able to expel them," but if they were citizens of the Jewish state, "we will be able only to jail them. And it is better to expel them than jail them." So it was better not to facilitate their receipt of Jewish state citizenship. But Ben-Gurion feared that they would prefer this citizenship. Eliʿezer Kaplan, the Jewish Agency's treasurer, added: "Our young state will not be able to stand such a large number of strangers in its midst."[77]

Much of the lobbying and diplomacy surrounding Subcommittee One focused on the exact contours of the two states. In the end, Britain and the Arabs, assisted by the US State Department, managed to persuade the Ad Hoc Committee to reduce the size of the UNSCOP-proposed Jewish state.

The British and the State Department made vigorous efforts to consign the Negev—which the UNSCOP majority had earmarked for the Jews—to Arab sovereignty. The personal intervention of Weizmann with Truman, on 19 November, was required—as well, perhaps, as Truman's perception that the Negev represented for the Jews what "the Frontier" had represented for the Americans a century before[78]—to save the bulk of the desert for the Jews,[79] though they had to give up Beersheba and a strip of territory along the Sinai-Negev border. In addition, Jaffa was removed from the prospective Jewish state and awarded to the Arabs as a sovereign enclave. The Jews were compensated with additional territory in the Galilee. With these changes to the original UNSCOP majority plan, the prospective Jewish state was reduced to 55 percent of Palestine, with a population of some half a million Jews and an Arab minority of around 450,000. (Another hundred thousand or so Jews lived in Jerusalem, which was to be part of the international zone.)

On 26 October, Zionist officials assessed that there were twenty-three votes for partition and thirteen against.[80] Matters slightly improved by 25 November, when Subcommittee One's report was finally adopted by the Ad Hoc Committee. The vote was twenty-five for, thirteen against, and seventeen abstentions. This was still short of the necessary two-thirds majority in the General Assembly.

The numbers triggered alarm bells in Jerusalem, and the Jewish Agency Political Department, assisted by local branches of the World Zionist Organization, embarked on a world-embracing campaign to bring in the votes. The campaign proceeded along two tracks: direct Zionist lobbying to persuade individual governments and indirect efforts to persuade Washington to pressure other governments to vote for partition. Both campaigns moved into high gear on 24–25 November.

On 23 November Jamal Husseini, the AHC representative, was optimistic (though another member of the Palestinian delegation, Wasif Kamal, seemed less so when he said, "The Jews are the most cunning people among the nations of the world and on top of that they have the means. They bribed most of the delegates, but we do not have the money to bribe").[81] The British estimated that there were "twenty-five–twenty-seven votes for partition and fourteen or fifteen against it";[82] on 26 November, their estimate was "30 . . . for partition . . . [and] 15 against," but this excluded "the Siamese delegation, which has disappeared, or the Liberian, which may possibly cast its vote with the Arabs."[83] It was touch and go.

Direct Zionist lobbying focused both on the governments at home and the delegations in New York, and a range of arguments, incentives, and disincentives were brought to bear. The underlying argument was the two-thousand-year history of Jewish suffering and statelessness, culminating in the Holocaust, and the international community's responsibility to make amends.

The Zionists faced a major challenge in the twenty-member Latin American bloc, the United Nations' largest, where the anti-Zionist influences of the Catholic Church—the Vatican opposed partition and Jewish state-hood—and local Arab and German communities were strong, and where anti-American feeling, which affected attitudes to Zionism, was widespread, though the regimes themselves were dependent on and aligned with Washington. During April–May, the Latin Americans appeared to support the Zionist cause, or so it seemed to Jewish Agency officials. But by October, many were wavering or even antagonistic, due, the Zionists believed, to "a very intensive campaign [by the Arabs "and their friends" of] . . . commercial pressure, diplomatic pressure, bribery"[84] and to apparent US irresolution. Of the bloc, only "five or six" were definitely for partition, and two, Argentina and Cuba, were "committed" on the Arab side. Of the remaining thirteen, about half were leaning toward partition, and the rest were "inclined to abstain."[85]

In the Ad Hoc Committee vote of 25 November six Latin American countries abstained, Paraguay absented itself, and one (Cuba) voted against, as against twelve "ayes." In the following days, the Zionist directed their efforts toward the recalcitrant countries' UN representatives, who seem largely to have been left to their own devices on the Palestine question.[86]

Pecuniary considerations apparently affected the votes of one or two Latin American ambassadors (though documentation in this regard is hard to find). According to reports, one Latin American delegation voted for partition after receiving seventy-five thousand dollars; another, perhaps Costa Rica, turned down a forty-five-thousand-dollar bribe but nonetheless voted for partition.[87] More telling, apparently, were promises and threats directed at individual governments by American Jewish businessmen and politicians. Apparently prominent in this lobbying effort was Samuel Zemurray, head of the United Fruit Corporation, which had large plantations in the Carribean.[88]

One of the most vocal pro-Zionist ambassadors to the United Nations was Jorge García Granados, the Guatemalan; he had led the pro-partition camp in UNSCOP and, during the General Assembly meeting, had lobbied his fellow Latin Americans relentlessly. The British believed that he was "receiving money from American-Jewish organizations" and alleged that he was "living extravagantly at the Waldorf Astoria Hotel."[89] American diplomats had reported that Granados enjoyed "'a beautiful friendship' with a Jewess named 'Emma.'"[90] Perhaps these reports were true. But he also, as he put it in his memoirs, believed in "the justice and historic necessity" of the creation of a Jewish state.[91]

The black African vote—Ethiopia and Liberia—was also important. Zionist officials in Britain approached Lorna Wingate, the widow of Orde Wingate. During the late 1930s, Orde Wingate was a passionate philo-Zionist and, as a young British army captain, trained and led Haganah troops in counterinsurgency operations during the Arab Revolt in Palestine. He died in an air crash in Burma in 1944 while commanding the Chindit guerrillas against the Japanese. In between, in 1940–1941, he had led British forces that reconquered Abyssinia from the Italians and restored Ethiopian independence and the rule of Emperor Haile Selassie.[92] The emperor "owed" Wingate, and in November 1947, the Zionists decided to call in the debt. Lorna Wingate cabled Selassie: "Fate of world may well hang on United Nations Palestine decision. . . . Partition only hope of ultimate peace. . . . I cast myself before you in name of Orde Wingate to ask that you stand again in history as man of God and man of destiny."[93] In the end, Ethiopia abstained; apparently Arab threats concerning the well-being of Egypt's large Coptic minority carried the day.[94]

By contrast, Liberia was subjected to the stick. Both former US secretary of state Edward Stettinius, who headed an American-Liberian development company, and Harvey Firestone, whose Firestone Rubber Company owned plantations in Liberia and imported rubber, Liberia's main (or only) export, were mobilized to threaten a boycott unless Liberia voted for partition. Jan Smuts, prime minister and foreign minister of South Africa, was also recruited to pressure Monrovia.[95] Liberia duly switched from abstention to "aye."

India, represented on UNSCOP, was vigorously lobbied from summer 1947, even though its pro-Arab stance was stark and consistent.[96] Even Albert Einstein was mobilized. Hayim Greenberg, a member of the American Section of the JAE and a man of letters, approached the physicist and then drafted Einstein's letter to Prime Minister Jawaharlal Nehru.[97] Einstein brandished morality rather than political interests or legalisms. The Jews, he wrote, had been history's victims "for centuries." Now the United Nations was considering compensating this "pariah" nation. The Holocaust only underlined the urgent need for a sovereign Jewish state. And this would not infringe on the rights of others—because the Jews would bring material benefit to their Arab neighbors, as they had in the past. In any event, the Arabs held sway or were assured sovereignty in over 99 percent of the areas liberated from the Turks in World War I; it was only moral that the Jews receive the remaining sliver of land in which they had once been sovereign, as Nehru well knew (Nehru in his years in a British prison had written a history of the world). "In the august scale of justice, which weighs need against need, there is no doubt as to whose [need] is more heavy," wrote Einstein.

Nehru responded with both realpolitik and ethics. He asserted that in India there was "the deepest sympathy for the great suffering of the Jewish people." But "national policies are unfortunately essentially selfish policies.

Each country thinks of its own interest first"—and India's interests, he implied, necessitated siding with the Arabs. But he added that in Palestine the conflict was between two sets of "rights," and he was not convinced that Jewish aspirations could be fulfilled without impinging on Arab rights. He declined to embrace Jewish statehood.[98]

During September–November, Zionist officials repeatedly met Indian diplomats and journalists at the United Nations; they were still eager to convert the giant of the subcontinent. Vijayalakshmi Pandit, Nehru's sister, who headed the delegation, occasionally threw out hints that something might change. But Shertok was brought down to earth by historian Kavalam Panikkar, another member of the Indian delegation: "It is idle for you to try to convince us that the Jews have a case. . . . We know it. . . . But the point is simply this: For us to vote for the Jews means to vote against the Moslems. This is a conflict in which Islam is involved. . . . We have 13 million [sic] Moslems in our midst. . . . Therefore, we cannot do it."[99] In a sign of the panic that overtook the Zionist leadership at the eleventh hour, one further effort was made to "convert" India. On 27 November Weizmann cabled Nehru that rejection of partition would spur the Palestinians to war: "[I] cannot understand how India can wish [to] obstruct such [a fair two-state] settlement," he argued.[100] But India would not budge.

China was also wooed, and perhaps Zionist lobbying contributed to the shift from outright rejection of partition to what Silver called "benevolent neutrality."[101] In the end, China abstained. The Chinese ambassador to the United Nations, V. K. Wellington Koo, though sympathetic to Zionism, explained: "[China] has her own difficulties. . . . The Chinese Republic . . . [has] twenty million Moslems many of whose leaders hold important positions in Nanking and throughout China."[102]

Nor, through most of October–November, was Western Europe, from the Zionist viewpoint, in the bag. "Our last hope is France," said Jamal Husseini, the AHC representative in New York, a few days before the crucial vote.[103] France was to remain a major Zionist headache until the last minute. And its vote, it was understood, would influence that of Belgium, Holland, Luxembourg, and Denmark. France had to take account of its traditional alliance with Britain and the sixteen million Muslims under its rule in North Africa.[104] And the winds from the Vatican affected French thinking. Initial French utterances did not bode well. True, France had helped the Zionists in the Exodus Affair. But Paul Ramadier, the French prime minister, told Zionist officials who came to lobby him in August that "Britain was in serious difficulties" and that the Arab League was "a force to be reckoned with [and France 'could not ignore the Arab population within the French Union']. . . . He wondered whether some interim arrangement might not be made. After all, there were two ways of getting the Jews to Palestine—the way of Moses and the way of Esther [to which Berl Locker, the chief Zionist interlocutor, replied that 'as far as he knew, Esther did not lead the Jews to Palestine']." Perhaps a "suitable country" could be found for Europe's Jewish DPs "within the French Union," Ramadier suggested.[105]

Weizmann gave the French UN delegation a persuasive pep talk in New York on 25 September. But pro-Arab French officials and a stream of anti-partition cables from the French consulate in Jerusalem and the French Legation in Damascus dampened its effect[106]—and, in any case, the matter was to be decided in the French cabinet.

By October, France's position had crystallized into abstention. One Zionist official reported from Paris that "the chances of changing the position of the French Foreign Ministry were very slim."[107] But the key lay with the cabinet. The Zionists, spearheaded by Weizmann, mobilized Léon Blum, the former prime minister and elder statesman of French socialism, to lobby the government.[108] The fall of the Socialist-led Ramadier administration and its replacement on 19 November by one led by Robert Schuman, with a Socialist minority, only aggravated matters. France abstained on 25 November in the Ad Hoc Committee. But intense Zionist lobbying, and pangs of Holocaust-related conscience, at last persuaded the cabinet the following day to instruct Alexandre Parodi, the head of the French UN delegation, to vote "aye."

According to British diplomats, it was the threat of resignation by three members of the cabinet—Finance Minister René Mayer, Labor Minister Daniel Meyer, and Interior Minister Jules Moch—buttressed by their announcement that American Jewry would organize a congressional campaign against continued US economic aid to France should it abstain, that clinched the decision, causing "consternation in the Quai d'Orsay" and prompting Parodi to ask the General Assembly, on 28 November, for a twenty-four-hour delay in the voting, a hiatus in which he sought, and failed, "to get the instructions reversed."[109] The delay, which caused palpitations among the Zionists, who feared that the two-thirds majority they believed they had in hand would slip away, was misinterpreted by them as stemming from machinations initiated by Harold Beeley and the Arab camp.[110]

Belgium, Holland, and Luxembourg also caused the Zionists unease—until they finally voted "aye." From September through November they had "adopted the attitude that they would vote for [partition] only if America, England and France would vote for it."[111] Less than two weeks before the vote, the Luxembourg delegate said that his government had given him complete freedom of action and that he intended to vote against partition; the Arabs had persuaded him that "partition would lead to the outbreak of war."[112] The Belgian government, with Paul-Henri Spaak at its head, generally favored partition—or so Spaak told Zionist officials. But he was under strong pressure, in the contrary direction, from his UN delegation and from the country's Catholic Party. As well, there were fears for the future of Belgian commercial interests in Arab countries, especially Egypt, and a desire not to offend Britain.[113] But Spaak seems to have cut his sail according to each interlocutor. On 26 November he told the British ambassador, George Rendel, that he was unhappy with partition, which would lead to war. Moreover, he disapproved of the American and Soviet position in favor of partition coupled with an unwillingness to provide forces to implement it. And yet, that was the only ballgame in town—so how could Belgium abstain? He asked Rendel for "advice," and the ambassador, "purely personally," recommended abstention. More formally, London declined to offer advice and added high-mindedly that it deprecated attempts by any power "to influence others."[114]

Holland referred to the problem posed by "her [Muslim] population of 16 million"—in Indonesia—but assured the Zionists that it would stick to its UNSCOP representative's pro-partition position.[115] Speaking of all three Benelux countries, a Zionist diplomat concluded, after the vote: "Their affirmative vote at the end came with some relief."[116]

Britain itself decided to abstain[117]—and indeed, in the final days before the vote instructed its diplomats to refrain from influencing other countries one way or another. But without doubt British diplomats around the globe, and especially in New York, "privately" advised various countries on the best course of action.

From the Zionist standpoint, the Anglo-Saxon Dominions—Canada, South Africa, Australia, and New Zealand—were an easier sell, and in the event, all four voted for partition. But it was not all smooth sailing.[118] Public opinion after the Holocaust strongly supported Jewish statehood. But the governments all had economic and political interests that militated in the opposite direction, and the traditional alignment of their foreign policies with London's seemed to indicate abstention. In June 1947 the Jewish Agency's Michael Comay discovered that the New Zealand UN deputy head of delegation, J. S. Reid, was "strongly anti-Zionist." Reid left him with the impression that "the New Zealand Legation is completely under the sway of the British Embassy." Comay was somewhat reassured by the South African minister, H. T. Andrews, who said that although "for 90% of the time, the Dominions' views roughly coincided with those of Britain," occasionally they took an independent tack and that the British "would not insist on unanimity" in the Palestine vote. London, for its part, was careful not to be seen to be "pushing" the Dominions.[119]

South Africa, with Smuts firmly at the helm, consistently championed the Zionist cause. But Australia and Canada—Australia's UNSCOP representative had abstained—were not completely firm, and New Zealand, almost down to the wire, caused the Zionists "anxiety."[120] Early on Wellington had assured the Jewish Agency that it would vote "aye."[121] But then it wavered, abstaining in the Ad Hoc Committee.[122] The alarmed Zionists dispatched a stream of telegrams, Chaim Weizmann and Henry Morgenthau, Jr., former US secretary of treasury and head of the United Jewish Appeal, writing to Prime Minister Peter Fraser and his finance minister, Walter Nash. The New Zealanders responded that in the absence of an adequate mechanism for implementation, the partition resolution would lead only to "bloodshed and chaos."[123] But in the end they, too, voted for partition.

The key, of course, was in Washington. Early on, Zionist officials commented, "Everything depends upon which way they decide to turn it."[124] Or, as AHC representative Jamal Husseini put it: "America is our greatest enemy."[125] But Washington's behavior, until the final seventy-two hours, was "never satisfactory" and "at times [downright] disheartening," reported one Zionist official. The Americans had waited weeks before publicly endorsing the UNSCOP majority report and in the Ad Hoc subcommittees "were the delegation most insistent on changes to our detriment." At the General Assembly, the American refusal to pressure other countries "did us great damage." The climax of this "policy of indifference" was on 26 November, when Greece, the Philippines, and Haiti, all "completely dependent on Washington—suddenly came out one after another against its declared policy." It was only then, after frantic Jewish lobbying, that Washington "exerted itself to rally support and the situation improved. . . . It was only in the last 48 hours . . . that we really got the full backing of the United States."[126]

From September, the Jewish Agency began applying pressure, directly and through American Jewish organizations and prominent public figures, on Washington to firm up its commitment to partition and to persuade its allies to fall into line. The Zionists were fairly certain that Truman and the White House would stay the course, but they worried about members of the American UN delegation and, even more, about certain State Department officials in Washington: "Men like [Loy] Henderson [director of State's Office of Near Eastern and African Affairs] and those behind him are *momzerim* [bastards] of the first order," as Dr. Abba Hillel Silver, chairman of the American Zionist Emergency Council, put it.[127] Another *bête noire* was State's Arabist George Wadsworth, a former ambassador to Iraq—"[our] bitterest enemy . . . a slinky, suave man," as Rose Halprin, a member of the JAE, put it.[128]

During September–early October, and despite Secretary of State George C.

Marshall's endorsement on 17 September of the majority report, Zionist hearts fluttered. With some State Department officials still privately proclaiming opposition to partition, the Americans projected irresolution—certainly in all that related to partition's implementation—and this sowed irresolution among the other delegations.[129]

Once Marshall had publicly endorsed partition, the Jewish Agency began pressing Washington to push or at least nudge other countries in the same direction. "I am not suggesting that the United States should convert itself into a steamroller and flatten them all out," Shertok told Henderson. But "a friendly word spoken in good time by United States representatives can do a great deal and can decide the issue." Shertok gave Henderson a list of Latin American governments he thought the United States should speak to.[130]

The United States maintained that it was "canvassing discreetly" but was avoiding any semblance of pressure so as not to put "up the backs of the other states." Or so Assistant Secretary of State Robert Lovett told Shertok.[131] Down to 25 November, the Americans declined to twist arms. Part of the explanation is that almost all the relevant State Department officials were either critical of or opposed partition. But it was also a matter of policy. As late as 24 November, Truman instructed Lovett not "to use threats or improper pressure of any kind on other Delegations to vote for the majority report."[132]

Some Zionist officials empathized with the American reluctance to twist arms. In private, several Latin American diplomats complained "very bitterly of the high-handed and brutal methods used by American[s] generally in regimenting the Latin American countries."[133] And American diplomats argued that "the US can't say you [do] this, this and this. . . . We are not in a position to say, do this."[134]

But following the Ad Hoc Committee vote of 25 November, the Zionist officials became desperate. Only a direct order from Truman, it was understood, could move the State Department—its officials in Washington and New York and its diplomats abroad—to exert real pressure. Weizmann, the Zionist big gun, was wheeled out. Twice he cabled Truman that he was beset by "grave anxiety lest [the partition] plan fail" to obtain the two-thirds majority and he reminded the president of his past "assurances" that the United States would "rally necessary support for UN endorsement partition plan." Specifically, he asked Truman to see what could be done about "France, China, Greece, Turkey, India, Siam, Philippines, Liberia, Ethiopia, Mexico, Cuba, Honduras, Nicaragua, Haiti, Paraguay, Colombia, El Salvador, Ecuador." Without at least some of these states, the resolution would not pass, he warned.[135] Weizmann also appealed directly to Secretary of State Marshall.[136]

Weizmann's intervention was probably a major contributor to the last-minute policy switch in Washington. In addition, the White House and various officials were bombarded with "letters, telegrams and telephone calls" from the American public.[137] Truman later recalled that he had never been subjected to "as much pressure and propaganda . . . as I had in this instance";[138] it had all left him "very upset."[139] On 25 November Truman's special assistant, David Niles, instructed the delegation in New York, in Truman's name, "to get all the votes they could, that there would be hell to pay if the voting went the wrong way."[140] And Niles and another presidential aide, Special Counsel Clark Clifford, appear to have intervened directly with several countries.[141] Particular pressure was put on Haiti and the Philippines (both in the end voted "aye") and Greece (which remained a "nay").

Senators and congressmen also interceded. Twenty-eight senators cabled a dozen wobbling governments to vote for partition, copies going simultaneously to the heads of the delegations to the United Nations and their representatives in Washington.[142]

Lebanon's delegate, Camille Chamoun, condemned American influence in the General Assembly as a "dark and obscure tyranny," and the Arabs were later to denounce the Zionists methods of "promising and threat, temptation and deception" in mobilizing the two-thirds majority.[143] Had the vote been taken secretly, as demanded by the Arabs, the Jews, said Iraq's leading politician Nuri Saʿid, would have won "no more than three or four votes."[144]

But the Arabs had failed to understand the tremendous impact of the Holocaust on the international community—and, in any event, appear to have used the selfsame methods, but with poor results. Wasif Kamal, an AHC official, for example, offered one delegate—perhaps the Russian—a "huge, huge sum of money to vote for the Arabs" (the Russian declined, saying, "You want me to hang myself?").[145] But the Arabs' main tactic, amounting to blackmail, was the promise or threat of war should the assembly endorse partition. As early as mid-August 1947, Fawzi al-Qawuqji—soon to be named the head of the Arab League's volunteer army in Palestine, the Arab Liberation Army (ALA)—threatened that, should the vote go the wrong way, "we will have to initiate total war. We will murder, wreck and ruin everything standing in our way, be it English, American or Jewish."[146] It would be a "holy war," the Arabs suggested, which might even evolve into "World War III." Cables to this effect poured in from Damascus, Beirut, Amman, and Baghdad during the Ad Hoc Committee deliberations, becoming "more lurid," according to Zionist officials, as the General Assembly vote drew near.[147] The Arab states generally made no bones about their intention to support the Palestinians with "men, money and arms," and sometimes hinted at an eventual invasion by their armies.[148] They also threatened the Western Powers, their traditional allies, with an oil embargo[149] and/or abandonment and realignment with the Soviet Bloc.

Zionist officials, aware of the potency of the fear of the outbreak of war, tended during September–November to pooh-pooh these threats. "There is a very great deal of bluff in it," Shertok told American Zionist leaders. "These countries have much more serious worries in their own homes than to start hazardous military operations . . . [in] Palestine. [And] the Arabs of Palestine are extremely unwilling to engage in any new adventure."[150] At the end of September, the American Zionist Emergency Council even issued a four-page memorandum analyzing, and discounting, the threats: "John D. Rockefeller would sooner turn to Stalin to ask for aid in the reduction of his income tax than Ibn Saʿud and other Arab kings would call for Soviet inter-vention in the Middle East. . . . An analysis of the military situation . . . will prove that there is no danger of any large-scale Arab attacks upon public or-der in Palestine. . . . The military potential of the different Arab-speaking states is notoriously weak. . . . Saudi Arabia's troops are picturesque horse-men. . . . It is inconceivable that any of these forces could interfere in Pales-tine without the consent and active cooperation of Great Britain. . . . Ridicu-lous is the assumption that an armed conflict between Arabs and Jews . . . would lead to World War III."[151]

But in general, until the last three days before the vote, Arab diplomats at the United Nations, and their governments, refused to believe that partition would gain a two-thirds majority and made no concerted effort to mobilize votes. Clear evidence of Arab desperation exists only for 27–29 November. The old Foreign Office Middle East hand Harold Beeley tried to orchestrate a last-minute postponement and compromise.[152] But the AHC declined to "consider . . . any concessions" after replacing their more moderate spokes-men, such as Henry Kattan, Albert Hourani, and Musa al-ʿAlami, with hard-liners.[153] And the Arab states, given the shortness of time, their varying agendas, the poor communications between New York and their capitals, and fears of being branded soft on Zionism, failed to rally around a unified proposal. The Lebanese delegate, Chamoun, independently put forward a five-point "federal" proposal based on the minority report but won no ku-dos, or agreement, from his fellow Arabs.[154] And Pakistan's delegate, For-eign Minister Muhammad Zafrulla Khan, who had led the Arab camp in the previous weeks' deliberations—"one of the ablest and most impressive dele-gates present from any country," according to a Zionist diplomat[155]—made himself scarce during those final days.[156]

One last point: delegates with no firm instructions from their govern-ments were no doubt influenced by the prevalent atmosphere in New York and Flushing Meadow, where the media broadcast "that an opponent of partition was an enemy of the American people. . . . [At Flushing Meadow the] almost exclusively Zionist audience . . . applauded declarations of support for Zionism. They hissed Arab speakers. They created the atmosphere of a football match, with the Arabs as the away team."[157]

On the afternoon of 29 November, the General Assembly presidium at last put draft Resolution 181 to the vote. The hall was packed. In alphabetical order each country was asked "yes," "no," or "abstains." The procedure was broadcast live on radio around the world. When the tally was complete, thirty-three states had votes "yes," thirteen "no," with ten abstentions.[158] Partition had narrowly passed with a two-thirds majority. The "nays" consisted of the Arab and Muslim states, Greece, Cuba, and India, the "ayes" of the United States, the Dominions, Western Europe, the Soviet Bloc, and most of Latin America. Among the abstainers had been Britain, Chile, and China. The Chilean delegate resigned in protest.[159]

Resolution 181[II] called for the partition of Palestine into two sovereign states, one Jewish, the other Arab. The Mandate was to terminate and the British pullout to be completed "not later than 1 August 1948." The two countries were to be bound in an economic "union." The Jewish state, on about 55 percent of Palestine's territory, was to consist of the bulk of the Negev, the central and northern Coastal Plain between Rehovot and Haifa, and the Jezreel and Jordan Valleys, including the Galilee Panhandle. The Arab state, on about 42 percent of Palestine, was to consist of the northwestern corner of the Negev and the southern Coastal Plain around Gaza, the hill country of Samaria and Judea as far south as Beersheba, and central and western Galilee. The Jerusalem area—including the city itself, outlying villages ('Ein Karim and Abu Dis), and Bethlehem—was designated a "*corpus separatum*," to be governed by the UN Trusteeship Council. The borders were set out in adjoining maps. The resolution provided for the establishment of a five-member "Commission," which, under "the guidance of the Security Council," would "take over and administer" the areas progressively evacuated by the British authorities. The British were specifically enjoined not to "prevent, obstruct or delay" the commission's work. The commission was to delineate and finalize the borders and help in the establishment of the two provisional governments, which would transitionally operate under the commission's supervision. The commission was also to oversee elections in the two states. The resolution assured all of access to religious sites and provided for the fair treatment of minorities.

The Zionists and their supporters rejoiced; the Arab delegations walked out of the plenum after declaring the resolution invalid.[160] The Arabs failed to understand why the international community was awarding the Jews any

The UN General Assembly partition plan, 29 November 1947

part of Palestine. Further, as one Palestinian historian later put it, they could not fathom why 37 percent of the population had been given 55 percent of the land (of which they owned only 7 percent).[161] Moreover, the Jews had been given the best agricultural lands (the Coastal Plain and Jezreel and Jordan Valleys) while the Arabs had received the "bare and hilly" parts, as one Palestinian politician, ʿAwni ʿAbd al-Hadi, told a Zionist agent.[162] More generally, "the Palestinians failed to see why they should be made to pay for the Holocaust. . . . [And] they failed to see why it was *not* fair for the Jews to be a minority in a unitary Palestinian state, while it *was* fair for almost half of the Palestinian population—the indigenous majority on its own ancestral soil—to be converted overnight into a minority under alien rule."[163]

On 2 December the ʿulema, or council of doctors of theology and sacred law, of Al-Azhar University in Cairo—one of Islam's supreme authorities—proclaimed a "worldwide jihad in defense of Arab Palestine."[164] The Arab UN delegates denounced the resolution and declared that any attempt to implement it would lead to war. Bevin described the Arab reactions to the vote as "even worse than we had expected." A particular worry of Bevin's was the safety of the hundreds of thousands Jews scattered around the Arab world, and particularly the hundred thousand Jews of Baghdad, who were at "risk of having their throats cut."[165]

Ben-Gurion, too, believed that war would ensue. But still, he argued: "I know of no greater achievement by the Jewish people . . . in its long history since it became a people."[166] Though the Arabs could not, or refused to, see it, Resolution 181, besides geopolitically redesigning a sliver of eastern Mediterranean coastline, was an emphatic ethical statement, one of those crossroads in history where morality and realism come together. Or as one Jewish historian later put it: "[It was] Western civilization's gesture of repentance for the Holocaust . . . the repayment of a debt owed by those nations that realized that they might have done more to prevent or at least limit the scale of Jewish tragedy during World War II."[167] Viewed in the longer span, the vote represented humanity's amends for two thousand years of humiliation and persecution—both by the Christian and Islamic worlds—of the Jews, the world's eternally stateless people, the world's eternal minority. This was the point made by the Jews of Rome when they celebrated the UN decision on 1 December beside Titus's Arch, "the symbol of our destruction 1877 years ago."[168] The Zionists had managed to obtain an international warrant for a small piece of earth for the Jewish people; it remained to translate the warrant into statehood.

When the Arab UN delegates threatened war if partition was endorsed they knew what they were talking about.

In May 1946, a summit of Arab heads of state at Inshas, Egypt, resolved that Palestine must remain "Arab" and that Zionism "constituted a threat not only to Palestine but to the other Arab states and to all the peoples of Islam."[169] The following month, at the special Arab League meeting at Bludan, Syria, the delegates, alongside a public rejection of the recommendations of the Anglo-American Committee and a demand for the cessation of all Jewish immigration to Palestine, secretly decided to help the Palestinian Arabs with funds, arms, and volunteers should it come to an armed struggle.[170] The League demanded independence for Palestine as a "unitary" state, with an Arab majority and minority rights for the Jews. The AHC went one better and insisted that the proportion of Jews to Arabs in the unitary state should stand at one to six, meaning that only Jews who lived in Palestine before the British Mandate be eligible for citizenship.[171]

At Inshas and Bludan, as in the get-togethers that were to follow, the Arab leaders were driven by internal and interstate considerations as well as by a genuine concern for the fate of Palestine. All the regimes, none of them elected, suffered from a sense of illegitimacy and, hence, vulnerability. All the leaders, or almost all (Jordan's ʿAbdullah was the sole exception), lived in perpetual fear of the "street," which could be aroused against them by opposition parties, agitators, or fellow leaders, claiming that they were "selling out" Palestine. As Shertok quoted the Syrian UN delegate Faris al-Khouri as saying in October 1947, the Arab states know they "may be heading for a disaster but they have no choice. They are committed up to the hilt vis-à-vis their own public. The position of all these governments was very weak. They were all tottering; they were all unpopular." They had no choice but to adopt a "firm, unequivocal, uncompromising attitude" on Palestine.[172]

The interstate feuding was in large measure fuelled by expansionist ambitions and real or imagined fears of others' expansionist ambitions. Throughout his reign, Prince, later King, ʿAbdullah had sought to establish a "Greater Syria" (comprising today's Israel–Palestine, Lebanon, Syria, and Jordan) under his aegis. The heads of the newborn Republic of Syria also hoped to establish a similarly contoured "Greater Syria"—but ruled from Damascus. The Lebanese Christians lived in perpetual fear of a Muslim, and Syrian, takeover (as, in fact, gradually occurred after summer 1976). ʿAbdullah (and the Hashemite royal house of Iraq) also harbored a deep-seated grudge, and expansionist ambitions, vis-à-vis King Ibn Saʿud, who had supplanted the Hashemites in Hijaz. Moreover, ʿAbdullah often talked of "uniting" Jordan and Iraq (again, under his tutelage). For their part, the Saudis regarded Jordan covetously, as did the Egyptians Sudan and, occasionally, southern Palestine. In general, the postwar Arab Middle East was divided into two loosely aligned and antagonistic blocs, one comprising Egypt, Syria, and Saudi Arabia, the other Jordan and Iraq. The internal Arab League arguments during 1946–1948 tended to follow this coalitional divide (though, on Palestine, the lines of demarcation often blurred, with Iraq and Syria usually taking a harder tack and Egypt and Saudi Arabia pressing for caution).[173]

All the Arab leaders distrusted and, in some cases (notably King ʿAbdullah), hated AHC leader Haj Amin al-Husseini and opposed the establishment of an al-Husseini-led Palestinian Arab state; al-Husseini was seen as an inveterate liar and schemer. The mufti, for his part, reciprocated ʿAbdullah's feelings and distrusted the other Arab leaders, suspecting them of seeking to partition Palestine among themselves.

With the approach of the UN General Assembly deliberations in autumn 1947, Arab thinking grew more focused and military. The League's Political Committee met in Sofar, Lebanon, on 16–19 September, and urged the Palestine Arabs to fight partition, which it called "aggression," "without mercy." The League promised them, in line with Bludan, assistance "in manpower, money and equipment" should the United Nations endorse partition. Indeed, warned the committee, the Arab states themselves "would be forced to take decisive action"; the governments, explained the committee, "would be unable to suppress the turbulent passions of their people resulting from the wrong that would be done them [by the passage of the partition resolution] and sit still."[174] (The fear of the Arab "street" would figure prominently in the decision-making of most of the Arab regimes as they inched toward the invasion of May 1948.) Secretly, the Political Committee recommended—at Iraq's urging[175]—that a "technical committee," immediately renamed the Military Committee, be established by the League to oversee the material assistance to the Palestinians. A million pounds were earmarked for the Palestinian Arabs' struggle.[176] In another secret decision, the committee instructed the League's members "to open the gates . . . to receive children, women and old people [from Palestine] and to support them in the event of disturbances breaking out in Palestine and compelling some of its Arab population to leave the country."[177] The Political Committee's decisions were then endorsed by the Arab heads of state, meeting as the League Council, at Aley, in Lebanon, in the second week of October. (The idea of a mass evacuation from Palestine may already have been doing the rounds among Arab decision-makers more than a year before. ʿAzzam reportedly [or mis-reportedly] declared in May 1946 that "Arab circles proposed to evacuate all Arab women and children from Palestine and send them to neighbouring countries, to declare 'Jehad' and to consider Palestine a war zone.")[178]

Meanwhile, the Military Committee, consisting of representatives of Iraq, Syria, Lebanon, and the AHC, began functioning under the chairmanship of

Ismail Safwat, an out-of-work Iraqi general described (somewhat unfairly) by the British ambassador in Baghdad as a "typically . . . old-fashioned Turkish officer, extremely brave and unutterably stupid."[179] Safwat submitted a prescient preliminary report to the League Council on 9 October. He asserted that the Zionists in Palestine were well organized politically, administratively, and militarily, and well armed, and the poorly organized and poorly equipped Palestinians "could not withstand them." The 350,000 Arabs living "in isolated villages and pockets" in the areas earmarked for Jewish sovereignty were facing "destruction." He recommended that the Arab states immediately mobilize, equip, and train volunteers, deploy forces along Palestine's borders, and set up a "general Arab command" that would control all the Arab military forces inside and around Palestine; supply the Palestinian Arabs, as a first stage, with "no less than 10,000 rifles," and machine guns and grenades; and give the Military Committee one million pounds and provide it with officers and noncommissioned officers who could train the volunteers. He also recommended that the Arab states purchase additional weapons for the forces that would be engaged in Palestine.[180]

The Arab states failed to set up a "general command" to run the prospective war, leaving the supervision of the assistance to the Palestinians in the hands of the Military Committee. But in line with the committee's recommendations, the League Council secretly resolved that the member states "take military measures," meaning mass troops along the frontiers to intimidate and deter the United Nations and the Great Powers from endorsing partition.[181] During late October–November the Syrians and Egyptians duly deployed several thousand soldiers near the borders, the Syrian "exercises" along the Jaulan (Golan) slightly alarming the British; indeed, a small Syrian force actually crossed the border near Dan, probably inadvertently, on 20 October and was promptly driven back by British troops (without casualties).[182]

More significantly, the council endorsed the Military Committee's recommendations regarding the mobilization and training of volunteers and the equipping of the Palestinians. Registration offices were set up in the Arab states under the auspices of local committees "for the defense of Palestine," and a training camp was organized by the Syrian army at Qatana, near Damascus. In November, hundreds of volunteers, mainly from Syria, Iraq, and Palestine, arrived. During the following weeks, some of the trainees, organized in platoon and company formations, were sent off to Palestine's towns to bolster local militias. But most of the volunteers were organized as an embryonic "army," the Arab Liberation (or Salvation) Army (*al-Jaish al-Inqadh*)—a name apparently coined by Syrian president al-Quwwatli, the army's patron and founder—to be commanded by Fawzi al-Qawuqji. Al-

Quwwatli was driven at least partly by a desire to offset a prospective Hashemite takeover of Palestine, suspecting that this would be only a stage in realizing King ʿAbdullah's vision of a "Greater Syria" with Amman as its capital. Egypt and the Saudis, too, were no doubt driven to support al-Qawuqji's appointment and the formation of the ALA from similar anti-Jordanian considerations.[183]

The Tripoli-born al-Qawuqji had served as an officer in the Ottoman army, had participated in the Druze revolt against the French Mandate authorities in 1925–1927, and in 1936 had led a band of several hundred volunteers, mainly from Iraq and Syria, who assisted the Palestine Arabs in their revolt against the British Mandate. He had well-established anti-imperialist credentials. In 1941 he had resurfaced in Rashid ʿAli al-Kilani's Iraqi rebellion against the British and, with the rebellion's demise, had removed to Berlin, where he had sat out the war serving the Nazis by recruiting Muslim volunteers and broadcasting German propaganda. After the war, he returned to Syria and, early in December 1947, was appointed to command the ALA. The appointment was endorsed by the League at its meeting in Cairo in the second week of December—though, somewhat contradictorily (probably to appease the Iraqis and Jordanians), the League also designated Safwat "commander of the national forces," meaning all the local Arabs and foreign volunteers fighting in Palestine.[184] In effect, al-Qawuqji ended up in full command of the ALA—its training and operations—and the local Palestinian Arab commanders (ʿAbd al-Qadir al-Husseini, Hassan Salame, and others) ended up commanding the various local militias. Safwat was left with a more or less nominal role advising the Arab League on the progress of the war.

Haj Amin al-Husseini was forever turning up uninvited at Arab League summit meetings. Through September–November 1947 he had demanded that the League establish a Palestinian government-in-exile with himself at its head. The League, advised by veteran Palestinian activists (including ʿIzzat Darwaza and Subhi al-Khidra, sometime members of Safwat's Military Committee),[185] rebuffed him, as it did his demand that his cousin, ʿAbd al-Qadir al-Husseini, be appointed overall commander of forces in Palestine. Haj Amin had bitterly opposed al-Qawuqji's appointment, mindful of 1936, when al-Qawuqji had contested his leadership of the revolt. In Berlin, the mufti had apparently vilified al-Qawuqji as a "British agent."[186] The two hated each other, and the continuing animosity was significantly to contribute to undermining the Palestinian Arab war effort in 1948.[187] The militia forces raised by, and aligned with, the Husseinis during the first months of the 1948 War were to operate without coordination with, and often at cross-purposes to, the ALA.

During the League deliberations of September–October 1947, the Iraqis appear to have been the most militant of the member states, "breathing brimstone for home consumption."[188] They called for the Arab states to intervene in Palestine even before the Mandate ended. The Egyptians and Saudis led the moderate camp, reluctant to get involved in a war for which they were unready and whose outcome was unpredictable.[189] They also suspected that a Jordanian or Jordanian-Iraqi invasion would be geared to territorial aggrandizement and nothing else. The League took no operational decisions.

The UN vote on 29 November changed all that. The Arab leaders were now called upon—each by his conscience and his peers and all by internal opposition factions and the "street"—to put their money where their mouths were. Already before the UN vote, Arab politicians had warned that "if a satisfactory solution of the Palestine case was not reached, severe measures should be taken against all Jews in Arab countries."[190] On 24 November the head of the Egyptian delegation to the General Assembly, Muhammad Hussein Heykal, said that "the lives of 1,000,000 Jews in Moslem countries would be jeopardized by the establishment of a Jewish state."[191]

With the passage of the UN resolution, the Arab "street," given its head, spoke unequivocally. There were massive demonstrations in cities across the Middle East and North Africa. In Cairo, there were daily protests, with "riffraff" quickly joining secondary school students. They vandalized European shops and cafés. But police prevented the mob from storming the Jewish Quarter.[192] On 4 December police fired on mobs in Cairo and Mansoura[193] before the government finally banned all demonstrations.[194] In Damascus, the demonstrators called for "Jihad" and arms; the prime minister "promised" that the government would "comply and be in the forefront of the liberation of Palestine."[195] "The Syrian Government were [sic] largely responsible for organizing and directing the demonstrations . . . [making] use of agents amongst the teachers, the Ulema [the religious authorities], the Ikhwan al Muslimeen [Muslim Brotherhood], and the leaders of the various city quarters," the British concluded.[196] Damage was done to the American and French legation buildings.[197] The Syrian Muslim Brotherhood denounced the UN decision, called for volunteers for Palestine and contributions, and announced that "it is a . . . battle either for life or death to a nation of 70 million souls . . . whom the vilest, the most corrupt, tricky and destructive people wish to conquer and displace."[198]

In some Arab states, the regimes—while issuing inflammatory statements—kept the mobs in check. But where the reins were loosed, or where the police joined the rioters, there was bloody mayhem. In pogroms in British-ruled Aden and the Sheikh Othman refugee camp outside the city, seventy-five Jews were murdered, seventy-eight were wounded, and dozens of homes, shops, and synagogues and two schools were torched during 2–4 December by Arabs and local Yemeni levies before British troops restored order.[199] Dozens of Jewish homes and a synagogue were also destroyed or looted, one woman was killed, and sixty-seven Jews were injured in rioting on 2 December in Bahrain.[200] In Aleppo, Syria, there was widespread anti-Jewish rioting on 30 November and 1 December, with dozens of houses, including the town's synagogues and Jewish schools, being torched. It is unclear how many Jews, if any, were injured or killed;[201] three thousand reportedly fled to Beirut.[202] In Damascus, Jews were set upon, as were nationals of Western states identified with the UN decision.[203] In Egypt, mobs torched the British Institute in Zagazig and attacked the British consulate general and Anglican cathedral in Cairo.[204]

The Arab governments weighed and responded to the partition resolution at the League Political Committee meeting in Cairo in the second week of December. Hostilities between the Arab and Jewish communities in Palestine had already begun. Five prime ministers, of Egypt, Iraq, Syria, Lebanon, and Jordan, attended. On the table was Safwat's second report, of 27 November, a thorough analysis of the military situation. Safwat bluntly concluded that "a victory over the Jews was not possible . . . by means of [armed] bands and irregulars alone. Therefore regular forces must be thrown into the battle, trained and equipped with the best weapons, who will be assisted by Palestinian [Arab] bands. . . . Because the Arab states lack sufficient means for a long war, everything must be done to assure that the war in Palestine will be over as quickly as possible."[205]

The Iraqi delegation, backed by Safwat, proposed that the regular Arab armies intervene, to "save Palestine," even before the British departed and the Jews proclaimed a state. The Iraqi prime minister's aides privately pointed to the "street" and explained that had the prime minister taken a "more reasonable line," it was doubtful whether he could have survived "for more than five minutes."[206] The clear-eyed prime minister of Lebanon, Riad al-Sulh, reportedly "very depressed," told British diplomats that "public opinion in Arab countries was so strong that it would be impossible for any Government to prevent volunteers coming to assist the Arabs [in Palestine] once serious fighting had begun."[207] The Egyptian foreign minister, Khashaba Pasha, said the same—but added, perhaps with a touch of humor, that the "elements who would volunteer [for Palestine] were those among whom excitability was greatest and it was better for the sake of law and order in Egypt that they should be out of the country."[208]

Al-Husseini, who was left out of the deliberations, was well informed—and deeply unhappy with Safwat's proposal for external military intervention. He believed (or at least argued) that Palestine's Arabs could take care of themselves. He feared that such intervention would result in shunting Palestine's Arabs—and himself—aside and provide an opportunity for land grabs by Jordan, Syria, and Egypt.[209] (He was, of course, right.)

Less hotheaded than the other Arab leaders and more reluctant to anger London, the Jordanians favored intervention—principally Jordanian intervention—but only after the British left. The Syrians were (rightly) suspicious that Jordan intended to annex Palestine or part of it. The other member states demurred, the Saudis and Egyptians leading the opposition. But the Egyptians announced that they themselves lacked the means to intervene.

In the end, the Arab League proved unable to agree on a clear goal for the unofficial war or to define a strategy by which it might be won. Instead, the leaders decided on something more modest. The League vowed, in very general language, "to try to stymie the partition plan and prevent the establishment of a Jewish state in Palestine," and the member states pledged to give the Palestine Arabs ten thousand rifles (Jordan and Lebanon a thousand each, and Syria, Iraq, Saudi Arabia, and Egypt two thousand each, each rifle to be supplied with five hundred bullets) as well as other light weapons. In addition, three thousand volunteers were to be trained in Syria by 15 January 1948. The League promised an additional million pounds for the war effort.[210] British observers commented that although some Arab leaders were eager to avoid conflict, "popular feeling" was such that they were "convinced, probably with considerable justification, that if they accepted [a compromise] solution, their positions, and possibly in some cases their lives, would be most insecure."[211] But the prime ministers were also driven by a desire to avoid a clash with the British and by the knowledge that they were not yet prepared for war. "The mood of the prime ministers was desperate rather than gasconading," stated one British intelligence report. Yet the Arab leaders were certain that the Jews would not make do with the area allotted them and were uplifted by the support they were receiving "not only from the Moslem world . . . but from Arab sympathizers, and anti-Jews in many countries."[212]

The prime ministers agreed to help the Palestine Arabs but understood that they could not solve the problem on their own. The question in Cairo was not really whether the Arab states would go to war but when and how. The emergent, vague consensus was that they would have to march when the Mandate ended, in mid-May 1948. This was implied in Iraqi foreign minister Jamali's query to officials in Whitehall: "What would be the attitude of HM Government if the Arab States sent their armies into Palestine on the termination of the mandate? The assumption would be that the [Arab] armies would occupy the whole of Palestine, but without molesting the Jews."[213]

The Arab get-togethers from Bludan onward had been marked by disunity, mutual suspicion, and cross-purposes. The antagonisms and suspicions undermined any hope of firm, realistic decision-making in the League councils. At the same time, in order not to appear weak-kneed and hesitant, moderate rulers—such as ʿAbdullah—allowed themselves to be pressed into extremist policies (or at least utterances), lest they be seen as insufficiently zealous. All paid lip service to Arab unity and the Palestine Arab cause, and all opposed partition. But all were at a loss about how to prevent it. Most, though they could not admit it to the others (or, perhaps, to themselves), knew that their armies were weak. Egypt and Jordan's military commanders estimated that the Haganah would prove formidable; other Arabs may have been more optimistic. One thing was clear, however: there could be no intervention so long as the British were in Palestine. None wished to fight the British, with whom most were aligned and who all understood were too powerful to challenge.

Still, having committed themselves to oppose partition, the Arab leaders felt they had to do something. The public bluster, the fear of their own populations whom they had helped whip up with militant rhetoric into a frenzy, and the pressure of fellow Arab politicians and leaders all combined to egg them on. The Arab states had embarked on a course leading to war. What remained to be seen was who exactly would take part and how it would all end.

The British response to the UN resolution was formulated at the cabinet meeting of 4 December 1947 on the basis of a joint memorandum submitted by the foreign and colonial secretaries. Whitehall had begun to plan the withdrawal—a vast logistical and political enterprise, given the hundred thousand Britons in the Mandate's military forces and civilian bureaucracies and the more than a quarter of a million tons of stores and ammunition and fourteen thousand vehicles[214]—soon after Bevin's withdrawal announcement of February 1947. Britain had been impoverished by the world war (indeed, by the two world wars), and a pullout had become "an economic as well as a political and ethical imperative."[215] Maintaining the army and police in Palestine had cost the Labour government more than two hundred million pounds sterling in the eighteen months after it assumed office.[216] Starting in June 1947, military manpower in Palestine was gradually reduced, the numbers declining from seventy-eight thousand to fifty-five thousand by 1 December. The rest would be gradually withdrawn during the following months.

The planning and pace of the withdrawal needs to be viewed against the dual backdrop of developments in Palestine and the international arena. Bevin regarded the UNSCOP majority report of 1 September 1947 as unjust and immoral. He promptly decided that Britain would not attempt to impose it on the Arabs; indeed, he expected them to resist its implementation. The publication of the report significantly invigorated British planning for the withdrawal. The army argued that it would need a minimum of eighteen months.[217] But the international political momentum was inexorable, and in October the British authorities began hurriedly to plan the wind-down of the Mandate. The UN partition resolution had stipulated 1 August 1948 as the deadline for both the termination of the Mandate and the completion of the military withdrawal. The British cabinet went one better: in the meeting on 4 December 1947 it resolved that the Mandate would end on 15 May and the withdrawal would be completed by 1 August.

But the cabinet decision added a fatal twist to its apparent conformity to international will. It decided, in a sop to the Arabs, to refrain from aiding the enforcement of the UN resolution, meaning the partition of Palestine. And in an important secret corollary, in line with the recommendation of the foreign and colonial secretaries, it agreed that Britain would do all in its power to delay until early May the arrival in Palestine of the UN (Implementation) Commission.[218] The Foreign Office immediately informed the commission "that it would be intolerable for the Commission to begin to exercise its authority while the [Mandate] Palestine Government was still administratively responsible for Palestine." Britain asked—in effect, it was an order—that the commission delay its arrival until "May 1st."[219]

This sealed the commission's fate and nullified any possibility of an orderly implementation of the partition resolution. Though an "Advanced Party" of the commission arrived in Palestine at the start of March 1948, the commission itself never reached the country or functioned. British hostility, Arab boycott, and the descent of the country into full-scale civil war assured that the partition resolution would not be implemented and that the commission would be redundant. The Advanced Party, headed by Spanish diplomat Pablo de Azcárate, was effectively isolated in a house in the British-guarded security zone near the King David Hotel, with its two secretaries forced to do the cooking and cleaning. The British made their stay "as uncomfortable . . . as possible."[220] The Jewish Agency's liaison officer to the commission, Walter Eytan, reported that "the poor man [Azcárate] simply did not know where to turn."[221] Azcárate spent the following weeks meeting with British and Jewish officials (Arabs refused to see him), but to no purpose. On 14 May, with the conditions on the ground radically transformed, the commission was formally disbanded by the General Assembly. Azcárate had spent most of late April and early May trying to assist the UN (Consular) Truce Commission, appointed by the UN Security Council on 23 April, to achieve a ceasefire. The Truce Commission proved as effective as the Implementation Commission.

3

The First Stage of the Civil War, November 1947–March 1948

THE WAR BEGINS

David Shaltiel, the commander of the HIS, wrote on the night of 29 November: "None of us knows what may happen tomorrow."[1] For months, the Yishuv had vaguely expected war, but at some ill-defined point in the future. The prevalent view in the HIS was that the Arab states were disunited and the Arabs of Palestine unprepared; they would not go to war on the passage of the partition resolution.[2]

The night of 29–30 November passed in the Yishuv's settlements in noisy public rejoicing. Most had sat glued to their radio sets broadcasting live from Flushing Meadow. A collective cry of joy went up when the two-thirds mark was achieved: a state had been sanctioned by the international community. The young poured into the streets and danced and celebrated around bonfires through the night. In the National Institutions compound in Jerusalem, Golda Myerson (Meir), acting director of the JA Political Department (Moshe Shertok was in New York), addressed the crowd from the balcony: "For two thousand years we have waited for our deliverance. Now that it is here it is so great and wonderful that it surpasses human words. Jews, *mazel tov* [good luck]."[3]

But some, like Yosef Nahmani, a veteran of Hashomer and a Tiberias city councilor, were more sober. That night, the celebrants carried him aloft through the streets of the lakeside town. But in his diary he jotted down: "In my heart there was joy mixed with sadness: joy that the peoples [of the world] had at last acknowledged that we were a nation with a state, and sadness that we lost half the country, Judea and Samaria, and, in addition, that we [would] have [in our state] 400,000 Arabs."[4] Nahmani's friend from the Second ʿAliya, Ben-Gurion, was also gloomy, but for another reason: "I could not dance, I could not sing that night. I looked at them so happy dancing and I could only think that they were all going to war."[5]

Not far from each celebrating throng was an Arab village or neighborhood. There the mood was grim. What the Palestinian Arab national movement, backed by the surrounding Arab societies and states, had for decades tried to stymie, what Palestine's Arabs had most feared, had now come to pass.

At 8:20 am on 30 November 1947, an eight-man Jaffa-based armed band, led by Seif al-Din Abu Kishk, ambushed a Jewish bus in the Coastal Plain near Kfar Syrkin, killing five and wounding others. Half an hour later the gunmen let loose at a second bus, southbound from Hadera, killing two more. Later that morning, Arab snipers began to fire from Jaffa's Manshiya neighborhood into southern Tel Aviv, killing at least one person. These were the first dead of the 1948 War. Shots were also fired at Jewish buses in Jerusalem and Haifa.

It is almost certain that the two fatal roadside ambushes were not ordered or organized by the AHC, and it remains unclear whether the gunmen were, in fact, reacting to the UN resolution. One HIS report says that the attacks "were planned in a coffee shop in Yahudiya on the night of 29 November after hearing the news [from New York]" but that "the aim was robbery under cover of a response to the UN resolution."[6] But the majority view in the HIS—supported by an anonymous Arab flyer posted almost immediately on walls in Jaffa—was that the attackers were driven primarily by a desire to avenge an LHI raid ten days before on a house near Raʿanana belonging to the Abu Kishk bedouin tribe.[7] The raiders had selected five males of the Shubaki family and executed them in a nearby orange grove.[8] The raiders believed (apparently mistakenly) that the Shubakis a few days earlier had informed the authorities about an LHI training session nearby. This had led to a British raid in which five Jewish youngsters were killed.[9]

Be that as it may, there was also a clear, organized Palestinian Arab response to the UN resolution. Guided by Husseini from Cairo, the AHC on 1 December declared a three-day general strike in Palestine to begin the following day. On 2 December a large Arab mob, armed with clubs and knives, burst out of Jerusalem's Old City and descended on the New Commercial Center at Mamilla Street, attacking Jewish passersby and shops. A number of people were injured, one seriously, and the district was set alight. The mob then proceeded up Queen Mary Street and into Jaffa Street. Haganah intelligence identified two AHC officials, Muhammad Ali Salah and Mahmoud ʿUmari, as leading the crowd.[10] Small Haganah units fired above and into the mob as Mandate police and troops generally looked on. Indeed, several policemen joined in the vandalizing and looting, though others helped evacuate the Jewish wounded.[11] The mob eventually turned back and dispersed. But the war had begun.

Yet that day, and for the next few weeks, no one really understood this. For most, the sporadic violence appeared to be just another wave, akin to the Arab outbreaks of 1920, 1921, and 1929; it would pass. This view affected both sides. The Palestinian notable Hikmat al-Taji al-Faruqi told an HIS agent two months after the start of hostilities: "When the business began . . . we did not expect it to begin. More accurately, we were not at all sure that it would develop and take on the dimensions of a war. . . . So we armed ourselves with stones, sticks, rented rifles and pistols."[12] But the violence was gradually to snowball into full-scale war, in which Palestinian Arab society would be shattered and the Arab world traumatized and humiliated.

THE CIVIL WAR: 30 NOVEMBER 1947–14 MAY 1948

The 1948 War—called by the Arab world the First Palestine War and by the Palestinians *al-nakba* (the disaster), and by the Jews the War of Independence (*milhemet haʿatzmaʾut*), the War of Liberation (*milhemet hashihrur*) or the War of Establishment (*milhemet hakomemiyut*)—was to have two distinct stages: a civil war, beginning on 30 November 1947 and ending on 14 May 1948, and a conventional war, beginning when the armies of the surrounding Arab states invaded Palestine on 15 May and ending in 1949. The civil (or ethnic or intercommunal) war between Palestine's Jewish and Arab communities, the latter assisted by a small army of volunteers from the wider Arab world, was characterized by guerrilla warfare accompanied by acts of terrorism. The subsequent conventional war, which ended officially only in July 1949 but in fact stopped, in terms of hostilities, the previous January, saw the armies of Syria, Egypt, Transjordan, and Iraq, with contingents from other Arab countries, attacking the newborn State of Israel and its army, the Haganah, which on 1 June 1948 became the Israel Defense Forces.

The civil war can roughly be divided into two parts or stages. From the end of November 1947 until the end of March 1948, the Arabs held the initiative and the Haganah was on the strategic defensive. This stage was characterized by gradually expanding, continuous, small-scale, small-unit fighting. There was terrorism, and counterterrorist strikes, in the towns and ambushes along the roads. Arab armed bands attacked Jewish settlements, and Haganah units occasionally retaliated. It was formless—there were no front lines (except along the seams between the two communities in the main, mixed towns), no armies moving back and forth, no pitched battles, and no conquests of territory. Then, in early April, the Haganah went over to the offensive, by mid-May crushing the Palestinians. This second stage involved major campaigns and battles and resulted in the conquest of territory, mainly by the Jews. At its end emerged clear front lines, marking a continuous Jewish-held piece of territory, with the areas beyond it under Arab control.

In describing the first, civil war half of the war, it is necessary to take account of three important facts. One, most of the fighting between November 1947 and mid-May 1948 occurred in the areas earmarked for Jewish statehood (the main exception being Jerusalem, earmarked for international control, and the largely Arab-populated "Corridor" to it from Tel Aviv) and where the Jews enjoyed demographic superiority. Almost no fighting occurred in the almost exclusively Arab-populated central and upper Galilee and Samaria, and the hostilities in the hill country south of Jerusalem were confined to the small ʿEtzion Bloc enclave and the road to it.

Two, the Jewish and Arab communities in western and northern Palestine were thoroughly intermingled. In the main cities and in some towns—Haifa, Jaffa–Tel Aviv, Jerusalem, Safad, Tiberias—the populations were mixed, with Arabs often sitting astride routes to the Jewish areas and Jews dominating the routes to and from Arab neighborhoods. In the countryside, Jewish and Arab settlements flanked most of the roads, enabling each side to interdict the other's traffic. This meant that Jewish settlers could cut off Arab villagers and the villagers, equally, could cut off and besiege Jewish settlers.

And three, the civil war took place while Britain ruled the country and while its military forces were deployed in the various regions. The British willingness and ability to intervene in the hostilities progressively diminished as their withdrawal progressed, and by the second half of April 1948 they rarely interfered, except to secure their withdrawal routes. Nonetheless, throughout the civil war, the belligerents had to take account of the British presence and their possible reaction to any initiative. Down to mid-April, this presence seriously affected both Arab and Jewish war-making.

Through the war, each side accused the British of favoring the other. But in fact, British policy—as emanating both from Whitehall and from Jerusalem, the seat of the high commissioner—was one of strict impartiality, generally expressed in nonintervention in favor of either side while trying to maintain law and order until the end of the Mandate. Both Whitehall and Jerusalem were eager to keep British casualties down. But at the same time,

Whitehall was bent on quitting Palestine with as little loss to its power and prestige in the Middle East as possible.

This implied a number of contradictions. The most important related to nonintervention versus the maintenance of law and order. Maintaining law and order often necessitated intervention. Moreover, intervention almost inevitably led to British casualties, and this ran afoul of the desire and intent to avoid them.

The military's guidelines were explicit: "Our forces would take no action except such as was directed towards their own withdrawal and the withdrawal of our stores; i.e., they would not be responsible for maintaining law and order (except as necessary for their own protection)."[13] But the high commissioner, Alan Cunningham, was also interested in leaving behind him as orderly a country (and reputation) as he could, and this required the maintenance of law and order for as long as possible. His boss, Colonial Secretary Arthur Creech Jones, had told the House of Commons on 3 December 1947 that "the British Government must remain responsible for law and order" for as long as it administered Palestine.[14] Cunningham put it this way: "It is our intention to be as impartial as is humanly possible. . . . [But] we wish to protect the law-abiding citizen."[15] This meant that the British would try to protect those attacked.

In practice, British troops intervened in the fighting quite frequently from November 1947 down to March 1948, and occasionally in April as well. This was one reason for the precipitous increase in British casualties during the Mandate's last five months. (Another was attacks on British troops by LHI and IZL gunmen, usually triggered by Arab attacks on Jews in which Britons were known to have assisted.) In all of 1947, British forces in Palestine suffered sixty dead and 189 wounded; in the period 1 January–14 May 1948, British losses were 114 dead and 230 wounded.[16]

The further contradiction, between strict impartiality and a desire to maintain Britain's standing in the Middle East, which required a pro-Arab tilt, led to inconsistent behavior, causing confusion among British officials and officers and among many Arabs and Jews.

British military interventions down to mid-March 1948 tended to work to the Yishuv's advantage since during the war's first four months the Arabs were generally on the offensive and the Jews were usually on the defensive. British columns repeatedly intervened on the side of attacked Jewish settlements and convoys. And the British regularly supplied escorts to Jewish convoys in troubled areas, such as the road to Jerusalem. This led to Arab accusations that the British were pro-Zionist.

But strategically speaking, during this period the massive British military presence and Haganah suspicions that the British in fact favored the Arabs—

"there is a sort of secret coalition between ʿAzzam Pasha and Bevin," said Ben-Gurion[17]—tended to inhibit Haganah operations. The Haganah could not contemplate large-scale operations, of which it became growingly capable as the war advanced, or conquest of Arab territory, out of fear of British intervention; and it understandably shied away from fighting the British while its hands were full with the Palestinian Arab militias and their foreign auxiliaries (though, to be sure, the IZL and LHI were far less cautious). Until April 1948, the Haganah operated under the assumption that the British military would block or forcefully roll back large-scale operations.

To a lesser extent, however, the British presence also inhibited Palestinian Arab attack at certain times. Moreover, the British military presence, and continued sovereignty over the country, certainly deterred the regular Arab armies from crossing the frontiers and interfering in the fighting before 15 May. The Arab leaders' periodic threats to this effect during the civil war remained empty bluster.

The guideline of impartiality, authorized by British cabinet decision on 4 December 1947, translated during the following months into a policy of quietly assisting each side in the takeover of areas in which that side was demographically dominant. In practice, this meant the handover, as the British successively withdrew from each area (Tel Aviv in December 1947, Gaza in February 1948, and so on), of Mandate government installations—police forts, military camps, utilities—to the majority community's control. The police forts and camps in the hill country of Judea, Samaria, and Galilee generally were turned over to Arab militia commanders; installations in the Coastal Plain and the Jordan and Jezreel Valleys went to the Haganah. This policy sometimes occasioned a more radical expression—British advice or urging to specific threatened or defeated communities to evacuate. For example, on 18 April 1948 the British urged the Arab inhabitants of Tiberias to evacuate the town; a week later they proffered the same advice in Balad ash Sheikh, an Arab village southeast of Haifa. In the course of January through May 1948, the British periodically urged the small Jewish communities north of Jerusalem (Neve Yaʿakov and ʿAtarot) to clear out, as they did the inhabitants of the four kibbutzim of the ʿEtzion Bloc, south of Bethlehem.

British troops did not always abide by the guideline of impartiality. Occasionally they indulged in overt anti-Jewish behavior (usually immediately following LHI or IZL attacks on them). During the war's first months British troops occasionally confiscated arms from Haganah units protecting convoys or manning outposts in urban areas (the British argued that they also seized arms from Arab militiamen).[18] And on a number of occasions British units disarmed Haganah men and handed them over to Arab mobs and "justice." For example, on 12 February 1948 a British patrol disarmed a Haganah roadblock and arrested its members on Jerusalem's Shmuel Hanavi Street. The four men were later "released" unarmed into the hands of an Arab mob, which lynched them and mutilated their bodies.[19] A similar incident occurred a fortnight later, on 28 February, when British troops disarmed Haganah men at a position in the Hayotzek Factory near Holon. Eight men were "butchered."[20] (The next day, LHI terrorists blew up a British troop train near Rehovot, killing twenty-eight British troops and wounding dozens more.)

Moreover, Whitehall's fears that the circumstances of the withdrawal from Palestine might subvert Britain's standing in the Middle East occasioned a number of major, organized British interventions against the Jewish militias, or noninterventions in face of Arab attack, in the dying days of the Mandate (see below for the cases of Jaffa and the ʿEtzion Bloc in April and May).

THE RELATIVE POWER OF THE TWO SIDES

At the start of the civil war, Whitehall believed that the Arabs would prevail. "In the long run the Jews would not be able to cope . . . and would be thrown out of Palestine unless they came to terms with [the Arabs]," was the considered judgment of the Chief of the Imperial General Staff (CIGS).[21] And indeed, the battle between the Yishuv and the Arab community seemed, at least on paper, extremely unequal. The Palestinian Arabs enjoyed a rough two-to-one population advantage—1.2 or 1.3 million to 630,000—and physically populated more of the country's surface than did the Jews. They also generally enjoyed the advantage of the high ground, whereas the Jews lived principally in the lowlands. Moreover, they benefited from a vast hinterland of neighboring, sympathetic states, which could supply them with volunteers, supplies, and safe havens. The Zionists' "hinterland"—Jewish and Zionist groups in the Diaspora—lay hundreds and thousands of miles away, and supplies and volunteers to the embattled Yishuv had to penetrate the British naval and air blockades of Palestine.

These factors aside, however, the Yishuv enjoyed basic advantages over the Palestine Arabs in major indexes of strength: "national" organization and preparation for war, trained military manpower, weaponry, weapons production, economic power, morale and motivation, and, above all, command and control. Moreover, despite the general demographic tilt, the Yishuv had a disproportionate number of army-age males (twenty- to forty-four-year-olds)[22] as, during the 1930s and 1940s, the Zionist leadership had taken care, as a matter of policy, to ship to Palestine, legally and illegally, young, fit males—deemed "good pioneering material."

Facing off in 1947–1948 were two very different societies: one highly motivated, literate, organized, semi-industrial; the other backward, largely illiterate, disorganized, agricultural. For the average Palestinian Arab man, a villager, political independence and nationhood were vague abstractions: his affinities and loyalties lay with his family, clan, and village, and, occasionally, region. Moreover, as we have noted, Palestinian Arab society was deeply divided along social and religious lines. And, among the more literate and politically conscious, there was a deep, basic fissure, going back to the 1920s, between the Husseinis and Nashashibis.

The 1936–1939 revolt had both irreparably deepened this divide (the rebellion ended with something like civil war between the two factions) and left Palestine Arab society largely decapitated, politically and militarily. The years of the Husseinis' anti-Opposition terrorism—which continued into 1946–1947[23]—had driven the Nashashibis and many of their allies out of political life altogether; come 1948, they abstained from joining the fight against Zionism. At the same time, the British suppression of the revolt had left many Husseini stalwarts and activists dead, wounded, or in exile. A general weariness of armed struggle had set in. The rebellion had also devastated the Arabs economically, though the war years had seen the economy bounce back. But in general, Palestinian Arab society had failed to overcome the trauma of the rebellion years.

During the Mandate, the Arab community had periodically tried, but failed, to develop self-governing institutions, and not because of British obstructionism. The community's sole veteran executive body was the Supreme Muslim Council, which dealt with religious affairs. The AHC, dominated since its inception in 1936 by the Husseinis, was unelected and unrepresentative; in its remodeled form, during 1946–1948, it completely sidelined the Opposition. Although it possessed a large network of supporters and agents in the localities and to some degree oversaw the workings of the local National Committees, which were resurrected with the start of the hostilities, the AHC failed to establish working national "governmental" structures.

The AHC theoretically functioned as a cabinet, with the exiled Haj Amin al-Husseini as president and Jamal Husseini as his deputy. Other committee members were responsible for particular areas of interest (Sheikh Hassan Abu Saʿud—the establishment of the National Committees) or localities (Rafik Tamimi–Jaffa; Muʿein al-Mahdi–Haifa). In 1946–1947, the AHC had six "departments"—lands, finances, economics, national organization, prisoners and casualties, and press—which, according to the HIS, made "theoretical sense" but, "in truth, there was chaos [andralmusiya] in most of" them. At the end of 1947, the AHC restructured the departments to face the challenges of war and statehood. But according to the HIS, by early

1948, only the Finance Department (or "Treasury") remained. The national organization, economic and prisoners and casualties departments had merged to become the Emergency Committee (*lajnat al-tawari*), composed of Saʿad al-Din ʿAref (a nephew of ʿAref al-ʿAref) and Ghaleb al-Khalidi (brother of Hussein Fakhri al-Khalidi, Jerusalem's mayor and a member of the AHC). The functional borders between the AHC, which theoretically managed the war on the national level, and the Emergency Committee were blurred. The HIS described the members and officials of the Emergency Committee as "murderers," "swords for hire," and "thieves" but, paradoxically, rated the committee itself as efficient. However, the members all took part in the various activities, with no lines of demarcation between them ("all buy weapons, all deal with supplies . . . all hand out military and civil instructions—and the confusion is great").[24]

By the start of the war, the AHC had signally failed. A major reason, as in 1936–1939, was its inability to raise funds. Palestine's Arabs were generally poor, and the wealthy—many of them identified with the Opposition and, disproportionately, Christian—were reluctant to part with their money. The AHC's chief fund-raising agency was the Treasury Department, headed by ʿIzzat Taunus. But Taunus's crash effort, starting in June 1947, to assemble funds, through taxation (one mil per packet of cigarettes, five mils per bus ticket) and "voluntary" contributions from the more prosperous, was a dismal failure. The department was also tainted by corruption. By 1 November it had managed to raise only twenty-five thousand Palestine pounds.[25]

The Palestinian leadership during the 1930s and 1940s may have talked often and loudly about "independence," but it had done little in terms of nuts-and-bolts preparations for self-government. The reasons were historical, cultural, and sociological. The centuries of Ottoman rule had failed to instill in the aʿyan a tradition of public service; rather, the wealthy vied for personal wealth, land, and power. Decades of cooperation with the Ottomans had rendered the aʿyan corrupt and venal. Under the British, it appeared easier to rely on the Mandatory institutions, which functioned efficiently, than to embark on the pioneering, difficult task of creating their own. Few Arabs acquired governmental or military experience during the Mandate. And a giant question mark hangs over the "nationalist" ethos of the Palestinian Arab elite: Husseinis as well as Nashashibis, Khalidis, Dajanis, and Tamimis just before and during the Mandate sold land to the Zionist institutions and/or served as Zionist agents and spies. In addition, during 1936–1947, the Palestinians developed a political and psychological reliance on the Arab states to pull their chestnuts out of the fire.

The contrast with Zionist society is stark. No national collective was more self-reliant or motivated, the Holocaust having convincingly demonstrated that there was no depending for survival on anyone else and having implanted the certainty that a giant massacre would as likely as not be the outcome of military defeat in Palestine. By the late 1940s, the Yishuv was probably one of the most politically conscious, committed, and organized communities in the world. It was also highly homogeneous: close to 90 percent Ashkenazi and 90 percent secular; only about 3 percent of the Yishuv was ultra-Orthodox and anti-Zionist. Hesitantly during the Ottoman years, and with increasing intensity during the beneficent Mandate, as Jewish numbers swelled, the Yishuv fashioned the infrastructure of a state-within-a-state or a state-in-embryo. By 1947, in addition to the Haganah, the Yishuv had a protogovernment—the Jewish Agency for Palestine—with a cabinet (the JAE), a foreign ministry (the agency's Political Department), a treasury (the agency's Finance Department), and most other departments and agencies of government, including a well-functioning, autonomous school system, a taxation system, settlement and land reclamation agencies, and even a powerful trades union federation, the Histadrut, with its own health service and hospitals, sports organization, agricultural production and marketing agencies, bank, industrial plants, and daily newspaper and publishing house.

Unlike the Palestinian Arabs, the Yishuv had a highly talented, sophisticated public service–oriented elite, experienced in diplomacy and economic and military affairs. Most of the twenty-six to twenty-eight thousand Palestinian Jews who had served in the Allied armies during World War II were, or became, Haganah members.

The Yishuv also enjoyed the effective backing of the World Zionist Organization, which had powerful branches in the United States. The Zionist movement had grown by leaps and bounds, and acquired popular support, during and after World War II, as a result of the Holocaust. At crucial junctures, the Zionists were able to tap the goodwill and political and financial resources of the large Diaspora Jewish communities. In an emergency fundraising tour of the United States in January–March 1948, Golda Myerson raised fifty million dollars for the Haganah, twice the sum that Ben-Gurion had asked her to bring back—"a brilliant success," in the words of Abba Hillel Silver, who praised her "eloquence and persuasion."[26] In a second whirlwind tour of American Jewish communities in May and June, she raised another fifty million dollars.[27] These funds paid for the Czech arms shipments that proved decisive in the battles of April through October 1948.

Theoretically, the Palestinians had the whole Arab world to fall back on. But that world, less organized and less generous than world Jewry, gave them little in their hour of need in money and arms. More robust was the contribution in terms of volunteers. But in this sphere, too, the pan-Arab contribution was actually meager in all but bluster. There appears to have been great reluctance to actually go and fight, especially among the more prosperous and educated. As one British intelligence official put it in December 1947: "Among the younger men . . . there is a great deal of temporary enthusiasm and exhibitionism, especially in Egypt, but very many of the youths who have so bravely smashed the windows of defenseless [Jewish] shopkeepers have little intention of undertaking anything so hazardous and uncomfortable as warfare in the stark Judean hills."[28]

Nonetheless, six to eight thousand volunteers reached Palestine, mainly from Iraq, Syria, and Egypt, and served alongside the local Arab militia units in the towns, with the Arab Liberation Army, and in the Muslim Brotherhood contingents in the south. But although the call for "jihad" reverberated through the Arab world, the frontline states, essentially poor and badly organized, proved unable to accommodate or deploy many of the volunteers. Indeed, the thousands who poured into Egypt and British-ruled Tripolitania-Cyrenaica from the Maghreb (Morocco, Algeria, and Tunisia) from early May were seen as "restive and argumentative" and, vaguely, a threat to the regimes—and most were incarcerated and then deported home. In mid-June the Egyptians, under British and French prodding, closed their borders to further Maghrebi volunteers.[29] More successful in penetrating Palestine were the hundreds of Egyptian Muslim Brotherhood volunteers, who entered the Gaza District in March–April 1948[30] and fought alongside local militiamen. They were superficially trained by the Egyptian army in camps in Marsa Matruh and Hakstap.[31]

Several dozen Britons, most of them former British army or police officers (by mid-March 1948 some 230 British soldiers and thirty policemen had deserted),[32] also served in Palestinian Arab ranks,[33] as did some volunteers from Yugoslavia and Germany. The Yugoslavs, possibly in their dozens, were both Christians, formerly members of pro-Axis Fascist groups, and Bosnian Muslims;[34] the handful of Germans were former Nazi intelligence, Wehrmacht, and SS officers.[35]

The Yishuv was reinforced, mostly after mid-May, by "more than 4,000" volunteers, Jewish and non-Jewish, from abroad. Most were idealists who supported the Zionist cause; a few came for the pay and adventure. Almost all had served in the Allied forces in World War II. A fair number were pilots and navigators, air force ground personnel, sailors, and experts in communications and armored warfare. A large contingent, of about eight hundred, arrived from South Africa; many came from North America. Of the IAF's 193 pilots in the 1948 War, 171 were foreign volunteers, about a hundred of them Americans.

The case of Milton M. Rubenfeld, "Captain USAAF Reserve, 0-940081 Serial Number," was not unusual. In early December 1947 he contacted the

Jewish Agency, writing: "In 1939 I enlisted in the Royal Air Force (UK) and fought for England because I thought I was helping the cause of the Jews. I desire to do the same thing now. . . . I could fly thousands of Jews into Palestine a month." He also suggested buying mothballed American fighter aircraft. "If the US Gov. refuses permission to fly these [aircraft] to Palestine . . . I will do so anyway," he wrote.[36]

Much of the senior staff of the Haganah/IDF Seventh (Armored) Brigade, including its commanding officer, Ben Dunkelman, and two of his battalion commanders (Joe Weiner and Baruch Friedman-Erez), were Anglo-Saxon volunteers. One American volunteer, David (Mickey) Marcus, of Eisenhower's staff in World War II, briefly served as an adviser to Ben-Gurion and on the IDF General Staff, with the rank of general, before being accidentally killed by an Israeli sentry in June 1948. (He is the only American soldier who died serving in a foreign army to be buried at West Point.) About 20 percent of the IDF Medical Corps at the end of 1948 were foreign volunteers.[37]

The Yishuv entered the civil war with one large militia and two very small paramilitary or terrorist organizations: the Haganah, the military arm of the mainstream Zionist parties, especially the socialist Mapai and Mapam, with thirty-five thousand members; and the IZL, the military arm of the Revisionist movement and its youth movement, Betar, and the LHI, which was composed, somewhat unnaturally, of breakaways from the IZL and left-wing revolutionaries who regarded the British Empire as their chief enemy. The IZL had between two and three thousand members and the LHI some three to five hundred. During the civil war, the three organizations occasionally coordinated their operations and did not clash with one another.

The Haganah, which as of 1 June 1948 was renamed the Israel Defense Forces, was the organization that counted. During the first months of the civil war, while defending the Jewish settlements and lines of communication, it reorganized. In a sense, the reorganization—from an amateur, territorially based militia into a relatively professional army—was carried out behind the shield provided by the Palmah, the Haganah's strike force. In November 1947 the Palmah had twenty-one hundred soldiers, with a thousand reservists. During the following months, while battling the Palestinian Arabs and suffering severe losses, it expanded into a force of six thousand troops, subdivided into three brigades.

Before the war, the Haganah fielded territorially based infantry companies in the Yishuv's towns and settlements. There was a skeletal General Staff, with specialized branches (intelligence service, manpower, logistics, medical corps, and so on) and an embryonic "Air Service." The reorganization and expansion of November 1947–May 1948 resulted in the creation and deployment of twelve brigades, three of them Palmah and two armored.

The Haganah's chief of operations, Yigael Yadin, had formulated the reorganization order on 7 November 1947. Its preamble read: "The danger of an attack on the country by the armies of the neighboring states . . . necessitates a different structure and deployment. Opposite regular armies there is a need to deploy with a trained, [regular] military force, armed and built along [regular] military lines."[38]

The seeds of the transformation were planted already in December 1946, when Ben-Gurion, the JAE's chairman (effectively the Yishuv's prime minister), took over the agency's defense portfolio. During the following months he studied the Yishuv's defense needs. Unlike others in the Zionist leadership, Ben-Gurion understood early on that the decisive battle for Jewish statehood would be waged not against the British or in the international arena but on the ground, against the Arabs, inside Palestine and along its borders. He realized that the Palestinian Arabs would not constitute a major military threat, but he feared the armies of the Arab states. As he told the Twenty-second Zionist Congress: "Until recently there was only the problem of how to defend [the Yishuv] against the Palestinian Arabs. . . . But now we face a completely new situation. The Land of Israel is surrounded by independent Arab states that have the right to purchase and produce arms, to set up armies and train them. . . . Attack by the Palestinian Arabs does not endanger the Yishuv, but there is a danger, that the neighboring Arab states will send their armies to attack and destroy the Yishuv."[39]

The Yishuv's military capabilities improved significantly during the immediate postwar years. One element was the establishment of a clandestine arms industry. The plants were usually built under cowsheds and other agricultural installations. The industry was based on machine tools purchased in the United States by Haganah representatives in 1944–1946. By the end of 1947, the Haganah's arms factories were producing two- and three-inch mortars, Sten submachine guns, and grenades and bullets in large numbers. Their contribution was not insignificant. Between 1 October 1947 and 31 May 1948 the secret plants produced 15,468 Sten guns, more than two hundred thousand grenades, 125 three-inch mortars with more than 130,000 rounds, and some forty million 9 mm (Sten gun) bullets.[40]

Another element was planning. Before 1946, the Haganah General Staff (HGS) had prepared plans for resisting a renewed Arab rebellion—with the Haganah seen as an auxiliary to the British military. In May 1946, the HGS formulated *tochnit gimel* (Plan C or the May Plan), addressing the possibility of mass, organized Arab attacks on the Yishuv. The plan included guidelines for Haganah retaliation against Arab leaders, villages, and urban districts; addenda, from October and December 1946, related to possible British assistance to the Arabs. In doctrinal terms, the Haganah from this point on took on sole responsibility for the defense of the Yishuv.[41]

During the countdown to 1948, a behind-the-scenes struggle for dominance in the reorganizing defense apparatus raged between the veteran Haganah commanders and the regular Allied—mostly British—army veterans who had returned from Europe. Ben-Gurion preferred the army veterans, arguing that the impending war would be mainly a conventional war while the Haganah brass had trained for a guerrilla struggle against irregulars. But the incumbent Haganah commanders effectively resisted "the Old Man," and although some former British army officers received important commands—such as the brigadiers Haim Laskov and Shlomo Shamir—the HGS and the brigade and battalion headquarters were manned predominantly by Haganah veterans, with Palmah officers (Yigal Allon, Yitzhak Rabin, Yitzhak Sadeh, and Shimon Avidan) figuring prominently.

At the end of November 1947 the Haganah's armory consisted of 10,662 rifles, 3,830 pistols, 3,662 submachine guns, 775 light machine guns, 157 medium machine guns, sixteen antitank guns, 670 two-inch mortars, and eighty-four three-inch mortars. Much of the weaponry was dispersed among the settlements, where it was needed for self-defense. In addition, the Jewish Settlement Police, officially under British command but in fact loyal to the Haganah, had some 6,800 rifles and forty-eight machine guns. Most Jewish settlements entered the war with well-prepared trench works, bunkers and bombproof shelters, with barbed wire perimeter fences and lighting, and minefields. The 250-odd rural settlements doubled as small fortified encampments. But the Haganah had no artillery or tanks, used makeshift armored cars (essentially trucks with steel plating), and had no combat aircraft, only light spotter planes. Ammunition was in short supply (some fifty rounds per rifle and six to seven hundred rounds per machine gun). The IZL and LHI together had another thousand or so light arms.

The Palestinian Arabs had nothing comparable to the Haganah. During its brief existence, the Palestinian national movement failed to establish a national militia, but not for want of trying. On paper, the Palestinian Arabs in 1946–1947 had two paramilitary youth organizations, the Najjada and the Futuwwa. Their chief activity consisted of noisy parades in town squares; little, if any, military training took place.

The Najada was founded in Jaffa in November–December 1945 by Muhammad Nimr al-Hawari, a Nazareth-born lawyer of bedouin origin who had served in the Mandate administration and had broken with the Husseinis in the early 1940s. Its founding proclamation declared that the Zionist Movement was "the most heinous crime known to history" and defined the organization's aims as instilling national consciousness and discipline in Palestine's youth. Al-Hawari tried to model the Najjada on the Haganah.[42] By mid-1946 it had, on paper, "8,000" members.[43]

The Futuwwa was founded at the end of 1935 by Jamal Husseini as the Arab Party's youth corps; the Nazi Party or the Hitlerjugend appear to have been his model.[44] It was disbanded during the Arab Revolt and resurrected by Husseini in early 1946 as a counterweight to the Najjada.[45] Kamal Erikat, a retired Mandate police officer, was its commander. The two organizations vied for recruits. The Husseinis then tried to take over the Najjada. Hawari resisted but, fearing assassination, fled to Jordan at the end of 1947. By the start of the war, neither the Futuwwa nor the Najjada in effect existed. The Palestinians entered the war without a national military organization.

Rather, the Arabs followed the pattern set at the start of the 1936 revolt. A number of large, organized armed bands, which the Jews called "gangs," sprang up in December 1947 in more or less spontaneous fashion. As in 1936–1939, they were most active in the hill country of Judea, Samaria, and Galilee and consisted largely of local peasants. The most important bands were ʿAbd al-Qadir al-Husseini's "al-Jihad al-Muqqadas," which operated in the hills around Jerusalem; Hassan Salame's group, based in the villages around Lydda and the Judean foothills to the east; and the band led by Abu Ibrahim al-Sghir, in lower Galilee. Each band had a hard core of two to five hundred fighters, who moved about the countryside quartering in successive villages. Some villages refused to host them, for fear of Jewish retribution. The bands were lightly armed, their heaviest weapons running to two- and three-inch mortars and medium machine guns. Each band was able to call on varying numbers of local volunteers for short, specific engagements. The Haganah's opinion of the bands' abilities was low, as was al-Qawuqji's; he reportedly described them as "unreliable, excitable and difficult to control and in organized warfare virtually unemployable."[46] The bands in fact often fought with tenacity and skill, but they rarely cooperated with one another and tended, by high-handed and often brutal behavior, to alienate the villagers among whom they "swam," in Mao Tse-tung's phrase. From the first, the bands encountered great reluctance among the villagers to volunteer or help, and occasionally villages refused them entry.[47] The unwillingness to join in the hostilities, out of fear, was occasionally matched by secret, specific ceasefire agreements between Arab villages and neighboring Jewish settlements.[48] This led one historian to conclude that "Palestinian society . . . during this period did not have that national spirit, which Benedict Anderson said constituted a 'fraternity that makes it possible . . . for so many millions of people not so much to kill, as willingly to die.' . . . One can conclude that Arab nationalism in Palestine was expressed in the existence of national consciousness and national emotions, but without the readiness to act or sacrifice."[49]

The largest and best-organized Arab formation fighting in Palestine until the pan-Arab invasion of May 1948 was the ALA, consisting mainly of volunteers from Syria, Iraq, and Palestine mustered by the Arab League in Syria. The volunteers were trained in Syrian army camps in Qatana, near Damascus, beginning in November 1947, and the ALA was officially established on 1 January 1948, with Fawzi al-Qawuqji at its head. Al-Qawuqji told his volunteers that "they were going off to Jihad to help the persecuted Arabs of Palestine. . . . We must expel the Jews from the Arab part of Palestine and limit them in that small area where they live and they must remain under our supervision and guard. Our war is holy. Women, children and prisoners must not be harmed."[50]

Syria initially supplied the money and arms. But during the following months the other Arab states contributed to the ALA's upkeep. At its height, in April and October 1948, the ALA had four to five thousand troops and could call on the services of hundreds of local volunteers in its areas of operation. The bulk of the army's officers were retired or seconded Syrian and Iraqi army personnel, with a sprinkling of Jordanians, Lebanese, Egyptians, and Bosnians.[51]

Company- and battalion-sized ALA formations entered Palestine from Lebanon and Jordan starting in December 1947–January 1948 and fanned out in the mixed towns, to bolster local Palestinian militia contingents, and in the hill country of Samaria and Judea. They were equipped with a diverse collection of light weapons, light and medium-sized mortars, and a number of 75 mm and 105 mm guns, with a small stock of shells. In mid-May, with the invasion of Palestine by the regular Arab armies, the ALA withdrew to Qatana to reorganize. During the following weeks the army returned to Palestine, this time to the Galilee, now armed with additional mortars and field pieces and a handful of antiquated armored cars.[52] On paper, in October 1948, the ALA consisted of eight "battalions" (Yarmuk 1, Yarmuk 2, Yarmuk 3, Ajnadin, Husayn, Qadisiya, Hittin, and the Druze Battalion). But in reality it mustered no more than three to four more or less regular-sized battalions (the three Yarmuk battalions and possibly the Hittin Battalion). The other "battalions" were in effect company-sized units that, before 15 May, were posted in towns to reinforce local militias.[53] Though nominally part of an "army," each ALA battalion usually operated on its own. The ALA was crushed and finally ejected from Palestine at the end of October.

In the main, Palestinian Arab military power was based on the separate local militias in the country's seven to eight hundred Arab villages and towns.

Of these, only some four hundred were involved in the war. The remainder, almost all in the territory that became the West Bank, were untouched by hostilities and barely contributed to the war effort. Each village had its own "militia" of ten or fifty or a hundred able-bodied men with pistols or rifles and a small stock of ammunition. The weapons were of diverse makes and ages, sometimes obsolete. Usually, each village militia was on its own. There was no "national" framework. At best, neighboring villages might help each other. Occasionally, the militias of a cluster of villages would mount a joint attack, usually as appendages of an armed band or an ALA unit, on a Jewish convoy or settlement. The firefight over, the militiamen would disperse to their homes until the next *faz'a* (summons). The faz'a might last a few hours or a day or two. In defense, each village was almost always on its own; when the Haganah went on the offensive, it was able to pick the villages off one at a time.[54]

Many villages tried to stay out of the fray, and some even preferred to assist the Jews out of a deep-seated antagonism toward their neighbors or because they believed that the Jews would win. By the beginning of summer 1948, the Druze villages of the Carmel and Western Galilee had thrown in their lot with the Jews. A few weeks later, the IDF set up a Druze unit, which participated in its offensives.[55]

All the Palestinian forces—armed bands, ALA, and village militias—suffered from acute supply problems. Especially badly off were the villages. In terms of food, they were largely autarchic. But they needed guns, ammunition, fuel. Yet most received no outside supplies of any kind during the war: the ALA and the bands had no supplies to spare, and when the Arab states or the Arab League Military Committee sent arms and ammunition, they almost invariably ended up in the hands of the bands or ALA; some arms reached the larger urban militias. Through the civil war, the villages sent purchasing missions to nearby towns or to Arab states to acquire a machine gun or a few rifles. But it was all a drop in the bucket.

The ALA, the bands, and the urban militias relied on supplies from neighboring Arab countries. But these states were poor, corrupt, badly organized, and not particularly generous, and the Military Committee, which "supervised" the war effort, and the AHC leaders in exile proved unable to raise the necessary funds or to organize the dispatch of war materiel to those in need. Haganah/IDF intelligence files are littered with intercepted messages from Palestinian towns and villages, from the bands, and from ALA units desperately calling upon this or that state, the Military Committee, or the AHC to rush supplies. Almost invariably the response was: "Soon, God willing."

According to one report, by 23 March 1948 the Arab states had sent 9,800 rifles and almost four million rounds of ammunition to Palestine.[56] But the bulk of the weaponry reached the ALA; a small part was distributed among the urban militias and the bands; the villages got nothing or almost nothing.

Much of the weaponry in or reaching Palestine between November 1947 and 14 May 1948 was of different types and calibers, and many of the rifles were unusable (particularly decrepit were the Saudi contributions). Only the ALA enjoyed the benefit of fairly standardized weaponry and ammunition. The arms shipments, which were illegal, had to get around British patrols and check posts. Moreover, the Haganah, well informed, occasionally interdicted arms convoys—as happened to a large shipment from Beirut heading for Haifa, near Kiryat Motzkin, on 17 March. A dozen Arabs were killed, including Haifa's militia commander, the Jordanian Muhammad bin Hamad al-Huneiti, and most of the arms and ammunition were destroyed.[57]

More critical than the supply problem was that of command and control. There were simply too many diverse Arab units and too many bodies pulling the strings from outside. There were the ALA units, some of them semi-independently garrisoning towns, the armed bands, and the individual village militias. The larger towns each had a number of militias (Jaffa had three or four), owing allegiance to different political controllers—the local National Committee, the AHC, a nearby armed band, the ALA, the Military Committee in Damascus, or even specific Arab governments. The Jordanians, for example, sent a number of large bedouin volunteer contingents that were directly controlled by Amman; the Muslim Brotherhood contingents were loosely managed from Cairo. The nominal coordinator of this disparate war effort, the Military Committee, beyond loosely controlling the ALA (al-Qawuqji was never particularly obedient), proved incapable of coordinating the different military groups. Indeed, the committee itself spent much of its time fending off challenges from the AHC, which sought to supplant it in the direction of the war. Inside Palestine, the ALA and most of the local National Committees rebuffed AHC efforts at intrusion or control, fearing that AHC directives could embroil them in unwanted or premature hostilities with the British or the Jews.

Aware of the problem, the Military Committee, ALA leaders, Haj Amin al-Husseini, and Palestinian band leaders met in Damascus, under the chairmanship of Syrian president Shukri al-Quwwatli, on 5 February 1948 to sort out the mess. A plan, providing for cooperation and a division of Palestine into zones of responsibility, was hammered out: Galilee and Samaria were placed under al-Qawuqji (ALA); the Jerusalem District under ʿAbd al-Qadir al-Husseini; the Lydda area under Salame; and the South under an Egyptian commander. The Military Committee was nominally given overall charge and the mufti was effectively sidelined—but the problem of the rival militias, especially in the big towns, and the rival interests of the patron Arab states, was left unresolved.[58] And the death of ʿAbd al-Qadir in early April left the crucial Jerusalem area bereft of central command for the crucial remaining five weeks of the civil war. In effect, through February until 14 May, the various bands and militias and the ALA fought separately and without real coordination. This was probably the most important factor in the eventual Palestinian defeat and in the Haganah's relative ease in accomplishing it.

THE FIRST PERIOD OF THE CIVIL WAR

The civil war half of the 1948 War, which ended with the complete destruction of Palestinian Arab military power and the shattering of Palestinian society, began on 30 November 1947 and ended on 14 May 1948, by which time hundreds of thousands of townspeople and villagers had fled or been forcibly displaced from their homes. But the disintegration of Arab Palestine, which underlay the military collapse, began well before the Haganah went on the offensive in early April 1948; indeed, there were telling signs even before the UN partition vote and the start of the accelerated British evacuation. The trigger appears to have been the UNSCOP partition proposals and Britain's announced intention to leave. Already in early November 1947, an official reported chaos in the largely Arab-staffed Nazareth District administration; the offices had ceased to function. The Christians, who manned the senior posts, were "living in fear for their property and lives (in this order). . . . The Husseini terror has increased lately and large sums of money are extorted from the Christians. Christians with means are trying to flee the country, especially to Lebanon and the United States."[59]

At base, many Palestinians entered the war knowing that they would lose—though, to be sure, some trusted that the Arab world, once mobilized, would ultimately overcome the Jews as it had the medieval Crusader kingdoms.[60] "The fellah is afraid of the Jewish terrorists. . . . The town dweller admits that his strength is insufficient to fight the Jewish force and hopes for salvation from outside. . . . The . . . majority . . . are confused, frightened. . . . All they want is peace, quiet," reported one HIS agent.[61]

Though the Arabs had initiated the violence, they were quickly evincing signs of demoralization. "In general there is fear in the Arab public of the Jews and this is one of the reasons for the depression and quiet in many areas," stated a Haganah report. "This fear is prominent among the Arabs in places hit by the dissident [that is, IZL and LHI] terrorist actions. Many areas, especially near Jewish population concentrations, are being evacuated out of fear of Jewish reprisals. On the other hand, there is a lack of confidence in the existing Arab leadership and their organizational abilities, especially because of their inability to deal with the masses of refugees and economic problems."[62] In Jaffa by early February, there was no "housing for the refugees and no hospitalization for the wounded, and commerce was paralyzed. . . . In Jerusalem there was complete chaos."[63] The fighting had deepened the traditional Muslim-Christian rift. In Jerusalem, the Christians were eager to leave, but the Muslims threatened to confiscate or destroy their property.[64] Outside the town, Muslim villagers overran the monasteries at Beit Jimal and Mar Saba, in the former "robbing and burning property," in the latter "murdering [monks] and robbing."[65] The daughter, living in England, of one middle-class Muslim, identified as "Dr. Canaan"—possibly Tawfiq Canaan, a well-known physician, political writer, and folklorist—of Musrara (Jerusalem), wrote to her father: "Yes, daddy, it is shameful that all the Christian Arabs are fleeing the country and taking out their money."[66]

Flight was the earliest and most concrete expression of Palestinian demoralization. Within twenty-four hours of the start of the (still low-key) hostilities, Arab families began to abandon their homes in mixed or border neighborhoods in the big towns. Already on 30 November 1947 the HIS reported "the evacuation of Arab inhabitants from border neighborhoods" in Jerusalem and Jaffa.[67] Arabs were also reported leaving the area around the Jewish Quarter of Safad (the town was predominantly Arab) and fleeing the villages of Jammasin and Sheikh Muwannis, bordering Tel Aviv.[68] By 9 December, the HIS was reporting that "Arab refugees were sleeping in the streets [of Jaffa]" and "wealthy families were leaving the [coastal] cities—heading inland. [Many initially fled to the family's village of origin.] Rich people are emigrating to Syria, Lebanon, and even Cyprus."[69] In one or two sites, there was deliberate Jewish intimidation of Arab neighbors to leave.[70]

Despite the haphazard efforts of some Arab local authorities, the following months were marked by increasing flight from the main towns and certain rural areas. By the end of March 1948 most of the wealthy and middle-class families had fled Jaffa, Haifa, and Jerusalem, and most Arab rural communities had evacuated the heavily Jewish Coastal Plain; a few had also left the Upper Jordan Valley. Most were propelled by fear of being caught up, and harmed, in the fighting; some may have feared life under Jewish rule. It is probable that most thought of a short, temporary displacement with a return within weeks or months, on the coattails of victorious Arab armies or international diktats. Thus, although some (the wealthier) moved as far away as Beirut, Damascus, and Amman, most initially moved a short distance, to their villages of origin or towns in the West Bank or Gaza area, inside Palestine, where they could lodge with family or friends. During this period Jewish troops expelled the inhabitants of only one village—Qisariya, in the Coastal Plain, in mid-February (for reasons connected to Jewish illegal immigration rather than the ongoing civil war)—though other villages were harassed and a few specifically intimidated by IZL, LHI, and Haganah actions (much as during this period Jewish settlements were being harassed and intimidated by Arab irregulars). Altogether some seventy-five thousand to one hundred thousand Arabs fled or were displaced from their homes during the first stage of the civil war, marking the first wave of the exodus.[71]

Through the civil war there was no clear Arab "policy" regarding the exodus. Almost from the start of hostilities, the AHC and the National Committees evinced ambivalence concerning the movement of Arabs out of battle zones or potential battle zones. This ambivalence was to characterize their thinking and behavior down to mid-May 1948. Advice and orders changed from month to month and place to place. In general, the AHC and some of the National Committees were annoyed and, as the months passed, increasingly alarmed, by the exodus and repeatedly instructed particular communities to curb it. In late December 1947, the AHC apparently issued a general, secret directive "forbidding all Arab males capable of participating in the battle to leave the country."[72] In late January 1948, British intelligence reported that the mufti had ordered departees to return home.[73]

But the AHC appeared far less worried about inhabitants moving from one part of Palestine to another than by flight out of the country. The National Committees, in contrast, were simply worried about departure from their towns. Already on 9 December, Haifa's NC "comprehensively discussed" the problem and inveighed against the "cowards" who were leaving the town. It resolved to appeal to the AHC to "prohibit departure."[74] A week later, the NC published a communiqué blasting the would-be fleers, who were "more harmful than the enemy."[75] In January 1948, militiamen in Jerusalem prevented flight and the local NC punished departing families by burning their property or confiscating their homes.[76] In February, the Tulkarm NC ordered the inhabitants to "stay in their places" in the event of Jewish attack.[77]

But AHC instructions to the localities down to the end of February 1948 to prevent flight appear to have been limited, hesitant, and infrequent. Things changed in March, probably due to the growing volume of the exodus and complaints from neighboring states. Husseini ordered the NCs of Tiberias and Jerusalem to halt the exodus. "The AHC regards this as flight from the field of honor and sacrifice and sees it as damaging to the name of the holy war movement and . . . the good name of the Palestinians in the Arab states and weakens the aid of the Arab peoples for the Palestinian cause, and leaves harmful traces in the economy and commerce of Palestine."[78] The HIS summarized AHC and NC efforts to stem the exodus during the civil war thus: "The Arab institutions tried to combat the phenomenon of flight. . . . The AHC decided . . . to adopt measures to weaken the flight by restrictions, punishments, threats, propaganda in the newspapers, radio, etc. . . . They especially tried to prevent the flight of army-age youths. But none of these actions was really successful."[79]

Anti-exodus AHC and NC "orders" were not always obeyed and were themselves often subverted by contrary AHC and NC "orders" and behavior. The fact that almost all AHC and NC members were either out of the country before the outbreak of hostilities or fled Palestine with their families in the first months of the war undermined the remaining officials' ability to curb the exodus. And perhaps even more tellingly, the AHC, local NCs, and various militia officers often instructed villages and urban neighborhoods near major Jewish concentrations of population to send away women, children, and the old to safer areas. This conformed with Arab League secretary-general ʿAzzam's reported thinking already in May 1946 ("to evacuate all Arab women and children from Palestine and send them to neighboring Arab countries," should it come to war)[80] and the Arab League Political Committee resolution, in Sofar in September 1947, that "the Arab states open their doors to absorb babies, women and old people from among Palestine's Arabs and care for them—if events in Palestine necessitate this."[81]

Almost from the start of hostilities frontline Arab communities began to send away their dependents. For example, already on 3–4 December 1947 the inhabitants of Lifta, a village on the western edge of Jerusalem, were ordered to send away their women and children (partly in order to make room for incoming militiamen).[82] Dozens of villages in the Coastal Plain and Jezreel and Jordan Valleys followed suit in the following months. The cities, too, were affected. In early February, the AHC ordered the removal of women and children from Haifa,[83] and by 28 March about 150 children had been evacuated, at least fifty to a monastery in Lebanon.[84] On 4–5 April 1948, a fifteen-vehicle convoy left Haifa for Beirut; on board were children and youths from the Wadi Nisnas neighborhood.[85]

Of course, the Arab exodus was not propelled only by the war-making and direct Arab and Jewish policies or actions. The changing economic circumstances also contributed. Almost from the first, the less-organized Arab economy was hard-hit. And the situation worsened as the war progressed. The separation of the two populations during the first weeks of fighting resulted in an economic divorce—cutting off many Arabs from their Jewish workplaces and closing the Jewish marketplace to Arab goods, especially agricultural products. Already in late December 1947, Haganah intelligence was reporting that Arab agricultural produce in Beit Sahur, southeast of Jerusalem, was rotting or selling for a farthing and there was no food for the animals.[86] By early March 1948, commerce in Jaffa was reported at a standstill and fuel was scarce; speculation and acts of robbery were rife (though there was no food shortage).[87] By early April, flour was in short supply in Jaffa and Haifa (and Acre).[88] Unemployment soared. The flight of the Arab middle class, which resulted in the closure of workshops and businesses, contributed to unemployment, as did the gradual shutdown of the British administration. All the Arab banks had closed by the end of April.

Prices—of flour, petrol, and other basic goods—also soared. A can of petrol, which cost eight hundred mils[89] or less before the war, cost five Palestine pounds in mid-May.[90] The hostilities led to supply problems, especially in the towns. Arab public transportation gradually ground to a halt. In May 1948, Jewish economic analysts wrote that the Arab economy in Palestine had been pushed back "more than twenty years," with the relatively "modern," advanced Coastal Plain hardest hit.[91]

Through the civil war, the mufti and the AHC never issued a general call to arms or a blanket order to attack "the Yishuv." Neither did the Arab states. British intelligence assessed that at the Arab League's Cairo Conference in December 1947 the Arab leaders agreed that "the campaign must not start prematurely, for the Arabs are not ready, neither organized nor armed. The first real move should be made in May, by when the Mandate will have terminated."[92] It appears that the Arab leaders were primarily motivated by fear of antagonizing the British.

The mufti and AHC desisted from ordering a general assault on the Yishuv, at least in the civil war's first three or four months, probably in large measure because of their inability to raise another full-scale military enterprise so soon after their crushing defeat in 1939 and because of Palestinian military unpreparedness.[93] But they also took account of the needs of the Palestinian peasantry—to defer large-scale fighting until after the harvests of citrus fruit in the Coastal Plain in winter 1947–1948[94] and, perhaps, the start of the grain harvest in spring 1948[95]—and the minatory British presence. The mufti repeatedly told visiting notables to keep their powder dry until a general assault was ordered several months hence. But the order was never issued. The mufti was probably preempted by the start of the Haganah offensives in early April 1948.

In mid-December 1947, one HIS informant told his controller that "the AHC had had no intention of starting disturbances on the scale that they had reached. . . . But they had made a mistake in announcing a three-day strike without taking account of the character of the Arab public; because the Arab going on strike for a protracted period is [prone to be] sucked into all sorts of acts of hooliganism and criminality [*pirhahut uviryonut*]."[96]

In late December, Husseini reportedly sent Jerusalem NC leader Hussein al-Khalidi a letter explicitly stating that the purpose of the present violence was "to harass (and only to harass)" the Yishuv, not full-scale assault.[97] In January 1948, High Commissioner Cunningham assessed that "official [Palestinian] Arab policy is to stand on the defensive until aggression is ordered by the national leadership. That widespread assaults on Jews continue and are indeed increasing illustrates the comparatively feeble authority of most of [the National] Committees and of the AHC. . . . The latter is anxious to curb Arab outbreaks but probably not to stop them entirely."[98] During the winter, perturbed by appeals from the notables of Jaffa and Haifa, Husseini appears to have agreed to nonbelligerency in the towns[99] and to have ordered a shift of the focus of hostilities from the main towns to the countryside.[100] On 22 February, the Haifa NC ordered a "cessation of shooting, and a return of each man to his regular workplace."[101] It is unlikely that such an order was issued without prior AHC endorsement.

Many of the Arab attacks in November 1947–January 1948 were "spontaneous" and even contrary to the mufti's wishes.[102] Others were "incited" or led by Husseini agents, but in unconcerted fashion.[103] Gradually, however, and partly because of Haganah, IZL, and LHI retaliatory attacks, the whole country—or at least the areas with Jewish concentrations of population— was set alight. And, occasionally, Husseini himself, approached by notables from this or that area of Palestine, would order the initiation of hostilities. But at other times he seems to have ordered local militias to desist. In February–March 1948 the orders were generally to refrain from mass attack and wait either for the British withdrawal or intervention by the Arab armies.

Despite the absence of a concerted effort, in the first stage of the civil war the Arabs had, or appeared to have, the edge, especially along the main roads, the lifelines to Jewish West Jerusalem and clusters of isolated settlements. Acting individually, armed bands attacked convoys and settlements, often recruiting local militiamen to join in. Gunmen sporadically fired into Jewish neighborhoods and planted bombs. The Haganah, busy reorganizing, and wary of the British, adopted a defensive posture while occasionally retaliating against Arab traffic, villages, and urban neighborhoods. The Haganah mobilized slowly, at first hobbled by the belief—shared by much of the Yishuv[104]—that it merely faced a new round of "disturbances." Only in early January did the Yishuv's leadership wake up to the fact that the war that they had long predicted had, in fact, begun—as Ben-Gurion told the JAE.[105]

The outbreak of hostilities had caught the Haganah on the hop, "in the very midst of the process of reorganization. The . . . brigades have not yet deployed, the mobilization of the 17–25-year-olds has only just begun," complained one senior official in mid-December 1947.[106] Going into the civil war, Haganah policy was purely defensive or, as Yisrael Galili, Ben-Gurion's deputy in the political directorate of the organization, put it: "Our interest . . . is that the hostilities don't expand over time or over a wide area." There should be Haganah retaliation, but preferably in the area in which the Yishuv had been hit and against perpetrators. "The Haganah is not built for aggression, it does not want to subjugate, it values human life, it wants to hit only the guilty . . . [it] wants to douse the flames."[107]

During the first ten days of disturbances, the Haganah desisted almost altogether from retaliation, and Ben-Gurion instructed that only property, not people, be hit.[108] But with the Jews, as Cunningham (somewhat unfairly) put it, in a "state of mixed hysteria and braggadocio,"[109] the Haganah decided, on 9 December, to shift from pure defense to "active defense, [with] responses and punishment."[110] The following month, the HGS decided to target individual Husseini military and political leaders[111]—though only one, Muhammad Nimr al-Khatib, of Haifa, was actually attacked (and badly wounded) in the civil war. One consideration behind this shift to a policy of limited retaliation was that the Arabs would interpret inaction as a sign of weakness; another, that the international community would stop supporting Jewish statehood in the belief that the Jews would "not be able to hold out."[112] The Haganah informed its members: "There is no thought of returning to the policy of restraint [*havlaga*] that seemingly existed during the disturbances of 1936–39."[113]

Yadin instructed the brigades to initiate retaliatory strikes against Arab transportation.[114] Two days later, on 11 December, Alexandroni Brigade troops ambushed Arab trucks on the Qalqilya–Ras al-ʿAyin road. A young lieutenant, Ariel Sharon, who commanded the detail, reported: "We jump on the truck and set it alight with Molotov Cocktails. Three wounded Arabs are burning inside. It is the blood of the [Jewish casualties in the] Ben-Shemen and Yehiam convoys [attacked by Arabs a few days earlier] that ignites this hatred in us."[115]

Ben-Gurion cabled his finance chief, Eliʿezer Kaplan, that the situation was "increasingly grave" and that acquiring additional arms had become a "matter [of] life [and] death." He instructed Kaplan to provide "all necessary funds" to Ehud Avriel, the Haganah's purchasing agent in Czechoslovakia.[116] In January 1948, Avriel signed the first of a string of arms contracts with the Czech government.

The Haganah still refrained from aggressive operations in areas not yet caught up in the conflagration. The policy was to "hit the guilty" and to avoid harming nonbelligerent villages, "holy sites, hospitals and schools," and women and children.[117] The following instruction is indicative: "Severe disciplinary measures will be taken [against those] breaching [the rules of] reprisals. It must be emphasized that our aim is defense and not worsening the relations with that part of the Arab community that wants peace with us."[118] Though Haganah reprisals increased in size and frequency during the following months, the organization remained strategically on the defensive until the end of March 1948.

This was reflected in Haganah policy toward specific villages. Orders went out to the field units that villages interested in quiet or in formal nonbelligerency agreements were to be left untouched.[119] Flyers were distributed calling on villagers to desist from hostilities.[120] During February and March 1948 the HGS attached "Arab affairs advisers" to each brigade and battalion to advise the commanders on the "friendliness" or "hostility" of specific villages in their zones of operation.[121] As late as 24 March 1948, Galili instructed all Haganah units to abide by standing Zionist policy, which was to respect the "rights, needs and freedom," "without discrimination," of the Arabs living in the Jewish State areas.[122]

The policy changed only in early April, as reflected in the deliberations of the Arab affairs advisers in the Coastal Plain. At their meeting of 31 March, the advisers acted to protect Arab property and deferred a decision about expelling Arabs or disallowing Arabs to cultivate their fields.[123] But a week later the advisers ruled that "the intention [policy] was, generally, to evict the Arabs living in the brigade's area."[124]

But this description of Zionist policy requires several caveats. From the first, the IZL and LHI did not play along. Almost immediately, they responded to Arab depredations with indiscriminate terrorism (to the ire of the Haganah chiefs).[125] "Enough [with restraint]. From now on—we [shall attack] the nests of murderers," announced Kol Zion Halohemet (the Voice of Fighting Zion), the IZL radio station, on 7 December 1947.[126] During the following days a series of attacks by IZL and LHI bombers and gunmen claimed several dozen lives. The most notable were two IZL bomb attacks outside the Jerusalem Old City Damascus Gate (on 12 and 29 December)[127] and a LHI grenade and machine gun attack (on 28 December) on coffee shops in Jerusalem's Romema district. The coffee shops, according to the LHI commander's later account, "were jammed with Arabs hatching schemes, sipping coffee and playing backgammon."[128] Similar IZL attacks were launched that month in Yazur and Yahudiya, in the center of the country, in Tira, south of Haifa, and in Jaffa, and on 4 January 1948 the LHI detonated a large truck-bomb at the old Jaffa municipality (*saraya*) building, which housed the NC offices, killing dozens.[129] The local leader, Rafik Tamimi, called the mufti and reported: "The situation in Jaffa is so bad, it's hard to describe."[130] Without doubt, the terrorist attacks sowed panic. But they also deepened Arab hatred and contributed to turning what was sporadic Arab violence into a bitter, full-scale war.

Second, the mainstream Zionist leaders, from the first, began to think of expanding the Jewish state beyond the 29 November partition resolution borders. As Shertok told one interlocutor already in September 1947, if the Arabs initiate war, "we will get hold of as much of Palestine as we would think we can hold."[131] He seemed to be referring particularly to the clusters of Jewish settlements left by UNSCOP outside the partition borders, such as that in Western Galilee, from which, even before 29 November, there was growing pressure on the Yishuv leadership for inclusion in the Jewish state.[132] Moreover, the Haganah's limited retaliatory policy itself contributed to the spread and escalation of the hostilities, in one or two cases igniting a fire where none had been before.

Last, to be sure, the Haganah's defensive policy during the first months of the war was dictated in part by a lack of means; the Haganah was not yet ready for large-scale offensive operations, in terms of both unit readiness and armaments. Indeed, in early February 1948 Galili hinted that matters would change once large arms shipments from Czechoslovakia arrived: "We are interested in holding on for two months, [after which] the situation might fundamentally change. In two months we will have different equipment, and then we will be able to deliver a decisive blow against them."[133]

Much of the fighting in the first months of the war took place in and on the edges of the main towns—Jerusalem, Tel Aviv–Jaffa, and Haifa. Most of the violence was initiated by the Arabs. Arab snipers continuously fired at Jewish houses, pedestrians, and traffic and planted bombs and mines along urban and rural paths and roads. Movement in certain areas and streets became unsafe. From the second week of December, Jewish traffic was organized in convoys, with Haganah and, occasionally, British escorts, and concrete anti-sniper walls were erected at the entrances to Jewish buildings and streets in the mixed towns. As the weeks passed the hostilities spread.

The first organized Arab urban attack was launched against the Jewish Hatikva Quarter, on the eastern edge of Tel Aviv. Following several days of sniping and Haganah responses in kind, British troops intervened, killing two Haganah men and arresting others. The Haganah then blew up a house on the outskirts of the neighboring village of Salame. The following day, 8 December 1947, hundreds of irregulars, led by Hassan Salame, assaulted the Hatikva Quarter. The Haganah resisted fiercely. A few of the quarter's houses fell as British troops looked on. The Arabs looted and set them alight. Haganah reinforcements arrived, infiltrating between British patrols, and the

Arabs retreated. The Arabs suffered some sixty dead, the Jews two dead. Afterward, a British officer returned a Jewish baby abducted by the attackers. The British suspected that the assault had been carried out on direct orders from Haj Amin al-Husseini.[134]

A second urban attack took place two months later, in Jerusalem, the seat of the Mandate government. The attackers ran the risk of British interference but claimed that they were retaliating for a Jewish attack on a bus. On 10 February 1948, about 150 Arabs poured out of the Old City and attacked the Yemin Moshe neighborhood to the west, across the Vale of Hinnom. They were protected by covering fire from the city walls. The Haganah, eventually aided by British troops, beat them off. Sixteen Arabs died and dozens were wounded (some by friendly fire); the Jews suffered one dead and five wounded.[135]

Attacks by Arab irregulars on rural settlements also began in early December 1947. On 4 December a band of 120–150 gunmen from Salame attacked Ef'al, a small kibbutz northeast of Tel Aviv. The settlers, helped by Palmah reinforcements, beat them off. A more forceful attack was launched on 27 December against nearby Kfar Yavetz by militiamen from Qalansuwa and Taiyiba. They were responding to provocative Haganah patrolling and the demolition of a nearby well. Haganah reinforcements reached the settlement in time and a British armored column also intervened. The attackers withdrew, leaving behind a number of dead. Several Haganah men were also killed.

A more extensive attack, also resulting from local friction, took place on 11 January 1948, against Kfar Uriah, near Ramla. A Palmah force and a column of British armor routed the attackers, who came from neighboring Beit Jiz and Khirbet Beit Far. Three Haganah men were killed and thirteen were wounded; twenty-five Arabs died.

Like most intercommunal wars, this one, too, was marked by cycles of revenge. On the morning of 30 December, an IZL squad threw bombs from a passing van into a crowd of casual Arab laborers at a bus stop outside the Haifa Oil Refinery, killing eleven and wounding dozens. In a spontaneous response inside the plant, Arab refinery employees (reinforced by laborers from outside), using "sticks, metal bars, stones, etc.," turned on their Jewish coworkers, mostly white-collar employees, and, in an hour-long rampage, butchered thirty-nine and wounded another fifty. Several Arab employees protected Jews. The British refinery executives and security officers refused to intervene or give the Jews arms from the plant's armory, though a number of British workers saved Jews. The massacre was halted by the arrival of British forces, who then allowed the Arabs to be bussed out. No one was arrested. The subsequent investigation by leading Haifa Jewish figures found that the massacre was spontaneous and triggered by the earlier IZL attack and that the Arabs had not planned the outbreak.[136]

But the HGS felt that the massacre could not go unpunished, whatever its trigger, and targeted the large village of Balad ash Sheikh and its satellite village, Hawasa, southeast of Haifa. Many of the refinery workers lived there. Indeed, an HIS report immediately named three Balad ash Sheikh villagers who had participated in the massacre.[137] On the night of 31 December–1 January, the Haganah sent in a Palmah company and several independent platoons. The orders were to "kill as many men as possible"—or, alternatively, "100" men—and "destroy furniture, etc.," but to avoid killing women and children. The raiders moved from house to house, pulling out men and executing them. Sometimes they threw grenades into houses and sprayed the interiors with automatic fire. There were several dozen dead, including some women and children. During the raids, nearby British and Arab Legion units fired from afar at the raiders. The Haganah suffered three dead and two wounded.[138] Mapam leaders criticized the indiscriminate nature of the retaliation. Ben-Gurion responded that "to discriminate [in such circumstances] is impossible. We're at war. . . . There is an injustice in this, but otherwise we will not be able to hold out."[139]

A second revenge cycle occurred in Eastern Galilee. On 2 December 1948, several Arabs attacked a Jewish guard buying cigarettes in a kiosk in the village of Khisas, at the tip of the Panhandle. The guard shot one of them dead. The British arrested the guard, but local villagers began to snipe at Jews cultivating nearby fields. On 18 December a group of Arabs ambushed and shot dead a Jewish cart driver near Kibbutz Ma'ayan Baruch.[140] The local Palmah contingent requested permission to retaliate against Khisas and other villages. Local Jewish leaders, led by Nahum Hurwitz, a veteran of Hashomer, opposed the idea, arguing that the area was largely quiet. But Yigal Allon, the Palmah OC, approved a reprisal (apparently without HGS approval), and that night the Palmah hit Khisas and a nearby mansion belonging to the local effendi, Emir Fa'ur. In Khisas, the Palmahniks stormed a house, killing three men, a woman, and four children, and then blew it up, also damaging an adjacent building; at the mansion, they killed four men. None of the dead appear to have been involved in the death of the cart driver. Much of Khisas's population fled—and those who remained sued for peace.[141]

The raid triggered a protracted dispute among the Yishuv's political leaders. A few, backed by Arab experts, condemned the raid, saying that it had "spread the conflagration." Yosef Sapir, a liberal leader, called for "severe punishment" of the officers responsible.[142] 'Ezra Danin, one of the HIS's founders, complained that the Haganah "does what it pleases despite our advice."[143] No one was punished. But the Arabs were bent on exacting revenge: on 9 January 1948, several hundred bedouin, mostly from Syria, directed by Emir Faʿur, attacked Kibbutz Kfar Szold on the Syrian border. They were driven off with the (eventual) help of a British armored column. One Haganah man was killed and four were wounded; twenty-four Arabs died and sixty-seven were wounded.[144]

The Haganah made other mistakes. On the night of 5–6 January 1948, a squad of sappers penetrated West Jerusalem's Katamon neighborhood and blew up part of the Semiramis Hotel, suspected of housing an Arab irregulars headquarters. Twenty-six civilians died, including the Spanish deputy consul, Manuel Allende Salazar y Travesedo. The explosion triggered the start of a "panic exodus" from the prosperous Arab neighborhood.[145] Jewish sources later claimed that one or two of the dead were irregulars.[146] Several JAE members criticized the Haganah,[147] and the British were irate, calling in Ben-Gurion for a dressing down. He subsequently removed the officer responsible, Mishael Shaham, from command.[148]

But generally Haganah retaliatory strikes during December 1947–March 1948 were accurately directed, either against perpetrators or against their home bases or hostile villages and militiamen. Relatively few women and children were killed. In mid-May, HIS summarized the results of the Jewish reprisals of December 1947–March 1948: "The main effect of these operations was on the Arab civilian population . . . [leading to] economic paralysis, unemployment, lack of fuel and supplies because of the severance of transport. They suffered from the destruction of their houses and psychologically their nerves were badly hit, and they even suffered evacuations and wanderings. . . . [All this] weakened the Arab rear areas and made the operations of the militiamen more difficult, and also led to clashes between the Arab population that was hurt and the Arab combatants whom the civilian inhabitants saw as the source of the disaster. The Jewish attacks forced the Arabs to tie down great forces in protecting themselves. . . . The [reprisals also caused] . . . doubt about their own strength. This war of nerves had great value in undermining to a large extent the confidence of the enemy. But these are phenomena suffered by each side in the conflict and they did not yet reach the extent of decisively affecting the staying power of the Arabs and their morale."[149]

Attacks on Jewish transport were one of the main features of the civil war. From early December 1947, Jewish traffic began to move in Haganah-protected convoys, sometimes accompanied by British armored cars. The Haganah cladded trucks and pickups with armor plating. But Arab ambushes grew in number and potency. On 11 December, a convoy from Jerusalem to the isolated ʿEtzion Bloc of Jewish settlements south of Bethlehem was ambushed by a fazʿa of Arab villagers; ten Jews died. On 14 December, a second convoy, headed for Ben Shemen, near Lydda, was shot up near the Beit Nabala military camp: fourteen Jews were killed and ten injured—shot by Arab Legionnaires serving with the British army in Palestine.[150]

The Jews retaliated in kind. On 12 December, for example, a unit of the Palmah's Third Battalion ambushed a bus, apparently filled with irregulars, at Nabi Yusha, near Safad, killing six and wounding thirty.

Within a month of the outbreak of hostilities, the stakes increased considerably, with the arrival of foreign volunteers who reinforced the Palestine Arab militias. Toward the end of December, some six hundred crossed into Palestine from Lebanon and Syria and fanned out in Jaffa, Haifa, Gaza, Safad, Acre, and Jerusalem.[151] A fortnight later, the advance units of the ALA—having completed their (superficial) training in Qatana—crossed the border. The ALA's Second Yarmuk Battalion (the Yarmuk River was the site of a famous Muslim victory over the Byzantines in 636), with just over three hundred troops, crossed over from Rmaich, Lebanon, on 9–10 January 1948 and headed for Tarshiha in the Galilee. The battalion was commanded by a Syrian army major, Adib Shishakli, and was composed mostly of Syrians.[152]

The First Yarmuk Battalion crossed from Transjordan a few days later and pushed inland, bivouacking in Tubas, near Nablus. The six-hundred-man battalion was commanded by Captain Muhammad Safa.[153] The British quickly learned of these illegal crossings and were much embarrassed (Cunningham was furious).[154] But they did nothing—other than exacting from Safa a worthless promise that the ALA would not engage the Jews until after they, the British, had left the country. A third ALA unit, the Hittin Battalion (named after Saladin's victory over the Crusaders at the Horns of Hittin in 1187), crossed into Palestine from Jordan (with King ʿAbdullah's permission) at the end of January and joined the First Yarmuk.[155] It was commanded by an Iraqi, Madlul Abbas, and was composed mostly of Iraqis, with a sprinkling of Palestinians.

The ALA commanders immediately proved both mendacious and incompetent. On 20 January the Second Yarmuk, supported by Abu Ibrahim al-Sghir's irregulars and local villagers—perhaps four hundred men, armed with obsolete rifles, three medium machine guns, and a light mortar—attacked Kibbutz Yehiam, in Western Galilee (an area earmarked for Arab sovereignty), which was defended by its members, a handful of Palmahniks, and a unit of the Twenty-first Battalion of the Levanoni (later, Carmeli) Brigade—in all, about seventy men, with one medium machine gun, and two light mortars. The defenders were well organized, and the attackers tipped their hand by prematurely blowing up a nearby bridge. Wave after wave of assaults failed to crack the defenses and the ALA withdrew, after suffering thirty dead and sixty wounded; Yehiam sustained four dead—and six more were killed in a nearby ALA ambush.[156]

The First Yarmuk went into action a month later, on 16 February. It had spent weeks preparing, and Haganah intelligence picked up the signs. The HGS guessed that Kibbutz Tirat-Zvi, in the Beit Shean Valley, was the target. The kibbutz was reinforced, and on the night of 15–16 February, a Palmah force blew up the Sheikh Hussein Bridge over the Jordan River, to cut off the ALA units from their Syrian bases. (That night Palmah units also blew up three bridges along the Lebanese-Palestinian border and houses in Jaffa and its suburb, Abu Kabir, and launched a daring raid deep in Arab territory, on the village of Sasa, in northern Galilee, killing some sixty villagers and destroying twenty houses.)[157] Haganah wiretappers had picked up coded messages: "The sheikh is on his way, everything is ready," and "A warm rain fell tonight near Beisan."[158] Soon after midnight, ALA units opened diversionary fire on neighboring kibbutzim and blew up bridges on approach roads. When mortars and machine guns opened up on Tirat-Zvi, the Haganah was ready. There were 115 defenders and about six hundred assailants. But Jewish counterfire, new barbed wire perimeter fences, and pouring rain and mud proved too much for the ALA. The main assault went in at dawn—and was broken. The Arabs retreated, and a British armored column arrived on the scene. The British ordered Safa to leave the area. He agreed—but only if the British first let loose with mortars and machine guns so that he could later explain that he had withdrawn under (British) duress. The British complied, and the First Yarmuk Battalion withdrew. The ALA left behind some forty to sixty dead. News of the defeat swiftly spread through Arab Palestine, causing demoralization. Tirat-Zvi had suffered one dead and one wounded.[159]

The failure of Arab attacks on urban neighborhoods, fear of British intervention, and the incessant appeals by urban notables (especially from Jaffa, motivated by the citrus harvest, which was exported through the port, and Haifa) to Husseini to sanction a cessation of urban violence had led to a switch in focus to the countryside. But this had produced mixed results, with many villagers refusing to host or cooperate with the armed bands and with a general failure to overrun any Jewish settlements. The Haganah troops were too skilled and highly motivated, the bands and the ALA too poorly equipped, trained, and led.

But the roads were another matter, and the Palestinian irregulars focused on them from January through March. Here they enjoyed relative success, and here, so it appeared, was the area of maximum Jewish vulnerability. Along the roads the Arabs usually enjoyed the advantages of the initiative, high ground, surprise, numbers, and firepower. And the results of successful large roadside ambushes could be far-reaching if not decisive. If supplies failed to get through, especially to Jewish Jerusalem, the Yishuv's morale and war effort might collapse. And the gradual withdrawal of British troops from successive regions of Palestine meant that in more and more areas it was possible to attack traffic without fear of British interference.

Already on 31 December 1947 the HIS reported: "The Arabs intend to paralyze all Jewish traffic on the roads within the next few days." In early February 1948 the service learned that ʿAbd al-Qadir al-Husseini intended to halt all Jewish traffic on the Tel Aviv–Jerusalem highway.[160] Supplies to Jerusalem were clearly a major target. But there were other Jewish areas of vulnerability. One of the severest blows to the Haganah resulted from the Palestinian blockade of the Jerusalem–ʿEtzion Bloc road, which early in the hostilities had witnessed the devastation of several convoys. On 15–16 January 1948, a reinforced thirty-five-man platoon, composed mainly of Hebrew University students, tried to bypass the road and reach the besieged bloc by foot through the Judean Hills. The column was spotted and ambushed by a fazʿa. The villagers killed all of them in a drawn-out battle (and then, according to some reports, mutilated their bodies).[161]

Side by side with ambushes along the roads, the Husseini-affiliated irregulars turned to large-scale urban terrorism, despite an increasing difficulty in penetrating Jewish neighborhoods, which were patrolled by the Haganah and cordoned off and separated from Arab neighborhoods with barbed wire and British and Jewish check posts. The Arabs had noted the devastating effects of a few well-placed Jewish bombs in Jerusalem, Jaffa, and Haifa[162] and enjoyed the services of an accomplished bomb-maker, the blond and blue-eyed Fawzi al-Kutub, who learned his craft with the SS in Nazi Germany.[163]

There was a string of bombings during January–March 1948. On the night of 1–2 February two British deserters, Eddie Brown and Peter Madison, and an Arab, Abu Khalil Janho, working for ʿAbd al-Qadir al-Husseini, drove a British army truck and a police car to the entrance of the *Palestine Post* building in downtown West Jerusalem. The three fled and at 10:55 PM the truck exploded, gutting the building and damaging the adjacent Himmelfarb Hotel, which housed Palmah troops. One man died and more than twenty were injured.[164]

The next attack was the war's worst. Despite ample forewarning, Husseini managed on 22 February to introduce three stolen British trucks and an armored car, driven by six British army deserters and ex-policemen, into the heart of Jewish Jerusalem. The small convoy stopped outside the Atlantic and Amdursky hotels, which housed Palmah troopers, on Ben-Yehuda

Street. Kutub had rigged the trucks with explosives in the village of Imwas (New Testament Emmaus), near Latrun. The Britons primed the bombs, shot dead a suspicious Jewish guard, and drove off in the armored car. The trucks blew up at 6:30 AM, leveling four buildings. The Palmahniks were out on operations. But fifty-eight people died, almost all civilians, and thirty-two were seriously injured. There was shock and anger. Ben-Gurion said that he had been in London during the Blitz, "but such a thing I never saw, I couldn't recognize the street." But, he added, "we were the first to commit [such acts] . . . the Jews were the first." He was referring to previous LHI and IZL bombings.[165] Vengeful IZL and LHI gunmen immediately took to the streets, killing sixteen British troops and policemen. A week later, on 29 February, an LHI bomb planted near Rehovot derailed a British troop train from Cairo to Haifa, killing twenty-eight and wounding others.[166]

The third Arab bombing of the series was the most audacious. On 11 March, a Husseini agent, Anton Daoud Camilio, who doubled as an HIS informer, drove a car bomb into the courtyard of Jerusalem's National Institutions compound, the headquarters of the Jewish Agency and the Jewish National Fund. Camilio was an American-born Armenian who worked as a driver for the American consulate. He was supposed to deliver three Bren machine guns to the Haganah. The guards were instructed to allow him in. He parked the consular vehicle and walked out of the compound. A few minutes later, the car exploded. Twelve people were killed and ten seriously wounded. The Haganah and the American consulate were badly embarrassed, and morale in Jewish Jerusalem was shaken.[167]

Ultimately, though, the bombings were a sideshow; the roads were far more important. The Arab ambushes during December 1947–mid-March 1948 had taken a heavy toll and supplying the isolated outposts in the Galilee, the Negev, and Judea, and Jerusalem's Jews, became a major headache for the Haganah. Most of the Palmah was deployed guarding the convoys, and the casualty rate was appalling. Jewish defensive tactics and means steadily improved. Yet so did the Arabs' organization and firepower. Often the convoys barreled through. But in the end it was an unequal struggle between small Haganah units in lightly armed, cramped, highly inflammable, makeshift armored cars and masses of Arabs enfilading the road from behind rocks on surrounding hills. Narrow roads made maneuver all but impossible. Communication between vehicles was often lost, and occasionally poor equipment impaired communications between the convoy and Haganah headquarters. Once a convoy was ambushed, there was usually nowhere to retreat to: Jewish settlements were often far away, and unfriendly Arab villages lay in all directions.

British troops often protected convoys and interfered in firefights.[168] But this ceased in March as more and more units were withdrawn to the Haifa enclave, from which they boarded ships to Britain. And the government's willingness to protect Jewish traffic was dampened by the dissidents' continuing attacks on its troops. In any event, assuring the safety of the withdrawing forces had become Whitehall's chief concern—though, to be sure, a second major interest was maintaining good relations with the Arabs so that Britain's position in the Middle East would remain robust after the withdrawal from Palestine.

Jewish pressure on Arab traffic was maintained throughout. In some areas, such as Haifa, topography and demography combined to give the Jews the upper hand. But ultimately, the Yishuv proved more vulnerable, because whereas most Arabs lived in autarchic or semi-autarchic villages, most Jews lived in towns that required continuous supply.

In late March, the Haganah endured a series of major disasters on the roads. They appeared to portend defeat in the war—and demonstrated the imperative for a basic change in strategy that would shift the initiative to the Yishuv and allow a diversion of energies from protecting convoys to smashing the Arab militias in their home bases. In less than a fortnight the Haganah lost most of its armored vehicles and dozens of its best troops.

First came three serious setbacks in the Jerusalem area—near Har-Tuv (18 March), ʿAtarot (24 March), and Saris (24 March)—in which the Haganah suffered twenty-six men killed and eighteen vehicles destroyed.[169] Greater disasters followed. On the morning of 27 March a large convoy—three dozen supplies-laden trucks accompanied by five busloads of troops and seven armored cars—snaked its way from Jerusalem to the ʿEtzion Bloc. A Haganah spotter plane flew overhead. Kamal Erikat, ʿAbd al-Qadir al-Husseini's deputy, decided to attack the convoy on its way back and mobilized thousands of armed villagers and townsmen from Hebron, Bethlehem, and Jerusalem. It would be the biggest convoy ambush of the war. The British warned the Jewish Agency that they would not intervene and advised that the convoy postpone its return. But the men and vehicles were needed in Jerusalem, the Haganah responded, and the convoy set out.

A Haganah spotter aircraft warned that Arabs were massed along the route and had set up roadblocks. But the commanders believed that they could push through. A British colonel in an armored car drove southward through the roadblocks and warned the convoy what to expect. The trucks and buses plowed on. Just south of Bethlehem, at Nabi Daniyal, the Arabs let loose. The convoy's obstacle-busting vehicle, mounting a steel "V," cleared six of the barriers but came to a halt at the seventh. Heavy fire rained down from the hillsides on the stalled vehicles. An armored relief column sent from Kibbutz Ramat Rachel, south of Jerusalem, was unable to reach the convoy and turned back after it, too, sustained casualties. The British declined to intervene.

Most of the 186 Haganah troopers, men and women, left their vehicles, which had become death traps, and took refuge in an empty stone house by the road. The armored cars, like a western wagon train, took up positions around the house (which served as a summer dorm for Arab grape harvesters). A handful of Haganah men managed to retreat to the ʿEtzion Bloc, six miles to the south. For thirty hours the rest of the troopers were under siege, several thousand Arabs pouring down fire from the rock-strewn hillsides. The attackers repeatedly tried to edge nearer. Haganah spotter planes, mounting Bren guns, periodically strafed them and dropped primitive bombs and supplies. In Jerusalem, the Haganah tried unsuccessfully to assemble a large relief force or prod the British into action. One defender, Aharon Gilad, recorded: "Depression took hold . . . all fear death." The surrounding Arabs shouted: "Where is your mother, where is Ben-Gurion? We shall soon cut your throats."

An Arab militiaman, a barber, later wrote: "I took part in the battle from 4 in the afternoon until midnight. Then we had supper. . . . At 4 in the morning it was very cold, but I felt as if it was a summer night. At 04:30 we received the order to assault. . . . Then two Jewish airplanes . . . threw down ammunition to the besieged but . . . not on target. Several [Arab] fighters went to collect the parcels. The aircraft fired on them with machineguns and threw bombs. Several fighters were lightly injured. The fighters fired on the airplanes, which fled the area."

On the morning of 28 March, a British armored column at last set out from Jerusalem, brushed aside the roadblocks, and halted a mile from the house. A three-way negotiation followed. Eventually, the Haganah agreed to stop the strafing runs, the Arabs stopped firing, and the besieged troops handed their weapons to the British. They then boarded British trucks and left, and the army handed over the weapons to the Arabs. Haganah losses were fifteen dead and seventy-three wounded, as well as ten armored cars, four buses, and twenty-five armor-clad trucks. The HIS estimated Arab losses at sixty dead and two hundred wounded. The engagement left a trail of bitterness in the Haganah command. The commander in the besieged house, Arye Tepper (Amit), later implicitly blamed the Haganah chiefs for the fiasco and proposed that the isolated outposts around Jerusalem, including the ʿEtzion Bloc, be evacuated; the price of holding on was too high.[170]

Almost simultaneously, an even deadlier ambush raged in Western Galilee. On 27 March, a seven-vehicle convoy, carrying eighty-nine men and women, was attacked on the road to the besieged Kibbutz Yehiam by units of the

ALA's Second Yarmuk Battalion and local militiamen. The HIS had received specific information from a Druze agent and had warned that the Arabs were massing—but in light of Yehiam's plight, the convoy's commander had decided to proceed. The ambush was sprung near the village of Kabri. The lead armored car managed to break through to Yehiam. But the remaining vehicles were stopped and subjected to withering fire. By late evening, all were burning, though some three dozen Haganah men escaped on foot to Jewish settlements. The Carmeli Brigade had no ready relief force, and although a British unit managed to reach the area and shell Kabri, it failed to link up with the convoy. The following morning, the British and Haganah found forty-seven bodies, many of them mutilated. Arab losses were reportedly three to six dead and a handful of wounded.[171]

A further disaster followed four days later. The situation of Jewish Jerusalem was precarious. "There is panic. . . . There may be food riots," wrote the head of the Jerusalem HIS, Yitzhak Levy.[172] The city verged on collapse. The Haganah readied a thirty-seven-vehicle convoy, loaded with reinforcements and supplies. It set out from Kibbutz Hulda on the morning of 31 March. But the previous night Haganah troops had blown up a house and killed fifteen Arabs in the nearby village of Abu Shusha. And the convoy itself, as it started out, encountered an Arab bus and fired shots, killing the driver and wounding several passengers. The alarm was sounded in the surrounding villages and the militiamen were mustered. The convoy was to be targeted.

The Arabs began sniping, trucks were overturned, and battle was joined. The fighting was confused. A number of Arab armored cars raced to the scene. Palmahniks occupied dominant hilltops while some vehicles retreated back to Hulda; others, though, were stuck and under ferocious attack. The occupants of one vehicle committed suicide with dynamite rather than fall into Arab hands. (Jews captured in convoy battles were normally put to death and mutilated.) By nightfall, most of the Palmahniks extricated themselves and reached Hulda. But twenty-two Haganah men had died and sixteen were wounded, and four more vehicles were lost. Arab losses were eight dead. It was the first time a whole convoy had failed to make it to Jerusalem.[173] In the last week of March, 136 supply trucks had tried to reach Jerusalem; only forty-one had made it.[174]

Cunningham keenly noted the Zionists' desperation: "It is becoming increasingly apparent that the Yishuv and its leaders are deeply worried about the future. The intensification of Arab attacks on communications and particularly the failure of the Kfar ʿEtzion convoy . . . to force a return passage has brought home the precarious position of Jewish communities, both great and small, which are dependent on supply lines running through Arab-controlled country. In particular it is now realized that the position of Jewish Jerusalem, where a food scarcity already exists, is likely to be desperate after 16th May. The loss of Jewish armoured vehicles has shaken confidence in the belief that they are the answer to most problems of supply by road. . . . The balance of the fighting seems to have turned much in favour of the Arabs."[175]

By the end of March, the Yishuv had suffered about a thousand dead.[176]

4

The Second Stage of the Civil War, April–mid-May 1948

The crisis the Zionist leadership faced was not only military: "It is becoming generally realized . . . that the United States aim is to secure reconsideration of the Palestine problem by the General Assembly *de novo*," wrote Sir Alan Cunningham.[1] He was referring to the fact that the spiraling hostilities and the Arab successes had bitten deeply into international support for partition and Jewish statehood—as the Arab initiators of the violence had hoped.

Surprisingly, the first to get cold feet were the Americans. Already on 2 December 1947, Truman was gently cautioning the Zionists and their supporters: "The vote in the United Nations is only the beginning and the Jews must now display tolerance and consideration for the other people in Palestine with whom they will necessarily have to be neighbors."[2] A few weeks later, Secretary of State George Marshall put it more starkly when he reportedly told his staff that "he thought US Government may have made a mistake supporting partition."[3]

The hint at a reversal of course on partition, quite naturally, immediately stoked strong Zionist counterpressure—and American reaffirmations of support for partition, perhaps, as the British suggested, linked to electoral considerations (Truman and most members of Congress were up for election or reelection in November 1948).[4] Nonetheless, by January the escalating Arab attacks and threats to intervene from outside Palestine began to take their toll in Washington. The British soon began toying with the idea of a formal "suspension of the partition plan" and the institution, in its stead, of a "trusteeship scheme." But they understood that this would become a realistic proposition only "after continued deterioration of situation in Palestine."[5] Curiously, the idea may have been introduced to Whitehall by Lord (Herbert) Samuel, the pro-Zionist first Palestine high commissioner (1920–1925), at a meeting with Clement Attlee sometime in December 1947 or early January.[6]

By late January 1948, Zionist officials assessed that the US position was as it had been on 29 November 1947—meaning, great reluctance regarding "partition" overcome at the last minute by Truman's direct intervention.[7] But by February, the State Department seemingly had won over the president who, somewhat equivocally, informed Marshall that he approved "in principle this basic position"—that is, given the failure of a peaceful partition, to place Palestine under UN trusteeship.[8] Inching toward trusteeship, Warren Austin, the US representative to the United Nations said that the Security Council was obliged to preserve peace, not force partition on the Arabs.[9] The State Department may even have envisioned London remaining in control, with the British "keeping their troops in Palestine until a final and peaceful settlement is achieved," in the words of James Reston of the *New York Times*.[10] The Policy Planning Staff of the State Department argued that "the maintenance . . . of a Jewish state" was contrary to the American "national interest" or "immediate strategic interests."[11] During the following weeks, Truman may still have been wavering, but Marshall was under the impression that the president had plumped for trusteeship. He authorized Warren Austin to proceed with the formal announcement.[12] Austin himself was somewhat reluctant[13] but in the end acceded[14] and on 17 March formally broached the possibility at the Security Council.[15]

Zionist lobbyists frantically maneuvered to parry the expected blow. At the last moment, they arranged a meeting between the great persuader, Chaim Weizmann, and the president. They met in the White House on 18 March. It is not completely clear what transpired. According to Margaret Truman, the president's daughter and biographer, and Zionist sources, Truman reiterated his support for partition, in which the Negev would be included in the Jewish state.[16]

So Austin's anti-partition statement at the Security Council the following day came as a bombshell, and not only for the Zionists. The American representative was no longer hesitant and suggestive; he spoke clearly and forthrightly, announcing a major policy volte-face: "There seems to be general agreement that the [partition] plan cannot now be implemented by peaceful means. . . . We believe that a temporary trusteeship for Palestine should be established under the Trusteeship Council . . . without prejudice . . . to the character of the eventual political settlement." He called on the council to instruct the Palestine Commission "to suspend its efforts to implement the proposed partition plan" and asked for a special session of the General Assembly to replace the partition resolution formally with one endorsing trusteeship.[17]

The Arabs were jubilant. The Jewish Agency rejected Austin's proposal as "a shocking reversal of [the US] position. . . . We are at an utter loss to understand the reason." It was apparently a capitulation to Arab violence, said Abba Hillel Silver, a spokesman for American Zionism.[18] The Soviets supported the Zionists.

Truman himself appears to have been genuinely shocked and unhappy with Austin's announcement. "The State Department pulled the rug from under me today," he jotted down. "The State Department has reversed my Palestine policy. The first I know about it is what I see in the papers! Isn't that hell? I am now in the position of a liar and a double-crosser."[19] But Marshall and the State Department later maintained that Truman had approved the Austin statement.[20] Clearly there had been some crossed wires—but also, it appears, some crass insubordination. Truman's strong reaction may also have been influenced by the immediate, adverse American press responses to Austin's speech.[21] In any event, Truman quickly reassured the Zionists that he stood by partition.

In the Yishuv, the Austin statement, which was followed by the terrible reverses along the roads, triggered a sense of catastrophe. "This is the most terrible day since the beginning of the war,"[22] David Ben-Gurion cabled Moshe Shertok, in New York, on 28 March. Nowhere was the sense of looming disaster more acute than in West Jerusalem. "There is starvation [$ra'av$]," reported Yitzhak Ben-Zvi from the embattled city.[23] In veiled language, Yitzhak Levy, head of the Jerusalem HIS, hinted at a specific problem. "The character of the Yishuv [that is, Jewish community] in Jerusalem is special. The multiplicity of [ethnic Jewish] communities and asocial modes of life among the poor classes, create a very weak background for this type of bloody warfare that we [now] face. Bread riots, the incitement of the masses, robbery and extortion are likely to develop rapidly and to destroy the city's defenses."[24] He was referring to the town's large ultra-Orthodox and Sephardi communities. Even abroad, the desperate straits of West Jerusalem—"the empty shelves in the shops, the queues whenever there is anything to buy and the general panicky feeling"—was attracting diplomatic and press attention.[25] Jerusalem, in short, was—or appeared—on the verge of collapse.

On 31 March Ben-Gurion summoned his military and political aides for a nightlong series of meetings. Yadin pointed to the Haganah's difficulties in different parts of the country. But Ben-Gurion's mind remained focused: "The fall of Jewish Jerusalem could be a deathblow to the Yishuv, and the Arabs understand this and will concentrate great forces to interdict traffic [to the city]." He demanded that the HGS scrape together a large force and send it to the besieged city.[26]

Yadin tried to calm the Old Man. Jerusalem was not in dire peril; the reports, perhaps, were exaggerated. In any case, the Haganah could not afford to deplete other sectors. As a compromise, he proposed mustering five hundred additional troops for Jerusalem.

Ben-Gurion: "Why not 5,000"?

Yadin: The Haganah hasn't that many available, or arms, to spare.

The argument grew heated.

Ben-Gurion: "We'll take men, arms, and mortars from the settlements."

Yadin: "I can't agree that someone [that is, Ben-Gurion] who's never seen a mortar in action, who doesn't know how many mortars there are . . . can give an order to send them."[27]

But in the end, Yadin caved in. The HGS spent the following hours organizing what was to be known as Operation Nahshon, geared to pushing one or more large convoys to the city and clearing the road of enemy bases, meaning the villages on either side that served as the militia assembly and jump-off points. Fifteen hundred men—three battalions—were mustered and placed under the command of Shimon Avidan, the Giv'ati Brigade's officer in command.

At the time, Ben-Gurion and the HGS believed that they had initiated a one-shot affair, albeit with the implication of a change of tactics and strategy on the Jerusalem front. In fact, they had set in motion a strategic transformation of Haganah policy. Nahshon heralded a shift from the defensive to the offensive and marked the beginning of the implementation of *tochnit dalet* (Plan D)—without Ben-Gurion or the HGS ever taking an in principle decision to embark on its implementation.

But the Haganah had had little choice. With the Arab world loudly threatening and seemingly mobilizing for invasion, the Yishuv's political and military leaders understood that they would first have to crush the Palestinian militias in the main towns and along the main roads and the country's borders if they were to stand a chance of beating off the invading armies. And there was an ineluctable time frame. The Palestinians would have to be defeated in the six weeks remaining before the British departure, scheduled for 15 May.

An additional reason for the start of implementation and the shift from defense to offense was the calculation that British military power had been, by early April, so depleted and British resolve, with eyes riveted on the impending withdrawal, so weakened that intervention against the Haganah was highly unlikely. By 1 April, British troop numbers in Palestine had diminished to 27,600.[28]

No doubt, too, the Haganah switched to the offensive in early April also, simply, because it could. For four months, under continuous Arab provocation and attack, the Yishuv had largely held itself in check, initially in the hope that the disturbances would blow over and, later, in deference to international—particularly British—sensibilities. In addition, the Haganah had lacked armed manpower beyond what was needed for defense. But by the end of March, recruitment and the reorganization of the militia in battalion and brigade formations were fairly well advanced. And Czech arms at last began to arrive.

The first shipment—of two hundred rifles, forty MG-34 machine guns, and 160,000 bullets—secretly landed during the night of 31 March–1 April at a makeshift airfield at Beit Daras in a chartered American Skymaster cargo plane.[29] A second and far larger shipment, covered with onions and potatoes—of forty-five hundred rifles and two hundred machine guns, along with five million bullets—arrived at Tel Aviv port aboard the *Nora* on 2 April. When the equipment was offloaded and reached the units, "some of the boys couldn't restrain themselves and kissed the guns, which were still coated with grease," Yisrael Galili recorded.[30] (A third shipment—consisting of ten thousand rifles, 1,415 machine guns, and sixteen million rounds—reached the Yishuv by sea on 28 April.)[31]

Before this, the Haganah high command had had to "borrow" weapons from local units for a day or two for specific operations, and the units (and settlements) were generally reluctant to part with weapons, quite reasonably arguing that the Arabs might attack while the weapons were on loan. Now, at last, the Haganah command had at hand a stockpile of thousands of weapons that it could freely deploy. The two shipments proved decisive. As Ben-Gurion put it at the time, "After we have received a small amount of the [Czech] equipment . . . the situation is radically different in our favor."[32] Without doubt, of all the shipments that subsequently reached the Yishuv, none was to have greater immediate impact or historical significance.

Until the end of March, Haganah policy had been to defend the existing Jewish settlements and protect the convoys supplying them. Occasionally, its troops carried out retaliatory strikes against Arab militia units and bases. But no territory was conquered and no village—with two exceptions over December 1947–March 1948 (ʿArab Suqreir and Qisariya)—was destroyed. But henceforward, Haganah policy would be permanently to secure roads, border areas, and Jewish settlements by crushing minatory irregular forces and destroying or permanently occupying the villages and towns from which they operated. The Arab militias and their ALA reinforcements had to be crushed; the main roads had to be permanently secured; and the Haganah's brigades had to be freed to deploy along the borders to fend off the expected pan-Arab invasion. In addition, the world, and particularly the United States, had to be persuaded that the Yishuv could and would win and establish its state. Victory over the Palestinian Arabs would assure the world community's continued adherence to the decision to partition Palestine and establish a Jewish state.

Plan D, formulated in early March and signed and dispatched to the Haganah brigade commanders on 10 March, was Yadin's blueprint for concerted operations on the eve of the final British departure and the pan-Arab invasion that was expected to follow hard on its heels. It was scheduled to be implemented in the first half of May, as the British convoys were due to converge on Haifa and Rafah on their way out and as the Arab states' armies deployed for invasion along the frontiers. The Haganah brigades were expected to move more or less simultaneously in the various sectors.

But a variety of factors, chief of which were the debacle on the roads, the specific threat to West Jerusalem and the American retreat from partition, persuaded Ben-Gurion and the HGS to launch this series of campaigns—which, in retrospect, can be seen as the implementation of Plan D—prematurely and in piecemeal fashion. Operation Nahshon was the first step.

Palestinian Arab strengths and weaknesses were well suited to the nature of the early months of the war, when fighting was dispersed, disorganized, small-scale, and highly localized. The moment the Haganah switched to the offense and launched large-scale, highly organized, and sustained operations, the Arab weaknesses came to the fore—and their militias, much like Palestinian society as a whole, swiftly collapsed, like a house of cards.

But in analyzing the war, and especially its course in the months December 1947–May 1948, it is well to remember that the Yishuv's leaders had failed fully to grasp the weakness of Palestinian society and were for the most part (pleasantly) surprised, even astonished, by the ease of the Haganah victories and by the swiftness of the collapse.

The Haganah shift of strategy was decided on incrementally during the first half of April: each decision appeared to be, and in large measure was, a response to a particular, local challenge. But by the end of the period it was clear that a dramatic conceptual change had taken place and that the Yishuv had gone over to the offensive and was now engaged in a war of conquest. That war of conquest was prefigured in Plan D.

Glimmers of the prospective change in strategy were apparent in the first months of 1948. In January, planning in the Haganah Jerusalem District provided for "the destruction of villages . . . dominating our settlements or endangering our communications routes."[33] And in Tel Aviv, one senior officer recommended destroying Jaffa's water reservoir "to force a large number of Arabs to leave the town."[34]

But such suggestions or "plans" were not, in fact, activated before the implementation of Plan D in April and May. And Plan D itself was never launched, in an orchestrated fashion, by a formal leadership decision. Indeed, the various battalion and brigade commanders in the first half of April, and perhaps even later, seemed unaware that they were implementing Plan D. In retrospect it is clear that the Haganah offensives of April and early May were piecemeal implementations of Plan D. But at the time, the dispersed units felt they were simply embarking on unconcerted operations geared to putting out fires in each locality and to meeting particular local challenges (the siege of Jerusalem, the cutoff of the Galilee Panhandle from the Jezreel Valley, and so on). The massive Haganah documentation from the first half of April contains no reference to an implementation of Plan D, and only rarely do such references appear in the Haganah's paperwork during the following weeks.

Plan D called for securing the areas earmarked by the United Nations for Jewish statehood and several concentrations of Jewish population outside those areas (West Jerusalem and Western Galilee). The roads between the core Jewish areas and the border areas where the invading Arab armies were expected to attack were to be secured. The plan consisted of two parts: general guidelines, distributed to all brigade OCs, and specific orders to each of the six territorial brigades ('Etzioni [Jerusalem], Kiryati [(Tel Aviv], Giv'ati [Rehovot-Rishon Lezion], Alexandroni [the Coastal Plain], Carmeli [Haifa], and Golani [Jezreel Valley]). The preamble stated: the aim "of this plan is to take control of the territory of the Jewish State and to defend its borders, as well as [defend] the blocs of settlement and the Jewish population outside these borders against a regular enemy, semi-regular[s] [that is, the ALA], and irregulars."

Previous Haganah master plans had referred either to the British or the Palestinian Arab militias or a combination of the two, possibly aided by Arab volunteers from outside, as the possible enemy. Plan D was geared to an invasion by regular Arab armies. It was to be activated when "the forces of the

[British] government in the country will no longer be in existence"—meaning that it was to be activated somewhere in the hiatus between the British withdrawal and the Arab invasion. When it emerged that no such hiatus would exist, the HGS prepared to activate the plan during the last week or two of (by then largely nominal) British rule.

The plan called for the consolidation of Jewish control in and around the big Jewish and mixed towns (Tel Aviv, Jerusalem, Haifa), the sealing off of potential enemy routes into the country, the consolidation of a defense line along the borders, and the extension of Haganah protection to Jewish population centers outside the UN-sanctioned borders. In doing this, the plan called for the securing of the main interior roads, the siege of Arab towns and neighborhoods, and the conquest of forward enemy bases.

To achieve these objectives, swathes of Arab villages, either hostile or potentially hostile, were to be conquered, and brigade commanders were given the option of "destruction of villages (arson, demolition, and mining of the ruins)" or "cleansing [of militiamen] and taking control of [the villages]" and leaving a garrison in place. The commanders were given discretion whether to evict the inhabitants of villages and urban neighborhoods sitting on vital access roads.[35] The individual brigades were instructed in detail about which British police stations and army camps they were to occupy, the particular roads they were to secure, and the specific villages and towns they were to conquer and either depopulate, destroy, and mine or garrison.[36]

Plan D has given rise over the decades to a minor historiographic controversy, with Palestinian and pro-Palestinian historians[37] charging that it was the Haganah's master plan for the expulsion of the country's Arabs. But a cursory examination of the actual text leads to a different conclusion. The plan calls for securing the emergent state's territory and borders and the lines of communication between the Jewish centers of population and the border areas. The plan is unclear about whether the Haganah was to conquer and secure the roads between the Jewish state's territory and the blocs of Jewish settlement outside that territory. The plan "assumed" that "enemy" regular, irregular, and militia forces would assail the new state, with the aim of cutting off the Negev and Eastern and Western Galilee, invading the Coastal Plain and isolating Tel Aviv and Jewish Haifa and Jerusalem. The Haganah's "operational goals" would be "to defend [the state] against . . . invasion," assure "free [Jewish] movement," deny the enemy forward bases, apply economic pressure to end enemy actions, limit the enemy's ability to wage guerrilla war, and gain control of former Mandate government installations and services in the new state's territory.

The plan gave the brigades carte blanche to conquer the Arab villages and, in effect, to decide on each village's fate—destruction and expulsion or occupation. The plan explicitly called for the destruction of resisting Arab villages and the expulsion of their inhabitants. In the main towns, the brigades were tasked with evicting the inhabitants of resisting neighborhoods to the core Arab neighborhoods (not expulsion from the country). The plan stated: "[The villages] in your area, which have to be taken, cleansed or destroyed—you decide [on their fate], in consultation with your Arab affairs advisers and HIS officers." Nowhere does the document speak of a policy or desire to expel "the Arab inhabitants" of Palestine or of any of its constituent regions; nowhere is any brigade instructed to clear out "the Arabs."[38]

In retrospect, Operation Nahshon marked the start of the implementation of Plan D. The operational order for Nahshon, issued by Avidan on 4 April, defined the objectives as (1) "to push [a] convoy" from Kibbutz Hulda to Jerusalem and (2) "to open the road to Jerusalem by means of offensive operations against enemy bases" along the road to assure the passage of future convoys. The order's preamble noted that "all of 'shem's' [that is, the Arab] villages along this route are to be regarded as enemy assembly points or bases of operation."[39] Most of these villages lay in the territory designated in the partition resolution for Palestinian Arab sovereignty—which meant that securing the road or "Corridor" to Jerusalem would involve an expansion of the prospective Jewish state's territory.

In effect, the operation began on the night of 2–3 April, even before the operational order was issued. A Palmah company, reacting to clashes between Jewish and Arab militiamen in the Motza area, conquered the small village of al-Qastal, just west of Jerusalem, overlooking the road. The company met negligible resistance and suffered no casualties.[40] Two days later, on the night of 4–5 April, a company of Givʿati Brigade troops blew up the four-story headquarters in an orange grove near Ramla of Hassan Salame, who commanded the irregulars at the western end of Nahshon's operational area. Though the commander emerged unscathed, some two dozen Arabs and a German officer who served as Salame's adviser died in the explosion. The operation dealt a mortal blow to Salame's reputation and to Arab morale countrywide; Arabs fled from nearby villages.[41] Givʿati had suffered only three lightly wounded.[42]

The operation effectively neutralized the main Arab band at the western end of the Jerusalem Corridor, paving the way for the Haganah conquest, on 6 April, of the Arab villages of Khulda and Deir Muheizin. With these and al-Qastal secured, the Haganah successfully relaunched the sixty-vehicle convoy, with reinforcements, food, fuel, and ammunition, from Kibbutz Hulda, where it had been stuck for a week, toward the capital. It reached West Jerusalem the following day, cheered by onlookers lining the sidewalks.

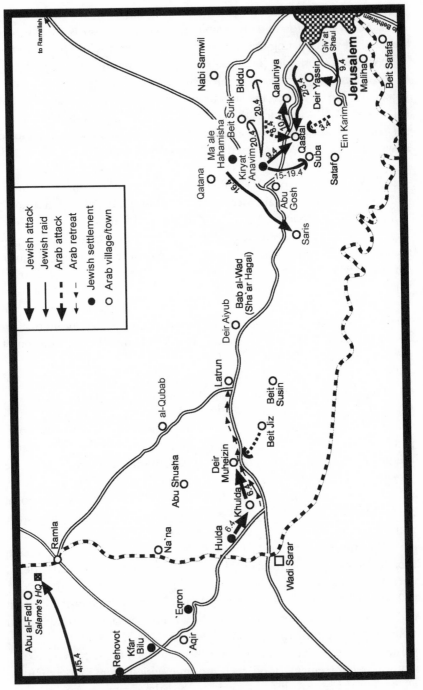

Operation Nahshon, April 1948

But if the destruction of Salame's headquarters grabbed instant, large headlines, the conquest of al-Qastal triggered major long-term effects. The Haganah garrisoned the empty village with a second-line infantry platoon from the 'Etzioni Brigade. Some of the troops had no combat experience; others knew no Hebrew. But HGS had misread the situation. During the following days Jerusalem Haganah and Palmah commanders bickered over who was responsible for holding and/or reinforcing al-Qastal. But 'Abd al-Qadir al-Husseini, the Arab Jerusalem Hills sector commander, understood its importance: al-Qastal dominated the western entrance to the city. Hundreds of militiamen and Iraqi volunteers massed to retake the village; irregulars arrived from as far away as Nablus. They sniped at the defenders and slowly inched toward al-Qastal. British armored cars initially helped the 'Etzioni troops with cannon fire but then withdrew. For the next three days, the 'Etzioni platoon was hit with mortars and machine guns from the surrounding hills. They continuously pleaded for reinforcements. But none materialized, though Haganah light aircraft periodically overflew the area and (ineffectively) lobbed grenades and strafed the Arabs. The 'Etzioni men held on.

Meanwhile, 'Abd al-Qadir al-Husseini journeyed to Damascus to plead for ammunition and arms, especially artillery. He argued that al-Qastal and the road were crucial. But he came away empty-handed. At one point, he reportedly chided Ismail Safwat, the head of the League's Military Committee, after flinging a map of Palestine in his face: "You traitor. History will condemn you. I am returning to al-Qastal, with or without heavy arms. I'll take al-Qastal or die fighting." That night, he composed a poem for his seven-year-old son, Faisal (who was to serve in the 1990s as the PLO's Jerusalem affairs "minister"):

> This land of the brave is the land of our forefathers.
> The Jews have no right to this land.
> How can I sleep while the enemy rules it?
> Something burns in my heart.
> My homeland beckons.[43]

He then set off for Palestine to organize what he hoped would be the decisive assault.

On the night of 7–8 April hundreds of irregulars, led by Ibrahim Abu Diya, of Surif village, reached al-Qastal's perimeter houses. The 'Etzioni unit fought them off with grenades and submachine guns. The assault bogged down, and the attackers withdrew.

'Abd al-Qadir al-Husseini had watched from a nearby hill but could see little. Just before dawn, he climbed the al-Qastal slope with two or three aides, one of them his deputy Kamal 'Erikat, either to see what was happening or to lead a fresh assault. Fog enveloped the hilltop village. ʿAbd al-Qadir and his colleagues wended their way through the first outlying houses. As they approached the mukhtar's house, an ʿEtzioni sentry mistook them for the first of long-promised reinforcements and hailed them in Arabic slang in common use in the Haganah: "Up here boys." ʿAbd al-Qadir called back, in English: "Hello boys." The sentry, Meir Karmiyol, sensed that it was an Arab's English—or he may have seen something amiss. He fired off a burst in the direction of the voices. ʿAbd al-Qadir fell to the ground and his aides fled down the hillside. ʿAbd al-Qadir muttered: "Water, water." A Haganah medic approached and tended him, but he expired. Karmiyol looked through al-Husseini's clothes and discovered documents, a miniature Qurʾan, gold pens, an ivory-handled pistol, and a gold watch. He realized that he had bagged a big shot. Yet the man's identity was still unclear.

Meanwhile, al-Qastal was peppered with sniper fire. The weary defenders expected a renewed assault momentarily. But the airwaves were soon filled with Arabic chatter and anxiety about their missing commander. Soon convoys with reinforcements were making their way to the area from Hebron and Nablus. They were bent on saving, or retrieving the body of, their leader. "I saw thousands of Arabs. Buses, trucks and donkeys brought them from Suba," one of the al-Qastal defenders later recalled.[44]

By noon, the village was under heavy attack. The defenders were low on ammunition and exhausted. A platoon of Palmah soldiers at last reached the area via the Jerusalem road. But it was too late. The ʿEtzioni troops had had enough. Many fled down the slope northward, toward the road—just as the Palmahniks, led by Nahum Arieli, were climbing up. The Arabs, coming from the south and west, "attacked like madmen."[45] They occupied some houses and laid down a barrage of mortar and machine gun fire. Arieli managed to reach the ʿEtzioni command post. But dozens of Haganah and Palmah men were already dead or wounded, and a mass of Arab militiamen was pressing up the alleyways toward the mukhtar's house.

Arieli ordered his men, and the remaining ʿEtzioni troops, to retreat eastward. As they withdrew, the dead and dying were left on the slopes. There was a lull in the shooting. "I saw a lot of Arabs, like flies, and then realized why it was quiet. They had taken the village. They started to celebrate. . . . I fled to the orchard [at the base of the hill] with part of my squad," an ʿEtzioni veteran recalled.[46] Arabs began to push down the slope, giving chase. Arieli and a handful of other officers took up positions nearby to cover the retreat. Their bodies were later found there, either felled by Arab bullets or by their own hand, with grenades, to avoid capture.

The Arabs spent the afternoon hunting and killing stray and wounded Haganah men. Eventually they found what they were looking for—Husseini's body. Arab command and control—and morale—broke down; they had lost their leader, and several of his lieutenants, including ʿErikat and Abu Diya, were wounded. ʿAbd al-Qadir's body was taken to Jerusalem and the following day, a Friday, was buried on the Temple Mount next to his father, Musa Kazim al-Husseini, the late mayor. The massive procession included most of East Jerusalem's notables, foreign consuls and Arab Legion officers, as well as most of those who had fought at al-Qastal, who abandoned their posts and accompanied the body to Jerusalem. "The whole country walked after his coffin. . . . Not a shop was open," wrote one diarist.[47] Abu Diya spoke over the open grave; Haj Amin al-Husseini, in Cairo, sent a eulogy. It was read out: "One thing shall not die, Palestine."[48] There was an eleven-cannon salute.

Meanwhile, Yadin—set on sending the empty convoy back from Jerusalem to Tel Aviv to reload—ordered the Palmah to retake al-Qastal, "immediately," and to reopen the road. The Harel Brigade officer in command, Yosef Tabenkin, balked, arguing insufficient forces. Yadin was enraged. Tabenkin backed down. Just before dawn, 9 April, two of Tabenkin's companies stormed into al-Qastal—which they found completely deserted, save for dozens of corpses.[49] The Palmahniks buried the dead. Some of the Jewish corpses had been badly mutilated.[50] The Palmahniks blew up most of the houses and organized a perimeter defense. The convoy, meanwhile, wound its way down the hills to Hulda, unmolested.

At al-Qastal, between 3 and 9 April, the Israelis had lost seventy-five men. The Arabs had lost ninety, but they included the Palestinian Arabs' foremost military commander. And they had lost a crucial battle and a vital strategic position on the road to Jerusalem.

The original operational order of 2 April for the conquest of al-Qastal had forbidden the Haganah troops from razing the village. In the same spirit, Yadin had initially instructed the Nahshon commanders to "occupy [sites], if possible, near villages and not to conquer them."[51] But the follow-up order, of 8 April, to recapture al-Qastal, specifically ordered the destruction of its houses. This was indicative of the radical change of thinking in the HGS. In line with Plan D, Arab villages were henceforward to be leveled to prevent their reinvestment by Arab forces; the implication was that their inhabitants were to be expelled and prevented from returning.

Simultaneously with the recapture of al-Qastal, IZL and LHI units, marginally assisted by the Haganah, conquered the village of Deir Yassin, between al-Qastal and Jerusalem. The village was militarily insignificant, and it was not much of a battle—but it proved to be one of the key events of the war.

The relations between Deir Yassin and the adjacent Jewish Jerusalem neighborhood of Giv'at Shaul had been checkered. In 1929, gunmen from Deir Yassin had attacked the neighborhood. In August 1947 and again the following January representatives of the two communities had signed mutual nonaggression pacts. The villagers subsequently turned away roving Arab irregulars, denying them aid, a haven, and a base of operations.[52] But it is possible that a band of Iraqi or Syrian irregulars bivouacked in the village just before its fall, and irregulars from the village reportedly fired on West Jerusalem and participated in the battle for al-Qastal.

When the battle for al-Qastal erupted, the Jerusalem Haganah command asked the IZL for assistance. The IZL chiefs declined, saying they wanted to launch an independent operation. In the end, they proposed to conquer Deir Yassin, and David Shaltiel, the Jerusalem Haganah OC, agreed. But he demanded that the IZL afterward hold the site permanently. The prospective operation loosely meshed with the Nahshon objective of securing the western approaches to Jerusalem. In planning their attack, the IZL and LHI commanders agreed to expel the inhabitants; a proposal to kill all captured villagers or all captured males was rejected. According to Yehuda Lapidot, the IZL deputy commander during the battle, the troops were specifically ordered not to kill women, children, and POWs.

Early on 9 April the IZL and LHI troops—altogether about 120 men—advanced on the village from the western edge of Jerusalem in two columns, with a van carrying a bullhorn between them. The van blared a message calling on the villagers to put down their weapons and flee. But the van quickly overturned in a ditch; the villagers may not have heard the broadcasts. As the attackers moved in, they encountered unexpectedly strong fire from the village's stone houses and were repeatedly pinned down. Haganah machine gunners provided intermittent covering fire from nearby hills, and two squads of Palmahniks in armored cars arrived to help extricate the wounded and neutralize key positions. The IZL and LHI troopers moved from house to house, lobbing in grenades and spraying the interiors with small arms fire. They blew up houses and sometimes cut down those fleeing into the alleyways, including one or two families. The operation lasted into late afternoon. The attackers suffered four dead and several dozen wounded, including the operation's commander.

It quickly emerged that the fighting had been accompanied, and followed, by atrocities. In part, these were apparently triggered by the unexpectedly strong resistance and by the (relatively) high casualties suffered by the attacking force. Some militiamen and unarmed civilians were shot on the spot. A few villagers may have been trucked into Jerusalem and then taken back to Deir Yassin and executed; a group of male prisoners were shot in a nearby quarry; several of those captured were shot in Sheikh Bader, a temporary LHI base in West Jerusalem. As the town's HIS commander, Yitzhak Levy, reported on 12 April, "The conquest of the village was carried out with great cruelty. Whole families—women, old people, children—were killed. . . . Some of the prisoners moved to places of detention, including women and children, were murdered viciously by their captors."[53]

In a follow-up report, Levy said that LHI participants later charged that IZL troops had "raped a number of girls and murdered them afterwards (we [that is, the HIS] don't know if this is true)."[54] The mukhtar's son, who had been a Haganah agent, was among those executed. The IZL and LHI troopers systematically pillaged the village and stripped the inhabitants of jewelry and money.[55] Altogether, 100–120 villagers (including combatants) died that day[56]—though the IZL, Haganah, Arab officials, and the British almost immediately inflated the number to "254" (or "245"), each for their own propagandistic reasons. Most of the villagers either fled or were trucked through West Jerusalem and dumped at Musrara, outside the Old City walls. The atrocities were condemned by the Jewish Agency, the Haganah command, and the Yishuv's two chief rabbis, and the agency sent King ʿAbdullah a letter condemning the atrocities and apologizing[57] (which he rebuffed, saying that "the Jewish Agency stands at the head of all Jewish affairs in Palestine").[58]

But the real significance of Deir Yassin lay, not in what had actually happened on 9 April, or in the diplomatic exchanges that followed, but in its political and demographic repercussions. In the weeks after the massacre the Arab media inside and outside Palestine continuously broadcast reports about the atrocities—usually with blood-curdling exaggerations[59]—in order to rally Arab public opinion and governments against the Yishuv.[60] Without doubt, they were successful. The broadcasts fanned outrage and reinforced the Arab governments' resolve to invade Palestine five weeks later. Indeed, ʿAbdullah was to point to the massacre at Deir Yassin as one of the reasons he was joining the invasion and why he could not honor his previous assurances of nonbelligerency vis-à-vis the Yishuv (see below).[61]

The most important immediate effect of the media atrocity campaign, however, was to spark fear and further panic flight from Palestine's villages and towns. The broadcasts may, in part, have been designed to reinforce Palestinian Arab steadfastness. Yet their effect was quite the opposite: hearing of what the Jews had done tended to sap morale and precipitate panic. Indeed, the IZL immediately trotted this out in justification of the original attack: Deir Yassin had promoted "terror and dread among the Arabs in all the villages around; in al-Maliha, Qaluniya, and Beit Iksa a panic flight began that facilitates the renewal of [Jewish] road communications . . . between the capital [that is, West Jerusalem] and the rest of the country."[62] "In one blow we changed the strategic situation of our capital," boasted the organization.[63] Menachem Begin, the leader of the IZL, who denied that a massacre had taken place, was later to argue that "the legend [of Deir Yassin] was worth half a dozen battalions to the forces of Israel. Panic overwhelmed the Arabs."[64]

The IZL commanders, then and later, may have had an interest in exaggerating the impact of Deir Yassin. But they weren't far off the mark. HIS officers around the country immediately reported on the fear- and flight-sowing impact of Deir Yassin.[65] Ben-Gurion himself noted—probably not unhappily—that Deir Yassin had propelled flight from Haifa.[66] British intelligence commented that "the violence used [at Deir Yassin] so impressed Arabs all over the country that an attack by [the] Haganah on [the Arab village of] Saris met with no opposition whatsoever."[67] Mapam's leaders later assessed that Deir Yassin had been one of the two pivotal events (the other was the fall of Arab Haifa) in the exodus of Palestine's Arabs.[68] The HIS-AD, in summarizing the Arab flight to the end of June 1948, pointed to Deir Yassin as a "decisive accelerating factor."[69]

But Deir Yassin was also, in an immediate, brutal sense, to harm the Jews. On the morning of 13 April, hundreds of militiamen from Jerusalem and surrounding villages, taking revenge for Deir Yassin and the death of ʿAbd al-Qadir, descended on the road running through the East Jerusalem neighborhood of Sheikh Jarrah, which linked Jewish Jerusalem and Mount Scopus, and ambushed a ten-vehicle Haganah convoy carrying mostly unarmed Jewish lecturers, students, nurses and doctors on their way to the mountaintop Hadassah Hospital–Hebrew University campus. Ironically, the convoy was also carrying two IZL fighters wounded at Deir Yassin. During the previous months, the Arabs had left these convoys—which were often accompanied by British armored cars—alone.

But on 13 April there was no British escort. Perhaps, as they later claimed, the British were shorthanded; perhaps they regarded revenge for Deir Yassin as fitting. It was a classic ambush: at 9:30 AM a large mine blew a hole in the road, halting the convoy. The attackers then let loose with light weapons and grenades. The six smaller, lighter vehicles managed to turn around and flee back to West Jerusalem. But the two armor-plated buses, packed with medical staff and students, and the two escort vehicles, were caught, able neither to advance nor to turn back. For hours the Haganah guards kept the attackers at bay while Haganah HQ pleaded with the British to intervene.

The government reacted lackadaisically if not with utter cynicism. As a Jewish Agency official put it, "British soldiers witnessed at close quarters university professors, doctors and nurses being shot down or roasted alive in the burning vehicles without doing anything."[70] Ben-Gurion was to define the event as "an English massacre. They were there, didn't lift a finger and prevented others from helping."[71] At around noon, a British officer, Major Jack Churchill, possibly on his own initiative, drove up but was unable to cajole any of the passengers to leave the buses and run for it to his armored car and an accompanying pickup; they preferred to await Haganah rescue. But the Haganah was warned off by the authorities and, in any case, lacked an effective relief force. Three Palmah armored cars that reached the area were hit and driven back by the ambushers. Distant Haganah outposts intermittently let loose with machine guns and mortars but to little effect.

The shooting went on for more than five hours. The defenders' fire slowly tapered off as their ammunition ran out. The ambushers inched toward the buses, eventually dousing them with gasoline and setting them alight. A British column reached the scene at 3:45 PM. But it was too late. By then, seventy-eight academics, doctors, students, nurses, and Haganah men were dead, many roasted alive. Only thirty bodies were recovered and buried; the rest had turned to ashes.[72] The Arabs had had their revenge.[73]

The ambush had a curious political consequence: Hebrew University president Yehuda Leib Magnes, a pillar of the Ihud Association, which had for years promoted a binational solution to the Palestine problem, was in effect forced to quit his job. For years, he had promoted this non-Zionist alternative; and for weeks, before the ambush, he had stridently criticized Jewish attacks on Arabs (Deir Yassin and others) and defended the British. But the killing of the convoy's passengers, many of them Hebrew University employees, coupled with the government's protracted inaction, thoroughly discredited Magnes, already under attack by right-wing professors. Four days later he left Palestine for the United States, ostensibly in search of funds for his beloved university. He never returned and died there a few months later.

The primary, limited objective of Operation Nahshon, to push a large convoy through the hills to Jerusalem, was almost immediately achieved. The twenty-five supplies-laden trucks, accompanied by five armored buses and eighteen armored cars, had started out from Kibbutz Hulda in the early hours of 6 April and reached the capital later that morning, almost without incident. The recapture of al-Qastal had enabled the Haganah to send the emptied vehicles safely back down the road to Hulda, to reload for a further trip. Several more convoys reached Jerusalem during the following fortnight.

But the brief lifting of the siege had not been achieved only through the protracted fight for al-Qastal; other villages along the road had served as operational bases for the Arab irregulars. On 6 April Palmah and Givʿati forces took Arab Khulda and neighboring Deir Muheizin almost without a fight. Arab militiamen from the Ramla area mounted counterattacks, but the Jewish garrison in Deir Muheizin, reinforced from Kibbutz Hulda, beat them off. However, on the evening of 7 April a British armored column drove up to the village—and demanded that the Haganah pull out (the British promised that they would not allow the irregulars to return). The Haganah complied. During the following days, the Haganah captured the villages of Qaluniya (11 April), whose militiamen had repeatedly attacked positions around al-Qastal, and Saris (16 April), just south of the road. But repeated attacks, on 15, 18, and 19 April, on the village of Suba, southwest of al-Qastal, were unsuccessful.

On 13 April Ben-Gurion had cabled Avidan: "The battle is not yet over, but this great operation—the largest of all our operations during the past four months, means that if we want—we can beat the enemy."[74] In fact, Nahshon had been only partially successful: several convoys had made it through and a number of villages had been taken and either permanently occupied or leveled. (Nahshon HQ orders, between 8 and 15 April, were consistent: to level the villages and drive out their inhabitants.)[75] But the Haganah forces allocated were insufficient to permanently clear and hold such a swath of territory. Arab villages and militia units remained in situ and continued intermittently to block passage along the road. For all intents and purposes, Jerusalem remained cut off.

The Haganah then launched a number of smaller, follow-up operations to "lift the siege"[76] and secure its hold on West Jerusalem. In Operation Harel (16–21 April), it managed to push three convoys up to Jerusalem, and on 20 April, the villages of Biddu and Beit Suriq, just north of the road, were raided and partially destroyed.

The following day, the bulk of the Harel Brigade moved to Jerusalem to undertake Operation Yevussi; segments of the Jerusalem–Tel Aviv road were left at the mercy of the Arab militias. During Yevussi (1), Palmah units took the village of Beit Iksa and the suburb village of Shuʿfat (22 April), respectively northwest and north of Jerusalem, and partially destroyed them (the order was to "destroy" the villages)[77] before withdrawing, but failed to take the dominant heights of Nabi Samwil, where several dozen Jewish fighters were killed in a disorganized retreat.[78]

In Jerusalem itself, in Yevussi (2), the Palmah was more successful. On 25 April Harel units conquered the Sheikh Jarrah neighborhood and the neighboring Police School fort, north of the Old City, establishing territorial continuity between West Jerusalem and Mount Scopus. But the British, bent on maintaining control of the road from Jerusalem northward, demanded that the Haganah leave. When the Haganah refused, they let loose with cannon and mortar fire, injuring about two dozen Jewish troopers and forcing a hasty Palmah withdrawal.[79] A similar Haganah effort to bolster the Mount Scopus position by taking the Augusta Victoria Hospital compound to its south failed after encountering unexpectedly strong resistance and after a Palmah mortar exploded.[80]

But the southern arm of Yevussi (2), designed to establish territorial continuity between the center of Jewish Jerusalem and the isolated southern Jewish neighborhoods of Mekor Hayim and Talpiyot, fared better. Almost all the Arabs living in West Jerusalem, including the inhabitants of Talbiyeh, Bak'a, and the German Colony and the Greek Colony, had fled to the Old City or farther afield during the previous months.[81] The problem remained Katamon, the prosperous neighborhood near Rehavia that sat astride the road south, to Mekor Hayim. Many of its inhabitants had already fled, but the neighborhood was strongly held by a band led by Abu Diya. The Haganah attack on Katamon was partly triggered by sniping from Katamon at Jewish areas and, perhaps, by the British evacuation of the Alamein Camp, just east of the neighborhood, which was then occupied by Arab militiamen.[82]

An initial Palmah attack on Katamon, on the night of 26–27 April, failed. Dominating the neighborhood was the Saint Simeon Monastery, at its southern edge. On the night of 29–30 April two Harel Brigade companies crept up on the monastery and in a sudden assault took it along with several outlying buildings. But the Palmahniks suffered serious losses.

The troopers understood—as, apparently, did Abu Diya—that the fate of the monastery "would decide the fate of Jerusalem."[83] The following morning he counterattacked; wave after wave of Arabs assaulted the monastery. Jewish casualties mounted steadily. By noon, most of the Palmahniks were either dead or wounded. A large relief column failed to break through, though sixteen Jewish fighters reached the besieged building.

Abu Diya's forces suffered serious losses, but they kept up the attack. By noon, the Palmah commanders had decided on retreat; the badly injured were to be left behind, to die in a planned demolition of the building. (The commanders assumed that the wounded, if captured, would be slaughtered.)[84] But at the last moment, around 1:00 PM, HIS signals intelligence officers intercepted an Arab militia transmission from Katamon to the HQ in the Old City saying that Abu Diya had fled—in order "to bring reinforcements," he later claimed—and that, in the absence of reinforcements, they would be forced to retreat.

The Saint Simeon defenders were informed of the intercept—and decided to hold on. The Arab assaults tapered off, and the militiamen began to retreat, with the remaining civilian inhabitants of Katamon fleeing in their wake.[85] Jewish relief columns at last reached the monastery at 5:00 PM, and the following morning, 1 May, ʿEtzioni Brigade troops occupied Katamon itself, chasing out a small Arab Legion unit that had protected the Iraqi consulate building. The occupation was followed by massive looting of the abandoned houses by the troops and Jewish civilians who pounced on the neighborhood. Jewish losses had amounted to twenty-one dead and eighty-three wounded.[86] Arab losses were probably higher.

Yet the Jewish success inside Jerusalem did nothing to open the road to the city. On 3–4 May, Harel's units, with reinforcements from the ʿEtzioni Brigade, moved out of Jerusalem and launched Operation Maccabbi. The aim was to reopen the road; the focus was on the hills south and north of the road between Saris and Latrun.

But Harel had suffered sixty-seven dead and 155 wounded in the previous fortnight and was in poor shape. The brigade took the hilltops and dug in; Beit Mahsir, the main village just south of the road, fell on 11 May. The following three days were characterized by confusion and wasted effort. ALA units, backed by 75 mm artillery pieces and (unusually) a squadron of British armored cars, counterattacked, but the Palmahniks in the hilltop positions held on. Crucially, however, Harel, briefly supported by Givʿati troops, failed to occupy the Bab al-Wad–Latrun stretch, even though the British pulled out of Latrun on 14 May and the ALA, on King ʿAbdullah's orders, left the following day. The HGS was riveted to Palestine's borders and the invading Arab armies—and on late 17–18 May, the Arab Legion reached Bab al-Wad—Latrun and occupied the area in force. The door to Jerusalem once again slammed shut. The Israelis had failed to understand the area's importance or to exploit the momentary power vacuum.[87]

Nonetheless, Nahshon (and its follow-ups) marked the turning point in the civil war. For the first time, the Haganah had deployed a large (brigade-sized) force and had shifted to the strategic offensive—the mode in which the Haganah and its successor organization, the IDF, was to remain, almost consistently, for the duration of the war. And for the first time the Haganah had embarked on a campaign of clearing areas of Arab inhabitants and militia forces and conquering and leveling villages, which was to contribute significantly to the collapse of Palestinian military power and society. Moreover, Haganah troops had killed the leading Palestinian military commander of 1948, and dissident troops had committed atrocities in Deir Yassin that, amplified through radio broadcasts, were decisively to encourage a mass Arab exodus from the Jewish state-to-be.

THE BATTLES OF MISHMAR HAʿEMEK AND RAMAT YOHANAN

While the Haganah was trying to break the back of the irregular formations in West Jerusalem and the Jerusalem Corridor, two battles took place in the north in which the new policy, of permanently occupying and/or razing villages and of clearing whole areas of Arabs, was given its head. As with Nahshon, which was a response to attacks on the Haganah's Jerusalem-bound convoys, so with these two battles: both were initiated by the Arabs but resulted in Jewish counteroffensives that ended in Haganah victories and the wholesale flight of Arab communities; both, retrospectively, were seen as stages in the implementation of Plan D.

The battle for Kibbutz Mishmar Haʿemek, from 4 to 15 April, was the more important. The kibbutz, one of the left-wing Mapam's oldest and largest, home to a succession of the party's leaders, sat astride the road from Jenin to Haifa, which would figure large the following month in the Arab states' invasion plans. It was surrounded by Arab villages.

From January through March 1948 units of the ALA had repeatedly failed to conquer any settlements, and al-Qawuqji had promised Cunningham that he would desist from further offensive action until 15 May.[88] In early April, possibly prodded by the Military Committee in Damascus—who may have sought to relieve the pressure on the Palestinians in the Jerusalem area—or by jealousy of ʿAbd al-Qadir al-Husseini's successes in late March,[89] al-Qawuqji decided to violate his pledge. He targeted Mishmar Haʿemek, a prestigious target and one whose capture might assist the prospective invading Arab armies in achieving a major objective—the conquest of Haifa.

Al-Qawuqji appears to have been certain of victory before firing the first shot—and this in part accounts for his premature announcements of victory during the first twenty-four hours of battle.[90] The kibbutzniks were not completely surprised when, on the afternoon of 4 April, al-Qawuqji's seven 75 and 105 mm field guns—in the first use of artillery during the war—let loose; Haganah scouts had noted the positioning of the guns, and mortars, around the kibbutz that morning.[91] The kibbutz's children were rushed through the trenches to safety in a cave just above the settlement. A handful of members were killed or wounded; dozens of cows and horses died. Most of the settlement's buildings collapsed or were badly damaged. But a follow-up infantry assault failed to breach the perimeter fence or the trench works, which were manned by the members. A company of Golani infantrymen arrived during the night of 4–5 April to reinforce the defenses.

Al-Qawuqji kept up the shelling during the following thirty-six hours, but the kibbutz held out. A British armored column arrived on 6 April and mediated a twenty-four-hour truce. The wounded and most of the women and children were evacuated—much as the settlement's noncombatants had been evacuated during the attacks of 1929 and 1936–1939. (This was one of the first evacuations of noncombatants from a Jewish settlement—a phenomenon that would characterize most front-line kibbutzim during the following weeks. Altogether, about ten thousand children were evacuated from the settlements during the spring and summer. In some cases, the separation from parents and homes lasted for more than a year.)

Cunningham described the ALA's performance at Mishmar Ha'emek as "an ignominious fiasco."[92] But al-Qawuqji tried to put the best face on it. He demanded the kibbutz's surrender and a handover of arms. When the Haganah brushed this aside, he proposed to withdraw—provided the Jews promised to desist from attacking the neighboring villages, which had served as his bases. The kibbutz responded with bravado: al-Qawuqji should compensate the kibbutz for the damage he had inflicted and must wheel his artillery pieces into the kibbutz and destroy them.[93] More realistically, the local leaders said that they would have to consult Tel Aviv. Meanwhile, they "agreed to nothing," as a Golani Brigade transmission put it.[94]

On 8 April, the ALA announced that Mishmar Ha'emek had been conquered and that "the Arab flag" was now flying above its water tower.[95] This was pure fantasy. Indeed, that day (or the next) a delegation of the settlement's members, probably including Ya'akov Hazan, Mapam's coleader, traveled to Tel Aviv and pleaded with Ben-Gurion—according to Ben-Gurion—to order the Haganah "to expel the Arabs [in the area] and to burn the villages. . . . They said that they were not sure [the kibbutz could hold out] if the villages remained intact and [if] the Arab inhabitants were not expelled." Ben-Gurion agreed. He recalled: "They faced a cruel reality . . . [and] saw that there was [only] one way and that was to expel the Arab villagers and burn the villages."[96] The local forces, now commanded by Yitzhak Sadeh and reinforced with Palmah, Alexandroni, and Carmeli companies, rejected a British suggestion to prolong the truce and on the night of 8 April took the offensive. Al-Qawuqji's units were gradually pushed out of the area—though al-Qawuqji continued to issue reports claiming to have won a famous victory,[97] confusing anyone who might have sent him aid. King 'Abdullah observed al-Qawuqji's "discomfiture" with "equanimity."[98]

Subsequently, one of al-Qawuqji's company commanders tellingly criticized the ALA's performance: "1. There was no plan behind the management of the battle . . . 2. There was no communication link, written or oral, between those directing the front and the management of the battle. 3. No one was responsible for the distribution of food. As a result our soldiers in the front line did not receive their meal until 14:30 and [received no] water between three in the afternoon and three [after] midnight. Those responsible

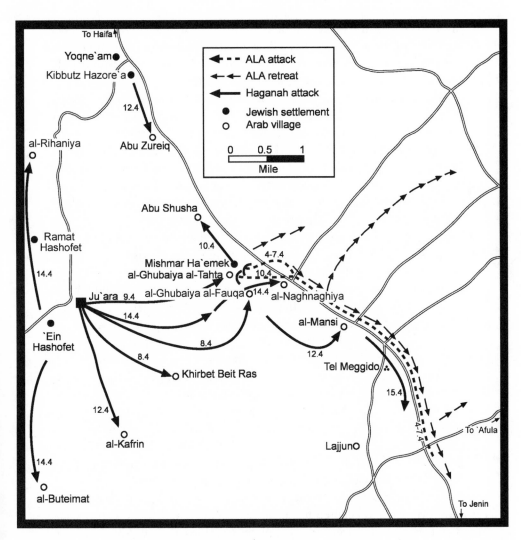

The Battle of Mishmar Haʿemek, April 1948

also did not ease the soldiers' suffering from the fierce cold. . . . There was no cooperation between the forces. The artillery fired without discrimination and the armored cars wandered [around the battlefield] as if they were independent agents, without any connection to us [infantry]."[99]

The Haganah troops first raided neighboring villages (Ghubaiya al-Tahta, Ghubaiya al-Fauqa, and Khirbet Beit Ras). Then, emboldened by success, they went on to conquer and permanently occupy village after village—Abu Shusha (10 April), al-Kafrin (12 April), Mansi and Abu Zureiq (12–13 April), and then al-Naghnaghia, Buteimat, and Rihaniyya (14 April). Some ALA equipment fell into Haganah hands, including, it was reported, al-Qawuqji's own Oldsmobile limousine (which was then transferred to Tel Aviv and used by Ben-Gurion).[100] By 16 April Arab Legion intelligence was reporting "a general collapse of Arab morale in Palestine extending to Army of Liberation [that is, the ALA] whose commander is stating his position is critical."[101] Al-Qawuqji complained—falsely—that "Russian non-Jews were assisting [the] Haganah . . . and that in combat area there were ten twin-engined bomber aircraft of American type."[102] In reality, according to Ben-Gurion, some 640 Haganah soldiers had faced about twenty-five hundred ALA troops, with superior firepower—and bested them.[103]

A wide swath around Mishmar Ha'emek was cleared of Arab inhabitants. Most simply fled, disheartened by al-Qawuqji's defeat or demoralized by Jewish attack. The remainder were expelled, toward Jenin.[104] A few prisoners were executed. The villages were then systematically leveled. According to the Mishmar Ha'emek logbook, by 15 April "all the villages in the area as far as the eye can see [had] been evacuated."[105] The flight and expulsion of inhabitants around Mishmar Ha'emek radiated panic farther afield, leading to flight from villages in the Hills of Ephraim and the Hefer Valley.[106]

The displaced villagers subsequently appealed to the AHC: "Thousands of poor women and children from the villages of Abu Zureiq and Mansi and Ghubaiya and al-Kafrin and other places near the colony of Mishmar Ha'e-mek, whose houses the Jews have destroyed and whose babies and old people [the Jews] have killed, are now in the villages around Jenin without help and dying of hunger. We ask you to repair the situation . . . and do everything to quickly send forces of vengeance against the Jews and restore us to our lands."[107]

The expulsions and accompanying acts of brutality had left a bitter taste in the mouths of some kibbutzniks. Eliezer Be'eri (Bauer), a Middle East scholar and member of Kibbutz Hazore'a, a neighbor of Mishmar Ha'emek's to the northwest, wrote to his Mapam colleagues: "Of course, in a cruel war such as we are engaged in, one cannot act with kid gloves. But there are still rules in war which a civilized people tries to follow." He detailed the atrocities and described how the neighboring villages were conquered and pillaged.[108]

Al-Qawuqji's ALA withdrew to the hill country to the east, around Nazareth. Mishmar Ha'emek had suffered losses and had been virtually leveled—but it had survived. The surrounding Arab villages in the western Jezreel Valley and the Hills of Ephraim to the west, abandoned by al-Qawuqji, had been leveled and their inhabitants driven into exile in northern Samaria.[109]

The Battle of Mishmar Ha'emek had had an adjunct. On 11 April, as his situation grew critical, al-Qawuqji had fired off a cable to the ALA's Druze Battalion, based in Shafa-'Amr, east of Haifa, to begin operations around Kibbutz Ramat Yohanan. He hoped it would ease the pressure around Mishmar Ha'emek. The battalion, commanded by the Druze warrior Shakib Wahab, who had fought against the French in the Syrian Druze revolt of 1925–1927, was only nominally under al-Qawuqji's command, the Druze community having insisted that the battalion retain its operational independence in Palestine.[110] Indeed, once in the country, Wahab opened secret peace negotiations with the HIS.

Nonetheless, Wahab acceded to al-Qawuqji's request. His troops occupied two semiabandoned villages, Hawsha and Khirbet Kayasir, west of Shafa-'Amr, and began to shell Ramat Yohanan and harass the neighboring settlements.[111] The Haganah responded. After an initial failure, which nonetheless chipped at the Druze Battalion's morale,[112] a battalion-sized Carmeli force on the night of 15–16 April overran the two villages. Wailing refugees fled to Shafa-'Amr, spreading rumors of Jewish atrocities.[113] For the Druze Battalion, recapturing the villages became a matter of honor. On 16 April they assaulted the Carmeli positions—they advanced "with large knives sparkling between their teeth in the sunlight"[114]—nine times. Some of the assaults were mounted to extricate casualties from previous assaults. Wahab had pleaded for artillery support, but the ALA HQ had sent only a brace of 2.5-inch mortars—and only one in ten of the mortar bombs used "had been serviceable, which heightened the despair."[115] Hundreds of local militiamen had joined in. But the Carmeli troops fought back steadfastly. By late afternoon, Wahab pulled his exhausted troops back to Shafa-'Amr.[116] The battalion had lost twenty-four men, and more than forty-two were "missing-in-action" (or "wounded"). Dozens of local Arab militiamen were also killed and wounded;[117] nineteen Carmeli soliders had died. One Haganah report praised "the [well-]trained and very brave enemy forces."[118] But the Haganah had won. During the following days most of Wahab's soldiers deserted and returned to Jebel Druze, in Syria; by 2 May, he was complaining that his battalion had only "190" soldiers left (of an original complement of five hundred): "the morale is very low . . . and [the local militiamen] are collaborating with the Jews in these days of harvest and are working together with them, they want good neighborly relations with the Jews."[119] "Why aren't you helping us?" Wahab complained to the ALA HQ.[120] But Wahab himself was—again—secretly negotiating a separate peace with the Haganah.[121] The defeat resulted in "mass flight" from Shafa-ʿAmr[122] and no doubt demoralized the Arab inhabitants of Haifa. The Carmeli troops razed Hawsha and Khirbet Kayasir, and "the whole area was cleansed [tohar]. Villagers fled and peace reigned in the whole area."[123] But more significantly, the battle had persuaded Palestine's own Druze community that the Arabs would lose. By summer, the community had thrown in its lot with Israel.

THE TOWNS

In Operation Nahshon and the battles around Mishmar Haʿemek and Ramat Yohanan, the Haganah had conquered and permanently occupied or destroyed clusters of Arab villages. During the following weeks, the Jewish forces assaulted and conquered key urban areas, in effect delivering a deathblow to Palestine Arab military power and political aspirations. Arab Tiberias and Arab Haifa, Manshiya in Jaffa, and the Arab neighborhoods of West Jerusalem all fell in quick succession.

Tiberias

Tiberias, on the western shore of the Sea of Galilee, was a mixed town, with some six thousand Jews and four thousand Arabs. The Arab neighborhoods sat astride the shore-hugging road linking the Jewish settlements in the (Upper) Jordan Valley and the (Lower) Jordan and Jezreel Valleys, which were supplied from the Coastal Plain. Relations between the communities had been relatively good in the first months of the war, and the Arab leadership—basically the Tabari clan, which hailed originally from Irbid in Transjordan—had kept out foreign irregulars. In February, the Tabari-dominated National Committee and local Jewish leaders concluded a nonbelligerency agreement.

In March, in large measure because of Haganah provocations, relations deteriorated.[124] There were sporadic firefights between local militiamen, and the small Jewish Quarter in Tiberias's Arab-dominated Old City, by the lake, was cut off from the Jewish neighborhoods up the slope to the west. Many of the quarter's inhabitants moved out. For their part, the Arabs suffered from food shortages and their shops closed. By the end of the month several dozen foreign irregulars, apparently Syrians with "a German officer," had moved in.[125] The Arabs periodically interdicted Jewish traffic along the south-north road. An explosion seemed inevitable. The British, with a small base nearby and about to withdraw, tried to maintain order but were disinclined to intervene forcibly. The Jews feared an influx of foreign irregulars and attack, the Arabs, Jewish conquest.

At some point during 9–11 April, against the backdrop of a new flare-up, in which the local Haganah for the first time used mortars, the HGS decided to resolve the "problem" once and for all. On 12 April, a Golani Brigade company raided the hilltop village of Khirbet Nasir al-Din, which overlooked Tiberias's Jewish districts from the west. Twenty-two villagers died—the Arabs alleged "a second Deir Yassin"; atrocities apparently had been committed—and the rest of the inhabitants fled down the slope to Tiberias, sowing panic and fear in the population.[126] The fall of Nasir al-Din vitiated the possibility of reinforcement of Arab Tiberias by the ALA.

The Haganah brought in the Palmah Third Battalion and Golani units, some arriving by boat from Kibbutz ʿEin-Gev, on the eastern shore of the lake, and, on the night of 16–17 April, struck hard. The troops dynamited a series of houses along the seam between the communities and barraged the Arab area with mortars. The British declined to intervene, and Arab pleas for help from outside went unheeded. It was all over in twenty-four hours. Some eighty Arabs were dead, "18" of them women;[127] the Haganah suffered a handful of casualties. The Haganah occupied key Arab areas and demanded surrender. The Jewish commanders vetoed the idea of a "truce," and the Arab notables, perhaps on their own initiative, perhaps heeding British advice, decided on an evacuation of the population.[128] The British imposed a curfew and assembled a fleet of trucks. Then, on 18 April, escorted by British armored cars, the Arab population was trucked out in separate convoys eastward to Jordan and westward to ALA-held Nazareth. The empty Arab quarters were then thoroughly looted: "[It was as if] there was a contest between the different Haganah platoons stationed in Migdal, Ginossar, Yavniel, ʿEin-Gev, who came in cars and boats and loaded all sorts of goods, refrigerators, beds, etc. . . . Quite naturally the Jewish masses in Tiberias wanted to do likewise. . . . Old men and women, regardless of age . . . all are busy with robbery. . . . Shame covers my face," recorded one local Jewish leader.[129] Arab Tiberias was no more.[130] The evacuation of Arab Tiberias within days triggered the complete evacuation of a string of neighboring villages, among them al-ʿUbeidiya, Majdal (the birthplace of Mary Magdalene), and Ghuweir Abu Shusha.

Haifa

Next to fall, and most significant, was Haifa. It had the second largest and most modern Arab community in Palestine and served as the country's major seaport and the unofficial "capital" of the north. What happened in Haifa would radiate across the Galilee. The city's Arab neighborhoods were concentrated along the seashore and around the port, at the foot of Mount Carmel. The newer, Jewish neighborhoods were perched up the slopes.

Tens of thousands of the city's original seventy thousand Arabs had fled during the previous months, and the Haganah had originally intended to occupy the Arab parts only when the Mandate ended. The Yishuv's leaders were keenly aware of Haifa's importance to the British—it was their main point of exit from Palestine—and realized that a premature offensive could result in Jewish-British clashes. In any case, once the British left, the town's Arab neighborhoods, by then probably demoralized, would surrender or fall in short order.

Yet as with the Haganah's general timetable, so with Haifa: the offensive was brought forward, partly because of the feeling that time was running out and the expected pan-Arab invasion was fast approaching; the Palestinian militias had to be subdued beforehand. On 18 April Galili told the Defense Committee that the Haganah was preparing "an operation . . . in Haifa."[131] And on 19 April a local Haganah representative, Abba Khoushi, had sounded out General Hugh Stockwell, the British commander in the north, about his attitude to a possible Haganah offensive in Haifa. The general had warned against it, implying that the army would have to respond.[132]

Khoushi's soundings had been made in part in response to the increased pressure during the previous days by Arab militiamen against Haganah positions along Herzl Street and the Jewish neighborhood of Hadar behind it. Stockwell himself implied as much in his subsequent report. But the immediate, concrete trigger of the Haganah offensive was the abrupt withdrawal on 21 April of British troops from their positions between the Jewish and Arab neighborhoods.

Just before dawn, the First Guards Brigade and auxiliary units abruptly pulled out of their downtown positions and withdrew to the harbor and to the neighborhood of French Carmel. Stockwell later explained that he had ordered the redeployment partly because of an increase in Arab and Jewish operations that had threatened the safety of his troops and partly because of the steady reduction in the number of troops he had available (as a result of the general withdrawal from Palestine). Immediately, spontaneous firefights erupted as Arab and Jewish militiamen jockeyed to occupy the abandoned British positions, which dominated key thoroughfares. Haganah troops oc-

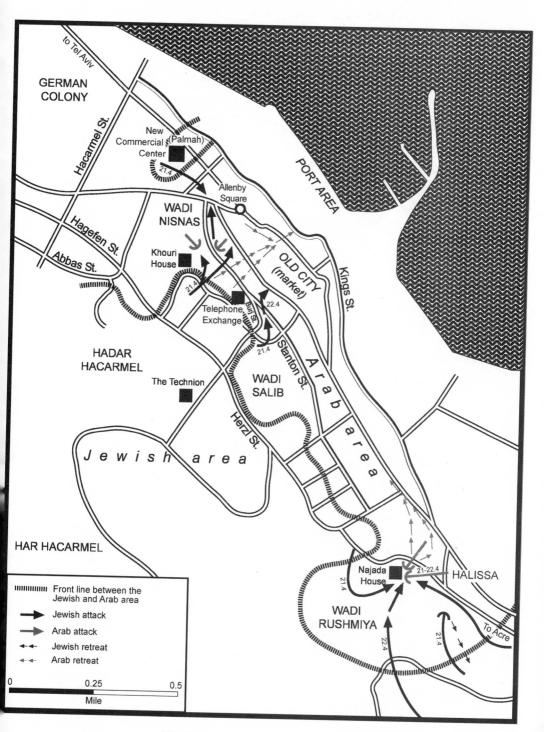

The Battle for Haifa, 21–22 April 1948

cupied Haifa's airfield and the Kishon Railway Workshops; the Arabs took over the railway offices.

But the local Haganah brass, headed by Moshe Carmel, the commander of the Carmeli Brigade, while taken by surprise, immediately understood that the British redeployment afforded a strategic opportunity and reacted accordingly;[133] the Arab response was disorganized and lackadaisical. Arab Haifa was defended by five hundred to a thousand armed militiamen; Carmel, with two battalions, had roughly the same number of troops[134] but enjoyed centralized and effective command and control and better arms. The Haganah also enjoyed topographically dominant starting positions.

During the morning, Carmeli's commanders hastily hammered out a plan—*mivtza bi'ur hametz* (Operation Passover Cleaning)—to "break the enemy" by launching two efforts at once: one, from several directions, against the Arab-populated Lower City, and the other, toward Wadi Rushmiya, the Arab neighborhood to the southeast that sat astride the road linking Haifa and the Jewish settlements of Western Galilee. Troops and equipment were frantically mobilized and deployed.

The minor, easterly effort proved the more difficult. At 1:30 PM an enlarged Haganah platoon, but with little ammunition and no food and water reserves, was sent to capture Najada House on Saladin Street, which dominated the Wadi Rushmiya quarter and bridge. The three-story stone-faced building was swiftly occupied. But for the next seventeen hours, the platoon was under constant sniping, machine gun, and grenade attack—indeed, under siege—from surrounding Arab buildings. The battle for Najada House precipitated a panic flight of inhabitants from Wadi Rushmiya westward, into the Lower City. Yet efforts by the Haganah command to link up with the platoon, whose losses mounted steadily, proved unavailing; the few armored cars that reached the building were unable to take out the wounded or silence the surrounding positions and, after delivering ammunition, withdrew. Carmel concluded that the platoon could be saved only if the more general, main operation soon to be unleashed against the Lower City was successful.

The Carmeli Brigade spent the rest of 21 April preparing the battle. A crucial shipment of new Czech rifles arrived from Tel Aviv that afternoon. They were quickly cleaned of grease and test-fired in the courtyard of Reali High School in Hadar. The troops then marched out, "through the streets of Hadar-Hacarmel. Along the way crowds watched . . . [and] women threw flowers." The Haganah had emerged from underground and was behaving like an army.[135] Soon after midnight, though short of ammunition, especially detonators and mortar bombs, the brigade was ready. At around 1:00 AM, 22 April, three-inch mortars and Davidkas (the Yishuv's homemade, largely ineffective heavy mortars) let loose with a fifteen-minute barrage on the Lower City. Arab morale plummeted—though it was a relatively light barrage and not all the bombs actually exploded. (Indeed, as Carmel later wrote, "Whenever a bomb exploded and a column of black smoke rose above the city's alleyways—the members of the [mortar] team would go wild, dance, rejoice, hug each other, throw their hats in the air.")[136] At the same time, a relief company set off for Najada House, on foot, battling through the alleyways. Arab militia resistance gradually collapsed and civilian morale cracked, the Arab population fleeing from the whole Halissa–Wadi Rushmiya area northwestward, into the Lower City. Shortly after dawn, the relief column reached the besieged platoon. The shooting there died down at 11:00 AM.[137]

Meanwhile, three other companies, one of them Palmah, in the early hours of 22 April, launched simultaneous assaults from Hadar northward and from the New Commercial Center (where the Palmah company was stationed) southward against major Arab strongpoints—the Railway Office Building (Khouri House), the telephone exchange, and the Arab militia headquarters, overlooking the Old Market—in the Lower City, and reached Stanton Street. The fighting, often bitter and hand-to-hand, inside buildings and from house to house, tapered off during the late morning. All the while, Haganah mortars peppered the Lower City with what one British observer called "completely indiscriminate and revolting . . . fire."[138] By noon there was a general sense of collapse and chaos; in the Lower City and in Halissa smoke rose above gutted buildings and mangled bodies littered the streets and alleyways. The constant mortar and machine gun fire, as well as the collapse of the militias and local government and the Haganah's conquests, precipitated mass flight toward the British-held port area. By 1:00 PM some six thousand people had reportedly passed through the harbor and boarded boats for Acre and points north.

A Palmah scout (disguised as an Arab) who had been in the Lower City during the battle later reported: "[I saw] people with belongings running toward the harbor and their faces spoke confusion. I met an old man sitting on some steps and crying. I asked him why he was crying and he replied that he had lost his six children and his wife and did not know [where] they were. I quieted him down. . . . It was quite possible, I said, that the wife and children had been transported to Acre, but he continued to cry. I took him to the hotel . . . and gave him £P22 and he fell asleep. Meanwhile, people arrived from Halissa."[139]

Haj Muhammad Nimr al-Khatib, a prominent Haifa Muslim preacher (who was not in Haifa during the battle but spoke with refugees from the town), later described the scene: "Suddenly a rumor spread that the British Army in the port area had declared its readiness to safeguard the life of anyone who reached the port and left the city. A mad rush to the port gates began. Man trampled on fellow man and woman [trampled] her children. The boats in the harbor quickly filled up and there is no doubt that that was the cause of the capsizing of many of them."[140]

Cunningham took a jaundiced view of the Haganah's tactics, as of the mindset of the Yishuv, which he saw them as reflecting. "Recent Jewish military successes (if indeed operations based on the mortaring of terrified women and children can be classed as such) have aroused extravagant reactions in the Jewish press and among the Jews themselves a spirit of arrogance which blinds them to future difficulties. . . . Jewish broadcasts both in content and in manner of delivery, are remarkably like those of Nazi Germany."

But he was equally critical of the Palestinians: he regarded them as incompetent and their elite as cowardly and ineffectual.[141] Both in Wadi Rushmiya and in the Lower City, the militiamen were poorly coordinated, lacked heavy weapons, and were short of ammunition. And through much of the battle, they were leaderless. Rashid Haj Ibrahim, the head of Haifa's NC, had left the city in early April. Ahmed Bey Khalil, the town's chief magistrate and sole AHC member (in effect, Ibrahim's successor as local leader), left "early on 21 April by sea." He was followed by Amin Bey ʿIzzadin, Haifa's militia commander, on the afternoon of 21 April, after the battle had begun, and by his deputy, Yunis Nafaʿa, who left sometime (probably early) on 22 April.[142]

Repeated pleas by the Arab political and military leaders for reinforcements from outside the city were stymied. At one point, British troops turned back a column attempting to reach the city from the village of Tira, to the south—"in the interests of humanity," said Stockwell (he argued that the reinforcements would merely have prolonged the fighting and increased the bloodshed, not altered the result).[143] Throughout, the Haganah had had the advantages of the initiative, topography, command and control, and firepower (mortars). Nonetheless, its commanders were surprised by the speed of the Arab collapse. Stockwell estimated Arab losses during 21–22 April at a hundred dead and 150 to two hundred wounded, Jewish losses at sixteen to twenty killed and thirty to forty wounded.[144]

During the morning of 22 April, the remaining Arab leaders called for a "truce." But the Haganah, having won, sought outright "surrender." Stockwell asked for its terms (which, to save Arab face, the Haganah agreed to call "truce terms"), amended them, and then arranged for a meeting—which all three sides understood was a surrender negotiation—at the town hall. Meanwhile, Thabet al-Aris, the local Syrian consul, prodded by local Arab notables, fired off a series of cables to Damascus asking for help; he warned that "a massacre of innocents is feared" or, alternatively, was already taking place. Responding, the Syrian and Lebanese governments called in the British heads of mission and demanded that the army step in and halt "this Jewish aggression." Syrian president al-Quwwatli hinted that, otherwise, the Syrian army might intervene.[145] But the diplomatic footwork accomplished nothing. The Syrian army was not going to move before the end of the Mandate.

Haifa's Arab notables were ferried to the town hall in British armored cars. The meeting convened at 4:00 PM. The Jewish leaders, who included Mayor Shabtai Levy, Jewish Agency representative Harry Beilin, and Haganah representative Mordechai Makleff, were, in Stockwell's phrase, "conciliatory," and agreed to further dilution of the truce terms. "The Arabs haggled over every word," recorded Beilin.[146] The final terms included surrender of all military equipment (initially to the British authorities); the assembly and deportation of all foreign Arab males and the detention by the British of "European Nazis"; and a curfew to facilitate Haganah arms searches in the Arab neighborhoods. The terms assured the Arab population a future "as equal and free citizens of Haifa."[147] Levy reinforced this by expressing a desire that the two communities continue to "live in peace and friendship."

But the Arab delegation, headed by Sheikh ʿAbdul Rahman Murad, the local Muslim Brotherhood leader, and businessmen Victor Khayyat, Farid Saʿad, and Anis Nasr—a mixture of Muslims and Christians—declined to sign on and requested a break, "to consult." The Arabs were driven to Khayyat's house, where they tried to contact the AHC and, possibly, the Arab League Military Committee; they wanted instructions. Israeli officials were later to claim that the notables made contact and that the AHC had instructed them to refuse the surrender terms and to announce a general evacuation of the city.[148] But there is no credible proof that such instructions were given, and it seems unlikely.[149] Indeed, a few weeks later, Victor Khayyat told an HIS officer: "There are rumors that the Mufti, the Arab Higher Committee, ordered the Arabs to leave the city. There is no truth to these rumors."[150] It appears that beyond Syrian and Lebanese efforts to persuade the British to intervene, no response was forthcoming from the AHC or Damascus to the notables' appeal.

When the notables reassembled at the town hall at 7:15 PM, they appear to have had no guidance from outside Palestine and were left to their own devices. The Arabs—now all Christians—"stated that they were not in a position to sign the truce, as they had no control over the Arab military elements in the town and that, in all sincerity, they could not fulfill the terms of the truce, even if they were to sign. They then said as an alternative that the Arab population wished to evacuate Haifa . . . man, woman and child."[151] Without doubt, the notables were chary of agreeing to surrender terms out of fear that they would be dubbed traitors or collaborators by the AHC; perhaps they believed that they were doing what the AHC would have wished them to do. One Jewish participant at the meeting, lawyer Ya'akov Solomon, was later to recall that one of the Arab participants subsequently told him that they had been instructed or browbeaten by Sheikh Murad, who did not participate in the second part of the town hall gathering, to adopt this rejectionist position.[152]

Be that as it may, the Jewish and British officials were flabbergasted. Levy appealed "very passionately . . . and begged [the Arabs] to reconsider." He said that they should not leave the city "where they had lived for hundreds of years, where their forefathers were buried, and where, for so long, they had lived in peace and brotherhood with the Jews." The Arabs said that they "had no choice."[153] According to Carmel, who was briefed, no doubt, by Makleff, his aide de camp, Stockwell, who "went pale," also appealed to the Arabs to reconsider: "Don't destroy your lives needlessly." According to Carmel, the general then turned to Makleff and asked: "What have you to say?" But the Haganah representative parried: "It's up to them [the Arabs] to decide."[154]

During the following ten days, almost all of the town's remaining Arab inhabitants departed, on British naval and civilian craft to Acre and Beirut, and by British-escorted land convoys up the coast or to Nazareth and Nablus. By early May, only about five thousand Arabs were left.

The majority had left for a variety of reasons, the main one being the shock of battle (especially the Haganah mortaring of the Lower City) and Jewish conquest and the prospect of life as a minority under Jewish rule. But, no doubt, the notables' announcement of evacuation, reinforced by continuous orders to the inhabitants during the following days by the AHC to leave town (accompanied by the designation of those who stayed as "traitors"), played their part.[155] In addition, the attitude and behavior of the various Jewish authorities during the week or so following the battle was ambivalent.

As the shooting died down, the Haganah distributed a flyer cautioning its troops not to loot Arab property or vandalize mosques.[156] On 25 April, Haganah troops clashed with IZL men, who had moved into the (largely Muslim) neighborhood of Wadi Nisnas and were harassing the locals and looting, and ejected them. Two days before, several Haganah officers went down to Wadi Nisnas and Abbas Street and appealed to the inhabitants to stay,[157] as, on 28 April, did a flyer issued by the Haifa branch of the Histadrut: "The Haifa Workers Council advises you for your own good to stay in the city and return to regular work."[158] American diplomats and British officials and officers, at least initially, reported that the Jews were making great efforts to persuade the Arabs to stay, whether for economic reasons (the need for cheap Arab laborers) or to preserve the emergent Jewish state's positive image.[159]

But more representative, at least after the first few days, was Beilin's response to the Arab notables' request for help in organizing the departure: "I said that we should be more than happy to give them all the assistance they require."[160] The Jewish authorities almost immediately grasped that a city without a large (and actively or potentially hostile) Arab minority would be better for the emergent Jewish state, militarily and politically. Moreover, in the days after 22 April, Haganah units systematically swept the conquered neighborhoods for arms and irregulars; they often handled the population roughly; families were evicted temporarily from their homes; young males were arrested, some beaten. The Haganah troops broke into Arab shops and storage facilities and confiscated cars and food stocks. Looting was rife. A week passed before services—electricity, water pipelines, and bakeries—were back in operation in the Arab areas. These factors no doubt influenced the decision during 23 April–early May by most of the town's remaining Arab families to leave, especially since Arab radio stations were continuously announcing an imminent Arab invasion and the defeat of the Zionists, after which, believed the refugees, they would return to their homes.

In the days after the fall of Arab Haifa the Haganah moved to secure the city's approaches. On 24 April Carmeli troops attacked the villages of Balad ash Sheikh, Yajur, and Hawassa, to the east. A British relief column arrived and advised the inhabitants to leave—which they promptly did, under British escort. No doubt, the fall of Haifa had dispirited and prepared them for their own evacuation. Two days later, the Haganah mortared Tira. The British intervened—but many villagers left nonetheless. (The village fell to the Haganah and was completely depopulated only in July.) On the night of 25–26 April Carmeli troops took a hill overlooking Acre and mortared the town, but here, too, British troops forced a Haganah withdrawal, and the townspeople held on.

Without doubt, the conquest of Arab Haifa and the evacuation of its inhabitants had a resounding effect on all the communities in the north, as well as farther afield. The Jewish Agency commented: "The evacuation of Haifa [and Tiberias] was a turning point," which "greatly influenced the morale of the Arabs in the country and abroad."[161]

Jaffa

Palestine's largest Arab city, Jaffa, was assaulted and largely depopulated a few days after Arab Haifa (though it finally passed into Jewish hands only on 13–14 May). Tens of thousands of Jaffans had fled during the preceding months, and by April, the remaining inhabitants were "insecure . . . and hopeless."[162] The town suffered from a multiplicity of militia groups, with no unified command. By mid-April, most of the local leaders had left.[163] But at

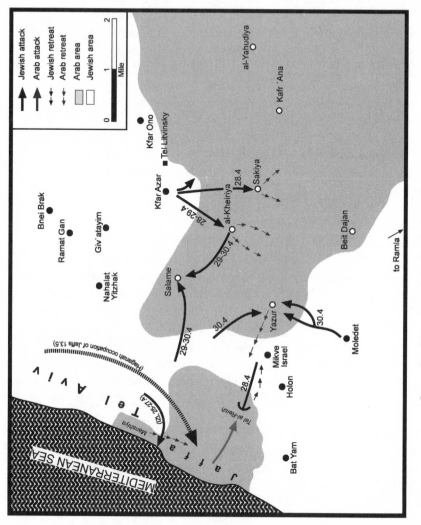

Operation Hametz and the Battle for Jaffa, April 1948

least two-thirds of the original seventy to eighty thousand inhabitants were still in place.

This time, it was the IZL rather than the Haganah. The Haganah brass had always regarded Jaffa, an Arab enclave in the midst of Jewish-earmarked territory, as a ripe plum that would eventually fall without battle; there was no need for a potentially costly direct attack. But news of the Haganah conquest of Haifa (and Tiberias) spurred the IZL to seek a victory of its own,[164] and no objective was more attractive than Jaffa, which bordered on Tel Aviv, the IZL's main base of recruitment and operations, which for months had endured sniping from Jaffa's northern neighborhoods.

The IZL mustered its Tel Aviv area forces, some six companies, and on 25 April (without coordination with the Haganah) hurled them against Jaffa's northernmost, newest neighborhood, Manshiya. Much of the population had already fled to central Jaffa or farther afield. The poorly trained IZL fighters—who, though perhaps conversant with the terrorist arts, had never experienced combat—battled for three days from house to house, usually advancing by blowing holes through walls and pushing from house to house rather than along the enfiladed alleyways. The Arab militiamen, British observers noted, fought more resolutely than in Haifa.[165] The IZL suffered forty dead and twice that number wounded—but the Arab militias were crushed, their remnants, along with Manshiya's inhabitants, fleeing to the center of Jaffa. Haganah intelligence scouts subsequently found among the ruins Arab corpses "badly" mutilated by the IZL.[166] The arrival in Jaffa on 28 April of ALA reinforcements failed to save Manshiya. That morning the IZL troopers reached the sea at the southern end of Manshiya, cutting the district off from Jaffa's core.[167]

The battle, and the arrival of Manshiya's refugees, no doubt demoralized Jaffa's remaining inhabitants—as did the quickly spreading rumor that it was the IZL, the authors of Deir Yassin, that was at the gates. But even more important in triggering the mass flight of the population southward, toward the Gaza Strip, was the ceaseless three-day mortaring of the town center, which accompanied the fight for Manshiya.

In 1946 IZL guerrillas had captured two 3-inch mortars and plentiful ammunition from the British. These were now taken out of their hideaway, and during 25–27 April IZL mortarmen rained down twenty tons of ordnance on the town's center. An HIS report described what happened during the first hours of the bombardment: "A terrible panic arose and all the inhabitants began to run towards the ʿAjami [Quarter]. The spectacle was shocking. Those running trampled each other underfoot, others left their shops open. . . . Even the armed men fled. . . . Jaffa's inhabitants were confused and helpless. One gold jeweler . . . cursed the leaders and said that they had

abandoned the Palestinians to stand alone against the Jews. . . . It were better to have accepted the partition agreement peacefully and not to surrender
to the enemy in war."[168]

The bombardment was "indiscriminate," according to Cunningham;[169]
the aim was "to break the spirit of the enemy troops [and] to cause chaos
among the civilian population in order to create a mass flight."[170] "Our
shells . . . fell on many central sites including the post office, near the municipality . . . and near the port. A coffee shop in the vegetable market was hit
and tens of gang members were killed and injured. . . . The barrage stopped
the movement of buses . . . and paralyzed completely the supply of food to
the city and in it. Hotels turned into hospitals. . . . The port filled up with
masses of refugees and the boarding of boats took place in confusion," IZL
intelligence was to report.[171] Among those fleeing by boat was Michel Issa,
the local ALA commander.[172]

The Red Cross representative in Palestine, Jacques de Reynier, was later to
recall: "Soon the flight started. In the hospital, the drivers of cars and ambu-
lances took their vehicles, collected their families and fled without the slightest regard to their duty. Many of the . . . nurses and even doctors left the hospital with [only] the clothes they had on."[173] By 8 May, only one doctor and
one nurse remained in the main, government hospital.[174]

The assault on Jaffa, following hard on the heels of the fall of Arab Haifa,
had placed the Mandate government and London in a quandary. Several
companies of British troops were still strung out along the seam between
Jaffa and Tel Aviv. They came under fire and briefly engaged the IZL during
the battle for Manshiya.[175] But the main problem was political. "There must
be no repetition there of what happened last week in Haifa," Sir Henry Gurney, chief secretary of the Mandate government, jotted down in his diary.[176]
Arab leaders inside and outside Palestine were blaming the British for Haifa:
they charged Stockwell with conspiring with the Jews or at least doing nothing about the Haganah offensive while preventing Arab reinforcements from
reaching the city, and with promoting the Arab surrender.[177] The British argued that the Arab leaders trotted out these charges "to excuse their own in-
eptitude" and "inefficient and cowardly behaviour." But, be that as it may,
they understood that Anglo-Arab relations had "considerably deteriorated"
as a result.[178] This triggered a major tiff in Whitehall—as well as, eventually,
intervention in the battle for Jaffa.

Late on 22 April, Field Marshal Bernard Montgomery, chief of the Imperial General Staff, had been summoned to 10 Downing Street, where he was
forced to admit that he had not been kept abreast of developments in Haifa.
Bevin "became very worked up; he said 23,000 [sic] Arabs had been killed

and the situation was catastrophic."[179] The following day Attlee, Bevin, and
Montgomery reconvened. Bevin, according to Montgomery, was "even
more agitated." "The massacre of the Arabs had put him in an impossible position with all the Arab states," Bevin had argued; the army had let him
down.[180] Incensed, Montgomery demanded that Bevin retract the charge
and attacked his handling of the Palestine crisis, saying that the foreign secretary was "now . . . trying to make the Army the scapegoat." Montgomery,
according to his own account, threatened to resign and tell all, "fairly [set-
ting] the cat among the pigeons." A fortnight later, Attlee convened a further meeting and succeeded in making peace: everyone, according to Montgomery, ended up "laughing."[181]

But, following Haifa (and Tiberias and Deir Yassin), Whitehall was seriously alarmed about Britain's position in the Middle East. And the army was
worried about the safe completion of the withdrawal from Palestine along
routes that passed through Arab-populated territory;[182] increased Arab antagonism might result in attacks. These considerations resulted in forceful
British intervention in Jaffa. Here the British could stop the erosion of their
image and position in the Middle East. Here they could vigorously demonstrate that they were not "pro-Zionist."

When news of the IZL attack reached London, Bevin "got very ex-
cited . . . and [instructed] the CIGS . . . to . . . see to it that the Jews did not
manage to occupy Jaffa or, if they did, were immediately turned out."[183]
The British rejected Arab demands to allow Arab Legion units to help the
embattled town[184]—or, more widely, to allow Arab armies to cross into
Palestine to defend its Arab inhabitants. But they immediately dispatched reinforcements—in all, more than four battalions of infantry, armor, and naval
commandos, from Cyprus, Libya, Egypt, Malta, and Iraq[185]—to Palestine,
despite the general evacuation that was under way. The troop reinforcement
was geared to freeing units already in Palestine to deploy in Jaffa (and, more
generally, to facilitate the evacuation, which required covering infantry, air,
and armored units).[186] Such was Bevin's fear of a reenactment of Haifa that
he bypassed normal channels (the defense minister and the high commissioner) in prodding the army to act.[187]

Already on 25 April, hours after the start of the IZL assault, the British
Lydda District commissioner, William Fuller, asked Tel Aviv mayor Yisrael
Rokah to get the IZL to call off the attack. Fuller persisted in these efforts
during the following two days, warning that the army would be forced to intervene.[188] On 28 April, the British, via Rokah, demanded that the IZL
cease fire and withdraw immediately from Manshiya—or they would "bomb
Tel Aviv from land, sea and air"; they intended to "save Jaffa for the Arabs at

all costs, especially in the light of the fact that the Jews had conquered Haifa."[189] The IZL rejected the demands.

But British forces were already on the move. Early on 28 April infantry units and squadrons of tanks pushed into Jaffa. Most of the British activity was merely demonstrative. Royal Navy destroyers sped up and down the coast and RAF aircraft flew dry runs over southern Tel Aviv and Jaffa. But one foursome of RAF Spitfires attacked with cannon and machineguns a Haganah position in a factory in nearby Bat Yam, forcing its abandonment, and British artillery and tanks hit suspected IZL positions in and around Manshiya. The IZL mortars fell silent.[190] Next day, the British tanks and infantry pushed into Manshiya itself, meeting stiff IZL resistance. Gurney sent Ben-Gurion a minatory message—which the Jews called an "ultimatum"—threatening to bomb Tel Aviv if he did not rein in the IZL and Haganah (see Operation Hametz below).[191] Montgomery had instructed the army to make sure that the Arabs remained in possession of Jaffa, to "bomb the Jews and shoot them up": "The more armed members of the IZL and Stern gangs that you can kill the better," he ordered.[192]

But Cunningham had already told the army what to do. Late on 29 April and repeatedly the following day British commanders met Amos Ben-Gurion, a Jewish Agency liaison officer (and Ben-Gurion's son), and Jaffa mayor Yusuf Heikal, and a ceasefire agreement was hammered out: the British would halt their attacks, the Haganah would stop Operation Hametz (see below) and promise not to attack Jaffa before the end of the Mandate, and the IZL would evacuate Manshiya, with Haganah troops replacing them and British troops patrolling its southern end and occupying its police fort.[193] The agreement went into effect on 1 May, the IZL troops finally pulling out of Manshiya—but only after blowing up the fort and a string of nearby buildings. Jaffa—or, more accurately, its fringe areas—were once more under British rule. But it was only until 13 May.

The British show of force may briefly have kept the Jews at bay. But it did little to stem the outward flow of refugees. Without doubt, contributing to the exodus was the Haganah offensive, *mivtza hametz* (Operation Unleavened Bread), of 28–30 April, just east of Jaffa, and the behavior inside the town of the Arab militias, especially recently arrived ALA troops commanded by Mahdi Salah.

In Hametz, conducted by units of the Giv'ati, Alexandroni, and Kiryati Brigades, the Haganah aimed at "completely surrounding and cutting off" Jaffa from its hinterland by conquering a string of Arab villages—Yazur, Yahudiya, Sakiya, Salame, Kafr 'Ana, and Beit Dajan—and the suburb-village of Tel al-Reish. The orders spoke generally of "cleansing the area [*tihur hashetah*]" and "permitting civilian inhabitants . . . to leave after they are searched for weapons." Women and children were not to be harmed, and looting was forbidden.[194]

Salame, Sakiya, Al-Kheiriya, and Yazur, heavily outgunned, fell almost without a fight, HIS attributing their general nonresistance to the effect of the prior Arab defeats in Haifa, Mishmar Ha'emek, and Tiberias: "It is clear that the inhabitants have no stomach for war."[195] Most of the villagers fled as the Haganah columns approached. A number of prisoners, who were suspected of killing Jews, were executed.[196] When Ben-Gurion visited Salame on 30 April he found "only one old blind woman."[197]

The killing of the prisoners was not unusual. Until April, neither side generally took prisoners, partly because they had no adequate facilities to hold them. The British, the country's nominal rulers, would not have countenanced Haganah or Arab militia POW camps, certainly not in areas under their control. In practice neither side, after capturing enemy positions, houses, or traffic, kept prisoners. Captured combatants were usually shot out of hand or, less frequently, after a brief incarceration and interrogation, freed.[198] During the first stage of the civil war, Jews probably killed more POWs than vice versa simply because Jews overran more Arab positions.

April and May were characterized by confusion and inconsistency. From the start of April onward, the Haganah captured villages and Arab urban neighborhoods and towns; and Arab combatants fell into Jewish hands in growing numbers, especially in Haifa. HGS ordered the brigades to set up temporary detention centers, and a number were established. But some units continued to shoot POWs or to release them for lack of holding facilities. Noncombatants almost invariably were freed.

In effect, prisoners were incarcerated in orderly fashion only from 26 May, when the Haganah set up a central POW camp in the abandoned village of Jalil al-Qibliya (Gelilot), just north of Tel Aviv. By 12 June, the camp held more than four hundred prisoners. From the Arab side, Jews captured before 15 May were often executed, though the large batch of POWs taken in the 'Etzion Bloc by the Arab Legion (see below) were transferred to a camp in Jordan. After 15 May, POWs usually ended up in detention camps in Arab states, though a few were murdered before they reached them.[199]

Without doubt, the rapid collapse of Jaffa's hinterland villages owed much to the prior IZL conquest of Manshiya and the demoralization of Jaffa's militiamen and inhabitants. In turn, the fall of the villages further undermined the morale of Jaffa's remaining residents, precipitating further flight.[200] But so did the chaos and rapine in Jaffa itself. "The shops, the markets and the banks were closed. . . . The sick, the wounded, and the dead who have been left without care . . . reinforce the dread. The fear of a renewal of the [Jewish] attack [while] they are without arms, is terrible," reported one Haganah intelligence source.[201] Electricity, water, and fuel were in short supply, and the recently arrived ALA and irregulars, mostly Iraqis, subjected the dwindling number of locals to robbery and rape, and systematically plundered the abandoned houses, shops, and warehouses—a task that "was completed by British troops. All is permitted as there is no government."[202] One Arab commentator later wrote that, as daily convoys of refugees were departing for Gaza, the ALA troops "acted as if the town was theirs, and began to rob people and loot their houses. People's lives became worthless and women's honor was defiled."[203] Mayor Heikal fled on 4 May or just before, as did most of the other remaining notables.[204]

Jaffa's agony ended on 14 May, when Haganah troops, accompanied by token IZL units, drove into the almost empty town; only about four thousand inhabitants remained. Ben-Gurion visited four days later and commented: "I couldn't understand: Why did the inhabitants . . . leave?"[205] The Haganah's peaceful entry followed two days of negotiations between Kiryati Brigade OC Michael Ben-Gal and a handful of Jaffa notables. The Haganah promised that there would be "no military trials and acts of vengeance" and that peace-minded inhabitants who had fled would be allowed to return.[206] In the formal agreement signed on 13 May, the Jaffa notables promised to hand over arms and keep the peace and the Haganah, to abide by the Geneva conventions and allow the return of women, children, and, after a security screening, males.[207]

But the following weeks were not untroubled. The Haganah screening of the remaining inhabitants was unpleasant; refugees were not allowed back; and property was vandalized and looted by soldiers and civilians from Tel Aviv, on a massive scale. One Haganah document graphically describes the events in Manshiya on 18 May: "There I found a large crowd of women, children and men who were looting everything: Chairs, cupboards, and other furniture, household and kitchen utensils, sheets, pillows." Haganah units tried to halt the looting, occasionally firing into the air or beating miscreants, but with incomplete success.[208] The problem was that the troops, too, were involved, as one official reported a week later: "I saw soldiers, civilians, military police, battalion police, looting, robbing, while breaking through doors and walls."[209]

And during the first few days, there were even more serious problems. A twelve-year-old girl was raped by soldiers, and there were a handful of cases of attempted rape.[210] The bodies of fifteen Arabs were found on a Jaffa beach, apparently executed by Haganah troops or the HIS.[211] Gradually matters improved. But the harassment of Arabs and the vandalization of their property appears to have ended only in August.

The mass flight from the towns and villages of Palestine at the end of April triggered anxiety and opposition among the Arab leaders. Victor Khayyat, the Haifa notable, who then toured the Arab capitals, was told by the prime ministers of Syria and Lebanon of their displeasure,[212] and in the first week of May, apparently in coordination with the British, the Arab leaders launched a campaign to persuade the refugees to return. The emphasis was on young, able-bodied males. On 5 May King ʿAbdullah publicly called on "every man of strength and wisdom . . . who has left the country, let him return to the dear spot. No one should remain outside the country except the rich and the old." He thanked those who had remained in Palestine "in spite of the tyranny now prevailing."[213] A few days before, he had specifically pressed bedouin refugees from the Beisan (Beit Shean) Valley to return.[214] On 5–7 May, the ALA, in radio broadcasts from Ramallah and Damascus, forbade villagers from leaving, threatening that their homes would be demolished and their lands confiscated. Inhabitants who had fled were ordered to return.[215] The broadcasts were monitored by the Haganah: "The Arab military leaders are trying to stem the flood of refugees and are taking stern and ruthless measures against them."[216]

At the same time, the British appealed specifically to the Arabs of Haifa to return to their homes; the AHC joined the campaign in the second week of May. Faiz Idrisi, the AHC's "inspector for public safety," ordered Palestinian militiamen to fight against "the Fifth Column and the rumor-mongers, who are causing the flight of the Arab population." The AHC specifically ordered officials, doctors, and engineers to return.[217]

The fall of Arab Tiberias and Arab Haifa cleared the way for a further, major Haganah offensive, the conquest of the villages of Eastern Galilee and the area's main town, Safad. A Syrian-Lebanese invasion was expected and clearing the rear areas of actively or potentially hostile Palestinian Arab bases— that could facilitate the invasion—became imperative. Yigal Allon, the Palmah OC, had reconnoitered the area in a spotter aircraft on 21 April and the following day recommended that the Haganah launch a series of operations, in line with Plan D, to brace for the invasion: Eastern Galilee had to be pacified, and the Arab inhabitants of the towns of Beit Shean (Beisan) and Safad had to be "harassed" into flight.[218] The HGS agreed, and Allon was put in charge. The orders initially defined the objective as "taking control of

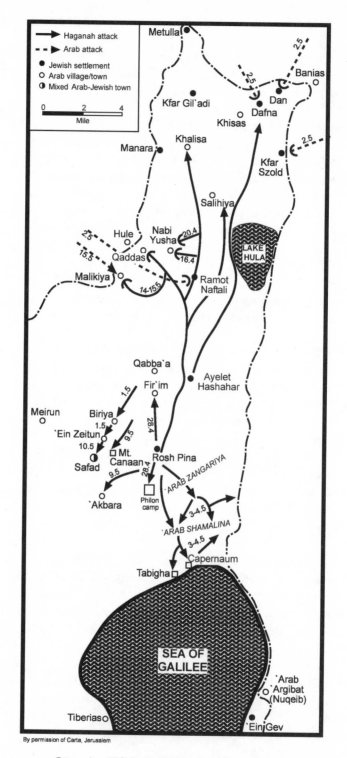

Legend:
- → Haganah attack
- ⇢ Arab attack
- ● Jewish settlement
- ○ Arab village/town
- ◑ Mixed Arab-Jewish town

Scale: 0 — 2 — 4 Mile

Metulla

Kfar Gil`adi

Banias

Dan

Khisas

Dafna

Khalisa

Manara

Kfar Szold

Salihiya

Hule · Nabi Yusha · 20.4

Qaddas · 16.4

LAKE HULA

Malikiya · 15.5

14-15.5

Ramot Naftali

Qabba`a

Fir`im

Ayelet Hashahar

Meirun

Biriya · 1.5

`Ein Zeitun · 9.5

10.5

Mt. Canaan

Rosh Pina

`ARAB ZANGARIYA

Safad

9.5

28.4

`Akbara

Philon camp

`ARAB SHAMALINA

3-4.5

Tabigha

Capernaum

3-4.5

SEA OF GALILEE

`Arab Argibat (Nuqeib)

Tiberias

`Ein Gev

By permission of Carta, Jerusalem

Operation Yiftah, Galilee Panhandle and Safad,
April–May 1948

the Tel Hai area and its consolidation in preparation for [the] invasion."[219] Two battalions, the Palmah's Third and Golani's Eleventh, as well as local militia contingents, were to take part.

The immediate trigger to Operation Yiftah, as it was to be called, was the staggered pullout of Britain's forces from Eastern Galilee from 15 to 28 April. Both sides rushed to occupy the abandoned Tegart forts and army camps or to eject occupying enemy forces. Operation Yiftah was preceded by stubborn, if abortive, Palmah attempts, on 16 and 20 April, to take the Nabi Yusha police fort.[220] The fort dominated the Hula Valley from the heights to the west.

Yiftah proper got under way on 28 April, with the Palmah occupation of the Tegart fort in Rosh Pina and the nearby army camp. On 3–4 May, the Palmah's First Battalion, in a suboperation named *mivtza matate* (Operation Broom), cleared of Arab inhabitants—mainly the Arab al-Shamalina and Arab al-Zangariya bedouin, who for weeks had sniped at Jewish traffic along the main south-north road—the area between the Sea of Galilee and Rosh Pina: "The tents were burned and most of the houses were blown up."[221] The Palmah had defined the aim as "the destruction of bases of the enemy . . . and to destroy points of assembly for invading forces from the east [and] . . . to join the lower and upper Galilee with a relatively wide and safe strip" of territory.[222] A Catholic priest, Boniface Bittelmeier, described what he witnessed: "There was a terrible explosion in Tabigha [on the northwestern shore of the Sea of Galilee]. We rushed out and saw pillars of smoke rising skyward. House after house was bombed and torched . . . smoke and fire were visible; in the evening, the 'victors' returned [to base?] with trucks loaded with cattle. What they couldn't take they shot."[223] In parallel, mortars were used to neutralize and clear a cluster of villages (Firʿim, Mughar al-Kheit, Qabbaʿa) north of Rosh Pina,[224] securing the road to the Galilee Panhandle, where, on 1–2 May, armed bands from Syria had attacked the kibbutzim Dan, Dafna, Kfar Szold, and Lehavot Habashan and ALA forces from Lebanon were attacking Kibbutz Ramot Naftali.[225]

But all this was merely a prelude to the battle for Safad, the strategically important mixed town that served as the "capital" of Eastern Galilee. Safad, with fifteen hundred Jews and ten to twelve thousand Arabs with a tradition of anti-Yishuv violence, was evacuated by the British on 16 April. They handed over to the Arabs the two dominant positions—the hilltop "Citadel" at the center of town and the large Tegart fort on Mount Canaan, to the east. That night the Arabs assailed the Jewish Quarter. The local Arab militia, of two hundred men, had been joined by more than two hundred ALA troops and Jordanian volunteers; the Haganah contingent, of some two hundred men and women, had been reinforced by an oversized Palmah platoon. The Jews drove back the Arab attack, and the Arab militias began to fall apart.[226]

The town's largely ultra-Orthodox Jewish community still feared annihilation.[227] And the Arab town's militia commander, the Syrian al-Hassan Kam al-Maz, seemed to give credence to their fears. He cabled Adib Shishakli, the ALA regional commander: "Morale is [still] very strong, the young are enthusiastic, we will slaughter them."[228]

But the tables were beginning imperceptibly to turn. Turf struggles created bad blood between the various Arab militias. Shishakli replaced Kam al-Maz with the Jordanians Sari al-Fnaish and Amil Jmai'an, who Kam al-Maz charged were "selling out to the Jews."[229] Kam al-Maz and his men left, and the remaining militiamen complained of a shortage of ammunition.[230] Operation Broom then cut Arab Safad off from any hope of aid from Syria.

On 1 May, Palmah Third Battalion troops, in a separate suboperation, captured two villages north of Safad, Biriya and 'Ein Zeitun, cutting off the town from the west. The troops executed several dozen male prisoners from 'Ein Zeitun in a nearby wadi.[231] Palmah sappers proceeded to blow up the two villages as Safad's Arabs looked on. The bulk of the Third Battalion then moved into the town's Jewish Quarter and mortared the Arab quarters.[232] Many Arabs fled, wending their way down Safad's eastern slopes toward the Syrian border.

Taken together, these operations, coming after Deir Yassin and the fall of Tiberias and Haifa, discouraged the population and paved the way for Safad's fall. An abortive Third Battalion attack on the Citadel on 6 May,[233] which included a mortar barrage, had the same effect.[234] Already on 5 May the commanders of the Jordanian volunteer force radioed al-Qawuqji that if reinforcements, including artillery, failed to arrive, they would leave; the town could not hold out for "more than two hours."[235]

After 6 May, the "terrified" Arabs sought a truce. Allon, who visited the Jewish Quarter the next day, rejected terms,[236] and the Arab states failed to provide the militias with assistance (apart from pressing Britain to intervene, which Whitehall declined to do). Allon ordered Moshe Kelman, the Third Battalion OC, to renew the assault and solve the problem of Safad immediately; the pan-Arab invasion was just days away.[237] Shishakli, who also visited the town, ordered an attack on 10 May and reinforced the militias with a further company of Jordanians. Meanwhile, his artillery began intermittently to shell the Jewish Quarter from a nearby hill.

Some local Jews sought to negotiate a surrender and demanded that the Haganah leave town. But the Haganah commanders were unbending and at 9:35 PM, 9 May, preempted Shishakli, launching a multipronged attack. The timing was immaculate: a few hours earlier, al-Fnaish, Jmai'an, and much of the Jordanian contingent had slipped out of town, severely undercutting the Arab defenses. (Some Arabs subsequently charged al-Fnaish with treachery, and he was briefly jailed in Syria. But some sources claim that the Jordanian volunteers were ordered to leave by King ʿAbdullah, who perhaps sought to prevent a Husseini victory that might result in the installation in Safad of a mufti-led Palestinian government.)[238]

The Palmahniks, backed by Davidka and 3-inch mortars, and PIATs, that night, under a heavy rain, managed to take the Citadel as well as the town's police fort (where the battle was particularly prolonged and severe) and other Arab positions, including the village of ʿAkbara, just south of town.[239] The Haganah successes and the Davidka bombs, which exploded with tremendous noise and a great flash, triggered a mass panic, "screams and yells."[240] According to Arab sources, cited by an HIS document, the first Davidka bomb, which killed "13 Arabs, most of them children," triggered the panic—intended by the Palmah commanders when unleashing the mortars against the Arab neighborhoods.[241] A rumor then spread that the Jews were using "atom" bombs (which, some Arabs believed, had sparked the unseasonably heavy downpour).[242] A Haganah scout plane, flying overhead, reported "thousands of refugees streaming by foot toward Meirun"; another report depicted the inhabitants "loaded down with parcels, women carrying their children in their arms, some going by foot, others on ass and donkey-back."[243] The Arab neighborhoods, literally overnight, turned into a "ghost town," and the Jewish inhabitants went "wild with joy and danced and sang in the streets."[244] The Palmahniks spent 10–11 May scouring the abandoned neighborhoods. During the following weeks, the few remaining Arabs, most of them old and infirm or Christians, were expelled to Lebanon or transferred to Haifa.[245]

During late April and early May, a handful of villages along the Syrian border were ordered, by the Syrian authorities or local Arab commanders, to evacuate their houses or to move out their women and children, either to facilitate their takeover by Arab militiamen or to clear the area in advance of the impending invasion.[246] This dovetailed with the Yiftah Brigade's efforts, immediately after the fall of Arab Safad, to clear out the villagers from the Hula Valley and Galilee Panhandle in advance of the expected invasion. According to Allon, Safad's demise had badly shaken the morale of the villagers; the Palmah sought to exploit the effect:

We only had five days left . . . until 15 May. We regarded it as imperative to cleanse the interior of the Galilee and create Jewish territorial continuity in the whole of Upper Galilee. The protracted battles had reduced our forces and we faced major tasks in blocking the invasion routes. We therefore looked for a means that would not oblige us to use force to drive out the tens of thousands of hostile Arabs left in the [Eastern] Galilee and who, in the event of an invasion, could strike at us from behind. We tried to use a stratagem that exploited the [Arab] defeats . . . a stratagem that worked wonderfully.

I gathered the Jewish mukhtars [headmen], who had ties with the different Arab villages, and I asked them to whisper in the ears of several Arabs that giant Jewish reinforcements had reached the Galilee and were about to clean out the villages of the Hula, [and] to advise them, as friends, to flee while they could. And the rumor spread throughout the Hula that the time had come to flee. The flight encompassed tens of thousands. The stratagem fully achieved its objective . . . and we were able to deploy ourselves in face of the [prospective] invaders along the borders, without fear for our rear.[247]

To reinforce this "whispering," or psychological warfare, campaign, Allon's men distributed fliers, advising those who wished to avoid harm to leave "with their women and children."[248]

During the following days villages that had not been abandoned, or had been abandoned briefly and then partially refilled with returnees (often because the refugees began to suffer from "hunger"),[249] were conquered, the battalion HQs usually instructing the attacking units to expel the inhabitants.[250] Palmah troops also mounted raids into Syria and Lebanon, blowing up, among other targets, the mansion, near Hule, of Ahmad al-As'ad, a leading south Lebanese Shi'ite notable.[251] A newly established bedouin unit, commanded by Yitzhak Hankin, took part in the operations.[252] Yet many Hula Valley villagers who fled or were driven out did not cross the border but encamped, often in swampland, along the Palestine side of the line, fearing that if they crossed into Syria they would be conscripted by the Syrian Army.[253] By the fourth week of May, the Palmah was "systematically torching the Hula [Valley] villages."[254]

While the Palmah was busy with Operation Yiftah, the Golani Brigade, to the south, also moved to seal potential entry points for the invaders. The brigade cleared the southern shore of the Sea of Galilee, with the large village of Samakh at its center, and the Lower Jordan and Beit Shean Valleys, including the town of Beisan.

The battle for Samakh, on 29 April, was short and relatively costless. The fall of Tiberias had gravely undermined the villagers' morale. As in Jaffa, an initial Haganah attack on 23 April, in which the British intervened in support of the villagers,[255] resulted in the flight of many of the inhabitants and the arrival of foreign Arab volunteers, who systematically plundered the empty homes and shops. A small force of Jordanian volunteers established itself in the police fort. A Golani sapper team blew a hole in one of the fort's walls, and perhaps with some bribery-driven connivance, the Haganah took the fort and then the nearby village, the remaining militiamen and population fleeing to Jordan and Syria.[256]

Beisan's turn came a few days later. As Yosef Weitz had put it on 4 May, "The emptying of the valley is the order of the day."[257] Tiberias and Haifa had triggered a partial flight of Beisan's population; the Haganah occupation on 27–28 April of the Gesher police fort, to the north, and a neighboring army camp further eroded morale. On the night of 10–11 May, Golani conquered two neighboring villages, Farwana and al-Ashrafiya, the inhabitants fleeing to Jordan. Golani blew up the houses and, the following night, occupied a dominant hillock, Tel al-Husn (biblical Beit Shean), from which it mortared the town. One of the town's two militia commanders, Ismail al-Faruqi, fled, followed by most of the ALA contingent. A short negotiation with the remaining notables resulted in a surrender, and Golani troops moved in on 13 May.[258] The townspeople were told that they could, if peaceable, stay.[259] The occupying troops were well behaved. A kibbutznik from the area was appointed military governor, and local Arab "inspectors"—who donned "yellow armbands," as a reporting HIS officer sadly noted—were selected to supervise water allocation and hygiene.[260] Nonetheless, within days the remaining one thousand to twelve hundred inhabitants were expelled—most on 15 May across the Jordan and a handful, mainly Christians, on 28 May, to Arab-held Nazareth.[261] The Haganah had feared that "the inhabitants might revolt" behind the Israeli lines.[262] Following Beisan's fall, neighboring bedouin tribes moved to Jordan. "The valley was almost completely cleansed of its Arab inhabitants. . . . This was the first time that the Beit Shean Valley had become a purely Hebrew valley," noted the Golani Brigade's official history.[263]

Together, the Yiftah and Golani Brigades, over late April–mid-May, had conquered Eastern Galilee and largely cleared out its Arab inhabitants.

Safad and Beisan were, in effect, part of the Haganah's countrywide effort to improve its position in preparation for the prospective Arab invasion—"to block as far as possible the way for [enemy] armor," as Yadin told the People's Administration (*minhelet ha'am*).[264] Beside improving defenses—trenches and bunkers in and around towns and rural settlements[265]—local offensive operations were launched, in line with Plan D, to gain last-minute advantages before the impending onslaught.

In the south, Giv'ati and the (Palmah) Negev Brigade expanded their area of control by capturing and depopulating a series of villages. On 4–6 May, Giv'ati troops surrounded the villages of 'Aqir and Qatra, demanding that the inhabitants hand over their weapons. Some were handed over, but the Israelis suspected that the villagers were holding back—and in Qatra a Jewish officer was killed—so Giv'ati took a handful of villagers hostage until more arms were produced. 'Aqir's inhabitants promptly fled, perhaps fearing that, if they stayed, fellow Arabs would accuse them of treacherously accepting Jewish sovereignty. At Qatra, the inhabitants were either intimidated into flight or expelled a few days later (after the start of the Egyptian invasion).[266]

On 9–10 May, Giv'ati launched *mivtza barak* (Operation Lightning). The objective was "to deny the enemy [the prospective Egyptian invaders] a base for future operations . . . by creating general panic. . . . The aim is to force the Arab inhabitants 'to move.'" The villages initially targeted were Beit Daras, Bash-shit, Batani al-Sharqi, and Batani al-Gharbi. The planners hoped that their fall would also trigger the abandonment of their smaller satellites.[267] Beit Daras offered serious resistance, and some twenty villagers were killed (along with four Israelis) and forty wounded before the village was conquered. Giv'ati's official history notes that "the attackers took care not to harm noncombatants, old people, women, and children [even though Beit Daras was considered] a village of murderers, the hands of its inhabitants covered in blood."[268] The conquest and destruction of Beit Daras triggered flight from neighboring Batani al-Sharqi, Ibdis, Julis, and Beit 'Affa. At Batani al-Sharqi Giv'ati troops executed four men.[269]

In the second stage of the operation (codenamed Operation Maccabbi), which began on 13 May, Giv'ati units stormed the village of Abu Shusha, near Ramla, and, after taking some notables hostage, disarmed the nearby village of Na'na without battle. At Abu Shusha some villagers apparently were executed.[270] During the following days, Giv'ati captured the large village of Mughar, which the troops found almost completely abandoned, al-Qubab, Sawafir al-Sharqiya, and adjoining Sawafir al-Gharbiyya. Giv'ati's Fifty-first Battalion had been instructed "to clear the front line . . . to cleanse [the Sawafir villages] of inhabitants . . . [and] to burn the greatest possible number of houses."[271] The brigade's official historian noted the troops' penchant to loot conquered villages.[272]

With the Egyptian invasion just hours away, the Negev Brigade's Ninth Battalion conquered the village of Burayr, apparently committing atrocities and killing several dozen villagers, and drove out the inhabitants of the nearby villages of Sumsum and Najd. A fortnight later, the brigade also raided the neighboring villages of Muharraqa and Kaufakha, driving out the inhabitants, and conquered Beit Tima and Huj, a "friendly" village that the brigade commanders nonetheless believed posed a danger.[273]

Observers understood the grim logic behind the Haganah operations: the Jews, complained Arab League secretary-general 'Azzam, were "driving out the inhabitants [from areas] on or near roads by which Arab regular forces could enter the country. . . . The Arab armies would have the greatest difficulty in even entering Palestine after May 15th."[274] He was right.

In Jerusalem, the 'Etzioni Brigade, aided by IZL troops, mounted a major push, *mivtza kilshon* (Operation Pitchfork), designed "to safeguard the Jewish area of Jerusalem . . . in face of the [expected] penetration by . . . mechanized and armored forces of the regular armies of the Arab states."[275] The operation, which ran from 14 to 18 May, involved three thrusts—the conquest of the Police School and the Arab neighborhood of Sheikh Jarrah, north of the Old City; the takeover in the center of the city of the large building complexes fortified by the British during the last two years of the Mandate (known collectively as "Bevingrad" or "Bevingrads"), including the central post office, the "Russian Compound" police fort and court buildings, as well as the Notre Dame monastery—French Hospital complex overlooking the Old City's northern wall, the YMCA and the King David Hotel; and, in the south, the occupation of the abandoned Allenby Barracks, the wholly or partly Arab neighborhoods of Talbiyeh, the German Colony, the Greek Colony, and Abu Tor, and the train station and adjacent Government Printing Office building.

The Bevingrads were occupied without a fight, due to prior British-Haganah agreement. The core of the agreement was reached in meetings on 12 May. At 7:00 AM, 14 May, the town commander, Brigadier Charles Jones, called in the Haganah liaison and told him that by 4:00 PM, no British troops would be left in the city. It was, in fact, a nod to begin operations and was accompanied by a Godspeed: "I am sure," said Jones, "that your State will be established. . . . I wish you good luck and success." Yosef Schnurman, the Haganah officer, expressed "appreciation" for Britain's work "during the past 26 [sic] years" and a hope that "the differences will be forgotten."[276]

The occupation of these areas was followed by large-scale looting and vandalizing of Arab property by Jewish troops and neighbors. Walter Eytan, dragged by acting American consul general William Burdett to look at a house in Bakʿa, reported: "Every single room in the house had been smashed up. . . . The whole place looked as if a band of savages had passed through it. It was not merely a question of ordinary theft, but of deliberate and senseless destruction. . . . A portrait had been left hanging on the wall with the face neatly cut out with a knife. As we went from room to room I felt more and more speechless and more and more ashamed. . . . I could only express my great regret."[277]

Jerusalem Haganah Home Guardsmen topped up their fortifications, prepared Molotov cocktails and booby-trapped buildings for the event of a successful Arab penetration. But the Haganah refrained from planning, or mounting, a major assault on the Old City, apparently guided by political considerations. As Ben-Gurion put it, "Jerusalem is different. It could antagonize the Christian world."[278]

In the Coastal Plain, the Alexandroni Brigade cleaned out a number of pockets of resistance. On 13 May, units of the Thirty-second and Thirty-third battalions attacked and overran Kafr Saba, between the Jewish settlement of Kfar Saba and the Arab town of Qalqilya. The local village militia, supported by an enlarged platoon of ALA troops, had intermittently attacked Jewish traffic and Kfar Saba during the previous months. The inhabitants fled the village as the Haganah troops entered; on the road out to Qalqilya the ALA extorted five Palestine pounds from each fleeing refugee.[279]

Somewhat belatedly, on the night of 22–23 May the Thirty-third Battalion also conquered the large fishing village of Tantura, which lay northwest of Zikhron Ya'akov along the Tel Aviv–Haifa coast road. The village had spurned Haganah demands to surrender. During the nightlong battle, the villagers put up stiff resistance, killing thirteen Alexandroni troops and a sailor before giving up. More than seventy villagers died. In the 1990s Arab journalists charged that the Israeli troops had carried out a large-scale massacre of disarmed militiamen and villagers in the hours after Tantura fell, a charge expanded in a master's thesis by an Israeli student, who, on the basis of Arab oral testimony (and the distortion of testimony by Alexandroni veterans), argued that up to 250 villagers had been systematically murdered.[280] Although some Alexandroni veterans hinted at dark deeds, most flatly denied the massacre charge. Documentary evidence indicates that the Alexandroni troops murdered a handful of POWs—and expelled the inhabitants—but provides no grounds for believing that a large-scale massacre occurred.[281]

The major last-minute, Plan D—generated operation in the North was *mivtza ben-ami* (Operation Ben-Ami), geared to coopting Western Galilee to the territory of the Jewish state and to blocking a major potential invasion route, the coast road, from Lebanon into Palestine[282]—though the initial operational order spoke more modestly of breaking through to the isolated kibbutzim Hanita and Eilon, pushing through supply convoys, bringing out their children, and, to assure the convoys' safety, conquering the villages of Sumeiriya, Zib, and Bassa along the way.[283] Intelligence assessments spoke of widespread demoralization in the villages and in Acre, the regional urban center, with many families fleeing the area.[284] The operation, commanded by Carmel, proceeded smoothly, with Carmeli's three-battalion column advancing rapidly during 13–14 May from Haifa's northern suburbs through Sumeiriya (which was immediately leveled), Zib, and Bassa to Eilon, Matzuba, and Hanita. Simultaneously, troops were landed by boat near Sumeiriya. Carmel described Arab fatalities in the "29-hour" operation as forty. Three Israelis died, one went missing, and five were wounded.[285]

Carmeli then shelled and stormed Acre, which raised a white flag on 18 May. The town was ripe for the taking, thoroughly demoralized by the fall of

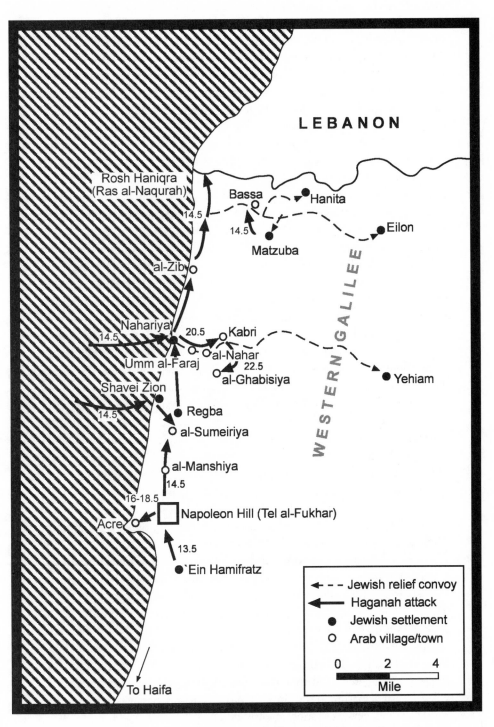

LEBANON

Rosh Haniqra
(Ras al-Naqurah)

14.5

Bassa

Hanita

14.5

Matzuba

Eilon

al-Zib

Nahariya

14.5

20.5

Kabri

al-Nahar

Umm al-Faraj

al-Ghabisiya

22.5

Yehiam

Shavei Zion

14.5

WESTERN GALILEE

Regba

al-Sumeiriya

al-Manshiya

14.5

16-18.5

Napoleon Hill (Tel al-Fukhar)

Acre

13.5

`Ein Hamifratz

To Haifa

- - ◄ Jewish relief convoy
◄━━ Haganah attack
● Jewish settlement
○ Arab village/town

0   2   4
Mile

Operation Ben-Ami, Western Galilee, 13–22 May 1948

Haifa the previous month and by repeated attacks on its outskirts. After one attack, on 26 April, one resident wrote to his son, Munir Effendi Nur, then in Nablus: "The shells . . . fell inside the city. . . . This attack caused panic among the inhabitants, most of who left or intend to leave. We may travel to Beirut. The preparations for flight from Acre encompass all levels [of society]: the rich, the middle class, and the poor—all . . . are selling everything they can."[286] By the end of April, Acre was crowded with refugees from Haifa. By 7 May, there was "no electricity or fuel. . . . There was an outbreak of typhus. . . . Many of the permanent inhabitants . . . had fled."[287] The locals wanted a ceasefire but the AHC refused to permit it,[288] and by 11 May most of the NC members had fled.[289] The commanders of the militia, the Haifa "expatriates" Amin ʿIzz al-Din and Yunis Nafaʿa, with some of their men, fled by boat to Lebanon on 14 May; their successor, Mahmoud Saffuri, fled on 16 May.[290] So when Carmel's troops attacked late on 16 May, the inhabitants responded promptly to the brigade's demand to surrender (otherwise "we will destroy you to the last man and utterly").[291] Shortly after midnight, between 17 and 18 May, a party of notables appeared at Carmeli's forward HQ and signed an instrument of unconditional surrender.[292] On 18 May, the troops moved in and scoured the town for weapons and militiamen: "The town . . . looked like after a war. [There were] bodies everywhere. Their number is estimated at 60."[293] Carmel cabled the General Staff: "Western Galilee is in our hands."[294] Some officers suggested that Acre's inhabitants be expelled.[295] But this was never acted on. Four soldiers of Carmeli's Twenty-second Battalion raped an Arab girl and murdered her father (they were later sentenced to three years in jail).[296] Otherwise, the Israeli military government rapidly reorganized the town's services and a substantial population stayed put, becoming Israeli citizens.

Subsequently, the Carmeli Brigade embarked on what was defined as "stage 2" of Ben-Ami, during 20–22 May conquering the villages of Kabri, Umm al-Faraj, and al-Nahar, slightly expanding eastward the coastal strip already in Israeli hands. The order defined the objectives as breaking through to Kibbutz Yehiam with three months of supplies and "attacking with the aim of conquest; to kill adult males; to destroy and torch [the villages]."[297] The villages were rapidly conquered. Kabri was leveled with explosives[298] after a handful of inhabitants were apparently executed.[299] At Ghabisiya, south of Kabri, the villagers—with a tradition of collaboration with the Yishuv—greeted Carmeli with white flags. But the troops opened fire, hitting several villagers, and then executed six more (allegedly because of the villagers' participation in the ambush of the Yehiam Convoy two months before). The villagers were subsequently expelled.[300]

Elsewhere, at a number of sites, Haganah Home Guard units readied for the prospective invasion by disarming or clearing out neighboring villagers. They feared that the villages would help the invaders and serve as bases for attack. Thus, on 13–14 May ʿEin-Gev, an isolated kibbutz on the eastern shore of the Sea of Galilee, demanded that neighboring Arab Argibat (Nuqeib), whom the Jews had earlier persuaded to stay put, accept Jewish rule and hand over their weapons. But the villagers opted for evacuation, probably fearing Arab charges of treachery if they stayed. The kibbutzniks demolished their houses.[301] A fortnight later, the kibbutz evicted the Persian Zickrallah family, who owned a large farm just south of the kibbutz, along with their thirty Arab hands. "In war, there is no room for sentiment," explains the ʿEin-Gev logbook. The Zickrallahs were later resettled in Acre.[302]

The Yishuv was not alone in trying to gain last-minute advantage on the eve of the invasion. Two Arab formations launched operations to clear the way for the expeditionary forces: a battalion of Muslim Brotherhood volunteers, commanded by Egyptian army officers, attacked Kibbutz Kfar Darom, and more tellingly, units of Jordan's Arab Legion, while still part of the British army in Palestine, conquered the ʿEtzion Bloc between Bethlehem and Hebron.

Kfar Darom sat astride the coast road between Rafah and Gaza. Brotherhood volunteers from Egypt had previously—and unsuccessfully—attacked the settlement on 10 April. Just before dawn on 11 May the battalion, which had infiltrated into Palestine two weeks before, launched an artillery barrage. Smoke bombs followed, behind which infantry advanced. The defenders held their ground and the Egyptians failed to break through the perimeter fence. According to the historian of the Muslim Brotherhood volunteers, the attackers' confusion was compounded by their own artillery volleys that landed among them. The volunteers retreated, leaving behind some seventy dead.[303]

Far more significant was the attack on the ʿEtzion Bloc, in which the four settlements were destroyed. The area had first been settled in 1927 and was then repeatedly abandoned because of Arab harassment and economic difficulties. In the early 1940s Jews affiliated to the nationalist religious Mizrahi Party returned to the area and established three kibbutzim: Kfar ʿEtzion, Massuʾot Yitzhak, and ʿEin Tzurim. A fourth kibbutz, Revadim, was added by Hashomer Hatzaʿir settlers. By 1948 there were some five hundred settlers and Haganah members in the bloc. Though the land had been purchased from the Arabs, the locals saw the settlers as aliens and invaders. Indeed, three weeks before the UN partition resolution, the mayor of Hebron, ʿAli Jaʿabri, warned Kfar ʿEtzion that the region's Arabs had resolved to "remove the Jews from the area in the event of the outbreak of hostilities."

Ja'abri advised them "to leave voluntarily . . . as in any event you will be re-moved by force" and promised that the settlers would be compensated for their lands.[304]

Starting on 12–14 January 1948—when a convoy from West Jerusalem to the bloc was ambushed by villagers and an attack on the kibbutzim by several thousand local militiamen was repulsed[305]—the bloc was effectively under siege. The Haganah retaliated, mainly by ambushing Arab traffic along the Hebron-Bethlehem road. On 15 January a thirty-five-man Haganah relief column was destroyed to a man.[306]

During the following months the Yishuv leadership repeatedly debated the possible evacuation of the bloc (as the British recommended). But a de-cision in principle was taken against: "No Jewish point or settlement should be evacuated and they [must] be held until the last man."[307] This principle, coupled with strategic considerations linked to the fate of Jewish Jerusalem, proved decisive. It was argued that the 'Etzion Bloc siphoned off Arab fighters who otherwise would have been free to attack West Jerusalem. In ad-dition, the bloc was a strategic asset because it was able to interdict Arab traffic between Hebron and the capital.[308]

In early April, the fighters in the bloc—on orders from the Haganah com-mand, who sought to reduce the pressure on Jerusalem—repeatedly am-bushed traffic, including Arab Legion and British army vehicles, along the Hebron-Bethlehem road. On 12 April Legion armored cars attacked Kfar 'Etzion's outposts, and then withdrew.[309] Further Haganah attacks fol-lowed, with the Legion taking casualties. As the British withdrawal deadline from Jerusalem drew near, they worried that the Haganah would block the road, along which their Second Brigade was due to proceed, via Beersheba and Rafah, to the Suez Canal.[310] The Legion's newly formed Sixth Regi-ment was placed in charge of security along the road.

The Haganah attacks along the road persuaded the British to allow the Legion to solve the problem, though they never admitted, then or later, to having taken such a decision. At first, a punitive attack was ordered. On 4 May, a Legion infantry force, with armored cars, Bren-gun carriers, and can-non, perhaps supported by a few British tanks and armored cars,[311] assaulted and took Haganah positions, principally the "Russian Monastery," on the eastern edge of the bloc, from which traffic had been attacked. But the Le-gionnaires failed to take and destroy other key positions and withdrew. Twelve Haganah soldiers died and thirty were wounded, and some light mortars and machine guns were lost. Several dozen Arabs died, mainly local militiamen who had joined in.

The local Legion commanders, led by 'Abdullah Tall, OC Sixth Regiment, began to plan the bloc's conquest. The attack went home on 12 May. Tall implies that he initiated the assault without authorization and that General John Glubb, the commander of the Legion, only gave it a post facto endorsement.[312] This appears unlikely. The assault was grounded in clear strategic rather than tactical considerations. The Legion seems to have been motivated in part by revenge for the casualties it had previously suffered at the hands of the bloc's fighters, in part by its obligation to secure the road for British traffic, in part by pressure from the Hebron notables to uproot what they had long regarded as an unwanted presence, in part—this was Glubb's subsequent justification for intervening[313]—by a desire to enable a last convoy of British-supplied vehicles and stores from the Suez Canal to reach the Legion. But, no doubt, Glubb also calculated that the advance removal of the obstacle posed by the bloc would facilitate his takeover of the Bethlehem-Hebron area in the forthcoming invasion, while its continued existence would hamper his operations.[314]

On the eve of the battle, the bloc was defended by some five hundred Haganah fighters and kibbutz members, who were armed with light weapons, two two-inch mortars, one three-inch mortar, a number of medium machine guns, and several PIATs. They had little ammunition, especially for the mortars and PIATs. The attacking force consisted of the bulk of two Legion infantry companies (the sixth and twelfth garrison companies), a company of ALA irregulars, two dozen armored cars, some of them mounting two-pounders, a battery of three-inch mortars, and possibly one or two six-pounders. These were supported by more than a thousand militiamen.

The Legion attacked just before dawn, 12 May, with an effective mortar and artillery barrage on Kfar ʿEtzion's outer redoubts and buildings. Armored cars then moved in, infantry following. The defenders had no answer to the Legion's armor and artillery and were killed or ejected from position after position. By noon, the Legionnaires had taken the "Russian Monastery" and had reached the crossroads at the center of the bloc, isolating Kfar ʿEtzion from the other settlements and occupying the landing strip, through which the besieged bloc had been supplied during the previous months. The radio messages from Kfar ʿEtzion grew desperate: "We are being shelled heavily. Our situation is very bad. Every minute counts. Send aircraft [to parachute supplies] as quickly as possible."[315]

After a pause, the Legionnaires renewed their artillery attack. That night the defenders radioed Haganah headquarters: "Send immediately belts for Spandau machine guns. Extricate us immediately. There is no hope of holding out. . . . The situation in men, weapons, and ammunition grave. Do everything tonight."[316] But all Jerusalem could do was ask the British and the Red Cross to intervene.[317]

The Legion renewed the assault just before dawn. A preliminary shelling was followed by armored cars and infantry attacking the perimeter trench works. Reinforcements arrived from Massu'ot Yitzhak and light aircraft dropped makeshift bombs without effect; ground fire forced them to stay too high. In any event, there was no way to stop the armored cars or to neutralize the artillery and mortars. That morning, the armored cars and infantry breached Kfar 'Etzion's defenses from the north. Just before noon, the order went out from the kibbutz's commanders to the outlying outposts and trenches to surrender. Groups of defenders carrying white flags emerged from bunkers and trenches. But elsewhere, unaware of the surrender order, the defenders still fired off the odd shot.

The bulk of the defenders, more than a hundred men and women, assembled in an open area at the center of Kfar 'Etzion. Arab soldiers "ordered [us] to sit and then stand and raise our hands. One of the Arabs pointed a tommy gun at us and another wanted to throw a grenade. But others restrained them. Then a photographer with a *kaffiya* arrived and took photographs of us. . . . An armored car arrived. . . . When the photographer stopped taking pictures fire was opened up on us from all directions. Those not hit in the initial fusillade . . . ran in various directions. Some fled to the [central] bunker. Others took hold of weapons. A mass of Arabs poured into the settlements from all sides and attacked the men in the center of the settlement and in the outposts shouting wildly 'Deir Yassin.'"[318] Almost all the men and women were murdered. All witnesses agree that the militiamen who poured into the settlement looted and vandalized the buildings, "leaving not one stone upon another."[319] (Afterward, they did the same in the three other settlements: they apparently were driven by a desire for revenge and "a desire to prevent the Jews' return to the bloc.")[320]

Not all the Legionnaires participated in the massacre. Indeed, the Legion subsequently variously denied that there had been a massacre or ascribed the slaughter to the local militiamen.[321] One officer saved and protected "Aliza R.," a Haganah radiowoman who had jumped into a trench during the initial fusillade. Two Legionnaires who heard her scream pulled her out and took her aside and (apparently) tried to rape her. A Legion officer shot the two with his tommy gun and led her to an armored car and safety.[322] In all, only a handful of the defenders survived: three were saved by Legion officers; another managed to reach Massu'ot Yitzhak, still in Jewish hands. The rest, 106 men and twenty-seven women, died in the battles that day or were murdered in the slaughter that followed. Another twenty-four defenders had been killed on the first day.[323] In the two-day battle, the Legionnaires apparently suffered twenty-seven dead and the local militiamen, forty-two dead.[324]

The fall of the bloc's main settlement clinched the fate of the other three, as the Haganah command immediately understood. The three kibbutzim were short of manpower, weapons, and ammunition and had no prospect of rescue by Jewish or British intervention. The Haganah in Jerusalem, with the invasion imminent, was too hard-pressed; and the British, with two feet out the door, were certainly not going to intervene and prevent an Arab victory—indeed, a victory by their Jordanian clients—bare hours before their exit from Palestine.

In hectic negotiations with the British and the Red Cross, the Jewish Agency on 13 May arranged the orderly surrender of the three settlements, which were subjected to continuous attacks during the afternoon and evening. The settlements had pleaded with Jerusalem to organize their surrender, fearing massacre the following morning.

On the morning of 14 May, as the leaders in Tel Aviv were putting last-minute touches to the new state's Declaration of Independence, a Red Cross convoy reached the bloc. The Legion had pulled back a few hundred yards. But thousands of militiamen surrounded the three settlements. Firefights broke out; a number of disarmed Jews were murdered. Another massacre loomed. But the Red Cross representatives, aided by Arab policemen from Jerusalem, negotiated the entry of small Legion units into the settlements to effect an orderly submission. Revadim, then ʿEin Tsurim, then Massuʿot Yitzhak surrendered. At each site the arms were handed over to the Legion, and the defenders were loaded onto trucks. Firefights broke out between the Legionnaires, bent on protecting the Jews, and the militiamen, who wanted to kill and loot. In the end, the Legionnaires loaded 357 POWs onto trucks and ferried them to Transjordan, where they remained until war's end. The Legion violated the surrender agreement by not releasing the females and the wounded, who were to have been transported to Jewish Jerusalem. But Chaim Herzog, the senior Haganah liaison officer with the British, reported that "the behavior of the Arab Legion vis-à-vis the prisoners from the ʿEtzion Bloc was exemplary [*hayta lemofet*]. They displayed great civility and obstructed the Arab mob's attempts to harm them."[325]

In the general landscape of the second stage of the civil war, the events at the bloc had been an exception. The hostilities of April through mid-May had resulted in a resounding Jewish victory and the crushing of Palestinian Arab military power and Palestinian society. In mid-May the HIS summarized:

> The big Jewish offensives . . . instilled fear also in the Arab fighters and exaggerated rumors, influenced by the Oriental imagination, spread about Jewish secret weapons and great damage and losses that the Arabs suffered. The fear and depression grew with each new . . . offensive. . . . After these victories the Arabs reached the conclusion that there is no place in the country where they

are safe, and flight began also from purely Arab areas. . . . A psychosis of flight [took hold] and massive flight and a complete evacuation of Arabs settlements [began], even before any [military] action was taken against them, or solely on the basis of rumors that they were about to be attacked . . . .

The influence on the Arab fighters was great because in large measure their military forces were directly hit, [and] they suffered many hundreds of casualties. They lost arms and ammunition and important bases, they moved from a position of attack to a condition of defense in the midst of demoralization. . . . The Arab population in large parts of the country was destroyed in every way, many Arab settlements ceased to exist, economic life was paralyzed and a vast amount of property was lost. Tens of thousands of Arabs fled from their places of residence into the interior of the country and to neighboring Arab countries. . . . They have almost no bases which they once had from which to attack the contiguous Jewish areas. [They suffered from] vast economic losses, the undermining of their military forces, anarchy and chaos because of the large number of refugees, and lack of [provisions] and diseases and a danger of epidemics.

But in mid-May what figured large in the Jewish leadership's minds was not Palestinian defeat or refugeedom but the looming pan-Arab invasion. The plight, and then fate, of the bloc seemed to prefigure what might happen when the invasion was unleashed. Indeed, Gush ʿEtzion was prominent in the crucial deliberations of the People's Administration on 12–13 May, in which the leadership finally resolved on the establishment and declaration of Jewish statehood. It was the first time a large Haganah contingent and settlement bloc had confronted a regular Arab army—and the result had been swift and disastrous.

As the struggle for dominion between the Haganah and the Palestine Arab militias was winding down, the political and diplomatic struggle over the emergence of the Jewish state was reaching a crescendo.

Following Warren Austin's Security Council declaration calling for a "temporary trusteeship" for Palestine, the Americans engineered a UN Security Council resolution on 1 April 1948 calling for (1) a truce in Palestine and (2) the convocation of a "special session" of the General Assembly to discuss "the future government of Palestine."

Both the Arab states, egged on by Palestine's Arabs—who were "vehemently opposed to even a temporary solution on these lines"[326]—and the Zionists rejected trusteeship. To be sure, many Arabs regarded the American proposal as "a considerable victory."[327] But this did not translate into support of the idea. The Arabs sought immediate independence and sovereignty over all of Palestine, not a prolongation of international rule, as embodied in an open-ended trusteeship; the Zionists were focused on declaring statehood on the termination of the Mandate, in line with the November 1947 partition resolution. They submitted a series of detailed rebuttals of trusteeship and mobilized for diplomatic battle. One overeager Jewish Agency official in New York, Dorothy Adelson, proposed to Shertok that a number of "brown, black or even coffee-colored Jews (the hue of an Egyptian could do)" be added to the Zionist delegation to the General Assembly, where the "non-white group" had nineteen votes, some of which could be mobilized to vote against trusteeship. This would "provide a visible answer to the canard that we are 'white aggressors,' that we are the servants of white imperialism, or that we are currying favor with the western world by hiding our dark-skinned oriental component."[328] It is unlikely that Shertok acted on the advice.

Abba Eban, the Jewish Agency representative at the United Nations, was delegated to present the case against trusteeship: that the General Assembly had already endorsed partition and undercutting Resolution 181 would weaken the United Nations; that both communities in Palestine were sufficiently mature to govern themselves; that a prolongation of British rule in Palestine was unthinkable and contrary to the will of the British public; that a trusteeship administration would fail to impose its authority in Palestine and would be actively resisted by Jews and Arabs—it swam "against every current of political sentiment in the country"; and that the physical partition of Palestine was so far advanced, as a result of events on the ground since November, that nothing could reverse it.[329]

On 17 April the Security Council called for a truce. The day before, the General Assembly convened in special session. There, during the next four weeks, the trusteeship proposal as well as separate proposals for a truce in Jerusalem were debated. American diplomats, maneuvering phlegmatically (perhaps with deliberation), proved unable to muster a two-thirds majority, and trusteeship was never brought to a vote. As one diplomat put it: "Trusteeship was so dead that if it were dropped on the floor, it would not bounce."[330]

During late April and into early May, the State Department increasingly saw the truce proposals as an alternative to trusteeship or at least as a cover through which the idea could be reintroduced. As Shertok said: "The [anti-Zionist] school in the State Department did not despair and tried to obtain through a truce what it hadn't succeeded in obtaining through the [appeal for a] trusteeship."[331] The assumption was that a truce, which would include a deferment of the declaration of Jewish statehood, would be matched by an Arab postponement of the invasion. But the Americans were unwilling to commit troops to enforce a truce.

United Nations representatives and local diplomats (under the rubric of

"the Consular Truce Committee," established by UN Security Council resolution of 24 April 1948) working in Jerusalem tried to negotiate a truce
throughout Palestine or at least in the holy city, but to no avail, despite
official Jewish and Arab agreement to many of the proposed clauses. The
truce proposals included a cessation of fighting, prohibition of entry of foreign troops into Palestine, and a limitation of Jewish immigration. In the
course of the General Assembly deliberations, the Syrian delegate, Faris al-
Khouri, against the backdrop of the battles for Tiberias and Haifa, charged
on 22 April that the Jews were massacring and expelling the Arabs. Shertok
responded that there had been no massacres and that the Arab flight was engineered by the Arab leaders, designed to blacken the image of the Jews and
clear the ground for the prospective invasion.

From the last week of April, the State Department focused on obtaining a
deferment of a Jewish declaration of statehood, arguing that the declaration
would precipitate an invasion. The consensus in the US government departments was that the Arab states would attack the Jewish state and persist in a
guerrilla war for as long as it took: "It is extremely unlikely . . . that the Arabs
will ever accept a Zionist state on their doorsteps." Without "diplomatic and
military support" from at least one Great Power, the Jewish state would go
under within "two years," they believed. Their advice against American intervention in support of a Jewish state was unequivocal.[332]

The Americans submitted a series of draft proposals to the Jewish Agency
and the AHC, linking the proposed three-month deferment of statehood
(by both sides) to an extended ceasefire.[333] During April and early May, the
Americans drafted and redrafted comprehensive truce proposals, which included a military and political standstill that required the Jews to curb immigration severely.[334] Article 6 of the proposals of 29 April read: "During the
period of the truce, no steps shall be taken by Arab or Jewish authorities to
proclaim a sovereign state in a part or all of Palestine."[335] Israel consistently
rejected the linkage and the deferment of statehood,[336] but the proposals—
against the backdrop of intense fighting in Palestine and Arab threats to invade—triggered a painful debate in the Zionist leadership about whether to
postpone statehood.

Shertok initially, very guardedly, favored acceptance of the truce and, implicitly, a deferment of the declaration, as (in qualified fashion) did several
senior Zionist figures in the American Section of the JAE.[337] They were
principally moved by a desire to improve the Yishuv's standing in the international arena, primarily in Washington. But Ben-Gurion consistently opposed any postponement. He bluntly vetoed several provisions in the truce
proposals (such as the limitation on ʿaliya).[338] Shertok's position hardened.

At the showdown with Marshall and Assistant Secretary of State Lovett on 8 May in Washington, Shertok flatly declared that the Yishuv "would not commit suicide to gain friendship." The Yishuv would not defer the declaration of statehood: "There was a feeling of either now or never. . . . Who can say what would happen during and after the three months' period? How can we be expected to be a party to our own undoing?"

Lovett responded that in November, in supporting partition, the United States had envisaged a peaceful transition from the Mandate to two states. But war had ensued. A truce could prevent the widening of the conflict, "and the position of the Jewish state [has been] rendered most precarious." To declare statehood would be a "gamble." Marshall warned against following the advice of soldiers "flushed by victory. . . . If we [the Jews] succeed, well and good. He would be quite happy; he wished us well. But what if we failed?"[339] Marshall may have had in mind the CIA report of August 1947, which predicted that if war broke out between a newborn Jewish state and the Arab states, the Arabs would win. The prognosis had been "coordinated" with the intelligence arms of the departments of State, the army and navy, and the US Air Force. At most, the Jews could hold out for "two years," the report concluded. (The report added that the eruption of such a war would unleash a wave of anti-Zionist, and perhaps anti-Western, jihadist "religious fanaticism.")[340]

The State Department had said its piece. It was now up to the Yishuv's leaders. The proponents of "statehood now" were doubtless encouraged by messages from Bartley Crum, a member of the Anglo-American Committee and a friend of Truman's—he reported that Truman's aide, Clark Clifford, "advised go firmly forward with planned announcement of State" and that he, Crum, "has definite impression President considering recognition"[341]—and by Sumner Wells, the former secretary of state, against postponement.[342]

The mood in Tel Aviv during those last days of the Mandate—as the prospective invasion loomed ever larger—was far less resolute than Shertok had appeared in Washington. It was pendular and uncertain. A hesitant joyfulness at the prospect of British departure and liberation from the colonial yoke was accompanied by a mixture of boundless hope and fear of the future. There was certainty that there would be an invasion. But no one knew which countries would invade, and with what force or ferocity.

The crucial meeting of the Yishuv's leadership—the thirteen-member People's Administration, which in mid-April had succeeded the JAE as the fount of power and which, on 14 May, was to become the Provisional Government of the State of Israel—took place on 12 May. The People's Administration, like the Provisional Government, was a coalition body consisting of representatives of the Yishuv's main political parties, including the non-Zionist Agudat Yisrael, but excluding the Revisionists and the Communist Party. The coalition, as the state's first general elections, in January 1949, were to demonstrate, represented about 85 percent of the Yishuv. The chief components of the People's Administration–Provisional Government were the two socialist parties: the social-democratic Mapai (four representatives) and the Marxist Mapam (two representatives). Mapai held the chairmanship-premiership and the defense, foreign affairs, and finance portfolios, effectively the main levers of power in the new state. Together, the two socialist parties, along with their affiliate, the representative of the Sephardi community, Bechor Shitrit (police and minority affairs minister in the Provisional Government), enjoyed a controlling seven-seat bloc in the thirteen-member body, and they could usually rely on the centrist Progressive Party and General Zionists Party representatives to go along with their decisions. During the following months, only rarely was Ben-Gurion unable to mobilize a solid majority in support of his policies.

On 12 May, the situation appeared far from rosy. To be sure, the Yishuv had just vanquished the Palestinian Arabs. But the immediate military background was ominous. That morning, the Arab Legion had attacked Gush ʿEtzion. "The situation there is very bad," Yigael Yadin, Haganah chief of operations, told the gathering. And, he added, the Haganah assumed that there would be a pan-Arab invasion within days.

After reviewing in detail the balance of forces between the Arab states and the Yishuv, Yadin concluded cautiously that "at this minute, I would say that the chances are very even [*hashansim shkulim*]. But to be more candid, I would say that they have a big advantage, if all this force is deployed against us."[343] Ben-Gurion was more optimistic: "We can withstand [an invasion] and defeat it, [but] not without serious losses and shocks."[344]

All the assembled knew that the state's fate hinged on the speed with which the heavy weaponry recently purchased in Europe and the United States could be brought over and deployed. "We have a large stock of weapons," said Ben-Gurion, who kept detailed tabs on the arms purchases. "But it is a bit far. Were it all in the country . . . we could then stand with confidence. . . . But it is not easy bringing it to the country. . . . The length of time [needed] to bring it . . . and how much we will succeed in bringing—this will play a major role not in the final outcome, but . . . in the number of casualties and the length of time it will take [to win]. . . . It won't be a 'picnic.'"[345]

In Czechoslovakia, ten S-199 Messerschmitt Avia fighters were waiting on the tarmac, as were thousands of "Czech" (Mauser) rifles and MG-34 and ZB-37 machine guns and millions of rounds of ammunition. In the United

States were a handful of B-17 decommissioned bombers, C-46 Commando transport aircraft, dozens of half-tracks (repainted and defined as "agricultural equipment"). In Western Europe, Haganah agents had amassed fifty 65 mm French mountain guns, twelve 120 mm mortars, ten H-35 light tanks, and a large number of half-tracks. All waited for the lifting of the British blockade of Palestine's shores and skies on 15 May. The Haganah had readied twelve cargo ships in European harbors. It was to this equipment that Ben-Gurion and Galili referred in trepidation, almost in Messianic terms, that morning.

"The Thirteen," as the People's Administration was called—and only ten were present that day (two were stuck in besieged Jerusalem and one was in New York)—then turned to the questions of the truce and the declaration of statehood. Most spoke out against both the general truce proposals and a limited truce in Jerusalem alone. The matter was decided by a vote of six to four.[346] As to declaring statehood, Ben-Gurion was adamant about not defining the new state's borders, arguing that if "our strength proves sufficient," the Yishuv will conquer Western Galilee and the length of the Tel Aviv—Jerusalem road—and, it was implied, coopt West Jerusalem—"and all this will be part of the state. . . . So why commit [ourselves to a smaller state?]"[347] By a vote of five to four it was decided not to define the borders; the name, "Israel," was decided by seven votes to zero. The text of the declaration was approved unanimously. No vote was apparently taken on a postponement; it was clear that Ben-Gurion, backed by Shertok, enjoyed majority support.[348]

On the afternoon of 14 May, just after High Commissioner Cunningham and his staff had left Jerusalem and flown from Kalandiya airstrip to Haifa, the leaders of the Yishuv—members of the National Council, the People's Administration, the Zionist General Council, and party politicians, local leaders, and journalists—gathered in a hall in Tel Aviv Museum. Some officials were stranded in Jerusalem; others remained outside the hall, which was too small to accommodate all the invitees. The Palestine Philharmonic Orchestra, which was to play the national anthem, "Hatikva" (the hope), was relegated to the floor above the hall. The preparations had been hectic, everything arranged at the last minute; and everything was overshadowed by the impending invasion. "We moved about our duties . . . as if in a dream. . . . The days of the Messiah had arrived, the end of servitude under alien rulers," was how Ze'eve Sharef, Ben-Gurion's assistant, later described it.[349]

An honor guard of spruced-up Haganah cadets, "white belts gleaming from afar," lined the sidewalk by the entrance. Ben-Gurion's limousine drew up, and he vigorously strode past them up the stairs into the building. The hall itself had been hastily redecorated: a cluster of historically apt paintings—Marc Chagall's *A Jew Holding a Scroll of the Law,* Maurycy Minkowski's *Pogroms,* Shmuel Hirshenberg's *Exile*—had been freshly hung. A large portrait of Herzl, flanked by blue and white flags, dominated one wall. The hall was packed, and the heat—photographers' arc lights and flash bulbs contributing—intense. At the dais sat eleven members of the People's Administration; along a table perpendicular to it sat fourteen additional members of the National Council. Behind them sat row upon row of other dignitaries.

At 4:00 PM all rose, spontaneously, and sang "Hatikva." Ben-Gurion—sixty-two, a five-foot, three-inch pragmatist with rock-hard convictions, who had devoted his life to amassing power, for himself and his people, with the aim of resurrecting Jewish self-determination in Palestine, a land he had reached (from Poland) in 1906 on the back of an Arab stevedore who carried him from skiff to shore—then read out the declaration, the "Scroll of the Establishment of the State of Israel": "The Land of Israel was the birthplace of the Jewish people. . . . Here their spiritual, religious and national identity was formed." They had ruled the land for centuries but then had been crushed and exiled. For centuries, they had yearned to return. They began to return at the end of the nineteenth century, and the international community had gradually come to support their claim to the land and sovereignty. The Holocaust had energized the Zionist struggle. On 29 November 1947 the United Nations had formally endorsed their quest. "Accordingly . . . We hereby proclaim the establishment of the Jewish State . . . the State of Israel." The audience rose and clapped: "all were seized by ineffable joy, their faces irradiated."[350] The proclamation was adopted by acclamation, and the leaders signed the document. "Hatikva" was sung once more, and Ben-Gurion proclaimed: "The State of Israel is established! This meeting is adjourned."

The ceremony had lasted thirty-two minutes. Those gathered—of Zionism's prominent leaders, only Chaim Weizmann was missing; he was abroad; later, Ben-Gurion vindictively refused Weizmann's request to add his signature to the document—fell on each others shoulders, cheered, and wept. Outside, in the streets, the crowds broke into celebration: "the city danced and made merry."[351] Eleven minutes later, Truman announced de facto recognition of the new state, shocking most State Department officials, who had been given no inkling of the move.[352] Truman had been spurred to action by a letter from Weizmann pleading that "the greatest living democracy" be "the first to welcome the newest into the family of nations."[353]

"In the country there is celebration and profound joy—and once again I am a mourner among the celebrants, as on 29 November," Ben-Gurion jotted down in his diary.[354] A few hours later, the Royal Navy flotilla, with the bulk of the Mandate administration on board, sailed out of Haifa harbor. By midnight, the aircraft carrier HMS *Ocean,* the flagship, the cruiser HMS *Euryalus,* carrying Cunningham, and the accompanying destroyers and frigates, were outside territorial waters, making for Malta. On *Ocean*'s windswept flight deck the band played "Auld Lang Syne."

The result of the five and a half months of fighting between the Palestinian Arab community, assisted by foreign volunteers, and the Yishuv was a decisive Jewish victory. Palestinian Arab military power was crushed, and Palestinian Arab society, never robust, fell apart, much of the population fleeing to the inland areas or out of the country altogether.

The Haganah, after holding its own on the defensive for four months while it transformed from a militia into an army, launched a series of offensives—most precipitated by Arab attacks—that, within six weeks, routed the Arab militias and their ALA reinforcements. Important pieces of territory assigned in the UN Partition Resolution to Palestinian Arab or international control—including Jaffa and West Jerusalem—fell under Zionist sway as hundreds of thousands of Arabs fled or were driven out. Meanwhile, the prestate Zionist institutions transformed themselves into solid, relatively effective departments and agencies of state, and the Haganah managed to consolidate its hold on a continuous strip of territory embracing the Coastal Plain, the Jezreel Valley, and the Jordan Valley, which it would prove able to hold against combined Arab attack from outside and from which it was able, eventually, to conquer additional territory. In the process, the Yishuv convincingly demonstrated that it was militarily formidable and capable of self-rule and that the emergent State of Israel was viable, persuading an initially hesitant United States, and in its wake, others around the world, to support it. Moreover, the decisive victory over the Palestinian Arabs gave the Haganah the experience and self-confidence necessary subsequently to confront and defeat the invading armies of the Arab states.

5

The Pan-Arab Invasion,
15 May–11 June 1948

Motto: "He said that the Arabs were not afraid of our expansion. They resented our very presence as an alien organism. . . . 'Politics were not a matter for sentimental agreements; they were resultants of contending forces. The question is whether you can bring more force for the creation of a Jewish State than we can muster to prevent it. If you want your State, however, you must come and get it. It is useless asking me for the Negev. . . . You can only get your Negev by taking it. If you are . . . strong enough to do this, or if you enlist strong partners—Britain, America . . . —you may well succeed. If you cannot, then you will fail.'"
—ʿAzzam Pasha, secretary-general of the Arab League, September 1947

THE ARAB STATES DECIDE TO INVADE

In November 1947, days before the eruption of hostilities, General Ismail Safwat, head of the Arab League Military Committee, wrote: "Victory over the Jews—who are well trained and well equipped—by gangs and irregular forces alone is not feasible. So regular forces must be thrown into the battle, trained and equipped with the best weaponry. . . . As the Arab states do not have sufficient means for a protracted war, everything must be done so that the war in Palestine will be terminated in the shortest possible time."[1]

As the months passed and the Palestinian Arabs, beefed up by contingents of foreign volunteers, proved incapable of defeating the Yishuv, the Arab leaders began more seriously to contemplate sending in their armies. The events of April 1948—Deir Yassin,[2] Tiberias, Haifa, Jaffa—rattled and focused their minds, and the arrival of tens of thousands of refugees drove home the urgency of direct intervention. By the end of April, they decided to invade. The following fortnight saw the leaders and their generals trying to hammer out agreed objectives, a coordinated strategy, and a unified command structure. They failed.

But the invasion, propelled by the combined momentum of their own rhetoric and pressure from below, went ahead. (As General John Bagot Glubb later recalled: "The Arab statesmen did not intend war. . . . But in the end they entered [Palestine] and ordered their commanders to advance as a result of pressure of public opinion and a desire to appease the 'street.'")[3] The American Legation in Damascus described the mechanism thus: "Government appears to have led public opinion to brink of war and now unable to retreat. Demand for war led by students, press and Moslem religious leaders. . . . Manifestos of students and ulemas . . . alike uncompromising."[4]

In the preceding two years of summitry, though occasionally hinting at the possibility of direct intervention, the Arab leaders, warned off by Britain and the international community, had shied from committing themselves to sending in their armies (though intermittently Syria and Iraq had privately and publicly threatened to do just that, even before the Mandate was terminated). In general, in private they appreciated and admitted their military weakness and unpreparedness.[5] But in public, militant bluster was the norm. Knowledgeable British observers opined that "the Arab states should [that is, would] receive some nasty surprises" if they invaded Palestine.[6] Indeed, Alan Cunningham dismissed talk of invasion as so much hot air—because, he reasoned, "these armies have neither the training, equipment nor reserves of ammunition . . . to maintain an army in the field far from their bases for any length of time, if at all."[7] But Cunningham was ignoring the possibility of irrational decision-making—and underestimating Arab resolve and capabilities.

Political and military developments in the last days of 1947 and early 1948 tended to cloud Arab judgment. The UN partition resolution threw all the leaders into a frenzy. But no major change of policy was immediately required since Jewish statehood was not yet a tangible reality; perhaps the Palestinian Arabs would yet thwart it. The battles of April 1948 and the imminent prospect of British evacuation and Jewish statehood changed all that. During April and early May there were nonstop deliberations, mainly in Cairo, Damascus, and Amman, among the Arab kings, presidents and prime ministers, and military commanders. Alec Kirkbride, the all-knowing British minister in Amman, described those last days before the invasion as "bedlam, the like of which I have never yet experienced. I cannot attempt to recount or record the numerous conversations which I have [had] with Arab leaders go- ing over the same ground again and again advocating caution . . . only to have all the work undone by desperate appeals for help from somewhere in Palestine or by the arrival of a new batch of refugees with new rumors."[8]

The consensus favoring invasion began to crystallize at the meeting in Cairo, starting 10 April, of the Arab League Political Committee. In the air was the ever-worsening news from Palestine—ʿAbd al-Qadir al-Husseini's death, Deir Yassin, and the failure of the Arab Liberation Army at Mishmar Haʿemek—and the growing pleas by Palestine Arab notables to the Arab governments to intervene.[9] Safwat said that Palestine was lost unless the armies invaded; Jordan indicated that the Legion would go in when the British left (though not before).[10] Syria and Lebanon, seemingly chafing at the bit, pressed Egypt to commit its army. But Prime Minister Mahmoud Nuqrashi argued, as before, that Egypt could not participate because the British army, in its bases along the Suez Canal, sat astride its lines of supply to Palestine; who knew what perfidious Albion might do?[11] As late as 26 April Foreign Minister Ahmed Muhammad Khashaba was saying that although Egypt could not and would not prevent "volunteers" from joining the fight, it "did not intend, and would not, send regular forces into Palestine."[12]

Yet the momentum of Jewish victories, Palestine Arab defeats, and the mi- natory rumblings of the Arab street proved inexorable. Public opinion was "all in favor of the war, and considered anyone who refused to fight as a trai- tor."[13] As Muhsin al-Barazi, Syria's foreign minister, put it in April: "[The] public's desire for war is irresistible."[14] By May, Syrian leaders were hysteri- cal; public opinion, they said, was "very excited," and there was talk—at least for the benefit of Western diplomatic ears—that "the whole country might go Communist and . . . our [that is, Britain's] friends would be swept away."[15] The same considerations applied in Baghdad, where the leaders looked both downward, at a turbulent politically involved middle class and an excitable "street," and sideways, at fellow Arab leaders; a failure of mili- tancy would enhance the position of the anti-Hashemite bloc (Egypt, Saudi Arabia, and Syria) in inter-Arab jockeying and rile the masses to the point of dangerous disturbances or worse.[16] None could ignore the Palestinian Arab tales of massacre and exodus. Nor could the Arab leaders, especially Egypt's, remain indifferent to the pressure of the Muslim religious establishment's call for "the liberation of Palestine [as] a religious duty for all Moslems with- out exception, great and small. The Islamic and Arab Governments should without delay take effective and radical measures, military or otherwise," pronounced the ʿulema of Al-Azhar University, a major religious authority, on 26 April.[17] Both King Farouk and Khashaba repeatedly stressed that, for "the whole Arab world," the struggle was religious. "It was for them a matter of Jewish religion against their own religion";[18] the Arab masses, said Farouk, were gripped by "widespread religious fervour . . . and men of the people were keen to enter the fray—as the shortest road to Heaven."[19]

The decision to invade was finally taken on 29–30 April, at the simultaneous meetings of the Arab heads of state in Amman and the military chiefs of staff in Zarka. Egypt still held back. But the die was cast. And on 11–12 May Egypt would also commit itself to invasion. Yet the pan-Arab decision papered over a basic lack of preparation and deep rifts between the states regarding the political and military goals and strategy, the unity of command, and political-military coordination.

For all their bluster from Bludan through Cairo, the Arab leaders—except Jordan's—did almost nothing to prepare their armies for war. They may have prodded one another into ever greater fervor, and they most certainly whipped up their "streets" into hysteria over their suffering brothers in Palestine. But in concrete military terms, they failed to prepare.

Britain and France had established the Arab armies to help maintain their imperial grip, to prop up unpopular client regimes, and to maintain internal order; the armies had never been intended or structured for external warfare. Only in 1945–1946, against the backdrop of the emergent Cold War, did the British begin to prepare or help in the conversion of the Egyptian, Iraqi, and Jordanian armies into modern fighting forces, capable of serving as auxiliaries in a fight with the Soviet Union. But lack of funds, incompetence, poverty, and suspicion of Britain's intentions frustrated the conversion in Egypt and Iraq. Similar problems discouraged the development, under French tutelage, of the newborn Syrian and Lebanese armies. Only the Jordanian army, and this very late in the day, began a real upgrade as May 1948 approached.[20]

Most of the Arab generals seem to have assumed that war would never come, or that their country would not participate, or that it would be a walkover. None of their armies had ever fought a war (except part of the Arab Legion, which had assisted the British army's conquest of Iraq and Syria in May–June 1941), and none really knew what war would entail. In the days before the invasion, the military and political leaders, gripped by a war psychosis, oscillated between complete contempt for the Jews and fatalism. Without doubt, "cultural misperceptions and racist attitudes toward Jews in general blinded and entrapped Arabs," as one historian has put it.[21]

Gamal ʿAbdel Nasser, who fought in Palestine, later summarized the Egyptian preparations and intentions: "There was no concentration of

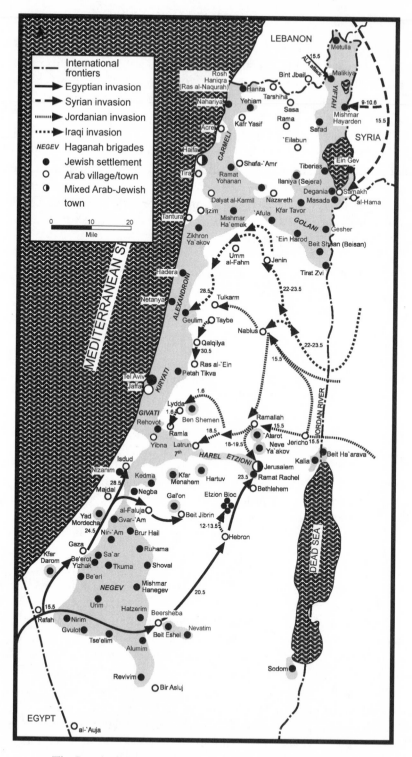

The Pan-Arab Invasion of Palestine/Israel, May–June 1948

forces, no accumulation of ammunition and equipment. There was no reconnaissance, no intelligence, no plans. . . . [It was to be a 'political war.'] There was to be advance without victory and retreat without defeat."[22] In the Egyptian high command, there was an absence of realism and clear-headedness.

"A parade without any risks" and Tel Aviv "in two weeks," was how the Egyptian army chiefs in May presented the coming adventure to their political bosses[23]—even though, just weeks before, they had spoken firmly against intervention, arguing lack of training, arms, and ammunition. In January 1948, the British, who were helping reorganize the army, assessed: "The Egyptian Army hardly warrants consideration as a serious invading force." Two months later the Egyptian war ministry offered the same evaluation.[24] "We shall never even contemplate entering an official war. We are not mad," the Egyptian defense minister, General Muhammad Haidar, told one journalist before the invasion.[25] Yet several days later, he reportedly said: "The Egyptian military is capable on its own of occupying Tel Aviv . . . in fifteen days, without assistance."[26] But the commander-elect of the Egyptian expeditionary force, General Ahmed ʿAli al-Muwawi, told Haidar that his troops were not ready. Al-Muwawi's deputy, Colonel Mohammed Neguib, also spoke bluntly about Egyptian unpreparedness—"Why court disaster?"[27] But Prime Minister Nuqrashi believed, or, as 15 May approached, pretended to believe, that "the whole affair would be a military picnic."[28] He reassured the officers that "there was no need for undue alarm. There would be very little fighting for the United Nations would intervene." He spoke of a "political demonstration" rather than of real battles.[29] Nuqrashi, against his better judgment, seems simply to have bowed to King Farouk's will. Farouk was driven by a hatred of Zionism, fear of the "street," a quest for glory, and a desire to stymie or at least counterbalance expected Hashemite gains in Palestine.

Only one prominent Egyptian raised his voice in protest. Ahmed Sidqi Pasha, a respected former prime minister, who in the past had (at least privately) supported partition,[30] called out in the secret debate in the Egyptian senate on 11–12 May, when Nuqrashi requested a vote for war: "Is the army ready?"[31] But nobody listened. The "aye" votes were unanimous. Sidqi alone walked out of the chamber without voting[32]—and, a few days later, in a newspaper interview, courageously cast doubt on "whether Egypt was fully prepared to face a situation created . . . 'by misplaced enthusiasm and a hastily improvised policy.'"[33]

In the wider Arab world, Sidqi was not alone. King ʿAbdullah had always acknowledged Arab (as distinct from Jordanian) weakness, and his son, Prince Talal, openly predicted defeat.[34] At the last moment, several leaders, including King Ibn Saʿud and ʿAzzam Pasha—to avert catastrophe—secretly appealed to the British to soldier on in Palestine for at least another year.[35] Egypt's foreign minister, Khashaba, had already done so. He "wished they would remain, and suggested that it was their duty to do so."[36]

Of course, the pessimists were right. The Arab military had done no proper planning or intelligence work (as one Arab participant-chronicler of the war put it, "the Arab intelligence services displayed complete contempt in assessing the enemy's strength"),[37] armaments and ammunition were in short supply, and logistics were inadequate, especially in those armies— Egypt's and Iraq's—that had to travel hundreds of miles before reaching the battlefields. Neguib, the deputy commander of the Egyptian expeditionary force, later recalled that he had had personally to hire twenty-one trucks from Palestinian Arabs to haul his troops from Rafah to Gaza.[38] And the Egyptians invaded without sufficient ammunition, spare parts, or food stocks, and with defective weapons. (Indeed, during the Revolution of July 1952, Neguib, in his letter to Farouk demanding the king's resignation, specifically charged the king with responsibility for "the traffic in defective arms ammunition" in 1948.)[39] Officers and soldiers alike were unprepared for what faced them—a tenacious, highly motivated enemy, well dug-in and fighting on home turf, with short, internal lines of communication and already superior to them in organization and numbers; eventually, the Israelis would also, at least in some categories of weaponry, be better equipped.

But realistic military considerations and evaluations had little effect on the political decision-making. The invasion was decided on despite the Arab regimes' overarching political priorities: for Egypt and Iraq, the eviction of the "imperialist" (British) presence; for most of the governments, the maintenance of power in the face of potentially lethal internal social and political unrest. Only for Jordan's ʿAbdullah was the invasion—viewed as a means to expand his kingdom—an immediate political priority.

Around the Arab world, flights of fancy and boastful militant rhetoric were given their head. By the start of May, the Arab leaders, including ʿAbdullah, found that they were trapped and could do no other—whatever the state of their armies. "The politicians, the demagogues, the Press and the mob were in charge—not the soldiers. Warnings went unheeded. Doubters were denounced as traitors," Glubb recalled.[40] In most Arab states the opposition parties took a vociferous, pro-war position, forcing the pace for the generally more sober incumbents. From late November 1947 until mid-May 1948 the streets of Cairo, Alexandria, Beirut, Damascus, and Baghdad were awash with noisy "pro-intervention" demonstrations, organized at least in part by the governments themselves. The press, too, both reflecting and fashioning opinion, chimed in with belligerent rhetoric, growing in stridency as 15 May approached. The leaders found themselves ensnared in their own rhetoric and that of their peers. By 15 May, not to go to war appeared, for most, more dangerous than actually taking the plunge. ʿAzzam Pasha put it in a nutshell: "[The Arab] leaders, including himself, would probably be assassinated if they did nothing."[41]

What was the goal of the planned invasion? Arab spokesmen indulged in a variety of definitions. A week before the armies marched, ʿAzzam told Kirkbride: "It does not matter how many [Jews] there are. We will sweep them into the sea."[42] Syrian president Shukri al-Quwwatli spoke of the Crusades: "Overcoming the Crusaders took a long time, but the result was victory. There is no doubt that history is repeating itself."[43] Ahmed Shukeiry, one of Haj Amin al-Husseini's aides (and, later, the founding chairman of the Palestine Liberation Organization), simply described the aim as "the elimination of the Jewish state."[44]

But officially and publicly, the Arab states were more circumspect and positive. Most described the aim of the invasion as "saving" the Palestinian Arabs. Typical was the Egyptian government invasion-day announcement: it had ordered its army into Palestine "to re-establish security and order and put an end to the massacres perpetrated by Zionist terrorist bands against Arabs and humanity."[45] Less carefully, al-Quwwatli told his people: "Our army has entered Palestine with the rest of the Arab states' [armies] to protect our brothers and their rights and to restore order. We shall restore the country to its owners, we shall win and we shall eradicate Zionism."[46]

But the actual military planning had been less ambitious. The Arab armies appear not to have had an agreed plan when they invaded Palestine on 15 May, even of a most general kind.[47] Certainly, there was nothing that can be considered a detailed plan. Safwat, in Damascus, had spent weeks trying to hammer out a joint strategy and, perhaps, a detailed plan: "A swarm of Syrian and Iraqi officers buzzed around the building seemingly more familiar with the science of political intrigue than with that of warfare. The distribution of funds, of commands, of rank, of operational zones, of arms and materials, all were objects of bargaining as intensive as any displayed in the city's souks."[48]

Yet some sort of draft plan was apparently produced by Captain Wasfi Tal, a young Arab Legionnaire serving as Safwat's head of operations. The plan foresaw an eleven-day campaign, with the Lebanese army pushing down the coast from Ras al-Naqurah to Acre; the Syrian army, in two separate columns, thrusting southward from Bint Jbail in southern Lebanon and westward from the Yarmuk Valley, through Samakh just south of the Sea of Galilee, eventually converging on Afula; the Iraqi army crossing the Jordan at Beisan and thrusting northwestward toward Afula; and the Arab Legion, crossing the Jordan, and driving for Afula from Jenin. The pincer around Afula would then, in a second stage, turn into a combined drive on Haifa. (Haifa had figured in Jordanian invasion thinking as early as October 1947;[49] for the Iraqis, the port's importance was enhanced by the presence of the oil refinery through which its chief export flowed to Europe.) At the same time, other Legion units would drive westward through Judea toward Lydda and Ramla and perhaps from there to the Mediterranean coast. Last, the Egyptian army, the Arab world's largest, would push up the coast road from Rafah through Majdal toward Jaffa–Tel Aviv, drawing Jewish forces away from the main Arab thrusts in the north.[50] One report has it that King Farouk, at a meeting with Haidar and senior officers three days before the invasion, spoke of "help[ing] the [Arab] Legion occupy" Tel Aviv.[51] The plan as originally envisaged called for far larger forces—as Safwat put it, "not less than 5 well-equipped divisions and 6 squadrons of bombers and fighter aircraft"[52]—than were actually committed by the Arabs on 15 May. Haganah intelligence picked up two variants of the plan in the days before the invasion.[53]

The "plan" was approved by the chiefs of staff in their meetings in Jordan on 29–30 April and endorsed by the Arab League Political Committee in Damascus on 11–12 May,[54] which, brushing Safwat aside, appointed the Iraqi general Nur al-Din Mahmud as commander of the regular and irregular forces about to descend on Palestine (albeit under the nominal "Supreme Command" of King ʿAbdullah). Just after the meeting, ʿAzzam traveled to Amman, where he tried to persuade Glubb to replace Mahmud as commander of the invasion. Glubb declined. "I could not help laughing," he recalled. "'I am unfit to command the Arab Legion—much less several different armies,'" he recollected having responded.[55] Perhaps he regarded ʿAzzam (and the plan) as "naive and impractical";[56] perhaps he sensed a trap: although he would not have any real control of the Arab armies, he most certainly would be blamed for whatever failure ensued.[57]

Nonetheless, it is worth noting that the core plan—a limited invasion, focusing on the north—made strategic sense. The relatively small expeditionary forces were not being asked to take over the whole country, with its 250-odd Jewish settlements or, at least initially, to conquer large, built-up urban centers, such as Tel Aviv. Instead, the core plan envisaged a limited objective, to sever Eastern Galilee from the rest of the country by converging from north and south on the junction town of Afula. And this would necessitate a preliminary passage mainly through friendly Arab areas before moving on to Afula (four miles from Nazareth, six miles from Jenin).[58]

During the following days, Mahmud—perhaps influenced by Glubb's skepticism—appears to have scaled down the grand design marginally, with Afula and severing Eastern Galilee, rather than Haifa, figuring as the main goals.[59] But, in one sense, this was mere shadowboxing; no one actually accepted Mahmud's military overlordship or desires. Each country was bent on going, or not going, its own way.

At the last minute, Lebanon decided not to participate in the invasion. The decision, taken on 14 May, no doubt shook the Syrians. But even more unsettling for the whole Arab coalition was Jordan's last-minute announcement of changed intentions and objectives. That day Jordan informed its partners that its army was heading for Ramallah, Nablus, and Hebron, to take over the area later known as the West Bank; it had no intention of thrusting northwestward, toward Afula, or of driving westward, to the sea. The goal of the Arab Legion—the Arab world's best army, as all acknowledged and as it emerged—was the (peaceful) takeover of the core Arab area of Palestine, not war with the Jews. As a result, Syria's (and Egypt's) war plans were, a t the last minute, radically and unilaterally altered.

From the first, King ʿAbdullah recognized Jewish strength and the limitations of his efficient but small army; and he knew, and despised and feared, his fellow Arab leaders and belittled their military capabilities. ʿAbdullah did not want Afula and did not really want his army operating in conjunction with the Syrians and Egyptians; he distrusted them. He wanted the West Bank, if possible including East Jerusalem. On 13 May, unilaterally changing plans, he instructed Glubb (and informed his Hashemite Iraqi allies) that the West Bank was the objective. He probably approved the one element in Mahmud's plan that remained intact, the prospective Iraqi assault across the Jordan into Israel at Gesher, in the Jordan Valley.

Perhaps the Iraqis insisted on this point; perhaps, unlike ʿAbdullah, they were loath to break openly with their coalition partners. After all, they had all along championed a pan-Arab assault on the Zionist entity, sometimes even insisting—or pretending to insist—on opening the assault before the British left. Perhaps they hoped to conquer the length of the Iraq Petroleum Company pipeline through the lower Jordan and Jezreel Valleys to the sea at Haifa. Or perhaps they merely sought a localized "symbolic" victory, unconnected to any grand design to gain the whole of Eastern Galilee or the pipeline's route.[60]

But, from ʿAbdullah's perspective, an Iraqi offensive just north of the West Bank meant pinning down Israeli troops who might otherwise be free to engage his own. Meanwhile, his legion would cross the river at Jericho and fan out toward Nablus, Ramallah, and Hebron, and then take over Lydda and

Ramla, thus occupying the core area of Arab Palestine—while refraining from attacking the territory earmarked by the United Nations for Jewish statehood.

ʿAbdullah's last-minute change of plans was not whimsical. It was deeply rooted in history—in decades of frustrated geopolitical hopes and in months of secret negotiations with the British and the Jewish Agency. Since arriving in the small village of Amman—population two thousand—in November 1920, the young Hashemite prince, son of Hussein Ibn ʿAli, the sharif of Mecca and king of Hijaz, had sought to rule a vast and important domain. Transjordan, awarded him by Colonial Secretary Winston Churchill in March 1921, was always too small for his britches. He wanted, at the least, to be king of "Greater Syria," encompassing present-day Syria, Lebanon, Israel/Palestine, and Jordan. But the French, the British, and assorted Arab politicians were forever frustrating his expansionist ambitions. Then, in 1937, a way forward at last seemed to open up, as embodied in the Peel Commission partition recommendations, which posited the union, under ʿAbdullah, of Transjordan and the bulk of Palestine (side by side with a minuscule Jewish state in the remaining 20 percent of the country). If he couldn't get "Greater Syria," perhaps he could at least have a "Greater Transjordan." But the Palestinian Arabs, backed by the rest of the Arab world, objected, and nothing came of the proposal. ʿAbdullah, however, remained enchanted with the idea of annexing Palestine, or parts of it, to his emirate; Palestine would accord his godforsaken desert realm some import and prestige.

World War II, with its tantalizing promise of Transjordanian territorial aggrandizement as compensation for ʿAbdullah's loyalty and services to Britain, came and went, with nothing gained. But when partition reemerged at the end of the war as a possible solution to the Palestine conundrum, ʿAbdullah was back on board. He saw his chance. Of course, he sought a partition not between the Jews and the Palestine Arabs but between the Jews and himself. Optimally, the Palestine Arabs would abandon al-Husseini and the notion of Palestinian Arab independence and call for union with Jordan under Hashemite rule (and during the 1940s ʿAbdullah persistently tried to organize such Palestine Arab support, with only minor success). But he could also manage without such endorsement. The Palestine Arabs, crushed by Britain in 1936–39 and still weak, could be ignored. Palestine or parts of it could be fused with Transjordan—if only there was agreement with Britain and the Jews, respectively ʿAbdullah's political-military patron and his powerful neighbors. From the summer of 1946 to early 1948 ʿAbdullah gradually hammered out the relevant agreements.

Of course, ʿAbdullah preferred to coopt all of Palestine, with the Jews receiving an "autonomous" zone (a "republic," he called it) inside his expanded kingdom. He repeatedly offered this to the Jewish Agency. But the Jews wanted a sovereign state of their own, not minority status. So partition it would have to be. This was agreed in principle in two secret meetings in August 1946 in Transjordan between ʿAbdullah and Jewish Agency emissary Eliahu (Elias) Sasson.[61] (Incidentally, ʿAbdullah and his prime minister, Ibrahim Hashim, believed—as had the Peel Commission—that such a partition, in order to be viable and lasting, should be accompanied by a transfer of the Arab inhabitants out of the area of the Jewish state–to–be.)[62]

There matters stood until UNSCOP proposed partition—but between Palestine's Arabs and Palestine's Jews—as the preferred solution. Neither ʿAbdullah nor the Jewish Agency wanted a Husseini-led Palestinian Arab state as their neighbor; both preferred an alternative partition, between themselves. On 17 November 1947, twelve days before the passage of the partition resolution, Golda Myerson (Meir), acting head of the Jewish Agency Political Department, secretly met ʿAbdullah at Naharayim (Jisr al-Majami), to reaffirm the agreement in principle of August 1946. ʿAbdullah at first vaguely reiterated his preference for incorporating all of Palestine in his kingdom, with the Jews enjoying autonomy. Meir countered that the Jews wanted peaceful partition between two sovereign "states." The Jews would accept a Jordanian takeover of the West Bank as a fait accompli and would not oppose it—though, formally, the Jewish Agency remained bound by the prospective UN decision to establish two states. ʿAbdullah said that he, too, wanted a compromise, not war. In effect, ʿAbdullah agreed to the establishment of a Jewish state in part of Palestine and Meir agreed to a Jordanian takeover of the West Bank (albeit while formally adhering to whatever partition resolution the General Assembly would adopt). Both sides agreed not to attack each other. The subject of Jerusalem was not discussed or resolved. The assumption was that the holy city would constitute a corpus separatum under UN jurisdiction, in line with the UNSCOP recommendation. Or, simply, the subject was too sensitive and complex to resolve.[63]

For ʿAbdullah, this was sufficient; he had the Yishuv's agreement. There remained Whitehall. ʿAbdullah since the early 1920s had intermittently badgered his British patrons to allow him to take over "Greater Syria" or at least Damascus; World War II and the dissolution of the French Mandate seemed to afford a major new opening. Yet once again the British, fearful of alienating the French and of inter-Arab entanglements, kept ʿAbdullah at bay. But the steady advance of the international community toward accepting a partition of Palestine following Britain's renunciation, in February 1947, of the Mandate laid the groundwork, as ʿAbdullah saw things, for his acquisition of parts of the country. During the second half of 1947, as the UNSCOP recommendations hardened into a General Assembly resolution, ʿAbdullah mounted a persistent campaign to persuade Whitehall to support a Jordanian takeover of Arab Palestine.

Already in August 1947 Christopher Pirie-Gordon, the acting British minister in Amman, endorsed the attachment to Transjordan of "the Arab areas of Palestine. The advantages to Transjordan . . . are obvious" and it would "immensely strengthen [Britain's] Hashemite Alliance."[64] In October, Kirkbride, the British minister, told visiting journalists that ʿAbdullah wanted "to rule Nablus and Hebron" and that "in his own view it was the logical solution" for the Palestine problem. Glubb also thought it was "the obvious thing" to do.[65] Both men lobbied Whitehall directly and vigorously: "strategically and economically Transjordan has the best claim to inherit the residue of Palestine and . . . the occupation of the Arab areas by Transjordan would lessen the chances of armed conflict between a Jewish state and the other Arab states. . . . A greater Transjordan would not be against our interests, it might be in their favour," argued Kirkbride.[66] And Glubb, at a meeting with Britain's director of military intelligence, Major-General C. D. Packard, laid out the Jordanian intentions more concretely: "The main objective of the invading force would be Beersheba, Hebron, Ramallah, Nablus and Jenin, with forward elements in Tulkarm and the area just south of Lydda."[67] ʿAbdullah was also keen on annexing the Negev or a large part of it, arguing that he "could not possibly agree to the Jewish State . . . cutting off Transjordan from Egypt" and, more widely, "the Arabs of Africa from . . . the Arabs of Asia."[68] In addition, Jewish possession of the Negev would threaten ʿAqaba, Transjordan, and the West Bank and would block the pilgrimage route to Mecca.[69]

Gradually, against the backdrop of the UN partition resolution and Britain's formal need not to be in violation, Whitehall was persuaded, though for months it played its cards very close to its chest. The culmination of the Jordanian lobbying campaign, and its success, was marked in the meeting between the new Jordanian prime minister, Tawfiq Abul Huda, and Foreign Secretary Ernst Bevin in London on 7 February 1948. It was attended by Glubb though the Jordanian foreign minister, Fawzi al-Mulki, at Abul Huda's request, was not informed of the meeting or its content and was not present. Abul Huda, conveying "the point of view of King ʿAbdullah," suggested that it would be to "the public benefit" for the Arab Legion, on the termination of the Mandate, to enter "the Arab areas of Palestine to maintain law and order." He added that he did not want or expect a "reply" from Bevin.[70]

Bevin, describing the meeting, said that, indeed, he had not replied, save for warning the Jordanians against any attempt to invade the Jewish-designated areas of Palestine. (Abul Huda had agreed.)[71] The Jordanian understood, as Bevin had meant him to, that his silence signaled consent. But Glubb later recalled, possibly inaccurately, that Bevin's response had gone beyond mere silence. Bevin, he wrote, had replied: "[Occupying the West Bank] seems the obvious thing to do. . . . [Bevin] expressed his agreement with the plans put forward."[72]

Following the meeting, Abul Huda cabled ʿAbdullah: "I am very pleased at the results."[73] There was a green light. Jordan had won British consent to occupy of the West Bank with the termination of the Mandate—so ʿAbdullah, Abul Huda, and Glubb believed—and nothing the British did or said thereafter was to contradict this impression.

But the months of intercommunal fighting, capped by the Jewish victories and the refugee exodus of April and early May, bit severely into the Jewish Agency–Hashemite understanding. "Tremendous public pressure is being brought to bear on the King [ʿAbdullah] and on the [Iraqi] Regent [ʿAbd al-Ilah] to intervene with troops in Palestine immediately. The fact that Amman is crowded . . . with Palestinian refugees . . . does not make matters any easier," Kirkbride reported.[74] But ʿAbdullah (and the Iraqis) resisted the pressure; invading Palestine while the British were still there was simply not an option. Yet not to invade immediately after they left also receded as an option: increasingly desperate Palestinian Arab appeals, the threat of Haganah conquest of the West Bank and East Jerusalem, the demands of Arab honor, and the temptation of territorial aggrandizement, as well as the beckoning lights of Jerusalem, the site of his father's tomb and Islam's third holiest shrine, combined to leave the king little choice.

Thus it was that when Golda Meir, disguised in an Arab robe, arrived on the night of 10–11 May in Amman for her second secret meeting with ʿAbdullah, the previous months' understanding about a peaceful Jewish-Hashemite partition was not reaffirmed. On the contrary. ʿAbdullah, cordial as always but "tired and depressed," now asked Meir to reconsider his original proposal, of an autonomous Jewish canton within a Hashemite kingdom. Why this rush toward statehood? he asked. Meir countered that back in November, they had agreed on a partition with Jewish statehood. Why not abide by the agreement? ʿAbdullah replied that the situation had changed. There had been Deir Yassin, and he was now only one of a coalition of five war-bound Arab rulers, no longer a free agent. "He is going to this business [that is, war] not out of joy or confidence, but as a person who is in a trap and can't get out," Meir later explained.[75]

She returned from the meeting depressed. Her aides were impressed that a clash between the Yishuv and Jordan was unavoidable. Or at least, as Yaʿakov Shimoni, of the Arab Division of the Jewish Agency Political Department, put it, 'Abdullah would choose a middle course: "[He] will not remain faithful to the 29 November [UN Partition] borders, but [he] will not attempt to conquer all of our state [either]."[76]

But 'Abdullah's bellicose tone and Meir's gloomy report notwithstanding,[77] the king had decided—as became clear from the Legion's subsequent actions—to move into Arab Palestine while trying to avoid war with the Yishuv and refraining from attacking the territory of the UN-defined Jewish state.

This actually emerged from an earlier secret meeting, in Naharayim on 2 May, at Glubb's behest, between the Legion's Colonel Desmond Goldie, OC First Brigade, and Shlomo Shamir and Nahum Spiegel, two senior Haganah officers. Goldie had stressed the Legion's desire to avoid conflict with the Haganah as it deployed in the West Bank.[78] At the Meir-'Abdullah meeting a week later, the king, while making no promises, had likewise affirmed his wish to avoid an all-out clash and implied that the Legion would not invade Jewish territory.

It is clear that 'Abdullah was far from confident of Arab victory and preferred a Jewish state as his neighbor to a Palestinian Arab state run by the mufti. "The Jews are too strong—it is a mistake to make war," he reportedly told Glubb just before the invasion.[79]

'Abdullah's aim was to take over the West Bank rather than destroy the Jewish state—though, to be sure, many Legionnaires may have believed that they were embarked on a holy war to "liberate" all of Palestine.[80] Yet down to the wire, his fellow leaders suspected 'Abdullah of perfidy (collusion with Britain and/or the Zionists). 'Azzam reportedly told Taha al-Hashimi on 13 May that he "smells a rat in the policy of King 'Abdullah. So he ['Azzam] will go to him and spur him on, saying . . . 'Either you will attack the Jews like Saladin attacked the Crusaders, or the curse of the world will fall upon you.'"[81]

'Abdullah took no notice. But once he had radically restricted the planned Jordanian (or Jordanian-Iraqi) contribution to the war effort, the other invasion participants had felt compelled to downgrade their own armies' objectives. The Syrians shifted their point of invasion from Bint Jbail to the southern tip of the Sea of Galilee, which forced the Syrian expeditionary force to spend 14 May driving from southern Lebanon to the southwestern edge of Syria, opposite al-Hama. The shift secured the northern (or right) flank of the Iraqi thrust across the Jordan at Gesher. The Lebanese army appears to have been affected to the extent of moving its point units from Ras al-Naqurah to the central and eastern sectors of south Lebanon—though with defense, not offense, in mind.

But the chief change occurred in the south. The altered Hashemite dispositions and intentions posed a dilemma for King Farouk: he was not about to allow his archrival, 'Abdullah, to make off with the West Bank (and possibly East Jerusalem) while completely avoiding war with the Israelis (something, incidentally, that all along he had suspected 'Abdullah intended). The Egyptian response was to change the planned single-prong offensive up the coast road into a two-pronged offensive. Now the left prong would proceed up the coast road toward Majdal and Isdud, and perhaps toward Tel Aviv, while a newly added right prong would veer eastward, via Beersheba, and occupy as much as possible of the southern West Bank, perhaps as far northward as Jerusalem. The Egyptians would thereby ensure that 'Abdullah would not get all of the West Bank and that they themselves would emerge from the war with a substantial and important part of central Palestine (Hebron and Bethlehem) under their control.[82]

Thus, in the days before and after 15 May the war plan had changed in essence from a united effort to conquer large parts of the nascent Jewish state, and perhaps destroy it, into an uncoordinated, multilateral land grab. As a collective, the Arab states still wished and hoped to destroy Israel—and, had their armies encountered no serious resistance, would, without doubt, have proceeded to take all of Palestine, including Tel Aviv and Haifa. But, in the circumstances, their invasion now aimed at seriously injuring the Yishuv and conquering some of its territory while occupying all or most of the areas earmarked for Palestinian Arab statehood.

From the start, the invasion plans had failed to assign any task whatsoever to the Palestinian Arabs or to take account of their political aspirations. Although the Arab leaders vaguely alluded to a duty to "save the Palestinians," none of them seriously contemplated the establishment of a Palestinian Arab state with Husseini at its head. All the leaders loathed Husseini; all, to one degree or another, cared little about Palestinian goals, their rhetoric notwithstanding. It was with this in mind that Jordan, on the eve of the invasion, ordered the ALA out of the West Bank[83] and subsequently disarmed the local Arab militias.

The Arab states' marginalization of the Palestinian Arabs was in some measure a consequence of their military defeats of April and the first half of May. These had also rendered them politically insignificant.[84] But the Jordanian occupation of the West Bank and the other invaders' early defeats (see below) marginally changed thinking vis-à-vis the Palestinian Arabs, especially in Cairo. Through the first half of 1948, the Arab League had consistently rejected al-Husseini's appeals to facilitate the establishment of a Palestinian Arab government in exile. But in mid-September 1948, under strong pressure from Egypt, which feared complete Hashemite dominance of the Palestinian Arabs, the Arab League Political Committee authorized the establishment of a Palestinian Arab "government." Ahmad ʿAbdul Baqi Hilmi, a Sidon-born Palestinian Arab banker, was named "prime minister," to head a "Cabinet" of twelve, which included Jamal Husseini as "Foreign Minister" and Raja al-Husseini as "Defence Minister." On 22 September the AHC proclaimed the establishment, in Egyptian-ruled Gaza, of the "All-Palestine Government," and on 30 September a constituent assembly, the "Palestine National Council," with some eighty delegates, was convened in the town. Momentarily escaping his Egyptian "protectors," Haj Amin managed to reach Gaza and was named "President" of the council.

It was all farce. Responding with alacrity in Amman, ʿAbdullah on 30 September convened the "First Palestinian Congress" as a counterweight; indeed, the "Congress" immediately denounced the Gaza "Government." The Egyptians, for their part, on 6–7 October bundled Haj Amin back to Cairo. In reality, the Gaza "Government" and "Council" did not long outlast his departure. Though most Arab governments rapidly recognized the hastily put-together, skeletal administration, it carved out no real fiefdom. Under tight Egyptian military administration, it had no real powers or funds and ruled no lands. Moreover, most of the small territory nominally under its control (that is, the area of Palestine occupied by the Egyptian army) in mid-October was overrun by the Israel Defense Forces in Operation Yoav. The Arab Legion, meanwhile, disarmed the Arab militiamen in the West Bank. The Egyptians hastily sent the few "ministers" left in Gaza back to Cairo. Within weeks, the farce was over, the Palestinian "government's" only achievement having been to print fourteen thousand Palestinian passports (which no one recognized). The "All-Palestine Government" maintained a paper existence as a subdepartment within the Arab League until 1959, when Nasser disbanded it.[85]

If Arab war aims were disparate, the Yishuv's initial goal was clear and simple: to survive the onslaught and establish a Jewish state. This was the chief aim both when Palestine's Arabs attacked and when the Arab states invaded. But gradually, from December 1947 onward, one and possibly two aims were added. The first is unarguable and clear: to expand the new state so that it emerge from the war with more defensible borders and additional territory. The second was, at least among some of the leadership, to reduce the number of Arabs resident in the Jewish state. As David Ben-Gurion obliquely put it in February 1948, after a visit to West Jerusalem: "From your entry to Jerusalem through Lifta-Romema . . . there are no strangers [that is, Arabs].

One hundred per cent Jewish. . . . I do not assume that this will change. . . . What has happened in Jerusalem . . . could well happen in great parts of the country—if we [the Yishuv] hold on. . . . And if we hold on, it is possible that in the coming six or eight or ten months of the war there will take place great changes . . . and not all of them to our detriment. Certainly there will be great changes in the composition of the population of the country."[86]

The Yishuv's expansionism was driven at first by survivalist, military considerations. The key problem was West Jerusalem, with its hundred-thousand-strong Jewish community. As the war unfolded, the community came under siege and mortal threat, and the historic attachment to Jerusalem—religious and nationalist—came to the fore. By April, the Haganah, while trying to lift the siege, was in fact pushing to attach the city to the Coastal Plain.

The Zionist leadership initially was chary about violating the UN partition borders, lest this bolster the Arabs' more general desire to overturn the resolution or give offense to the international community. The Zionist shift from unreserved adherence to the UN borders to expansionism was slow and hesitant. The pan-Arab invasion of mid-May ended the hesitancy: if the Arabs were defying the United Nations and were bent on destroying the Jewish state, the Jews would take what was needed for survival, and perhaps a little more. As Moshe Shertok put it on 16 June 1948: "It is clear that it would be good if we could achieve two things: (A) Not to give up an inch of the land within the borders of 29 November [1947]. . . . (B) To add to this territory those areas we have captured and not out of a desire merely to expand, but under pressure of bitter necessity. That is, those areas that bitter experience has taught us that we must dominate in order to provide the state with protection . . . (Western Galilee, the road to Jerusalem and Jerusalem itself)."[87]

On the eve of the pan-Arab invasion, each side enjoyed strategic advantages and disadvantages. The Arabs held the initiative and could count on a measure of strategic and tactical surprise: they would be striking first, and when and where they chose, and could expect to enjoy at least temporary local superiority, in manpower and weaponry. The planned simultaneity of the assaults, across a number of borders, boosted the advantage of the initiative and surprise. Moreover, from the beginning, the invaders held much of Palestine's high ground: the Arab-populated and controlled hill country of Galilee, Samaria, and Judea. Jewish concentrations and control, on 14 May, were largely limited to the lowlands: the Coastal Plain and the Jezreel and Jordan Valleys. The Arabs also had an overwhelming preponderance in heavy weapons: artillery, armor, and combat aircraft.

Counterweighing these Arab advantages, the Haganah enjoyed a superi-

ority in both quality and quantity of manpower, unity of command, and relatively short lines of communications that facilitated, at least theoretically,
resupply and the rapid shift of forces and weapons from front to front to
meet successive threats. By and large, the Haganah had better trained, more
capable commanders—though the Arab Legion's (mostly British) senior officers were probably as good, if not better. Initially on the defensive, the Haganah enjoyed the home court advantage, consisting of greater familiarity
with the terrain and the morale-boosting stimulus of fighting for one's own
home and fields and in defense of one's loved ones. Moreover, as during the
civil war, the Jews felt that the Arabs aimed to reenact the Holocaust and that
they faced certain personal and collective slaughter should they lose. Most
Haganah troops had lost relatives in the Holocaust, a loss fresh in their
minds, and they were imbued with boundless motivation and a measure of
fury ("once more we are under attack and threat of annihilation").

The soldiers of the Arab armies were less motivated. Though keen on defeating the Jews—seen as religious infidels and political usurpers—and helping their Palestinian "brothers"—they did not view the war as an existential
proposition. Their states, villages and towns, and families were not under real
threat; in defeat, they could still return to hearth and home. The Arab soldiers were invaders fighting a long way from home for a remote and somewhat abstract cause. This gap in motivation was to tell on the battlefield, especially in May and June, when small Jewish units with rifles and Molotov
cocktails staved off far larger Arab forces backed by armor and artillery (as in
Kibbutz Nirim and Kibbutz Degania Aleph).

Last, the Haganah enjoyed an unquantifiable though very real advantage
because of its victory in the civil war. In crushing the Palestinian militias, it
had gained combat experience and self-confidence. Conversely, the Arab
armies had no such victory under their belts, no tangible reason for self-
confidence, and good reason to fear the Haganah.

THE YISHUV PREPARES

A month before the invasion, Ben-Gurion told his colleagues, "We are
[still] quite far from having the force we need to meet the 15th of May. We
lack almost half the necessary manpower, we lack 80% of the transport, and
we lack the rest of the [necessary] equipment in no small measure. . . . There
is no food, there is no fuel, and a thousand other things."[88]

The mobilization of the Yishuv for the invasion was a giant and fateful undertaking; its existence hung in the balance, as all realized. But some had understood earlier than others, and Ben-Gurion was among the first. Back in

December 1946, when taking over the Security (or Defense) Department of the Jewish Agency, he told the Twenty-second Zionist Congress, meeting in Basel: "We now face a completely new situation. Palestine is surrounded by independent Arab countries. . . . [They] can buy and produce weapons, establish armies and train them. . . . An attack by the Arabs of Palestine does not endanger the Yishuv. But there is a danger that the neighboring Arab states will send their army [sic] to attack the Yishuv and destroy it. . . . We must prepare immediately. . . . This in my opinion is the primary task of Zionism."[89] (Already a decade earlier, against the backdrop of the Arab Revolt and the gathering storm of World War II, Ben-Gurion had jotted down in his diary: "The danger we face is not riots—but destruction. Because the attackers will not be only the Arabs of Palestine but perhaps [also] Iraq and Saudi [Arabia], and they have aircraft and artillery. And we must draw a political and military conclusion [from this]."[90]

Ben-Gurion understood that the political struggle against Britain would be won; and it was a matter of months, not years. The British would leave, and the Yishuv would face a pan-Arab onslaught. Yet the Yishuv, perturbed by daily economic, political, and military problems, failed to begin preparing in time.

Ben-Gurion spent much of 1947 learning the Yishuv's defense problems and pondering a reorganization of the Haganah. The organization had to be expanded and restructured in order to change from a collection of locally based, albeit centrally controlled, militias into an army. Its command structure needed to be reorganized and manned with experienced professionals (in Ben-Gurion's eyes meaning mainly by veterans of the Western armies of World War II), and it had to acquire the arms necessary for waging conventional war (tanks, artillery, aircraft, armored personnel carriers, gunboats).

But the key steps to achieving this reorganization and rearmament were set in train only at the end of 1947. The Haganah had some thirty-five thousand members, but only two thousand—organized in the Palmah—were full-time soldiers. The mobilization of members for full-time service and the recruitment and training of additional manpower began in late 1947. A mobilization committee was established in October, and recruitment offices were set up and began to operate in the towns in November and December.[91] By the end of December, some seventy-five hundred men were under arms (twenty-five hundred of them Palmahniks); by April, twenty-four thousand; by mid-May, about thirty thousand, about half of them veteran Haganah members; by early July (by then the Haganah had become the Israel Defense Forces), about sixty-four thousand.[92]

Alongside the start of mobilization, the Haganah began to reorganize structurally. Initially, there was talk of establishing a fourteen-battalion army. On 7 November 1947, Ya'akov Dori, the chief of general staff, and his political superior, Yisrael Galili, head of the Haganah National Staff, issued "the Order for a National Structure." It stated: "The danger of an attack on the country by the armies of the neighboring Arab countries . . . necessitates a different structure and deployment. Opposite regular armies it is imperative to prepare in a military [as distinct from militia] force—trained, armed, and structured along military lines." The order called for the establishment of four brigades, with fifteen battalions, based on the existing Palmah battalions and newly formed Haganah units. The brigades were seen as administrative rather than operational frameworks.[93] But the restructuring took on a life of its own, fueled by the spread of the hostilities that began at the end of November and the prospect of pan-Arab invasion, and by March 1948 nine brigades had begun to form, with expanding brigade and battalion HQs, recruitment centers, training camps, logistical services, and armories. It was a race against time, and everything was in flux; in every sphere there were shortages. In mid-February one of the Golani Brigade's incipient battalions reported that it had "195" soldiers with "100" personal weapons, "one pickup truck and five motorcycles," and eight rented cars.[94] In late April, the 'Etzioni Brigade, responsible for Jerusalem, still had only one fully operational battalion; in late May one of the Tel Aviv area Kiryati Brigade's battalions, the Forty-third, had no personal weapons.[95] The organization and equipping of the brigades was hampered by the continuous operational burdens to which each was subjected by the ongoing war against the Palestinian Arab militias—though participation in combat also provided the units and soldiers, most of them new recruits, with experience and self-confidence. By May the Haganah had reorganized into nine fully operational if underequipped brigades—three of them Palmah—each with two to five battalions, with a small territorial Home Guard defending the towns and rural settlements to the rear. By the end of April into early May, some battalions had participated in brigade-size operations.

(During the following six weeks, the Haganah General Staff established three additional brigades, two of them designed to serve as a strategic reserve. The order to establish the semiarmored Seventh Brigade was issued on 14 May. It was hastily assembled and equipped and, within days, thrown into battle at Latrun. Two weeks later, HGS began the again hasty establishment of a second semiarmored brigade, the Eighth—initially with one armored battalion, the Eighty-second—under the command of the founder and first commander of the Palmah, Yitzhak Sadeh. The brigade, as a fully operational unit, first saw action in mid-July. During June the IDF also set up, in the Galilee, the Oded Brigade, the last established of the twelve Israeli brigades that fought the 1948 War. By July, almost all IZL and LHI members had been inducted into the IDF.)

During 1947–1948 the Haganah scoured the globe for arms. It was a massive effort, involving locating the needed arms, purchase (and, in the case of aircraft, training the crews), and shipment to Palestine (before 15 May circumventing the British blockade and after 29 May in defiance of the UN embargo). The effort involved Haganah agents and networks of Zionist officials and sympathizers, subterfuge and chicanery, dummy companies and counterfeit letters of authorization and accreditation, and large sums of money. The world was awash with decommissioned armaments from World War II. The arms were bought from both states and private dealers.

In the United States, Ben-Gurion in 1945 had secretly recruited eighteen Jewish millionaires, organized as, and misleadingly titled, the Sonneborn Institute, to help provide the Haganah's needs in money and equipment, including machine tools needed for the Haganah's embryonic arms industry. The group hired dozens of experts for the acquisition or transport of equipment or for establishing particular contacts (with Latin American dictators or underworld dealers). Many of the group's activities were illegal; it operated outside the framework of the official Zionist organizations. The Institute created and used dummy companies, such as the New England Plastic Novelty Company. But much of the equipment it purchased failed to reach Palestine because of intervention by the American authorities, who on 14 December 1947 imposed an embargo on all arms shipments to the Middle East. Thereafter, the Federal Bureau of Investigation regularly arrested Institute and Haganah agents and impounded purchases. The Institute's most ambitious project, handled by Haganah agent Yehuda Arazi, was the purchase of the decommissioned aircraft carrier *Attu*—for $125,000—on which Arazi hoped to load hundreds of armored vehicles, artillery pieces, and aircraft and convey them en masse to Palestine. The plan fell through, for reasons of expense and American interference, and the carrier was sold as scrap metal. The Institute's major successes were providing the Haganah with machine tools for making ammunition and with field communications equipment that became the backbone of the brigades' communications from May 1948; and (through Al Schwimmer, a Trans World Airlines engineer) the provision of a cluster of C-46 Commando cargo planes, four B-17 bombers, several Harvards, and a lone serviceable Mustang, and more than five hundred thousand gallons of (also embargoed) aviation fuel.[96]

Haganah agents purchased a variety of weapons, some of them useless, in Western Europe during 1947–1948. Most important were the purchases in France or with French assistance of thirty 65 mm guns, twelve 120 mm mortars, and 75 mm antitank and field artillery pieces, as well as ten H-35 Hotchkiss light tanks (which served from summer 1948 as the core of the Seventh Brigade). The Yishuv's first "artillery" pieces were a batch of His-pano-Suiza 20 mm antiaircraft cannon (purchased from Switzerland), the first twelve reaching Tel Aviv by sea on 23 April.[97]

The Arab Division of the Jewish Agency Political Department had care-fully monitored the Arab League's deliberations during 1947 and early 1948 with one question in mind: Were the Arab states going to invade? ʿAbdullah and Iraq's leaders repeatedly told British diplomats from autumn 1947 that they would march: ʿAbdullah, delimiting the message, spoke of a takeover (by the Legion, with or without Iraqi support) of "the Arab part of Pales-tine"; the Iraqis, led by Prime Minister Salih Jabr, spoke of occupying "the whole (repeat the whole) of Palestine."[98] And, occasionally, Jordanian lead-ers, such as Prime Minister (until December 1947) Samir Rifaʿi, also spoke of "the whole of Palestine."[99] When, in the second half of April 1948, the die was cast, the Yishuv's intelligence executives took note. Or, as Shertok told the UN Security Council (a little presciently) in mid-April: " The Govern-ments of the Arab League . . . are now reliably reported to be preparing plans for the occupation of the whole area of Palestine by their armies, which would cross its frontiers from north, east and south immediately after the ter-mination of the . . . Mandate."[100]

King ʿAbdullah's "declaration of war" on the Yishuv of 26 April (which was followed by a formal endorsement by the Jordanian National Assembly on 6 May of the prospective Legion invasion)[101] were public gestures that, if somewhat premature, quickly registered with HIS—and were interpreted as an exertion of pressure on the other Arab states to fall into line.[102] In early May ʿAzzam told the London *Daily Telegraph* that intervention by the Arab states was "inevitable"; Lebanese interior minister Camille Chamoun told a press conference in Beirut on 7 May, after returning from a meeting with Syr-ian president Shukri al-Quwwatli, that "all the Arab armies will invade Pales-tine."[103]

In the last weeks of April and the first weeks of May, invasion was palpably in the air. But, down to the last moment, the Yishuv's leaders did not know which armies would invade (would Egypt really participate?), when they would attack, what their military objectives would be, what routes they would take, and how many troops would participate and how effectively. As late as 7 May, Ben-Gurion jotted down in his diary: "Will the neighboring states fight [that is, invade]?"[104] The Haganah appears to have gotten word of the "plan" put together by the Military Committee in Damascus and of its core goal, to cut off Eastern Galilee and the Jezreel Valley from the Coastal

Plain and an advance on Haifa. HIS also understood, or guessed, that the armies would meet up before jointly assaulting Haifa. It was also clear, or at least likely, that the invasion would begin on 15 May.[105]

But that was it. By 12–13 May, that there would be an invasion was certain. But the aims, participants, and routes were all uncertain: "I can only summarize feelings, not authoritative reports," HIS and Jewish Agency Political Department official Shimoni told his colleagues. He said that there would certainly be a Legion invasion, assisted by the Iraqis. He also believed the Syrians would invade, "and something symbolic [would be contributed by] Lebanon." As to Egypt, Shimoni was uncertain whether it would go beyond monetary contributions "and advice." He also assessed that Jordan would "not try to conquer all of our state." However, he noted that "French intelligence officers" had told the Jewish Agency a day or two before that the armies of Egypt, Jordan, Iraq, Syria, and Lebanon would all invade on 15 May, with the aim of occupying all of Palestine, "and their arrows would be directed at Tel Aviv."[106]

THE BALANCE OF MILITARY FORCES

The civil war had ended with the Haganah in control of two continuous, connected north-south strips of Palestine, which were more or less contiguous with the Jewish settlement concentrations. The shorter strip consisted of the Galilee Panhandle and the Jordan and Beit Shean Valleys. The longer one, along the Mediterranean coast, ran from the Lebanese border at Rosh Haniqra (Ras al-Naqurah) through Western Galilee, Haifa, and Tel Aviv–Jaffa, and ended around Rehovot. The two strips were thinly linked by the Jewish-held Jezreel Valley. In addition, two Jewish-held appendages jutted out of the southern end of the Jewish-held Coastal Plain. A thin strip of land ran, from west to east, to Jewish-held Western Jerusalem; and in the south there was the larger appendage of the northern Negev settlement bloc, running from Gvar-ʿAm in the north to Nirim in the southwest to Alumim in the south, connected to the Jewish-dominated coastal area by a sliver of land around Negba.

The Palestinian Arabs, though having lost the civil war, continued, with the help of the ALA and other foreign volunteer units, to hold the central Galilee from the Lebanese border southward to (and including) Nazareth; the southern Coastal Plain, including Isdud, Majdal, and the area later known as the Gaza Strip; a somewhat expanded West Bank (Judea and Samaria), which stretched westward to Lydda and Ramla and southward to Beersheba; and the bulk of the Negev Desert, which was inhabited by bedouin. They also held a small ALA-supported enclave along the coast just south of Haifa, which included the villages of Tira, Ijzim, and Tantura.

Nine Haganah brigades, composed of some 16,500 troops, defended the Jewish areas.[107] The Eleventh, Yiftah (Palmah) Brigade in the Galilee Panhandle and Jordan Valley; the First, Golani, Brigade in the Beit Shean and Jezreel Valleys; the Second, Carmeli, Brigade in Western Galilee and Haifa; the Third, Alexandroni, Brigade in the Coastal Plain; the Fourth, Kiryati, Brigade in the greater Tel Aviv area; the Sixteenth, ʿEtzioni, Brigade in West Jerusalem; the Tenth, Harel (Palmah), Brigade in the Jerusalem Corridor; the Fifth, Givʿati, Brigade in the Rehovot-Hulda area, southeast of Tel Aviv; and the Twelfth, Negev (Palmah), Brigade in the northern Negev pocket. Three more brigades—the Seventh, Eighth, and Ninth (Oded)—were added in the following weeks.

About half the Haganah's manpower served in service, headquarters, and Home Guard units. On 15 May only 60 percent of Haganah troops had arms.[108] But large shipments soon arrived, and by the start of June, according to Ben-Gurion, the IDF had "reached a saturation" in small arms, including thirty-six thousand rifles, sixty-five hundred light machine guns, and more than thirty-three million bullets.[109] The Yishuv's own arms factories also helped out: by the start of June, the weapons plants had produced seven thousand Sten submachine guns; by October, sixteen thousand. The Yishuv's plants also produced Sten gun ammunition, light and medium mortars, antitank projectiles, grenades, mines, and crude bombs.

The Haganah's main problem during the first weeks of the invasion was a lack of heavy weapons. It had managed to steal or buy from the departing British units two or three tanks, twelve armored cars (four of these mounting cannon), three half-tracks, and three coastal patrol vessels. By the end of May, ten additional tanks and a dozen or so half-tracks had arrived, as had forty-five light artillery pieces, twenty-four antiaircraft or antitank cannon, and seventy-five PIATs. Dozens of makeshift armored trucks and cars had been built in Tel Aviv's workshops. By 31 May, the Haganah also had about seven hundred two-inch mortars and one hundred three-inch mortars, plus a dozen or so locally made crude heavy mortars (Davidkas)—all of which compensated, to some degree, for the initial lack of artillery. The Haganah Air Service, which became the Israel Air Force (IAF), had twenty-eight light reconnaissance and transport aircraft but no combat aircraft. By 29 May, Israel had received, assembled, and sent into action four Czech-made Messerschmitt Avia S-199 fighters; seven more arrived, in parts, by 11 June.[110]

Just as the Arabs tended to exaggerate Jewish strength, the Jews tended to exaggerate Arab strength—and Yishuv strategy cannot be understood without taking account of this. Jewish fears of defeat and possible annihilation were very real, and they began to dissipate only after the Arab armies proved to be much smaller and, by and large, less competent than anticipated.[111]

On paper, according to Haganah estimates, the Arab states possessed armies comprising 165,000 troops.[112] In mid-1947, Ben-Gurion believed that the Arab Legion alone consisted of no less than "15–18,000" troops, with "400 tanks."[113] (In truth, the Legion had no tanks and only seven to eight thousand soldiers.)

The Arab armies were much smaller and severely underequipped—and they deployed only part of their strength in Palestine, usually leaving large numbers of troops at home to guard against internal upheaval by minorities (for example, Iraq's Kurds) or political opponents.[114] All the same, the Arab states sent their best, and best-equipped, formations, and these were supplied and supported by many thousands of logistical and base camp troops to the rear.

The invading forces consisted, on 15 May, of about twenty thousand combat troops:[115] some fifty-five hundred Egyptians (two brigade groups), forty-five hundred to sixty-five hundred Arab Legionnaires,[116] 2,750 from Syria (one brigade), and twenty-seven hundred from Iraq (one reinforced brigade). To this number one should add air force personnel in Syria, Iraq, and Egypt and some two thousand Lebanese army troops, who applied pressure on, and posed a constant threat along, the northern border, pinning down Haganah troops, and thousands of irregulars (ALA, Muslim Brotherhood, and local militiamen) inside Palestine.[117] During the following two to three weeks, an additional three to four brigades (one each from Egypt, Syria, and Iraq, with further Jordanian troops organized as a new brigade), numbering at least eight thousand troops, arrived at the fronts.

On paper, according to Haganah estimates, the Arab armies had some seventy-five combat aircraft, forty tanks, three hundred armored vehicles, 140 field guns, and 220 antiaircraft and antitank guns.[118] But, in practice, they had far less, much of the equipment (especially the aircraft) being unserviceable. Some of the other weaponry never reached the Palestine theater.[119]

Following the invasion, both sides substantially increased their forces, the Israelis handily winning the manpower race. In 1948, twenty-to-forty-four-year-old males constituted a full 22 percent of the Jewish population. In the end, Israel proved able to put 13 percent of its population into uniform.[120] By mid-July, the IDF was fielding sixty-five thousand troops; by October, eighty-eight thousand; by January 1949, 108,000.[121] The Arab armies, joined by contingents from Yemen, Morocco, Saudi Arabia,[122] and Sudan, probably had forty to fifty thousand troops in Palestine and Sinai by mid-July and sixty-eight thousand in mid-October,[123] the numbers perhaps rising slightly by the end of winter.

A major reason for the relative decline in Arab strength in the course of the war and the concomitant increase in Israeli strength, which by September and October 1948 resulted in clear Israeli superiority, was the Israeli "victory"—and Arab "defeat"—in the handling of the international arms embargo. In line with the UN Security Council decision, the international community imposed a blanket arms embargo on all the combatants from 29 May 1948 until 11 August 1949. (This followed the unilateral American embargo, imposed already from 14 December 1947, and the British curtailment of arms and munitions exports to the Middle East that began in February 1948.)[124] The embargo was applied with great rigor by the United States, as well as by Britain, the traditional supplier of Egypt, Iraq, and Jordan, and France, the traditional supplier of Syria and Lebanon. As it turned out, the embargo had an asymmetrical effect—badly hurting the Arabs but hurting the Yishuv only minimally. This was a major factor in the gradual, steady decline of Arab military power and the relative, steady increase in Israeli military power.

The Arab states had not expected the embargo and had failed to prepare large stockpiles of weaponry, ammunition, and spare parts before 15 May. Nor had they nurtured alternative sources of supply from Eastern Europe or from private arms dealers or an independent capability to buy and ship arms to the Middle East clandestinely. Once the UN embargo was imposed, the Arab states, for lack of funds and an appropriate procurement apparatus, proved by and large unable to purchase weapons, munitions, and spare parts. And, after expending vast quantities of munitions in the invasion weeks of May and June, the Arab armies, from July onward, increasingly found themselves short of war matériel. For example, in October 1948 the Egyptian air force, which nominally had thirty-six fighters and sixteen bombers, was able to fly less than a dozen fighters and only three or four bombers, and these with ill-trained aircrews and inadequate munitions.[125]

The embargo also had a dire psychological effect on the Arab world. As ʿAzzam put it, "The Arabs [felt that they] were in fact without a friend in the world."[126]

By contrast, the Haganah,—an underground organization well versed in the clandestine arts—fashioned secret arms procurement networks in Europe and the Americas during 1947 and early 1948. Yishuv fundraisers managed to raise some $129 million, in cash and pledges, from Jews abroad to bankroll the war effort. The Yishuv spent some $78.3 million of this on arms purchases between October 1947 and March 1949.[127] As we have seen, these networks concluded a series of deals with Czechoslovakia, which was hungry for American dollars, and with private dealers, and shipments began to arrive in Palestine from the end of March 1948, the bulk of the arms, including heavy weaponry, arriving after Israel's declaration of statehood. The arrival of the Czech light weapons in March through May and of artillery pieces and armored vehicles in May through July proved crucial to the Haganah/IDF victories both over the Palestinian Arabs and the invading armies. Obversely, the failure of the Arab states to obtain additional armor, aircraft, guns, and ammunition, particularly for its artillery and mortars, proved crucial in the Arab shift after May and June to the defensive and to the subsequent Arab defeats. Similarly, the embargo-violating arrival in Israel of thousands of trained Jewish and non-Jewish volunteers from abroad, including hundreds of air and ground crew, was not matched by a similar increase in expert military personnel in the Arab armies. (More than three hundred Americans and Canadians—mostly with World War II experience—served in 1948 in the IAF, 198 of them aircrew.)[128] By the last months of 1948, the IAF had far more trained aircrew than were needed; the Arabs had far too few. Thus, in October 1948 the Israel Air Force, flying only a dozen or so fighters, proved able to gain immediate air superiority against the Egyptians, flying in Operation Yoav some 240 missions to the Egyptians' thirty to fifty missions. The surfeit of experienced personnel and the availability of spare parts and munitions made all the difference.

THE JORDANIAN FRONT

The army the Yishuv (rightly) feared most was the Arab Legion. The Jews had come to respect it during the months its units had served with the British army in Palestine. It was professional and efficient. Its strength in May 1948 was around nine thousand, of whom some twelve to thirteen hundred were tribal auxiliaries.[129] The Legion was highly mechanized, with effective service units, and was led by a complement of some fifty to seventy-five experienced British officers and noncommissioned officers, mostly seconded from the British army or mercenaries.[130] They included Glubb, the Legion's commander, and most of the senior staff—his deputy, Norman Lash, the brigade commanders Teal Ashton and Desmond Goldie, and most battalion OCs. The Legion—officially renamed the Jordan Arab Army—had a highly professional artillery arm.

Most of the Legion's combat troops—Glubb says "4,500"[131]—crossed into Palestine on 15 May. But a number of Legion companies had been left behind in Palestine when the bulk of the Legion, which had been seconded to the British army, withdrew to Jordan as part of the general British withdrawal from the country in late April and early May. The British had promised the Jewish Agency and United Nations that all of the Legionnaires would withdraw by the end of April. But in the second week of May, the

British conceded that several Legion companies, for technical reasons, had not been able to pull out. These units, in Jericho, ʿEin Karim, Latrun, Ramallah, Nablus, and Hebron, "greeted" the Legion as it crossed the Jordan westward and facilitated its smooth entry into parts of Palestine on 15–17 May.[132]

The British had established the Arab Legion in 1921 as a small, mobile border patrol unit. Glubb reorganized it in the 1930s when he became its deputy commander, and he was named commander on 21 March 1939. During World War II the Legion was considerably expanded to assist the British campaigns in Iraq and Syria in 1941. By war's end it numbered some eight thousand troops, mostly organized in garrison companies guarding British bases.

The Legion underwent a substantial reorganization during October 1947–early May 1948. It absorbed many of the two thousand troopers of the Transjordan Frontier Force (TJFF), the Palestine Mandate's border patrol force, and its manpower was otherwise expanded. Additional arms were acquired, and new units were created with an eye to establishing a force that could either help Britain and the United States should there be a showdown with the Soviet Union or, alternatively, occupy parts of Palestine after the British withdrew. By mid-May 1948, the original, single mechanized brigade, along with some independent guard companies, was reconstituted as two truck-borne mechanized brigades, the First and Third, each consisting of two one-battalion regiments. The brigades were run by a divisional headquarters commanded by Glubb's deputy, Lash. Each brigade had two four-gun artillery batteries of twenty-five-pounders. Each battalion had twelve to fourteen Marmon Harrington or Humber IV armored cars, each mounting a two-pounder gun. The Legion also had several dozen armored cars armed with machine guns, twenty-four six-pounder antitank guns, and forty three-inch mortars, all dispersed among the battalions.[133] During the second half of May and into early June, nine of the remaining "garrison companies" were reorganized into a third infantry brigade, the Fourth, consisting of the Fifth and Sixth regiments. This brigade, with two batteries of twenty-five-pounders, was largely unmechanized and underequipped, and was composed of recruits drawn largely from the kingdom's villages and towns rather than from the bedouin tribes, which were the mainstay of the Legion's original infantry battalions.[134] The Legion had no tanks or aircraft. By May 1949 it consisted of fourteen thousand soldiers.

The Legion was short of ammunition, especially for its artillery and mortars, and suffered severely from the British arms embargo.[135] A large, last-minute supply of artillery shells and mortar bombs—altogether some 350 tons—was confiscated by the Egyptians at Suez on 22 May.[136] But during the initial weeks of the invasion, the Legion's officers, perhaps unaware of the supply problem, were profligate in their use of artillery and mortars. On 30 May, the Fourth Battalion, fighting in Latrun, ran out of artillery shells.[137] During the following months, especially in the fighting in mid-July, Glubb pleaded with Whitehall for resupply, only to be rebuffed with the argument that if Britain violated the embargo, the Americans would do likewise and supply arms and ammunition to Israel in even more significant quantities. Nonetheless, during September and October Britain surreptitiously supplied the Legion with limited quantities of spare parts and ammunition, including artillery shells.[139]

The Jewish force facing the Legion initially consisted of three brigades. The ʿEtzioni Brigade defended West Jerusalem and what remained of the Palmah Harel Brigade, which had suffered severe casualties in the battle for the roads during February through May, held the area around Jerusalem, especially to its west. The Alexandroni Brigade was responsible for the Coastal Plain area opposite the West Bank, along the line from Tulkarm to Qalqilya. A few miles to the south, at Latrun, the Jordanians were to encounter, from the third week of May, an additional unit, the newly formed Seventh Brigade.

ʿAbdullah, flanked by Glubb, spent 14 May visiting the Legion's units in their assembly areas east of the Jordan River. The king addressed the troops: "He who will be killed will be a martyr; he who lives will be glad of fighting for Palestine. . . . I remind you of the Jihad and the martyrdom of your great-grandfathers."[139]

Kirkbride left a good description of the first shot fired during the Legion's entry into Palestine:

"At a few minutes before the hour of midnight on May 14–15th, 1948, King ʿAbdullah and members of his personal staff stood at the eastern end of the Allenby Bridge across the River Jordan waiting for the mandate to expire officially. . . . At twelve o'clock precisely the King drew his revolver, fired a symbolical shot into the air and shouted the word "forward." The long column of Jordanian troops which stretched down the road behind the bridge . . . moved off at the word of command, the hum of their motors rose to a roar. They passed [through] Jericho and went up the ridgeway [westward]."[140]

"The troops themselves were in jubilation. . . . Many of the vehicles had been decorated with green branches or bunches of pink oleander flowers, which grew beside the road. The procession seemed more like a carnival than an army going to war," Glubb later recalled.[141] Some soldiers appear to have been disappointed with the populace's reaction to the impending invasion.

Captain Mahmud al-Ghussan, a staff officer in the Legion's Fourth Regiment, for example, later recalled that the inhabitants of Amman had virtually ignored the troops as they passed through on their way to Palestine "in order to save it from the Zionists and the West."[142] But others came away with different recollections. Maʿan Abu Nowar, another young officer, recalled that "emotions ran high. . . . I remember my father and mother among the crowd . . . in Amman. As I was passing by in my GMC light armoured car, my mother shouted: 'God be with you, my son. Don't come back. Martyrdom my son.' I was shocked, not because my mother wished me to be killed . . . but because her head and face were bare. . . . In Jordan, conservative and devout women like her did not usually appear in public without a scarf covering their heads and faces."[143]

The push into Palestine was straightforward and unopposed: the First Brigade, consisting of the First and Third regiments, headed northwestward for Nablus, fanning out around the town; the Third Brigade, with the Second and Fourth regiments, headed from Jericho north and then west, deploying by nightfall in and around Ramallah. Two days later, its units would push westward to Latrun and Bab al-Wad, astride the western approach to Jerusalem. The Legion's aim was to take control of key Arab areas of eastern Palestine. There was no Jewish or Palestinian Arab resistance. In most areas, cheering Arab crowds showered the Legionnaires with rice.

The original Legion plan had been to avoid Jerusalem.[144] They had promised the British a nonbelligerent takeover of the West Bank, without Jerusalem. The United Nations had earmarked Jerusalem for international rule, and occupation of the city would be a clear violation of the will of the international community; and Britain, Jordan's patron, would be seen as complicit. Moreover, Jerusalem had a hundred thousand Jewish inhabitants, and the Legion's entry might spark Jewish-Jordanian hostilities, which Britain had specifically warned against and which Prime Minister Abul Huda had promised Bevin to avoid.

But military developments and King ʿAbdullah's private political and personal inclinations ultimately overwhelmed such considerations. On 13 May the British pulled out of the Old City, and the Haganah defenders of its Jewish Quarter immediately occupied some abandoned positions, expanding their area of control (in *mivtza shefifon,* Operation Viper). On 15–16 May, the Old City's Arab irregulars attacked and conquered most of these strongpoints, including the Greek Orthodox church, on the western edge of the quarter. But Jerusalem's Arabs began to panic.

The panic was mainly triggered by the Haganah's Operation Pitchfork (*mivtza kilshon*) in West Jerusalem, launched on 14 May. Within hours, the Haganah had taken the series of abandoned British strongpoints ("Bevingrads") in the city center (the Central Post Office, the Russian Compound, the King David Hotel, and the adjacent YMCA, and the Notre Dame de France monastery complex, overlooking the Old City's northwestern wall) and Arab or partly Arab quarters to the south and north, including the German and Greek "colonies," Bak'a, and the Allenby Camp in the south and the Sheikh Jarrah neighborhood (occupied by the IZL) and the adjacent Police School to the north. On 17–18 May the Haganah added the Arab Abu Tor neighborhood and the city's train station, just south of the Old City, to its conquests.[145] Masses of Arabs fled into the Old City. "We have conquered almost all of Jerusalem apart from [the] Augusta Victoria [Hospital, bordering the Mount of Olives] and the Old City. The Old City is besieged by the Jews from almost all sides," Ben-Gurion, exaggerating, told his cabinet.[146]

Operations Shefifon and Kilshon were mounted at least in part because of Haganah fears that the Legion would also target Jerusalem.[147] But their result was "a terrible panic . . . many [East Jerusalemites] began fleeing the city," reported Haganah intelligence.[148] The town's notables fired off a stream of cables to 'Abdullah and Glubb: "S.O.S. The Jews are near the [Old City] walls, tell the Arab Legion to give help immediately," and "Save us! Help us! They are up to the Jaffa Gate! They have occupied Sheikh Jarrah! They are scaling the walls of the Old City! Save us!"[149] In their desperation they even cabled al-Qawuqji to "Send help immediately."[150]

The only realistic potential "savior," however, was the Legion. And 'Abdullah could not stand aside. On 16 May he cabled Glubb: "I . . . order that everything we [that is, the Arabs] hold today must be preserved—the Old City and the road to Jericho. This can be done either by using the reserves which are now in the vicinity of Ramallah or . . . the general reserves. I ask you to execute this order as quickly as possible."[151] Further cables followed the next day, one from Abul Huda, who had initially opposed entering Jerusalem as contravening the UN decision:[152] "His majesty . . . is extremely anxious and indeed insists that a force from Ramallah with artillery be sent to attack the Jewish neighborhoods of Jerusalem. The Jews are attacking . . . the Old City. . . . An attack on the Jews would ease the pressure."[153]

But Glubb was reluctant to commit his army to prospectively costly and indecisive street fighting. He had too few troops, and his armored cars—the Legion's key mobile asset—would be both vulnerable and relatively useless in urban warfare. Until the last minute he hoped that a truce would be agreed or imposed that would leave Jerusalem out of it.[154] He tarried. Crossing into the West Bank on 16 May and moving from unit to unit, Glubb deliberately stayed "out of contact" with Amman—to avoid receiving the order to move on Jerusalem.[155]

But he could stall for only so long. At nightfall on 17 May he ordered two twenty-five-pounders to take up positions overlooking northern Jerusalem "from which they could support an advance if ordered." And two infantry companies were dispatched to the Mount of Olives.[156] Early on 18 May one of the companies moved into the Old City[157] to man the walls—from which, Glubb reminded the readers of his memoirs, ever with an eye to history, "nearly 1,900 years ago the Jews themselves had cast their darts at the advancing legions of Titus." But these were token forces and could not be expected to hold off a serious Haganah assault. "The King was haggard with anxiety lest the Jews enter the Old City and the Temple [Mount] area . . . [where] his father the late King Husayn of Hijaz, was buried." That night, Glubb ordered a massive push from Ramallah through Sheikh Jarrah into the Old City. "The die was cast," he recorded.[158]

'Abdullah's decision to intervene in Jerusalem was propelled by the Palestinians' appeals. And, without doubt, he feared that if East Jerusalem fell, his fellow Arabs would blame him. But he was also driven by other considerations, chief of which was the political and religious importance of the city to the Islamic world (as well as to the Christian West and the Jews). East Jerusalem was the jewel of Palestine. Annexed by Amman, it would turn 'Abdullah's godforsaken desert kingdom into a major player. Alternatively, the loss of the Old City would gravely undermine Arab morale. Moreover, the king was loath to allow the graves of his father and brother Faisal to fall into Jewish hands.[159] No doubt, the unopposed occupation of the bulk of the West Bank whetted the king's appetite for bigger and better conquests; for a few days, he even talked about conquering West Jerusalem and Tel Aviv.[160]

And, to be sure, there was a major strategic consideration, which Glubb quickly appreciated: if East Jerusalem fell, the road to the Jordan River would be open, and if Haganah units reached Jericho, they would cut off the Legion from its supply bases and threaten it with encirclement. The Legion's position in Nablus, Ramallah, and Hebron would become untenable; the army would face "disaster." To hold the West Bank, the Legion had to secure East Jerusalem.[161]

On the morning of 19 May, a battalion-sized Legion force of infantry and armor, with six-pounder and mortar batteries, hastily patched together from the brigades that had fanned out in the northern West Bank, set out down the main road from Ramallah to the Old City. At Sheikh Jarrah and the Police School, the Legionnaires brushed aside the IZL defenders—killing six and wounding fifteen—and proceeded southward, reaching the Old City's Damascus Gate in the afternoon. A linkup had been achieved.[162] But the route from Shu'fat through Sheikh Jarrah and Musrara to the Old City was still enfiladed by Haganah (and IZL) light weapons and mortars from West

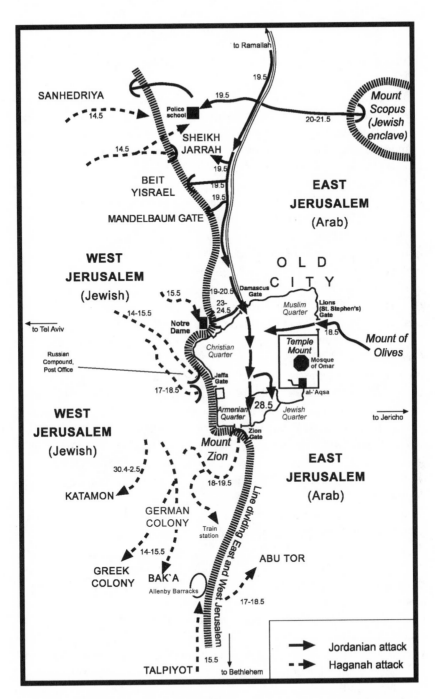

Operation Kilshon and the Jordanian attack of Jerusalem, 13–28 May 1948

Jerusalem's easternmost districts and, from the east, from the Hebrew University–Hadassah Hospital campus on Mount Scopus, a Haganah enclave in Arab territory. A Legion effort to break into Mount Scopus that day was repulsed by the Haganah, as were small armored thrusts westward, into the Sanhedria, Beit Yisrael, and Mandelbaum Gate areas. The main thrust, at Mandelbaum Gate, was beaten off, with three Legion armored cars disabled, by a mélange of Home Guard and Gadna (Haganah youth corps) fighters, brandishing a PIAT and Molotov cocktails, supported by one Haganah armored car mounting a two-pounder.[163]

The success boosted Yishuv morale; the Haganah had demonstrated, after the defeats in the ʿEtzion Bloc and the Police School, that the Legion's armor and artillery could be stopped.[164]

On 20 May Legion armored cars attacked the Haganah and Gadna positions on the top floors of Notre Dame, which dominated the northern wall of the Old City. "The Haganah soldiers seem to be mostly little boys and girls of 15 or 16 and quite irresponsible," reported one British woman who was in the complex.[165] But the Legionnaires failed, abandoning several burned-out cars, hit by Molotov cocktails, by the monastery walls.[166]

In all these attacks, the Legion was trying to secure the Ramallah–Old City road—or "do [nothing more] than protect the Old City," as Kirkbride, briefed by Glubb, informed Whitehall.[167] But Israeli leaders, including Ben-Gurion,[168] not privy to Glubb's plans, interpreted the attacks as the start of an effort to penetrate and conquer West Jerusalem. (Subsequently, Israel's interior minister, Yitzhak Gruenbaum, could not fathom "why the Arab Legion, when it took Sheikh Jarrah, didn't proceed further. Had it continued, it is possible it could have conquered all of Jewish Jerusalem or a large part of it. But we had a miracle."[169] Gruenbaum assumed that conquering West Jerusalem was Jordan's objective.)

Indeed, the Israeli prime minister believed that the Jordanian invasion was part of a pan-Arab design, supported by Britain, "to destroy within a few days the [Jewish] state."[170] His suspicions went so far as to report (mistakenly) that the Legion was about to use British-supplied poison gas.[171] Even the Anglophile and generally cool-headed foreign minister, Moshe Shertok, suspected Jordan and Britain of complicity in an "unmistakable inexorable line of crushing [the] Jewish State or reducing it to [the minuscule 1938] Woodhead [Commission proposals] size and letting neighboring beasts devour large part of Palestine."[172] The Legion push in Jerusalem—and the IZL's flight from Sheikh Jarrah—had resulted in an order by David Shaltiel, the Haganah Jerusalem District OC, to all commanders "to shoot anyone . . . who was not obeying his orders or was trying to flee the battlefield."[173]

One reason the Yishuv leaders believed that the Jordanians were bent on taking West Jerusalem was the intermittent artillery barrages the Jordanians unleashed during the battles around the Old City. Although some shelling was directed at Israeli mortar batteries or government buildings, much was indiscriminate, and Jewish civilian casualties were extensive. Reporting from Jerusalem, a senior official—probably Walter Eytan—wrote that "in [the northern West Jerusalem neighborhoods] there is scarcely a single home that has not been shelled, scarcely a family that has not suffered some loss in dead or wounded . . . [and the inhabitants] go hungry. . . . One Hadassah Hospital alone . . . treated one thousand shell casualties in the two weeks between May 15th and 31st. . . . Because they are mostly . . . poor people, people without influence, one does not hear much about this mass suffering."[174]

The war was not confined to the northern neighborhoods. At the southern edge of Jerusalem, hundreds of local irregulars were joined on 19 May by eight hundred Egyptian regulars and Muslim Brotherhood fighters—the van of the right arm of the Egyptian invasion via Beersheba and Hebron—and several platoons of Legionnaires. The combined force deployed 3.7-inch howitzers and three-inch mortars and six armored cars. Their target was Kibbutz Ramat Rachel, which controlled the Jerusalem-Bethlehem road and the southern entrance to Jerusalem. For three days, the force bombarded the kibbutz, almost leveling it. Then, on 22 May, after an infantry assault, the eighty weary and outgunned defenders abandoned the site and fled to Jerusalem. The Arabs systematically looted the buildings, then torched them. But that evening, in a surprise attack two Haganah platoons from Jerusalem retook the kibbutz. The following day the Arab forces retook the settlement; and that evening, the Haganah returned.

The final battle began on 24 May. Again the Arabs attacked. But this time, the Haganah force, reinforced by fifty IZL members, held grimly onto the western half of the kibbutz. A company from the Harel Brigade arrived. The following day the Arabs made one last effort, and failed. The Palmah, using flamethrowers, counterattacked that night, drove the remaining Arabs out, and conquered the nearby monastery of Mar Elias. The Arabs retreated to Sur Bahir. In the weeklong battle, more than a hundred Arabs died; among the Israelis, twenty-six were killed and eighty-four were wounded. The Israelis had secured the southern entrance to Jerusalem.[175]

But the key to Jerusalem lay north of the city. The Legion's position remained precarious. It firmly held only the area around the Damascus Gate; but the Ramallah-Jerusalem road was still enfiladed by Israeli fire, and the entrance to the Old City and its northwestern wall were dominated by the Haganah-occupied, five-hundred-room, stone-faced complex of Notre Dame.

Glubb ordered the Third Regiment, which had deployed in Samaria, to head for the capital. For six days, its bedouin soldiers "had fretted and cursed in inaction" around Nablus;[176] now, at last, they were joining battle.

In the early morning hours of 22 May the regiment, commanded by Lieutenant Colonel William Newman, an Australian World War II veteran, dismounted from their trucks and advanced, under a blazing sun, from Shuʿfat through Sheikh Jarrah to the Old City's northern walls, all the while taking fire from Haganah positions in Sanhedriya, Mea Shearim, and Mount Scopus. The Legion responded with artillery, mortars, and small arms; the whole area was enveloped in thick smoke; many Legionnaires, by now exhausted, went astray in the streets and alleyways north of the Old City walls. But the core of the Third Regiment, backed by gun-mounting armored cars, launched a desultory attack on Notre Dame. As the shells crashed into the stonework, the defenders moved from room to room and fired back. One of the cars was ignited and disabled by Molotov cocktails hurled by Gadna youths. The Legionnaires backed off. The next day, the regiment tried again. This time, it was a well-organized assault, with infantry, armored cars, and artillery. The shells "came thick and fast," as one compound resident noted.[177] But "the Holy Catholic Church seemed to have built for eternity," wrote Glubb; the Legion's two- and six-pounders and mortars were of little use against the stout walls. The infantry failed to enter the compound. A twenty-five-pounder was brought up and fired point-blank. It felt like "a continuous earthquake," recalled one of the defenders.[178] An Israeli PIAT knocked out two armored cars. At one point, a Legion company managed to penetrate the ground floor. The fighting was hand-to-hand, from room to room; both sides lobbed grenades and fired tommy guns. The defenders, most of them sixteen- and seventeen-year-old Gadna youths—one (Mordechai Rotenberg) was fourteen—held on.[179] Most of the regiment, pinned down by Haganah fire, failed to reinforce the penetration. In the end, Lieutenant Ghazi al-Harbi, a native of Saudi Arabia, and his Fourth Company were ordered to withdraw; the Haganah reoccupied the ground floor. Fighting around the building continued for several hours. By evening the Legion had had enough and withdrew to the Damascus Gate. The Third Regiment had suffered dozens of dead and wounded.[180]

Glubb later visited the regiment and met al-Harbi: "The tears ran down his wrinkled and weather-beaten face as he begged for permission for one more try to take Notre Dame. 'We'll do it this time, O father of Faris,' he assured me," recalled Glubb. "I vetoed any more attempts."[181]

But the regiment had managed to link up with the Old City, and by 24 May, a continuous, thin Legion line stretched from Ramallah through Sheikh Jarrah and the empty area between West and East Jerusalem.

The battle had not gone all the Haganah's way. During 14–16 May the Jewish settlements of ʿAtarot and Neveh Yaʿakov, north of Sheikh Jarrah, were attacked by irregulars and Legion units and abandoned, the defenders withdrawing to Mount Scopus. And on 17–20 May, the militarily untenable settlements of Kalia and Beit Haʿarava, at the northern end of the Dead Sea, south of Jericho, were abandoned. The women and children left by air and the rest by sea, southward, to Sodom.

But the most significant Israeli defeat occurred within the Old City itself, with the fall of the Jewish Quarter. Before the war, most of the inhabitants— almost all ultra-Orthdox—had been "on good terms with their Arab neigh-bours," resented the Haganah presence, and "were loath to see their homes sacrificed to Zionist heroics," as one British diplomat put it.[182]

Following an unsuccessful attack by Arab militiamen on 11 December 1947, British troops took up positions around the quarter, forming an outer cordon sanitaire around the Haganah-defended perimeter. The British occa-sionally impounded Haganah weapons. On 28 March there was a skirmish as the British tried to confiscate Haganah weapons; there were several dead— but the British stopped harassing the defenders.

Until 13 May, when the British evacuated, ninety men, mostly Haganah, had defended the Jewish Quarter. In the following days, about a hundred more joined them. On 16 May Arab irregulars attacked the quarter, captur-ing several positions and mortaring the houses. Many inhabitants fled into synagogues and cellars. The quarter's rabbis demanded that the Haganah surrender; they feared a massacre. But Haganah Jerusalem headquarters or-dered the defenders to hold on, promising reinforcements. The battle raged the next day, too. The defenders suffered heavy losses, and the Haganah was left with ten bullets per rifle. But it held on. A Haganah effort on 17–18 May to break into the Old City at Jaffa Gate was beaten off.[183] But a simultane-ous effort, by the Harel Brigade's Fourth Battalion outside the southern wall ended with the conquest of Mount Zion after fierce fighting inside the Dor-mition Abbey.

The Haganah decided to exploit the success and take Zion Gate and link up with the besieged quarter. But the planning was slapdash, and the Fourth Battalion was given insufficient reinforcements to carry it through. That night, 18–19 May, a platoon of twenty-four exhausted Palmahniks (two of them women)—led by David Elʿazar (IDF chief of general staff, 1972–1974)—took Zion Gate after blowing in the doors with an eighty-eight-pound charge.[184] The Arab defenders fled. A handful of Palmahniks, fol-lowed by eighty middle-aged Haganah conscripts—defined by the quarter's defenders as "useless"—carrying boxes of ammunition and extra weapons, reached the quarter.

The small Palmah force felt unable to hold the gate and the alley to the Jewish Quarter unless substantially reinforced. Owing to incompetence or a misunderstanding, Shaltiel failed to send the additional troops, and just after dawn, 19 May, the Palmahniks abandoned Zion Gate without a battle and returned to Mount Zion. For five hours, no one held Zion Gate. Indeed, two Israelis from West Jerusalem walked through it to the quarter, bringing food for their relatives. The area was quiet, no one stopped them, and they saw no one.[185] Around noon, a Legion unit occupied the gate; once again, the quarter was sealed off.[186]

Now it was seasoned Legionnaires—ʿAbdullah Tall's Sixth Regiment— not disorganized Palestinian militiamen, who were doing the besieging. The assault on the Jewish Quarter was renewed. The Legionnaires were assisted by irregulars, half of them ALA. The defenders were outnumbered five to one and completely outgunned. Starting on 19 May, the Legionnaires, heavily supported by cannon and mortars, steadily reduced the quarter. The attackers methodically blew up each house and position they conquered. Armored cars with two-pounders were deployed in the alleyways.

On 22 May the quarter's rabbis, Zeʾeve Mintzberg and Ben-Zion Hazan, cabled Israel's two chief rabbis: "The community is about to be massacred. In the name of the inhabitants [this is] a desperate appeal for help. The synagogues have been destroyed and the Torah scrolls have been burned. . . . Misgav Ladakh [Hospital] is under a hail of shells and bullets. . . . Save us."[187]

The Harel Brigade tried to break back in, but the attempts were poorly planned, undermanned, and half-hearted. Daily the Legion broadcast a demand to surrender, and by the end, most of the inhabitants were pressing the Haganah to accede. On 26–27 May, the Legionnaires took the Hurvat Israel (or "Hurva") Synagogue, the quarter's largest and most sacred building, and then, without reason, blew it up. "This affair will rankle for generations in the heart of world Jewry," predicted one Foreign Office official.[188]

The destruction of the synagogue shook Jewish morale.[189] Jerusalem Haganah headquarters ordered the defenders to hold on "for a few more hours"—but was unable to mount a serious relief effort. Israeli historians would later charge Shaltiel with incompetence and even indifference. But West Jerusalem itself was under siege—the Legion had blocked the Tel Aviv–Jerusalem road at Latrun and Bab al-Wad—and he was extremely shorthanded. He understood that the quarter was a sideshow. And its anti-Zionist ultra-Orthodox inhabitants were not exactly the Haganah's cup of tea.[190]

On the morning of 28 May a delegation of rabbis arrived at the quarter's Haganah command bunker and announced that they intended to surrender.

The commander, Moshe Roznak, agreed that they open "truce negotiations." Glubb described what followed: "Two old rabbis, their backs bent with age, came forward down a narrow lane carrying a white flag." In no man's land they met a Jordanian officer and said that they were empowered to negotiate. Tall demanded to see the quarter's mukhtar, Rabbi Mordechai Weingarten. Weingarten, accompanied by his daughter, Yehudit, duly appeared, and the negotiations began in a nearby café.

A brief ceasefire was agreed, and Weingarten returned to the Jewish Quarter, where representatives of the inhabitants and the defenders voted almost unanimously in favor of surrender; only the IZL representative abstained. Shaltiel was not consulted or informed. Rosnak, Weingarten, and Tall then signed an instrument of surrender. Tall agreed that the civilian inhabitants and all the women would be free to leave for West Jerusalem; army-age males (or "combatants") would become prisoners of war. Seriously wounded combatants were to be set free.[191] By then, of the 213 defenders, thirty-nine were dead, and 134 were wounded.[192]

The fears of the quarter's inhabitants proved groundless; the Legion had learned its lesson from Kfar ʿEtzion. The Legionnaires deployed in force and protected the Jews from the wrath of the gathering Arab mob. The soldiers shot dead at least two Arabs and wounded others as they guarded the Jews. One POW recalled: "We were all surprised by the Legion's behavior toward us. We all thought that of the soldiers [that is, Haganah men] none would remain alive. . . . [We feared a massacre. But] the Legion protected us even from the mob, they helped take out the wounded, they themselves carried the stretchers. . . . They gave us food, their attitude was gracious and civil."[193]

The Legionnaires took prisoner 290 healthy males, aged fifteen to fifty—two-thirds of them, in fact, noncombatants—and fifty-one of the wounded. The other wounded and twelve hundred inhabitants were accompanied by the Legionnaires to Zion Gate and freed.[194] The quarter was then systematically pillaged and razed by the mob.[195] The fall of the Jewish Quarter, an important national site, dealt a severe blow to Yishuv morale.

As the battle in Jerusalem unfolded, the importance of the Tel Aviv–Jerusalem road and the vital sector at Latrun and Bab al-Wad dawned on the two sides.[196] But the penny dropped first for Glubb. In Jerusalem, the fighting had ended more or less in stalemate: Israel held West Jerusalem and the Arabs, the eastern part of town, including the Old City. Glubb understood that if he was to continue holding East Jerusalem (and, perhaps, the West Bank as a whole), he must prevent the Israelis, who had a far larger army, from reinforcing the underequipped ʿEtzioni and Harel Brigades. He had to block the road from Tel Aviv—and Latrun–Bab al-Wad was the place, where the narrow road begins the climb up through the Judean Hills to the capital.[197] Occupying Latrun–Bab al-Wad would also draw off or pin down Israeli troops who might otherwise be deployed in Jerusalem.[198]

The Israelis saw the situation in a mirror image. The Haganah feared that the Legion was intent on conquering West Jerusalem or shelling and starving it into submission; ʿEtzioni and Harel had to be reinforced and the city resupplied; the Haganah had to take Latrun–Bab al-Wad and open the road. And some commanders no doubt thought about a further, offensive stage, in which the Haganah would conquer East Jerusalem and push down to Jericho and the Jordan, leaving the Legion cut off and stranded in the West Bank.

The small hillock at Latrun, topped by the large Tegart police fort, and the surrounding Arab villages of Latrun, Deir Aiyub, Imwas, Yalu, and Beit Nuba, sat astride the junction of the Tel Aviv–Jerusalem and Ramallah-Majdal roads. The fort had been held from the end of April, when the British abandoned it, until mid-May by units of the ALA and assorted militiamen. On 14 May the Jordanians ordered al-Qawuqji to withdraw from the West Bank, and the ALA pulled out. A platoon of left-behind Legionnaires, of the Eleventh Infantry Company, and dozens of Jordanian tribal militiamen, under Lieutenant ʿAbd al-Majid al-Maaita, took over the Latrun fort—but the road to Jerusalem remained open. For two days, the Haganah failed to exploit the vacuum, and on 17 May, the door began to slam shut: Glubb ordered in the Fourth Regiment, commanded by Habas al-Majali. The troops began to deploy between Bab al-Wad and Latrun that night. On 18 May the road to Jerusalem was severed.

Once again West Jerusalem was besieged and under dire threat; along its eastern edges, the Legion was mounting continuous attacks. Ben-Gurion feared a collapse. He demanded that the Haganah "take Latrun and all the surrounding villages and break through . . . to Jerusalem."[199] It was to be the first time Israel breached the tacit nonaggression agreement with ʿAbdullah; the area had been earmarked by the United Nations for Arab sovereignty. During the following weeks, Israel made three major efforts to take Latrun—and failed each time, with heavy losses. And, in the end, the IDF built a bypass road that demonstrated that the attacks had not, after all, been necessary and that an alternative supply route to Jerusalem was available.

The HGS hastily assembled a plan and task force. The Seventh Brigade, in charge of the operation, had been slapped together from scratch during the previous fortnight: its men and officers were poorly trained, and its equipment was seriously deficient. The Seventh was in no shape to take on the Legion. And the state of Alexandroni's Thirty-second Battalion, loaned to the

Seventh for the attack, was not much better. It arrived at the assembly point, Kibbutz Hulda, at the last minute.[200] Shlomo Shamir had some twenty-four hundred troops, with twelve armored cars, ten three-inch mortars and two 65 mm field artillery pieces.[201]

The Haganah went in blind; its eve-of-battle intelligence spoke of irregular "local forces" rather than of a Legion presence.[202] In fact, by the evening of 24 May, the Fourth Regiment had been joined by the Second Regiment, commanded by Major Geoffrey Lockett. The area had turned into a reduced-brigade redoubt, the Fourth Regiment holding Latrun village and fort and the neighboring village of Imwas, and the Second Regiment deployed immediately to its east, between Beit Nuba, where its two batteries of twenty-five-pounders were dug in, and Yalu, and Deir Aiyub to the south. The two-regiment brigade, the Third, commanded by Colonel Teal Ashton, consisted of twenty-three hundred soldiers, plus eight hundred auxiliaries, with sixteen three-inch mortars, eight six-pounders, ten two-pounders, thirty-five armored cars (half of them with two-pounders), and the twenty-five-pounders.[203] Israeli scouts had noted the arrival of the new battalion—but the information had failed to reach operation HQ.

Yadin sensed his forces' unreadiness. He tried to obtain a postponement. But Ben-Gurion refused; the prime minister, acting the generalissimo, feared a collapse in Jerusalem within hours or days. He ordered Yadin to go ahead.

Though not optimistic, the Haganah commanders believed that surprise and the fact that the main assault would take place at night, when the Legion's artillery would be less effective, would offset the Jordanians' obvious advantages. The operation was codenamed Bin-Nun, after Joshua Bin-Nun, who had commanded the Israelite forces battling the Canaanites at the same spot, the Ayalon Valley, some thirty-two hundred years before. In command was OC Seventh Brigade Shamir. The soldiers were told that they were tasked "to save Jerusalem."[204]

Two battalions, the Thirty-second and the Seventh Brigade's Seventy-second, were to go in, with the Seventy-third in reserve. All were unready in almost every way. There was only meager artillery support—two pre–World War I 65 mm French mountain guns, four homemade Davidka heavy mortars, which failed to work, and a battery of 81 mm mortars. There was no armor. Only a quarter of the Thirty-second's soldiers had canteens; ammunition was low; there were few light mortars and machine guns. And only part of the Seventy-third Battalion was at Hulda; the rest was still equipping southeast of Haifa.

But their defeat was assured by another factor: the Thirty-second and Seventy-second set out five to six hours later than planned, which meant that the battle would take place in daylight. The Thirty-second's B and A companies were ordered to sweep, undetected, south of Latrun and head northward, taking the hilltops overlooking Latrun village and Imwas. If successful, the battalion was then to loop westward and take Latrun village and the police fort. Meanwhile, the Seventy-second Battalion, in a wider southeasterly sweep, was to take the chain of hills to the southeast, eventually conquering Deir Aiyub and the hilltops overlooking Bab al-Wad. In effect, the plan called for a frontal attack on a well-entrenched brigade complex.

The attack never really took place. The Thirty-second and Seventy-second battalions crossed the starting line at 3:00–4:00 AM, on foot, moving parallel to and just south of the Tel Aviv–Jerusalem road. First Platoon, B Company, Thirty-second Battalion, commanded by Lieutenant Ariel ("Arik") Sharon, acted as point. An hour after setting out, B Company was spotted just south of Latrun village and hit by Legion mortars and artillery. A Company, to their south, was also hit. With sunrise, the Jordanian fire became extremely accurate. The Israelis had no answer. The battalion took heavy casualties. Hiding behind rocks, both companies replied with light weapons, ineffectively. Equally ineffective was the brigade artillery, which was out of range for counterbattery fire. The Seventy-second Battalion, moving a half-mile or so to the south of the Thirty-second, was hit by artillery from Legion positions at Latrun and Deir Aiyub and by hundreds of Arab militiamen who, summoned for the kill from nearby villages, engaged them from the south. The sun was up and it grew hot.

A Thirty-second Battalion veteran later described what happened: "We took a heavy Jordanian barrage, the likes of which I had never experienced. The shelling had a terrible effect. All my men were new immigrants. They lost their heads. . . . Some shouted to retreat, others pleaded for water. The wounded were covered in blood. The gnats and the *hamsin* [that is, hot easterly desert winds] in the Ayalon Valley were almost as bad as the artillery. . . . Terrible was the cry of the new immigrants, many of whom were Holocaust survivors: '*Wasser, wasser*' (water, water) [they shouted]." The barrage ignited the brush, adding smoke to the melange.[205]

In both battalions, the cry went up to retreat, and, in disorderly fashion, groups of soldiers began to turn back, some carrying wounded and dead, sprinting from rock to rock, hiding behind folds of earth. A Company, Thirty-second Battalion, managed to establish a temporary position on a slope south of the main road, from which it opened up on the Jordanian positions near Latrun village and on squads of Legionnaires who sortied south of the road to pick off the Israelis. Jordanian artillery ranged in on the slope and harried the retreating troops. At 11:30 AM, Shamir, who never left Hulda and lost control over his units, issued a general order to retreat. But the

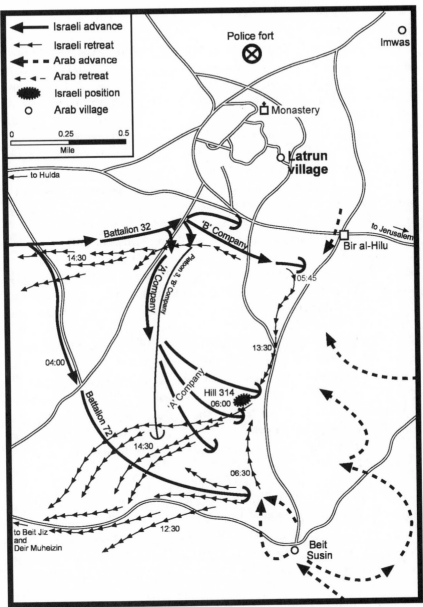

Legend:
- Israeli advance
- Israeli retreat
- Arab advance
- Arab retreat
- Israeli position
- Arab village

0   0.25   0.5
Mile

Police fort
Imwas
Monastery
Latrun village
to Hulda
Battalion 32
'B' Company
14:30
Platoon 3, 'B' Company
'A' Company
04:00
13:30
to Jerusalem
Bir al-Hilu
05:45
'A' Company
Hill 314
06:00
Battalion 72
14:30
06:30
to Beit Jiz and Deir Muheizin
12:30
Beit Susin

By permission of Carta, Jerusalem

The First Battle of Latrun (Bin-Nun aleph), Central Front, 25 May 1948 brigade's artillery cover was completely ineffectual, as Jordanian casualty figures were to demonstrate.

It was 95 degrees Fahrenheit, with 38 percent humidity. The retreat under heavy, accurate fire, with many already dead and wounded, and some over-whelmed by thirst, was difficult and disorganized.[206] Many soldiers discarded their equipment; the Jordanians were later to collect 220 rifles, dozens of Sten guns, and fifteen machine guns.[207] Among the seriously wounded was Sharon, hit in the stomach and leg (he later recalled mumbling "imah," mommy);[208] he was eventually pushed and dragged to safety by a (badly wounded) sixteen-year-old subordinate.

Jordanian irregulars, screaming "Idbah al yahud" (slaughter the Jews), pressed southward from Latrun and northward from the village of Beit Susin in an effort to surround and pick off the Israelis.[209] Shamir ruled against sending his few armored vehicles into the killing fields. A handful of Israeli machine-gunners, with great heroism, stayed put and kept the irregulars at bay as the Thirty-second's survivors ran and crawled their way to safety. Some, noted witnesses, were in such a stupor that they walked upright, slowly, as if oblivious to the machine gun fire and shells. Arab irregulars and Legionnaires killed off stragglers. By late afternoon, most had reached safety or had been picked up by rescue squads in cars and armored vehicles. Alexandroni had suffered fifty-two dead; the Seventh Brigade, twenty dead. The Legion took six prisoners. About 140 Israelis were wounded and saved.[210] The dead included some killed off or left to die after the Legionnaires and irregulars had occupied the battlefield. The Legion and irregulars suffered no more than five dead and six wounded.[211] Ben-Gurion wrote: "The blow was so harsh that also those not physically injured were badly affected. . . . It was a very bad blow."[212]

Israeli intelligence subsequently was full of praise for the Legion's performance, noting especially the quality of the infantry and mortar crews.[213] But the Jordanians failed to exploit their success and attack the headquarters at Hulda, which they could easily have done. Nonetheless, the defeat left a lasting scar on the psyche of the IDF General Staff—and, conversely, a feeling of elation among the Jordanians.[214]

The road remained closed, and West Jerusalem on the verge of starvation. As the city's military governor, Dov Yosef, wrote to Ben-Gurion: "I don't want to add to your difficulties and I am trying to keep up the morale of the inhabitants, but we have food left for only a few days."[215]

The Legion was wary of an Israeli follow-up attempt and asked Iraq and Egypt to help out. Both sent aircraft to strafe Israeli positions west of Latrun, and the Iraqis launched a local assault at Geulim, near Netanya, which the

Haganah command initially interpreted as an effort to drive to the sea and cut Israel in two. The Egyptian advance from Majdal to Isdud during 27–29 May (see below) may also have been, at least in part, a response to the Jordanian request.

But the Israelis were not to be deflected from a second try. The Seventh Brigade was eager to neutralize the effects, on morale and unit prestige, of the debacle. More important, West Jerusalem cried out for relief (especially after the fall of the Jewish Quarter). And there was an international-political imperative: on 29 May the UN Security Council issued a call for a four-week ceasefire—which threatened to freeze the front lines from the moment it went into effect. Ben-Gurion feared that if the road remained blocked, the political settlement that might follow would leave West Jerusalem outside the Jewish State.[216] The road had to be opened.

The Seventh Brigade, now reinforced by the Fifty-second Battalion, Giv-ʿati Brigade (which replaced the decimated Thirty-second, which had been returned to Alexandroni), had five days to plan a second attack. But again it incorrectly assessed the Jordanian deployments; it failed to fathom the quantity and quality of the Legion's positions in the Yalu–Deir Aiyub sector, held by the Second Regiment.[217] And the operational planning was defective. In effect, the Haganah repeated the first attack. Again, instead of mounting a brigade-sized attack on the key objective, the Latrun fort, the Israeli assault was diffuse. The plan called for an eastern effort, by the Seventy-second Battalion and the Fifty-second Battalion—an experienced infantry force—setting out from Beit Susin, to take Deir Aiyub and Yalu, from there hitting Latrun village from the east, and a western effort, by the Seventy-first and Seventy-third battalions, to take the fort and Latrun village from the northwest.

This time (Operation Bin-Nun Bet) it would be a night attack. At about midnight, 30–31 May, the eastern arm silently crossed the road at Bab al-Wad and, dividing in two, began the climb, on foot, to Deir Aiyub (Seventy-second Battalion) and Yalu (Fifty-second Battalion). They hoped to achieve surprise. One company passed through Deir Aiyub, which was empty, but then, climbing the hillock overlooking the village—the site of the tomb of Job—was spotted by Jordanian sentries, and all hell broke loose. Grenades and light weapons, artillery and machine gun fire poured down on the Israelis. Thirteen men were killed and several wounded. The company, mainly composed of new immigrants, broke and ran, retreating southward to Bab al-Wad.

Meanwhile the Fifty-second Battalion, on the right, prepared to assault the spur ("Artillery Ridge") just above Yalu. But the eastern arm's headquarters, hearing of the shambles at Deir Aiyub, ordered the battalion to pull

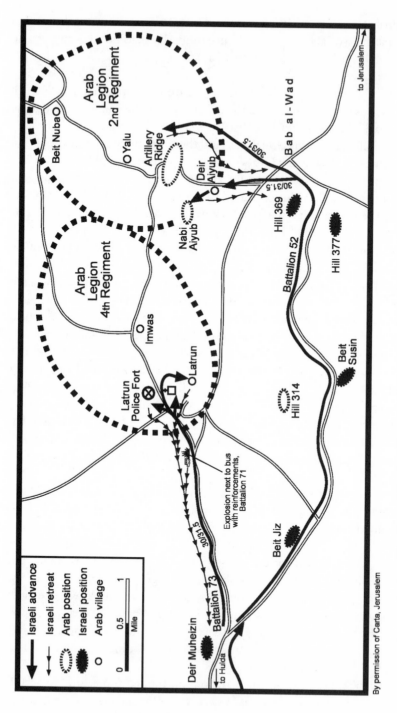

Legend

- → Israeli advance
- ↓ Israeli retreat
- ⬭ Arab position
- ⬬ Israeli position
- ○ Arab village

0   0.5   1
Mile

Map labels:

Arab Legion 2nd Regiment

Arab Legion 4th Regiment

Beit Nuba ○

○ Yalu

Artillery Ridge

Deir Aiyub ○

Nabi Aiyub ○

Bab al-Wad

Hill 369

Battalion 52

Hill 377

Hill 314

Beit Susin

Imwas ○

○ Latrun

Latrun Police Fort ⊗

Explosion next to bus with reinforcements, Battalion 71

30/31.5

30/31.5

Beit Jiz

Deir Muheizin

Battalion 73

to Hulda

to Jerusalem

The Second Battle of Latrun (Bin-Nun bet), Central Front, 30–31 May 1948

By permission of Carta, Jerusalem

back, which it did in orderly fashion, taking only a handful of casualties from Jordanian gunners.[218] By dawn it, too, was back in Bab al-Wad.

The eastern arm of the offensive had failed. Meanwhile, at Latrun, the main, western arm got under way, with an artillery barrage on the fort and the village. The mixed column—the Seventy-third Battalion, with half-tracks, two mounting flamethrowers, and armored cars, some with cannon, and the Seventy-first Infantry Battalion—achieved tactical surprise. Again, though, the effort was dispersed, with one unit heading toward the fort, and two companies heading eastward, for Latrun village and the wood around the adjoining Trappist monastery. The efforts against the village and the monastery were successful: the monastery fell, as did about half the village, pinning down Legion forces that could otherwise have been sent to aid the fort.

Nonetheless, the fort, the main objective, proved too much, though the initial omens were good. A preliminary artillery barrage effectively neutralized the guns inside the complex—the Legionnaires deployed two-pounders on the roof—and the Israeli armored column, composed of five half-tracks and several armored cars, an infantry platoon, and sappers, breached the perimeter fence and reached the fort's walls, spewing fire from the flamethrowers. For a moment, the defenders—Legionnaires and militiamen—were stunned. But the flames afforded clear targets for their six-pounders, overlooking the fort, and grenades. One by one the half-tracks burst into flames, including the one carrying Hadassah Lempel, the radiowoman, who was keeping HQ abreast of the battle. She died. The sappers, with 550 pounds of explosives, managed to blow a hole in the fort's outer wall, but the accompanying infantrymen, in the confusion, did not follow through, and the sappers were eventually overpowered and killed in the ground-floor rooms, the defenders shouting "Allahu Akbar." The operation commander, Haim Laskov, ordered his reserves, D Company, Seventy-first Battalion, to join in. But as they disembarked from their buses at the assembly point, a soldier accidentally detonated a mine. Three soldiers died, and several were wounded. The rest of the company, uncertain about what happened, panicked and fled westward. The explosion attracted heavy Jordanian artillery fire.[219] Colonel Mickey Marcus, the American volunteer and adviser who had just been appointed head of Central Front, summarized: "Artillery cooperation was okay. The armor was fine. The infantry [was] very poor."[220]

The battle was not yet over; Israeli companies still had a foothold outside the fort and in Latrun village. But the news from the eastern arm, at Deir Aiyub, was bad, and, most important, dawn was fast approaching. Laskov understood that even if his troops somehow took the fort and village, they could not hold out against a daylight Legion counterattack backed by ar-

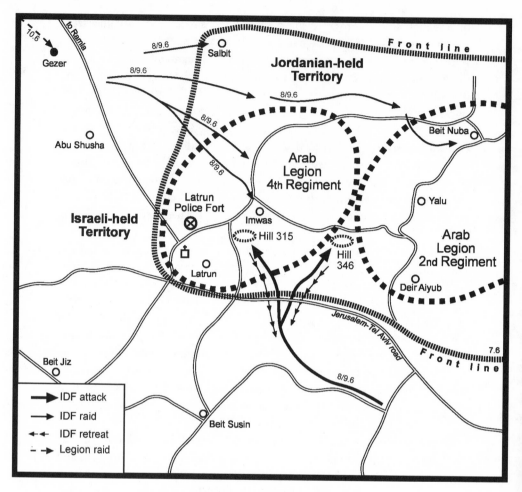

The Third Battle of Latrun, 8–10 June 1948

tillery. He ordered a retreat, directing it from a nearby field.[221] He was the last to leave the area. He later recalled: "I didn't want to come back. . . . I wouldn't have. I no longer cared; if they shot me—they shot me. . . . Suddenly the American photographer Robert Capa arrived with a canteen full of brandy. We sat together. We drank. He said: 'Mickey Marcus orders you back.' I couldn't go. I couldn't understand Jews retreating, fleeing. I couldn't do it. And then Capa said: ' "Mickey" told me to tell you that what this nation now needs is honor, integrity and justice. Move back!' [So] I went back."[222]

The Seventy-third battalion had suffered about 50 percent casualties. Altogether, the two arms of Bin-Nun Bet had forty-four dead and twice that number wounded. Legion casualties are unknown.[223] The Legion's main loss was Lieutenant al-Maaita, the fort's commander, killed either during the battle or in an artillery strike in its wake.

The IDF made one more major attempt against Latrun, on 8–9 June, codenamed Operation Yoram. The Seventh Brigade, sent to the rear to reorganize, was replaced by the Yiftah Brigade. This time the General Staff decided on a concentrated, two-battalion night attack—by Harel's Fifth Battalion and Yiftah's Third Battalion—in the seam between the Legion's Fourth and Second regiments. A third battalion was to provide decoy sorties around the Fourth Regiment's perimeter. The Fifth Battalion was to take the major position—Hill 346—overlooking Latrun and Imwas from the east; the Third Battalion was then to pass through it, take nearby Hill 315, and attack Latrun village and fort.

The operation kicked off with a barrage by four 65 mm cannon and four 120 mm mortars on the fort, Latrun village, and surrounding positions. Hills 346 and 315, each held by a company of the Fourth Regiment, were left untouched to avoid alerting the Legion. The Fifth Battalion set off on foot from Bab al-Wad, took the wrong wadi, and mistakenly approached 315. Near midnight, the Fourth Regiment's sentries spotted them and opened up. The whole front came alive with illumination rounds and artillery. The Fifth Battalion pushed up the slope and, in hand-to-hand combat, successively took 315's two peaks. But the Legion subjected them to withering fire from neighboring positions and then counterattacked. The battle continued for hours, the Legionnaires even calling down artillery on their own positions. The Fifth Battalion sustained heavy casualties.

Meanwhile the Third Battalion, which had set off an hour late, began its climb. It lost eye contact with the Fifth Battalion. When it finally reached the slope of 346, it expected to find the Fifth Battalion in place. Instead, it was met by small arms fire and grenades, then artillery. The battalion radioed HQ and asked that the Fifth be told to cease fire; the Third assumed that the Fifth took them for Jordanians. But HQ refused to believe that this was what was happening, and the Third Battalion's radiomen failed to raise the Fifth directly. So the Third Battalion held its fire and stayed put. It didn't understand what was happening and had no way to solve the problem. It was night and all around were the sounds of battle, from the Fifth Battalion engaged on Hill 315 and from Yiftah's raids along the Fourth Regiment's perimeter, at Salbit, Imwas, and Beit Nuba, which caused little damage but sowed consternation in the Legion brigade HQ.

The Fifth Battalion had taken a key position at the center of the Fourth Regiment's perimeter, causing a partial retreat of Legionnaires from nearby positions. The confusion in Jordanian ranks was probably as great as among the Israelis. But Yiftah HQ decided to call it a day: with daylight fast approaching and without a clear picture of what was happening, in addition to the Fifth battalion reporting heavy casualties and the Third Battalion still out of the fight, Yiftah HQ probably had little choice. Third Battalion was ordered back to Bab al-Wad and at 5:30 AM, the Fifth Battalion was also ordered to retreat. It did so under Jordanian harassment, carrying its casualties through rocky, mountainous terrain to safety.[224] The four-hundred-man battalion had suffered sixteen dead and seventy-nine wounded, all from the lead two companies.[225] The Third Battalion suffered a handful of dead and injured. The Legion suffered several dozen casualties.[226]

Operation Yoram had a painful—for the Israelis—appendage. On 10 June, with the UN-imposed truce to begin the following day, the Legion mounted a last-minute raid; perhaps it was a private initiative of a British Third Brigade officer, Captain T. N. Bromage.[227] A battalion-size force, composed of Legionnaires and irregulars, with a dozen armored cars, attacked Kibbutz Gezer. The settlement was defended by sixty-eight Haganah members (thirteen of them women). After a four-hour fight, the assaulting force, shouting "Deir Yassin, Abu Shusha," overran the kibbutz.[228] A dozen defenders managed to flee; most surrendered. One or two were executed. The Legionnaires protected the rest from the irregulars. The next day, the Legionnaires released the female prisoners. Altogether, twenty-nine Haganah men and two Legionnaires died. The settlement was looted by the irregulars and neighboring villagers.[229] The large IDF forces in the area had failed to intervene because of poor communications. That evening, after the Legionnaires withdrew, Yiftah troops retook the kibbutz from the irregulars.[230]

Operation Yoram had been, in a very real sense, superfluous. There had been no overwhelming need to capture Latrun. On 10 June, an alternative supply route to West Jerusalem was fully functioning, skirting south of the Tel Aviv–Jerusalem road and Latrun. The "Burma Road"—named after a road that bypassed Japanese positions in the Far East in World War II—followed a series of dirt paths linking the Israeli-held abandoned villages of Deir Muheizin, Beit Jiz, Beit Susin, Beit Mahsir, and Saris before returning to the main road at Neve Ilan.

The possibility of an alternative route had first surfaced three weeks before when Palmah scouts had hiked from Kiryat 'Anavim to Hulda without encountering Arabs. On 28 May, the Haganah occupied Beit Jiz and Beit Susin. Their capture in effect gave the Haganah a continuous corridor from Tel Aviv to Jerusalem. The problem would be to render the stretch south of Latrun transport-worthy. On the night of 29–30 May two jeeps, one from the Harel Brigade, heading westward, and the other, from the Seventh Brigade, heading eastward, met just south of Bab al-Wad. During the following days, while engineers flattened out the rocky, steep stretches, jeep convoys from Hulda, hauling 65 mm cannon and mortars, reached the outskirts of West Jerusalem. The Jordanians heard the engineers and the convoys and from Latrun sent salvos of artillery and patrols to disrupt the work—but these efforts were half-hearted and unsuccessful.

Still, though useful in moving equipment, the rough route did not solve West Jerusalem's civilian supply problem, which grew more acute by the day. Starting on 5 June, IDF engineers began resurfacing the route for civilian trucks. By 10 June, it was ready. Thereafter a steady trickle of trucks reached the capital.[231] At the same time, an alternative water pipeline was laid, from Na'an to Bab al-Wad (and from there to Jerusalem), replacing the old pipeline that the Jordanians blocked at Latrun.

By the end of the first month, both sides, though licking their wounds, were generally satisfied. Partition, as they had envisioned back in November 1947, had taken place. 'Abdullah had taken control of much of Arab-populated eastern Palestine, stretching from Jericho to Lydda-Ramla in the west and Tulkarm, Nablus, and Jenin in the north. He had also managed to save East Jerusalem for the Arabs and take the Jewish Quarter, and had administered severe setbacks to the Yishuv. The Haganah/IDF, for its part, had managed to deny the Legion a toehold in West Jerusalem and, despite defeats in Latrun, had found a solution for resupplying Jerusalem. It had held its own against a professional, British-led army and, more important, had regained the initiative. The Jordanians were to remain completely on the defensive for the rest of the war.

Both sides had managed to avoid a war to the finish. Indeed, the Legion had avoided attacking the territory of the UN partition plan Jewish state.[232] But the Legion had suffered serious losses—one intelligence source put them at "some 300 dead and 400–500 wounded"[233]—and its stocks of ammunition, particularly for artillery and mortars, were extremely low. The minuscule Legion could ill afford such a level of casualties or ammunition expenditure. By August, the Legion had shells left for only five days of combat. Indeed, for the six twenty-five-pounder batteries, the mainstay of its artillery, it had only two thousand shells left.[234] And Glubb had no idea if and when more shells, mortar bombs, and bullets would arrive. Jordan, and its patrons in London, henceforward lived in constant fear that the IDF would turn its attention eastward and encircle and destroy the Legion, which all understood was the main prop of the monarchy as well as the only serious obstacle to Israeli conquest of the West Bank.

On the other hand, the IDF—five times larger than the Legion and steadily resupplied from Czechoslovakia—more than made up for its losses in men and ammunition. Within weeks, the IDF was far stronger than it had been on the eve of the battle with the Legion.

THE EGYPTIAN INVASION

Muhammad Mamun Shinawi, the rector of Al-Azhar University, wished the Egyptian expeditionary force, initially consisting of some six thousand troops,[235] Godspeed as it crossed the border at Rafah on 15 May: "The hour of 'Jihad' has struck. . . . A hundred of you will defeat a thousand of the infidels. . . . This is the hour in which . . . Allah promised paradise. . . . Fighters, this is a war there is no avoiding, to defend your women, homes, and the fatherland of your fathers and forefathers."[236] The Egyptian invasion, of course, was geared not—at least in any immediate sense—to defending Egypt but to preventing Israel's establishment or perhaps destroying the Yishuv, and to "saving" the Palestinian Arabs. But, perhaps understandably, Farouk rejected Haj Amin al-Husseini's request to accompany the expeditionary force (or to support the establishment of a Palestinian Arab provisional government).[237]

During the run-up to the war, the Egyptian army had failed to prepare. In line with the Anglo-Egyptian treaty of 1936, the British equipped and helped train the Egyptian army. But during World War II, with its loyalties in doubt, the British did not expand or modernize the force.

But at the end of the war—to meet British Cold War needs—a plan was set in motion to vastly expand the army to three divisions. A team of fifty British officers advised and trained it. In reports home, however, they wrote that the Egyptians were "corrupt," "lazy" "egotists" and "stupid." The initial target, for 1949, was a one infantry-division army with auxiliary armored and artillery contingents and a small navy and air force. But Anglo-Egyptian political tensions, centering on Cairo's demand for the closure of Britain's Canal-side bases, stymied progress. Indeed, in December 1947–January 1948 the Egyptians sent the British military mission packing. Inevitably, this affected not only training but arms deliveries. Except for some Spitfire fighter aircraft, little new equipment reached Egypt during the countdown to the invasion.

At the end of 1947, the Egyptians pressed London, along with requests for heavy equipment—tanks, planes, and artillery pieces—for "a small quantity of mustard gas, phosgene cylinders and tear gas capsules for training purposes." The British said "no."[238]

Though on paper the Egyptian ground forces consisted of four brigades—three infantry and one armor—they were in fact far smaller in May 1948. There were two infantry brigades and one undersized tank battalion (some thirty tanks in all, but without guns), and several dozen armored cars, most of them Bren gun carriers, with some Humber IIIs and IVs and half-tracks dispersed among the infantry battalions. Egyptian artillery consisted of thirty twenty-five-pounders and two dozen or so undependable older pieces (eighteen-pounders and 3.7-inch and 4.5-inch howitzers). There were also some antitank guns.

On paper, the Egyptian air force—the Arab world's largest—consisted of seven squadrons, two of them (with thirty-two serviceable aircraft) of Spitfire IX fighters and two of bombers (mainly converted Dakota C-47 transports). The withdrawal of the British mission rapidly reduced the effectiveness of the force, which lacked qualified pilots, ground crews, and spare parts.[239]

On 26 April General Ahmed Ali al-Muwawi was appointed to command the expeditionary force, whose lead elements were deployed that day in El ʿArish in eastern Sinai; Colonel Mohammed Neguib was his deputy. The force, which crossed into Palestine on 15–16 May and (in Allenby's footsteps) pushed northward into the "Gaza Strip," up the coast road, consisted of a reinforced brigade group, composed of the First, Sixth, and Ninth battalions; a support battalion of three-inch mortars and machine guns; an artillery battalion consisting of twenty-four twenty-five-pounders, a battalion of twenty-four armored cars, and support units, including antitank and antiaircraft guns. During the following three weeks, the Egyptians reinforced the column with an additional regular battalion, the Second, and three reserve battalions, the Third, Fourth, and Seventh, and the battalion of light tanks and some old howitzers,[240] and restructured the expeditionary force into two brigade groups, the Second and Fourth.

But the invasion was preceded by the entry into Palestine, while still under British rule, of two smaller forces, one of Muslim Brotherhood volunteers in April, and the other of regular Egyptian army volunteers on 6 May. These regulars (designated the Light Forces), initially 124 men and four officers, were charged with reconnaissance tasks preceding the invasion. With the invasion, the Light Forces, beefed up with more regulars (and, later, reserve units), were joined to the Muslim Brotherhood volunteers, whose number also substantially increased (some of the additional recruits hailed from the Maghreb),[241] and improvised battalions were organized. The whole force was placed under the command of the Light Forces commander, Colonel Ahmed ʿAbd al-ʿAziz, and was to constitute the right wing of the invasion.

Some of the Muslim Brotherhood volunteers had been in the northern Negev for weeks and had twice unsuccessfully attacked Kibbutz Kfar Darom (on 14 April and 10 May).[242] On 19 May ʿAbd al-ʿAziz's force headed eastward, occupying Beersheba, and then veered northeastward, into the Hebron Hills, passing through Hebron and reaching the Bethlehem area and the outskirts of Jerusalem three days later. On 22–24 May the force joined the Legion and local irregulars in the attack on Kibbutz Ramat Rachel.

It is just possible that this force split from the main Egyptian thrust up the coast road and, "contrary to orders," advanced toward Hebron-Bethlehem because ʿAbd al-ʿAziz refused to accept al-Muwawi's authority and because Palestinian Arab notables from the Hebron-Bethlehem area had pleaded with him to come and protect them.[243] But it is more likely that, at the last minute, Cairo decided to split the expeditionary force and dispatch ʿAbd al-ʿAziz's slapdash brigade northeastward to occupy as much as possible of the West Bank to avert a complete Jordanian takeover. Moreover, installing the brigade in the Hebron-Bethlehem area had the advantage of threatening the left flank of the Israeli forces trying to bar the main Egyptian push northward.

Al-Muwawi's main force advanced slowly and cautiously, up the coast road. The tardiness was due in part to severe logistical disabilities.[244] Nasser, then a major, later recalled that his troops had gone into Palestine without combat rations or a field kitchen: he was given a thousand pounds, and "I bought all the cheese and olives I could lay hands on in Gaza. My heart ached at the thought of the soldier who was to attack fortified positions with his bare body and then sit in a hole like a mouse nibbling away at a piece of cheese. . . . My heart cried out with every beat: 'This is no war.'"[245] Al-Muwawi was also worried by the threat posed by the kibbutzim along his route of march: they could harry his supply convoys and might try to cut off his forward units. He was to expend great resources in subduing the kibbutzim—at the expense of pressing speedily northward.

The Haganah held the northern Negev approaches and the settlement enclave in the northern Negev with two brigades, Givʿati, in the north, with five battalions, and the (Palmah) Negev Brigade, in the south, with two battalions (the Second and Eighth); two additional battalions, the Seventh and Ninth (the latter constituted as a raider force, based on thirty jeeps, each mounting two machine guns), were hastily organized and reached the Negev in the third week of May. Together, the two brigades had some four to five thousand troops. Giv'ati was organized in regular battalions; some of the Negev Brigade's troops, especially from the original two battalions, were dispersed among the settlements. The brigades had several dozen Israeli-made armored cars and two- and three-inch mortars but, in the first days of the invasion, no field artillery or proper armor.

In classic fashion, the Egyptians heralded the invasion with a dawn attack by a foursome of Spitfires on 15 May on Tel Aviv's airfield, Sdeh Dov—where the bulk of the Haganah aircraft were concentrated—and the neighboring Reading Power Station. A number of Israeli aircraft were destroyed and others hit, and five Israelis were killed. The antiaircraft gunners were caught with their pants down.[246] During the following hours additional waves of Egyptian aircraft bombed and strafed targets around Tel Aviv, but with little success. One Spitfire was downed and its pilot captured.[247] (The Egyptian air force continued raiding Tel Aviv during the next six days, the most severe attack, on 18 May, killing forty-two civilians and wounding one hundred in the central bus station.[248] The attacks, and the complete absence of Israeli interceptors, severely, if briefly, shook civilian morale and caused serious economic harm. But Egyptian losses, including five Spitfires shot down by British airmen on 22 May when the Egyptians mistakenly bombed Ramat David Airfield, east of Haifa, which was still in British hands,[249] and more effective anti-aircraft defenses, brought the Egyptian air raids—which were never more than extremely light, by World War II standards—to a halt. By the end of May, the Egyptians had lost almost the whole Spitfire squadron based in El 'Arish, including many of their best pilots.)

Just as the first Egyptian Spitfires were on their way to Tel Aviv, two infantry battalions, reinforced with armor and artillery, crossed the border just south of Rafah and—one battalion for each—attacked the settlements of Nirim, on the western edge of the Negev settlements enclave, and Kfar Darom, which sat astride the Rafah-Gaza road. The two kibbutzim and several neighboring settlements were the Yishuv's first line of defense. They were to prove exceptionally hard nuts to crack; waves of Egyptian troops were severely bled and stalled at each outpost.

When Yitzhak Sadeh, Ben-Gurion's military adviser, proposed immediately abandoning a few of the isolated southern settlements (which, ultimately, were militarily untenable), Ben-Gurion responded: "There is no hurry. Gaining time is a big thing."[250] Ben-Gurion was proved right. The Egyptian thrust lost momentum, and the Haganah gained time in which to reposition its forces and absorb and deploy the heavy weapons that it had purchased in Europe and the United States but had been unable to bring in before 15 May.

Nirim (in Arabic, Dangour) was defended by forty-five well-entrenched Haganah members, twelve of them women, armed only with light weapons (their heaviest armaments were two machine guns and a two-inch mortar with twelve bombs, six of them, as it turned out, duds). The perimeter was mined and well fenced. The local bedouin left the area a few days before on Arab orders; like the bedouin, HIS knew that the kibbutz would be targeted.

The Egyptian Sixth Battalion attacked that morning, pounding the settlement first with artillery and mortars and then with an infantry assault. The Egyptians went in without adequate intelligence or planning.[251] The infantry, perhaps four to five hundred strong, were backed by two batteries of twenty-five-pounders, a battery of three-inch mortars, twenty Bren gun carriers, and half a dozen armored cars mounting two- and six-pounders. But the armor failed to reach, and break through, the perimeter fence, perhaps fearing land mines. The infantry was "slow and . . . appeared lethargic and without energy." The attackers were halted at the perimeter fence and retreated, leaving behind twelve to thirty-five dead; additional casualties were taken to the rear. Nasser, who joined the battalion just after the attack, later recalled: "I felt that the dead left behind at Dangour symbolized the battalion's [lack of] faith in the cause for which it was fighting."[252] Israeli observers estimated that "40%" of the Egyptian casualties were caused by their own mortars.

After the attack, the infantrymen sat down for "lunch," some 650 yards away, within sight of the settlement. The Egyptians then resumed their barrage—and withdrew to Rafah, where they held a "victory rally." Egyptian radio announced that "Dangour" had been taken.[253] During the next two days the Egyptians repeatedly bombed and shelled the settlement, but there were no further infantry assaults. A Palmah squad, with a doctor, reached the settlement between bombardments. The defenders had suffered seven dead and a handful of wounded, and "the settlement [buildings] were completely destroyed."[254]

By the end of that first day, one Negev Brigade officer, Haim Bar-Lev (IDF chief of general staff, 1968–1971), concluded that "the outcome of the war had been settled, because if 45 defenders had withstood about 1,000 [sic] Egyptians, who were aided by fighter aircraft, artillery, and armor, and beat them—then the whole Yishuv would hold out in the war."[255]

Something similar happened at Kfar Darom, which Muslim Brotherhood fighters had previously attacked.[256] On 15 May, the kibbutz was defended by forty members (ten of them women) and twenty Palmah Negev Brigade regulars, who had light weapons, PIATs, and Molotov cocktails. A Palmah relief column was ambushed a mile short of the kibbutz on the night of 14–15 May, and more than a dozen were killed or wounded.

The Egyptian First Battalion, backed by more than a dozen armored vehicles, attacked after dawn. Dozens of infantrymen, and perhaps a few vehicles, were hit, and the battalion, commanded by Said Taha, withdrew—and then, bypassing the settlement, headed for Gaza. Three of Kfar Darom's defenders were killed, and thirty were wounded.[257] A number of Israeli settlements to the east—Nir-ʿAm, Beʾeri, and Beʾerot Yitzhak—were heavily shelled but not assaulted.

That evening, the Ninth Battalion joined the First in Gaza, where al-Muwawi established his headquarters. The next three days were spent reorganizing, while air and artillery forces pounded the Jewish settlements to the east. The Egyptians also dropped leaflets, calling on the settlements to surrender "in the name of the merciful Allah . . . for Allah sides with the Good."[258]

On 19 May the Egyptians resumed their advance northward, immediately taking fire from the roadside Kibbutz Yad Mordechai (in Arabic, Deir Suneid), which, perched on a hill, dominated the coastal road midway between Gaza and Majdal (today Ashkelon). The Hashomer Hatzaʿir kibbutz was founded in 1943 and named after Mordechai Anielewicz, the commander of the Warsaw Ghetto Uprising. Many members were expartisans: "Among us were many whose homes had once before been demolished around them, in the ghettoes of Poland, in Stalingrad," one veteran of the impending battle was to write.[259]

The kibbutz was in territory the United Nations had earmarked for Arab sovereignty. Unlike Nirim and Kfar Darom, the Egyptians could not afford to leave it behind as they advanced northward. The Negev Brigade understood this—and ordered the defenders to stand fast and delay the invaders for as long as possible. The time was needed to bolster the defenses further north and to absorb new weaponry. As Ben-Gurion put it: "This is a race in [that is, against] time. If we hold out for two weeks—we will win."[260] An assembly of the kibbutz members decided on the evacuation of women and children and to fight to the last. On the night of 18–19 May, a small Israeli armored column reached the kibbutz and extricated its ninety-two children (contrary to orders from OC Negev Brigade Nahum Sarig). Left behind were 110 members (twenty of them women) and two squads of Palmahniks, with light weapons, a medium machine gun, and a PIAT.

The Egyptians attacked just after dawn, 19 May, when fighters, batteries of twenty-five-pounders and mortars pounded the settlement. But the First Battalion's assault, supported by a company of armor, just after noon, was driven back after initially breaching the perimeter fence. The Egyptians suffered dozens of dead; the kibbutz, five dead and eleven wounded. Cairo Radio announced that the settlement had fallen.[261] The next morning, 20 May, the assault was resumed by the (fresh) Seventh Battalion, this time supported by gun-mounting armored cars. In desperate hand-to-hand fighting along the perimeter, with much of the kibbutz on fire behind them, the defenders beat back seven assaults. But thirteen more Israelis died and twenty were wounded; dozens of Egyptians also died. That night the Palmah sent in a platoon of reinforcements (which included six British army deserters who had thrown in their lot in with the Jews), with another PIAT and three machine guns.

The Egyptians spent 21–22 May licking their wounds and shelling the kibbutz; the Egyptian air force prevented a relief column from reaching the site. The settlement's buildings were leveled, and the defenders had become "inhabitants of caves and tunnels."[262] By 22 May with dozens of wounded, the defenders were pleading for permission to withdraw. At 7:30 AM they radioed HQ: "Fear a second Kfar ʿEtzion [that is, massacre]. Allow [us] to evacuate, or send help. Extricate the women and wounded." At 11:00 they radioed: "No water. Exhausted." At 2:00 PM they threatened to evacuate that night: "We haven't the strength to defend the settlement."[263]

The Egyptians were determined to take Yad Mordechai. They added another battalion, the Second, and artillery and a tank, which hit the kibbutz through 23 May. Just before sunset, the battalions mounted a joint assault, "preceded by a destructive broom of fire and shells. Four waves . . . tried . . . and four waves fell back as they left behind them a trail of blood of [sic] two hundred dead. . . . They had tanks and artillery and aircraft. . . . And we— we had a few grenades and machine guns. . . . We pressed our human advantage. We had what to fight for—for our beloved settlement, for the children who would come back to the site, and, yes, also for the name . . . of Mordechai Anielewicz. . . . It is possible we did not know it—but our war was a sort of reprisal for his death, there, on foreign soil, in a war without a future."[264]

By nightfall, half the defenders were dead or wounded. Under cover of darkness, the Negev Brigade sent a company of Palmahniks in armored vehicles to extricate the wounded. The column was spotted and attacked, but some vehicles made it through and linked up with the kibbutz. The relief force informed the kibbutzniks that only the wounded were to be extracted; the fit were to fight on. All realized, however, that the situation was hopeless. Contrary to orders, the kibbutzniks decided to break out during the night, on foot. They were assisted by the armored cars, who took out the seriously wounded. The Egyptians haphazardly shelled the area but failed to halt the evacuation. But two members, one of them a woman, Laika Shafir, carrying a wounded Palmahnik, were spotted and surrounded by Egyptian troops, who bayoneted all three. Ben-Gurion subsequently criticized the evacuation.[265]

By morning, the kibbutzniks and Palmahniks had reached Israeli territory. Unaware, the Egyptians continued to shell the kibbutz through the early afternoon of 24 May. Then, hesitantly, they entered the ruins and raised a celebratory cheer; it was the first settlement they had actually vanquished. The price had been heavy; hundreds had died or been seriously wounded, and the Haganah had forced a four-to-five-day delay in the Egyptian advance northward, giving the Giv'ati Brigade time to prepare.[266]

During the last week of May, flying columns of the Negev and Giv'ati Brigades harried the Egyptians. The embryonic IAF also took part, periodically bombing, with converted civilian aircraft, Gaza—the Egyptian headquarters—and its environs. On the night of 25–26 May, sixteen townspeople were reportedly killed by incendiaries and fifty-five- and 110-pound bombs.[267] The Israelis believed that the Egyptian advance "was directed at Tel Aviv."[268] Israeli desperation was such that two Palmah Arab Platoon scouts, David Mizrahi and ʿEzra Afgin (Horin), were sent to Gaza reportedly to poison wells (as well as gather information). They were caught on 22 May near Jibalya with "thermos flasks containing water contaminated with typhoid and diphtheria [or dysentery] germs," according to King Farouk. Mizrahi and Afgin had apparently poured the concoction into one well before being captured and confessing.[269] The two were executed on 22 August.[270] The Egyptians complained to London, but the Foreign Office thought it prudent "to keep out" (though one official minuted that the matter was so "obnoxious" that perhaps, if the opportunity arose, Britain could "express [its] disgust" to the Israelis).[271]

The Egyptians reached Majdal on 24 May and made it their headquarters, setting up a defensive perimeter. Some observers thought that the Egyptians—"wisely"—had, at this stage, in view of their logistical problems, "decided . . . to advance no further."[272]

But on 28 May they renewed their push northward, reaching Isdud (Ashdod), their van digging in less than two miles beyond the village. This last leapfrog may have been prompted by a Jordanian request to relieve the pressure on Latrun—so, at least, the Haganah suspected.[273] (Ben-Gurion said, "The Egyptian army sent to Ashdod doesn't understand what it is fighting for.")[274] But the Egyptians may equally have sought to advance as far as possible toward Tel Aviv or, alternatively, to reach the northern edge (that is, Isdud) of the southern portion of Palestine allotted in the UN partition resolution to the Palestinian Arabs. In any event, the Egyptians never advanced further and quickly lost the initiative—which they were never to regain during the war. In less than a week, two Israeli efforts changed the strategic picture in the south.

In the first action, just before sunset, 29 May, a foursome of Israeli Messerschmitts—the first assembled[275] and sent into action—took off from ʿEqron Airfield, less than ten miles from Isdud. Givʿati Brigade's "Cultural Officer," the poet (and former anti-Nazi partisan) Abba Kovner, witnessing the take-off, wrote: "All that the Jewish people had . . . was sent aloft."[276]

One of the pilots was ʿEzer Weizman (who was to command Israel's air force in the 1960s and was later to serve as the state's president). He later recalled: "As soon as we got up into the air, we could see anti-aircraft fire directed at us from . . . Ashdod. We swung out to sea, climbing to 7,000 feet, and swooped toward the Egyptian column. The sight took my breath away. The Egyptian Army, in all its power and glory, was spread along the road and knew, more or less, what stood between it and Tel Aviv—two and a half companies of the Givʿati Brigade, anxiety-stricken and exhausted. I must confess I had a profound sense of fulfilling a great mission."[277] The lead pilot, Lou Lenart, who had flown in the US Air Force in the Philippines, was quoted by Ben-Gurion as saying that "he had never encountered such AA fire."[278] Each pilot made three passes, bombing the center of Isdud and strafing the Egyptian troops. By conventional standards, the attack was a failure. Few if any Egyptians were killed; all three planes' 20 mm cannon stopped firing after the first burst. One plane was shot down and another crash-landed, badly bending a wing. But the attack had a strong psychological impact. One intercepted Egyptian radio message stated: "We have been heavily attacked by enemy aircraft, we are dispersing."[279] Conversely, the watching Israeli troops nearby were uplifted by the spectacle; for the first time, they were receiving real air support.[280] Thereafter the Egyptians felt that they had lost air supremacy and remained fearful of air attack.

The next blow was on the ground. Fearing a resumption of the advance on Tel Aviv, HGS ordered the Givʿati and Negev Brigades to attack and "destroy" the Egyptian vanguard.[281] In *mivtza pleshet* (Operation Philistia) or the Battle of Isdud—mistakenly portrayed in traditional Zionist historiography as the crucial action in which the Egyptian advance was stymied—some two thousand IDF soldiers faced a slightly larger force of twenty-five hundred entrenched Egyptians, of the First, Second, and Ninth battalions. Moreover, the Israelis dispersed their effort in a way that increased their numerical disadvantage at most points of contact.

Elements of the two Israeli brigades, supported by a battery of 65 mm artillery and a pair of 120 mm mortars, attacked Isdud and the Isdud (or Suqreir) Bridge to the north on 2–3 June. They briefly captured houses on the village outskirts but were driven off with serious losses.[282] Elsewhere, the

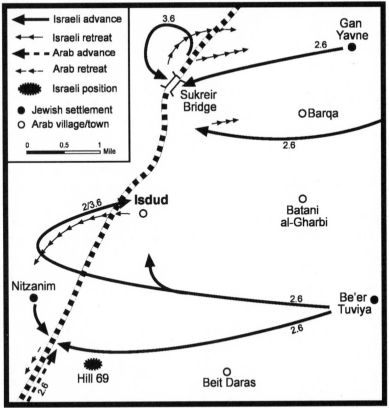

The Battle of Isdud, Operation Pleshet, 1–3 June 1948

attackers were firmly repulsed by the Egyptians; many were hit during the retreat. Some fifty Israelis were killed or went missing, and another fifty were wounded; Egyptian losses are unknown.

But the unsuccessful attack caused alarm, amounting almost to panic, in the Egyptian command, which feared that their forces north of Majdal were overstretched and might be cut off. One Egyptian diarist recorded: "Front commander [Neguib] reports that his forces were bombarded from the air, by artillery and by mortars and that the Jews launched an assault which was barely beaten off. The headquarters was badly damaged and the telephone lines were cut."[283] The fear of being cut off was exacerbated by a Giv'ati ambush just south of Isdud, which shot up a supply column from Majdal. An additional reason for Israeli joy was the success that day, 3 June, of the lone operational Israeli Messerschmitt, piloted by Mordechai Allon. He intercepted and downed two converted Egyptian Dakotas on a bombing mission over Tel Aviv.[284]

The Egyptian advance had come to a halt before Operation Pleshet. But the attack nonetheless had serious—and, from the Israeli perspective, positive—consequences. An Arab chronicler, Kamal Ismail al-Sharif, was to write: "In accordance with the plan worked out by the Arab states, the Egyptian army was to have advanced to Yibna [Yavneh], but immediately upon the arrival of the Egyptian van at Isdud, the enemy . . . launched a strong attack. . . . Though it was repulsed, the enemy achieved at least one objective—the pinning down of the Egyptian army . . . in Isdud. It would be no exaggeration to say that the Jewish attack on Isdud was a turning point in the Israeli-Egyptian struggle. . . . The Egyptian command was forced to change its plans: instead of continuing to chase after the Zionist gangs, the command decided to limit itself to severing the Negev from the rest of the country."[285] In other words, all thought of driving on Yavneh and onward to Tel Aviv was driven out of Egyptian minds. Al-Muwawi radioed Cairo that, lacking men and equipment, and already overextended, he "could not advance one step further" without courting disaster.[286]

But the Egyptians had achieved one important success before coming to rest at Isdud: during the battle for Yad Mordechai, the First Battalion had advanced eastward, from Majdal, along the road through Faluja to Beit Jibrin, linking up with the right arm of the invasion force in the Hebron hills. The troops dug in and established a chain of positions on either side of the road, thus both securing the west-east axis and linking the invasion's two arms, and cutting off the two dozen Jewish settlements south of the road, effectively besieging them and the Negev Brigade. At the same time, as Nasser later pointed out, this also had the effect of further dispersing the Egyptian expeditionary force "at the end of long lines of communication. [The battalions] became so scattered that their main concern was to defend themselves and protect their lines of communication. . . . We had lost all power of initiative."[287]

During the following months Egyptian energies were devoted to maintaining, and even expanding, the west-east chain of positions and to assuring the continued siege of the settlement enclave—while Israeli energies were devoted to breaking through, lifting the siege, and linking up with the settlements while driving a wedge between the western and eastern arms of the Egyptian army.

About halfway between Majdal and Beit Jibrin stood the ʿIraq Suweidan police fort, which dominated the west-east road as well as a (secondary) north-south road running east of and parallel to the coast road. The Israelis were to dub the fort at the crossroads "the monster on the hill." With its evacuation by the British on 12 May, it had been occupied by Muslim Brotherhood irregulars. On 22 May, Egyptian regulars replaced them and then unsuccessfully attacked the well-fortified Kibbutz Negba, about a mile to the north.[288] Negba was to remain a focus of Egyptian attention until the start of the First Truce on 11 June.

On 1–2 June the Egyptian First Battalion attacked in force, with hundreds of infantrymen back by fighter-bombers, a company of light tanks, a company of armored cars, and three batteries of field artillery. The settlement's seventy members, reinforced by seventy Givʿati troopers, beat them off. At one point Egyptian armor broke through the perimeter fence but was driven off by Molotov cocktails and a lone PIAT. The defenders were helped, at a crucial moment, by the arrival of a column of machine-gun mounting Negev Brigade jeeps, which struck the attackers from the flank. The Egyptians retreated. The defenders suffered eight dead and eleven wounded; the Egyptians, more than a hundred casualties.[289]

After Isdud and the failure at Negba, all thought of further aggressive action seems to have vanished in the Egyptian command. Indeed, Kirkbride conjectured that the Egyptians had "entered into a tacit mutual non-interference pact with the Jewish Colony [that is, colonies] in the area of Palestine which they occupy . . . a case of live and let live."[290]

But this was far-fetched. The Egyptians were to take one more settlement, Kibbutz Nitzanim, between Majdal and Isdud. The Egyptians had bypassed it in their advance northward. But with a truce just days away, they could not afford to leave it astride their main supply route. On 6–7 June, the Ninth Battalion, supported by troops from the Seventh Battalion, armor, artillery, and fighter-bombers, launched a determined assault and, despite an initial repulse, penetrated the perimeter fence. Gradually they rolled up the 140 defenders. Among the attackers was ʿAbd al-Hakim ʿAmr (Nasser's friend and colleague, later the Egyptian army's chief of staff and defense minister, who committed suicide, or was murdered by Nasser's agents, in 1967 following the Egyptian defeat in the Six Days' War). The IDF command failed to send reinforcements, and the settlement's lone PIAT was put out of action early in the battle. Thirty-three of the defenders were dead and sixteen wounded when the outpost's commanders realized that further resistance was useless and opted for surrender. The Egyptians prevented their local auxiliaries from massacring the POWs. One hundred and five Israelis surrendered.[291] Three or four were subsequently murdered by the Egyptians or irregulars. Among them were Avraham Schwarzstein, the settlement OC, and his radiowoman, Mira Ben-Ari. The two, carrying a white flag, had left their bunker and walked toward a group of Egyptian officers. One Egyptian, ʿAbd al-Munʿim Khalif, drew a pistol and emptied it into Schwarzstein. Ben-Ari shot Khalif dead, and the other Egyptians then shot Ben-Ari.[292]

The unauthorized surrender was regarded by the IDF command as "shameful": "It is better to die in the trenches of [our] homes, than to surrender to the murderous invader," insisted the Givʿati battle broadsheet, written two days later by Abba Kovner. [293]For their part, the kibbutz members and the political body the kibbutz belonged to, the liberal Haʿoved Hatzioni, charged that the high command, dominated by socialists, had been indifferent to Nitzanim's fate and had failed to arm the kibbutz adequately or to send a relief force. Kovner's attack was seen as adding insult to injury. At war's end, the kibbutzniks demanded a committee of inquiry. In April 1949, the committee ruled that the kibbutzniks and soldiers had fought bravely and that the high command should have reinforced the settlement. It "rehabilitated" the fighters and criticized Kovner—but also cleared Givʿati's commanders of any political bias in their dealings with the kibbutz.[294]

To be sure, the stubborn resistance of the kibbutzim along the Egyptian line of advance had demonstrated that the expeditionary force lacked the wherewithal even to push beyond Isdud, let alone reach Tel Aviv. By the end of May, al-Muwawi had hunkered down just north of Isdud, eighteen miles short of Tel Aviv. Perhaps those had been his orders from the first, or perhaps the resistance and the size and incompetence of his forces and supply problems had been decisive.

By the start of the First Truce, the Egyptian battalions were strung out and entrenched along the road between Rafah and Isdud, between Majdal and Beit Jibrin, and between Beersheba and Bethlehem; its lines were long and vulnerable and its forces dispersed. The Egyptians were no longer capable of mounting a serious offensive.

THE INVASIONS IN THE NORTH

The Iraqis

As with the Egyptian army, at the end of World War II, under British tutelage, plans were tabled for the modernization and expansion of the Iraqi army, which had been established with British assistance in the 1930s. The five-year plan called for a three-division army with an armored brigade and a five-squadron air force. Here, too, the thinking was geared to a possible Soviet threat. But Anglo-Iraqi relations were seriously subverted in January 1948 when riots erupted in Baghdad after the signing of a new Anglo-Iraqi defense agreement in Portsmouth. These halted cooperation in the five-year plan and the supply of additional British weapons, though a last-minute transfer of ammunition was completed in early spring.

On the eve of the invasion the Iraqi army consisted of two underequipped, undersized infantry divisions and a poorly equipped armored brigade, with some 120 armored cars, about seventy of them Humber IVs and Daimlers mounting two-pounder or six-pounder guns. The army had two operational artillery battalions, one equipped with modern twenty-five-pounders and the other, with obsolescent 3.7-inch and 4.5-inch howitzers. There were also two batteries of six-inch howitzers in extremely poor condition. Most of the artillery ammunition was old and undependable; some of it dated from 1916–1917, though the twenty-five-pounders had a stock of eighteen thousand modern shells. The army also had seventeen-pounder antitank guns and some antiaircraft artillery. In March 1948 the Iraqi air force boasted sixty-two aircraft, about half of them Anson transport planes that were convertible to bombers and Gladiator fighter-bombers. Only three were modern Fury fighter-bombers. All the rest were old and in poor maintenance. Another seven Furies reached Iraq during April and May, but without guns, ammunition, or spare parts.[295]

In April and early May, Iraq prepared three brigade groups for dispatch to Palestine. The expeditionary force, initially numbering some forty-five hundred soldiers, was commanded by Major General Mustapha Raghib (who was replaced, in effect, in September by the army's commander-in-chief, Saleh Saib al-Juburi). Iraq decided to intervene at a cabinet meeting on 22 or 23 April; the news of the fall of Arab Haifa had apparently been decisive.[296] The Iraqis told Britain that, "in face of the continued Zionist aggression ['Deir Yassin, Tiberias and . . . [the] terrible massacre at Haifa'], she must take necessary measures to prevent a disaster which would threaten the very life of Palestine Arabs and be fraught with danger to Iraq itself";[297] she was "bound" to do so "as an Arab State" and "also because public opinion in Iraq insisted that some action should be taken."[298] But the expeditionary

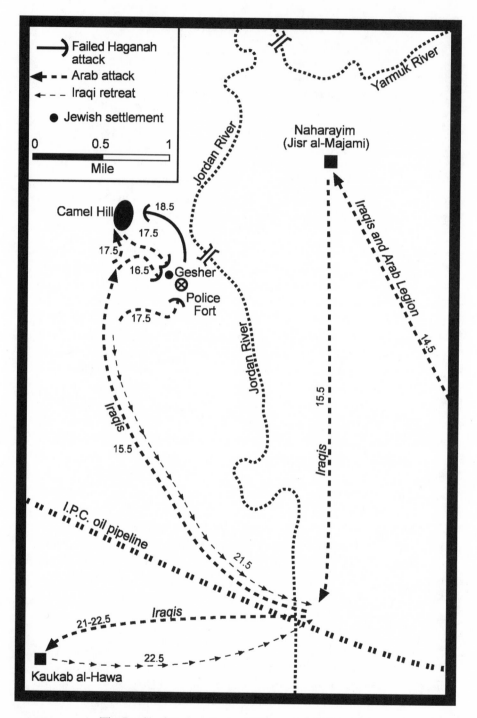

The Battle of Gesher, Jordan Valley, 15–22 May 1948

force, crossing through Jordan with ʿAbdullah's agreement, moved very slowly, owing to logistical problems and poor roads.

Iraq's Second Brigade Group, consisting of two infantry battalions, an armored car battalion, and a battalion of twenty-five-pounders, began arriving in Mafraq, Jordan, at the end of April.[299] The Iraqi force was to constitute the Legion's "junior partner" and right wing, first in the Jordan Valley and subsequently in the hills and foothills of northern Samaria. But it had come with an agenda of its own. Apart from helping to crush the Jewish state, the Iraqis appeared interested in reaching Haifa, on the way conquering the area on either side of the length of the Iraq Petroleum Company pipeline that conveyed oil from fields near Mosul through the Lower Galilee to Haifa.[300]

On the evening of 14 May, the brigade occupied the Naharayim (Jisr al-Majami) electricity plant, an Israeli enclave just east of the Jordan. But finding the two bridges across the river demolished, they turned south. On the morning of 15 May they forded the river, their objective Kibbutz Gesher and the neighboring police fort, which overlooked the river. The kibbutz was pounded by artillery through the day. "We are surrounded since last night. 3″ mortars are intermittently hitting us. Two aircraft dropped bombs. It is not known to whom they belong," radioed Gesher.[301] The Israelis opened the floodgates at the Degania and Dalhamiya dams, raising the level of the Jordan, but without real effect; the Iraqis kept crossing.

On 16 May the Iraqis captured Camel Hill, northwest of Gesher, and launched simultaneous infantry attacks on the kibbutz and the fort. Israeli Piper Cubs pinpricked the Iraqis from the air, and the defenders repulsed the Iraqis, inflicting heavy losses. The following day the Iraqis renewed the assault, this time with armored cars and infantry. The armored cars broke into the fort's courtyard but were beaten back by a hail of Molotov cocktails. Six cars were put out of action. The Iraqis then besieged the settlement for five days. Israeli counterattacks, under a hot Jordan Valley sun (on 18 May more than a dozen troopers fainted from the heat),[302] failed to dislodge them from the Camel. The Iraqis tried one more direct assault and then, on 22 May, attempted indirection—by scaling the heights of Kaukab al-Hawa, the site of the Crusader fortress of Belvoir, dominating the area from the west. But Golani Brigade troops who had dug in on the crest the day before beat them off.[303] Witnessing the Iraqi fiasco was the regent, ʿAbd al-Ilah.[304] The Haganah had made effective use of two of the 65 mm cannon that two days before had been used so tellingly against the Syrians a few miles to the north (see below).

The Iraqis' situation, stranded on the west bank of the Jordan without bridges for resupply and with Gesher and Golani robustly fighting back, was unproductive and, in the long run, precarious. And Glubb needed them elsewhere. Under IDF pressure in Jerusalem and in desperate need of the Legion's First Battalion bivouacked around Nablus, Glubb pressed the Iraqis to leave Gesher and to redeploy in Samaria.[305]

On 22 May the Iraqis threw in the towel and withdrew back across the Jordan. The brigade group, now joined by the forward elements of two further brigade groups, the First and Third, drove southward along the east bank and then crossed the river westward at the Damiya Bridge into Samaria. During the First Truce, in June and July, two further scratch brigades, the Fourth and Fifth, joined the Iraqi force in the West Bank.[306] By September, the Iraqi expeditionary force, with five brigades, consisted of eighteen thousand soldiers, making it the largest Arab army in Palestine.[307] A handful of British officers "advised" the Iraqi army until they were ordered home in early June 1949.[308]

Once in Samaria, the Iraqis were largely inactive. But renewed Haganah pressure on the Legion at Latrun resulted in a minor Iraqi attack, at Glubb's request, to disperse Haganah energies. On 28 May an Iraqi battalion attacked and took part of the Coastal Plain settlement of Geulim, southeast of Netanya. Alexandroni troops counterattacked—while the Iraqis were busy looting—and retook it.[309] A handful of IAF aircraft periodically bombed and strafed the Iraqis during the next three days.[310] The Iraqis hunkered down in Samaria and made no further offensive efforts, except the capture on 30–31 May of Ras al-ʿEin water pumping station, midway between Geulim and Lydda.

The IDF decided to take on the Iraqis at the northern tip of their perimeter, in Jenin. It is unclear what motivated the General Staff: a desire to preempt a possible Iraqi push toward the Jezreel Valley or to the Mediterranean through Israel's narrow "waist" (at places a mere ten miles wide from the Arab lines to the sea); a desire to draw Legionnaires away from Latrun or to prevent Iraqi assistance to the Legion; or merely to grab additional land before the UN truce came into effect.[311]

In preliminary operations, on 28–30 May, Golani units advanced southward from the Jezreel Valley and captured a string of Palestinian villages: Zirʿin, Nuris, and al-Mazar, in the Gilboʿa foothills, and the crest of Mount Gilboʿa itself, as well as Tel Meggido and the village of Lajjun to the west. The area had been held only by a ragtag collection of militiamen. Its conquest paved the way for the advance on Jenin.

On 1–2 June Moshe Carmel launched the core of the offensive, using the Carmeli Brigade's two battalions, the Twenty-first and Twenty-second, and Golani's Thirteenth Battalion, with additional Golani companies in reserve. The objective was to conquer Jenin and surrounding villages and "to kill and destroy the enemy."[312] Golani swiftly overran the villages of Sandala, Muqei-

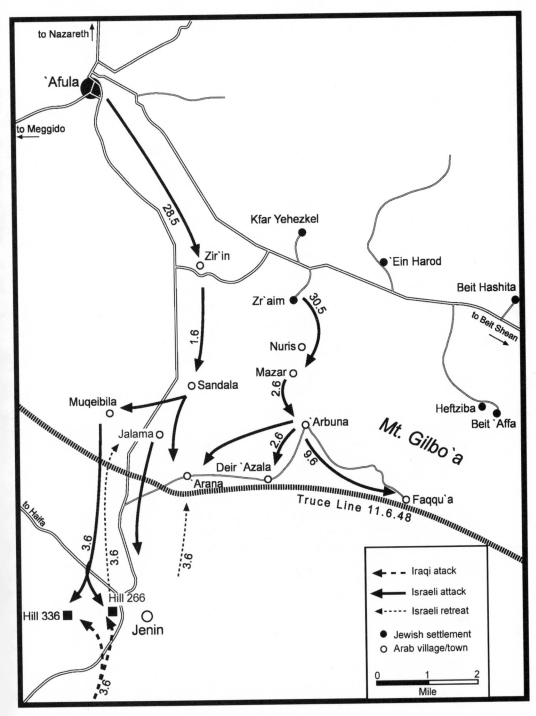

The Battle of Jenin, 1–3 June 1948

bila, Jalama, and ʿArana, and on the morning of 3 June Carmeli, in three columns, moved on Jenin itself. But although the Twenty-first Battalion managed to occupy three hills overlooking the town from the west, the Twenty-second and an armored bus column failed to take some of their objectives, including the key Jenin police fort to the east, and parts of the town itself. The troops suffered from the intense heat and from an inability to dig in on the rock-encrusted hills.

Jenin's defenders, consisting of several companies of Iraqi troops and local irregulars, resisted stubbornly until a fresh battalion of Iraqis—apparently commanded by Lieutenant Colonel ʿOmar ʿAli[313]—and a battery of artillery arrived from Nablus. A confused seesaw battle ensued. Iraqi air attacks and the arrival of the reinforcements, who mounted a determined counterattack, broke the back of the Twenty-first Battalion. The battalion had bad luck. A chance shell hit its command post and killed and injured several officers, including the battalion's deputy commander, Shraga Mustobolski, who reportedly muttered "how awful and difficult to be wounded in such a place" before dying;[314] and a rumor spread that a retreat had been sounded. The companies in the hilltops west of Jenin, having taken severe losses, broke and fled from one hilltop position after another. Flight proved infectious. Some of the retreating troops reached Twenty-second Battalion positions, which also began to crumble.

Throwing in his reserves, Carmel managed, by nightfall, to occupy the center of Jenin, now mostly abandoned. But the retreat of the Twenty-first Battalion and the precarious situation of the Twenty-second to the east of town, while the Iraqis held onto the police fort and harassed all IDF movement to the north, left the troops in the town center badly exposed. Carmel informed the General Staff that his situation was critical and offered a choice: if the IDF mounted an assault on Tulkarm, to relieve the pressure in Jenin, he would order his troops to stand fast; otherwise, he would retreat.

The General Staff responded that no attack could or would be launched against Tulkarm; Alexandroni wasn't up to it. He must decide. Carmel ordered a general retreat, and the units in Jenin, along with the Twenty-second Battalion, on the night of 3–4 June withdrew northward. By morning the IDF had redeployed along a line just south of ʿArana.[315] The Israelis had suffered thirty-four dead and one hundred wounded; the Iraqis and irregulars, perhaps some two hundred dead.[316] The IDF had narrowly missed delivering a major blow to the invaders.[317]

Jenin had been a nasty defeat; superior IDF forces had been routed by a small number of Iraqis and irregulars. But as often happens in war, defeat can sometimes produce strategic dividends. The abortive attack on Jenin (coupled with a minor success by Alexandroni troops at Qaqun, northwest of

Tulkarm) had persuaded the Iraqis—much as had happened with the Egyptians after Yad Mordechai and Isdud—to sit tight and not to venture again out of the Arab-populated "Triangle." The nightmare scenario of an Iraqi thrust to the Mediterranean across Israel's narrow waist had been averted.

The Syrians

With independence in 1946, the Syrian government had planned to enlarge its army to division size, with three brigade groups. But as with the Egyptian and Iraqi military plans, May 1948 caught the Syrians on the hop. On paper, the army mustered some ten thousand soldiers.[318] In reality, owing to a lack of weapons, ammunition, and trained manpower, only one brigade, the First, commanded by Colonel ʿAbd al-Wahab Hakim, was more or less ready; Hakim, indeed, apparently argued that it was not.[319] The brigade had about two thousand troops and consisted of two infantry battalions, an armored battalion with a company of light Renault 35 and Renault 39 tanks (mounting 37 mm cannon), and two companies of armored cars, some mounting light cannon. The brigade had four-six batteries of 75 mm and 105 mm guns.[320]

Another brigade, the Second, was still being organized and would consist of two infantry battalions and a battalion of armored cars. The infantry was equipped mainly with obsolescent French rifles, though some of the soldiers carried British and German makes. The Syrian air force consisted of about twenty Harvard trainers, converted for use as fighters or bombers, and a number of light aircraft. A large proportion of the planes were unfit for action, as were many of the pilots. The Syrians suffered from a shortage of ammunition.[321]

The Syrian invasion got off to a poor start because of the last-minute change in the Arab war plan and because of the army's low "work standards" (as one Israeli observer was to put it: "The Syrians would generally fight in the morning. During the afternoon they would take a light siesta, and at night they would go to sleep in orderly fashion").[322]

Instead of pushing into northern Galilee from southern Lebanon, the First Brigade made tracks on 14 May for the Golan, from which it was to cross into Palestine at the southern tip of the Sea of Galilee. The Syrians aimed to help "save Palestine" and destroy Israel. But their immediate military objectives are less clear. Apparently, they had the vague aim of reaching Afula, linking up with the Iraqi army and heading for the Mediterranean at Haifa or Netanya, thus cutting the Jewish state in two or at least isolating the north.[323] But it is also possible that the Syrians intended only limited local gains, such as the conquest of Tiberias or even the whole of the Sea of Galilee shoreline, which they could then tout as a "victory."

The Syrian Invasion and its rebuff, 15–20 May 1948

Back in February, Syrian politicians apparently told the visiting Palestinian leader Musa al-ʿAlami—in line with traditional "Greater Syria" ambitions—that they were interested in gaining control of "all Palestine" or at least its "Arab areas."[324] But by mid-May, their ambitions appear to have been reduced substantially. On 18 May, the British minister in Damascus reported that the "combined Syrian-Iraqi objective is Tiberias."[325] To judge from the Syrians' actions, he may have been right (at least as regards Syria).

Early on 15 May, elements of the ill-equipped Syrian Second Brigade attacked Kibbutz ʿEin-Gev, on the Sea of Galilee's eastern shore. At dawn, a lone fighter-bomber dove on the kibbutz and released a brace of bombs; they missed. Syrian infantry opened up with machine guns. The children and many of the women were already in shelters, and the men were in the perimeter trenches. The following night, after a heated debate, the kibbutz sent its 150 children, accompanied by seventy older members, by boat to Tiberias and safety. The Haganah regional commander reacted angrily; ʿEin-Gev had not received permission. ʿEin-Gev's poorly armed defenders awaited the ground assault.[326] But none came.

In fact, ʿEin-Gev was a diversion. The main, First Brigade's, assault, commanded by Colonel Hakim, was mounted at the southern end of the lake, into the lower Jordan Valley. Facing the Syrians was Golani's Twelfth (Barak) Battalion and local militiamen, dispersed in the kibbutzim. A company of the Palmah's Yiftah Brigade, and militia platoons from settlements farther afield, joined the fray during the following days.

The Syrians began crossing the border at al-Hama in the early hours of 15 May, shelling the kibbutzim to its west throughout the day. One infantry company attacked Kibbutz Shaʿar Hagolan but was beaten back. A kibbutz member described what she saw that evening, when she left her guard post and went to the shelter: "The children were wet with sweat. Inside it was crowded, all the noncombatant inhabitants were inside. Girls, members' parents, pregnant women, it was impossible to reach and see [my] girl. . . . I returned to the post."[327] (Later that night, the children and many women were evacuated.) Half a mile to the north, a Syrian battalion occupied the ridge of Tel al-Qasir and pushed westward, taking the former Animal Quarantine Station, on the eastern edge of Samakh, and then attacked the village itself. The situation was confused; Haganah platoons from Jordan Valley settlements hastily deployed in the empty village. Two 20 mm cannon, a PIAT, a handful of bombing missions by Haganah Air Service Piper Cubs, and a company from the Golani Brigade were to prove crucial, and the Syrians were beaten back. Outside Tiberias, the Jews built barricades and fortifications; they believed the town was next. "The situation was very grave.

There aren't enough rifles. There are no heavy weapons," Ben-Gurion told the Cabinet.[328]

The Syrian brigade, spearheaded by cannon-mounting armored cars, attacked Samakh again on 16 May. Again, the attack was beaten back, though the Syrians gained a toehold by occupying the former British army camp on the village's eastern edge. Syrian President al-Quwwatli, flanked by Prime Minister Jamil Mardam and Defense Minister Taha al-Hashimi, visited the front that day. Al-Quwwatli instructed his troops "to destroy the Zionists."[329]

At dawn on 18 May, the First Brigade, now reinforced by an additional infantry battalion, renewed the attack on Samakh. Advancing in two columns, led by armored vehicles, this time including light Renault 35 tanks, and backed by artillery, the Syrian infantry outflanked the village from the south. The fire from the Syrians' 75 mm cannon and 81 mm mortars was accurate and devastating—while the Israeli 20 mm guns jammed.[330] The defenders retreated in confusion, westward, to Kibbutz Degania Aleph, leaving wounded and dying in Samakh's rubble. Syrian artillery "chased" the retreating troops. But al-Quwwatli reprimanded his officers for wasting shells.[331] By noon, the Syrians had reached, and taken, the police fort on the western edge of the village. Israeli losses that morning were three captured and fifty-four dead, most of them Jordan Valley kibbutzniks.[332] (The Syrian general staff had a poor picture of what was happening. They appear to have believed that the Lebanese army had—also—crossed the border and conquered three settlements south of Ras al-Naqurah.)[333]

The fall of Samakh shook the morale of the Jordan Valley Haganah—and precipitated a minor crisis in HGS. There was even confusion about the identity of the invaders. Ben-Gurion jotted down in his diary: "We have received word that the Legion has occupied Samakh. . . . There is something of a panic in the Jordan Valley."[334] Moshe Dayan, the Haganah's Arab affairs officer, was appointed OC of all forces in the area. The Syrian advance now threatened the kibbutzim Sha'ar Hagolan and Masada, south of Samakh, and Degania Aleph (Dayan's birthplace and the first kibbutz) and Degania Bet, to the west. Without permission from headquarters, the members of Sha'ar Hagolan and Masada abandoned their homes and fled to nearby Kibbutz Afikim.[335] The abandoned sites were immediately looted by local Arabs. The Deganias evacuated their women and children.

That night, 18–19 May, a newly arrived company of Yiftah Brigade troops counterattacked at Samakh but was driven back. The company came across "tens of bodies" of Jews who had died in the Syrian assaults on the village.[336] That same night, a seaborne platoon from 'Ein-Gev landed at Samra, to the south, and raided the Syrian concentration on Tel al-Qasir. Though unsuccessful, the raid may have delayed the subsequent Syrian push on the Deganias by twenty-four hours, which were well used by the Israelis to prepare.[337] That night, another Yiftah company crossed the Jordan eastward and attacked the Syrian camp at the Customs House, near the main Bnot Yaʿakov Bridge, north of the Sea of Galilee. The raid was a major success. The Syrian defenders, one or two companies, fled after a brief firefight, and the Palmahniks, without loss, destroyed the camp and a number of vehicles, including two armored cars.[338]

But commando raids do not win battles, and by 19 May morale in the lower Jordan Valley had plummeted. The events at Samakh, Shaʿar Hagolan, and Masada had badly affected the inhabitants. "In several settlements the spirit of resistance had collapsed because of the strength and armor of the enemy," reported two veteran kibbutzniks. They added that without further reinforcements, the remaining settlements could not hold out.[339] A delegation of kibbutz members set out for Tel Aviv. But even without seeing them, the Haganah high command set about repairing the damage. Reinforcements were readied, and a back-stiffening order was issued by Yadin: "No point should be abandoned. [You] must fight at each site."[340] Yadin and Ben-Gurion faced off over the Yishuv's only available asset, the battery of four pre–World War I 65 mm mountain guns (without proper sights). Ben-Gurion wanted to send them to Jerusalem; Yadin insisted on the Jordan Valley. Ben-Gurion backed down, and to the valley they went, arriving in the nick of time on the slopes to the west of the Deganias.[341]

The denouement of 20 May came as something of a surprise—and not only to the Syrians. As anticipated by the Haganah, the Syrians launched a major push against the two Deganias. The defenders—about seventy in Degania Aleph and eighty in Degania Bet, the majority kibbutz members, with a leavening of Haganah and Palmah squads[342]—were ordered to fight, and die, where they stood; there could be no retreat.

The defenders enjoyed the support of three 20 mm guns at Beit Yerah, enfilading the road from Samakh to Degania Aleph, and four 81 mm mortars, three of them positioned in Kinneret, a kibbutz just to the north, and the fourth at Degania Aleph itself. The kibbutz also had a Davidka mortar, but it exploded during the battle, injuring a crewman. Each of the Deganias also had a PIAT with fifteen projectiles. And the Haganah had the battery of 65 mm mountain guns.

The Syrians attacked at dawn. First there was a half-hour artillery barrage on the two kibbutzim. Then the Third Infantry Battalion, backed by eight to twelve Renault 35 tanks and about twenty armored cars, in three columns, advanced across the seven hundred yards separating the Samakh police fort from Degania Aleph's eastern redoubts.

The Israelis let loose with all they had—and the Syrian infantry halted. But the tanks and their train of armored cars inched forward. "I waited for the [lead] tank to reach 35–40 meters [from me] and I fired one shot from the shoulder. I think the projectile was a dud. I had no choice but to straighten up [out of the trench]. I fired one shot from the hip and I hit him," recalled Yitzhak Eshet, the PIAT man at Degania Aleph. The tank was immobilized. (In the tank's logbook, later found inside by the Israelis, its commander, Lieutenant Faiz Khadfi, had jotted down a few minutes earlier: "We attacked a settlement west of Samakh.")[343] The 20 mm cannon then hit two armored cars behind the tank. Another two tanks were set alight by grenades and Molotov cocktails after they had trampled the kibbutz's outer perimeter fence. The armored column was still operational. But it had left its infantry, pinned down, hundreds of yards behind. The remaining tanks and armored cars turned around and pulled back.[344] By 7:45 AM the assault had halted, though Syrian troops, digging in, still held most of the territory between the Samakh police fort and Degania Aleph's fence.

Then it was the turn of Degania Bet. Artillery and tanks shelled the out-works. Around noon the Syrians advanced. They were stopped about a hundred yards from the perimeter fence. The defenders fought grimly, their homes just yards behind them. The Syrians began to dig in.

The Deganias had stopped the Syrians, but they were still just beyond the perimeter fences, harassing the settlements with cannon fire and light arms. The stalemate didn't last. The five-truck convoy, with the four 65 mm mountain guns, had slowly made its way northward from Pardes Katz in the coastal plain. They reached the heights of Alumot, above the Deganias, soon after noon. At 1:20 PM they were ready and began firing into Samakh. Until then, the Syrians were certain that the Israelis possessed nothing that could reach their forward HQ; now their commanders had to scramble for shelter. A lucky hit blew up a Syrian ammunition depot inside the village. The 65 mm's then lowered their sights and began to rake the infantry and armor strung out between Samakh and the Deganias. The dry fields began to burn,[345] and panic took hold. The Syrian infantry fled eastward in confusion,[346] shells nipping at their heels. The armor followed. Syrian officers apparently shot some of the fleeing soldiers.[347]

All in all, they had had a very bad day: the fight at the Deganias had been bloody and frustrating; now they were being subjected to a barrage no one had warned them of. They retreated all the way back to Tel al-Qasir, aban-doning the ruins of Samakh, Masada, and Shaʿar Hagolan on the way. The following day, the Haganah reoccupied Samakh, its police fort, and the two kibbutzim,[348] and sifted through the bodies—of the fifty-two Jewish dead, left behind in the retreat from Samakh, and the dozens of newly dead Syrians.

The Syrians attributed their defeat to unpreparedness and the quality of the Israeli fortifications. They also pointed to the lack of coordination between various Syrian units and between the Syrians and the Iraqis, who—according to one Syrian historian—were supposed to have assisted them against the Deganias.[349] Within days, the Syrian defense minister, the chief of staff, and the commanders of the First and Second Brigades had resigned.[350] The defeat persuaded British observers that the Arabs would not win the war. Indeed, they spoke of the Luftwaffe's defeat in the Battle of Britain in 1940, after which it was clear that the Germans would not win the air war: "A greater edge than the [Syrians] enjoyed at Degania they won't have again," they commented.[351]

Having failed in their thrust south of the Sea of Galilee, the Syrian army rested and regrouped and, a fortnight later, reentered the Galilee, this time just south of Lake Hula, at Mishmar Hayarden, a moshav that dominated the Bnot Ya'akov Bridge. Elements of the Second Brigade joined the First in the offensive. Their aim was probably limited: to conquer one or more small chunks of territory in order to reach the start of the expected UN truce with an achievement in hand.[352] The attack was probably coordinated with the Lebanese army, which on 5 June surprised and attacked the small Jewish garrison at al-Malikiya and overwhelmed it (the village had been taken in a commando-style attack by the Palmah on the night of 28–29 May). A few days later, the ALA, which had withdrawn from central Palestine a fortnight before, returned to the country via al-Malikiya. Al-Qawuqji established his headquarters in Nazareth.

The Lebanese success at al-Malikiya marked their only real participation in the war and gave Beirut cover against accusations of indifference to the fate of Palestine.

The Syrians were initially less successful. The First Brigade, now commanded by Colonel Anwar Banud, attacked Mishmar Hayarden on 5–6 June, but without success. On 9–10 June they tried again, core elements of the Second Brigade, commanded by Colonel Tawfiq Bashur, fording the Jordan just north of the settlement. A mortar and artillery barrage preceded the assault.[353] The moshav, defended only by several dozen members, fell after a fierce fight. The Syrian assault was assisted by strafing runs by fighter-bombers. Some two dozen settlers were taken prisoner. A Syrian historian later wrote that the Jews had left "120" bodies dispersed among the fences, "and from their mouths there was the smell of wine, which the Jews used to give their soldiers during battle."[354] Elements of two IDF brigades, which were encamped in the area, failed to intervene, though a battery of 65 mm cannon halted the Syrian advance westward, just short of Kibbutz Ayelet Hashahar and the moshava Mahanayim. There the Syrians remained until the start of the First Truce on 11 June. They had gained a toehold west of the Jordan, giving them, on the military plane, the potential to renew offensive operations in the Galilee; on the political plane they had gained a bargaining chip for future negotiations.

The Lebanese Front

The Galilee Panhandle, bordered in the west and north by Lebanon and on the east by Syria, was defended by the Palmah's Yiftah Brigade. To the west was the Lebanese army, with thirty-five hundred troops in four infantry battalions, two artillery batteries (74 mm and 105 mm), and an armored battalion consisting of armored cars and some light tanks.[355] Two of the battalions, with the armored cars and the artillery batteries, were deployed in southern Lebanon in April and early May 1948.[356] According to the Arab League invasion plan, they were to advance down the coast road from Ras al-Naqurah toward Acre and Haifa.

But at the last moment, Lebanon—despite Prime Minister Riad al-Sulh's often fiery rhetoric—opted out of the invasion. On 14 May, President Bishara Khouri and his army chief of staff, General Fuad Shihab (both Maronite Christians), decided against Lebanese participation; Colonel Adel Shihab, commander of the army's First Regiment (battalion), designated to cross into Israel, apparently refused to march. The Lebanese parliament, after bitter debate, ratified the decision the same day.

The last-minute change of heart stemmed from the powerful Maronite community's disaffection with Arab League policy vis-à-vis Zionism. The Maronites had always been ambivalent, with many regarding the Jews as potential allies against the hostile sea of Muslims that surrounded, and threatened, both communities. As one Israeli agent put it, "in their hearts the Christians are happy with the establishment of the State of Israel."[357] The Shi'ites of southern Lebanon, generally friendly with the Jewish settlements across the border, also appear to have had misgivings about the Jihad against the Jews.[358] There was a general recognition that the army was too small and ill equipped to go to war and a fear that hostilities might result in Israeli conquest of southern Lebanon. American and French representatives in Beirut apparently warned the Lebanese to stay out.[359] Last, perhaps the Haganah's Operation Ben-Ami, in which the Carmeli Brigade on 13–14 May had advanced northward along, and taken, the very road the Lebanese had ear-marked for their push southward, had acted as a deterrent.[360]

Lebanon decided to deploy its army defensively. But to cover itself politically, in the inter-Arab arena, it also agreed to serve as a base for a small ALA "invasion" of Palestine and to provide that force with covering artillery fire, a handful of armored cars, "volunteers," and logistical support.[361] The force, the Second Yarmuk Battalion, composed of several hundred Lebanese, Iraqi, Syrian, and Yugoslav volunteers, was commanded by the Syrian officer Adib Shishakli, and its mission no doubt was coordinated with the Syrian army, which was about to invade from the east.[362] On the morning of 15 May, the ALA crossed the border and pushed into al-Malikiya, an abandoned Arab village that was a natural gateway from south Lebanon into the Galilee Panhandle. But the previous night, the Palmah, realizing its importance, had sent in the Yiftah Brigade's First Battalion, which, after an arduous climb, had fanned out in and around the village and the neighboring abandoned British army camp. The two battalions met head on in the alleyways of al-Malikiya and the surrounding hilltops.[363]

The ALA's advantage in artillery—the Palmahniks had none—and the rapid deployment of a company of Jordanian bedouin volunteers, counterattacking from the southwest,[364] proved decisive. By nightfall, the Israelis began to retreat eastward, carrying as many as 150 dead and wounded back down the slope to the Jordan Valley.[365] The Arabs dug in at al-Malikiya and the neighboring village of Qadis. Yet though victorious, they, too, had suffered serious losses; certainly they had lost the will to advance further. Indeed, their situation was such that Shishakli withdrew his garrison from the neighboring Nabi Yusha police fort to reinforce al-Malikiya.

Subsequently, Beirut Radio repeatedly announced that the Lebanese army had attacked Israel. The broadcasts were intended to fend off possible criticism of Lebanese nonparticipation in the pan-Arab effort. But the HIS had it right: one agent later reported that "the Lebanese army . . . did not join the invasion as its main forces were concentrated between Tyre and Ras al-Naqurah [to the west]";[366] another, that General Shihab had "refused to invade [Palestine] and argued that his army is only a defensive army and [incapable] of offense, but let loose against [Kibbutz] Hanita [in Western Galilee] with a mortar barrage in order to show that the Lebanese were also taking part in the war."[367]

Al-Malikiya had been a severe blow. But the Palmah refused to concede defeat. On the night of 15–16 May, its commandos destroyed a bridge over the Litani River, some six miles north of the border, impairing Lebanon's ability to supply the invading column and forcing the Lebanese to devote resources to guarding their rear.[368] The following night, Yiftah units occupied the (abandoned) Nabi Yusha police fort, just west of Qadis. The fort had previously withstood two determined Palmah assaults. And on the night of 28–29 May, Yiftah retook al-Malikiya itself. The brigade attacked the village simultaneously from Kibbutz Ramot Naftali in the east and from the rear, an Israeli mechanized column having crossed the border at Manara, some six miles to the north, and then driven down dirt tracks inside Lebanon, without lights, through a string of Lebanese villages, before reaching al-Malikiya from the rear. The villagers had cheered the column, believing it to be Arab. In all, the Palmah suffered two dead and three wounded in the operation.[369] But on 5–6 June, as we have seen, the Lebanese army, assisted by a Syrian battalion and the ALA, recaptured al-Malikiya, which had been left in the hands of a Haganah garrison company. The conquest reopened a major supply route from south Lebanon to the upper central Galilee, where the ALA was now concentrated. The attack—Lebanon's only success in the war—enabled Beirut to argue, at last, that they had participated in the assault on Israel. The Lebanese army withdrew from al-Malikiya, handing it over to the ALA, on 8 July, at the end of the First Truce.[370]

The invasion period ended with both sides attempting to gain local advantage on each front. "In preparation for the truce, which could mark the end of the period of battles, there is a need to create *facts [on the ground] of political importance* by capturing certain enemy bases and by capturing our sites that were conquered by the enemy," Southern Front instructed the Givʿati and Negev Brigades. Givʿati was told to take sites dominating the Egyptian-held area just north of Isdud; the Negev Brigade, "to 'clean up' all the Arab villages captured by the Egyptian military force, and to mount raids on Egyptian supply depots."[371] The Israeli troops proceeded to occupy hilltop positions and villages (Yasur, Batani Gharbi, Julis, Jusair) along the front lines—including the Bir Asluj police fort, on the road between ʿAuja al-Hafir and Beersheba, an Egyptian supply route from Sinai. But they failed, as ordered, to take the ʿIraq Suweidan police fort or retake Nitzanim. The Egyptians, for their part, on the night of 9–10 June captured Hill 69, west of Beit Daras, in a fierce battle[372] and, the following day occupied the main Majdal-Faluja–Bureir-Julis crossroads. The Jordanians raided Gezer, and the Syrians captured Mishmar Hayarden (as described above).

THE AIR AND NAVAL WAR BETWEEN 15 MAY AND 11 JUNE 1948

Air and naval operations during the first, civil war half of the 1948 war were peripheral and had almost no impact on the fighting. The Palestinian Arabs had no air arm, and the Haganah's Air Service was small and insignificant, employed in reconnaissance, ferrying commanders, resupply, and marginal ground-support missions. Neither side had "navies."

Air and naval operations were also of no great importance in most theaters of operation and battles between 15 May and 11 June 1948. Both Israel and the Arab states lacked serious air and naval capabilities. During the first weeks of the conventional war the Israelis' light aircraft continued to bomb Arab encampments and columns, usually at night to avoid enemy interception, and usually with little effect, except marginally on morale.

However, the Haganah had half a dozen combat-trained pilots, and soon they were joined by dozens of experienced North American, Commonwealth, and Western European flyers, who were to constitute the backbone of the IAF (formerly the Air Service).

The air forces of Egypt, Syria, and Iraq (Jordan and Lebanon had none), though relatively formidable on paper, in fact counted for little. Many of Egypt's fighters and bombers were unserviceable; few of its pilots were competent; ground control, aircraft maintenance, and air intelligence were all poor to appalling. The same applied for the much smaller Syrian and Iraqi air forces. Because of losses and diminishing stocks of ammunition and spare parts, all these air forces contracted during the war.

By contrast, the IAF grew steadily. The first four (Messerschmitt) fighters arrived in mid-May—and went into action on 29 and 30 May. By 11 June eleven Messerschmitts were operational and by 12 August twenty-five.

The Egyptian air force, using bombers and Spitfires, repeatedly attacked Israeli air fields, ground forces, rural settlements, and towns. Few casualties were caused, and these gradually fell off as Israeli air power grew and interception became more effective. In Tel Aviv, which was repeatedly hit by Egyptian air raids, more than forty civilians were killed. Most died on 18 May at the central bus station.

Following the Messerschmitt attacks on the Egyptian and Iraqi columns, Egyptian fighters repeatedly hit ʿEqron Airfield, where the Israeli fighters were based. On 30 May Egyptian bombers, aiming for ʿEqron, hit the center of the town of Rehovot, including the Sieff (later, Weizmann) Institute, killing seven and wounding thirty. The following day, they hit ʿEqron Air field, hitting two partially assembled Messerschmitts.[373]

In part a response to the Egyptian air attacks and in part a gut response to the Jordanian victories at Latrun, Ben-Gurion decided to bomb the Arab capitals. He seemed to think—based on his memories of the German Blitz against London—that air power could prove decisive (though given the poverty of Israeli resources, this was plain silly): "Our air force has to bomb and destroy Amman. The weak link in the Arab coalition is Lebanon. . . .

When we break the [Arab] Legion's power and we bomb Amman, we will also destroy Transjordan, and then Syria will fall. If Egypt will still dare to fight—we will bomb Port Said, Alexandria and Cairo. And thus we will end the war—and pay back for [the treatment of our forefathers by] Egypt, Assyria [that is, ancient Iraq] and Aram [that is, ancient Syria]."[374]

In the early morning hours of 1 June, two IAF Rapids and one Bonanza flew to Amman and dropped several dozen fifty-five- and 110-pound bombs on the town, the king's palace and the adjacent air field (under British control).[375] About a dozen persons died and a number of (British) aircraft were hit. The British warned Israel that if this recurred, they would hit its air fields and aircraft.[376] Israel did not bomb Amman again.

Ten days later, early on 11 June, hours before the First Truce came into effect, a lone Dakota, loaded to the gills with 176-pound bombs and incendiaries, took off from 'Eqron, heading for Damascus. It was crewed by seven Britons and South Africans. Flying northward, they could see Haifa to the west, "lit up like a Christmas tree." At 3:12 AM the first bomb was thrown out of the rear door by two crewmen. In all, the plane made six passes over the Syrian capital, delivering sixteen high explosive bombs and ninety four-pound incendiaries, dispersed indiscriminately. The Syrians were caught completely by surprise; they sent up no interceptors, and antiaircraft fire only began ten minutes after the plane had left the area. A Western journalist who witnessed the bombing later wrote that twenty-two Syrians died and more than a hundred were injured, and it "put the fear of God into the inhabitants of Damascus."[377] More significant, it forced the Syrians to think seriously about bolstering their air defenses and resulted in a diminution of their aerial activity over Israel during the following bout of fighting, in mid-July.

If air activity, on both sides, was largely of nuisance value and failed seriously to affect the ground fighting, naval operations were even of smaller significance during May and June 1948.

Both sides used boats to ferry supplies and reinforcements to advancing ground units: the Haganah landed 450 troops and tons of ammunition and fuel in Nahariya during Operation Ben-Ami, and the Egyptians ferried troops and equipment to Majdal and Isdud during their advance up the coastal road (indeed, the first landing of Egyptian troops at Majdal took place on 14 May, a day before the start of the ground invasion).[378]

The only significant offensive naval operation took place on 2–4 June. On 2 June, an Egyptian corvette briefly shelled Qisariya, where there was a small Israeli naval station, and then withdrew, causing no injuries and little damage. On the morning of 4 June, a three-boat Egyptian flotilla (a corvette, a landing craft, and an armed troop carrier) were sighted off Tel Aviv, apparently aiming to shell the city or launch a commando raid. The ships were engaged by the small frigate *Eilat,* the Israel Navy's only armed ship, but the larger Egyptian guns kept it at bay after scoring several hits. Three IAF light aircraft intervened, strafing and bombing the Egyptians as they maneuvered off Jaffa. One boat was hit by a bomb, and the Egyptians called it a day. Throwing up smokescreens, they sailed back to Port Said. One Israeli aircraft was shot down. [379]

The result of the four-week contest between the Haganah/IDF and the invading Arab armies was an Israeli victory. The Arabs had enjoyed major advantages (the initiative, vastly superior firepower), and in retrospect, this was the only period in which they could have won the war or made major territorial gains at Jewish expense. But they failed. In effect, they were stopped in their tracks—the Syrians establishing a line just west of the old international border at Tel al-Qasir, with a symbolic gain at Mishmar Hayarden; the Jordanians and Iraqis occupying territory allotted to the Palestinian Arabs (except for the Jewish Quarter of the Old City); and the Egyptians more or less reaching the northern limit of the southern chunk of Palestine allotted the Arabs, at Isdud—though they did cut off the northern Negev settlements enclave and the Negev Brigade.

The Israelis had suffered many casualties. But they had contained the four-pronged assault. And their army was far larger and better armed at the end of the four weeks than at the beginning. The invaders had failed to destroy any large Haganah/IDF formations. The Israelis had held on to much of the territory earmarked for their state, and in some areas—Jaffa, Western Galilee, the Jerusalem Corridor—had substantially added to their holdings. Moreover, after the first fortnight's containment battles, the Haganah/IDF had moved over to the offensive on all fronts. By early June, the Israelis had caused the Arabs sufficient casualties and shock to persuade them to shelve any thought of further advance. The Israelis may have been unsuccessful in their initial counterattacks (Latrun, Isdud, Jenin). But the strategic initiative had passed from Arab into Israeli hands and was to remain there for the duration of the war. And, politically, the Israelis enjoyed hesitant international support whereas the Arabs were commonly seen as the aggressors.

But, like the Arabs, the Israelis were thankful for the long breather provided by the truce. Subsequently, Moshe Carmel said: "The truce came down upon us like dew from heaven. The formations are tired, weary."[380]

6

The First Truce, 11 June–8 July 1948, the International Community, and the War

The First Truce came into effect on 11 June, the result of weeks of shuttle diplomacy by Count Folke Bernadotte, the United Nations' special mediator for Palestine.

On 14 May the UN General Assembly had voted for the appointment of a "Mediator" to assure the safety of the holy places, to safeguard the well-being of the population, and to promote "a peaceful adjustment of the future situation of Palestine." Achieving an Israeli-Arab peace settlement was to be the focus of Bernadotte's efforts during the following four months.

He was appointed mediator by UN Secretary-General Trygve Lie on 20 May. Though hampered by dyslexia, Bernadotte had been deputy head of the Swedish Red Cross and during World War II had saved thousands, including many Jews, from the Nazis. He knew next to nothing about the Middle East or Palestine, and the haste of his appointment had allowed him little opportunity for study.

When Bernadotte arrived in Paris on 25 May, on the first leg of his mission to the Middle East, Ralph Bunche, the black American intellectual appointed by Lie as his deputy, thought that Bernadotte and his elegant wife, Estelle, "gave the impression of going to a party."[1] Bunche had been a key (and highly effective) official on UNSCOP and was well versed in the affairs of Palestine. Bernadotte was to acquire a rudimentary knowledge about the problem, and its possible solution, during his two-day Paris stopover, where he met British, UN, Zionist, and French officials. On arriving at Le Bourget

Airport, Bernadotte, at their first meeting, asked Bunche: "What do they want me to do there, in Palestine?" Bunche: "To go and stop the war." Bernadotte: "How?" Bunche: "With bare hands." Bernadotte: "O.K., let's go."[2] The two men were to form an efficient team—the gung-ho Swedish aristocrat, "optimistic . . . and eager for action," and the "overcautious" and pessimistic African American from Detroit—the "humanitarian" Don Quixote and his faithful, ruminating Sancho Panza, as one historian was to put it.[3]

Meanwhile, the UN Security Council on 22 May had called for a truce, to begin forty-eight hours later—while, under British threat of veto, avoiding branding the Arab states the "aggressors." The Israelis agreed immediately. But the Arabs demurred, their generals still hoping for victory or at least to overrun more of Palestine. The British were unhappy: their Jordanian wards had occupied the territory agreed upon, more or less, in the February meeting between Prime Minister Tawfiq Abul Huda and Foreign Secretary Bevin but were now enmeshed in a war with the Jews that they might well lose. And the advance of the other Arab armies had bogged down—indeed, all were threatened with defeat, which the world might interpret as a British defeat and the Arab world as a fruit of British perfidy (the Arabs never tired of portraying the British as Zionism's patron and ally—much as leading Zionists never relented in depicting the British as the Arabs' patron and backer). Last, against the backdrop of the pan-Arab assault, the British feared that Zionist pressure on Washington would persuade the Americans to lift their embargo and arm the Israelis, with dire consequences for Arab arms and Anglo-American amity.

The British and Americans—ever worried about the possibility of Soviet penetration of the Middle East, which the hostilities, they believed, could facilitate—pressed the Arab states to agree to a truce. But the Arabs, with little to show for their efforts, were still in an aggressive mode—all but Jordan, which had been successful, and Iraq, which had been humiliatingly unsuccessful. The Iraqis blew successively hot and cold. Their thinking—or feelings—are embalmed in a cable from the British minister in Baghdad to the Foreign Office, reporting on a meeting with the regent, ʿAbd al-Ilah: "In regard to the future, the Regent said: 'We cannot be beaten by the Jews. We cannot afford to be beaten by them. We will fight to the last even if we are left with only knives in our hands. I am ready to go into the front line myself. But if fighting is stopped by the Great Powers or by the United Nations that would be a different matter.' I got the impression that Arab honor would then be satisfied," commented the British minister.[4]

This was the background to the Security Council's resolution of 29 May, calling for a four-week truce, to begin on 1 June and imposing a blanket embargo on arms and additional military personnel on Israel and the Arab states. Bernadotte was assigned the task of negotiating the truce.

Thus the mediator's tasks were amended and his order of priorities reset: to halt the fighting and then to negotiate a full peace settlement. He spent the next fortnight negotiating a truce. It proved no easy matter. And most observers were skeptical; after all, for six months the British, the United Nations, and others had tried to achieve a ceasefire without success. The *New York Times* gave Bernadotte "slim chances."[5]

The problem was the Arab side: all the regimes were fearful of the "street," and each leader feared his peers; agreement to cease fire would immediately be interpreted, and vilified, as weakness if not cowardice or complicity with the enemy. The publics believed what their newspapers and leaders had told them since 15 May—that the expeditionary forces were beating the Jews and driving on Tel Aviv and Haifa. They would not understand agreement to a ceasefire. As Lebanese prime minister Riad al-Sulh—who "invited himself to tea" on 27 May with the British minister in Beirut, Houstoun Boswall—put it: "Any Arab leader who had accepted the ceasefire appeal unconditionally . . . would, in the present state of public opinion, have done so at the risk of his life. (Iraqi Director General for Foreign Affairs has told me the same thing.) Result of anything that could be interpreted by peoples as weak would be chaos with students and workmen assuming the function of government in the Arab states." Moreover, the Arab leaders understood that a truce "would be more to the advantage of the Jews than it could be to the Arabs."[6]

But by the second week of June reality had begun to dawn; conditions were propitious. Both sides needed a respite. "The Arab forces are exhausted and lacking in ammunition," Yigael Yadin radioed his brigade commanders.[7] And on the Israeli side there was unanimity among the "military experts": all "strongly favored the truce," as Ben-Gurion told his Cabinet colleagues.[8]

As to the negotiator, Bernadotte's energy, obvious impartiality, and sense of mission served him in good stead. He kicked off with talks in Cairo, where—on 30 May—he was told by Egypt's leaders and ʿAbd al-Rahman ʿAzzam that the Arab states might consent to a short-term truce but would never agree to the existence of a Jewish state.[9] His meeting with Ben-Gurion the following day was no more upbeat, the Israeli prime minister raising a variety of problems. But though the meeting had been "unpleasant,"[10] Israel had agreed to the truce, in principle.[11] So, in the end, did the Arabs—who later said they regretted it, believing—or at least arguing—that they "had seen victory snatched from them."[12]

Bernadotte was left with two major concrete problems: the supervision of the arms embargo and the prevention, during the truce, of the entry of military personnel into Palestine and the combatant countries. The Arab states worried that the Jews would find ways to circumvent the embargo, and the Israelis insisted that immigration to Israel must not be completely halted. The Egyptians, absurdly, proposed that their navy patrol the Palestine coastline "for" the United Nations. The Israelis pressed to allow men of military age into Israel, especially from the British detention camps in Cyprus, where thousands had been languishing for months or years, many of them Holocaust survivors. The Arabs objected. A blowup occurred between Shertok and Bernadotte in Haifa on 6 June, with the Israeli "raising his voice," or shouting.[13] But Israel eventually gave way—as its military "manpower resources extremely strained and tired; many vital positions tenuously held . . . 4 weeks respite would be great boon."[14] Bernadotte had threatened that if his terms were rejected there would be no truce—and Israel would be held to account.

Bernadotte demanded acceptance by 9 June. Both sides complied, the truce to begin on 11 June. It was to last for four weeks, until 8 July. But Bernadotte and the United Nations had invested too little, too late in establishing a proper supervisory apparatus, and so the truce—which required close, continuous inspection of all the Arab Middle East's and Israel's sea- and airports, as well as the front lines between the armies—was never adequately maintained, especially in all that concerned the arrival of war matériel and additional manpower.

The Arabs violated the truce by reinforcing their lines with fresh units and by preventing supplies from reaching isolated Israeli settlements; occasionally, they opened fire along the lines. Above all, the situation of Jewish Jerusalem remained precarious—because of the military threat by the Arab Legion, the shortage of supplies, and the political separation from the Jewish state, which weighed heavily on the population—and the Israeli Cabinet anticipated mass flight from the town during the truce. Ben-Gurion declared, "We must prevent panic flight with all the means at our disposal."[15]

The Israelis, for their part, also moved additional troops to the fronts. But they dramatically changed the strategic situation in their favor by systematically violating the arms and military personnel embargoes, bringing in both clandestinely by air and sea.

At the start of the truce, a senior British officer in Haifa predicted that the four weeks "would certainly be exploited by the Jews to continue military training and reorganization while the Arabs would waste [them] feuding over the future division of the spoils."[16] He was right. As one British official subsequently put it: "The Arabs lost the initiative throughout Palestine during the four weeks and the Jews were able to re-equip themselves."[17] In his memoirs, Nasser highlighted this by recalling the situation on his front, around Isdud: the Israeli side "buzzed with activity" while on the Egyptian side there was lethargy, "laxity," and "laughter."[18] In addition, the Israelis exploited the truce for raiding and occupying sites along the lines that would give them advantage when and if fighting resumed.

During the invasion weeks and the First Truce, the Yishuv managed to convert its pre-state "national institutions" rapidly into the agencies and offices of a full-blown state. Nowhere was this more apparent than in the military domain. The Haganah quickly made the transformation from a semilegal underground/militia into a full-fledged army and by the end of the truce was far stronger, in terms of command and control, manpower, and weaponry. The IDF's manpower almost doubled between 15 May and 9 July, the number in uniform rising from some thirty to thirty-five thousand to sixty-five thousand. Perhaps as many as four thousand of the new recruits were veterans of the Allied armies (British, American, Canadian, Czech) of World War II who came from abroad to help out. Most went home after the war. These veterans included specialists in the crucial specialized branches—sailors, doctors, tank men, logistics and communications experts, air- and ground crews.

The Israelis also managed to bring in large quantities of arms. By the end of the truce, more than twenty-five thousand rifles, five thousand machine guns, and more than fifty million bullets had reached the Haganah/IDF from Czechoslovakia.[19] During the invasion weeks and the truce, the Haganah/IDF also began to receive some of the heavy weapons purchased earlier, principally in the United States and Western Europe. By the end of June, Israel had received and deployed some thirty Swiss-made 20 mm cannon. A number of Krupp 75 mm cannon also arrived in June.[20] Fighter aircraft trickled in, principally from Czechoslovakia. By the end of July, Israel had received twenty-five Messerschmitts—though the far more useful Spitfires began to arrive only in late September and into October. By February 1949, Israel had a dozen Spitfires. By mid-July 1948 a number of transport aircraft, some of them converted to combat use, and three B-17 bombers had also arrived.[21]

During June, most of the existing IDF brigades were substantially beefed up, the companies and battalions filling out more or less to standard size, and two new brigades, the Eighth (armored)—which began organizing in late May—and the Ninth (Oded)—which was commissioned on 17 June—were added to the roster. Many of the newly arrived armored vehicles—mostly World War II–vintage American half-tracks, some mounting guns or mortars—were deployed in the Eighth Brigade. Large quantities of ammunition arrived and were forwarded to the expanding units. The army that confronted the Arab states on 8–9 July was radically different from, and far stronger than, that which they had met on 15 May.

The Israelis also used the truce to establish new settlements and begin planning others, mostly on newly conquered territory. Ben-Gurion believed the time was propitious—but cautioned against publicizing these activities: "We should speed up settlement, and in more places, and it is possible, but this time we should maintain silence," he told the Cabinet.[22] But in fact the state was hard pressed on other fronts and devoted few resources to establishing new settlements, Weitz complained.[23]

The Arab armies also grew during the truce, but mainly in numbers. The Egyptian expeditionary force, for example, was beefed up with six companies of Sudanese regulars[24] in addition to Egyptian recruits and reservists. But little additional weaponry or ammunition reached the army in Palestine.

Once the truce was in place, Bernadotte turned his attention to achieving a political settlement. He also spent time trying to persuade the Arabs to extend the truce. He spoke of "peace by Christmas"[25] and hoped that negotiating peace would, of itself, generate Arab and Israeli interest in extending the truce.

The chief obstacles, as Bernadotte saw them, were the Arab world's continued rejection of the existence of a Jewish state, whatever its borders; Israel's new "philosophy," based on its increasing military strength, of ignoring the partition boundaries and conquering what additional territory it could; and the emerging Palestinian Arab refugee problem, the creation of which Moshe Shertok defined, with insight, as "the most spectacular event in the contemporary history of Palestine"[26] and which Bernadotte almost immediately sensed would become a key issue for the Arab side.

On 26 June the mediator set his signature to "preliminary" proposals—a "basis [for] . . . further discussion"—for a settlement. He recognized three basic facts: that (1) Israel existed (or as he put it a few weeks later: "It is there. It is a small state, precariously perched on the coastal shelf with its back to the sea, defiantly facing a hostile Arab world");[27] (2) that the Jordanian takeover of the core area of the proposed Palestinian Arab state—the West Bank—was irreversible; and (3) that the partition borders were dead. But he misread the military situation. He still believed that there was a "military balance" between Israel and the Arab states, which he could capitalize on—whereas in reality, the balance had already shifted and would progressively shift further in Israel's favor.[28] Bernadotte finessed the November 1947 UN decision to establish a Palestinian Arab state (alongside Israel) and proposed that a (vague) "Union" be established between the two sovereign states of Israel and Jordan (which now included the West Bank); that the Negev, or part of it, be included in the Arab state and that Western Galilee, or part of it, be included in Israel; that the whole of Jerusalem be part of the Arab state, with the Jewish areas enjoying municipal autonomy; and that Lydda Airport and Haifa be "free ports"—presumably free of Israeli or Arab sovereignty.[29] He also asserted that the refugees have the "right to return home without restriction and to regain possession of their property."[30] The proposals were transmitted to the two sides on 27 June.

The core idea, of reducing the size of the Jewish state by transferring the Negev to the Arabs while compensating Israel with (the much smaller) Western Galilee, was rooted in the British desire that the Arabs—preferably Jordan—hold the Negev so that territorial continuity between the eastern and western Arab lands—and between Britain's bases in Egypt and Iraq—would be maintained. This would have the added advantage of giving Jordan, Britain's most loyal regional client, an outlet, in Gaza-Majdal, to the Mediterranean.[31] Moreover, the "exchange" (roughly) reflected the military status quo, following Israel's conquest of Western Galilee in Operation Ben-ʿAmi and Egypt's (partial) conquest of the Negev. The Israelis and Soviets believed that Bernadotte's ideas emanated from the Foreign Office, but this is not clear from the available documentation.

A week later, the Israelis rejected the Bernadotte "plan," especially offended by the award of Jerusalem, with its majority Jewish population, to the Arabs. But they agreed to an extension of the truce by a month. The Arabs rejected both the plan, which included, of course, acceptance of the Jewish state, and a truce extension.

For the length of the truce, the Arab League had bitterly debated an extension. The Jordanians were dead set against the renewal of hostilities. After all, they had achieved their ambitions by occupying the West Bank, including Latrun, Lydda, and Ramla, and East Jerusalem. They feared that in renewed hostilities, the expanded IDF would overpower them and their allies. The Jordanians were also hardest hit by the embargo and suffered from an acute shortage of ammunition.

But the other Arab governments, having failed to attain their territorial objectives or the destruction of the Jewish state, and believing that the truce had favored the Jews, and egged on by opposition charges of weakness or treachery, pressed for a resumption of warfare. This or that Arab leader may have fathomed the real balance of forces—Syrian prime minister Neguib Armenazi, for example, was "personally convinced that the Arab States will all have to concede the existence of a Jewish State," reported one British interlocutor[32]—but none except the Jordanians were able to translate this into policy. As IDF intelligence explained, probably quoting an (unnamed) Arab agent: "The Arab states must continue the war for reasons of national pride, otherwise there is a danger of the collapse of their political regime[s]."[33] The Arabs were certain to renew the war at the end of the truce, "and possibly even before then," concluded Israeli intelligence.[34]

On 6 July Arab League representatives, meeting in Cairo, decided unanimously against the renewal of the truce.[35] "I was in a minority of one," Jordanian prime minister Abul Huda explained to John Glubb. "All the others wanted to renew the fighting. If I had voted alone against it, we should only have been denounced as traitors, and the truce [in any case] would not have been renewed. Jordan cannot refuse to fight if the other Arabs insist on fighting. Our own people here would not stand for that."[36] Egyptian foreign minister Ahmed Muhammad Khashaba offered one explanation for the League decision—which was spearheaded by Egyptian insistence: "It was a matter of life and death for them [that is, the Arab leaders] that there should be no Jewish state. They had no desire for renewed hostilities and no illusions about military risks involved but saw no alternative."[37] The stage was set for Egypt's renewal of hostilities and the Israeli offensives that followed.

DISMANTLING THE JEWISH DISSIDENT ORGANIZATIONS

One other important development occurred that June: the disbandment of the right-wing Zionist dissident organization the IZL. The crucial event was the "Altalena Affair."

On 1–2 June Ben-Gurion's aide, Israel Galili, and IZL commander Menachem Begin signed an agreement disbanding the IZL and providing for the transfer of the organization's troops to the IDF, where they were to constitute a number of separate battalions in the Alexandroni and Giv'ati Brigades. The IZL units in Jerusalem were left out of the agreement and maintained a separate, independent existence, Jerusalem officially not being part of the State of Israel.

But on 19–20 June there occurred what Ben-Gurion and his ministers were to regard—or said they regarded—as a mini-rebellion. An IZL ship, the *Altalena,* having embarked from France with some nine hundred immigrants and IZL members and a shipment of arms, arrived off Israel's shores. The IZL demanded that the arms be distributed among "its" IDF battalions and the independent IZL unit in Jerusalem. The government refused. Without obtaining government permission, IZL troops took control of a beach area near Kfar Vitkin, north of Netanya, and began to offload the immigrants and arms. IDF troops surrounded them, and a number of firefights ensued. On 21 June the IZL men on the beach surrendered, but the *Altalena* set sail for Tel Aviv. There, on Ben-Gurion's orders, IDF artillery fired on the ship. Hit and on fire, it soon sank. Most of the arms were lost. At the same time,

Palmah troops also took over the organization's headquarters in downtown Tel Aviv and arrested and disarmed the dissidents. Altogether, eighteen men died in the clashes, most of them IZL.

Begin refrained from igniting a civil war, and most of the IZL men returned to the IDF. But this time they were dispersed in the different units; there were no longer "IZL battalions." The IZL and LHI units in Jerusalem remained separate from the IDF until mid-September, when there, too, they were disbanded in the wake of the Bernadotte assassination, described in the next chapter.

Arab militiaman carries "captured" Jewish baby after attack on Hatikva Quarter, December 1947 (By permission of the Central Zionist Archives)

Jerusalem's Ben-Yehuda Street hours after an Arab multiple truck bombing, February 1948 (By permission of the Central Zionist Archives)

ʿAbd al-Qadir al-
Husseini, Palestinian
militia leader in the
Jerusalem area, c.
1948 (By permission
of the Central Zionist
Archives)

Encampment near Tel Aviv for Jewish "refugees" fleeing war zone, 1948
(By permission of the Central Zionist Archives)

Arab irregulars stand to in the Jerusalem Hills area
(By courtesy of IDF Archive)

From left to right, David Ben-Gurion, Golda Meir, and Moshe Shertok
(Sharett), May 1948 (By courtesy of Photography Department, Government
Press Office, State of Israel)

Haganah religious recruits in training (By courtesy of IDF Archive)

Egyptian plane downed over Tel Aviv, May 1948 (By courtesy of
Photography Department, Government Press Office, State of Israel)

Constructing the "Burma Road," June 1948 (By courtesy of
Photography Department, Government Press Office, State of Israel)

Harry Truman and Chaim
Weizmann (By permis-
sion of the Central Zionist
Archives)

Ramla prisoners of war, Operation Dani, 12–13 July 1948 (By courtesy of Photography Department, Government Press Office, State of Israel)

Haganah guards in Negev settlement, early 1948 (By permission of the Central Zionist Archives)

Givati Brigade cavalry operation at the abandoned Arab village of Nabi Rubin,
August 1948 (By permission of the Central Zionist Archives)

Dead Egyptian soldier at Huleikat, Operation Yoav, October 1948 (By courtesy
of Photography Department, Government Press Office, State of Israel)

An inhabitant of ʿAjjur in the Judean foothills southwest of Jerusalem surrenders, October 1948 (By courtesy of Photography Department, Government Press Office, State of Israel)

An Israeli soldier meets with Arabs in Majdal, c. 5 November 1948 (By courtesy of Photography Department, Government Press Office, State of Israel)

Egyptian prisoners of war captured at Huleikat, Operation Yoav,
October 1948 (By courtesy of Photography Department, Government Press
Office, State of Israel)

Israeli troops enter Beersheba, Operation Yoav, 21 October 1948 (By courtesy of
Photography Department, Government Press Office, State of Israel)

Egyptian prisoners of war captured in Beersheba, Operation Yoav,
October 1948 (By courtesy of Photography Department, Government Press
Office, State of Israel)

Yitzhak Sadeh (By courtesy
of IDF Archive)

Arab refugees leaving upper Galilee, Operation Hiram,
October–November 1948 (By courtesy of Photography Department,
Government Press Office, State of Israel)

Israeli troops enter Iqrit, upper Galilee, Operation Hiram, late October 1948 (By
courtesy of Photography Department, Government Press Office, State of Israel)

The IDF conquest of Sasa, upper Galilee, Operation Hiram,
late October 1948 (By courtesy of Photography Department,
Government Press Office, State of Israel)

The besieged Egyptian Faluja Pocket commander Colonel Saʿid Taha arrives for
talks with IDF General Yigal Allon (By courtesy of Photography Department,
Government Press Office, State of Israel)

Israeli troops take over Qalansuwa in the Little Triangle, May 1949, following the signing of the Israel-Jordan Armistice agreement (By courtesy of Photography Department, Government Press Office, State of Israel)

Arab Legion Colonel ʿAbdullah Tal (left) and aide (By courtesy of IDF Archive)

UN mediator Count Folke Bernadotte (in uniform) with Moshe
Shertok (Sharett); Ralph Bunche is on the left (By courtesy of IDF Archive)

From left to right, Yigal Allon, Yigael Yadin, David Ben-Gurion, and Ya῾akov
Dori (By courtesy of IDF Archive)

Instrument of surrender, signed by
local Arab dignitaries, Acre,
18 May 1948 (By courtesy of
IDF Archive)

King Farouk (By permission of
The Trustees of the Imperial
War Museum, London)

King ʿAbdullah and Glubb Pasha (By permission of The Trustees of the
Imperial War Museum, London)

"The Accomplished Fact": "The Jew" is trodden down under the boots of "the
Egyptian army," "the Arab Legion," and the armies of "Iraq," "Syria," and
"Lebanon" (*Rouse-al-Yusuf,* 20 October 1948)

7

The "Ten Days" and After

The First Truce was scheduled to end on 9 July. But, hoping to catch the IDF off guard, Egypt preempted and launched its offensive the day before, with the aim of bolstering its position along the Majdal–Beit Jibrin line. On 9 July Israel mounted offensives of its own on all three fronts. The IDF command hoped that they would be decisive and end the war. But they weren't, and the war would drag on for another half a year. The "Ten Days," as Israel called this brief, sharp bout of hostilities, ended on 18 July, following the UN Security Council's imposition of the Second Truce.

At the end of the First Truce, Israel was in a belligerent mood. It was still reeling from the impact and losses of the pan-Arab invasion. The country's feeling was encapsulated in David Ben-Gurion's statement in the Cabinet on 11 July: "I would like [the war] to continue for at least another month, because the war must end in the conquest of Shechem [Nablus], and I believe it is possible; the war must end with such a bombing of Damascus, Beirut, and Cairo, that they will no longer have a desire to fight us, and will make peace with us. Our goal is peace, what will happen if at the end of the war there will [still] be enmity around us [I don't know]. . . . If we do not blow up [that is, bomb?] Cairo, they will think, that they can blow up [that is, bomb] Tel Aviv and that we are powerless. . . . [If we bomb them] then they will respect us, I want it [to end] this way, and not by coercion by the UN in the middle of the war, [which will] enable the Arabs to say, [']had not England and America intervened, we could have destroyed the Jews.['] It is better that they see that this is not so."[1]

Ben-Gurion's confrontational mood may in part have been caused by the previous week's "rebellion" in the IDF General Staff, directed against his "overbearing" authority in all matters military. Over the previous weeks, Ben-Gurion had acted like a generalissimo, effectively usurping the powers of the chief of staff. Now, in the first week of July, in preparation for the impending battles, he was bent on appointing two British army World War II veterans, Shlomo Shamir and Mordechai Makleff, as Negev Brigade and Central Front OCs, respectively, over the heads of more experienced or incumbent Haganah/Palmah veterans. Yigael Yadin and other General Staff members responded by tendering their resignations. In part, it was a struggle over the management of the war, with Ben-Gurion dismissive of the Haganah/Palmah veterans' military abilities and the generals resentful of Ben-Gurion's autocratic (and amateur) interferences. It was also, in part, a political squabble between the Mapai leader and affiliated colonels and the nonpartisan or Mapam-linked veterans of the Haganah and Palmah, vaguely rallying in support of Mapam stalwart Israel Galili, the former head of the Haganah National Staff whom Ben-Gurion had effectively ousted back in May.

A ministerial committee, the Committee of Five, headed by Interior Minister Yitzhak Gruenbaum, was appointed to sort out the mess, but the compromise they proposed on 6 July, substantially curtailing Ben-Gurion's powers, resulted in the Old Man withdrawing to his bedroom in a huff (in "a state of collapse," as Moshe Shertok described it)[2] and himself threatening resignation. In the end, a settlement was reached, and Ben-Gurion was reinvested with almost complete control over the army. But his feathers had been ruffled, and he had been forced to accept the appointment of General Yigal Allon, the Palmah OC (and Mapam stalwart), as head of the planned operation in the central sector (albeit without the title of "front commander"). Nonetheless, Galili was now definitively ejected from the Defense Ministry, and a few weeks later, in September, the Palmah's separate HQ was disbanded, with the three Palmah brigades falling under the full control of the IDF General Staff (previously the Palmah HQ had exercised autonomous control in certain administrative matters, training, and appointments in the brigades).[3]

THE SOUTH

Even more markedly than during the invasion, the Ten Days were distinguished by a complete absence of cooperation and coordination between the different Arab armies, enabling the IDF to make the most of its unity of command, internal lines of communication, and superiority in manpower.

During the truce, the IDF had planned a major offensive against the Egyptian army. The Egyptians held a thin strip of territory on either side of the Majdal–Faluja–Beit Jibrin road, which connected their major holdings along the coast, from Rafah to Isdud, and the secondary arm of the expeditionary force, strung out between Beersheba, Hebron, and Bethlehem. At the same time, the Majdal–Beit Jibrin strip separated the coastal core of the Jewish state from the Negev settlements enclave, with its two dozen kibbutzim, guarded by the Negev Brigade. The aim of *mivtza an-far* (Operation An[ti]-Far[ouk]) was to reestablish the territorial link between the two areas, cut through the Egyptian-held strip, and serparate the right wing of the Egyptian expeditionary force from its main arm along the coast.[4] The intention, at least of one of the participating brigades, Giv'ati, was also to destroy and clear of inhabitants the villages that were to be captured and to demolish or drive out makeshift Arab refugee encampments.[5]

But the Egyptians, having used the truce to enlarge their expeditionary force to four brigades, preempted the IDF by striking at dawn on 8 July. In his memoirs, Gamal 'Abdel Nasser, a staff officer in the Sixth Battalion, noted "a spirit of indifference" and an absence of "conviction" in the Egyptian preparations. The Egyptian officers seemed to be playing at soldiering and "there was no trace of the authentic fighting spirit." "We spent the [truce] days as though we were in our barracks in Cairo. Our laughter filled the trenches and our jokes made the rounds throughout our positions," he recalled.[6] But Nasser himself, by his own admission, was behaving no better: he seems to have spent the time recruiting officers to the clandestine Free Officers Organization, which planned and eventually carried out the coup that overthrew the monarchy in 1952, instead of preparing for renewed hostilities.[7]

The main aim of the Egyptian offensive was to widen and strengthen the Majdal–Beit Jibrin wedge, deepening the isolation of the Negev settlements enclave, and to remove the threats to their supply lines along the coast and in the interior. Their minor effort, by the Second Brigade (Seventh and Sixth battalions, and the newly arrived Sudanese battalion), starting out from the Isdud area, targeted Beit Daras and the Sawafir villages[8] (perhaps with the ultimate aim of reaching the Masmiya Junction).[9] The attack on Beit Daras, held by Giv'ati's Fifty-third Battalion, was swiftly repulsed, the Sudanese and Israelis engaging with "bayonets and grenades"[10] on the outskirts of the village.[11] Nasser ascribes the Egyptian defeat to bungling by the Sudanese, who fired the wrong-colored flare into the air, precipitating an Egyptian artillery barrage on their own positions. In turn, this prevented the Sixth Battalion's planned follow-up attack on the Sawafirs.[12]

But the main Egyptian thrusts, by the Fourth Brigade (Second and Ninth battalions) from Majdal, supplemented by the Sixth Battalion, were partially successful. The poorly prepared attack by the Sixth Battalion on Julis was repulsed; Nasser emerged from it "in a state of revolt against everything . . . in revolt against the smooth, closely-shaven chins and the smart and comfortable offices at General HQ, where no one had any idea what the fighting men in the trenches felt or how much they suffered from orders sent out at random."[13] Nasser was lightly wounded in the chest: "I was not particularly frightened nor sorry for myself nor sad. . . . 'Is this the end?'[he asked himself.] I was not even upset by this question . . . for the first time since my arrival in Palestine I remembered my little daughters, Huda and Muna. . . . I then suddenly remembered my men."[14] But the Second and Ninth battalions took and held the vital crossroads of the Majdal-Faluja–Julis-Kaukaba roads southwest of Negba and Hill 113, which overlooked the crossroads, and the villages of Kaukaba and Huleikat.[15]

The IDF counterattacked that night, 8–9 July, unleashing Operation An-Far. The Negev Brigade's Seventh Battalion, commanded by Uzi Narkiss, supported by additional platoons, failed to take the ʿIraq Suweidan police fort, southeast of Negba, held by elements of the Egyptian First Battalion, and Givʿati briefly took, and then abandoned, the villages of ʿIraq Suweidan, east of the police fort, and neighboring Beit ʿAffa. But a company of the Fifty-third Battalion, supported by a platoon from the Fifty-fourth, striking from Negba, took the Ibdis position and village, north of Negba, and then on 9–10 July beat off determined counterattacks by the Egyptian Second Battalion, which enjoyed air support. The Fifty-first Battalion, striking southward from Kfar Menahem, took the village of Tel al-Safi. Givʿati's daily "combat pages," written by Abba Kovner, were headed "Death to the Invaders!" and were phrased in emotive language, such as "Killer dogs—their fate is blood [that is, death]" (echoing the language of Soviet broadsheets from the Eastern Front in World War II). Kovner enjoined the troops not to be deterred—"the more you run over bloody dogs, the more you will love the *beautiful*, the *good*, and *liberty*."[16]

After regrouping, the Egyptians, on 12 July, launched their most determined counterattack, using the Fourth Brigade. With diversionary assaults by elements of the Sixth and Second battalions at Julis and Ibdis, the main Egyptian force—the Ninth Battalion, commanded by Lieutenant Colonel Rahmani—struck at Kibbutz Negba itself, the hinge of the Israeli line. About a hundred kibbutzniks and Givʿati soldiers defended Negba. Beginning at dawn, repeated infantry assaults—"wave after wave,"[17] backed by armor and artillery—failed to breach the perimeter fences, and by sunset the Egyptians retired, leaving behind dozens of dead as well as a disabled tank and four Bren gun carriers. Kovner, his mind always dominated by his experiences in Eastern Europe during World War II, was to dub the steadfast settlement "Negbagrad." The Egyptians had poured some four thousand artillery and mortar rounds into the kibbutz, but the defenses had held. Negba suffered five dead and sixteen wounded; Egyptian losses were some two to three hundred dead and wounded (roughly half the Ninth Battalion). A battery of 65 mm guns had assisted the defenders.[18] Following the defeat, General al-Muwawi dismissed Fourth Brigade OC Mohammed Neguib, though he reinstalled him later at the head of another brigade. In his memoirs, Neguib castigated al-Muwawi but admitted that he had been insubordinate.[19] The battle proved to be the turning point of the Ten Days in the south.

In the following days, the initiative lay almost wholly with the IDF. One reason was the growing Egyptian lack of ammunition.[20] On 13–14 July the Fifty-fourth Battalion took Hill 105, just north of Negba. The following nights, other Giv'ati units raided Egyptian positions at Beit 'Affa, Hatta, and Beit Jibrin. And on 16–18, in Operation Death to the Invaders (*mivtza mavet lapolshim*), both Giv'ati and the Negev Brigade mounted a series of operations designed to expand their areas of control. Giv'ati's Fifty-first Battalion took a swath of villages around Kibbutz Kfar Menahem, including Zeita, Mughallis, Idnibba, Kheima, Jilya, and Qazaza, and "expelled their inhabitants, [and] blew up and burned a number of houses; the area is now clear [*naki*] of Arabs."[21] The Fifty-fourth Battalion occupied Beit 'Affa; the Fifty-second Battalion took Hatta; and Moshe Dayan's Eighty-ninth Battalion, diverted from the center to the south, with support from the Fifty-third Battalion, took Karatiya, just east of 'Iraq Suweidan, while elements of the Negev Brigade tried but failed to take Kaukaba and Huleikat.[22]

The Egyptians, for their part, attacked the kibbutzim Gal-On (14 July) and Be'erot Yitzhak (15 July)[23] but failed, as did their counterattack, led by half a dozen tanks, on 18 July against the Fifty-third Battalion entrenched at Karatiya. A lone PIAT operator managed to knock out a tank and the others took flight, the infantry following.[24] At 7:00 PM, 18 July, the renewed or Second Truce, ordered by the UN Security Council, went into effect. "Dirty, red-eyed from lack of sleep, with torn clothes, deathly tired," the Israeli and Egyptian troops, who had slogged it out for ten days, emerged from their foxholes.[25]

The upshot, in the south, had been indecisive, but the IDF had retained a slight edge. The Giv'ati and Negev Brigades had captured territory along the peripheries of their former holdings but had failed both to establish a perma-

nent link-up or corridor between the core of Jewish territory ending at
Negba with the Jewish settlements enclave of the northern Negev and, for
that matter, to cut off the Egyptian concentrations along the coast (the Gaza
Strip–Isdud) from their right wing in the Hebron Hills. The capture of
Karatiya had briefly disrupted traffic along the Majdal–Beit Jibrin road, but
the Egyptians established a bypass road immediately to the south. And yet,
the Egyptians had failed to conquer additional Jewish territory or settlements (except for Kibbutz Kfar Darom, whose situation as a lone, isolated
outpost along the Egyptians' main route of march had become untenable; its
defenders managed to slip out during the night of 8–9 July and reach Israeli
lines) or to roll back Giv'ati from Negba, which threatened their north-south
communications along the coast, or to widen their corridor. At the end of
the Ten Days, al-Muwawi "summarized the military situation in very gloomy
terms." He pointed to the shortage of weaponry and ammunition, to the
lack of coordination between the Arab armies, to the (politically dictated)
overextension of the Egyptian lines, and to the low morale of his troops.[26]
He was gravely worried about the future.

THE NORTH

In contrast with the south, in the northern and central theaters of operation the initiative lay wholly with the IDF: it was the Israelis who renewed
battle in the Galilee and the Jordan Valley (as well as in the Lydda-Ramla
area).

The main IDF offensive in the north was *mivtza dekel* (Operation Palm
Tree), designed to surround and destroy the ALA and to expand the Jewish-
held coastal strip of Western Galilee eastward into the mountains and to capture Nazareth and the surrounding area, in which much of the ALA was concentrated. The order stated that the units were to "completely root out
[*bi'ur*] the enemy from the villages" around Nazareth.[27] The operation was
also geared toward preempting a presumed offensive by Fawzi al-Qawuqji
against Afula.[28]

Northern Front (later, "Northern Command"), headed by Moshe Carmel, deployed a force equivalent to two undersized brigades, consisting of
the Seventh Brigade's Seventy-first (Armored) Battalion and the Seventy-
ninth (Infantry) Battalion, Carmeli's Twenty-first Battalion and Golani's
13th Battalion. Colonel Haim Laskov commanded the operation. Facing
these forces was a considerably smaller and weaker force of two ALA battalions (the Mahdi Salah "Brigade," consisting of the Hittin and Mahdi battalions), probably mustering about a thousand troops in all, backed by a small
number of local irregulars dispersed in the town and villages. (The ALA at

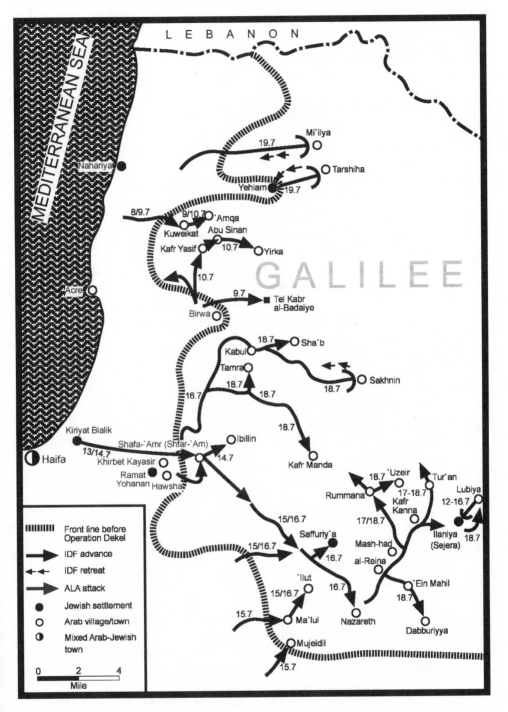

Operation Dekel, Galilee, July 1948

this time probably numbered altogether some three to four thousand troops, divided into three "brigades," each consisting of two battalions, and an additional independent Alawite battalion).[29] The desertion of most of the Druze irregulars further weakened the Arab side. Those from Syria returned home, and the bulk of the local, Galilee Druze had, soon after the Battle of Ramat Yohanan, covertly decided to throw in their lot with what they saw as the stronger side. This assured, during Dekel, the bloodless conquest of (partly Druze) Shafa-ʿAmr (Shfar-ʿAm) and a string of Druze villages in Western Galilee.[30]

Setting out a few hours before the official expiry of the First Truce, a company of the Twenty-first Battalion on the night of 8–9 July assaulted and took the village of Kuweikat. A few miles to the south, the Seventy-first Battalion took a series of positions just west of Majd al-Kurum. The following night, the Twenty-first Battalion took the village of ʿAmqa. Crucial in this series of successes was the IDF's use of field artillery and mortars, which laid down preliminary barrages, generally putting the defenders to flight. The Druze villages of Kafr Yasif, Abu Sinan, and Yarka—defined in IDF orders as "liaison base[s]" rather than enemy strongholds[31]—surrendered without a shot on 10 July. ALA counterattacks that day and the next were half-hearted and ineffective.

These speedy successes persuaded Dekel HQ to mount a deeper push into ALA-held territory to the south. On the night of 13–14 July elements of the Twenty-first, Seventy-first, and Seventy-ninth battalions captured the large mixed village of Shafa-ʿAmr. Representatives of the village's minority Druze population the day before had secretly met and worked out the details of the "conquest" with IDF officers. The IDF first mortared the village's Muslim neighborhoods. The next day, the Seventy-ninth Battalion took the village of Ibillin, to the northeast.

Emboldened by its successes and the weak ALA resistance, Northern Front decided to take the town of Nazareth, al-Qawuqji's headquarters since the start of the First Truce.[32] Al-Qawuqji had prepared for the Ten Days by trying to mobilize auxiliaries for the ALA from the surrounding villages (most young adult males seem to have been reluctant)[33] and by ordering the villagers to move out their women and children and/or sleep outside their villages.[34] Bedouin were ordered to pack up and moved out of the area.[35] According to the IDF, many of the townspeople were unhappy with the ALA, "who had behaved tyrannically toward them . . . especially toward the Christians."[36]

In part, the IDF push on 13–14 July was motivated by a desire to reduce al-Qawuqji's pressure on Ilaniya (Sejera) (see below). On 15 July, Golani Brigade units captured the villages of Maʿlul and al-Mujeidil, to the west of

Nazareth, and that night took the village of ʿIlut (where apparently two massacres of civilians took place during the following days),[37] while an armored column of the Twenty-first and Seventy-ninth battalions drove straight down the road from Shafa-ʿAmr, taking Saffuriya (Tzipori), a large village northwest of Nazareth. The inhabitants of Nazareth and its ALA garrison were instantly demoralized. Indeed, already on 15 July Israeli intelligence had predicted or reported that "the inhabitants were unwilling to fight."[38]

The day before, Ben-Gurion had instructed the army—taking account of Nazareth's importance to the world's Christians[39]—to prepare a task force to run the town smoothly, to avoid the looting that had characterized most previous conquests, and to avoid violating "monasteries and churches" (mosques were not mentioned). Attempts at robbery "by our soldiers should be met mercilessly, with machineguns," he instructed.[40] Carmel duly warned his troops not to enter or violate "holy sites."[41]

Against the backdrop of ALA demoralization and disintegration and the flight of Husseini-supporting families, Israeli agents maintained continuous contact with Nazareth's notables about a quiet surrender.[42] Nazareth, with its Christian majority, had traditionally been nonbelligerent toward the Yishuv (though sometime in June or early July some locals had murdered a Jewish farmer and dragged his body through the streets behind a motorcycle, to the cheers of bystanders),[43] and the IDF had no reason to unleash its firepower on the town.

Nazareth fell on 16 July, almost without a fight. Thousands of inhabitants, most of them Muslims, streamed out, in cars and by foot,[44] with many of the Fahoum clan, including town mayor Yusuf Fahoum, in the lead.[45] The two-brigade (Carmeli and Seventh) column had encountered an ALA squadron of nine armored cars at the entrance to town and brushed them aside with their 20 mm cannon. The column then drove into town. There was some sniper fire, but for all effects and purposes the fight was over.[46] Al-Qawuqji and the ALA had fled. The Israelis suffered one soldier wounded, the Arabs, sixteen dead. "A wave of true happiness passed over the town, joy mixed with dread in expectation of what was to come. The inhabitants really were joyful that they were rid of the regime of tyranny and humiliation of the [ALA] Iraqi [troops] who used to hit, curse, shoot, and jail the quiet inhabitants without reason. The dread stemmed from [fear] lest the reports they had received about Jewish behavior in previously occupied areas should prove true; they especially feared incidents of rape about which they had heard terrible stories from Acre and Ramla," reported the IDF Intelligence Service.[47] At 6:15 PM, "a delegation of town notables appeared bearing a flag of surrender";[48] a few hours later, an instrument of surrender was signed.[49] The IDF troops behaved unobjectionably. "Soon the [inhabitants] became aware that they were being well-treated and not being harmed," reported the Intelligence Service.[50] (Nonetheless, in the following weeks Muslim families steadily left the town, according to Israeli reports.)[51]

But the following afternoon, Carmel and Laskov ordered the town's new military governor, Seventh Brigade OC Colonel Ben Dunkelman—a Canadian volunteer with armored experience from World War II—to expel the inhabitants.[52] Dunkelman refused.[53] Laskov appealed to Ben-Gurion: "Tell me immediately, in an urgent manner, whether to expel [*leharhik*] the inhabitants from the town of Nazareth. In my opinion, all should be removed, save for the clerics."[54] Ben-Gurion backed Dunkelman.[55] Perhaps he was moved by possible world Christian reactions; perhaps he thought the idea objectionable as Nazareth's inhabitants had not resisted. Orderly administration was imposed under the new governor, Major Elisha Sulz. IDF troops—except those serving in the military government—were barred from the town,[56] and normal life was rapidly restored. Indeed, Nazareth soon filled with returning locals and refugees from surrounding villages.[57]

During the following two days, exploiting their success, Operation Dekel's battalions took a swathe of territory to the north, northeast, and northwest of Nazareth, including the villages of Mash-had, Kafr Kanna, Sha'b, Rummana, 'Uzeir, Bu'eina, Tur'an, al-Ruweis, Iksal, Dabburiyya, and Tamra.[58] Elsewhere, a thrust *eastwards* from Western Galilee toward Sakhnin ended in an ALA counterattack, with the Israelis withdrawing.

The speed of the IDF advance had been facilitated by al-Qawuqji's ill-timed diversion of most of the ALA's offensive energies and firepower to Eastern Galilee. On the night of 9–10 July, units of the Golani Brigade took Kafr Sabt, west of the Sea of Galilee. In response, al-Qawuqji mounted a series of counterattacks, amounting to a rolling offensive, to take Ilaniya (Sejera), which constituted a Jewish promontory deep in ALA territory. As with the attacks on Yehiam, Tirat Zvi, and Mishmar Ha'emek during the civil war, al-Qawuqji appears to have been driven by a desire to conquer at least one Jewish settlement to have something to show for his efforts. He deployed infantry, armored cars, and a battery of 75 mm artillery. Again he fell short. The ALA suffered from a shell shortage.[59] Repeated ALA assaults during 11–16 July failed to break the Golani Twelfth Battalion defenses; al-Qawuqji's men took heavy losses.[60] Indeed, his forces were so spent and demoralized after these failures and the fall of Nazareth that the battle ended on 18 July with Golani's capture, just before the Second Truce, of Lubiya, the large Arab village that was the ALA's main base in Central Eastern Galilee.[61] Northern Front, for its part, failed to take the large Western Galilee villages of Tarshiha and Mi'ilya.[62]

The upshot of Dekel and its appendages was the IDF conquest of a swathe of Western Galilee along with Nazareth and its satellite villages. The blow to the ALA was immense. Al-Qawuqji removed his HQ from Palestine to ʿEitaroun in southern Lebanon. And the flight of tens of thousands of townspeople and villagers into the interior of the Galilee, northern Samaria, and Lebanon aggravated the refugee problem. In Bint Jbail, in southern Lebanon, the joke was that refugees were "renting the shade of a fig tree for £P25."[63] For those who fled or were driven out there would be no return. As the terms of surrender dictated by Northern Front and accepted by the remaining inhabitants of ʿEin Mahal, an all-Muslim satellite village of Nazareth, put it: "[For] all the inhabitants . . . who have fled the village, [re-]entry . . . is forbidden, and they will be considered aliens, all their property will be confiscated, and if they are caught in the village they will be killed." As to those who had stayed put and behaved themselves, they "would enjoy the Government of Israel's protection."[64]

Following the Ten Days, the army carried out punitive operations in the newly captured villages. In Dabburiyya, three houses belonging to persons alleged to have murdered two Jewish girls at the start of the war were demolished.[65] The troops systematically disarmed the villages (Druze villagers were allowed to keep weapons) and rounded up and incarcerated adult males believed to have fought alongside, or helped, Qawuqji.[66] After the reinstitution of the truce, IDF units extended their areas of control and took over a string of Galilee villages (among them, Kabbul, Damoun, and Miʿar) on the periphery of the areas captured in Dekel.[67]

To the northeast, the IDF launched a brigade-sized effort, *mivtza brosh* (Operation Cypress), to destroy the Syrian bridgehead around Mishmar Hayarden.[68] Carmeli and Oded brigade units had concentrated in the area toward the end of the truce. The Syrians were estimated to be holding the three-mile-deep enclave west of the Jordan, about six miles from north to south, with a reinforced brigade, with more than three thousand troops, backed by artillery and a twelve-plane air force.[69]

The plan, based on a strategy of indirect approach (which was to characterize many of the IDF's operations during the following decades), was to send two battalions (the Twenty-third and Twenty-second) across the Jordan and Lake Hula into Syria, around the enclave's right flank, and then to veer southward towards the Bnot Yaʿakov–Quneitra road, cutting it off from Syria. The two battalions would then attack the enclave from the rear, from Syrian territory. At the same time, two battalions (the Twenty-fourth and Oded's Eleventh) would assault the enclave frontally, from the east.

But the Israelis had underestimated the power of the Syrian force, which had used the truce well. The Syrians had constructed a series of hilltop forti-

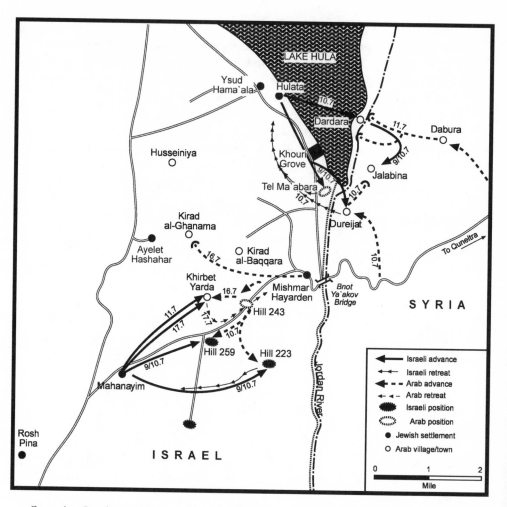

Operation Brosh, attacking the Syrian bridgehead at Mishmar Hayarden, 9–12 July 1948

fications the length of the enclave's perimeter. The IDF offensive kicked off on the morning of 9 July when a company of the Twenty-third Battalion, surprising the Syrians, crossed Lake Hula to the small Israeli settlement of Dardara (later renamed Kibbutz Ashmora) on its eastern shore and, encountering only light resistance, during the night took a hill overlooking Dardara and Khirbet Jalabina, just across the frontier inside Syria. The battalion's two other companies pushed down the southwestern shore of the lake and took additional positions, Tel Ma'abara and—fording the river in small boats—Khirbet al-Dureijat.

The Twenty-second Battalion, programmed to exploit the Twenty-third's successes, was to have crossed the Jordan in its wake and captured the Syrian base at the Customs House on the escarpment east of the Bnot Ya'akov Bridge, astride the road to Quneitra. But the engineers accompanying Carmeli failed to assemble the necessary pontoon bridge. The Twenty-second's troops began to cross over slowly and laboriously in rowboats, a squad at a time. But the battalion could not hope to reach its objective by dawn and was ordered to abandon its mission and return.

Meanwhile, on the night of 9–10 July, the Eleventh and Twenty-fourth battalions attacked the enclave head-on, from west to east, taking a series of hilltop positions. The Syrian ground forces, backed by aircraft, counterattacked the following morning. Syrian tanks repeatedly attacked Carmeli troops on Tel Ma'abara but were driven off by Molotov cocktails, artillery, PIAT, and machine gun fire. But the *tel* was abandoned during the night. The Syrians retook Khirbet al-Dureijat but were driven off by Carmeli at Khirbet Jalabina (which was subsequently, nonetheless, abandoned) and Dardara. At the western edge of the enclave a determined Syrian attack briefly resulted in the capture of Khirbet Yarda, but the position was retaken that night by a fresh company from Golani's Thirteenth Battalion.

Both sides had taken casualties in the seesaw battle. But the Syrians recovered first. At first light on 16 July they counterattacked with armor and infantry at the northern and western edges of the enclave. They took the Khouri Grove, at the southern end of the Hula Lake, and, briefly, Khirbet Yarda, but Carmeli Brigade troops recaptured the position,[70] which then remained in IDF hands until the end of the war.

The upshot of the Ten Days was that the IDF, while slightly reducing the size of the enclave, had failed to uproot the Syrian bridgehead, which was to remain in Arab hands until their withdrawal as part of the Israeli-Syrian armistice agreement of July 1949. In Operation Cypress, IDF casualties were ninety-five dead and some two hundred wounded; the Syrians, according to IDF estimates, lost twice those numbers.[71]

THE CENTRAL FRONT

Although substantial battles took place in the south and north, the IDF's major effort during the Ten Days was in the Central Front. Ben-Gurion was still anxious about the fate of West Jerusalem—militarily under threat by Jordan and politically endangered by Count Bernadotte and the UN partition resolution—and the road to it (despite the Burma Road bypass). After the repeated debacles at Latrun, he continued to hold the Arab Legion in deep respect.[72] And the Arab towns of Ramla and Lydda, which Ben-Gurion regarded as "dangerous in every respect"[73] and as "two thorns"[74] in Israel's side, sat astride the old main road and posed a constant threat to Tel Aviv, a bare ten miles away. They had to be "destroyed," he obsessively jotted down in his diary.[75] The IDF (wrongly) believed that the Legion intended to use the towns as a springboard for an offensive against Tel Aviv—and vastly overestimated the Jordanian force in the area. On 26 June, the IDF believed that the two towns were manned by 1,150–1,500 Legionnaires; in reality, there were about 150.[76]

Mivtza dani (Operation Dani, named after Dani Mass, the Palmah commander of the "35" killed on the way to the ʿEtzion Bloc in January) targeted Lydda-Ramla—but had a wider scope. It was geared to clearing all the remaining Arab-held sections of the Tel Aviv–Jerusalem road and the controlling ridge of hills to its north, stretching from Latrun to Ramallah. This meant taking on the Arab Legion.

Planning for the operation had begun in May. The operational order was finalized during the First Truce, initially called *mivtza larla"r* (Operation Larla"r—an acronym of Lydda-Ramla-Latrun-Ramallah), with General Allon in command. Dated 26 June, it read: "To attack in order to destroy the enemy forces in the area of the bases Lydda-Ramla-Latrun-Ramallah, to capture these bases and by so doing to free the city of Jerusalem and the road to it from enemy pressure."[77]

The IDF enjoyed superior numbers and firepower, concentrating its largest force ever: two Palmah brigades, Harel and Yiftah (together five battalions), the Eighth Brigade (Eighty-second and Eighty-ninth battalions), and several battalions of Kiryati and Alexandroni infantrymen, backed by some thirty artillery pieces.

"From the very beginning of hostilities, I had told both the King and the government [of Jordan] that we could not hold Lydda and Ramla . . . and had secured their consent to the principle that Lydda and Ramla would not be defended," Glubb recalled.[78] He reasoned that his main priority was defending the core hill area of the West Bank and (with faulty logic) that the IDF would have the advantage in a full-scale, mobile battle in the Lydda-

Ramla plain. So he positioned only a token force in the two towns. Aside from the Legion company divided between the towns' two police forts and a further company stationed to the north, at Beit Nabala, Lydda and Ramla were defended by ragtag militias, consisting of hundreds of armed locals[79] bolstered by several hundred Jordanian tribal irregulars. But large additional forces were close by. Late on 10 July, the Legion's strategic reserve, the (over-strength) First Regiment, with forty armored cars, half of them mounting cannon, and a battery of twenty-five-pounders and a battery of 4.2-inch mortars, joined the fight. The Legion's Third Brigade, consisting of the Second and Fourth regiments, held the Latrun area to the west but only marginally influenced the battle. Glubb refused to throw it in to defend the two towns, fearing for Latrun, the pivot of the Legion's hold on the West Bank.[80]

Glubb's unwillingness to fight for Lydda and Ramla was indicative of a more general Jordanian posture: 'Abdullah did not want to renew hostilities. He had achieved his territorial ambitions in the invasion's first weeks; now the task was to hold onto his gains. Renewed warfare would endanger them.

The Arab League's decision on 6 July to renew the war formally obligated 'Abdullah, yet he still hoped to stay out. Just before the start of the Ten Days, he secretly informed Israel "that he does not wish to fight and that we should not touch him." But, Ben-Gurion informed the Cabinet, "we could not accept his proposal [as] Lydda and Ramla were [still] in his hands."[81]

'Abdullah ordered the Legion "to assume a defensive role." On 10 July, Glubb toured his forward units, as he put it, "to make . . . arrangements for a phony war."[82] The Legion would not attack and would try to minimize hostilities. No doubt, 'Abdullah—and Glubb—were also motivated by their army's acute shortage of ammunition and by British pressure to avoid any display of belligerency.

The initial stage of the IDF offensive, a two-brigade pincer movement to surround Lydda and Ramla and the rural hinterland to their east, kicked off in the early morning hours of 10 July. The Eighth Brigade, assisted by the Thirty-third Battalion (Alexandroni) and the Forty-fourth Battalion (Kiryati), advanced southward from Kfar Syrkin and eastward from Kafr 'Ana, and took the villages of Qula, al-Tira, Rantiya, al-Yahudiya, and Wilhelma, and Lydda International Airport, south of Yahudiya. The Yiftah Brigade, advancing from al-Bariya northward, took the villages of al-Kunaiyisa, 'Innaba, Kharruba, Jimzu, Daniyal, and Khirbet al-Dhuheiriya, and linked up with the Jewish boarding school compound of Ben Shemen, east of Lydda, which had been under siege since mid-May. The Israelis encountered only light resistance. Indeed, the ease with which the IDF conquered Arab territory in

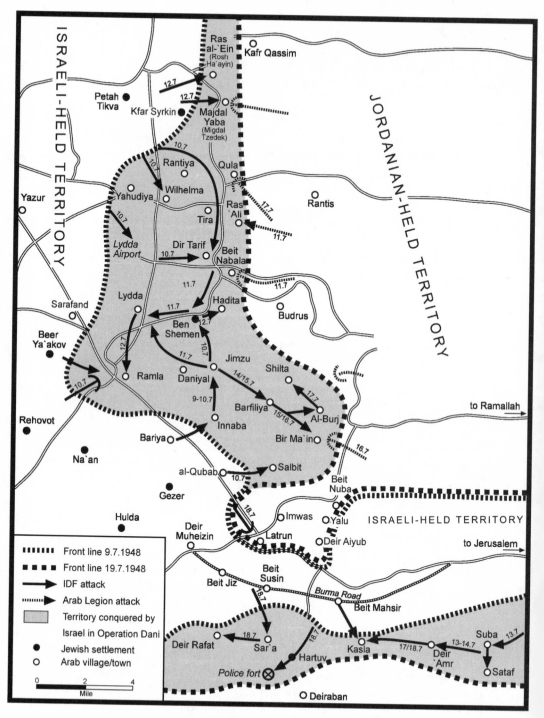

Operation Dani, Lydda and Ramla, July 1948

the first days of the operation prompted Ben-Gurion to remark that, until then, he had believed that the Israelis' "secret weapon" was their spirit. But, in fact, it "was the Arabs: they are such incompetents, it is difficult to imagine."[83]

Things turned difficult later that afternoon, however, when the Legion's First Regiment reached Beit Nabala and engaged the Eighth Brigade outside Deir Tarif, giving it a bloody nose. But the regiment made no subsequent effort to push toward Lydda: Glubb still refused to commit troops to defend the towns (and, indeed, the handful of Legionnaires in Lydda withdrew eastward on the night of 11–12 July).

The IDF renewed its advance on 11 July. The (Palmah) Third Battalion pushed from Daniyal toward Lydda itself but failed to penetrate the defenses. Allon threw in the Eighty-ninth Battalion (Eighth Brigade), under Lieutenant Colonel Moshe Dayan. Its half-tracks, an armored car, and machine gun-mounting jeeps sped southeastward down the road from Ben Shemen, into Lydda, turned south, reaching the outskirts of Ramla—and then turned around and drove back around Lydda to Ben Shemen. The raid lasted forty-seven minutes.[84] The troops appear to have shot at everyone in their path. One participant, "Gideon," later recalled: "[My] jeep made the turn and here at the . . . entrance to the house opposite stands an Arab girl, stands and screams with eyes filled with fear and dread. She is all torn and dripping blood. . . . Around her on the ground lie the corpses of her family. . . . Did I fire at her? . . . But why these thoughts, for we are in the midst of a battle, in the midst of conquest of the town. The enemy is at every corner. Everyone is an enemy. Kill! Destroy! Murder! Otherwise you will be murdered and will not conquer the town."[85]

The raid, which left dozens of Arabs (and nine Israelis) dead, coupled with the Yiftah attack on the Lydda defense line, sent the irregulars into shock;[86] they lost the will to fight. Their morale also probably suffered from having been abandoned by the Legion. That evening, in the Eighty-ninth Battalion's wake, the Third Battalion at last entered Lydda and took up positions in the town center after minor skirmishing.[87] The following morning, Kiryati's Forty-second Battalion moved into Ramla; its notables had surrendered the town the previous night without a fight. In both towns the troops began rounding up young adult males.

The battle for the two towns appeared to be over. But things abruptly turned sour. At around noon, 12 July, a squadron of Legion armored cars drove into Lydda, either to reconnoiter or to look for a stranded officer.[88] They came up against surprised Third Battalion troopers, who thought the town had been pacified. A firefight ensued, and locals joined in, sniping from windows and rooftops. The jittery Palmahniks responded by firing at anything that moved, throwing grenades into houses and massacring detainees in a mosque compound; altogether, "about 250" townspeople died, and many were injured, according to IDF records.[89] Ben-Gurion then authorized Allon to expel the population of Lydda, which had "rebelled," and Ramla. From the first, Ben-Gurion and the IDF commanders had thought in terms of depopulating the two towns.[90] Already on 10 July, the relevant units had been ordered "to allow the speedy flight from Ramla of women, old people, and children."[91] Just after noon, 12 July, Allon's operations officer, Yitzhak Rabin, issued the orders. Yiftah was instructed that "the inhabitants of Lydda must be expelled quickly without attention to age. They should be directed toward Beit Nabala";[92] a similar order reached Kiryati regarding Ramla[93]—despite the surrender instrument that implicitly allowed Ramla's inhabitants to stay (it stated: those "who wish may leave")[94]—though the brigade was instructed to take "all army-age males" prisoner.[95] Yiftah and Kiryati troops methodically expelled that day and the next the towns' fifty thousand inhabitants, and the refugees encamped in them—though, to be sure, many, having endured battles, a massacre, and Israeli conquest, were, by then, probably eager to leave for Arab-controlled areas.

From Lydda, the inhabitants left on foot, some being stripped of money and jewelry by IDF troops at checkpoints on the way out.[96] From Ramla, the population was trucked to a point near the village of al-Qubab, from which they proceeded eastward on foot.[97] During the following days, suffering from hunger and thirst, dozens probably died on the way to Ramallah. An Israeli trooper later described the spoor of the refugee columns, "to begin with [jettisoning] utensils and furniture and in the end, bodies of men, women, and children, scattered along the way. Old people sat beside their carts begging for a drop of water—but there was none."[98] Another soldier recorded vivid impressions of how "children got lost" and how a child fell into a well, and presumably drowned, ignored as his fellow refugees fought over water.[99] "Nobody will ever know how many children died" in the trek, wrote the Legion's commander, John Glubb.[100]

An Israeli commander, probably Allon, later explained that clogging the roads with needy refugees served Israel's strategic purposes by cluttering the main axes against a possible Legion advance westward, by burdening the Legionnaires with tens of thousands of people in dire need of succor, and by generally causing demoralization.[101] Making such military use of refugees was later criticized by Mapam's coleader, Meir Ya'ari.[102]

Without doubt, the refugee wave caused the Legion immediate major logistical problems.[103] The Fourth Regiment reported: "Some 30,000 women and children from among the inhabitants of Lydda, Ramla, and the area are dispersed among the hills, suffering from hunger and thirst to a degree that many of them have died."[104] Legion transport collected and ferried the refugees to Ramallah.[105] A week later, the Legion was reporting that "seventy thousand souls are dispersed in the streets [of Ramallah], most of them poor; they are suffering from a lack of basic goods and water [and] represent a serious health problem." The Ramallah city council appealed to King 'Abdullah to remove them.[106]

But 'Abdullah's (and Glubb's) troubles went beyond the refugees' supply problems. The towns' fall, compounded by the inrush of refugees, some of them crossing the river and reaching Amman itself, and the attendant shortage of ammunition, were to trigger a major military and political crisis; Glubb even spoke of the impending destruction of his army or, alternatively, of resigning or pulling back to the East Bank.[107] In Nablus, Salt, and Amman there were unprecedented street demonstrations. In Amman, "wives and parents" of Legionnaires tried to break into the king's palace; Glubb himself was subjected to spitting and catcalls of "traitor" as his car passed through West Bank villages.[108] In Nablus, the Palestinians in effect drove out the Jordanian governor, Ibrahim Pasha Hashim, and the Iraqi army had had to use force to suppress the demonstrations.[109]

Alec Kirkbride later graphically described the events in Amman on 18 July: "A couple of thousand Palestinian men swept up the hill toward the main [palace] entrance . . . screaming abuse and demanding that the lost towns should be reconquered at once. . . . The king appeared at the top of the main steps of the building; he was a short dignified figure wearing white robes and headdress. He paused for a moment, surveying the seething mob before, [then walked] down the steps to push his way through the line of guardsmen into the thick of the demonstrators. He went up to a prominent individual, who was shouting at the top of his voice, and dealt him a violent blow to the side of the head with the flat of his hand. The recipient of the blow stopped yelling . . . [and] the King could be heard roaring: 'so, you want to fight the Jews, do you? Very well, there is a recruiting office for the army at the back of my house . . . go there and enlist. The rest of you, get the hell down the hillside!' Most of the crowd got the hell down the hillside."[110]

Glubb and Kirkbride regarded the Palestinians as ungrateful. The Legionnaires, at that very moment doing battle "from Latrun to Deir Tarif," had suffered one in four dead or wounded of those who had crossed the river on 15 May—and here were the Palestinians maligning them as "traitors."[111]

But Glubb became the butt of pan-Arab anger. The Political Committee of the Arab League was in session in Amman during 12–13 July. Some participants, including the Iraqis, charged that Glubb was serving Britain, or even worse, the Jews, and that his arguments about ammunition and troop shortages were merely excuses.[112] And, at the same time, the "Syrian and Iraqi authorities and . . . ʿAzzam" were busy berating Britain for helping the Jews by withholding supplies from the Arab armies.[113] "Many" Iraqi expeditionary force officers seemed to feel that "both branches of the Hashemite house" (that is, in Jordan and Iraq) were "in the pay of the British and even working with the Jews."[114] Non-Jordanian Arab politicians seem to have been happy at last to have a stick with which to beat ʿAbdullah and his army, the only one to have registered a substantial success against the Israelis. "One cannot help feeling that many of the Arab leaders would rejoice in the downfall of Jordan," commented Kirkbride.[115] Egyptian journalists at Cairo airport later assailed Glubb—who immediately after the Ten Days went on extended leave to England, perhaps ordered by ʿAbdullah—with: "Why did you betray the Arab cause?" and "Why did you give Lydda and Ramla to the Jews?"[116]

ʿAbdullah, though aware of the true situation, bowed before the storm and summoned Glubb to a meeting of the Council of Ministers, where he was roundly upbraided. The king found it politic to shoulder him with the blame for the loss of the two towns. Talk of ammunition shortages was flippantly dismissed and Glubb's resignation was suggested (though not actually requested): "If you don't want to serve us loyally, there is no need for you to stay," was how ʿAbdullah reportedly phrased it.[117] But the Legion was still in the midst of battle; Glubb couldn't simply walk away. Besides, London pressed him to soldier on.[118]

Without doubt, the Ten Days severely undermined Britain's position. As Kirkbride later put it: "I am struck principally by the extreme precariousness of our position in Transjordan. . . . We have reached a degree of unpopularity which I would have described as impossible six months ago."[119]

Be that as it may, the Israelis believed that they had solved a strategic problem. Or as Ben-Gurion reported to the Cabinet—while completely failing to hint that he had authorized, or that there had been, an expulsion—"in Ramla and Lydda not one Arab inhabitant has remained."[120] Of course, this was wishful thinking—hundreds of Arabs had remained in hiding and hundreds more were to infiltrate back into the two towns during the following months[121] (and, today, the two towns have substantial Arab—and socioeconomically—minority populations).

Meanwhile, to the northeast, Alexandroni (in a suboperation of Dani, Operation Batak) captured Iraqi-held Majdal Yaba and Ras al-ʿEin, north of Qula. An effort on 11 July to take Deir Tarif from the Legion's First Regiment failed. So similarly did an effort that day by the Legion's Third Brigade, driving northwestward from Bir Maʿin, to dislodge Yiftah from Jimzu. During the following days, Alexandroni conducted a bloody seesaw battle with units of the Legion's First Brigade—sent to secure the seam area at the southern end of the Iraqi zone of control in western Samaria—over Qula, re-taking the village for the last time on 18 July, just before the Second Truce came into effect.[122] In place they found the bodies of sixteen Alexandroni troopers left behind when the Legion took the position two days before. One Israeli report read, "On most of them were signs of severe mutilation: stab wounds, some had had their genitals cut off, some were missing ears. One body was cut into many bits with its genitalia stuffed in its mouth. With-out doubt some of the dead fell into Arab hands while alive and were killed subsequently. . . . Their trousers [and] shoes were missing."[123]

The IDF advances of 9–13 July seem to have spent Operation Dani's of-fensive energies. Most of Israel's tanks and much of its other armor was in disrepair, and some units had taken serious casualties. The Israelis were also hamstrung by the expectation of a new UN-imposed truce and fear of a ma-jor Legion counterattack: "Where is the Legion?" Ben-Gurion asked his di-ary.[124] From the start, IDF intelligence had overestimated Legion strength, had no inkling of the Legion's severe ammunition shortages, and was obliv-ious to Jordan's decision to pursue a "phoney war" and abandon Lydda and Ramla to their fate.

So IDF operations from 13 to 18 July were desultory and localized: the idea of pushing on to Ramallah was, in effect, abandoned. Although on 14–17 July Yiftah and Kiryati forces made small additional gains, taking the unde-fended villages of Barfiliya and Salbit southeast of Jimzu, and al-Burj and Shilta, a renewed effort by Harel troops on the night of 15–16 July to take the hilly ridge to the east of Latrun, around Yalu village, failed, as did a last-minute frontal effort an hour or two before the start of the Second Truce led by two Cromwell tanks (driven by British defectors) to take the Latrun po-lice fort. A series of lapses, crowned by a direct hit on one Cromwell's gun,[125] or a stuck shell casing,[126] put paid to the effort. Once again, the IDF had failed to take Latrun. To the north, Yiftah troops suffered a serious re-verse—suffering forty-five dead—at Khirbet Kureikur, east of Shilta.[127]

Meanwhile, in a series of parallel, minor attacks, the Harel Brigade's Sec-ond and Fourth battalions expanded Israel's holdings in the Jerusalem Cor-ridor south of the Tel Aviv–Jerusalem road, taking a series of villages—Suba, Sataf, Khirbet al-Lauz, Khirbet Deir ʿAmr, and ʿAqqur (13–14 July) and Kasla, Beit Umm al-Meis, Beit Thul, Sarʿa, Deir Rafat, ʿIslin, Ishwa, and ʿAr-tuf (17–18 July). At the eastern end of the corridor, on the southern and western peripheries of Jerusalem, units of the IZL and the ʿEtzioni Brigade took the villages of Beit Safafa, ʿEin Karim, and al-Maliha. But a combined IDF-IZL-LHI attack on the Old City on 16–17 July failed, despite the tem-porary capture of a position adjacent to the New Gate. The failure was due partly to a major starting delay and the short time left before the start of the truce in Jerusalem, which was a day earlier than in the rest of the country.[128] The failed attack on the Old City had been initiated by ʿEtzioni Brigade (and Jerusalem district) OC David Shaltiel, contrary to orders by the General Staff, which had preferred that he take Sheikh Jarrah. He was dismissed a few days later and replaced by Dayan.

The upshot of these small successes was that a new, less vulnerable road to Jerusalem became available to the Israelis, paralleling and south of the Burma Road. At the end of the Ten Days, IDF units along the front lines were ordered "to prevent the return of the Arab inhabitants to their towns and villages conquered by us, also with live fire."[129] Refugees encamped near the front lines were driven off.[130]

In sum, by the end of Operation Dani the IDF had made substantial territorial gains, but it had failed in its major strategic objective. Lydda and Ramla and their rural hinterland to the east were in Israeli hands, yet the key fortress of Latrun (not to speak of the town of Ramallah) remained firmly in Legion hands. Glubb had managed to stabilize a south-north line along the Judean-Samarian foothills from Latrun–Beit Nuba to Beit Sira, Budrus, and Qalqilya and retain the bulk of the West Bank and East Jerusalem. Yet the Latrun police fort and its satellite villages—Latrun, Imwas, Deir Aiyub, Yalu, and Beit Nuba—though heavily defended, were now precariously held, constituting a thin wedge of land jutting into Israeli territory. And Glubb's position was doubly precarious, given his munitions shortages. Indeed, on 18 July, in the middle of the last skirmishes of the Ten Days, he had informed Kirkbride's deputy, Christopher Pirie-Gordon—who in turn informed London—that "his supplies of shells and mortars will finally give out some time today or tomorrow at the latest." Without a last-minute resupply, "there will be only the alternatives of the positions being overrun or a general withdrawal [from the West Bank]."[131]

During the Ten Days, as in previous bouts of the war, air operations had little impact on the battles, chiefly because all the air forces were extremely small and weak. Nonetheless, the appearance and actions of aircraft over battlefields and, even more, over capital cities had a certain, if ultimately unquantifiable, effect on military and civilian morale.

The most striking air operation was the attempted bombing on 15 July of King Farouk's ʿAbdeen Palace in Cairo by a lone IAF B-17. Three B-17 Flying Fortresses had been purchased by the Haganah in the United States before 15 May, had been flown to Czechoslovakia to be outfitted and armed, and on 15 July had set out for Israel. Their orders were to bomb Egyptian targets on the way. One headed for Cairo, where it failed to hit the palace but caused some damage nearby,[132] causing Ben-Gurion satisfaction if not joy.[133] The bombing certainly raised morale in Tel Aviv.[134] Some thirty Egyptians died and a railway line was hit.[135] The two other airplanes bombed Rafah (instead of El ʿArish, their ordained target) before landing at ʿEqron Airfield.[136] The Egyptians responded on 16 and 17 July by repeatedly bombing Tel Aviv with Dakotas, accompanied by a Spitfire fighter escort, killing at least fifteen Israelis. The Egyptians lost one Dakota.[137] In the following days the B-17s bombed El ʿArish and Syrian positions around Mishmar Hayarden. On the night of 17–18 July an IAF Dakota bombed Damascus itself, killing about sixty and injuring another eighty to one hundred people. The bombs blew out the windows of the Syrian parliament building.[138] A further bombing, by a lone B-17 bomber on the morning of 18 July, aimed at Maze Airfield but missed, hitting Damascus itself, with bombs and crates of large bottles (to "heighten panic"). Twenty persons were killed and eighty injured, and windows and doors in the apartment occupied by the US chargé d'affaires shattered. This provided "an unpleasant introduction" for the American minister, James Keeley, who had arrived in the Syrian capital the night before.[139] Rich families reportedly fled Damascus, and the Syrian government began building air raid shelters. The Syrians (and Iraqis) reacted that evening by bombing the Ramat David Airfield and Haifa but failed to hit anything.[140]

The IAF Messerschmitt Squadron flew ground-support missions and occasionally intercepted Egyptian aircraft. The Arab air forces were almost completely ineffective; only the Syrian air attacks around Mishmar Hayarden had a serious impact.

The UN Security Council resolution of 15 July brought hostilities to a halt, calling for the reinstatement of the truce no later than 18 July; failure to comply would trigger sanctions against the offender. The Arab media were outraged. One Arab newspaper greeted the announcement this way: "No justice, no logic, no right, no equity, no understanding, but blind submission to everything that is Zionist."[141] The Iraqis, too, argued—or pretended to argue—for continuing the war, mainly to assuage public opinion.[142] The Iraqi prime minister, Salih Jabr, had been remarkably honest about this to the British chargé in Beirut: "He [said that he had decided to speak out against accepting the truce as he had seen] an opportunity for increasing his political stature in Iraq, where public opinion was strongly in favour of continuing the fighting."[143] But for the more level-headed observers, the results of the Ten Days had demonstrated Israel's military superiority, and the Arab leaders were clearly eager that the world force them to comply (though the Arab media routinely broadcast "news" of "fictitious Arab victories to keep at fever heat the already inflamed imagination of the people," as one British diplomat put it).[144] Jordan argued that its lack of ammunition compelled it to cease fire. Indeed, the severe shortage of mortar and artillery rounds left Glubb and Kirkbride in grave doubt whether the Legion could hold the West Bank if fighting was renewed.[145] Pirie-Gordon feared that the Legion "would have difficulty even in protecting the road to Amman."[146] And Egypt, also severely short of ammunition,[147] hadn't the "stomach for further fighting."[148] In August, the British moved some military stores from the Suez area to their bases in Jordan, including twenty-five-pounder and mortar rounds, but they assured the Americans that these would not be handed over to the Legion unless Israel "threatened" to attack Transjordan itself.[149] In effect, Jordan was left with a grave shortage of ammunition that quashed any thought of participation in renewed hostilities. It appears that Iraq, too, was not resupplied.

And so the situation was to remain during the following months: the Arabs were reluctant to renew the war whereas the Israelis—at least in the Cabinet and General Staff—were at least agreeable to, if not eager for, war. In contrast with the First Truce, the Second thus witnessed a reversal of roles. The Arabs henceforward labored to prevent renewed hostilities while the Israelis, who wanted the invaders out of Palestine and the Arab leaders to agree to peace, increasingly understood that neither would be achieved through diplomacy.[150]

No major battles or strategic changes occurred during the Second Truce, which lasted until 15 October. But the period was marked by continuous eruptions of violence. Both sides, especially during the truce's first days, tried to improve their tactical position in various areas; large numbers of Arab refugees continuously tried to infiltrate through Israeli lines to return to their homes or reap crops; and the Egyptians, contrary to the truce terms, barred the passage of convoys to resupply Israel's Negev settlement enclave. All of these resulted in firefights and, occasionally, in skirmishes. Noteworthy in this connection were three large-scale Israeli attempts in late July and August to push convoys to the enclave (one of them was successful).

The biggest military operation during the truce was the Israeli conquest of a cluster of villages south of Haifa dubbed "the Little Triangle": Ijzim, 'Ein Ghazal, and Jaba. The villages repeatedly fired at Israeli traffic along the coast road and were supplied by the Iraqis from northern Samaria. During the Ten Days Ben-Gurion had brushed aside a call for immediate action: "These villages are in our pocket. We can act against them also after the [reinstitution of the] truce. This will be a police action. . . . They are not regarded as en-

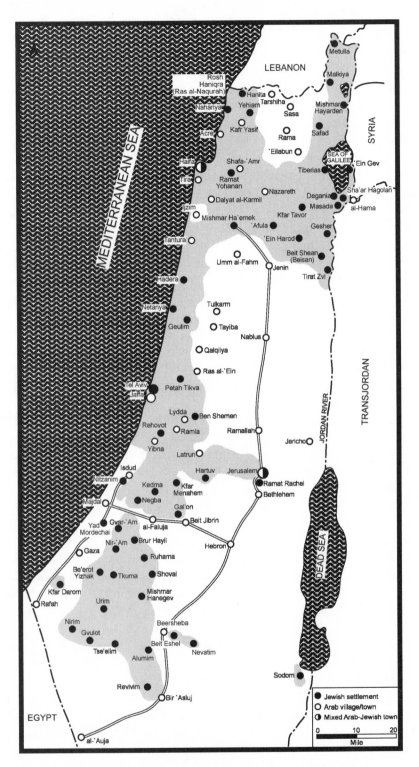

Israeli-held areas at the end of the Ten Days, 19 July 1948

emy forces as their area is ours [that is, inside Israeli territory as defined by the UN partition resolution] and they are inhabitants of the state."[151]

Sniping at traffic continued after the start of the Second Truce, and the villages refused to desist or surrender. The problem had to be resolved.

For several days IDF artillery and aircraft intermittently bombarded the villages, and on 24 July Israel launched *mivtza shoter* (Operation Policeman). The aim was "to gain control" of the coast road between Zikhron Ya'akov and Haifa "and to destroy all the enemy in the area."[152] Alexandroni deployed four infantry companies, armored cars, and several batteries of artillery and mortars. The troops also received air support.[153] By 26 July it was over. Most of the inhabitants fled before and during the attack, reaching northern Samaria; hundreds of others were forcibly expelled during the following days. At least a hundred militiamen and civilians were killed. The IDF blew up most of 'Ein Ghazal and Jaba. Bernadotte subsequently declared the attack unjustified and demanded that the villagers be allowed back. Israel refused.[154]

As with the First Truce, the Second Truce benefited the Israelis more than the Arabs. True, the Arab armies, like Israel's, expanded during the three months of quiet. By early September, according to Yadin, the Egyptian expeditionary force numbered "12,000" soldiers, with a 30 percent increase in armor and artillery and a supplement of three Saudi Arabian battalions and thousands of local auxiliaries; the Legion had recruited additional manpower so that its regiments now had "full complements"; and the Iraqi force had grown to sixteen battalions. All the Arab armies had improved their fortifications.[155]

Nonetheless, the truce favored the Israelis, who used the time more efficiently. The poor UN supervision of sea- and airports ended up working in Israel's favor, since it alone had the wherewithal to buy and transport arms and men into the area. The boost in light weaponry assured "the [Israeli] infantry platoon . . . more firepower than its Arab equivalent," Yadin said. In heavy weapons, such as tanks, combat aircraft, and antitank guns, the IDF remained abysmally deficient.[156] But there were rays of light. Between June and October, Israel's artillery had grown from five to 150 guns.[157] Foreign volunteers—Maha"l—and foreign conscripts—Gaha"l—accounted for about twenty thousand of Israel's eighty-five-thousand-strong army in October and November 1948; almost all arrived after 15 May.[158]

During the truce, the Arabs and Bernadotte pressed Israel to agree to a return of all or some of the refugees. But the Zionist leaders had decided against this. By late summer 1948 a consensus had formed that the refugees were not to be allowed back during the war, and a majority—led by Ben-Gurion and Shertok—believed that it was best that they not return after the war either. The Israelis argued that a discussion of refugee repatriation must await the end of hostilities: in wartime, returnees would constitute a fifth column. But, in private, they added that after the war, too, if allowed back, returnees would constitute a demographic and political time bomb, with the potential to destabilize the Jewish state.

The Arabs, for their part, began to speak of a refugee return as a precondition to opening peace talks. The Arab leaders argued that elementary justice demanded that the refugees be allowed to return to the homes from which they had fled or been ejected. In pressing this demand, they were also aware of the political and military harm to Israel that would attend a mass refugee return; it wasn't simply a matter of "justice."

The Israeli decision to bar a refugee return had consolidated between April and August. The April exodus from Haifa and Jaffa had brought the matter into focus. Initially, the leadership was of two minds. During April, when the Yishuv switched to the offensive, local military and civilian leaders gradually shifted to a "good-bye and good riddance" approach. For months, the Arabs had attacked settlements and traffic; once gone, it was felt, it was best that they not return. The switch in policy among Alexandroni's Arab affairs advisers, as recorded in the minutes of their meetings in late March and early April, is indicative.[159]

On the political plane, though, no policy decision had yet been taken. In early May, after a visit to Haifa, Golda Myerson (Meir), the powerful acting director of the Jewish Agency Political Department, noted the "dreadful" exodus of the town's Arabs and how they had left "the coffee and pita bread" on the tables. She told her colleagues, "I could not avoid [thinking] that this, indeed, had been the picture in many Jewish towns [that is, in World War II Europe]. . . . [Should the Jews] make an effort to bring the Arabs back to Haifa, or not [?] We have decided on a number of rules, and these include: we won't go to Acre and Nazareth to bring back [Haifa's] Arabs. But, at the same time, our behavior should be such that if, because of it, they come back—[then] let them come back. We shouldn't behave badly with the Arabs [who have remained] so that others [who fled] won't return."[160]

This was all pretty vague. But during the following weeks the leaders were compelled to take the bull by the horns as Arab leaders began to press the refugees to return and refugee spokesmen began to press Bernadotte to facilitate it.[161] Without doubt, the pan-Arab invasion of 15 May hardened Israeli hearts toward the refugees. The onslaught of the armies, which threatened to destroy the Yishuv, left the Israelis with little room for error or humanitarian misgivings. As one local official put it: "There are no sentiments in war. . . . Better to cause them injustice than that [we suffer] a disaster. . . . We have no interest in their returning."[162] A powerful anti-return lobby galvanized, consisting of local officials, army commanders, and senior executives in the national bureaucracies. Jewish leaders from Safad, the Mount Gilboʿa area, and Western Galilee wrote or traveled to Tel Aviv to demand that a return of refugees to their area be prevented.[163] The head of the IDF Intelligence Department wrote, "There is a growing movement by the Arab villagers . . . [to] return now. . . . There is a serious danger that they will fortify themselves in their villages . . . and with the resumption of warfare, will constitute at least a [potential] Fifth Column."[164] Yosef Weitz, head of the JNF Lands Department, Elias Sasson, head of the Foreign Ministry's Middle East Affairs Department, and Ezra Danin, an old intelligence hand soon to be named a senior adviser at the Foreign Ministry, banded together as a self-appointed Transfer Committee, advising the Cabinet to bar a return and how to do it. Shertok agreed with Weitz that "the momentum [of Arab flight] must be exploited and turned into an accomplished fact."[165] Weitz, Danin, and Sasson submitted a three-page proposal, "Retroactive Transfer: A Scheme for the Solution of the Arab Question in the State of Israel," to Ben-Gurion. The document set out the means—destruction of abandoned villages and fields, Jewish settlement of Arab sites, prevention of Arab cultivation, help in the orderly settlement of refugees in Arab countries—by which a return was to be prevented.[166] Indeed, the Transfer Committee, led by Weitz and using JNF equipment, in summer 1948 off its own bat leveled about half a dozen villages.[167]

But the lobbying may have been superfluous; the leadership probably needed little convincing. Already on 1 June, a group of senior officials, including Shertok, Cabinet Secretary Zeʾev Sharef, and Minority Affairs Minister Bechor Shitrit, had resolved that the Arabs "were not to be helped to return" and that IDF commanders "were to be issued with the appropriate orders."[168] It was feared that the refugees would try to exploit the impending truce beginning 11 June to infiltrate back to their homes. Front-line units were instructed to bar a refugee return. Oded Brigade HQ instructed its battalions "to take every possible measure to prevent" a return; this would "prevent tactical and political complications down the road."[169] The army, too, appears to have been thinking of both the military and political advantages of barring a return.

The Cabinet discussed the issue on 16 June. In speech after speech, with Ben-Gurion and Shertok setting the tone, the ministers spoke against refugee repatriation. "I believe . . . we must prevent their return at all costs," said Ben-Gurion, adding, "I will be for them not returning also after the war." Shertok agreed: "Had anyone arisen among us and said that one day we should expel all of them—that would have been madness. But if this happened in the course of the turbulence of war, a war that the Arab people declared against us, and because of Arab flight—then that is one of those revolutionary changes after which [the clock of] history cannot be turned back. . . . The aggressive enemy brought this about and the blood is on his head . . . and all the lands and the houses . . . are spoils of war. . . . All this is just compensation for the [Jewish] blood spilled, for the destruction of [Jewish property]."

Preventing a return was not just a national interest; it had personal implications for some of the ministers. Agriculture Minister Cisling, from Mapam (Ahdut Ha'avodah wing), said that the villagers of Qumiya, which overlooked his home in the Jezreel Valley kibbutz 'Ein Harod and from which it had been harassed with fire, should also not be allowed back.[170]

No vote was taken on 16 June—though orders immediately went out to all front-line units to bar refugee infiltration "also with live fire."[171] Within weeks the consensus turned into government policy, partly in response to Bernadotte's growingly persistent appeals to allow refugee repatriation. On 28 July the Cabinet formally resolved, by nine votes to two, that "so long as the war continues there is no agreement to the return of the refugees."[172] The decision was augmented in September: "A final solution to the refugee problem [would be reached] as part of a general settlement when peace comes."[173] During the following weeks, the Cabinet repeatedly reendorsed this position. But peace never came—and the refugees never returned.

During the Second Truce the IDF not only barred refugees from crossing back into Israeli-held territory but systematically scoured the newly conquered areas for returnees, preventing resettlement in the abandoned and semiabandoned villages. A few would-be returnees were killed along the front lines; many more were rounded up and shoved back across the borders. The degree of resolution and harshness in implementation varied from area to area and unit to unit. There was a perpetual cat-and-mouse struggle between the troops and the returning and resettling refugees.

On 20 July, Giv'ati's Fifty-first Battalion HQ cautioned its companies: "With the start of the [Second] Truce there is a fear of the return of the villagers to the conquered villages. Such a return could also be accompanied by the infiltration of a camouflaged enemy force." The companies were ordered to prevent infiltration to the villages of Summeil, Barqusiya, Bi'lin, Masmiya al-Saghira, al-Tina, Kheima, Idnibba, Jilya, Qazaza, and Mughallis, all close to the front line with the Egyptians. The units were told to "destroy" any "armed force" and "to expel . . . unarmed villagers."[174] The previous day, a patrol had visited Kheima, Jilya, Qazaza, Mughallis, and Idnibba to ascertain that they were empty. Near Kheima, it encountered a group of Arabs in a grove of carob trees, refugees from Masmiya and ʿAjjur. "They were warned . . . that if anyone entered areas under our control—they would be killed. They promised to obey and were released."[175] During the following days, patrols expelled refugees near Tel al-Safi, al-Tina, and Mughallis, apparently killing three of those initially detained.[176] At Tel al-Safi, the Fifty-third Battalion was left an unwelcome "dowry" by a previous unit—"fourteen Arab males, aged over sixty, four of them handicapped, and six old Arab women, all blind, and eight toddlers." The Fifty-third's intelligence officer complained and requested a vehicle to solve the "problem" (presumably by expulsion).[177] A fortnight later, Givʿati reported Arabs returning to several villages to harvest crops and resettle. Units torched Kheima and Mukheizin and scoured Idnibba, Mughallis, Jilya, Qazaza, and Sajd, killing a number of Arabs in firefights.[178]

Perhaps the most extensive rear-area Second Truce "cleansing" operation was carried out by Givʿati in the sand dunes around Yibna–Arab Sukreir–Nabi Rubin, just north of the Egyptian lines. The operation was named *mivtza nikayon* (Operation Cleaning); armed units were to be destroyed and unarmed civilians expelled.[179] The operation was mounted on 28 August. Shacks and huts were torched, ten Arabs were killed, three were injured, and three were captured (many others probably fled as the IDF approached). Twenty cows, camels, and mules were also killed. The refugees were from Zarnuqa, Yibna, and Qubeiba and were trying to harvest their fields. "The hunger rampant among the refugees forces them to endanger themselves [and] penetrate our area," stated the IDF report.[180]

Similar operations took place in other areas immediately behind the front lines. On 8 August, for example, a Golani Brigade company scoured the area of Umm al-Zinat in the Hills of Menashe, southeast of Haifa, "to seek out and destroy the enemy." The company encountered a band of fleeing Arabs and fired at them, killing one. Another group of Arabs was discovered in a nearby wadi. One man was interrogated and shot (the report does not say why). At Umm al-Daraj, the unit encountered another group, which included women. They said they were Druze, "[so] we did nothing to them."[181] Some miles to the east, another Golani unit ambushed a group of Arabs trying to enter the abandoned village of Hittin "to gather their belongings." The unit chased them off, killing some men and pack animals.[182] In the northern Negev enclave, cut off from the core of the Jewish state by the Egyptian expeditionary force, the Yiftah Brigade regularly scoured villages and bedouin encampments. On 22 September the troops entered the abandoned villages of Muharraqa and Kaufakha, detained four men, and blew up houses. A number of "elderly residents" were allowed to stay.[183]

The IDF units patrolling the newly conquered areas regularly drove off or skirmished with armed harvesters. The encounters in early August between one Golani patrol and harvesters in the Lower Galilee were typical. Near the abandoned village of al-Mujeidil the unit saw "groups of Arab women working fields. I [squad leader Shalom Lipman] ordered the machine gun to fire three bursts over their heads, to drive them off. They fled in the direction of the olive grove." But after the patrol left, the Arabs returned. The patrol came back and encountered "a group of Arab men and women. . . . I opened fire at them and as a result one Arab man died and one Arab man and one woman were injured. In the two incidents, I expended 31 bullets." The following day, 6 August, the patrol returned and witnessed two funeral processions; one of those injured the previous day presumably had died. A day or so later, the patrol again returned to the site and saw a large group of women harvesting. "When we approached them to drive them off, an Arab male [was found] hiding near them, [and] he was executed by us. The women were warned not to return to this area of Mujeidil." The company commander appended his comment to the squad's report: "I gave firm orders to stymie every attempt to return to the area of the village of Mujeidil and to act with determination."[184] At about the same time, Giv'ati's Fifty-second Battalion reported sending a patrol to the fields of Sawafir, Jaladiya, and Beit 'Affa, where "a large number of Arabs were seen reaping. . . . Most . . . were women and old men." The patrol killed eight Arabs and detained three.[185]

Alongside the roundups and expulsions and the prevention of harvesting, the Yishuv, starting in spring 1948, took a series of measures that helped assure the nonreturn of the refugees. Some of the procedures stemmed from immediate military necessity; others from economic requirements. But, taken together, all obviated any possibility of a return.

Probably the most important measure was the near-systematic destruction of villages after conquest and depopulation. While two villages, 'Arab Suqreir and Qisariya, had been demolished by Haganah troops in January and February 1948, the start of a policy of demolition can be pinpointed to the first half of April, when Haganah units involved in Operation Nahshon and in the battle around Mishmar Ha'emek were ordered to level the villages after conquest. "We intend to destroy the villages when we leave them," a Golani unit fighting around Mishmar Ha'emek informed Carmeli and Golani HQs on 9 April.[186] That day, the Palmah's First Battalion demolished the village Ghubaiya al-Fauqa.[187] The next day Haganah troops occupied and blew up thirty houses in al-Kafrin and additional houses in Abu Zureiq and Abu Shusha.[188] The last houses in Abu Zureiq, a large village northwest of Mishmar Ha'emek, were destroyed on 14 April.[189]

A similar pattern prevailed in Operation Nahshon, when the Haganah tried to secure the road to Jerusalem. While the original operational order, from 4 April,[190] did not call for the destruction of the villages, follow-up orders almost invariably included instructions to demolish houses. On 10–11 April the Palmah captured and destroyed the village of Qaluniya, west of Jerusalem.[191] "When I left," recorded an American journalist, "sappers were blowing up the houses. One after another, the solid stone buildings, some built in elaborate city style, exploded and crashed."[192] The Harel Brigade blew up the village of Saris on 16 April.[193] That day, Nahshon Corps HQ ordered the troops "to take and destroy" Beit Suriq,[194] Sajd,[195] and Beit Jiz, and part of Qubab.[196] The reasoning behind the demolitions was simple: the Haganah lacked troops to garrison every empty village and feared that, should they be left intact, they would be reoccupied by Arab irregulars, who would again cut off the road to Jerusalem, or be used as bases by the Arab armies when they invaded.

During the following weeks, Haganah/IDF units as a matter of routine destroyed—when they had sufficient explosives or caterpillars—captured villages, partially or wholly. Without doubt, an element of vengefulness and punishment underlay the destruction—to pay back villages for specific acts of aggression or "the Arabs" for the war they had unleashed upon the Yishuv. There were also economic considerations: the Jewish settlement institutions had always needed and wanted more land, for existing and projected settlements; destroying villages meant the nonreturn of the original inhabitants, which, in turn, meant that more land would become available for Jewish use. Above and beyond this there were general and specific military considerations, And from summer 1948, immediate and long-term political calculations came to the fore: the villages had to be destroyed to prevent a return in order to obviate the rise of a fifth column, to keep down Arab numbers, and to maintain Arab-free areas the Jewish state intended to coopt.

During June and July awareness of the destruction and dissent from it, on ideological grounds, surfaced in the Cabinet, largely from Mapam ministers, who in principle favored—or at least said they favored—the return of the refugees after the war. As Cisling put it in the Cabinet on 16 June, "it was one thing" to destroy villages in battle; it was quite another to destroy a site "a month later, in cold blood, out of political calculation. . . . This course will not reduce the number of Arabs who will return to the Land of Israel. It will [only] increase the number of [our] enemies."[197]

But a more powerful, and ultimately effective, source of opposition arose inside the Yishuv that summer: the Finance Ministry. Seen from an economic perspective, and against the backdrop of the massive Jewish immigration that began to flood the country, the destruction of rural and urban housing made no sense in terms of the new state's problems. The abandoned houses were needed for the new immigrants (*olim*). At the least, urged Yitzhak Gvirtz, director of the Arab (or Absentee) Property Department, the houses should be stripped of reusable assets such as doors, window frames, and tiles before being demolished.[198]

The problem was greater than window frames, however. The houses themselves needed to be preserved or at least those deemed habitable by olim. By autumn the country faced an acute, growing housing shortage. As Reuven Gordon, an inspector of abandoned property responsible for Isdud, complained in December: "A week ago [soldiers] . . . began to destroy buildings. . . . Of course, if the army has an order, they carry it out, but I ask, can't they find [another] solution . . . as these villages near Rehovot can be used to house new immigrants."[199] A few weeks earlier, Finance Minister Eliʿezer Kaplan told his fellow ministers: "Every possibility of accommodating [immigrants] must be exploited and a general order must be issued to the army not to destroy houses without a reason."[200] By early winter, Kaplan had his wish, and the army generally refrained from destroying villages and urban housing. But by then the country's rural and urban landscapes had been radically transformed.

More than the house demolitions ushered in this transformation. Also at work were the takeover and allocation of the abandoned agricultural lands, the establishment of new Jewish settlements in the countryside, and the settlement of olim in the largely abandoned Arab urban neighborhoods.

In spring 1948 Jewish settlements began to reap abandoned Arab fields around the country while preventing Arab farmers from harvesting their crops. This was a mirror image of Arab efforts to harass Jewish harvesters, but the Arabs were less efficient. The reaping was "crucial to the war effort," said Gvirtz.[201] It undermined the economy, self-confidence, and staying power of the rural Arabs, and it bolstered the Yishuv's war economy. The harvesting, carried out by Jewish settlements, was largely organized by Jewish regional authorities, and it gave rise to acquisitive urges. During May the line between asking for one-time permission to harvest abandoned fields and requesting permanent possession was imperceptibly crossed. By July, settlements were formally writing to the newly formed Agriculture Ministry for permanent leaseholds. As Kibbutz Neve-Yam, asking for the lands of neighboring Sarafand, south of Haifa, put it: the Arab exodus "opened up the possibility of a radical solution which once and for all could give us sufficient land for the development of [our] settlement."[202] Weitz, certain that the refugees would not be returning, jotted down in his diary that "a complete agrarian revolution" was under way.[203]

From early August, the Agriculture Ministry and the JNF began leasing the abandoned fields to settlements, usually for six to twelve months. The political and territorial situation was still unclear; the state might yet be forced to absorb returnees. It was also uncertain, in the flux of war and with manpower mobilized, how much additional land each settlement could handle after the expected demobilization. Besides, the settlement agencies wanted to retain their freedom to plan the country's agricultural future— and they needed to leave open their options, as between the expansion of existing settlements and the establishment of new ones, while taking account of the claims of the various political parties and their affiliated settlement associations. Indeed, during and immediately after the war there were repeated feuds—between established and new settlements, between private farmers and collective settlements, and among the settlement associations—over the confiscated lands. Kibbutzim usually fared better than private farmers and *moshavim* (cooperative villages), established settlements better than new ones.[204]

In 1949, Weitz was to summarize the agrarian revolution: "A great change has taken place before our eyes. The spirit of Israel, in a giant thrust, has burst through the obstacles, and has conquered the keys to the land, and the road to fulfillment has been freed from its bonds and its guardians-enemies [that is, the British]. Now, only now, the hour has come for making carefully considered [regional development] plans. . . . The abandoned lands will never return to their absentee owners."[205]

A major facet of this revolution was the establishment of new settlements. About 180 were set up in the course of 1948 and 1949, most on confiscated Arab lands. A handful were established on the actual sites of Arab villages (usually where the houses were of stone, rather than clay or mud, and deemed adequate for renovation and Jewish habitation).

Setting up settlements was a matter both of ideology and of strategy. Zionism from inception had held that agricultural settlement was the chief means by which the Jewish people would "return to the soil," fashion the "new Jew," and again become productive members of the family of nations. Settlement was also the means by which the Land of Israel would be "redeemed" from its centuries-old desolation and usurpation by foreigners. Last, the settlement grid would determine the envisioned state's contours and frontiers. Militarily speaking, the settlements, most of them kibbutzim, had proved their worth: they had successfully rebuffed Palestinian Arab assault and subsequently were a principal obstacle in the path of the invading Arab armies.

During the war's first, critical months Zionist energies were directed at defending the Yishuv. But in mid-April, within days of the strategic switch to the offensive, the national institutions began to establish new settlements, not only to assure control of the main roads linking the Yishuv's concentrations of population and the border areas but also to consolidate its hold on newly conquered territory. Initially, the new outposts were set up on Jewish-owned land within the November 1947 Jewish state partition borders. Kibbutz Brur Hayil, the first settlement, was established on Jewish land near the Arab village of Bureir in the northern Negev on 18–19 April.

Within months, though, such niceties were thrown to the wind, and settlements were established on Arab-owned land and outside the partition borders. This change can be traced to July, just after the Ten Days, when Weitz and his colleagues submitted to Ben-Gurion a plan for twenty-one settlements in Western Galilee and the Ramla-Lydda area, mostly on Arab-owned land outside the partition borders. Even so, in principle, the plan called for the establishment of the settlements outside actual village sites, so that the "houses and trees" would remain available for returning fellahin.[206]

The idea of leaving aside "surplus land" for returning villagers was pressed by Mapam, which supported a refugee return. But this was an exemplary case of having your cake and eating it: the idea allowed Mapam's affiliated kibbutzim (organized in two associations, the Kibbutz Artzi and Kibbutz Meuhad) to partake of the newly acquired Arab lands while maintaining their ideological principles. The three dozen settlements—almost all kibbutzim—that went up between September 1948 and January 1949 were mostly on Arab-owned land along the new state's borders.

This did not solve the problem of the now-empty areas in the interior of the state, captured and still to be captured—principally in the Galilee, Jerusalem Corridor, and northern Negev approaches. In September, Weitz proposed setting up "150" settlements in these areas. The plan was honed over the following weeks and resubmitted by Weitz, Yehoshua Eshel, the IDF's settlement officer, and Haim Gvati of the Agricultural Center, as a ninety-six-settlement plan. The plan embodied a new principle: "Wherever conditions make it necessary, the new settlement should be established [on the site of] the existing village." The idea of keeping, or leaving aside, "surplus" land for returnees was now abandoned.[207] Senior Mapam figures and Kaplan registered objections. Weitz, annoyed, dryly commented: "Many of the ministers were worrying more about [re-]settling the Arabs than settling the Jews."[208] But Ben-Gurion effectively terminated the argument about setting aside "surplus lands" when he said, in December, "Along the borders, and in each village we will take everything, as per our settlement needs.

We will not let the Arabs back."[209] Most of the hundred or so settlements established in 1949 were immigrant moshavim.

Between May 1948 and December 1951 Israel absorbed some seven hundred thousand Jewish immigrants—or slightly more than its total Jewish population at the dawn of statehood. A small proportion was settled in moshavim. The vast majority were installed in the abandoned Arab neighborhoods of the big towns, in the depopulated small towns, and, when the housing ran out, in vast transit camps (*ma'abarot*) on the peripheries of the towns (from which, after months or years, the immigrants were relocated to the towns once housing had been constructed).

The accommodation of immigrants in abandoned urban housing began hard on the heels of the Arab exodus from the various sites. Already in January 1948 Ben-Gurion had ordered Shaltiel, the Jerusalem District commander, "to settle Jews in every house in abandoned, half-Arab neighborhood[s], such as Romema [in West Jerusalem]."[210] During the following months, abandoned urban houses were often settled by Jewish refugees from Palestine's war zones (altogether some seventy thousand Jews had been displaced from rural and urban settlements during the war). By early May 1948, eighteen thousand Jewish "refugees" were living in the greater Tel Aviv area.[211]

But it was Weitz's Transfer Committee that first suggested as a matter of policy—with the main aim of preventing an Arab refugee return—the settlement of new Jewish immigrants in abandoned Arab housing. The first Arab town to be settled by olim was Jaffa, occupied by the Haganah in mid-May; the first batch of settlers moved into its "German Colony" in early July. By September, twenty-four hundred Jewish families, most of them immigrants, had moved into the town, while the remaining Arabs—some five thousand souls—had (during August) been concentrated in part of the central ʿAjami neighborhood. The concentration facilitated the settlement of Jewish families elsewhere in town and provided for the safety of the Arabs (who had become targets of intimidation and robbery by Jewish criminals). Certain IDF units also laid hold of Jaffa properties in which to house the homeless families of soldiers and officers.

By August, twelve to thirteen thousand olim had been settled in Haifa's empty neighborhoods (after the town's four thousand remaining Arabs had been concentrated in the Wadi Nisnas neighborhood and ʿAbbas Street). The Arab quarters of West Jerusalem were first settled in February and March 1948 with Jewish refugees from the town's front-line districts; new olim were settled in the abandoned districts beginning in September.

The settlement of the smaller towns began a little later. They initially lacked the infrastructure—running water, electricity, a sewage system—that allowed swift settlement. New olim were first settled in Acre, which still had a substantial Arab population, in early October 1948; Ramla and (the abandoned Arab districts of) Safad were settled in November; Beersheba in February 1949; and Beisan in April.[212]

Taken together, the destruction of the villages and parts of the Arab urban neighborhoods; the confiscation of Arab fields, orchards, and groves and their cultivation by Jews; the establishment of settlements on Arab lands and, occasionally, on Arab village sites; and the settlement of the Arab urban districts by Jewish immigrants all contributed to a vast revolution in Palestine's human and physical landscape, a revolution that was to continue and consolidate during the following years. By the early 1950s, the former Arab areas of the territory that had become Israel bore little resemblance to what they had looked like in 1947 (except for the handful of picturesque villages preserved more or less intact by the new owners, such as ʿEin Karim, outside Jerusalem, and ʿEin Hod, south of Haifa).

The condition of many of the four hundred thousand Arabs displaced by midsummer 1948 was "appalling."[213] They were temporarily housed in public buildings in towns and under trees on the outskirts of villages or in abandoned British army camps in the countryside (most of which became refugee camps) in Arab-held areas of the country. Some received local or international food aid; others did not. Except for Jordan, the Arab states did little for them, except make "unfulfilled promises," in King ʿAbdullah's phrase.[214] The aid that came arrived mainly from the West, through groups such as the International Committee of the Red Cross and the Quakers. Western observers feared the outbreak of epidemics before or with the onset of winter. The new US special representative (later ambassador) to Israel, James McDonald—in the 1930s he had served as League of Nations high commissioner for German refugees—estimated that "100,000 old men, women and children," "who are shelterless and have little or no food," would die when the rains came.[215] (Such jeremiads were to prove groundless. There were no major epidemics, and few refugees died that winter. The Palestinians, a largely agricultural people and used to the outdoors, proved hardy.)

Bernadotte organized immediate relief. He had Trygve Lie send Sir Raphael Cilento, the Australian director of the UN Division of Social Activities, to investigate. Bernadotte solicited aid from dozens of governments and organizations and set up a Disaster Relief Project (later called the Refugee Relief Project), naming Cilento as its head, to coordinate the contributions and their distribution. But corruption and mismanagement in the distribution centers (Beirut, Damascus) left most of the aid—such as thousands of tents donated by Britain—in warehouses. The Red Cross reported at the end of September that, despite the "hullabaloo," the "tragic fact is that substantially nothing in food or goods have reached refugees."[216] Lie next appointed Stanton Griffis, US ambassador to Cairo, to head up a newly created body, the UN Relief for Palestine Refugees in the Near East, effectively replacing Cilento. A year later, in December 1949, this organization was succeeded by the United Nations Relief and Works Agency for Palestine Refugees in the Near East (UNRWA), which continues today to provide food, education, and other aid to the refugees and their descendants.

The tilt in the balance of power in Israel's favor, the continuation of the no war, no peace, situation—with continuous truce infringements by both sides—and the grave strain the continued mobilization put on Israel's society and economy gradually persuaded the Israelis that they must act. "It is doubtful if we can hold up in this situation [for long] from a financial perspective," Ben-Gurion told his Cabinet colleagues on 1 August. "[And] our international position will be increasingly undermined. . . . The invaders must be forced to make peace or leave the country, or we ourselves will expel them. . . . In my opinion, the end of August or maximum the middle of September is the [deadline]. . . . If until then there isn't peace . . . and the invading armies haven't left the country, we ourselves will drive them out."[217] American Secretary of State George Marshall defined Israel's mood as growingly "chauvinistic and imperialistic."[218] Ben-Gurion put it bluntly: faced with a choice of the Palestine problem being resolved diplomatically, involving major territorial losses for Israel, or militarily, "I am for a decision by war. . . . Otherwise, we will be defeated," he told his Cabinet colleagues.[219]

But the Israelis were undecided about where to strike. Ben-Gurion, with his Jerusalem-centric perspective, generally focused on the West Bank, to safeguard Jerusalem and drive out or destroy the Legion. Other ministers, and the IDF General Staff, preferred a blow against the Egyptian army, regarded as the Arabs' most powerful and geopolitically most threatening force (its troops were on the outskirts of Jerusalem and, at Isdud, some twenty miles from Tel Aviv).

After the Ten Days, however, the Israeli populace seems to have lapsed into political torpor. The feeling was rife that Israel had won and the war had ended. As the weeks passed, this feeling, that Israel had assured its survival, deepened. Or as Yadin put it: "The impression has emerged among the public [that] . . . from a military perspective we are already 'on top' [al hasus, literally on the horse]. . . . This impression has been created by, on the one hand, the exaggeration of divisions of opinion, as it were, on the Arab side . . . and, on the other hand, the occasional exaggeration of our army's successes while hiding its defeats."[220]

Ben-Gurion and the military understood that the situation, with much of Israel's adult male population indefinitely mobilized and the Arab armies at the gates of Tel Aviv and Jerusalem, was untenable. On 9 September Ben-Gurion summoned the editors of the dailies "to explain that the war was not yet over, and that most difficult tests were, perhaps, still before us. . . . In the Yishuv there was no dread of the situation, no austerity, no readiness to bear the burden. There was a feeling of relief, that we have established a state and won and overcome the anarchy. But we are far from secure—and let us not underestimate the enemy's power or desire to win." The editors queried the military censorship, the continued "persecution" of the dissidents (the IZL and LHI), and wastefulness at IDF headquarters. Ben-Gurion responded that the war was a struggle of "the Jewish people against the whole world, and also against the history of the Dispersion, and if the newspaper editors felt this, they would know what not to write and what to write, and how."[221]

Matters hung fire through August and the first half of September. The IDF was not yet ready, and in any case, Israel could not strike before the Arabs offered a gross, clear provocation. Meanwhile, the American and British foreign ministries worked on a solution to supersede the partition resolution. They agreed that partition was now a fait accompli. But it had to be between a smaller Israel and the Arab states rather than the Palestinians. The foreign ministries of the Anglo-Saxon powers hammered out a rough plan. The Negev should go to Jordan (or Egypt) and Jerusalem should be internationalized.[222] But the Americans wanted to move slowly and covertly; presidential and congressional elections, in which the Jewish vote and America's generally pro-Israeli public opinion would play a part, were scheduled for early November. The new thinking was coordinated with Bernadotte—and its Anglo-American authorship was carefully concealed.

American and British representatives—Robert McClintock and Sir John Troutbeck, head of the British Middle East Office—in the second week of September separately and secretly flew to Rhodes, where Bernadotte was drafting proposals. Each came with his own nation's version of the plan.[223]

What emerged was the forty-thousand-word "Progress Report of the United Nations Mediator for Palestine," known as Bernadotte's "second plan." It was largely drafted and completed by Ralph Bunche on 16 September. Bernadotte was off to Israel and had signed blank pages for Bunche to fill in. Bernadotte fully trusted his deputy.[224] The mediator, who flew out of Rhodes early on 17 September, never actually saw the full, final text; by the afternoon he was dead.

The plan called for a straightforward partition of Palestine between Israel and Jordan (with no "Union" between them). Israel was to get the whole of the Galilee and the Mediterranean coastline and Jordan all the Negev, south of the Majdal-Faluja line, as well as the West Bank (including Lydda and Ramla). Jerusalem was to be internationalized under UN control, with separate communal autonomy for its Arab and Jewish communities. Lydda and Haifa were to be "free ports." The Palestinian refugees were to enjoy a right of return or, if they chose, to receive compensation for their lost property instead. The plan was to be implemented by a "Conciliation Commission," which was to replace the UN mediator (Bernadotte, frustrated and tired, had already decided to quit and return to the Swedish Red Cross).

Before the Israelis and Arabs could react, Bernadotte was assassinated in West Jerusalem by four LHI gunmen. The assassination, which had been authorized by the LHI high command or "Center" (composed of Yitzhak Shamir, Natan Yelin-Mor, and Israel Eldad), overshadowed all responses to the plan. It caught the Israeli government and security forces completely by surprise and was vastly embarrassing. Without doubt, however, the assassination was in part the upshot of the anti-Bernadotte, anti-UN atmosphere generated by the government and its spokesmen through the summer against the backdrop of continued truce violations along the front lines and restrictions on immigration and the supply of the Jewish Negev settlements. The Israeli populace increasingly viewed the UN-engineered truce as serving Arab interests and as an obstacle to an Israeli victory and an end to the war. By September, Bernadotte was seen as anti-Israeli, indeed anti-Semitic (despite his World War II reputation as a "savior" of Jews) and as a pawn of the (pro-Arab) British Foreign Office. One Israeli newspaper even ran an article titled "the Monster in Rhodes."[225]

The assassination triggered a massive Israeli crackdown on the LHI (and IZL) in Jerusalem. The police never found the actual killers; Ben-Gurion probably did not want them found for internal political reasons. But the two organizations ceased to exist. The IZL, which had already disbanded over May and June in the rest of the country, converted into a political party, Herut. The LHI, most of its troopers inducted into the army at the end of May, vanished altogether.

Bernadotte's plan was submitted to the UN General Assembly and published by Trygve Lie immediately after his death. The assassination effectively placed Israel in the dock and should have paved the way for the assembly's adoption of the plan. But it didn't. Secretary of State Marshall may have been persuaded that it offered "a fair basis for a settlement"[226] (though, to be sure, the White House, on the eve of the elections, could never have endorsed it in face of Israeli opposition)—yet both Israel and the Arabs immediately rejected it, for much the same reasons that they had opposed the first Bernadotte "plan." The Arabs were still unwilling to accept or recognize Israel's existence. Lebanese prime minister Riad al-Sulh told a British diplomat "not for the first time, that it had taken the Arabs over a century to expel the Crusader[s] but they had succeeded in the end";[227] and Egyptian foreign minister Ahmed Muhammad Khashaba said: "No Arab government could accept a settlement of this kind. . . . In due course [the Arabs] would be strong enough to accomplish what was at present impossible owing to their military weakness."[228] The Israelis, for their part, opposed anything less than the 1947 partition resolution borders and, indeed, now wanted better ones, which they knew to be militarily within reach. The General Assembly, at Arab urging, repeatedly postponed a debate on the plan.

In any case, the plan was quickly overtaken by events—principally the IDF offensive against the Egyptian expeditionary force that began on 15 October and the offensive against the ALA in the Galilee two weeks later. The resultant Israeli conquest of the northern Negev and Central Galilee killed any thought of a trade-off between the Negev (to the Arabs) and the Galilee (to the Jews), which was the core of the Bernadotte plan. So the assassination, as one historian has put it, "does not belong to . . . [those] which have 'changed history.' . . . The struggle for Palestine was decided elsewhere."[229]

Although Bernadotte's murder may have briefly delayed the launch of Israel's long-contemplated offensive to break the logjam created by the truce—Israel could not politically afford to violate the truce immediately after the killing—the plan itself almost certainly assured that the offensive would be directed against the Egyptians in the south rather than the Jordanians in the center of the country. The plan threatened to award the Negev to the Arabs; the IDF offensive in the south led to the conquest of the northern Negev and the link-up between Israel and the isolated settlement enclave, significantly reducing the possibility of an eventual transfer of the Negev to the Arabs through diplomacy.

In August and September Egyptian intelligence picked up hints of the IDF's preparations for an offensive. And the Egyptians may have understood that the plan's award of the Negev to the Arabs might well trigger an IDF offensive to produce a preemptive fait accompli.

Be that as it may, King Farouk—bypassing Foreign Minister Khashaba—hurriedly dispatched Kamil Riyad, a court official, to Paris to sound out the Israelis secretly about terms for a separate peace. Farouk appears to have feared that the United Nations would adopt the Bernadotte plan, which awarded the Negev to Jordan; he was loath to see further Hashemite aggrandizement. Indeed, the Hashemite-Egyptian rift only burgeoned in the months following the invasion. Egyptian and Jordanian officers and officials, and their local Palestinian supporters, were forever quarreling over control of the Bethlehem-Hebron area, where large Egyptian formations coexisted alongside smaller Jordanian units. Both sides had appointed military governors, though for the time being, the Jordanians pretended to accept Egyptian dominance. The two sides even bickered over the size of the flags their units flew in the towns, the Egyptians complaining to the United Nations that the Jordanians' was a couple of inches larger than their own.[230]

On 21 September, Riyad met Elias Sasson, the Israeli Foreign Ministry's chief Arabist, for four hours. Sasson had been sent to Paris by Shertok in early July specifically to meet Arab leaders and diplomats to try to initiate peace negotiations. He had written letters to Arab leaders and diplomats, but nothing came of them. The Arabs did not appear keen on direct negotiations, let alone peace.[231]

Now the Egyptians were interested, and Riyad's overture seemed promising. At their first meeting, Riyad described Egypt's worries, not least of which was the fractious Arab attitude toward the Palestine problem, and asked Sasson to submit "a basis" for a separate Israeli-Egyptian settlement.[232] Sasson formulated a fourteen-point proposal. It included Egyptian agreement to regard the establishment of Israel as a fait accompli and to withdraw its troops from Palestine. Israel would not occupy the areas vacated and agreed that the Palestinians could determine whether they wanted an independent state or preferred annexation by one or other of the Arab states.[233]

The palace and Egyptian officials in Paris looked over the draft and offered comments. Their language was a tad obscure. Shertok believed that the Egyptians were ready implicitly to recognize Israel and withdraw from UN-earmarked Israeli territory but that they also demanded retention of the Rafah-Isdud coastal strip and all the Negev or at least the Palestine-Egypt border area east of Sinai.[234] Sasson and Riyad met again on 30 September. The Egyptians wanted the southern part of Arab Palestine. They opposed a Jordanian takeover of the area and feared that the British would establish bases there. They also opposed Jewish control of the holy sites in Jerusalem and sought assurances about future Jewish immigration and guarantees against future Israeli expansionism and economic domination. The Egyptians were also worried about communist penetration of the region via Israel.[235] Israel responded with clarifications: it rejected any "formal limitation" on Jewish immigration and was willing to rule jointly with "the neighboring Arab State" over Jerusalem's Old City or allow "international rule" and to provide free transit for goods through Haifa port. The future Israeli-Egyptian border could be negotiated.[236]

The talks came to naught. It is probable that they were merely an Egyptian stratagem designed to stave off the expected Israeli offensive, as Ben-Gurion suspected, and that Cairo never seriously intended to negotiate peace, let alone make peace, with the Jewish state. Still, the Egyptians, for the first time, had talked with Israel.

The Israelis did not allow the talks to hamstring their military planning. During late September and early October the plans matured. The post–Ten Days situation, with Israel's Negev settlements enclave and the Negev Brigade, along with the uninhabited remainder of the Negev to the south and east, cut off from the coastal heartland and effectively besieged by the Egyptians, was unbearable. During the truce the Israelis had had to supply the Negev by air, mostly at night, stretching the IAF's resources. With winter approaching, weather conditions would hobble the airlifts.[237] And Israel could not indefinitely sustain the no war, no peace situation, with its manpower mobilized (unlike the Arabs, for whom the war-making required only a sliver of their populations). Last, Bernadotte's "award" of the Negev to the Arabs augured a permanent loss, with international endorsement, of the territory.

From August into early October, the Israeli leadership debated where and when to strike. As the truce dragged on and the likelihood that diplomacy could lead to an Arab withdrawal from Palestine decreased, the pressure to renew hostilities grew. The Israelis waited for an opportune moment.

But for months they wavered on the "where." Galili put it in a nutshell: "The choice is hard: [it is] between the center of gravity in the south . . . to capture the whole of the Negev, and the center of gravity in the Center vis-à-vis the Jordanians and Iraqis—to redeem Jerusalem completely and to move the eastern border as far as possible eastward. Each of our front commanders recommends and preaches to mount the offensive on his front."[238]

There were political considerations. King ʿAbdullah had for years been the only Arab leader willing to talk peace with the Yishuv; Ben-Gurion believed that the man really wanted peace. On the other hand, he had joined the invasion and engaged the Jews in battle around and in Jerusalem, giving the Haganah and IDF a trouncing. The question was whether an enlarged Jordanian kingdom, with its army poised along Israel's borders near West Jerusalem and Tel Aviv, was really an optimal situation. Would it not be better, perhaps, to push the Legion back across the river and help set up an Arab puppet state or autonomous area in the heartland of Palestine? This, at least, was how Shertok and some of his aides were leaning in summer 1948. As the foreign minister put it, "Without completely removing from the agenda the possibility of Transjordanian annexation of the Arab part of Western Palestine, we should prefer the establishment of an independent [Palestinian] Arab state in Western Palestine. In any event, we should strive to clarify this possibility and emphasize that it is preferable and desirable on our part as opposed to [Jordanian] annexation." He was thinking of Palestine Arab Opposition politicians figuring prominently in such a polity.[239]

There were good military reasons to strike eastward: the situation of Jewish Jerusalem was still precarious. Jordanian gunners sitting in East Jerusalem and along the southern and northern edges of the corridor from Hulda to the city were a perpetual threat, as was the Iraqi deployment in the northern West Bank, from whose western edges—Qalqilya-Tulkarm—it was a bare ten miles to the Mediterranean. The Jordan River was always seen as the country's "natural" defensible, strategic border. In addition, a Jordanian West Bank might eventually host British bases—and the British were seen as hostile. There were also good historical-ideological reasons: the West Bank, with Jerusalem's Old City at its center, was, after all, the crucible of Judaism, the historic heartland of the Jewish people. A renascent Jewish state without Hebron, Bethlehem (birthplace of King David), Bethel, Shechem (Nablus), and, above all, East Jerusalem, with the Wailing Wall, Temple Mount, and the necropolis to its east, was felt by many, and not only on the Revisionist Right, to be incomplete.

On the other hand, the West Bank and East Jerusalem had not been earmarked by the United Nations for the Jewish state; the bulk of the Negev had been. Taking the Negev would enjoy at least a measure of international legitimacy. The northern Negev settlements had to be relieved. And, last, the large—potentially the strongest—Arab army a mere 18 miles from Tel Aviv, was a standing mortal threat. If the war ended with the Egyptians still at Isdud, who knew what might happen ten or twenty years hence? This was the situation the status quo and the Bernadotte plan threatened to perpetuate.

The IDF believed that it had sufficient power to launch a major offensive on only one front. Its effort in July to launch simultaneous offensives had resulted in failure against the Egyptians and the Syrians and only partial success against the Jordanians. The IDF still lacked sufficient heavy weaponry. The General Staff plumped for the southern option. In early September it issued preliminary operational orders for a major assault against the Egyptians, *mivtza esser* (Operation Ten)—from the ten plagues meted out to Egypt by the Almighty in Moses' day—to be mounted later that month.[240] The planned operation was later renamed *mivtza yoav*, Operation Yoav.

But matters were delayed by the Bernadotte assassination—and by political indecision at the top. The Cabinet would have to resolve where and when to strike. The decision in effect was taken, in two stages, at the Cabinet meetings of 26 September and 6 October.

The precipitant to the first debate was an attack by Palestinian irregulars on 24 September on Position 219 near the ruins of ancient Modiʿin, the birthplace of the Maccabees, in which twenty-three Israeli soldiers were killed, and Arab Legion harassment of Jewish convoys near Latrun and along the Burma Road.[241] Position 219 was immediately retaken, but Ben-Gurion hoped to use the events as a fulcrum for a large-scale IDF assault against the Arab Legion at Latrun and points east, to firmly secure the length of the Tel Aviv–Jerusalem road. He understood that this could provoke Arab attacks along the whole West Bank front or even an Egyptian attack in the south, renewing the war. But he was not averse to this: "If as a result war will break out throughout the country . . . I see this as positive for a number of reasons." He explained that the IDF could then conquer the remainder of the Galilee, break through the Egyptian line between Majdal and Beit Jibrin, and link up with the Negev settlements enclave.

As to the center of the country, it is not completely clear whether Ben-Gurion wanted the IDF to conquer the whole of the West Bank or only a large part of it, with or without East Jerusalem. In the course of the 26 September meeting, he said different things. But the thrust of his thinking was probably embodied in the following passage: "We have [that is, there are] two sorts of *goyim* [non-Jews], Arabs and Christians. I don't know who are better. If I had to choose, I would choose the Christian world. But I have no choice. The Land of Israel is in this part of the world, surrounded by Arabs. And we will have to, to the extent it is up to us, to find a way to [coexist with] the Arabs—[find] a way to an agreement, to a compromise. . . . We are now full of bitterness toward the Arab world, but they are here and will remain here. And we must look to the future." Ben-Gurion seemed to be saying that the IDF should conquer the western edges of the West Bank, thus widening the Jewish-held Coastal Plain, and expand the Israeli-held Jezreel Valley southward, perhaps as far as Nablus, but leave in Arab hands the hilly spine from Nablus through Ramallah to East Jerusalem. He preferred that the Arabs retain East Jerusalem and Israel West Jerusalem rather than that all the city become a Christian-ruled international zone.

But the majority of the Cabinet opposed an offensive in the West Bank. Justice Minister Pinhas Rosenblueth (Rosen) reacted by saying: "I heard Ben-Gurion's words with dread, but also amazement." Renewing the war would result in the bombing "of our airfields, the bombing of Tel Aviv." He quoted Ben-Gurion as saying, only a few days before, that Bernadotte's assassination prevented an Israeli renewal of hostilities. Health Minister Haim Moshe Shapira argued that one could also lose in war. "We tried to conquer Latrun six times, and who knows what will happen on the seventh try." And renewing the war would hurt Israel's international position. Transport Minister David Remez said, "Both to murder Bernadotte and to defy UN decisions—that is a bit much." Minority Affairs and Police Minister Bechor Shitrit feared that the Americans would cut off economic aid. Religious Affairs Minister Yehuda Leib Fishman (Maimon) said that the Old City was a matter "for the Messiah. We will not conquer it." But he supported the campaign to secure the road to Jerusalem. The two Mapam ministers were divided—Bentov (Hashomer Hatza'ir) seemed to oppose any Israeli military initiative and sought to leave the way open for a deal with King 'Abdullah while Cisling (Ahdut Ha'avodah) supported both an attack on Latrun and "securing the Negev."

Ben-Gurion was adamant. He said, "Were it possible to achieve the minimum through an agreement with the Arabs—I would do it, because I am full of fear and dread of the militarization of the youth in our state. I already see it in the souls of the children, and I did not dream of such a people and I don't want it." He pressed his proposal to attack Latrun; the attack on Position 219 could not be left unanswered.

But the Cabinet voted seven to five against.[242] The ministers seem to have been motivated by the Bernadotte assassination and its repercussions on Israel's international standing; by fears that an attack in the West Bank would frustrate a deal with 'Abdullah; and by the possibility that the defeat of the Legion might suck in the British (via their mutual defense pact with Jordan) and/or result in the incorporation of hundreds of thousands of additional Arabs, resident in the West Bank, by Israel.

Ben-Gurion was subsequently to call the Cabinet's decision a *bechiya ledorot* (a cause for lamentation for generations), since he feared that it had put paid to any thought of acquiring Judea and Samaria, along with the Old City of Jerusalem, for Israel, perhaps forever.

Having nixed the "Jordanian option," the Cabinet in effect ushered in the offensive against the Egyptians. On 6 October it debated and decided on an offensive in the south—to be triggered by an Egyptian provocation. The aim was to link up with the settlements enclave and break the back of the Egyptian army. But Ben-Gurion still hoped that the renewed hostilities would result in Israeli conquest of the West Bank.

Ben-Gurion told the ministers that the IDF believed that it could "destroy the whole Egyptian force in seven days" (he was being wildly optimistic) and that the army could then take over the Bethlehem-Hebron area "unopposed." Indeed, such a victory would mean that the whole of the south, "from Jerusalem to 'Aqaba," would be in Israeli hands. There would then be no need to conquer Latrun; a road could be built, south of the current corridor, to Jerusalem that would run outside the range of Jordanian artillery.

Ben-Gurion (incorrectly) predicted that the other Arab armies, with the Iraqis in the lead, would intervene in the Israeli-Egyptian hostilities.

If the Arabs in the West Bank joined in, Ben-Gurion said, "the intention" was to send several brigades down the Jordan Valley to cut off and envelop the Iraqi force in Samaria (and perhaps the Legion in Judea, as well). But if the other Arab armies did nothing, Israel would leave the West Bank alone.

Ben-Gurion was not overly worried about the international reactions to an offensive in the south: "[Impending are] elections in America. This was not a decisive factor, but it is an important factor . . . and it would be a crime and idiocy to miss this [opportunity]. . . . [Pro-Israeli] cables [even] arrive from *goyim* [standing for election to Congress]. . . . They send greetings and want a reply and to use it in their electoral district. Therefore at this time the Americans won't rush to condemn us."[243]

What helped Ben-Gurion and the other ministers make up their minds was the arrival, earlier that day, of information from Washington and Paris that President Truman had instructed Marshall to cease pushing the Bernadotte plan—which Israel feared would be adopted by the United Nations—and to renew American support for the 29 November 1947 partition borders—which meant that the bulk of the Negev would remain Israeli.[244]

Bentov countered, "Our final objective, after all, is to make peace with the Arab world." The question was whether the contemplated offensive would bring this objective any closer. But most of the ministers backed Ben-Gurion. The Cabinet voted for the offensive,[245] with Shertok, away in Paris, joining the "ayes."[246] The ministers were not informed, by Shertok or Ben-Gurion, of the previous weeks' Egyptian peace feelers.

Following the meeting, the IDF General Staff refined the plan. Like Ben-Gurion, several generals felt that renewed hostilities in the south would enable the IDF to advance also in the center of the country, to take Beit Jala and Bethlehem, and possibly parts of the northern West Bank.[247]

8

Operations Yoav and Hiram

THE SOUTH

The Egyptians had no interest in renewing the war. By mid-October their high command was under no illusions. It was keenly aware of its army's weakness and vulnerability and of Israel's growing strength. The expeditionary force was overstretched—strung out along three axes, between El ʿArish and Isdud along the coast, with its back to the sea; between ʿAuja, Beersheba, and Bethlehem to the east; and between Majdal and Beit Jibrin— and short of manpower, weaponry, and ammunition. The high command knew that the other Arab armies would offer them no help. Months before, the Egyptians had abandoned any idea of further advance; they hoped merely to emerge with their gains intact. Their army was on the outskirts of Jerusalem and twenty miles from Tel Aviv and, entrenched along the Majdal–Beit Jibrin road, separating the Negev from the Jewish state. They had not destroyed the Jewish state or defeated the IDF. But they had "saved" a substantial part of Palestine for the Arabs.

From the Israeli perspective, things looked very different, indeed, grim. True, they had stopped the Egyptian advance. But the bulk of the territory allocated by the United Nations for Jewish statehood—the Negev and its northern approaches—was either in Egyptian hands or cut off, and the expeditionary force threatened the long-term security of the state's core. If the front lines of 14 October were to turn into permanent borders, Israel would be truncated and extremely vulnerable. Moreover, the no-peace, no-war situation was untenable. As David Ben-Gurion put it to his ministers on 26 September, "A protracted truce will break us."[1] The Egyptian expeditionary force had to be destroyed or, at the least, driven from Palestine. The IDF brass, keenly aware of Egypt's political isolation and military vulnerability, was chafing at the bit.[2]

The operational order for Operation Yoav called for "the routing [*migur*] of the Egyptian army." The IDF deployed four brigades—Giv'ati, the Eighth, Yiftah, and the Negev—later joined by elements of the Ninth Brigade (Oded), as well as assorted supporting units, including three battalions of artillery and mortars. In the first stage, the IDF intended to drive wedges between the Egyptian forward positions along the south-north Rafah-Isdud and west-east Majdal–Beit Jibrin axes, "open a corridor to the [besieged] Negev [enclave]," and capture Faluja and 'Iraq al-Manshiya, midway between Majdal and Beit Jibrin; in stages "two" and "three," the IDF hoped to conquer Majdal and Gaza, respectively.[3]

The plan was a compromise between the General Staff's desire to destroy the core of the Egyptian expeditionary force through main assault and the more subtle approach of the newly appointed OC Southern Command, Yigal Allon, who preferred a staggered, indirect approach based on disrupting the Egyptian lines of communication and isolating the Egyptian brigades in pockets, the pockets then to be reduced *ad seriatim*.[4] The Allon approach eventually prevailed. The originally envisaged frontal assaults on Gaza and Majdal were deferred, and the first stage of Operation Yoav, during 15–22 October, resulted in the separation of the main western and eastern wings of the Egyptian army, the severing of the Majdal–Beit Jibrin line, and the encirclement of a brigade-size force at Faluja. Israeli forces also severed the Rafah-Isdud road, imperiling the brigade strung out between Gaza and Isdud. In the following days, the eastern wing of the Egyptian army, between Beersheba and Bethlehem, crumbled, most of the units retreating, without battle, to Sinai, and the brigade deployed on the road to Isdud retreated to Gaza, abandoning Isdud and Majdal to the Israelis.

In the weeks before the operation, the IDF infiltrated most of the refurbished Yiftah Brigade—the troops by foot and in nighttime convoys, one of them consisting of eighty vehicles (Egyptian troops noticed the convoy but reasoned that it was their own and failed to interfere),[5] and their heavy equipment mostly by airlift—into the besieged northern Negev enclave so that the Egyptians could be assaulted from both north and south of the Majdal–Beit Jibrin line. Many of the Negev Brigade's troops were airlifted in the aircraft returning northward, out of the enclave, for rest and reequipment.

On the eve of Yoav, the Egyptian expeditionary force consisted of the equivalent of four brigades, with nine regular infantry battalions, three artillery battalions, and two armored battalions, and assorted auxiliary formations, including Saudi and Sudanese battalions and companies, several Egyptian reserve infantry battalions, and hundreds of Muslim Brotherhood and Palestinian irregulars.[6]

The area from El ʿArish to Gaza was held by the Third Brigade, which included the Third Infantry Battalion; the road from Yad-Mordechai northward through Majdal to Hamama and the western section of the west-east wedge, from Majdal to ʿIraq al-Manshiya, were held by the reinforced Fourth Brigade, which included the First, Second, Sixth, and Ninth battalions, a number of artillery battalions, and some Saudi, Sudanese, and local irregular companies; the coastal strip from Hamama northward to Isdud was held by the Second Brigade, which included the Fourth and Seventh infantry battalions and part of the Fifth Infantry Battalion; and the curving strip of territory stretching northeastward from ʿAuja al-Hafir on the old Negev-Sinai frontier through Bir ʿAsluj and Beersheba, to the Hebron Hills and Bethlehem, was held by the ragtag "Light Forces Command," which included the First (reserve) Infantry Battalion, part of the Fifth Infantry Battalion, and battalions of Muslim Brotherhood troops and other irregulars.[7]

The main Egyptian formations along the coast were supported by a battalion of sixteen light Mark VI tanks and a battalion of armored cars, including some Humber IIIs. The infantry was also supported by a battalion of twenty-five-pounders (twenty-four guns), batteries of eighteen-pounders, and a number of 4.5-inch and 6-inch Howitzers. The force had four antiaircraft batteries (of 3.7-inch and 40 mm guns). The infantry battalions had six-pounder antitank guns. The "Light Forces Command" had the support of six 6-inch Howitzers and four six-pounder antitank guns but no armored cars or other tracked vehicles. The Egyptian force was severely lacking in ammunition, and some of what it had was of World War I vintage.[8]

Ben-Gurion defined the Cabinet decision of 6 October to attack the Egyptians as "the gravest [that is, most important] since we decided [on 12 May] to establish the state."[9] He understood that the offensive would unfold in the shadow of almost certain and speedy UN interference: "[The battles] won't continue for more than four-five days, as one can assume that the Security Council will immediately intervene. Seven days will be the maximum." This meant that the IDF had to attack with great force and speed and achieve its objectives quickly.[10]

The Egyptians seem to have sensed that an Israeli attack was imminent: in the days before Yoav they canceled all leave, and the front line units were apparently placed on alert.[11] Still, they were inadequately prepared for what hit them.

For political reasons, the Israeli plan called for the Egyptians to fire the first shots; Israel must not be branded the aggressor. As Ben-Gurion told the Cabinet: "A giant effort must be made [to show?] that the initiative and the responsibility come from the Arab side or at least that the whole question of the initiative and responsibility will be blurred."[12]

Operation Yoav began on 15 October. During the previous weeks, the Egyptians had regularly blocked with fire the passage to the beleaguered northern Negev settlements of supply convoys, contrary to the truce terms. The IDF anticipated that they would continue to conform to pattern. A convoy was sent in from Karatiya, near Faluja, at around 3:00 PM. But "as the convoy covered every additional mile unmolested, our nerves were stretched to the breaking point," recalled Yitzhak Rabin, Allon's chief of operations. "The excuse for our attack was slipping out of our grasp." In the end, the Egyptians obliged with a few rounds. The Israelis responded and then blew up one of their own fuel trucks to cause a commotion, and the Egyptians let loose and sent six Spitfires to attack Israeli positions at Dorot.[13] "We had our pretext," Rabin recalled.[14]

The IAF—then consisting of eleven serviceable fighter aircraft (four Messerschmitts and seven Spitfires), three B-17s, and more than a dozen converted civilian aircraft[15]—went into action. In his order of the day, IAF commander Aharon Remez had written: "Let every soldier, every pilot and air crew member, every mechanic know . . . that the fate of the corps, the people and state [depend on him]. Our soldiers at the fronts are looking skyward. We will not disappoint them."[16] The assault by the whole of the IAF hit the main Egyptian airfield at El ʿArish and targets in Gaza and Majdal, the two Egyptian ground force HQs, at 6:00 PM. The aim was to catch the Egyptians on the ground and achieve air superiority, and to sow confusion in their command structure. At El ʿArish, the IAF achieved complete surprise and, together with continuous follow-up raids, rendered the airfield inoperative (the Israeli daily *Davar*, absurdly, compared the initial strike to "the blow launched by the Japanese against Pearl Harbor").[17] The raids on Gaza and Majdal were inaccurate and militarily ineffective. But the raiders hit the village of al-Jura, mistaking it for Majdal, with devastating effect; al-Jura served as a refugee way station. A follow-up raid on Majdal the following day was more effective. A captured Egyptian soldier described the raids: "In Majdal the IAF bombing hit an artillery communications position: four were killed, two were injured, and the signals truck was blown to bits. Terrible was the strike against the refugees living in al-Jura. He said that some 200–300 were

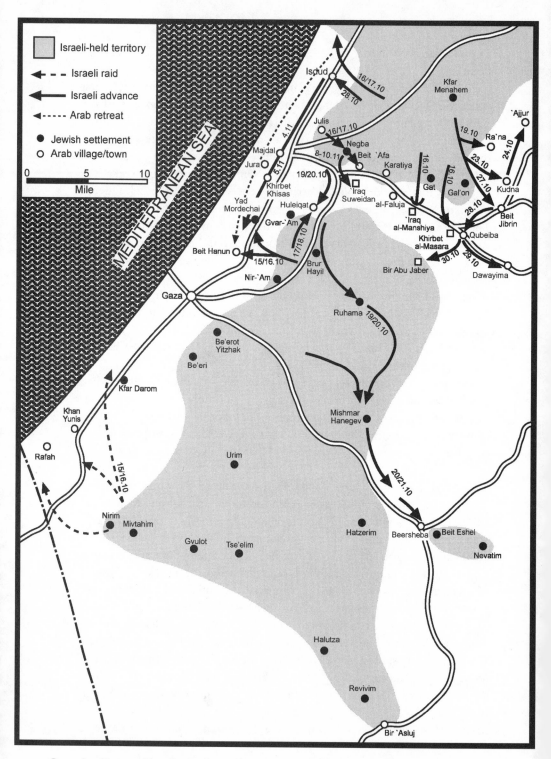

Legend:

Israeli-held territory

← - - Israeli raid

← Israeli advance

◄ · · · · Arab retreat

● Jewish settlement

○ Arab village/town

0   5   10
Mile

MEDITERRANEAN SEA

Isdud
16/17.10
28.10
Kfar Menahem
`Ajjur
19.10
Ra`na
23.10
24.10
Julis
16/17.10
Negba
Beit `Afa
8-10.11
Karatiya
16.10
Gat
16.10
Gal`on
27.10
Kudna
Majdal
Jura
5.11
4.11
19/20.10
Khirbet Khisas
Iraq Suweidan
al-Faluja
28.10
Beit Jibrin
Yad Mordechai
Huleiqat
`Iraq al-Manshiya
Khirbet al-Masara
Qubeiba
Gvar-`Am
17/18.10
Bir Abu Jaber
30.10
28.10
Dawayima
Beit Hanun
15/16.10
Brur Hayil
Nir-`Am
Gaza
Ruhama
19/20.10
Be'erot Yitzhak
Be'eri
Kfar Darom
Mishmar Hanegev
Khan Yunis
Urim
Rafah
15/16.10
20/21.10
Nirim
Mivtahim
Hatzerim
Beersheba
Beit Eshel
Gvulot
Tse'elim
Nevatim
Halutza
Revivim
Bir `Asluj

Operation Yoav and its aftermath, northern Negev, Majdal, 15 October–10 November 1948

killed and injured. In their second visit to Majdal [on 16 October] the aircraft hit 30–40 soldiers."[18]

One of the "bomb-chuckers"—usually air cadets—on board the Commando aircraft, Yoash Tzidon, later described the modus operandi: "[We] stood in a row in the cargo hold and rolled the bombs, whose detonators were neutralized by a pin, like a grenade, toward the open cargo door. The head of the team stood there, pulled out the pins, and then pushed out the ready bombs as quickly as possible. . . . We [eventually] reached a pace of [chucking out] a bomb per second. These were night missions and the targeting was done 'approximately' by the pilot. Surprisingly, we occasionally hit the targets. We flew at 20,000 feet . . . and we circled . . . over the target area without oxygen sometimes for more than two hours. . . . The Egyptian AA fire was always strong."[19]

Throughout Yoav, the IAF was to enjoy complete air supremacy. Though the two air forces were about even in the number of serviceable aircraft, the IAF had an overwhelming advantage in capable air- and ground crews. The IAF flew eight times as many missions as the Egyptians during Yoav. The Egyptians also suffered from a severe shortage in aerial munitions and spare parts.[20] But in all, given the smallness of the air forces involved, air capabilities and operations had little effect on the fighting.

The IDF's ground effort began on the night of 15–16 October and was pressed relentlessly for seven days. That first night, Giv'ati's Fifty-third Battalion cut the Majdal–Beit Jibrin road by capturing hilltop Position 224.9 and Khirbet al-Masara, between 'Iraq al-Manshiya and Qubeiba.[21] Simultaneously, units of the Yiftah and Negev Brigades, advancing from Kibbutz Nir-'Am, occupied a series of hilltop positions just east of Beit Hanun, from which IDF machine guns, mortars, and artillery henceforth dominated the Gaza-Majdal road. Repeated Egyptian counterattacks failed to dislodge the Israelis. Simultaneously, to keep the Egyptians guessing about the operation's strategic objectives, the Negev Brigade's Ninth Battalion mounted a series of (largely unsuccessful) raids to the southwest, harassing the Egyptians near Rafah, Khan Yunis, and the ruins of Kfar Darom.[22]

Allon's plan called not just for severing the Majdal–Beit Jibrin axis but also for chopping up the Egyptian forces deployed along it, isolating one unit from another. On 16 October, the IDF's Eighty-second and Seventh battalions failed to take the village of 'Iraq al-Manshiya, roughly midway between Majdal and Beit Jibrin, suffering more than a hundred casualties. But that night, 16–17 October, Giv'ati drove a second wedge through the Majdal–Beit Jibrin line, south of Negba. The Fifty-first Battalion in hard-fought battles took Egyptian positions "103," "113," and "100" and a fourth position overlooking the "Crossroads," effectively cutting the road between the ʿIraq Suweidan police fort and Majdal. The Israelis attacked with determination—and "hatred" of the invader, according to the battalion's OC Yehuda Wallach.[23] One soldier, Yaʿakov Arnon, wrote a letter to his parents just before the battle: "I was pampered at home, relatively spoiled. But you educated me to always to sacrifice on behalf of Zionism—and I am now off to fulfill the mission." He died later that day on Hill 113.[24] Follow-up efforts on the nights of 17–18 and 18–19 October by Givʿati to take the Huleikat positions and by Oded to cut the Egyptians' bypass road from ʿIraq Suweidan to ʿIraq al-Manshiya just south of Karatiya were beaten off.

By early 19 October it appeared that the IDF had been only partially successful. Ben-Gurion jotted down in his diary: "It is clear that we still don't have soldiers. Our boys are excellent, and they are good Zionists, but not yet soldiers."[25] He even vented his doubts about Allon: "I fear that Yigal Allon is unable to command such a wide front."[26]

But this was to misread the significance of what had happened. True, several units had failed to uproot well-entrenched, tenacious Egyptian infantrymen and gunners. But the IDF had driven powerful wedges between the western (coastal) and eastern (Hebron Hills) arms of the Egyptian army, effectively isolating the eastern arm, and had driven a second wedge, between Gaza and Majdal. These successes had knocked the Egyptian high command off balance, preparing the ground for the following days' clinchers. Indeed, already on 19 October General al-Muwawi hastily withdrew his command post—which he saw as threatened with entrapment—from Majdal back to Gaza, using a dirt track west of Beit Hanun.

Al-Muwawi had acted just in time. That night, 19–20 October, Yiftah units expanded the western wedge, occupying Beit Hanun astride the Majdal-Gaza road;[27] and a few miles to the east, Givʿati's Fifty-second and Fifty-fourth battalions completed the conquest of the north-south road from Julis through the "Crossroads" to Huleikat, taking the Huleikat positions,[28] forging continuity between the core Jewish state area to the north and the Negev enclave at Brur Hayil–Gvar-ʿAm. At Huleikat, the Egyptians and their Saudi auxiliaries had fought bravely, the Givʿati troops suffering twenty-eight dead and seventy wounded in seven hours of combat with bayonets and grenades.[29] A simultaneous effort by Givʿati's Fifty-first Battalion to take the ʿIraq Suweidan fort, immediately to the east, had failed. But the Egyptians strung out between Bethlehem and Hebron were now completely cut off from the western arm of the expeditionary force,[30] and four thousand Egyptian troops were surrounded in an enclave, to be known as the "Faluja Pocket," along the Majdal–Beit Jibrin line, between ʿIraq Suweidan and

Khirbet al-Masara. They were to remain there, under siege, until late February 1949.

General Al-Muwawi knew that the game was up. To save the two arms of his army he had to pull back from Isdud–Majdal–Beit Jibrin and Bethlehem-Hebron and regroup in a greatly reduced line between Beersheba and Gaza. At issue, he believed, was no longer the conquest or retention of (parts of) Palestine but "the defense of the Land of Egypt." This was the gist of his cable to Cairo in late afternoon, 20 October, and Cairo's response that evening; Israeli intelligence intercepted both communications.[31] Israeli intelligence also intercepted Egypt's request for Jordanian and Iraqi assistance—and their de facto responses, amounting to a "no."[32]

But if the Egyptians were hard-pressed militarily, the Israelis were running out of political time. Already on 16 October General William Riley, the American head of the UN Observer Mission, had demanded that Israel halt its assault and return to the 14 October lines. Ben-Gurion ignored him, but the unanimous Security Council's call on 19 October for "an immediate and effective ceasefire," to be followed by negotiations geared to achieving a "withdrawal" to 14 October, was a little more serious.[33] However, Israel, as expressed in a telegram from Eban that Ben-Gurion quoted in Cabinet, saw the démarche as "weak." Eban noted that the Americans had refrained from participating in the discussion[34] and that the Soviets had been instrumental in preventing an explicit demand for Israeli withdrawal to the previous lines. Ben-Gurion, without consulting the Cabinet, delayed a response to give the army more time. The al-Muwawi intercepts probably contributed to Ben-Gurion's resolve.[35]

Israel dragged its feet for two days. On 21 October it informed the United Nations of its readiness to comply. On 22 October Acting Mediator Ralph Bunche ordered the two sides to cease fire at 12:00 GMT that day. Israel's interior minister, Yitzhak Gruenbaum, concluded: "I have a feeling, that each time we succeed—someone stops us and prevents us from exploiting the situation to the end, and we do what that 'someone' wants. On the other hand—when the Arabs are winning—no one ever stops them."[36]

This sense, and reality, of last-minute UN interventions denying Israel full military victories was to hound Israeli policy-makers down the decades. Nonetheless, by 22 October the IDF was to achieve one additional, major success.

Sensing that he had hours rather than days, Allon on 19 October had a choice—to go for Majdal and Gaza or to take Beersheba, the Negev's capital, which would seal the fate of the eastern wing of the Egyptian army and bolster Israel's political claim to the Negev. He chose—the General Staff allowed him discretion—Beersheba, knowing that a head-on collision in the coastal towns would be costly and that their capture would probably not be accomplished in the relevant time frame. Allon had taken note of the Egyptians' impressive stamina in defense. He explained: "It emerged that the Egyptian command had instilled into their troops the belief that the Jews do not take prisoners, but rather kill the prisoners. Thus every position saw itself compelled to fight to the death. . . . Though we tried to circulate handbills and information [to the contrary] and to create bad blood between officers and men and between [Arab] locals and the [Egyptian] army, we failed to persuade them that we take prisoners and are hospitable [to POWs]."[37] (Ben-Gurion, incidentally, thought simply that "the Egyptians had fought with great courage"—on Hill 113, at Huleikat, and especially at ʿIraq Suweidan.)[38]

Ben-Gurion was skeptical about the IDF's ability to take Beersheba in twenty-four to forty-eight hours.[39] But Allon went ahead. Late on 19 October he sent off a flying column, consisting of the Eighty-second Armored and the Seventh Infantry battalions, through the newly established Huleikat passage. It covered the distance to Beersheba in less than two days. On the way, it was joined by elements of the Ninth Battalion. On 21 October the three battalions stormed into Beersheba, taking only a handful of casualties, though the town was defended by a regular infantry battalion (the First) with artillery and mortar batteries and hundreds of North African, Egyptian, and Palestinian auxiliaries. The first Ben-Gurion heard of the conquest, apparently, was from an Arab radio station.[40]

About 120 Egyptian soldiers were taken prisoner. Many of Beersheba's inhabitants had fled to Hebron days before, following IAF bombings; a few had stayed put. Palmah poet Hayim Guri was later to describe the battle's aftermath, the "corpses . . . lying face down, leaning against a wall, on all fours"; the looting ("the blinding gold of the spoils"); the "eruption of the black wolf of hatred"; "the eternal prisoners' face."[41] A number of POWs were murdered by Ninth Battalion troops bent on avenging fallen comrades (Guri's "wolf of hatred"?): they threw a grenade into the mosque where POWs were being held; a number of civilians were executed after being stripped of valuables.[42] Most prisoners were placed in detention centers and set to work cleaning up the town. The civilians, about 350 of them, were expelled to Gaza.[43]

Hard on the heels of the fall of Beersheba, the Egyptians suffered a second blow—the sinking of their flagship, the *Amir Farouk*, a 1,440-ton British-built sloop. The ship and a minesweeper were sighted by the Israelis on 21 October off the Gaza coast, and a squadron of three one-man, explosive-packed speedboats, accompanied by a pickup boat, were sent to intercept.

Leading the squadron was Yohai Bin-Nun, commander of the small naval commando unit. The two Egyptian ships were carrying troops. They had their lights on and apparently believed that the UN cease-fire was in effect. Two speedboats attacked the *Amir Farouk*, the seaman on each jumping off seconds before his boat rammed the Egyptian's hull. The flagship capsized and sank. The third speedboat, crewed by Bin-Nun, badly damaged the minesweeper, which the Egyptians later tugged back to Alexandria. The three commandos, swimming among hundreds of Egyptians, many of them dead or wounded, were retrieved by the pickup boat. Ben-Gurion later took the three commandos to lunch.[44]

While Allon's troops were attacking at Beit Hanun, Huleikat, and Beer-sheba, the IDF General Staff—to pin down unengaged Egyptian forces and widen the corridor to West Jerusalem as well as to secure the length of the Jerusalem–Tel Aviv railway line—authorized the Harel and ʿEtzioni Brigades to mount twin attacks on the Egyptians and local irregulars in the Beit Shemesh and Bethlehem areas. The two brigade commanders, Yosef Tabenkin and Moshe Dayan, had for weeks been pressing the high command to allow them to conquer East Jerusalem, the ruins of the ʿEtzion Bloc, and Hebron. The General Staff cautioned that the assaults must end by dawn 21 October or before the cease-fire took effect.

On the night of 19–20 October, in *mivtza hahar* (Operation the Hill), three Harel battalions swept southwestward and southeastward from Har-tuv, taking a string of villages—Bureij, Deiraban, and Deir al-Hawa, and the Beit Jimal Monastery—and driving out their inhabitants. The troops subsequently dynamited some of the villages.[45] One of the handful of Israeli casualties was the legendary Aharon Schmidt, known as "Jimmy," an operations officer in the Harel Brigade, a talented violinist and poet.[46]

The Egyptian, Muslim Brotherhood, and Sudanese defenders fled after the Egyptian command told them it could not supply them with ammunition "as the Gaza–Beit Jibrin road had been severed."[47] During the next two days the Israeli troops pushed southward and eastward and took Beit Natif, Jarash, Beit ʿItab and ʿAllar, Ras Abu ʿAmr, al-Qabu, Husan, and Wadi Fukin (though later abandoned the last two villages). At the same time, on Harel's left flank, the ʿEtzioni Brigade was scheduled, in Operation Yekev, to take the Beit Jala crest, on the outskirts of Bethlehem, and then possibly conquer Bethlehem itself. Brigade OC Dayan was optimistic. In his prebattle briefing he quoted Orde Wingate's epigram: if attacked from an unexpected direction, Egyptian troops will flee "like birds hearing a tin can being beaten." But a determined Egyptian machine gun crew pinned down the vanguard of ʿEtzioni's Sixty-first Battalion as it clambered up the slope toward Beit Jala. There was confusion and paralysis. The lead platoon's OC disappeared into the night, and the company, battalion, and brigade OCs were left without a clear picture. They failed to take any initiative. With dawn approaching and fearful of a diplomatic imbroglio, the attack was called off. Ben-Gurion—with the IDF General Staff divided—rejected Dayan's appeal to renew the offensive the following day, fearing that the United Nations would intervene and order the IDF out of Beersheba. Ben-Gurion also feared Christendom's ire were Israel to assault Bethlehem.[48]

Besides, Ben-Gurion had no wish to clash with the Jordanians, a conflict that might end the Egyptians' military and political isolation. In the hours before the cease-fire the Jordanians had organized and dispatched a flying column from Ramallah to Bethlehem-Hebron. The Jordanians pretended that its purpose, as Alec Kirkbride put it, was "to stiffen the Egyptians."[49] But its real goal was to beef up Jordan's token units in the area (which had coexisted alongside the Egyptians during the months of Egyptian control), take over from the departing Egyptians, and, above all, prevent IDF conquest of the southern West Bank.

Already on 16 October, the day after the start of Yoav, John Glubb had divined both the danger and the opportunity: "If the Jews break through to . . . Beersheba, the Egyptians in Hebron will be cut off. We don't want the Jews to capture Hebron too. If we step in and occupy Hebron . . . we shall appear as saviours. . . . The Jewish offensive may have good and bad sides. It may finally give the gyppies [that is, Egyptians] a lesson. . . . Perhaps we could send a regiment to Hebron," he had mused.[50]

On 21–22 October, as Mayor Muhammad ʿAli al-Jaʿabri appealed to King ʿAbdullah to save Hebron, Glubb sent in his column ("G Force"), consisting of two mechanized infantry companies and an armored car squadron, all from the First Regiment, and a battery of heavy mortars, 350 men in all, which fanned out in Bethlehem and Hebron. The force was commanded by Major Geoffrey Lockett, "an eccentric British officer who liked his pinch of snuff and tot of whiskey . . . [a] gallant man with a great love for fighting."[51]

But Lockett didn't get his fight, not immediately. The IDF did not respond. Bound by the UN cease-fire order and still engaged against the Egyptians, Ben-Gurion had no desire to renew the war with the Legion.

Just after noon on 22 October the guns (briefly) fell silent. Operation Yoav was officially over. It had ended in significant Israeli achievement, if not in a decisive victory. IDF radio interception had played an important part. The Israelis had broken the Egyptian cipher and, for example, decrypted in real time the order to withdraw and stabilize a new front along the Beersheba-Gaza line.[52] The victory, reported the Israeli representative in Washington, had "made [a] deep impression [on the American] Defense and State Departments."[53] In Cairo, the Egyptian leadership for days deluded itself—and tried to delude others, including their Arab allies—about the events in the Negev. Prime Minister Mahmoud Nuqrashi told Arab leaders, gathered in Amman, that his army was in excellent shape and that "there is no need to take Zionist propaganda seriously."[54] 'Azzam Pasha told journalists that the Egyptians had recaptured Beersheba.[55]

But outside observers were more clearheaded (or honest). They noted the fragmentation of the Egyptian army, the encirclement of the force at Faluja, and the dissolution of the eastern arm of the expeditionary force. "With their backs to the sea and incomplete control over their communications with Sinai, the Egyptians must be very uncomfortable," was how the British representative in Amman understatedly put it.[56]

Al-Muwawi was particularly concerned about his northernmost brigade, the Second, dug in around Majdal and Isdud. After the fall of Beit Hanun, Egyptian engineers rapidly laid down wire matting on the dunes along the Mediterranean shore, creating a makeshift bypass route from Gaza to Majdal. But it was built for retreat, not advance. In the fortnight after 22 October, al-Muwawi, in nightly convoys, gradually pulled back his northerly units, starting with Isdud, which was evacuated on 26–27 October. Most of the Palestinian population fled southward along with the Egyptians. IAF reconnaissance reported: "A giant stream of refugees, with cattle, sheep, mules, and carts is seen streaming along the whole shoreline between Isdud and Gaza."[57] At the same time, to the east, the Legion, fearing the spread of panic, was doing its best to bar the way to refugees fleeing eastward from Beit Jibrin–Tarqumiya toward Hebron.[58]

In most places, the IDF did not have to resort to expulsion orders. The inhabitants, with or without Egyptian advice, fled as the Israelis approached or let loose with mortars and machine guns. Most villages were found abandoned or almost completely empty when the IDF entered. The few remaining inhabitants—those left behind, because of handicap, carelessness, or age—were usually expelled. In some places, inhabitants initially removed themselves only a few hundred yards to wait and see what the IDF intended and only later moved on or were pushed toward the Gaza Strip. Elsewhere, with fleeing inhabitants infecting neighboring villages with panic, in a domino effect, the refugees moved directly toward the Gaza Strip. Without doubt, Allon wanted empty villages and towns behind the shifting front line and probably let his subordinates understand this (though explicit written expulsion orders from Southern Front to its subordinate units are rare).

Yoav had been a success. But Israel had sought a more comprehensive victory. During the days after 22 October its military and political leaders acted to bolster the operation's gains, in defiance, or circumvention, of the UN truce observers, especially in the east, where observers were thin on the ground.

Already on 22–24 October Giv'ati and Eighth Brigade units expanded the IDF's area of control and tightened the noose around the Egyptian Fourth Brigade, centered at Faluja–'Iraq al-Manshiya, by conquering a string of villages and positions in the Judean foothills, north of Beit Jibrin, including Kidna, Ra'na, Zikrin, 'Ajjur, and Zakariya, mostly after brief skirmishes.[59] On 27 October, IDF General Staff formally ordered Southern Front "during the truce" to "soften up" the besieged Egyptian units and to "gain tactical advantages" by harassing the 'Iraq Suweidan–'Iraq al-Manshiya pocket and the Majdal area, by conquering nearby villages (al-Qubeiba and Dawayima) and by employing "psychological warfare by means of flyers and 'treatment' of civilian inhabitants."[60]

The IDF reduced and tightened the noose around the Faluja Pocket. That day the Eighty-ninth Battalion, Eighth Brigade, took Beit Jibrin and its police fort, following the Giv'ati Brigade's failed attempt during the previous two days. The Egyptian and Sudanese troops apparently withdrew following the Giv'ati attack. Yet after taking the fort (with relative ease) and entering the village, the Eighty-ninth Battalion troopers—many of them LHI veterans—were attacked by a squadron of seven or eight Arab Legion armored cars that had ventured down the road from Hebron to Tarqumiya to scout out the situation. A firefight developed, with the Israelis pouring machine gun and mortar fire on the armored cars. But the Israelis were outgunned and took casualties in and around the village. "In the center of the village there was a small furry donkey, quietly cropping the grass, evidently not at all disturbed by the battle raging around him," recalled one British Legion officer. The battle was decided when Israeli antitank rockets hit two of the lead Jordanian armored cars: the Jordanians about-faced and withdrew up the road to Tarqumiya, leaving behind several stricken vehicles and three charred bodies. The Israelis had suffered three dead and fifteen wounded. This was to be the war's last serious clash between Jordan and Israel.[61] The battle had been a giant misunderstanding: the Israelis believed the Jordanians were attempting to retake Beit Jibrin; the Arabs, that the Israelis were headed for Hebron. "This gallant little action saved the city"—or, even more grandly, "an area of some six hundred square miles"—Glubb later recorded.[62] (Interestingly, half a year later, when Jordan and Israel were about to sign the armistice agreement—in which Jordan ceded a strip of land around Tulkarm-Qalqilya to Israel—formally ending their war, King 'Abdullah pleaded with Yadin: "Give me Beit Jibrin!" Yadin said "no.")[63]

The capture of Beit Jiibrin and the repulse of the Jordanian column definitively ended all hope of withdrawal eastward, or help from the Legion, for the Faluja Pocket's defenders. But the Egyptian commanders refused to surrender, the commander of the ʿIraq al-Manshiya fort responding to an Israeli overture that his "soldiers would fight to the last man."[64]

The next day, the Eighty-ninth Battalion captured al-Qubeiba and the dominant position atop Tel Lachish (site of the Israelite town besieged and conquered by Sennacherib, king of Assyria, in 701 BCE). The Egyptians had fled both locations without a fight. The Egyptian command asked the Fourth Brigade, trapped in the pocket and complaining of lack of "fuel and food and ammunition, and [with] a multiplicity of wounded," whether it could break out through al-Qubeiba.[65] It couldn't.

On 29 October the Eighty-ninth Battalion assaulted neighboring Dawayima, a village of four thousand. Three days before, Southern Front had warned all units "not to harm the population" (and to desist from looting and to safeguard "holy sites").[66] But things turned out differently at Dawayima. A reduced company, mounted on seven half-tracks, advanced on the village from three directions, all guns blazing. The attackers believed that the villagers had participated in the conquest of the ʿEtzion Bloc, "the blood of whose slaughtered soldiers calls for revenge."[67] The Israelis encountered only light resistance, and as the half-tracks approached, "the plain [eastward] was covered with thousands of fleeing Arabs." The half-tracks pursued the villagers with their machine guns.[68] Subsequently, the troops rounded up dozens of villagers and executed them in one or two batches. A Mapam activist later wrote a complaint, quoting an officer who had reached the village a day or so later: "The first [wave] of conquerors killed about 80 to 100 [male] Arabs, women and children. . . . One commander ordered a sapper to put two old women in a certain house . . . and blow it up. The sapper refused. . . . The commander then ordered his men to push in the old women and the evil deed was done. One soldier boasted that he had raped a woman and then shot her."[69]

Pressure by Mapam ministers resulted in a number of investigations. One investigator, Isser Beʾeri, head of the IDF Intelligence Service, concluded in November that about eighty villagers had been killed during the battle and another "22" afterward. Arab reports, which reached UN observers, exaggerated, speaking of "500" or even "1,000" victims. United Nations investigators were unable to find evidence of a massacre (though they tended to believe the survivors who reached Hebron who spoke of atrocities).[70]

The IDF also slowly nibbled at the Egyptian positions in the west, despite the UN cease-fire directive. On 28 October Israeli troops occupied Isdud and the devastated site of Kibbutz Nitzanim, to the south and on 4–5 November, took Majdal, without battle. The Egyptians had already withdrawn to Gaza, most of the region's inhabitants accompanying them. Some Egyptian officials bewailed the Palestinian penchant for flight: "Why do I see the people confused in their thoughts, packing to leave, wandering long distances to countries that are not theirs . . . ?" wrote Mustafa al-Sawaf, a local Egyptian administrator.[71] But other Egyptians had urged the local inhabitants to flee with them.

At Isdud, originally a town of five thousand inhabitants, the Israelis found a few hundred people, who greeted them with white flags and asked for permission to stay. Permission was granted, and a sergeant—one Sasson Gottlieb—was appointed governor. But Southern Command then reversed itself and ordered the inhabitants to leave.[72] A similar pattern seems to have been followed at Hamama, a large, refugee-filled village to the south. But Giv'ati behaved inconsistently. A week later, at Majdal, the conquering Giv'ati unit found in place fewer than a thousand of the town's original ten thousand inhabitants; the rest had fled. Their elders asked to surrender and stay. And here, contrary to precedent, inexplicably, the troops allowed the population to remain, even hanging on the walls posters cautioning soldiers against looting and improper behavior. The IDF sent patrols to the surrounding dunes and groves to beckon those hiding there to return home.[73] Hundreds streamed back to town. But during the following weeks, about five hundred nonlocal refugees were identified and expelled. By 1950, the town contained more than two thousand Arabs (alongside Jewish settlers who had begun to move in during 1949).[74] On 5 November Israeli troops occupied the ruins of Yad Mordechai, where they came to a halt. An old Arab woman told the Israelis that the area's inhabitants had fled "because fear of the Jews had fallen upon" them.[75]

By early November the Arab leaders understood that the Egyptian army "was 'broken.'"[76] Apparently, the Egyptian high command agreed. Despairing of the royal court, it launched a devious initiative designed to achieve a diplomatic exit from its predicament. Kirkbride reported that the Egyptian liaison officer in Amman delivered an oral message to 'Abdullah from the Egyptian defense minister asking the Jordanian king to suggest to King Farouk "that the time has now come to negotiate a settlement of the Palestine problem." The Jordanians "realized" that the Egyptian army wanted negotiations with Israel—but while being "able to meet public criticism in Egypt by blaming Transjordan for taking the initiative." (At the same time, the Iraqi military told 'Abdullah that the Iraqi prime minister was "anxious for a settlement.")[77]

But the Israelis still regarded the Egyptian army as very much in the field.

And the Faluja Pocket was a thorn in their side. On the night of 8–9 November the Eighth Brigade assaulted and at last took "the Monster on the Hill," as the Israelis dubbed the ʿIraq Suweidan police fort, with Givʿati taking the neighboring ʿIraq Suweidan village.[78] The ring around the Faluja Pocket, commanded by Colonel Said Taha, had further tightened: some three to four thousand Egyptian troops, of the First, Second, and Sixth battalions, were isolated in the enclave, which was now less than four miles from east to west and two and a half miles from north to south. On 11 November Taha cabled his superiors: "The situation of our forces has grown much worse because of the siege from all directions, because we are in range of light weapons, because of the cessation of supplies and the paucity of ammunition . . . because of lack of fuel for the vehicles . . . because of air attacks by heavy bombers and the lack of anti-aircraft weapons. . . . Our wounded are suffering and dying for lack of means to carry out operations." The Egyptian command permitted Taha to decide whether to hold on or agree to an orderly withdrawal, under UN supervision. It even implied that he could surrender.[79] Under a flag of truce, Taha met Allon on 11 November in Kibbutz Gat, in Israeli-held territory. The conversation took place in English, at Taha's insistence, and not in Arabic, as Allon, who knew Arabic well, had proposed. It went as follows:

Allon: Colonel, may I express my admiration for your brave soldiers' fighting abilities. The conquest of the ʿIraq Suweidan fort and half the 'Pocket' took a great effort, though not many casualties.

Taha: Many thanks, sir. I must say that your soldiers, who excelled in bravery, put us in quite a difficult situation.

Allon: Is it not tragic that both sides, who in fact have no reason to quarrel, are killing each other mercilessly?

Taha: Yes, it is tragic; but that is the way of the world. It is fate, sir, and one cannot evade it.

Allon: I hope you have noted that the war was forced upon us, as it is being fought on our land and not in Egypt. I believe the battle has already been decided and it is best to speed up the end of hostilities.

Taha: It is true. But I am an officer . . . and I must carry out orders.

Allon: It is best that you take note that while most of your army is pinned down in a hopeless war in Palestine, in your country the British army, which we have just gotten rid of, rules. Don't you think that you have fallen prey to a foreign imperialist plot . . . ?

Taha: You did well to throw out the British. It won't be long before we expel them from Egypt.

Allon: But how will you expel them if all your army is stuck here, after a big defeat and on the eve of an even bigger defeat? Isn't it better for you to return to Egypt and take care of your own business, instead of being entangled in an adventure in a foreign land?

Taha responded that he would do what he was ordered. Allon pointed out that the pocket's position was hopeless and offered Taha "surrender with honor . . . with the possibility of an immediate return home." But Taha refused to lay down his arms.

Indeed, he immediately cabled his superiors: "We have made contact with the Jews and it is now clear . . . that they insist on unconditional surrender. They will not allow us to withdraw until all the Egyptian army withdraws from Palestine. If you don't solve the problem in the [next] 24 hours, I am sorry to say, I will no longer control the situation."

Taking leave of Allon, Taha said that he hoped that the IDF would respect the cease-fire, as it had not when capturing ʿIraq Suweidan. Allon responded that he would obey international law but that such law did not protect an army that had invaded another country.

Farouk sent the pocket's defenders a letter of encouragement and promoted Taha to brigadier general.[80]

The cease-fire was effectively restored after the fall of ʿIraq Suweidan. But Southern Front continued operations geared to assuring that the area it had just conquered remained clear of Arabs. Its units periodically scoured the villages. The Lower Coastal Plain District HQ's order of 25 November to the Home Guard battalions under its command was typical: "[We] are aware of the movement of Arab civilians from Gaza northwards as far the village of Majdal. The Arabs have [re-]settled in a number of villages." The units were ordered to expel "the Arab refugees from the above-mentioned villages and to prevent their return by destroying the villages." The units were ordered to search Hamama, Jura, Khirbet Khisas, Niʿiliya, al-Jiya, Barbara, Beit Jirja, and Deir Suneid, round up inhabitants, and expel them to Gaza. The villages were then to be "burned and razed." The units were enjoined to "carry out the operation with resolution, accuracy, and energy but any unwanted deviation [from norms] . . . was to be restrained."[81]

The operation took place five days later: the villages were scoured and hundreds of inhabitants and refugees were expelled to Gaza; some of the villages were torched.[82] The expulsion from Khirbet Khisas was to serve Israeli novelist Yizhar Smilansky ("S. Yizhar") as the basis for his short story "The Story of Khirbet Hizʿa," one of the few pieces of dissentient fiction published in Israel in the wake of the 1948 War.

Side by side with driving or keeping out Arabs, Yoav also had appendages involving the consolidation of Israeli rule through further conquest. On 23–25 November the Negev Brigade, unopposed, enlarged Israel's holdings when two of its battalions, led by the brigade reconnaissance unit, pushed, in Operation Lot—named after Abraham's nephew, whose wife, according to the Bible, had turned into a pillar of salt some thirty-five hundred years earlier—from Beersheba to Sodom on the Dead Sea and to ʿEin Husub and Bir Maliha in the parched ʿArava. Both areas had been earmarked for Jewish sovereignty in the UN partition scheme. Sodom, the site of major chemical works, had been held through the civil war by Jewish troops, but the Jordanian invasion had cut it off from the Jewish heartland, and since May, it had been supplied only by air. The linkup now extended Israeli territory through the northern Negev to the southern sector of the Dead Sea.

Ben-Gurion had had his eye on ʿEin Husub since October, when he said that it had "the biggest spring in the Negev." "It is clear to me," he told his Cabinet colleagues, "that a settlement could be established there." Always aware of historical roots, he also noted ʿEin Husub's proximity to King Solomon's copper mines, some miles to the south, at Timna. At Kurnub, between Beersheba and Sodom, Ben-Gurion thought "30 thousand" families could be settled. Abba Eban, he said, had telegraphed from New York urging immediate settlement, to facilitate the perpetuation of Israeli rule in the area.[83] (In fact, the area was settled only in the 1950s.)

The limited defeat of the Egyptian army had political repercussions, as Ben-Gurion had intended and as he noted even before the fall of Beersheba: Israel had registered "an important political victory in the world."[84] Soldering together the northern Negev settlements enclave to Israel "proper" while also cutting off the Egyptian force in the Hebron-Bethlehem hills from the main body of the expeditionary force along the coast all but buried Count Bernadotte's proposed cession of the Negev to the Arabs. In general, Israel's stock soared.

The Egyptians, through diplomacy, tried to salvage what they could—or at least ward off a new IDF offensive. Kamil Riyad, of Farouk's court, renewed contact with Elias Sasson and offered an "armistice." It was not clear whether he was actually speaking for the king or, indeed, enjoyed the support of Prime Minister Nuqrashi. The Egyptians asked Israel to withdraw from all territory in the south earmarked by the partition resolution for the Palestinians (Beit Hanun to Isdud) and to agree to Egypt's continued retention of the territory from Beit Hanun south to Rafah and the land in the northwestern Negev adjacent to the old Egypt-Palestine international border. Riyad no longer demanded, as he had in September, all of the Negev. But neither was he offering Israel "peace" in exchange for these concessions, Moshe Shertok said.[85] The Egyptians assured Israel that if the deal was struck, they would remain neutral should hostilities be renewed between Israel and the other Arab states. They hinted that "political" talks might follow an armistice.[86]

On 4 November Shertok outlined the Egyptian proposal to the Cabinet. Israel responded—through Sasson—that it "tended not to agree to the attachment of the Gaza area to Egypt," fearing future Egyptian aggression, though it agreed to Egyptian retention of the northwestern Negev (an area allocated to the Palestinians in the 1947 partition resolution).[87]

Nothing came of all this. Yet the idea of an armistice was now in the air, as it had not been at any point since May. But the Egyptians were not quite there. The Security Council cease-fire call of 19 October had implied an Israeli return to the pre-15 October lines. Israel parried with reservations, clarifications, and queries—but, in practice, refused to budge. A new Security Council resolution, on 16 November, finessed the call for withdrawal and posited the opening of Israeli-Egyptian armistice negotiations. The Egyptians demurred. A British effort to bypass American objections and persuade the General Assembly to adopt the Bernadotte plan was defeated in behind-the-scenes maneuvering. But elements of the plan persevered. On 11 December, the assembly, in Resolution 194, formally adopted a number of Bernadotte's proposals, including recognition of the refugees' right of return and the establishment of the Palestine Conciliation Commission (PCC).

HIRAM

Back in 1937 the British Peel Commission had earmarked all of the Galilee for Jewish sovereignty. The commission had taken account both of Jewish history—for much of the first millennium BCE the area had been Jewish, and it had played a prominent part in the Great Revolt against Rome in the first century CE—and of contemporary needs. If emptied of Arab inhabitants by an agreed or compulsory transfer, the area could accommodate masses of Jewish immigrants. But the partition resolution of 1947 had earmarked Western and Central Galilee, largely populated by Arabs, for Palestinian Arab sovereignty. Subsequently, in the battles of May and July, Western Galilee had fallen under Jewish control. But upper central Galilee, from the Sakhnin–'Arabe–Deir Hanna line through Majd al-Kurum up to the Lebanese border, remained under Arab, specifically ALA, control. The Israelis wanted the area. As Shertok had told Andrei Vyshinskii, the Soviet deputy foreign minister, and Iakov Malik, the Soviet representative on the Security Council, the border in the Galilee "was a very plunging *décolleté.* . . . [In] its current state it is impossible to defend, and the line has to be righted [that is, pushed north to the old Palestine-Lebanon international border]."[88]

Much as the Egyptians had supplied the pretext for Operation Yoav, so al-

Qawuqji supplied the justification for Operation Hiram, in which the IDF overran the north-central Galilee "pocket" and a strip of southern Lebanon. IDF Northern Front OC Moshe Carmel was later to write that al-Qawuqji's provocation had been like "a match that ignited . . . [the] fire . . . in a dry, yellow field . . . but the fire quickly rose . . . [and] turned on him and he was unable to douse it."[89]

In truth, as with Yoav, Operation Hiram had been long in the planning.[90] Already in mid-May, Ben-Gurion had spoken of conquering southern Lebanon up to the Litani (which presupposed the prior conquest of central Galilee). Northern Front's operations officer, Mordechai Makleff (IDF chief of general staff, 1952–1953), had told Ben-Gurion during the Second Truce that it would take the army only two to three days to take the central Galilee "pocket."[91] Ben-Gurion clearly hoped that it would fall into Israeli hands— and "empty of Arabs," as he put it to the Cabinet on 26 September[92]—and Northern Front had meticulously planned the operation. In early September it had formulated an early draft of "Hiram," defining the operation's objective as "the clearing of central Galilee and the destruction of the enemy forces in it."[93] And on 6 October, at the IDF General Staff meeting, Carmel had pressed for authorization.[94] But the Cabinet held back.

The Arabs were shortly to give him his chance. Before dawn on 22 October, in defiance of the UN Security Council cease-fire order, ALA units stormed the IDF hilltop position of Sheikh ʿAbd, just north of, and overlooking, Kibbutz Manara, a new settlement in the hills west of the Hula Valley. The Home Guard garrison was caught by surprise and fled. Manara was imperiled. It is possible that the attack was launched by al-Qawuqji in direct or indirect response to Egyptian importunings that the other Arab armies relieve the pressure on them.[95] But he had acted without the support or agreement of the Lebanese government.

Ben-Gurion initially rejected Carmel's demand to launch a major counteroffensive. He was chary of antagonizing the United Nations so close on the heels of its cease-fire order. He agreed only to the relief of Manara.[96] But the hasty efforts by the Carmeli Brigade on 22–24 October to reinforce Manara and take back Sheikh ʿAbd failed, with heavy loss of life (thirty-three IDF dead, forty wounded). Indeed, ALA units strengthened their hold on the hilltops along the Yiftah-Manara road, knocking out an IDF armored column.[97] The kibbutz was now besieged, and the main south-north road through the Panhandle to Metulla was also under threat. During the 24–25 October ALA troops regularly sniped at Manara and at traffic along the main road. In contacts with UN observers, al-Qawuqji demanded that Israel evacuate neighboring Kibbutz Yiftah—that had been established two months before—and thin out its forces in Manara. The IDF demanded the ALA's withdrawal from the captured positions and, after a "no" from al-Qawuqji, informed the United Nations that it felt free to do as it pleased. Sensing what was about to happen, the Lebanese army "ordered" al-Qawuqji to withdraw from Israeli territory—but to no avail.[98]

Al-Qawuqji's provocation at Sheikh 'Abd made little military sense, considering that his "army" consisted of three undersized "brigades," each, in fact, amounting to a battalion, totaling some three thousand troops, who were backed by two to three companies of regular Syrian troops and several hundred local militiamen and foreign Moroccan volunteers. At the end of October the Syrians sent two battalions to reinforce the ALA, perhaps with an eye to eventual Syrian annexation of central Galilee.[99] But only one of these, the Ninth, ended up in Galilee, fighting the Israelis. Al-Qawuqji's troops suffered from acute shortages of supplies, especially ammunition; on 25 October one battalion informed him that it was down to seventeen rounds per rifle and lacked food.[100]

The impending conquest of central Galilee was obliquely debated in the Israeli Cabinet—though never actually put to the vote (unlike Operation Yoav). Shertok had earlier argued that the "pocket" was crowded with Arabs, many of them refugees from the areas of Eastern Galilee that had fallen to the Israelis in April and May, and if it appeared that it would become part of Israel, still more refugees would pour into it from Lebanon and Syria. He implied that, for demographic reasons, he was averse to conquering central Galilee.[101]

But the defense establishment, including Ben-Gurion, was eager to take the "pocket." As Carmel later put it, "There were among us those who were happy with [al-Qawuqji's] move, as they believed that his crass violation of the cease-fire gave us just cause, politically, to embark on a large-scale offensive."[102] Without doubt, Bernadotte's legacy (with its proposed trade-offs between the Negev and the Galilee), and the IDF successes in the south in the third week of October, helped Ben-Gurion make up his mind. He may have feared that the conquest of the Negev might induce the international community to "compensate" the Arabs with the Galilee or parts of it. Establishing a fait accompli in the north, in "Hiram," would remove the threat.

On 16 October, a week before the attack on Sheikh 'Abd, Carmel—prompted by the start of the IDF onslaught against the Egyptians the day before—had pressed Ben-Gurion to be allowed "to begin in the Galilee." Ben-Gurion had refused.[103] But on 24–25 October he gave the green light, [104] and on 28 October, wielding four brigades (Carmeli, Golani, the Seventh, and Oded, just rushed up from the south), Carmel unleashed "Hiram," named after the biblical king of Tyre, an ally of King Solomon. The aim, stated the final version of the operational order, was "to destroy the enemy in the central Galilee 'pocket,' to take control of the whole of the Galilee and to establish a defense line on the country's northern border."[105]

The order made no mention of the prospective fate of the civilian inhabitants of, and refugees in, the "pocket." But an earlier order, produced six weeks before the start of Hiram by Haifa District HQ, one of Northern Front's units, spoke of "evicting" the inhabitants from the conquered villages.[106] This would have been in line with Ben-Gurion's stated expectation that the "pocket" would be "empty [*reik*]" of Arab villagers after conquest.

The offensive began with air attacks just before dusk on 28 October by a lone B-17, Dakotas, Rapides, and Austers on key villages and ALA HQs at Tarshiha, Sukhmata, Mughar, Jish, and Sasa.[107] They were not particularly effective, though they "greatly encouraged" the IDF ground troops who were about to set off.[108] During the previous nights the four brigades had quietly mustered on the edges of the "pocket" (while maintaining normalcy along the roads during daylight hours). The ALA was caught completely off guard. On the night of 28–29 October the Golani, Seventh, and Oded brigades simultaneously stormed the "pocket" from west and east.

The offensive was designed as a pincer movement, with the Seventh (armored) Brigade attacking from the east and the Ninth (Oded) Brigade attacking from the west, with feints and minor help from Golani and Carmeli. The operation was conducted in mountainous terrain, with dirt tracks and narrow roads linking the various objectives. The key and decisive battle was fought on the first night, 28–29 October, between units of the Seventh Brigade and the ALA's Second Yarmuk "Brigade." Pushing northwestward from its bases in Safad–'Ein Zeitim, the Seventh stormed the key villages of Meirun, Safsaf, and Jish, with the newly organized IDF Circassian Company first occupying Qaddita. At all three sites the ALA fought with determination before being overpowered. On the morning of 29 October the brigade beat off a counterattack by Syrian and ALA units at Jish.[109] "The [Syrian] troops, well-dressed and well-equipped, ran hither and thither between the houses and in the alleyways and in the nearby fig groves, alone and in groups, and tried to fire back. . . . Qawuqji's troops fled in the direction of the Jermak. . . . We captured two . . . armored vehicles taken from us in the Yehiam Convoy and now decorated with the symbol of the ALA, a bent dagger dripping blood, stuck in the heart of a Shield of David. . . . Later the POWs started to reach us, broken-spirited Qawuqji men and frightened Syrian officers and

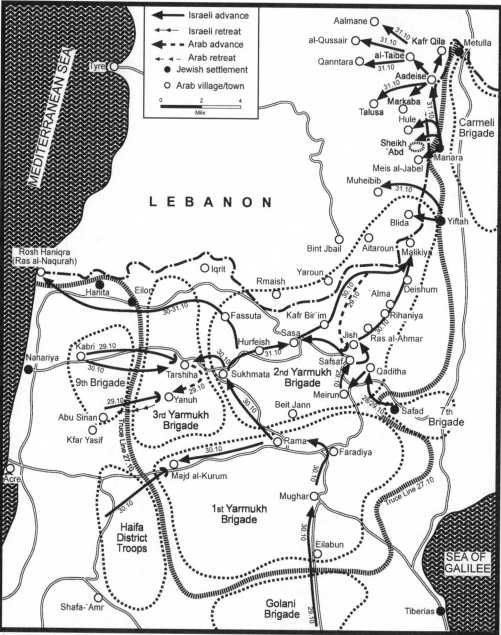

Operation Hiram, Northern Front, 27–31 October 1948

men who stood and looked on us with bewildered eyes. A young Syrian officer muttered continuously in English: 'I was in the Military Academy for two years.'"[110]

The other arm of the pincer, the Ninth Brigade, which set out from Kabri, did not fare as well. Its Ninety-second Battalion was stymied on 28–29 October on the road to Tarshiha, despite enjoying effective artillery support, and its auxiliary Druze Company was set upon by an ALA unit and local militiamen (in violation of a prior surrender agreement) inside the village of Yanuh and forced to retreat, suffering heavy losses (fourteen dead—eleven Druze soldiers and three Jewish officers).[111]

But the Ninth Brigade renewed its assault the following evening. Tarshiha fell early on 30 October. The inhabitants and the ALA had been thoroughly demoralized by the bombing raids, in which twenty-four persons had died and sixty were buried under the rubble.[112] The brigade then pushed eastward (and northwestward toward Fassuta and Deir al-Qasi), taking Sukhmata and Hurfeish and linking up with the Seventh Brigade at Sasa, which the Seventh had taken, without a fight, earlier that day, ALA HQ having just before ordered a retreat. At the same time, Golani units pushed northward from Lubiya and took the villages of ʿEilabun, Mughar, and Rama, joining up with the Ninth Brigade at Sukhmata. Seventh Brigade units later that day advanced northeastward along two axes, reaching the border with Lebanon and taking Kafr Birʿim and Saliha, and Ras al-Ahmar, Reihaniya, and Deishum. They completed their push at dawn on 31 October by taking Malikiya, from which the Lebanese and ALA defenders had fled hours earlier.[113]

The poor ALA showing in Hiram was due in part to incompetent command, which proved inflexible and unable to move troops to counter threats in a fast-changing situation. But, in general, the IDF deployed far greater firepower, mobility, and manpower, making the outcome a forgone conclusion. Moreover, the ALA—and the Galilee "pocket" inhabitants—appear to have suffered from a host of epidemics, including malaria, diphtheria, and typhoid, as three captured Arab doctors told the Israelis afterward. "All the [Arab] Liberation Army was in fact sick," one of them said.[114]

When the Seventh Brigade halted on the Lebanese border, OC Ben Dunkelman issued a communiqué to his troops: "With this ends the brilliant push by the 7th Brigade that took altogether 60 hours. The Galilee of the Jewish Revolt [that is, 66–70 CE] the Galilee of Yohanan of Gush Halav [John of Gischala, one of the revolt's commanders] and Rabbi Shimon Bar Yohai [a spiritual leader after the Bar-Kochba Revolt of the second century CE], has been liberated. The Galilee . . . is all in our hands." Yaʿakov Dori, sick through most of the war, congratulated him: "You have freed the Galilee from the hands of the invaders and given it back to the Jewish people forever."[115]

The Lebanese units and villages along the border had earlier been showered from the air with leaflets warning against intervention. If they stayed out, they would not be harmed, the IDF promised.[116] The Carmeli Brigade, held in reserve for the first two days, on 30 October pushed up the slopes westward and northward from Yiftah and Manara and took Sheikh ʿAbd, abandoned by the ALA without a fight. Around midnight 30–31 October, Carmeli crossed the frontier into southern Lebanon and occupied a string of fifteen (mostly Shiʿite) villages between the Panhandle's western border and Wadi Duba (Wadi Saluki), from Aalmane and Deir Siriane, along the Litani River, in the north to Qanntara and al-Qussair in the west to Meis al-Jabel and Blida in the south. The Lebanese Army faded away and the villagers welcomed the Israelis, some of them signing surrender instruments, others asking to be annexed by Israel.[117] Indeed, "many villages" west of Wadi Duba contacted the IDF and asked to surrender.[118] Early on 31 October Israel agreed to a ceasefire, which went into effect at 11:00 AM.[119]

Israeli troops remained in southern Lebanon until March 1949, when the two countries signed an armistice agreement. A key clause provided for Israeli withdrawal back to the international frontier. During the half-year-long occupation, the Israelis "controlled" the villages mainly through in-and-out patrolling rather than permanent garrisons.

Carmeli's move into Lebanon was the first time the Israelis had crossed a recognized international frontier and invaded a sovereign Arab state. Yet it is unclear why it did so or how the decision was taken. The matter had not been debated in the Cabinet or General Staff before Hiram or at its start, let alone resolved. Apparently, on 30 October, after Sheikh ʿAbd and other positions along the border had been occupied, Carmeli commanders had pressed Front OC Carmel for permission to cross into Lebanon and secure a defense line along Wadi Duba. Carmel had contacted Yadin, who apparently called Ben-Gurion, who gave the go-ahead. Carmel, according to his later testimony, was motivated by the consideration that the Litani River and Wadi Duba afforded natural, defensible boundaries for Israel and by a desire to gain what he saw as an asset in eventual negotiations with the Syrians, who still occupied a chunk of Israeli territory west of the Jordan River.[120] Be that as it may, Ben-Gurion, reporting on Operation Hiram, failed to inform his Cabinet colleagues on the afternoon of 31 October that the IDF had, hours earlier, crossed into Lebanon.[121]

During the takeover of the Lebanese border strip, Carmeli troops committed a major atrocity in the village of Hule. On 1 November, after conquest, they rounded up local males and POWs, crowded them into a house, shot them, and then blew up the building. Altogether thirty-four to fifty-eight persons died. The company commander involved was tried, convicted, and sentenced by an Israeli court to a seven-year prison term, which he never actually served.[122]

Hule was just one of a series of atrocities committed by the Golani, Seventh, and Carmeli Brigades, and auxiliary units, in the course of Hiram and in its immediate aftermath. Altogether, some two hundred civilians and POWs were murdered in about a dozen locations. There is no evidence that the killings were instigated or ordered by Northern Front HQ (indeed, Carmel subsequently condemned them) or that they were part of a policy designed to facilitate a civilian exodus from the conquered areas. Indeed, the haphazardness of the killings (Christians as well as Muslims were murdered; in some sites two or four persons were killed; in others, fifty or eighty) and the fact that in most of the villages, the atrocities were not followed by an expulsion would seem to undermine this conjecture. But, given the number and concentration of the atrocities and the diversity of the units involved, there are grounds for suspecting that the field commanders involved believed that they were carrying out an authorized policy probably designed to precipitate flight.

The main massacres, aside from Hule, occurred in Saliha, where sixty to eighty persons were blown up in the village mosque; Jish, where a dozen or more Moroccan or Syrian POWs and civilians were killed; and Safsaf, where fifty to seventy civilians and POWs were murdered (all three by the Seventh Brigade); ʿEilabun, where twelve (Christians) were executed (Golani Brigade); and ʿArab al-Mawasi, where another fourteen were executed (102nd Battalion). The massacres at ʿEilabun and ʿArab al-Mawasi were both, apparently, precipitated by the occupying troops' discovery of the decapitated bodies and one or both heads of two Israeli soldiers captured by ALA troops a month before in a skirmish near ʿArab al-Mawasi.[123] No Israeli perpetrators were tried or jailed for the atrocities (except in the case of Hule), despite a string of internal IDF and civilian investigations authorized by the General Staff and the Cabinet.[124]

Hiram apparently precipitated the flight, mostly to Lebanon, of about thirty thousand local inhabitants and refugees resident in the "pocket."[125] But at least as many, both Christians and Muslims, remained (today they and their descendants constitute the core of Israel's 1.3-million-strong Arab minority). As we have seen, no directive of expulsion was included in the main operational order by Northern Front to its brigades and other units issued before Hiram, and no such order was issued while the Galilee was being conquered. Indeed, a senior Israeli Foreign Ministry official, who later toured the Galilee, spoke with commanders and assessed the demographic denouement of the operation, wrote: "From all the commanders we talked to we heard that during the operations . . . they had had no clear instructions, no clear line, concerning behavior towards the Arabs in the conquered areas—expulsion of the inhabitants or leaving them in place . . . discrimination in favor of Christians or not."[126] And: "The attitude toward the Arab inhabitants of the Galilee and to the refugees [there] . . . was haphazard [*mikri*] and different from place to place in accordance with this or that commander's initiative. . . . Here [inhabitants] were expelled, there, left in place; . . . here, [the IDF] discriminated in favor of the Christians, and there [the IDF] behaved toward the Christians and the Muslims in the same way."[127] And although the official, Yaʿakov Shimoni, had favored expelling the refugees camped out in the Galilee, and perhaps many of the permanent inhabitants as well, this had not been conveyed in time to the IDF and had not been the army's policy.

Without doubt, many officers, perhaps including Carmel, had wanted the Galilee "pocket" depopulated; certainly this was the defense minister's wish. (After all, Ben-Gurion had told one interlocutor only days before the offensive: "The Arabs of Palestine have only one function left—to run away.")[128] But this had never been translated into policy or operational instructions, at least not in the relevant timeframe.

But on the morning of 31 October, rising early, Ben-Gurion drove up to Safad, Northern Front HQ, where he met Carmel. What exactly was said is unknown, but Ben-Gurion jotted down in his diary that he (or Carmel) expected "additional Arabs" to flee the area, above and beyond those who had already fled or been expelled,[129] and Carmel promptly—while Ben-Gurion was still with him or hard on the heels of the Old Man's departure—instructed all his units: "Do all in your power for a quick and immediate cleansing [*tihur*] of the conquered areas of all the hostile elements in line with the orders that have been issued[.] The inhabitants of the areas conquered should be assisted to leave."[130] Ten days later Carmel reiterated: "[We] should continue to assist the inhabitants who wish to leave the areas we have conquered. This matter is urgent and should be expedited quickly."[131] To this order Carmel had added that "a 5-kilometer-deep strip behind the border line between us and Lebanon must be empty of [Arab] inhabitants."[132]

But it is one thing to instruct units before they set out to conquer villages, or while conquering them, to expel the inhabitants; it is quite another to tell them, after they have conquered the villages and moved on, to go back and expel the inhabitants who have already been neutralized. The fact that the UN cease-fire had gone into effect at 11:00 AM on 31 October may also have contributed to the nonexpulsive behavior of most IDF units following their receipt of the expulsion directive, radioed to the units only an hour before.

Besides, the order was couched in very unimperative language. Carmel had pointedly avoided using the word "expel" (*legaresh*), perhaps hinting at his moral unease.

As a result, Carmel's units by and large failed to expel the inhabitants who had remained in place after Hiram had washed over them. And, indeed, Carmel later punished neither commanders who had expelled communities nor commanders who had failed to expel.

In the following weeks, IDF patrols between the conquered villages and the Lebanese border regularly prodded refugees to cross the border and prevented refugees from returning to the villages. For example, on 3 November the Eleventh Battalion reported: "On the way back [from Malikiya to Sasa] columns of refugees returning from Lebanon were spotted. . . . A number of bursts [of gunfire] were fired toward them. They disappeared."[133] Or: "Between 'Eilabun and Mughar . . . a bedouin encampment with 15 big tents has sprouted up. . . . We found only women and old men. . . . In line with the order not to allow Muslim inhabitants to return we told them that they must leave. We did not use force."[134] Occasionally the patrols were more violent: a Ninety-first Battalion patrol between Deir al-Qasi and Mansura encountered a group of refugees "heading for Lebanon. One of these refugees refused to say where he lived and where he originated, and as he tried to run away—was shot and killed."[135] Moreover, during the weeks after the operation IDF units uprooted villagers from a number of sites along the Lebanese border, including Kafr Bir'im, Iqrit, and Mansura, for security reasons (though, inconsistently, due to last-minute lobbying by Minorities Affairs Minister Bechor Shitrit, left in place Arab communities in Jish and Tarshiha, which were also within the border strip). Most were transferred inland, to still-populated villages in the Galilee; others were expelled to Lebanon.

Within days of the end of Hiram, Ben-Gurion began to press for the settlement of the Galilee. "It makes no sense," he wrote, "for the Galilee [now] in our hands to remain empty and desolate." Israel must establish "a chain of settlements along the [Mediterranean] coast to Rosh Hanikra and along the length of the Lebanese border and also around Safad."[136] The IDF's settlement officer, Lieutenant Colonel Yehoshua Eshel, was similarly minded. He presented Northern Front with a map on which he had marked sites for new settlements—Malikiya, Saliha, Sasa, Mansura, Tarbikha, and Bassa—"according to the national plan." Northern Front apparently wanted Malikiya to be first, and Eshel agreed. The plan was approved by the Cabinet.[137] But given Israel's other problems, including the continued state of war with Egypt, little was immediately done. Ben-Gurion again raised the matter before the Cabinet on 9 January 1949, arguing that the new immigrants faced "a catastrophic [housing] situation" and that the emptiness of the Galilee villages continued to present a security problem; establishing a chain of settlements along the Galilee frontier would serve as a "Maginot Line" that could frustrate renewed Arab invasion. The Cabinet approved Ben-Gurion's motion—"to encourage the settlement of olim in all the abandoned villages in the Galilee."[138] Dozens of sites were settled during the following months.

In Operation Hiram, the IDF completed the conquest and incorporation of the Galilee into Israel. This dovetailed with at least one element of Bernadotte's political legacy, that the Galilee be assigned to Israel. Thus it was that the UN Security Council, in its subsequent resolutions calling for IDF withdrawal, did so with respect to the pre-15 October lines in the south but not in the north; indeed, somewhat strangely, nothing at all was said about Israeli withdrawal from southern Lebanon.[139]

The demise of the ALA was probably welcomed by Lebanon's leaders, who had been unhappy with its presence and activities on Lebanese soil and certainly were uninterested in an ALA- or Palestinian-ruled area on its southern border. By 31 October, the ALA had collapsed, and its harried troops had fled to Lebanon. The IDF had failed to obliterate the ALA, as demanded in Hiram's operational order, but for all practical purposes the force had been knocked out of the war. The Israelis estimated that the Arabs had suffered four hundred dead—half of them Syrians and the rest ALA and local militiamen—and 550 prisoners, most of them ALA. After the retreat, many deserted from the ALA and headed for their homes in Lebanon and Syria. Part of the ALA was temporarily coopted into the Syrian army—but was finally disbanded in May 1949.[140] One ALA officer, Nimr abu Naaj, reportedly committed suicide following the rout.

It had been a one-sided affair. Israeli losses were about twenty dead (most at Yanukh).[141] Throughout the fighting, the Syrians, as Ben-Gurion noted, had failed "to fire a shot" along the Syrian-Israeli front, despite repeated calls for help from al-Qawuqji. "They are afraid [that we will attack them] and want to hold on to their positions [that is, gains]," Ben-Gurion concluded. The Lebanese, too, had not raised a finger to help the ALA.[142]

Moreover, Israel had emerged from the fray with a major card in any future negotiations with Lebanon (and possibly Syria)—its occupation of a swath of south Lebanon. The conquest had a downside, which Foreign Minister Shertok, in Paris, was quick to point out; many viewed it as an unprovoked Israeli aggression, which might undermine Israel's position in the West.[143] But still, Israel had emerged with a concrete bird in hand.

As was its wont in occupied Arab-populated areas, Israel imposed military government on the core of the Galilee.[144] The inhabitants, mostly deemed hostile or of doubtful loyalty, were subjected to a strict regimen of curfews and travel restrictions, which lasted, with a gradual easing of the strictures, until 1966. The Druze villagers were allowed to keep their weapons, and Christian villagers who had been transferred inland for security reasons were told that when conditions improved, a return to their villages would be considered. IDF units were instructed to bar the return of refugees from Lebanon.[145]

9

Operation Horev,
December 1948–January 1949

The fronts remained under truce and largely quiet during the second half of November and most of December. In Hiram and Yoav, the IDF had expanded Israel's holdings, demolished the ALA, badly hurt the Egyptians, and linked the Negev settlement enclave to Israel. But the Syrians still held three small enclaves, at Mishmar Hayarden, near Banias, and along the southeastern shoreline of the Sea of Galilee, at Samra–Tel al-Qasir, all in territory earmarked for Israel by the UN partition resolution. The Jordanians and Iraqis, though quiescent, firmly held the West Bank, surrounding Jewish Jerusalem on three sides and within a short tank-drive of Tel Aviv and the Mediterranean. More important, the Egyptians still held the Gaza Strip and the Faluja Pocket areas of Mandatory Palestine. They had established a continuous chain of fortified positions between ʿAuja al-Hafir and Bir Asluj, just south of Beersheba, which effectively left the central and southern Negev under their thumb and Beersheba itself under potential threat.

Israel, meanwhile, remained burdened by the crippling weight of mobilization: half its adult males were under arms, away from their families, offices, farms, and plants, and with no end in sight. The new state, ravaged by the war, needed its manpower and peace to pursue reconstruction and to absorb the masses of immigrants flooding its shores. Yoav had failed to resolve the strategic dilemma of "no war, no peace."

David Ben-Gurion was still powerfully drawn to Judea and Samaria by historical-ideological and strategic considerations,[1] but international diplomatic considerations dictated caution and restraint. Besides, the Jordanians had made it abundantly clear that they were out of the fight, and the Israelis still feared British military intervention should hostilities with Jordan be renewed. Zvi Ayalon, the Central Front OC, assured Ben-Gurion that it would take only "5 days" to conquer the West Bank or large parts of it. But Israel's representatives at the General Assembly meeting in Paris, Abba Eban and Reuven Shiloah, weighed in firmly against.[2]

But the south was another matter. The UN Security Council resolution of 4 November calling on the IDF to withdraw to the positions of 14 October in the south vaguely undermined Israel's geopolitical claims. The new resolution may have been illogical—it called for Israeli withdrawal from territory awarded to Israel by the United Nations, territory that had been conquered by Egypt in defiance of the United Nations, and then recaptured by Israel—but there it was.

Israel sought to have the resolution rescinded—or, at least, superseded and neutralized. It embarked on a diplomatic offensive. In yet another letter to President Truman, Chaim Weizmann asked that Washington dissociate itself from British machinations geared to obtaining the Negev for the Arabs and reinstating territorial continuity between British bases in Egypt and Iraq.[3] Truman responded that he deplored "any attempt to take [the Negev] away from Israel" and conceded that "what you have received at the hands of the world has been far less than was your due."[4]

But the Americans did more than just send a sympathetic letter. On 16 November, in a new resolution, the Security Council called on the Israelis and Arabs to open armistice negotiations to resolve the conflict, as Israel had long demanded. Shertok correctly assessed that it served to "blur" the significance of 4 November.[5] Israel immediately embraced the new resolution—and continued to quibble and stall over the implementation of 4 November (the Egyptians, for their part, demanded the installation of an Egyptian governor in Beersheba). Israel was especially keen on maintaining the stranglehold on the Faluja Pocket, which it viewed as a major stimulus to Egyptian agreement to open armistice or even peace negotiations[6] (though the Egyptians insisted that they would not open armistice talks until the siege was lifted and the Faluja garrison, or at least half of it, was allowed to withdraw to Egyptian lines).

Yoav had ended with a feeling in Cairo that the Egyptian army was on the verge of annihilation. On 11 November the Egyptian government even dismissed General al-Muwawi and replaced him with General Ahmad Fu'ad Sadiq. But this was cosmetics; it could have no effect on the military issue. To avoid defeat the Egyptians needed either to withdraw completely from Palestine or to agree to peace with Israel (which might conceivably leave them in occupation of a very small part of the country). But both were unthinkable; each alternative would be seen, and broadcast, by King Farouk's internal and external enemies, and fathomed by the Egyptian public, as a national humiliation. As it was, the Egyptian army's performance was widely lambasted, if only as a means of getting at the king. At the least, Egypt wanted to emerge from the war with enough of the Negev to assure territorial continuity between the Maghreb and Mashreq ("Egypt could not be separated from other Arab states by the Jewish state," was how Mahmoud Fawzi, a senior member of the Egyptian delegation to the United Nations, put it)[7] and to retain enough of Palestine to be able to argue that its army had something to show for its troubles. And it abhorred the idea of signing a peace agreement, and especially a separate peace, with Israel.

Of immediate and particular worry to the Egyptian General Staff—the public was left in the dark about the problem—was the fate of the four thousand trapped troops at Faluja: their destruction and/or surrender might be something the regime and the army command would not survive.

The Egyptians spent November and December searching frantically for a way out. Diplomatically, they pressed the British to save their army by urging the United Nations to achieve an Israeli withdrawal to the 14 October lines and by parlaying secretly with the Israelis to either stave off the expected military blow or emerge with some sort of agreement—far short of peace—that would leave major parts of Palestine in their hands. Militarily, the Egyptian General Staff frantically sought a way to save the brigade at Faluja. But the thinly stretched, ill-equipped Egyptian army could do nothing alone; and the Arab states—most relevantly Jordan—refused to cooperate.

There was a great deal of inter-Arab shadowboxing around the subject. In November, the Arab League Political Committee actually devised a "plan" whereby the Jordanians, Iraqis, and Syrians would each contribute a battalion for a relief force that would extricate "the heroes of Faluja." Alternately, the Jordanians nominally earmarked their Third Brigade to carry out the rescue effort—and even (twice) sent the "G Force" OC, Major Geoffrey Lockett, by foot, into the Pocket, to assess and coordinate a rescue operation.[8] But nothing came of all this; no Arab state had the troops to spare or the will to help the Egyptians. Indeed, ʿAbdullah was probably eager to see Farouk's complete humiliation. Thus the meeting of the Arab chiefs of staff in Cairo on 11–12 November ended without affording the Egyptians solace or hope. Meanwhile, the Egyptians managed to infiltrate some supplies to Faluja in camel caravans.

During November, Egypt again sent out diplomatic feelers to Israel—but demanded, in exchange for nonbelligerency, all the territory south of the Majdal–Beit Jibrin–Dead Sea line (that is, the Negev and more). The Israelis brushed this aside, arguing that Egypt had lost the war and was not "entitled [to a] territorial reward."[9] Then, in early December, the Egyptians informed the United Nations that they were willing to open armistice talks[10]—but proceeded to stall and stonewall. They demanded that Israel first comply with 4 November. They blithely told Ralph Bunche, who told Ben-Gurion, that they were "ready for peace." But they declined to enter into negotiations. All the while, their army remained in Palestine, on Israeli soil; occasionally, they attacked Israeli positions. "We will not stand for foreign armies [remaining on our territory, armies] with whom we have no peace and that represent a danger to our existence and security," Ben-Gurion told Bunche in early December.[11] Notice had been served.

Since the 1930s, a deep pessimism underlay Ben-Gurion's attitude toward the Arab world. Despite King 'Abdullah's real interest in peace and the (dubious) Egyptian overtures, Ben-Gurion, like many Israelis, was not hopeful, at least in the short and medium terms. Even signing a formal peace agreement with an Arab state, he feared, might not have a lasting or broader significance. "One must look not at decisions and documents but at the historical reality. What is our reality: The Arab peoples were beaten by us. Will they forget this quickly? 700,000 people beat 30 million. Will they forget this humiliation? One must assume they have feelings of honor. . . . Is there any assurance that they will not want revenge?"[12] he asked. And the Arab states continue to reject the idea and reality of a Jewish state in their midst, he could have added.

Ben-Gurion believed that only the successful application of force would change the status quo and perhaps jolt the Arab states toward acceptance of Israel, if not actual peace-making. By mid-December he felt that the time was ripe. "In a few days," he told the Cabinet, "we will try to end our conflict with Egypt by expelling them from the Negev." It depended on good weather. The only objection was raised by Bentov, from Mapam, who worried about the fate of the "100,000" Arabs he said lived in the area Ben-Gurion proposed to conquer.[13]

On 19 December the issue was brought to the vote. The debate was charged and revealing, about both the future and the past; the ministers even sortied into political philosophy, questioning the ultimate worth and consequences of military action.

Ben-Gurion opened with his usual, meandering, tour d'horizon. The Israeli public was always oscillating between extremes, he said. Now it was "drunk with victory," just as it had been in a trough of depression before 15 May. Be that as it may, the war had to be "brought to an end," and the new state had to focus its energies on "immigration and settlement." Economically, the situation was no longer tenable; we are "on the verge of a catastrophe," he declared. Israel's long-term security required a major increase in strength, and this depended on a massive boost in manpower and an improvement of infrastructure, through immigration and settlement. The Yishuv had to settle the conquered areas, especially the Galilee, both to house the immigrants and to assure its continued rule over them. But this, too, required a cessation of hostilities.

Ben-Gurion explained Israel's victories to date. He spoke of the manpower differential, in terms of both quality and quantity. "One of the chief factors in our victory was the spiritual composition of our people, the quality of our manpower. . . . [But there was also the factor of numbers.] Until now there was a view that the Arabs were many and we were few. But this view is incorrect. It is true in relation to the overall numbers of Arab inhabitants, but not in relation to the army fighting us." Ben-Gurion went on to argue that in the civil war, against the Palestinians, Arab numbers had been greater. But in the conventional war, Israel fielded more troops than the Arab states, though they had been better armed during the four weeks between the invasion and the start of the First Truce. "We mobilized the maximum, but the Arabs mobilized the minimum." Moreover, the Yishuv had received both money and experts from the Diaspora. But ultimately, the Arabs were vastly stronger in manpower, which is why massive immigration was necessary, "a matter, for us, of life [and death]." The Arabs could be expected to seek "revanche" and renew their assault on the Yishuv, when they felt stronger. So the Yishuv needed to grow stronger, to deter the Arabs or at least assure victory.

Ben-Gurion proposed a two-stage military effort: (1) to drive out the Egyptian army and (2) to conquer a strip of land along the West Bank's western edge, including Wadi 'Ara and Latrun, to widen the narrow coastal "waist" and secure the road to Jerusalem. Ben-Gurion hoped that this would be followed by a peace agreement with 'Abdullah, "who exhibits a will to peace." And peace with Jordan could conceivably pave the way to a wider peace between Israel and the Arab world (Ben-Gurion was not particularly hopeful on this score).

A lively debate followed. Interior Minister Yitzhak Gruenbaum, a liberal (the General Zionists Party) and one of the leaders of interwar Polish Jewry (he had been a member of the Polish parliament, the Sejm, before emigrating to Palestine in 1932), said that he agreed with Ben-Gurion, that "it was possible that the situation of no-peace and no-war" would continue indefinitely. But he questioned whether Israel should take Qalqilya and Tulkarm, on the western fringes of the West Bank, since their inhabitants might not flee and Israel should do nothing to enlarge its Arab minority. Israel had been able to hold onto the areas it had conquered because their inhabitants had fled; it could not hold territory packed with Arabs. As to the Negev, Gruenbaum feared that an attempt to conquer the whole Negev, down to ʿAqaba, might result in a clash with the British, which neither he nor Ben-Gurion wanted. Nonetheless, he supported an offensive against the Egyptians, including taking ʿAqaba. Ben-Gurion interjected that the IDF lacked the strength to both take and hold extended lines down to ʿAqaba. Gruenbaum also proposed that Israel formally declare Jerusalem part of Israel. Lastly, taking issue with Moshe Shertok, Gruenbaum opposed the establishment of a Palestinian Arab state in the West Bank. It would be ruled by the mufti or his allies and "would be a permanent enemy of the State of Israel" and a major obstacle to peace between the Jewish state and the Arab world. "All the aspirations and ideals of this [Palestinian] state would be directed against the State of Israel," and it would always strive to expand westward—"against us." Gruenbaum, like Ben-Gurion, preferred Jordanian annexation of the West Bank.

Minorities Affairs Minister Bechor Shitrit, while favoring both an offensive against the Egyptians and "expansion" eastward into the West Bank, doubted whether it was appropriate to engage in both simultaneously. He also feared that an Israeli attack on the West Bank might suck in the British.

David Remez, the minister of transport, argued that "opening [hostilities] on two fronts does not seem to me great progress on the road to achieving peace [or] . . . shortening the war." (Ben-Gurion interjected: "I did not mean the opening of two fronts simultaneously, but one after another.") He was against renewing the war with ʿAbdullah, but he also saw "no logic" in renewing hostilities in the Negev, unless directed at conquest of the whole of the area, including ʿAqaba, which the IDF was too weak to do.

Justice Minister Pinhas Rosenblueth thought that Ben-Gurion was ignoring "international factors," meaning not so much Britain as the United States. He, too, cautiously favored an offensive against the Egyptians but took issue with renewing the war against ʿAbdullah. Agriculture Minister Cisling, driven by his Marxist premises, argued that peace with ʿAbdullah was out of the question—the British, who controlled him, wouldn't allow it—and that only Lebanon was a potential peace partner. He favored offensives both against the Egyptians and in the West Bank. Peretz Bernstein, minister of trade and industry (General Zionists), was uncertain whether the proposed offensive in the south would bring nearer peace with Egypt or make it more remote. As to the West Bank, merely nibbling at its fringes would not improve Israel's strategic situation, he argued. But he fell short of recommending the complete conquest of the West Bank. He adamantly opposed the establishment of a Palestinian Arab West Bank state.

Finance Minister Eliʿezer Kaplan argued that achieving peace was vital for Israel. In principle, he opposed new campaigns of conquest. He was against conquering parts or all of the West Bank and was uncertain about the benefit of conquering more of the Negev. On the whole, he favored attempting to achieve peace on the basis of the existing territorial status quo. But he was willing to make an exception of the ʿAuja al-Hafir crossroads, which, if taken by the IDF, might help prod Egypt into making peace.

Mapam's Bentov, too, was doubtful about the value of further offensives; they would not necessarily bring Israel any closer to peace, which is what the country needed. Israel could not defeat the Arabs decisively, he reasoned. (Ben-Gurion interjected that the IDF could, were it not for international interventions. Bentov: "I am not sure. Would we have reached Cairo?" Ben-Gurion: "We would have reached Beirut, Damascus, and Amman and bombed Cairo. We have the power to halt all sea traffic to Egypt. We have a secret weapon." But Ben-Gurion did not elaborate. Bentov responded by citing the adage that one could do everything with bayonets but sit on them. Real security was achievable only through political agreements—peace—not conquests.) As to the fate of the West Bank, Bentov said that a Palestinian state there might be like "a bone lodged in the throat" of the Jewish state (as Gruenbaum had phrased it), but a West Bank ruled by ʿAbdullah would be like "a knife on the nape of our neck, and this is worse than a bone in the throat." He feared that an expanded Jordan would be swallowed up by Iraq—and such a large neighboring state might mortally threaten Israel. A small Palestinian state, which would be at peace with, and dependent on, Israel, would pose less of a threat. Bentov even suggested that Jews could settle in the West Bank.

Bentov's asseverations elicited an ideological outburst from Gruenbaum. He opposed peace on the basis of the territorial status quo: "A peace that doesn't guarantee Jerusalem for us, will not satisfy us, will not satisfy the will of the Jewish public . . . and will not give us the only possibility of consolidating our victory or the start of the [Messianic] redemption [*athalta di-geula*]. . . . We will not give up Shechem [Nablus]."

At this point, Walter Eytan, the director general of the Foreign Ministry, who "represented" Shertok, who was abroad, intervened. He said that one must both distinguish between the sacred (the West Bank) and the profane (the Negev) and between "sacred" and "sacred"—by which he meant that one had also to distinguish between those parts of the West Bank occupied by Iraq (Tulkarm, Qalqilya, Nablus, Jenin) and those occupied by ʿAbdullah. The implication was that attacking the Iraqi-held Qalqilya-Tulkarm area would not be an attack on Jordan.[14] Eytan implied that Shertok would probably support a new offensive against the Egyptians—but that it should take place before the Palestine Conciliation Commission reached Israel.

The three-man PCC had been established a few days before on the basis of

UN General Assembly Resolution 194, of 11 December. The resolution, hammered out in weeks of behind-the-scenes debate between Israel, the Arab states, Britain, and the United States, embodied elements of Count Bernadotte's plan but also drew on Resolution 181, of November 1947, and charted out principles and a mechanism for the resolution of the conflict. The new resolution endorsed the General Assembly partition resolution as the basis for a settlement. But it also posited the right of peace-loving refugees to return to their homes ("the right of return") or to receive adequate compensation in lieu of return. And it provided for the establishment of a conciliation commission that would mediate a settlement (replacing the dead Bernadotte). The United Nations quickly cobbled together the PCC, consisting of an American chairman and French and Turkish representatives. Eytan hoped that the Israeli offensive would start, and finish, before their arrival in the region.

Ben-Gurion wound up the debate by cleaving to the consensus. He had not advocated, he said, simultaneous assaults in the Negev and West Bank; there was no need to decide on the West Bank operation now. But the Egyptians did not want peace and would have to be evicted from Israeli soil. As to the West Bank, he argued that it was best to wait for the outcome of the offensive against Egypt and to see whether the "UN will swallow it as it swallowed the Galilee business [that is, Operation Hiram]." In any event, 'Abdullah was the only Arab leader interested in negotiating with Israel. Lebanon would not sign a separate peace because it was too weak; the Christians of Lebanon would not dare "betray the other [Arab] states. But 'Abdullah could betray [them]."

As to the Negev, Ben-Gurion understood that he had the backing of a solid Cabinet majority. The matter was not even put to the vote.[15] That evening Ben-Gurion went to the opera; the fare was *Manon*. On his left sat James McDonald, the American representative, with his daughter; on his right, two junior Soviet diplomats.[16] Israel knew, through wiretapping American diplomats' lines in Paris,[17] that the United States would prevent sanctions against Israel. And the Soviets were consistent supporters of an Israeli Negev, if only to deny the British a land bridge, and bases, between their main Middle East outposts in Egypt and Jordan and Iraq. Besides, they viewed all the Arab monarchies as enemies. The Soviet minister in Tel Aviv, Pavel Ivanovich Ershov, spoke of King Farouk as "a corrupt, contemptible young man."[18] (But Ben-Gurion's effort to use Operations Yoav and Horev to pry open the door to Jewish emigration from the Soviet Bloc—he argued that military conquests were all well and good but to hold on to the Negev, Israel would require massive settlement of Jewish immigrants in the area, and these could only come from behind the Iron Curtain[19]—acted like a boomerang. He antagonized his Russian interlocutors, who may have feared Zionist—possibly triggering other minority—agitation inside the Soviet Union. At any event, during the following weeks a frostiness crept into the Soviet attitude toward Israel; new limitations were imposed on Jewish emigration; and there was a gradual reduction in military supplies to Israel.)

The IDF offensive—Operation Horev (in Hebrew, Mount Sinai is also called Mount Horev)—began on the afternoon of 22 December. The Egyptians had reinforced their positions around Gaza, sensing that the Israelis were about to strike. They correctly estimated that the operation would begin between 20 and 25 December. But they weren't sure whether it would be directed at the Hebron Hills or Gaza.[20] The British, Egypt's ambivalent patrons, appear to have been taken by surprise, if only because they could not understand how the Israelis could regard the Egyptian army as a threat: "They would have been a menace [to Israel] had they been soldiers," Hector McNeil, the Minister of State at the Foreign Office, told an Israeli representative in London.[21]

Operation Horev—which aimed "to defeat the Egyptian Army in the Land of Israel,"[22] expel it from the country and force the Egyptians to sue for peace—began with air and artillery strikes on positions along the Mediterranean coast and inside the Gaza Strip. The IDF deployed elements of five brigades, and large auxiliary formations: Golani (battalions 12, 13, and 19); the Negev Brigade (Seventh and Ninth battalions); Harel (battalions 4, 5, and 10); and Eighth Brigade (Eighty-second, Eighty-ninth, and Eighty-eighth battalions). In addition, the Alexandroni Brigade and two undermanned Home Guard battalions (the Negev and Lower Coastal Plain districts) were also assembled around the Faluja Pocket, as were several artillery and mortar battalions.

Facing them were four Egyptian brigades: the Second Brigade, with three infantry battalions and armored and artillery support, strung out in an east-west line from Bir Asluj through ʿAuja to Abu Ageila in Sinai; the Third and Fourth Brigades, with more than ten battalions, strung out from Gaza westward to El ʿArish and southward from Rafah to ʿAuja al-Hafir; and, at Faluja, the Ninth Brigade HQ, with two infantry battalions, some armored and artillery units, and several hundred irregulars. With the Saudi and Sudanese battalions, there may have been in all twenty thousand troops.

On paper, the Egyptian air force mustered about sixty-five fighter aircraft and a dozen bombers, but many were not serviceable, due to a lack of parts and ground and aircrews. The IAF had about two dozen fighters and more than a dozen bombers, as well as several dozen converted civilian aircraft for light bombing and reconnaissance missions.

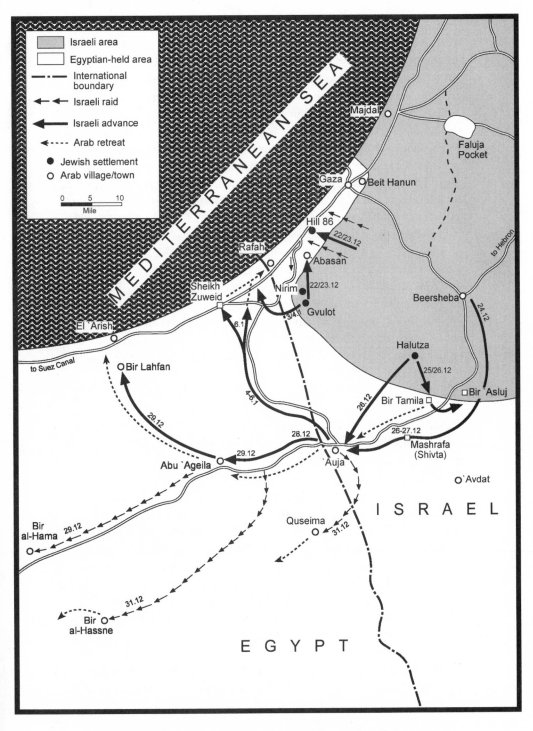

Operation Horev, Rafah and Sinai, 22 December 1948–7 January 1949

Rain caused the cancellation of many of the planned air raids and severely hampered the ground assault by Golani's Thirteenth Battalion, which at midnight took Hill 86, overlooking the main Rafah-Gaza road and railway line. Golani units raided other Gaza Strip positions, principally at 'Abasan. The aim was to confuse the Egyptians and rivet their attention to the Gaza Strip, where they had long feared a cut-off of their forward units.[23]

The main effort, at Hill 86, was addled from the start. Although the infantrymen took the hill and dug in, the rain and accurate Egyptian shelling prevented a convoy of artillery from arriving during the night. At dawn the Egyptians mounted a series of counterattacks. They were resolute; continued Israeli occupation of the hilltop would have left the Egyptians around Gaza cut off from Rafah and El 'Arish.

But, from the Israeli perspective, Hill 86 and 'Abasan were decoys. Horev was based, in conception, on the indirect approach and was far more ambitious. It aimed to trap the core of the Egyptian army, the two brigades strung out between El 'Arish and Gaza. Yigal Allon had no intention of ramming his head against the brick wall of Egyptian defenses. The main blow was to fall to the southwest, on the Bir Asluj – 'Auja al-Hafir line; Israel would threaten the Sinai Peninsula itself. If successful, the IDF was to swing northward from 'Auja to the Mediterranean coast, cutting off all the Egyptian units between El 'Arish and Gaza. Horev was to be supplemented by a separate effort against the Faluja Pocket.

The Egyptians sent wave after wave of infantry and armor up the slopes of Hill 86. One of their first casualties that dawn was Mohammed Neguib, OC of the Tenth Infantry Brigade Group (consisting of the Third and Fourth Brigades), effectively the deputy commander of the Egyptian expeditionary force. Neguib had led the counterattack. His tanks—equipped with "car batteries," as he tells it—stalled, and one was caught in an Israeli crossfire. "Feeling responsible . . . I left my jeep and driver and the staff officer who was accompanying us and crawled five hundred yards under heavy fire in the hope of pulling [a] wounded [tank man] to safety. As I was lifting him out of the hatch, he was hit in the head and instantly killed by two machinegun bullets, two more of which hit me before I could take cover. . . . I lay on my back and unbuttoned my overcoat and blouse. Blood was bubbling out of a hole in my chest, and there was a burning pain in my side. . . . [Eventually aides reached me and] wanted to carry me, but I insisted on walking with my arms around their shoulders in order to conceal from the rest of my troops how badly wounded I really was. It is never good for the morale of soldiers to see their commander being carried off the battlefield." Though initially pronounced dead, Neguib recovered.[24]

The Egyptians then repeatedly assaulted the hilltop, with armor, flamethrowers mounted on tracked vehicles, and infantry. Muslim Brotherhood volunteers played a key role.[25] The Israelis had only a diminishing number of PIATs with which to fend off the armor. One armored vehicle crew was overcome with grenades and bayonets. The Egyptian flamethrower troops reportedly were chained to their places inside the vehicles.[26] The pouring rain and mud caused the Israeli machine guns to jam, "and we lacked almost any functioning weapon. . . . Chaos reigned around us." In the end, the Israelis retreated helter-skelter "swept by machine gun and mortar fire."[27] Hill 86 was back in Egyptian hands. Thirteen soldiers of Battalion 13 were dead, thirty-five wounded. The Egyptians also took a handful of Israelis prisoner.

But the assault on Hill 86 and the auxiliary raiding around ʿAbasan, however costly to Golani, were a diversion well spent. The Egyptian command was certain that the IDF intended a frontal assault on the Gaza Strip[28] and concentrated its forces accordingly. But the main IDF thrust—by the Eighth and Negev Brigades (the latter now mechanized and partly armored)—went in to the south, against the Bir Tamila and ʿAuja al-Hafir positions, which guarded the southern entrance to the Sinai Peninsula (the ʿAuja–Abu Ageila road). Because of rain and mud, which caused logistical problems, the attack got off to a late start (on the night of 25–26 instead of 24–25 December), and air cover was inadequate. But the Israelis nonetheless were successful. The thrust southward unfolded like a classic desert operation. It marked the high point of Allon's generalship. The brigades faced a virtually static enemy in a chain of hilltop fortifications: it was tank and half-track against trench works and antitank gun, movement versus immobility. Given the paucity of Egyptian artillery, the result was a forgone conclusion.

The Negev Brigade had been sent on its way by Ben-Gurion, who arrived at the Ninth Battalion's assembly area at Halutza after adventurously trudging through rain-filled wadis with Yigael Yadin for two hours when their jeep convoy stuck in the mud west of Beersheba.[29] A small flying column of the battalion's troops, maintaining radio silence (they used carrier pigeons for communications), infiltrated south of the Egyptian lines and occupied two unoccupied positions at Mashrafa (the site of the Nabatean town of Shivta), midway between Bir Asluj and ʿAuja. Simultaneously, the bulk of the Ninth and Seventh battalions attacked and took, after a seesaw battle, the cluster of Egyptian positions at Bir Tamila, southwest of Bir Asluj. At one point in the battle, the "French Commando," many of them ex–Foreign Legionnaires and Moroccan Jews, retreated from one of the conquered positions under heavy Egyptian fire, leaving behind, under a railway bridge, a handful of wounded. When they retook the position a half-hour later, they found that all the wounded had been murdered, with their genitals mutilated and their penises stuck in their mouths. Some had been blinded with burning cigarettes. The troops drew their knives and murdered a number of Egyptian POWs. Southern Front reacted by disbanding the French Commando.[30]

Israeli blocking forces halted Egyptian efforts from ʿAuja to aid the embattled companies at Mashrafa–Bir Tamila. By early morning 26 December, all the Bir Tamila positions had fallen. The road from Beersheba to the outskirts of ʿAuja was in Israeli hands.

The way was now clear for the planned Eighth Brigade assault on ʿAuja al-Hafir itself, the last remaining Egyptian position in the Negev, and to advance into Sinai. ʿAuja was held by Egypt's First Infantry Battalion, reinforced by some border guard units, with a battery of 3.7-inch howitzers and mortars, in a number of hilltop positions around the oasis. The Eighth Brigade, with three battalions, attacked at dawn, 26 December. By noon the following day, after suffering serious losses (six LHI veterans of Battalion 89 were killed and two dozen wounded), the brigade had taken all the ʿAuja positions. Harel's Fifth Battalion and other Eighth Brigade units, deployed as a blocking force on the Rafah-ʿAuja road, beat back two determined Egyptian armored efforts to relieve ʿAuja. The Egyptians lost five armored cars and a deputy battalion OC.[31]

The original planning had called for the Eighth Brigade, after taking ʿAuja, to press forward into Sinai. But its losses and exhaustion precluded this. Instead, the Negev Brigade, which had advanced westward from Bir Tamila and linked up with the Eighth Brigade at ʿAuja, crossed the international frontier at noon, 28 December. The brigade's task, as set by Allon, was to conquer the Abu Ageila crossroads, the key to the Peninsula, and then to raid (or conquer) El ʿArish to the north and Bir al-Hama to the west. Allon's instructions to the Negev and Eighth Brigades, regarding Abu Ageila and El ʿArish, were given without receiving the consent of the General Staff. Allon suspected that political impediments might stay Yadin's hand when it came to crossing the frontier or conquering El ʿArish and cutting off the Gaza Strip. Best that he be informed of Southern Front's actions after the event.

"[We] left behind us hundreds of Egyptian soldiers and officers, dispersed and straying among the hills, looking for the remnants of their units or ready to surrender. We paid them no attention and continued on our way," recalled the Ninth Battalion's deputy OC, Micha Peri.[32] An Egyptian chronicler confirms that the retreat from the Bir Asluj–ʿAuja al-Hafir line into Sinai was in fact a "rout," with the Jews shouting, "Forward, to Cairo!" in the wake of the fleeing Egyptians.[33]

In the push into Sinai, the Negev Brigade's two battalions, the Seventh and Ninth, were accompanied by the Eighth Brigade's Eighty-second armored battalion and artillery units. The units, on trucks, armored cars, jeeps, and half-tracks, with a company of tanks, "sang" as they drove into Egypt. "We were suffused with a sense of Jewish power bursting into Egypt, after a long period of the Egyptian invaders' presence on our soil," recalled one Israeli soldier.[34] An Egyptian chronicler relates that a bedouin who witnessed the IDF entry into Sinai related that "as they crossed the border, the Jews halted their vehicles and got down to kiss the Egyptian soil. Many of the Jewish troops cried for joy and hugged one another."[35]

Both Ben-Gurion and Yadin seem to have been otherwise preoccupied during the crossing into Egypt; Yadin was in bed with the flu, and Ben-Gurion was busy finding accommodation for the newly arrived Soviet representatives to Israel, raising money in the United States, and directing the secret peace talks (see below) with the Jordanians. There is barely a word about the conquest of ʿAuja and the advance on Abu Ageila in his diary entries for 27, 28, and 29 December[36] (though at Cabinet meetings, biblical as always, Ben-Gurion told his ministers: "There are those who say that the children of Israel there [that is, at Abu Ageila] made the golden calf [egel]."[37] Strangely—as with the push into Lebanon in Operation Hiram two months earlier—the Israeli leadership seems initially simply to have ignored the possible political implications and consequences of the cross-border campaign. Perhaps the lack of international reaction in Hiram lowered their guard during Horev.

Just short of Abu Ageila the units were strafed by Israeli aircraft and then shelled by Egyptian antitank gunners. At 4:25 PM Yadin cabled Allon: "[You] are to refrain from advancing to Abu Ageila until you see me. If [your forces] have already moved, you are to carry out a raid only."[38] But Allon was keenly aware of the need for speed in the face of the crumbling Egyptian morale and defenses and possible international intervention. He responded: "The push on Abu Ageila cannot be stopped. After we take the place—we will be free to leave it, if that is what is decided." Allon declined to fly to Tel Aviv to discuss the matter (as Yadin had requested).[39] Meanwhile, he hastily organized the assault on the battalion-sized complex of fortifications at Umm Katef–Abu Ageila. Just after midnight 28–29 December the positions fell to Seventh Battalion assault. Palestinian prisoners held by the Egyptians at a nearby detention center were set free. But hundreds of Egyptians gave themselves up, preferring Israeli imprisonment to wandering in the desert without food or water.[40]

Abu Ageila was not Allon's real objective, though. He was after bigger game: El ʿArish. Its fall would close the trap on the bulk of the Egyptian army, in the Gaza Strip, and, no doubt, augur that army's collapse—and Allon wasn't going to allow diplomats or Yadin to stop him. Allon sent his deputy, Yitzhak Rabin, to tell Yadin that what was happening at Abu Ageila was a "raid." Rabin did not mention El ʿArish. As he later phrased it in his memoirs: "I had neglected to specify our entire plan and confined myself to the capture of Abu Ageila. I had reason to believe that if I were to reveal the whole plan, including the capture of El ʿArish, the General Staff might suspect we had gone mad."[41]

Just after dawn, 29 December, the Eighty-second and Ninth battalions pushed northward on the road to El ʿArish. That afternoon they took the "last stop" before El ʿArish, Bir Lahfan. A battalion OC was captured, the highest-ranking Egyptian officer to fall into Israeli hands. But most of the Egyptians fled into the desert. "The many shoes scattered by the roadsides testified to crumbling [Egyptian] companies and platoons that had turned into human dust," wrote one Eighth Brigade chronicler.[42] Allon cabled Yadin, hours after the fact: "Our forces are moving on a raid on El ʿArish. We have taken [Bir Lahfan] airfield [twelve miles south of El ʿArish]." He asked HQ to send pilots to fly out four captured Egyptian aircraft.[43] Meanwhile, he ordered the Eighty-second Battalion to press on. It encountered an antitank position and took it. The Egyptians fled. By evening, the Eighty-second and elements of the Negev Brigade were about six miles short of El ʿArish. With their airfields in eastern Sinai either lost or on the verge of capture, the Egyptians flew out their remaining planes to the Suez Canal area—leaving the expeditionary force completely without air cover.

Meanwhile, the Seventh and Tenth battalions mounted deep penetration raids into the heart of Sinai, against army camps in Bir al-Hassne and Bir al-Hama. The first raid netted more than two hundred prisoners.

At Bir Lahfan, as Allon contemplated the final push northward, a telegram from Yadin reached him and Rabin, stating: "I have learned from the [IDF] Intelligence Service and from [IAF] aerial reconnaissance that our forces have moved toward El ʿArish. . . . You are herewith ordered to halt all movement of your units without prior approval from me." A follow-up cable read: "What is happening here? Stop the advance!" And a third cable: "I repeat and emphasize that I forbid you to carry out any operation north of Abu Ageila without my permission."[44]

Allon boarded a plane for Tel Aviv. He hoped to persuade Yadin and Ben-Gurion to let him take El ʿArish. Perhaps he assumed that by the time the deliberations in Tel Aviv were ended, the Eighth and Twelfth Brigades would have taken the town.[45]

The meeting with Yadin, at home in bed, around midnight 29–30 December was stormy. Yadin refused to budge. Allon said that his forces could and would take El ʿArish and then turn eastward, attacking Rafah from the rear. Yadin demanded that the brigades return to Abu Ageila. Allon radioed his staff officers: "It's no use. Withdraw from El ʿArish."[46]

It is possible that Yadin feared that Allon's forces were too small to take and hold El ʿArish. More likely, he was moved by expectations of international pressure. Whatever the case, Yadin forced a withdrawal. But he agreed to allow Allon an alternative, to push from Abu Ageila toward Rafah along the international frontier, which could assure the envelopment of the Gaza Strip without taking El ʿArish.

Nonetheless, Allon made one last effort: the following morning he met with Ben-Gurion (and Yadin) and pleaded that they reconsider. But Ben-Gurion, too, refused to budge. Indeed, he went one better: if the British actually deployed forces threatening the IDF, Allon was ordered to withdraw back to ʿAuja, across the frontier.[47] As the prime minister told the Cabinet: "There is a consideration that has guided us from the start of the operation: through all the war we have been careful not to face off with the British army."[48] The Israelis remained genuinely fearful of British intervention, given—as they saw things—Foreign Secretary Bevin's "irrational" anti-Israeli "bias."[49]

It is not altogether clear why Yadin (and Ben-Gurion) were so adamant on late 29 December and early 30 December about pulling back from El ʿArish; international pressure had barely been unleashed. But ongoing diplomatic moves—and premonitions of worse to come—doubtless played a key role. Following the IDF thrust across the international frontier, the Egyptians, on 28 December, had demanded the immediate convening of the Security Council to halt what they—with brazen chutzpah—called Israeli "aggression." Previously, Bunche had submitted to the council reports condemning Israel for the impasse in the Negev as resulting from its intransigence over the Faluja Pocket. Now Britain submitted a resolution calling for Israeli compliance with the resolution of 4 November, which had called for withdrawal to the 14 October line. Egyptian War Minister Muhammad Haidar had informed London that the Israelis were "now within six miles of El ʿArish."[50] On 29 December the Security Council called for an "immediate ceasefire" and implementation of the 4 November resolution.

By morning 30 December, the Eighth and Twelfth Brigades were back in Abu Ageila. But by then, London was frenetic, breathing down Truman's neck. Pressed by Cairo, Britain was insistent on saving the Egyptian army—and understood that the IDF had to be prevented from completing its encirclement. The Egyptians were panic-stricken and transmitted the panic to London via the British embassy in Cairo. Egypt's leaders were "begging [Ambassador Sir Ronald Campbell] for war material." They even asked that "British aircraft, tanks and guns with British crews but with Egyptian markings" be sent to attack the Israelis.[51] Campbell opined that an Egyptian defeat would lead to grave instability in Egypt and that Britain's position in the

Middle East in general would be imperiled, especially if Britain rebuffed Egyptian pleas for help. The assassination of the Egyptian prime minister, Mahmud Fahmi Nuqrashi, two days earlier did not help. He was murdered by a young veterinary student and Muslim Brotherhood member, ʿAbdel Meguid Ahmad Hassan, disguised as a police lieutenant, in the Ministry of Interior building in Cairo, days after he had outlawed the organization. The defeat in Palestine was one of the reasons later cited by the assassin.[52]

In a series of almost hysterical telegrams, Campbell strongly urged London to authorize arms shipments to Egypt and to launch limited military intervention against Israel. Campbell hoped that this would force the IDF out of Sinai or even back to "the positions they occupied in [the] Negeb on October 14th." Such action could restore Britain's position in the Middle East, he argued.[53] Britain's minister to Beirut, Houstoun Boswall, concurred.[54]

But Britain's willingness to help Egypt was hampered by a lack of information about the true state of affairs in Sinai; its own reconnaissance aircraft had not yet supplied clear photographs, and the Egyptians could not be trusted to tell the truth. As Bevin put it (somewhat censoriously) to Campbell on 30 December: "We cannot understand the Egyptian reports of the fighting. Public statements from Cairo represent the battles as Egyptian victories. At the same time we receive [private] appeals for help. The public here will not understand. Is it not better for the Egyptian Government to give the true facts?"[55] Bevin agreed only to allow Egyptian aircraft to use Britain's Suez Canal–side bases for refueling.

But he sensed that the Egyptians were on the verge of defeat. He instructed his ambassador in Washington to "inform [the] State Department . . . that if Jewish forces are in fact attacking Egyptian territory our obligations under the Anglo-Egyptian [Defense] Treaty would of course come into play."[56] And he followed this up with something still firmer: "I trust that it may be possible for the United States Government to act on the Jews as to make any military action by us on Egyptian territory unnecessary. . . . This can only be ensured if the Jews immediately withdraw from Egyptian territory. . . . In view of the aggressive use to which the Jews had put arms obtained from Soviet satellite countries we shall no longer be able to refuse to carry out British contracts to the Arab countries."[57] The cat was now among the pigeons.

Initially, the Americans were uncertain whether Israel had actually invaded Sinai or had just carried out a small "unauthorised" and "mistaken" crossing of the frontier.[58] But by 30 December things were clear: Ben-Gurion was told that Truman was "deeply disturbed" by the "invasion [of] Egyptian territory." This was proof, said the State Department, of Israel's "aggressiveness" and "complete disregard" of the United Nations.[59]

At first, Israel denied that it had invaded Egyptian territory. But under the barrage of appeals and threats from London, Washington was propelled into action. At lunchtime on 31 December, McDonald, the US representative in Tel Aviv, was instructed to tell Israel to get out of Sinai. Shertok was summoned and told to inform Ben-Gurion and Weizmann that Britain had threatened that, unless the IDF withdrew from Sinai, London would be compelled to "take action" under the terms of the Anglo-Egyptian Defense Treaty. Washington, for its part, regarded the invasion of Sinai as "ill-advised" and as jeopardizing "the peace of the Middle East." This might require "reconsideration" of America's "relations with Israel." (By the way, the United States also criticized Israel's "threatening" attitude toward Jordan.)[60] As Shertok jotted down McDonald's statement, "his fingers tightened around his pen, and his face was white with tension," the American later recorded.[61]

McDonald then drove to Tiberias, where Ben-Gurion was holidaying, and once again read out the "statement." It was after midnight on New Year's Eve. Ben-Gurion responded that the IDF had not really invaded Egypt but had crossed the border for "tactical" reasons. In any case, it had already "received orders to return."[62] The prime minister added: "I am surprised by the harsh [American] tone. Is there any need for a friendly power to approach a small and weak nation in such a tone?"[63]

By then Israel's troops had pulled backed. On 30 December they had withdrawn from Bir Lahfan to Abu Ageila, and the following afternoon Yadin ordered Allon to pull out of Sinai back to ʿAuja by noon, 1 January 1949. He was to leave scorched earth behind (destroyed airstrips, roads, and so on). Allon again flew to Tel Aviv and pleaded with Yadin and Shertok (Ben-Gurion was on holiday) to give him more time and to retain several positions just inside Sinai. Yadin and Shertok refused: they said that Israel could not go back on its word and must pull out completely—but they gave Allon another seventeen hours to complete the pullback.

By morning 2 January 1949, "not an Israeli hoof remained in Egypt";[64] the IDF was back in ʿAuja. But Israel was both alarmed and annoyed by the diplomatic démarche that had forced its retreat. It was being pilloried as an aggressor—and threatened with British military intervention—when it was Egypt (and its fellow Arab states) who were the aggressors, who had clearly violated the UN Charter and a UN decision by invading Palestine and attacking the State of Israel (and the British, to judge from their internal correspondence, clearly understood this);[65] and all the Israelis had been doing since 15 May 1948 was attempting to drive out the invaders. Israel failed to understand Britain's threats of intervention or to lift its arms embargo or, for that matter, America's support of these threats. This was the gist of letters sent by Shertok to McDonald and Weizmann to Truman. The Israelis invoked the right of "hot pursuit" in defense of their penetration of Sinai and decried the inequitable treatment by the Security Council and the Great Powers of the two "invasions." And, to add insult to injury, the United States and Britain were sponsoring Egypt for a Security Council seat while Israel was being denied UN membership![66]

The IDF had withdrawn from Sinai. Yet the battle was nonetheless to be resolved not in the corridors of international diplomacy but in the desert sands. And this time Israel was not to be denied victory. If Britain and the United States had stymied Allon's wide, encircling sweep around the Egyptian rear, then he would go for a narrower, diplomatically less troublesome encirclement and close the trap at Rafah rather than at El 'Arish; the objective was the same.

Golani, Harel, and the Eighth Brigades (along with the Ninth Battalion, Negev Brigade) were assigned the conquest of Rafah; the Negev Brigade was assigned Gaza city (to be attacked after the Egyptians rushed troops from there to defend Rafah). The aim of Operation Horev, Stage Two, was to take Rafah and its surroundings and cut the road and rail links between the Gaza Strip and Egypt, isolating the expeditionary force between Rafah and Beit Hanun.

Rafah, which was to be attacked from the south and west by the Harel Brigade and by Golani from the east, was defended by an enlarged, well-dug-in in Egyptian brigade, backed by batteries of twenty-five-pounders and twenty Locust tanks. The Israelis struck on the night of 3–4 January. Golani's Twelfth Battalion, setting out from Nirim, took "Cemetery Hill," an important outpost south of Rafah, but failed to take Position 102 and the nearby army camps. Meanwhile, a mix of Harel and Negev brigade battalions began their push northward from 'Auja—most of the route ran along the Egyptian side of the international line—and during 4–6 January took a chain of Egyptian roadside positions.

The Egyptians sent reinforcements across the Suez Canal and mounted fierce counterattacks on the forward Israeli units, and a stalemate reigned along the hilly crests southeast of Rafah, though continuous Israeli aerial and naval bombardments of the towns and positions inside the Gaza Strip, which caused heavy civilian casualties (mainly among Palestinian refugees), sorely tried Egypt's staying power. The Egyptians tried to prevent fleeing soldiers from reaching the Nile Delta area and spreading demoralization to the heartland.[67] They managed to retake two key positions controlling the 'Auja–Rafah and Rafah–El 'Arish crossroads. However, Harel's Fourth Battalion, commanded by David El'azar, occupied an empty Egyptian position in sand dunes to the west, inside Sinai, near Sheikh Zuweid, at last cutting the El ʿArish–Rafah road on the evening of 6 January. The position, reinforced on 7 January by armored cars, artillery, and two tanks from Eighth Brigade, also dominated the Rafah–El ʿArish railroad track. Desperate Egyptian counter-attacks were repulsed, the attackers losing eight tanks and armored cars in one charge. Key to the victory was an antitank six-pounder manned by Russian-speaking Gahalniks.[68] On the night of 7–8 January, Ninth Battalion scouts raided the railway line, and a mine they planted blew up a train bound for El ʿArish carrying hundreds of Egyptian wounded from Rafah.

But by then the Egyptians had thrown in the towel. For days, General Sadiq, OC of the expeditionary force, feeling that the trap was closing, had pressed his government to agree to a cease-fire. On 5 January Cairo informed the United Nations, United States, and Britain that they were ready to begin armistice negotiations if Israel ceased hostilities. Israel was informed by the United Nations the following day.[69] The IDF's capture of the Sheikh Zuweid position and the sabotage of the railway tracks only reinforced Cairo's determination to halt the fighting and save its army.

Ben-Gurion was unhappy that yet again the IDF had, at the last minute, been prevented from demolishing the Egyptian army. But he viewed the Egyptian démarche to end the state of belligerency within the wider Middle Eastern context; Jordan and the other Arab states, he was sure, would follow suit.[70] Moreover, he was keenly attuned to Washington—where opinion was "dangerously tense, almost hostile" to Israel and where Truman was beginning to perceive Israel as a "trouble-maker." Israel's representative in Washington strongly urged acceptance of the cease-fire.[71] On 7 January Tel Aviv responded positively and ordered Allon to pull all his forces out of Egyptian-held territory by 10 January. The fighting was to have ended at 2:00 PM, 7 January, but went on for a few more hours as local Egyptian commanders tried, to no avail, to reopen the route to El ʿArish.

Once again, Allon was stupefied and angry; once more he had had the Egyptian Expeditionary Force by the throat and had been ordered to let go. But Ben-Gurion would brook no dissent. Chief of Staff Dori rebuked Allon: he "had no right . . . to criticize the political management of the war," which was the political leadership's prerogative.[72] Ben-Gurion reportedly told Allon: "You are a good commander but you have no political experience. Do you know the value of peace talks with Egypt? After all, that is our great dream!"[73] That night (9–10 January), the Harel and Eighth Brigade evacuated Sheikh Zuweid, reopening the Rafah–El ʿArish road. By the end of the day, all IDF units had quit Egyptian territory. Two days later, on 12 January, Egyptian and Israeli delegations arrived in Rhodes to begin UN-mediated armistice negotiations. The fighting war had ended.

But the battles of 4–7 January around Rafah had managed nonetheless to suck in the British. In November 1948 the Israelis had downed a British Mosquito reconnaissance aircraft over Israel. London suspended reconnaissance flights. But Operation Horev prompted a renewal of border-hugging flights, and between 30 December 1948 and 6 January 1949, the RAF flew seven reconnaissance missions over Sinai, principally to ascertain the positions of the Israeli columns and whether they were in violation of the international frontier. All the missions had ended without incident. The flights of 7 January were to be different.

That morning, the British sent two flights over the combat zones around and south of Rafah: a flight of two Mosquitos, accompanied by four Spitfires, to reconnoiter and photograph the situation on the ground; and a flight of four Spitfires whose mission was "tactical reconnaissance." Both were apparently ordered to fly over Abu Ageila and then veer northward, along the western side of the international frontier; not to cross into Israeli territory; and not to attack Israeli ground or air forces, being permitted to fire back only if attacked by aircraft. The photographic mission passed without incident. But the second mission, of four Spitfires—each armed with loaded 20 mm cannon—came to grief. Passing over an Israeli position southwest of Rafah, one of the aircraft was downed by Israeli ground fire. Seconds later, the other three were shot down by a pair of patrolling Israeli Spitfires. The "Israeli" pilots, incidentally, were an American and a Canadian, both non-Jews, who a few years before had fought alongside the RAF against the Germans. One of the British pilots was killed, two were captured by Israel, and the fourth was picked up by bedouins and returned safely to the Suez Canal. At the start of the battle, it was unclear to the Israelis to whom the intruding Spitfires belonged. All four had been shot down on the Egyptian side of the frontier. But the Israelis then dragged parts of the downed planes across the frontier into Israel—"for understandable reasons," as Allon put it.[74]

The British then sent a further patrol, consisting of nineteen aircraft—fifteen Tempests and four Spitfires—to find out what had happened to the missing foursome. Because they were on a search mission, the guns of all but one of the Tempests were not cocked before takeoff and could not be cocked in flight, which meant that they were virtually defenseless. They took approximately the same flight path as the original Spitfires, but it is possible that some of them strayed into Israeli airspace. At all events, four Israeli Spitfires, with Ezer Weizman in the lead, pounced on them. Again, the British—with their eyes pinned to the ground in search of wrecked aircraft—were caught by surprise. And again, the Israelis, coming out of the sun, were initially uncertain whom they were attacking. The British Spitfires, flying ahead of the Tempests, were not involved in the battle. A number of British Tempests were hit, and one of them crashed, ten miles inside Israel, with its pilot killed.[75] The Israelis suffered no losses.

The British military and political authorities, understandably angry, issued threats, and the IDF braced for a British revenge attack. Ben-Gurion jotted down in his diary, on hearing of the felled planes: "The information I received worried me"[76]—and he rushed back from Tiberias to Tel Aviv. Israel signaled London, via the United Nations, that it had had no intention of attacking Britain. London reconsidered. The British cabinet decided against lifting the arms embargo on the Arab states and limited its reaction to landing "Force O," consisting of a brigade HQ, an infantry battalion, an antitank battery, and an antiaircraft battery in ʿAqaba on 8 January (a move that, in fact, had already been decided in November, principally because of a possible Israeli threat to Jordan)[77]—and, perhaps surprisingly, awarding Israel de facto recognition.[78] The Israelis interpreted the ʿAqaba landing and other British troop movements in the region, and the threat to renew arms shipments to the Arabs, as minatory.[79] But the bulk of the British cabinet, perhaps restraining Bevin, reached the conclusion that Britain had been in the wrong or at least felt that now that the Arabs had agreed to negotiate an armistice, the war was at an end—and hardly a time for Britain to embark on a war of its own against the Jewish state.

Throughout, the British government received little comfort from Washington or its own public. McDonald later reported that Truman, at a meeting with the British ambassador to Washington, had been "firm": he had criticized the flights over the battle zone and the landing of the troops at ʿAqaba and had commended Israel's "prompt withdrawal" from Sinai and its readiness to negotiate an armistice.[80] The Americans appealed to Britain to refrain from escalation. In London, Winston Churchill and several British newspapers castigated the government's behavior.

But Israel took, and continued for several more days to take, the British threat, and its assumed designs on the Negev, seriously. Ben-Gurion instructed Dori and Yadin to beef up the Negev's defenses and plan a counterstrike, should the British attack in the Negev, the West Bank, or Jerusalem.[81] The IDF prepared Operational Plan Yefet to confront a possible British-Jordanian-Iraqi challenge and exploit an attack in the Negev to make gains in the center of the country. The Israelis expected the British to open with a preemptive air campaign against IAF bases.[82]

Nothing came of all this. Within days, British belligerency was replaced by conciliation. The British took note of Israel's military preparations. But they were probably more impressed by America's support for Israeli control of the

Negev and Washington's abandonment of the Bernadotte plan; Washington would certainly not countenance a British war on Israel to gain control of the Negev.

Whitehall, including Bevin, caved in. As Ben-Gurion put it in his diary: "Meanwhile, Bevin has been panicked by his Conservative critics and [criticism by] his party colleagues, and yesterday made a surprise announcement that it has been decided to free the Cyprus illegal immigration detainees (when?) and [that the Cabinet] is discussing recognition of the Israeli government. It seems that they have had enough."[83]

OPERATION HISUL

"From the Egyptian perspective, Faluja is their Tobruk, and their people are holding out with great courage," Ben-Gurion said on 29 December.[84] He was explaining the latest in the string of Israeli failures against the pocket. *Mivtza hisul* (Operation Liquidation), during 27–28 December, was a sideshow of Operation Horev. Much as the besieged pocket was an albatross and source of great anxiety for the Egyptians, it was a permanent thorn in the side of the IDF, sitting astride a main crossroads and necessitating the investment of large encircling forces, lest the Egyptians mount a breakout from, or a break-in into, the pocket. It had to be destroyed—the aim was "the liquidation of the pocket," as the operational order put it—and the General Staff allocated the Alexandroni Brigade, an additional infantry battalion, the 152nd, and a number of artillery and heavy mortar batteries, for the task. Operation Horev was seen as a natural "environment" for the action, when the main Egyptian forces, and air force, would be otherwise preoccupied.

After repeated bombing raids during 26–27 December, two battalions, the Thirty-third and Thirty-fifth, went in on the night of 27–28 December. The aim was to conquer the village of ʿIraq al-Manshiya and positions around it on the eastern edge of the pocket and then to assault Faluja and its environs. The Egyptians, with about four thousand troops, were well dug-in.

The initial moves went badly. The Thirty-fifth Battalion attacked before midnight. But its two companies failed to take the two-squad "Road Position," which dominated the road between Faluja and ʿIraq al-Manshiya, or to penetrate ʿIraq al-Manshiya from the east. Rain and mud hampered the attack, jamming weapons and limiting mobility. The battalion also failed to mine the road.

Two hours later, the Thirty-third Battalion succeeded in entering and occupying most of ʿIraq al Manshiya, despite stubborn Egyptian resistance. But the battalion's C Company failed to take the dominant hillock, Tel

Sheikh al-Areini, just north of the village. Meanwhile, inside the village, Israeli soldiers—"unable to control themselves," as one IDF report subsequently put it[85]—mowed down surrendering Egyptian troops. This may account for the powerful resistance offered by the Egyptian troops on the nearby tel. Battalion HQ lost contact with C Company and, eventually, with the two companies inside the village, whose component units continued fighting, in disorganized fashion, pockets of Egyptian resistance. Just after dawn, an Egyptian armored column with infantry support reached ʿIraq al-Manshiya from Faluja. Israeli reinforcements failed to reach the Thirty-third Battalion. The Egyptian armor picked off Israeli squads and platoons in the village's alleyways. The battalion HQ failed to provide the embattled companies with artillery support. At 9:30 AM, 28 December, brigade HQ ordered a general retreat. The companies withdrew in disorder; few from C Company, stranded north of the village, made it. Altogether, the Thirty-third and Thirty-fifth battalions suffered eighty-eight dead, five MIAs, and sixty wounded—the worst losses suffered by the Yishuv in a single engagement during the war other than in the fall of the ʿEtzion Bloc in mid-May.

The Egyptians probably suffered a similar number of casualties,[86] and after a series of telling IAF raids, in which some sixty-five Egyptian soldiers died, Saʿid Taha requested permission to surrender the Faluja Pocket: "The bodies of the dead are emitting a stench. . . . The whole town [Faluja] is continuously under fire. I see [that is, want] to agree to hand it over to the Jews." But the Egyptians managed to push several convoys with supplies into the pocket, and the Egyptians held on, despite the artillery harassment.[87] But here, too, the guns fell silent on 7 January.

Hisul had been a dismal failure, and the pocket remained intact until the signing of the Israel-Egypt General Armistice Agreement on 24 February 1949, after which the Egyptian troops peacefully withdrew to Sinai under Red Cross flags.

As in previous episodes during the war, aerial activity had a marginal effect on the ground operations in Operation Horev, though both sides had substantially reinforced their air forces. Both flew dozens of ground attack and interception sorties, and the Egyptian air force—now with new Italian-made Macchi and Fiat fighters—lost half a dozen to Israeli interceptors and ground fire. At least three Macchis were destroyed on the ground in IAF attacks on Bir al-Hama Airfield in Sinai. In aerial combat, the Spitfires proved superior to the Italian models. Nonetheless, the Egyptians bombed the ʿEqron Airfield, Jerusalem, and (apparently by mistake) the Allenby Bridge near Jericho. IAF aircraft repeatedly bombed the Egyptian forward airstrips around El ʿArish and Bir al-Hama as well as Egyptian positions in the Gaza Strip and Abu Ageila. At sea, an Egyptian flotilla on 1 January briefly shelled Tel Aviv and was driven off by IAF B-17s.

All in all, Horev had been a major Israeli victory. The IDF had failed to destroy or even permanently trap the Egyptian Expeditionary Force, which was saved by the UN bell. But it had cleared the Egyptians out of Palestine, except for the sliver of territory to be known as the Gaza Strip. And it had forced the army's political superiors, in order to save it, to sue for an armistice.

Moreover, Operation Horev triggered conciliatoriness beyond Egypt's borders. Once Egypt was out of the fight, its allies realized—if they hadn't before Horev—that it was pointless to battle on. Egyptian readiness to lay down arms had a domino effect in the Arab world. And some Arabs were even ready to go one better. Horev had severely alarmed the Jordanians; perhaps they feared that they were next in Israel's sights. They began to clamor for the start of formal peace negotiations. This echoed in Alec Kirkbride's cable to London of 29 December, calling on London to remove its veto on the start of such negotiations: "King ʿAbdullah should be allowed to make the best terms he can with the Jews without further restrictions on our part," he wrote Bevin.[88]

The stage was set for the start of the diplomatic termination of the war.

10

The Armistice Agreements,
January–July 1949

The war of 1948 formally ended with the signing of armistice agreements between Israel and four of the Arab belligerents: Egypt (on 24 February 1949), Lebanon (23 March 1949), Jordan (3 April 1949), and Syria (20 July 1949). The Iraqis refused to enter into armistice negotiations.

The Israeli-Egyptian armistice talks opened on the Greek island of Rhodes on 13 January 1949—six days after the start of the cease-fire, three days after Israel pulled its troops out of Sinai and Rafah—and lasted six weeks. In the chair, effectively mediating between the two sides, was the United Nations acting mediator for Palestine, Ralph Bunche, Count Bernadotte's successor.

The negotiation was between unequal parties. The Egyptians sorely felt their disadvantage: their army had just been thrashed, and in the absence of an agreement, Israel might renew hostilities, conquer the Gaza Strip, and perhaps drive once again into the Sinai Peninsula. The expeditionary force, still strung out between El ʿArish and Gaza, was highly vulnerable, and the fate of the regime was linked to the fate of the army. On the basis of the previous months' experience, the Egyptians knew that they could expect no help from their fellow Arabs or, most likely, from the Great Powers. And a brigade-size force remained trapped deep in Israeli territory, at Faluja, at the mercy of the IDF. Its situation was highly embarrassing for Cairo.

But not all the cards were in Israeli hands. On the table, in terms of international diplomacy, perched the 1947 UN partition resolution, a fundamental reference point for most officials involved in solving the Palestine problem, and in a number of sectors, the IDF occupied land beyond the UN-ear-marked borders of Jewish statehood. The Arabs, at a minimum, would demand that Israel withdraw to the 1947 lines. Moreover, the Israeli leadership and public profoundly desired peace; the troops, sick of the yearlong war, wanted to return to their loved ones; and the economy, starved of manpower, thirsted for their return. Masses of immigrants were pouring into the country, and the war-making hampered their absorption.[1] Peace was imperative.

Israel's leaders understood that an agreement with the Egyptians was crucial—"of far-reaching importance," in Walter Eytan's phrase[2]—in paving the way for similar agreements with the other belligerents. Politically, demographically, economically, and culturally, Egypt was the key Arab country. If it didn't sign, none would—leaving Israel embattled and mobilized, with the problem reverting to the UN Security Council for debate and resolution. The council would not necessarily rule in Israel's favor.[3] An agreement with Cairo was seen as crucial to Israel's "acceptance" in the Middle East and in the international community (it was not yet a member of the United Nations).

The Israelis were represented at Rhodes by a mixed political and military team, headed by Eytan, director general of the Foreign Ministry. His subordinate, IDF chief of operations Yigael Yadin, and his aides, who included Yitzhak Rabin, Southern Front's operations officer, thought Eytan too conciliatory—and occasionally the generals back in Israel, including OC Southern Command Yigal Allon, Rabin's direct superior (and friend), pressed the negotiators with hard-line advice.[4] In the end, disagreements between the team members were settled by David Ben-Gurion or the full Cabinet, which ultimately authorized the successive compromises that made the agreement possible.

The Egyptian delegation was formally led by a military man, Colonel Muhammad Seif el Dine, but the man in charge may well have been ʿAbd al-Munʿim Mustapha, a Foreign Ministry official.[5] Several colonels, a handful of Foreign Ministry officials, and a representative of the Court, Ismail Sherine, rounded out the delegation. It is not clear whether King Farouk's court, the army general staff, or the prime minister or foreign minister were calling the shots.

Entering the talks, Israel's negotiating position was based on the military realities on the ground and the fact of Egyptian defeat; the Egyptian position, on the pre-Yoav and pre-Horev front lines and on the UN Security Council resolutions, which had called on Israel to withdraw to the 14 October lines. The withdrawal-promoting Security Council resolution of 4 November was buttressed by a memorandum by Bunche defining and endorsing the truce lines of 14 October.[6]

Israel initially demanded that Egypt withdraw from the areas its troops still occupied in Palestine—that is, the Gaza Strip and the Bethlehem area—and that the future armistice boundary between the two countries be based on the old international Egypt-Palestine frontier, agreed between the British Empire (effectively governing Egypt) and the Ottomans (ruling Palestine) in 1906. The Egyptians initially sought what amounted to sovereignty over the central and southern Negev—partly in order to restore the historic territorial contiguity of the Arab and Islamic worlds—and demanded that Israel withdraw from the areas of Beersheba, Bir Asluj, and ʿAuja. The southern Negev and Beersheba, they said, could be demilitarized. The Egyptians also demanded that Israel allow the evacuation of the Faluja Pocket—"which weighed on them most heavily of all," as one Israeli delegation member put it[7]—before anything else was discussed or settled. Israel refused.

The six weeks of talks consisted of formal and informal Israeli-Egyptian meetings and trilateral negotiations, with Bunche receiving Israeli and Egyptian proposals, passing them on to the other side, receiving each side's comments on the proposals, passing those on, occasionally with his own bridging suggestions, and so on. Bunche repeatedly tried to mobilize American pressure on Israel to soften its positions. But Israeli diplomats in Washington and Lake Success, New York, managed to parry the pressure and, in fact, elicited countervailing pressures by the United States on Egypt to reduce its demands, especially in relation to Beersheba.[8]

There were recurrent crises. The chief final stumbling blocks were the fate of ʿAuja and strips of Israel-held territory on the northern and southern edges of the Gaza Strip, from which Israel in the end agreed to withdraw. The problem of ʿAuja was solved, at Bunche's suggestion, by turning the village and its environs—all on the "Palestine" side of the international line—into a demilitarized zone (DMZ).

In the eventual compromise, signed on 24 February, each side promised to refrain from military action against the other, and the Egyptian force trapped in Faluja, was permitted to withdraw, with all its equipment, beginning the following day. The agreed Armistice Demarcation Line—which was not, the accord said, to prejudice the final borders delineated in any future political agreement—followed the exact contours of the 1906 border, except for the inclusion on the Egyptian side of the Gaza Strip. The agreement allowed for continued Egyptian military occupation of the strip. Limitation of forces zones (allowing only "defensive forces") were instituted along the length of both sides of the border, on the Israeli side encompassing the western Negev and on the Egyptian side, the area to the east of the El ʿArish–Abu Ageila line. A mixed armistice commission (MAC), headquartered in the ʿAuja DMZ, was established, manned by Israeli and Egyptian officers and chaired by a UN officer, to supervise the implementation of the agreement.[9]

The agreement—like the armistice agreements between Israel and the other Arab states that followed—kicked off with a Preamble that placed the document squarely, as Israel insisted, within the context of bridging between "the present truce" and the institution of "permanent peace in Palestine." But because of the Arab states' fundamental unwillingness to make peace with the Jewish state, the agreement proved to be not an introduction to anything deeper and wider but a segue assuring only nonbelligerency (which in any event was only partially delivered as, during the following years, the borders between Israel and its three main Arab neighbors seethed with Arab infiltration, terrorist strikes inside Israel, and Israeli counterstrikes, and with clashes—with Syria and Egypt—over the DMZs instituted by the armistice agreements).[10] Nonetheless, the Egyptian-Israeli agreement was the first between Israel and an Arab country and may be seen as a forerunner to the first peace treaty between Israel and any of its neighbors, the Israeli-Egyptian accord of 1979.

The Israeli-Lebanese armistice talks, held in no-man's-land on the border near Rosh Haniqra (Ras al-Naqurah) on the Mediterranean coast, were a shorter and less disputatious affair. From the start, there was a friendly atmosphere. Indeed, as the Israelis reported, "the Lebanese [delegates] pretend / say that they are not Arabs and that they were dragged into the adventure [that is, the war] against their will. They maintain that, for internal reasons, they cannot openly admit their hatred for the Syrians."[11]

The talks began on 1 March, the Lebanese having insisted on waiting until the Israeli-Egyptian negotiations had been successfully concluded, and lasted three weeks. The main problem on the agenda was the strip of villages occupied by the IDF at the end of Operation Hiram. Five of them, never permanently occupied, had been "relinquished" by Israel, as "a goodwill gesture," already in mid-January.[12]

The delegations were headed by military men (Lieutenant Colonel Mordechai Makleff for Israel and Lieutenant Colonel Toufic Salem for Lebanon). The two sides agreed from the start that the international border, demarcated by France and Britain (the Mandatory rulers respectively of Lebanon and Palestine) in 1923, be reinstituted as the frontier between the two states.

The Lebanese demanded that Israel withdraw from their territory. Israel sought both a Lebanese withdrawal from the sole patch of Palestine they had

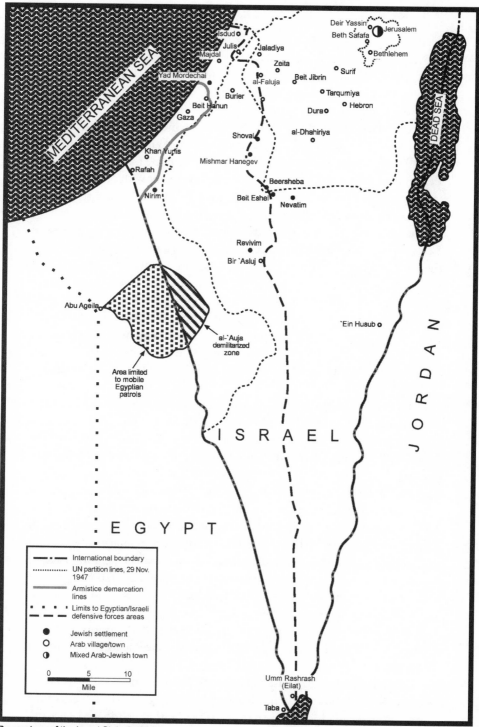

MEDITERRANEAN SEA

Deir Yassin
Beth Safafa
Jerusalem
Bethlehem

Isdud
Julis
Majdal
Jaladiya
Zeita
Surif
Beit Jibrin
al-Faluja
Yad Mordechai
Burier
Tarqumiya
Beit Hanun
Dura
Hebron
Gaza
Shoval
al-Dhahiriya
Khan Yunis
Mishmar Hanegev
Rafah
Beersheba
Nirim
Beit Eshel
Nevatim

Revivim
Bir 'Asluj

DEAD SEA

JORDAN

Abu Ageila
al-'Auja
demilitarized
zone
'Ein Husub

Area limited
to mobile
Egyptian
patrols

I S R A E L

E G Y P T

—·—·— International boundary
·········· UN partition lines, 29 Nov.
            1947
———— Armistice demarcation
            lines
· · · · Limits to Egyptian/Israeli
            defensive forces areas
● Jewish settlement
○ Arab village/town
◐ Mixed Arab-Jewish town

0   5   10
Mile

Umm Rashrash
(Eilat)

Taba

By courtesy of the Israel State Archives

Israel-Egypt general armistice agreement lines, 24 February 1949 occupied—several hundred square yards at Ras al-Naqurah—and the withdrawal of the Syrian army from the enclaves it had conquered west of the old Palestine-Syria border (chiefly the area around Mishmar Hayarden, north of the Sea of Galilee). The Israelis also sought minor changes in the eastern sector of the Lebanon-Israel border.

Henri Vigier, one of Bunche's assistants, who mediated, backed the Lebanese, who rejected both the Syrian "linkage" and any cession of territory. The Israelis eventually acquiesced—partly in the hope that agreement with Lebanon would clear the decks for a similar agreement with or, alternatively, military action against Jordan—but then insisted that Syrian troops stationed in Lebanon be withdrawn.[13]

The Lebanese countered that the presence of foreign (Syrian) troops in Lebanon was an internal Lebanese affair—but, in a separate undertaking to the United Nations, committed themselves to the withdrawal of Syrian troops to the "Tripoli-Aleppo line." This sufficed. Both sides agreed to limit themselves to "defensive forces" along the border.[14] The Israel-Lebanon General Armistice Agreement, to be supervised by a MAC similar to the MAC provided for in the Egyptian-Israeli agreement, was signed on 23 March 1949, with the IDF withdrawing back to the international line during the following days and the Syrian army quietly leaving Lebanon thereafter.

Israel and Jordan were next, signing an armistice agreement on 3 April. But midway between the two previous signings (of the Israel-Egypt and Israel-Lebanon accords), Israel decided to occupy the central and southern Negev and establish itself on the Gulf of ʿAqaba (Gulf of Eilat). The area had been earmarked for Israeli sovereignty in the UN partition resolution, was almost completely unpopulated, and since October–November 1948 had been patrolled occasionally by Jordanian reconnaissance squads. The Israeli move was facilitated by the conclusion of the armistice agreement with Egypt, which obviated the possibility of Egyptian military intervention against the IDF's march south, designated *mivtza ʿuvda* (Operation Fact, or fait accompli). Jordan, more or less isolated in the inter-Arab context and militarily no match for the Israelis, understood that it was in no position to resist, and this was recognized by Israel.[15] The operation was timed to precede the conclusion of the armistice deal with Jordan: Ben-Gurion wanted to establish the fact of Israeli control before the armistice negotiations moved into high gear.

Operation ʿUvda,[16] the last military operation of the war, began on 7 March and ended on 10 March, when a makeshift flag—a white sheet with a Star of David inked in—was raised by the IDF over the abandoned police sta-

Israel-Lebanon general armistice agreement lines, 30 March 1949

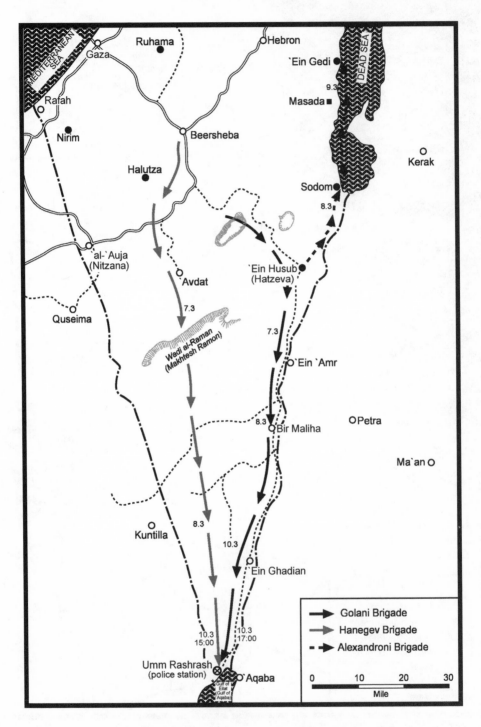

Operation ʿUvda, Negev, 6–10 March 1949

tion at Umm Rashrash, on the shore of the gulf across the way from ʿAqaba, where the port city of Eilat was built during the following years.

Ben-Gurion—and, to a somewhat lesser degree, the Zionist movement as a whole—had for decades been obsessed with the Negev and its southern maritime outlet, the coastline of the Gulf of ʿAqaba. The empty wasteland was seen as the country's only relatively large stretch of land available for the absorption of a mass of immigrants, and many suspected that it harbored mineral riches. Ben-Gurion had visited what the Bible (occasionally) and he called "Eilat" (or "ʿEtzion-Gaver") at least three times in the 1920s and 1930s. In 1935 he had written to the pro-Zionist US Supreme Court Justice Louis Brandeis of Eilat's "great significance," quoting the relevant biblical passage (1 Kings 9:26). "It is of the greatest economic and political importance that a Jewish settlement be established there as soon as possible, in order to create a political *fait accompli*."[17]

The IDF conquest of the northern Negev in October–November 1948 rendered reaching Eilat practical. In late November 1948, the IDF began to inch southward along the Negev's eastern periphery, occupying Kurnub and ʿEin Husub in the ʿArava (a patrol then drove as far south as Bir Maliha).[18]

But the Red Sea was what captivated the Cabinet's imagination. It held the promise of maritime links with Africa and Asia, helping to free Israel from the isolation imposed by Arab enmity. "And . . . there is no need for a special permit to enter Eilat. The permit was already issued by the UN, and when we will be capable of entering Eilat . . . we will have to do it," Ben-Gurion told the Cabinet in January 1949.[19] In the IDF, rumors had been rife that the Israeli Foreign Ministry, always attentive to international pressures, was the main obstacle to the march southward; Moshe Sharett (Shertok) denied this.[20] In truth, possible Egyptian intervention and serious logistical problems had always obtruded. The signing of the armistice with Egypt cleared away one obstacle. A succession of IDF reconnaissance patrols, the last of them in late February, to scout out possible axes of advance, resolved the second issue.[21]

On 7 March mechanized units of the Golani and Negev Brigades set out simultaneously from the Beersheba area—Golani taking the easterly route straight down the ʿArava (Wadi ʿAraba), along the old Palestine-Transjordan frontier, and the Negev Brigade pushing down the physically more trying route through the middle of the Negev via Ras al-Raman and Wadi ʿUkfi. Both reached Umm Rashrash on the afternoon of 10 March, the Negev Brigade winning the race by two hours. Golani's troops repeatedly had had to work around Arab Legion units that had taken up positions on the Israeli side of the ʿArava line, at ʿEin Amr and ʿEin Ghadian. Shots were repeatedly exchanged, but there were no casualties, and the Jordanians withdrew from each position as the Israelis approached or after they were outflanked. The Jordanians protested that the Israeli move was a violation of UN truce resolutions[22] but, given the balance of forces, offered no serious resistance. Both governments had ordered their troops to avoid hostilities.[23]

Britain reacted by reinforcing its garrison in ʿAqaba and threatened both to engage the Israeli forces, under certain circumstances,[24] and to turn to the United Nations. But the following day, 11 March, Israeli and Jordanian representatives signed a general cease-fire agreement.[25]

In a separate move, on 7–9 March, a company of Alexandroni Brigade troops advanced from Beersheba, via Kurnub and ʿEin Husub (Hatzeva), to Sodom and then, by boat, northward to ʿEin Gedi, occupying the area's springs as well as Masada, the hilltop site of the Jews' last stand against Rome during the Second Revolt, which ended in 73 CE. Thus, the central and southern Negev, down to the gulf coastline, and much of the western shore of the Dead Sea were physically joined to Israel, and without battle. Sharett called ʿUvda "a brilliant victory which didn't cost us one drop of blood."[26] "This is perhaps the greatest event in the past months, if not in the whole war of independence and conquest," Ben-Gurion, with his penchant for hyperbole, jotted down in his diary.[27]

The negotiation of the Israeli-Jordanian armistice agreement was drawn out and difficult. The talks, beginning informally on 26 December 1948, confronted the problems posed by long, unnatural, serpentine front lines; large Jewish and Arab concentrations of population, including refugees, close to the front lines; the presence of Iraqi troops in Samaria and Egyptian troops around Bethlehem; and the complex of issues raised by the divided city of Jerusalem and its holy sites. Israel's desire to widen its narrow "waist" by coopting strips of territory on the West Bank's western and northern fringes (parts of which had been included by the UN partition plan in Israel but had been occupied by Iraqi troops) and King ʿAbdullah's desire to annex the West Bank and the southern Negev to his kingdom added to the complexity of the geopolitical context of the talks.

Jordan initially called for an armistice based on the partition plan boundaries as amplified by Bernadotte's proposals of September 1948, with Jordan taking over much of the territory earmarked for Palestinian Arab sovereignty. Israel sought an agreement based on the postbellum military-territorial status quo. Specifically, Jordan wanted Israel to cede Lydda and Ramla (or at least allow the repatriation of their inhabitants) and Jaffa and to give up the southern Negev. Jordan also sought an exchange of tracts of land in and around Jerusalem.

Israel, for its part, demanded the 1947 partition borders in the Negev, a cession of the western fringes of the area held by the Iraqi army in Samaria, and Jordanian withdrawal from the Latrun Salient. Israel also sought freedom of passage between West Jerusalem and Mount Scopus, the site of the Hebrew University campus and the (main) Hadassah Hospital, the Mount of Olives (with its large Jewish cemetery), and the Wailing Wall.

Nothing had been finalized by the start of the formal Israeli-Jordanian talks that began in Rhodes on 4 March, with Bunche once again mediating. Heading the Israeli delegation was Reuven Shiloah (Zaslani), a Foreign Ministry man with deep roots in intelligence work (two years later he would found and direct the Mossad, Israel's foreign intelligence service), who was flanked by Lieutenant Colonel Moshe Dayan (IDF chief of general staff, 1953–1958) and Lieutenant Colonel Dan Lanner. The Jordanian delegation was led by Colonel Ahmed Sudki al-Jundi, who was backed by a team of Legion officers. In parallel, secret direct Israeli-Jordanian negotiations—where the real decisions were discussed and reached—were conducted in sites in Jordan, in effect sidelining Bunche.

In mid-March, after failing to reach agreement on Latrun and Jordanian and Israeli free passage to the sites in and around Jerusalem, the two sides decided to postpone discussion of all the territorial questions relating to the city and its environs until after the armistice was signed.

In the background, throughout, hovered the threat and possibility, in the absence of an agreement, of unilateral Israeli military action to alter the front lines—already roughly hinted at by ʿUvda, launched three days after the start of the formal negotiations, and by the Israeli occupation in mid-March of a series of positions in the foothills of western Judea.[28] In mid-March the IDF had been poised to conquer part of the West Bank but had been halted by Ben-Gurion in part because of warnings by Abba Eban about Washington's possible reaction.[29] Israel threatened to conquer the western foothills of Samaria if Jordan did not agree to cede them through diplomacy. At one point, Israel presented a twenty-four-hour ultimatum.[30] ʿAbdullah feared that if the IDF reopened hostilities, Israel would take the whole of the West Bank, not merely the strip of territory on its northwestern periphery. He made a last-minute effort to mobilize British and American support. But neither power was willing to guarantee the existing lines as international frontiers or, indeed, Jordanian control of the West Bank.[31] Britain was unwilling to extend its defense pact guarantee beyond the East Bank.

ʿAbdullah's fears were not unfounded. The IDF had prepared a plan, Operation Shin-Taf-Shin, "to rectify the border with 'the Triangle' in several places"—specifically, to conquer the Jenin basin, Wadi ʿAra, and the line of foothills southward to Bartaʿa[32]—and began to deploy its forces.[33] This meshed with the widespread regret over not having conquered Judea and Samaria in the course of the war and with the latent desire, still strong in IDF staff circles, to do so in the future.[34] Operationally, such a limited offensive could well have snowballed into a full-scale conquest of the West Bank, as both ʿAbdullah and many IDF officers understood.

Officers such as Allon, OC Southern Command, felt that the IDF during the war had missed the opportunity to establish a secure, natural frontier along the Jordan River. Allon, bypassing channels, took the unusual step, a moment before the conclusion of the Israeli-Jordanian armistice agreement, of urging Ben-Gurion to order the conquest of the West Bank. He wrote (saying he was conveying the thinking of "most of the army's senior officers"): "There is no need for a perfect military education to understand the permanent danger to the peace of Israel from the presence of large hostile forces in the western Land of Israel—in the [Jenin-Nablus-Tulkarm] Triangle and the Hebron Hills." The area could be conquered easily and "relatively quickly," given the balance of forces. And gaining the first line of foothills peacefully, through the prospective armistice agreement, "cannot be seen as a solution to the problem." Israel needed territorial "depth," argued Allon. He feared the long-term possibility of a Jordanian-Iraqi lunge, perhaps assisted by British troops stationed in the West Bank, across Israel's narrow waist to the sea, which would cut the state in half. Israel's strategic border should be along the Jordan River. Such a line, he argued, would also give Israel the added benefit of hydroelectric power, which could be derived from the river, and additional water for the development of the Negev. Britain, he assured Ben-Gurion, would not intervene to safeguard any area west of the river. "Time is working against us," he cautioned. Allon expected that "a large part" of the West Bank's population, refugee and permanent, would flee eastward across the river in the event of such an onslaught.[35]

ʿAbdullah (and John Glubb) were acutely aware both of this drift in IDF thinking and of the IDF's preparations in the third week of March to unleash Shin-Taf-Shin. ʿAbdullah sought both a face-saver and a measure of mutuality. He demanded that Israel also cede some territory—in the southern Judea foothills—and issue guarantees for the inhabitants living in the territory he was about to give up.

Israel nominally agreed to a token cession (apparently of territory it was not actually holding).[36] The two sides signed an in-principle agreement on 23 March and finalized it at Rhodes on 3 April.[37] In the Israel-Jordan General Armistice Agreement, the two sides agreed to limit their forces to a depth of six miles on both sides of the armistice line, including in Jerusalem. Jordan agreed to cede a continuous strip of territory, about three to five miles wide, running from just southwest of Qalqilya northward to Wadi ʿAra

The Israel-Jordan general armistice agreement lines, 3 April 1949

and from there eastward to a point just north of Jenin. Israel agreed to cede to Jordan a far smaller patch of territory south of Hebron, near Dhahiriya. Included in the Jordanian-ceded strip (known henceforward in Israeli historiography as "the Little Triangle") were fifteen or sixteen villages, adding some twenty thousand Arabs to Israel's minority population. Jordan agreed that Iraq's troops in Samaria would be withdrawn eastward, across the Jordan. The agreement provided for the establishment, in addition to a MAC, of a (bilateral) "Special Committee" that would work out the free- passage arrangements around and in Jerusalem and solve the Latrun Salient dispute. (It met during the following months but failed to reach agreement on any important issue. Jews were unable to reach the Wailing Wall or to reactivate the Mount Scopus campus and hospital; Arabs were barred from using the Jerusalem-Bethlehem road, which ran through West Jerusalem; the salient remained in Jordanian hands and Israel built a bypass road, while the Jordanians built a bypass road linking East Jerusalem and Bethlehem.)

The Syrians held out until last in agreeing to armistice talks—as if to underline their greater reluctance to take steps that might be construed as a willingness to acquiesce in Israel's existence (though in the course of the talks Colonel Fozi Selo, head of the Syrian delegation, said that although it was now "aiming at a temporary solution," Damascus looked forward to "advancing towards final peace").[38] And the Syrian-Israeli armistice negotiations were to be the most protracted, unfriendly, and difficult.

They began on 5 April near Khirbet Yarda, in no-man's-land on the western edge of the Syrian-held enclave at Mishmar Hayarden. Vigier mediated but on matters of substance (and often also in matters of minute detail) was guided from New York by Bunche. The Israeli delegation was led by Makleff, who was assisted by IDF officers and Foreign Ministry officials. Selo was flanked by army officers and a legal adviser. The lack of Syrian Foreign Ministry personnel underscored the nonpolitical, strictly military nature of the deliberations in Syrian eyes.

Israel, having neutralized the other belligerents with armistice agreements, had the advantage of facing an isolated and weaker interlocutor. But the Syrians were in possession of Israeli territory, after repeated IDF failures to dislodge them. The fact that a new Syrian regime, under Colonel Hosni Za'im, had taken power, by coup d'état, immediately before the talks began, complicated the negotiation to the extent that the new ruler had to establish his credentials as a steadfast opponent of Zionism.

Israel demanded that the Syrians withdraw back to the old international Syria-Palestine frontier delineated by the British and French in 1923 and reaffirmed in the 1947 partition resolution[39]—that is, pull back from the

Mishmar Hayarden enclave; the Tel al-Qasir strip southeast of the Sea of Galilee; a small strip of land between Kibbutz Dan and the village of Banias, at the northern edge of the Galilee Panhandle; and to a line a hundred yards east of the Jordan River and ten yards east of the northeastern Sea of Galilee shoreline—and constitute it as the armistice demarcation line. The Israelis relied on the just-set Lebanese precedent.[40] The Syrians at first demanded that Israel withdraw from the areas in the Galilee that it had occupied in Operation Hiram. Then—echoing the Israeli stance in the talks with Egypt and Jordan—Syria argued that the armistice boundaries should mirror the existing military-territorial status quo; Damascus sought to hold onto its conquests.

The Syrians wanted first to sign a general cease-fire agreement. The Israelis demurred, arguing that such an agreement would tie their hands in the armistice negotiations, when the threat of military action might prove necessary to eke out Syrian concessions. "The Syrians are not like the other Arab peoples and we cannot rely on [that is, trust] them, and we suspect that if we sign a cease-fire, they will withdraw from all future negotiations."[41] In the end, the two sides exchanged letters committing themselves to abide by previous UN resolutions.

The talks dragged on without result for more than a month. The IDF prepared for a renewal of hostilities (the plan, Operation Pine Tree, called for conquest of the Golan Heights, including Quneitra, threatening Damascus, and attacking the Mishmar Hayarden enclave from the rear).[42] But Ben-Gurion hesitated, for internal and diplomatic reasons. Bunche proposed a way out—again, by suggesting full withdrawal in exchange for demilitarization of the areas evacuated.[43] The Syrians countered by proposing to bypass the armistice with a full-fledged peace agreement, which would leave the Syrians in possession of half the Jordan River (the line running down its middle from north to south) and half the Sea of Galilee, along with the (Israeli) strip of territory along its eastern shoreline around ʿEin-Gev. Zaʿim proposed a face-to-face meeting with Ben-Gurion and expressed a willingness to absorb three hundred thousand Palestinian refugees within the context of a peace treaty.[44] Ben-Gurion refused to meet.[45] He regarded Zaʿim's proposals as most likely insincere and, at best, as designed to leave Syria in possession of Israeli territory and vital water resources. He demanded that the Syrians first agree to withdraw back to the international line; afterward, the two sides could negotiate "peace."

Haggling over the exact constitution of the DMZs followed, with Bunche proposing that these be expanded to include the Israeli-held eastern shoreline of the lake.[46] Israel agreed. The Syrians regarded the DMZs as areas in which neither country was to be sovereign; the Israelis, as Israeli territory

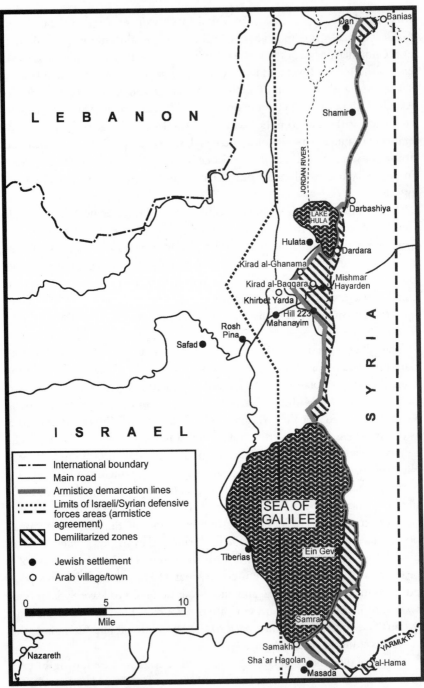

Israel-Syria general armistice agreement lines, 20 July 1949

from which the military were to be barred. The disagreement on this issue remained unresolved. The two sides agreed on limitation of forces zones along each side of the border. The two states signed the armistice agreement, to be supervised by a MAC, on 20 July.[47]

The Syrians withdrew back to the international frontier and the areas evacuated became DMZs. Local Jewish police administered the Jewish-inhabited areas (Mishmar Hayarden, ʿEin-Gev), and local Arab policemen the Arab-inhabited areas (Kirad al-Baqqara).

The signing of the general armistice agreements marked the formal end of the first Arab-Israeli war. The state of war had been replaced by a de jure state of nonbelligerency. Subsequently, the international community and, to a somewhat lesser degree, the former combatants themselves, were to recognize the armistice lines as de facto international frontiers. The agreements also provided for the establishment of four separate UN-chaired MACs to supervise the implementation of the agreements and to adjudicate in disputes relating to their provisions.

The armistice agreements were not peace treaties and did not provide for many of the features that normally govern the relations between neighboring states at peace with each other (diplomatic relations, trade ties, and so on). During the following years, Arab leaders made abundantly clear their uniform view that the armistice accords were merely elaborate cease-fire agreements, implicitly temporary and qualitatively different from and well short of full peace treaties.

In Israel, a more complex appreciation of the agreements took hold, with some leaders, including Ben-Gurion, viewing them as de facto peace accords, which effectively freed them from the need energetically to pursue full peace, while others took the Arab view that they were overblown cease-fire agreements that would have to be overtaken by peace treaties—or else they might issue in renewed fighting once one or both sides felt it to be in their interest. This, in fact, is what happened along both the Israeli-Syrian and Israeli-Egyptian frontiers as the three countries fought over control of the DMZs, a struggle that was one of the precipitants to the 1956 Suez-Sinai War between Egypt and Israel (and Britain and France) and between the Israelis and the Syrians in 1967.

Nonetheless, down to 1967 the armistice accords in large measure governed Israeli-Arab border relations, both through what they lacked and through what they stipulated.

11

Some Conclusions

"The Palestine problem is still in its infancy. The preface ended with the [end of the] Mandate and Chapter One began [in November 1947]. . . . Do not miss [the 'next installment']!" recommended the British consul general in Jerusalem midway through the 1948 War.[1]

"Chapter One," the first war between Israel and the Arabs, was the culmination of developments and a conflict that had begun in the 1880s, when the first Zionist settlers landed on the shores of the Holy Land, their arrival and burgeoning presence increasingly resented by the local Arab population. Over the following decades, the Arabs continuously inveighed, first with the Ottoman rulers, and then with their British successors, against the Zionist influx and ambitions, and they repeatedly attacked the new settlers, initially in individual acts of banditry and terrorism and then in growingly massive outbreaks, which at first resembled nothing more than European pogroms.

The Zionists saw their enterprise and aspirations as legitimate, indeed, as supremely moral: the Jewish people, oppressed and murdered in Christendom and in the Islamic lands, was bent on saving itself by returning to its ancient land and there reestablishing its self-determination and sovereignty. But the Arab inhabitants, supported by the surrounding, awakening Arab world, decried the influx as an aggressive invasion by colonialist, infidel aliens; it had to be resisted. The culminating assault on the Yishuv in 1947–1949 was a natural result of this posture of antagonism and resistance.

David Ben-Gurion well understood these contradictory perspectives. As he told his colleagues, against the backdrop of the Arab Revolt of 1936–1939: "We must see the situation for what it is. On the security front, we are those attacked and who are on the defensive. But in the political field we are the attackers and the Arabs are those defending themselves. They are living in the country and own the land, the village. We live in the Diaspora and want only to immigrate [to Palestine] and gain possession of [*lirkosh*] the land from them."[2] Years later, after the establishment of Israel, he expatiated on the Arab perspective in a conversation with the Zionist leader Nahum Goldmann: "I don't understand your optimism. . . . Why should the Arabs make peace? If I was an Arab leader I would never make terms with Israel. That is natural: We have taken their country. Sure, God promised it to us, but what does that matter to them? Our God is not theirs. We come from Israel, it's true, but two thousand years ago, and what is that to them? There has been anti-Semitism, the Nazis, Hitler, Auschwitz, but was that their fault? They only see one thing: We have come here and stolen their country. Why should they accept that?"[3]

To be sure, while mentioning "God," Ben-Gurion—a child of Eastern European social democracy and nationalism who knew no Arabic (though, as prime minister, he found time to study ancient Greek, to read Plato in the original, and Spanish, to read *Don Quixote*)—had failed fully to appreciate the depth of the Arabs' abhorrence of the Zionist-Jewish presence in Palestine, an abhorrence anchored in centuries of Islamic Judeophobia with deep religious and historical roots. The Jewish rejection of the Prophet Muhammad is embedded in the Qurʾan and is etched in the psyche of those brought up on its suras.[4] As the Muslim Brotherhood put it in 1948: "Jews are the historic enemies of Muslims and carry the greatest hatred for the nation of Muhammad."[5]

Such thinking characterized the Arab world, where the overwhelming majority of the population were, and remain, believers. In 1943, when President Franklin Roosevelt sent out feelers about a negotiated settlement of the Palestine problem, King Ibn Saʿud of Saudi Arabia responded that he was "prepared to receive anyone of any religion except (repeat except) a Jew."[6] A few weeks earlier, Ibn Saʿud had explained, in a letter to Roosevelt: "Palestine . . . has been an Arab country since the dawn of history and . . . was never inhabited by the Jews for more than a period of time, during which their history in the land was full of murder and cruelty. . . . [There is] religious hostility . . . between the Moslems and the Jews from the beginning of Islam . . . which arose from the treacherous conduct of the Jews towards Islam and the Moslems and their prophet."[7] Jews were seen as unclean; indeed, even those who had contact with them were seen as beyond the pale. In late 1947 the Al-Azhar University ʿulema, major authorities in the Islamic world, issued a fatwa that anyone dealing with "the Jews," commercially or economically (such as by "buying their produce"), "is a sinner and criminal . . . who will be regarded as an apostate to Islam, he will be separated from his spouse. It is prohibited to be in contact with him."[8]

This anti-Semitic mindset was not restricted to Wahhabi chieftains or fundamentalist imams. Samir Rifaʾi, Jordan's prime minister, in 1947 told visiting newsmen, "The Jews are a people to be feared. . . . Give them another 25 years and they will be all over the Middle East, in our country and Syria and Lebanon, in Iraq and Egypt. . . . They were responsible for starting the two world wars. . . . Yes, I have read and studied, and I know they were behind Hitler at the beginning of his movement."[9]

The 1948 War, to be sure, was a milestone in a contest between two national movements over a piece of territory. But it was also—if only because that is how many if not most Arabs saw it (and see it today)—part of a more general, global struggle between the Islamic East and the West, in which the Land of Israel/Palestine figured, and still figures, as a major battlefront. The Yishuv saw itself, and was universally seen by the Muslim Arab world, as an embodiment and outpost of the European "West." The assault of 1947–1948 was an expression of the Islamic Arabs' rejection of the West and its values as well as a reaction to what it saw as a European colonialist encroachment against sacred Islamic soil. There was no understanding (or tolerance) of Zionism as a national liberation movement of another people. And, aptly, the course of the war reflected the civilizational disparity, in which a Western society, deploying superior organizational and technological skills, overcame a coalition of infinitely larger Islamic Arab societies.

Historians have tended to ignore or dismiss, as so much hot air, the jihadi rhetoric and flourishes that accompanied the two-stage assault on the Yishuv and the constant references in the prevailing Arab discourse to that earlier bout of Islamic battle for the Holy Land, against the Crusaders. This is a mistake. The 1948 War, from the Arabs' perspective, was a war of religion as much as, if not more than, a nationalist war over territory. Put another way, the territory was sacred: its violation by infidels was sufficient grounds for launching a holy war and its conquest or reconquest, a divinely ordained necessity. In the months before the invasion of 15 May 1948, King ʿAbdullah, the most moderate of the coalition leaders, repeatedly spoke of "saving" the holy places.[10] As the day of invasion approached, his focus on Jerusalem, according to Alec Kirkbride, grew increasingly obsessive. "In our souls," wrote the founder of the Muslim Brotherhood, Hassan al-Banna, "Palestine occupies a spiritual holy place which is above abstract nationalist feelings. In it we have the blessed breeze of Jerusalem and the blessings of the Prophets and their disciples."[11]

The evidence is abundant and clear that many, if not most, in the Arab world viewed the war essentially as a holy war. To fight for Palestine was the "inescapable obligation on every Muslim," declared the Muslim Brotherhood in 1938. Indeed, the battle was of such an order of holiness that in 1948 one Islamic jurist ruled that believers should forego the hajj and spend the money thus saved on the jihad in Palestine.[12] In April 1948, the mufti of Egypt, Sheikh Muhammad Mahawif, issued a fatwa positing jihad in Palestine as the duty of all Muslims. The Jews, he said, intended "to take over . . . all the lands of Islam."[13] Martyrdom for Palestine conjured up, for Muslim Brothers, "the memories of the Battle of Badr . . . as well as the early Islamic jihad for spreading Islam and Salah al-Din's [Saladin's] liberation of Palestine" from the Crusaders.[14] Jihad for Palestine was seen in prophetic-apocalyptic terms, as embodied in the following hadith periodically quoted at the time: "The day of resurrection does not come until Muslims fight against Jews, until the Jews hide behind trees and stones and until the trees and stones shout out: 'O Muslim, there is a Jew behind me, come and kill him.'"[15]

The jihadi impulse underscored both popular and governmental responses in the Arab world to the UN partition resolution and was central to the mobilization of the "street" and the governments for the successive onslaughts of November–December 1947 and May–June 1948. The mosques, mullahs, and ʿulema all played a pivotal role in the process. Even Christian Arabs appear to have adopted the jihadi discourse. Matiel Mughannam, the Lebanese-born Christian who headed the AHC-affiliated Arab Women's Organization in Palestine, told an interviewer early in the civil war: "The UN decision has united all Arabs, as they have never been united before, not even against the Crusaders. . . . [A Jewish state] has no chance to survive now that the 'holy war' has been declared. All the Jews will eventually be massacred."[16] The Islamic fervor stoked by the hostilities seems to have encompassed all or almost all Arabs: "No Moslem can contemplate the holy places falling into Jewish hands," reported Kirkbride from Amman. "Even the Prime Minister [Tawfiq Abul Huda] . . . who is by far the steadiest and most sensible Arab here, gets excited on the subject."[17]

Nor did this impulse evaporate with the Arab defeat. On the contrary. On 12 December 1948 the ʿulema of Al-Azhar reissued their call for jihad, specifically addressing "the Arab Kings, Presidents of Arab Republics, . . . and leaders of public opinion." It was, ruled the council, "necessary to liberate Palestine from the Zionist bands . . . and to return the inhabitants driven from their homes." The Arab armies had "fought victoriously" (sic) "in the conviction that they were fulfilling a sacred religious duty." The ʿulema condemned King ʿAbdullah for sowing discord in Arab ranks: "Damnation would be the lot of those who, after warning, did not follow the way of the believers," concluded the ʿulema.[18]

The immediate trigger of the 1948 War was the November 1947 UN partition resolution. The Zionist movement, except for its fringes, accepted the proposal. Most lamented the imperative of giving up the historic heartland of Judaism, Judea and Samaria (the West Bank), with East Jerusalem's Old City and Temple Mount at its core; and many were troubled by the inclusion in the prospective Jewish state of a large Arab minority. But the movement, with Ben-Gurion and Weizmann at the helm, said "yes."

The Palestinian Arabs, along with the rest of the Arab world, said a flat "no"—as they had in 1937, when the Peel Commission had earlier proposed a two-state solution. The Arabs refused to accept the establishment of a Jewish state in any part of Palestine. And, consistently with that "no," the Palestinian Arabs, in November–December 1947, and the Arab states in May 1948, launched hostilities to scupper the resolution's implementation. Many Palestinians may have been unenthusiastic about going to war—but to war they went. They may have been badly led and poorly organized; the war may have been haphazardly unleashed; and many able-bodied males may have avoided service. But Palestinian Arab society went to war, and no Palestinian leader publicly raised his voice in protest or dissent.

The Arab war aim, in both stages of the hostilities, was, at a minimum, to abort the emergence of a Jewish state or to destroy it at inception. The Arab states hoped to accomplish this by conquering all or large parts of the territory allotted to the Jews by the United Nations. And some Arab leaders spoke of driving the Jews into the sea[19] and ridding Palestine "of the Zionist plague."[20] The struggle, as the Arabs saw it, was about the fate of Palestine / the Land of Israel, all of it, not over this or that part of the country. But, in public, official Arab spokesmen often said that the aim of the May 1948 invasion was to "save" Palestine or "save the Palestinians," definitions more agreeable to Western ears.

The picture of Arab aims was always more complex than Zionist historiography subsequently made out. The chief cause of this complexity was that fly-in-the-ointment, King ʿAbdullah. Jordan's ruler, a pragmatist, was generally skeptical of the Arabs' ability to defeat, let alone destroy, the Yishuv, and fashioned his war aim accordingly: to seize the Arab-populated West Bank, preferably including East Jerusalem. No doubt, had his army been larger and Zionist resistance weaker, he would have headed for Tel Aviv and Haifa;[21] after all, for years he had tried to persuade the Zionist leaders to agree to Jordanian sovereignty over all of Palestine, with the Jews to receive merely a small, autonomous zone (which he called a "republic") within his expanded kingdom. But, come 1948, he understood the balance of forces: the Jews were simply too powerful and too resolute, and their passion for self-determination was not to be denied.

Other Arab leaders were generally more optimistic. But they, too, had ulterior motives, beyond driving the Jews into the sea or, at the least, aborting the Jewish state. Chief among them was to prevent their fellow leaders (especially ʿAbdullah) from conquering and annexing all or too much of Palestine and to seize as much of Palestine as they could for themselves. This at least partly explains the diffusion of the Egyptian war effort and the drive of its eastern arm through Beersheba and Bethlehem to the outskirts of Jerusalem. It is possible that the commanders of the main, western wing of the Egyptian Expeditionary Force, advancing up the coast from Rafah, were instructed to halt, at least for a time, at Isdud, the northernmost point of the southern portion of Palestine allotted by the United Nations for Arab sovereignty. But had the Israelis offered minimal resistance and had the way been clear to push on to Tel Aviv, I have no doubt that the Egyptians would have done so, in line with their public rhetoric. Their systematic destruction of all the Jewish settlements along the way—a phenomenon that was replicated by the Arab armies in the West Bank and Jordan Valley—is indicative of the mindset of the armies and governments involved.

The Yishuv's war aim, initially, was simpler and more modest: to survive; to weather the successive onslaughts, by the Palestinian Arabs and the Arab states. The Zionist leaders deeply, genuinely, feared a Middle Eastern reenactment of the Holocaust, which had just ended; the Arabs' public rhetoric reinforced these fears. But as the war progressed, an additional aim began to emerge: to expand the Jewish state beyond the UN-earmarked partition borders. Initially, the desire was to incorporate clusters of Jewish settlements in the state. West Jerusalem, with its hundred thousand Jews, figured most prominently in the Zionist leaders' imagination. But as the war progressed, a more general expansionist aim took hold: to add more territory to the minuscule state and to arm it with defensible borders. By September, some spoke of expanding as far eastward as the Jordan River, seen as a "natural" frontier (both the UN partition borders and the new lines created by the May–July 1948 hostilities were a strategist's nightmare), while incorporating the historic heartland of the Jewish people, Judea and Samaria, in the new state. A third and further aim—which emerged among some of the political leaders, including Ben-Gurion and Moshe Shertok, and in the military, after four or five months of hostilities—was to reduce the size of Israel's prospective large and hostile Arab minority, seen as a potential powerful fifth column, by belligerency and expulsion.

Both Arabs and Israelis often argued during 1947–1948 that they were the weaker side, hoping to garner world sympathy and material support. (But occasionally, at the same time and somewhat confusingly, they argued the exact opposite—in order to frighten their enemies or magnetize support and recruits or generate public self-confidence.) During the civil war stage, the Palestinians rather shamefacedly pointed to their poverty and disorganization as opposed to the "power of international Jewry." The Israelis, reluctantly, often acknowledged Palestinian Arab weakness yet, during November 1947–mid-May 1948, argued (1) that the Palestinians enjoyed the support of the vast surrounding Arab hinterland and (2) that the Arab states would soon join in.

An honest appraisal of the balance of strength in the war requires a reassessment of the components of a state's or a society's strength and weakness and necessarily extends the discussion beyond the narrow parameters of military manpower and weapons rosters. The organization and unity of purpose of armies and the effectiveness of their command and control systems is of paramount importance. Measurable categories, such as financial resources, as well as less quantifiable elements, such as levels of motivation and morale, must also be considered. So, too, must details regarding types of weaponry and stockpiles of given types of ammunition and spare parts at different points in time in a protracted struggle as well as the combat experience and training of officers and men. A clear understanding of these and other factors goes a long way to explaining the Yishuv's victory.

In rough demographic and geopolitical terms, without doubt, the Arabs were far, almost infinitely, stronger than the Yishuv. The Palestinian Arabs outnumbered Palestine's Jews by a factor of two to one. And the surrounding Arab states mustered a total population of forty million, with an additional, vast demographic hinterland stretching into the Arabian Peninsula and across North Africa to the Atlantic Ocean, as compared with the Yishuv's paltry population of 650,000. The Yishuv, to be sure, received a small stream of volunteers from Diaspora Jewry (and the Christian West). But the Palestinian Arabs and the Arabs of the confrontation states, who both also enjoyed the services of foreign volunteers, were incomparably stronger in demographic terms. And the disproportion in terms of land mass and economic resources, or potential economic resources, was, if anything, even greater.

But the Yishuv had organized for war. The Arabs hadn't. The small, compact Jewish community in Palestine was economically and politically vibrant, a potential powerhouse if adequately organized and directed. And it enjoyed a unity of purpose and a collective fear—of a new Holocaust—that afforded high levels of motivation (as well as magnetizing international support). The fact that the Yishuv was the victim of aggression and that each Jewish soldier was almost literally defending hearth and home added to the motivational edge. This edge was amply demonstrated in places where a handful of poorly armed defenders beat back massive Arab assaults, as at Nirim and Degania in May 1948.

The Palestinian Arabs, with well-established traditions of disunity, corruption, and organizational incompetence, failed to mobilize their resources. They even failed to put together a national militia organization before going to war. Their leaders may have talked, often and noisily, about the "Zionist threat," but they failed to prepare. Perhaps, by the late 1940s, they had come to rely on foreign intervention as the engine of their salvation. Much as, throughout their history, the Palestinian Arabs displayed a knee-jerk penchant to always blame others—the Ottomans, the British, Europe, the United States, the Jews—for whatever ailed them, so, from the mid-1930s on, they exhibited a mindless certainty that, whatever they did or whatever happened, someone—the United Nations, the Great Powers, the Arab states—would pull their chestnuts out of the fire.

The Palestinians (like the surrounding Arab states) had a socioeconomic elite with no tradition of public service or ethos of contribution and sacrifice (typical was the almost complete absence of sons of that elite among the fighters of 1936–1939 and 1948); for many, nationalism was a rhetorical device to amass power or divert resentments rather than a deeply felt emotion. The Palestinian Arabs suffered from a venal leadership and a tradition of imperial domination as well a sense of powerlessness and fatalism. These combined to neuter initiative.

When war came—at their instigation—the Palestinians were unprepared: they lacked a "government" (indeed, almost all the members of the AHC, and many, if not most, NC members were outside the country for most of the civil war), and they were short of arms and ammunition. All told, the eight hundred Arab villages and dozen or so towns of Palestine, in December 1947, may have possessed more light arms than the Yishuv. But they were dispersed and under local control and not standardized, and most of them probably never saw a battlefield. The Palestinians lacked the economic or organizational wherewithal to import arms and ammunition in significant quantities once the hostilities commenced, and the Arab states were niggardly with material support.

The Palestinian militias performed moderately well, when they were on the offensive, between late November 1947 and the end of March 1948 (though they, and their ALA reinforcements, never conquered a single Jewish settlement). But once the Yishuv went over to the offensive, it was all over. From early April, the Haganah was able to concentrate forces and pick off Arab towns, villages, and clusters of villages in succession and in isolation; villages failed to assist their neighbors, and clusters of villages, neighboring clusters of villages. Almost no villagers came to the aid of townspeople and vice versa. In effect, each community was on its own. And the incompetent and small ALA, though deploying some heavy weapons, failed to make a difference.

Between early April and mid-May, Palestinian Arab society fell apart and was crushed by a relatively poorly armed and, in many ways, ragtag Jewish militia. One day, when the Palestinians face up to their past and produce serious historiography, they will probe these parameters of weakness and responsibility to the full (as well as the functioning of their leadership and society in the months and years before 1948). Among the things they will "discover" will be how few young men from the Hebron, Ramallah, and Nablus areas—largely untouched by the war—actually participated in 1948's battles and how few of them died in the fighting in Jaffa, Haifa, Jerusalem, and the Jezreel and Jordan Valleys. The Yishuv had fought not a "people" but an assortment of regions, towns, and villages. What this says about the Palestinian Arabs, at the time, as a "people" will also need to be confronted.

As to the conventional war, which began with the pan-Arab invasion of 15 May 1948, the Arab states were infinitely larger and more populous than Israel and possessed regular armies, with heavy weapons. Hence, they were "stronger." But Israel nonetheless won, and this requires explanation.[22] After the war, Arab commentators and leaders argued that the Arab states, too, were essentially "weak," given the "newness" of their state structures, their corrupt ruling classes, and the fractious heritage of colonialism. The aim was to score propaganda points in debates in the international arena as well as to "justify" what had happened in the face of criticism by the "street" or opposition parties. The Israelis, for their part, also intent on retaining the image of the underdog, trotted out maps of the Middle East, which highlighted the Yishuv's small size, and tables of comparative heavy weapons strengths, which underlined Israeli weakness. Often, Israeli spokesmen and commentators indulged in statistical acrobatics to prove their point.

But there was a large element of truth in the Israeli claim, certainly in mid-1948, to "weakness." The newborn state was assailed simultaneously from various directions, and Israeli troops in many sectors did end up battling far larger Arab contingents. And in the weeks before 15 May, the Yishuv's leaders could not know or guess how poorly the Arabs would organize for war or how incompetently and disunitedly their armies would perform. The Yishuv was genuinely fearful of the outcome—and the Haganah chiefs' assessment on 12 May of a "fifty-fifty" chance of victory or survival was sincere and typical.

Egypt, Iraq, Syria, Lebanon, and Jordan had all achieved independence (or semi-independence) a few years before, and most had new armies with inadequate training and no experience of combat. Their populations consisted largely of illiterate peasants for whom religion, family, clan, and village were the cores of identity and loyalty. They were relatively untouched by the passions of modern nationalism (though were easily swayed by Islamic rhetoric) and lacked technological skills, which bore heavily on the functioning of air and naval forces, artillery, intelligence, and communications. The states themselves were all poor and poorly organized and led by self-serving politicians of varied abilities and ethics; all, except Lebanon, were governed by shambling autocracies, and none, except perhaps Jordan's, enjoyed popular legitimacy or support.

Their armies were all small and poorly equipped. Come 1948, they—except Jordan—failed to mobilize properly, owing to a combination of inefficiency, lack of resources, and overconfidence. And their populations were more easily inclined to rowdy street demonstrations than actually to going off to fight in the harsh hills of Palestine.

In May 1948 all, except Jordan, found it prudent, when dispatching expeditionary forces to Palestine, to leave behind large units to protect the regimes or counter rebellious minorities (such as the Kurds in northern Iraq). Nonetheless, the four armies that invaded on 15 May were far stronger than the Haganah formations they initially encountered, if not in manpower—where they were roughly evenly matched—then in equipment and firepower. The invaders had batteries of modern twenty-five-pounders, tanks, dozens of gun-mounting armored cars, and dozens of combat aircraft. The Haganah had virtually no artillery and initially made do with mortars, no tanks, and no combat aircraft (until the end of May), and its improvised armored car fleet was inferior in every respect.

But the Haganah enjoyed home court advantages—internal lines of communication, higher motivation, familiarity with the terrain—and managed to hold on, even going over to the counterattack, albeit abortively, within days of the invasion. During the following weeks, owing to effective mobilization, the Haganah/IDF gradually overtook the Arab states' armies in terms of manpower. By war's end, the IDF outnumbered the Arab armies engaged in Palestine by a factor of almost two to one. Once the Yishuv had weathered the initial onslaught, the war, in effect, was won. All that remained was to see how much of Palestine it could conquer (or be allowed to hold by the Great Powers) and how severely the invaders would be trounced.

The Great Powers and the United Nations affected the course of the war in a number of significant ways. One was by way of armaments and the asymmetrical effects on the belligerents of the international arms embargos. The Americans imposed an arms embargo on the region starting in December 1947. The United Nations imposed a wider embargo in late May 1948, crucially affecting supplies to the Arab states, which had traditionally received their weapons and ammunition (on credit) from their former colonial masters, Britain and France. The embargo, to which Britain and France were obedient, at a stroke cut off the Arabs from almost all sources of weaponry, ammunition, and spare parts. And they lacked the agility, networks, knowledge, and funds to switch horses in midstream and begin procurement from alternative sources. In effect, the Arab states had to fight the war with what they had in stock, a stock they had failed to build up adequately in the preceding years and that rapidly diminished as the hostilities progressed.

It was otherwise with the Yishuv. The Yishuv had never bought or received arms from states and had developed no prewar dependencies. Instead, it had bought arms in the international black market. It had entered the war with experienced clandestine procurement networks and with the financial backing of American Jewry. In preparation for the war, the Haganah purchased arms or "civilian" equipment convertible to war purposes in the United States (including machine tools needed to produce arms) and in the world's black markets. Once the fighting began, the Yishuv/Israel discovered another, major source of equipment. The Americans and, by and large, the Western European states refused to sell the Haganah arms. But the Soviet Union and Czechoslovakia, for a combination of reasons—financial, political (anti-British), and ideological-humanitarian (many Czechs saw the Jews as fellow sufferers)—were willing to ignore the United Nations and sell arms to the Yishuv. (The Syrians also made some purchases from the Czech Skoda Arms Works, but they were meager—and they proved unable safely to transport them to Syria. Indeed, Israeli naval commandos twice managed to interdict these shipments in European waters.) From late March 1948 onward, Czech arms—and additional arms from black and gray market sources— poured into Palestine/Israel, enabling the Yishuv to neutralize the Palestinian Arab militias, go over to the offensive, parry the Arab armies' invasion, and, eventually, win the war.

The United Nations' embargo-enforcing machinery, from the start, was inadequate and ineffective. Israel proved adept at circumventing it; the Arabs, except in the matter of dispatching additional manpower to the fronts, never really tried. In terms of importing militarily professional manpower, the Yishuv also "beat" the Arabs. The Yishuv/Israel managed to attract and hire expert foreign military personnel—(mostly Christian) air- and ground crews, naval personnel, communications experts—and deploy them effectively. It was not primarily a matter of salaries: many came for the adventure, but most because of the Holocaust and sympathy for the beleaguered new state; for some, it was a repeat of the (tragic failed) effort to save the Spanish Republic. Of the Arab states, only the Jordanians, who increased their roster of Britons during the war, managed to recruit and deploy foreign military experts to any real effect. The handful of ex-Nazi Germans or Bosnian Muslims recruited by Syria, Egypt, and the Palestinian Arabs proved of little significance.

The Great Powers and the United Nations significantly affected the course and outcome of the war in other ways. From the start, the Yishuv enjoyed an immense moral advantage stemming from the overwhelming international support, which included the United States and Soviet Union, for partition and Jewish statehood. Without doubt this affected both the Palestinians and the Arab states in their political and military decision-making. Throughout, the Arab leaders were constrained by the thought that they were defying the will of the international community and that, should the Yishuv face defeat and massacre, the Great Powers might well intervene on its behalf. This certainly helped persuade King ʿAbdullah on the eve of the invasion that it was pointless to seek the Yishuv's destruction.

But through November 1947–May 1948 the Great Powers failed to intervene in the civil war and force partition down the Arabs' throats and failed again, in May and June 1948, when the Arab states launched a war of aggression, in defiance of the UN resolution, against the Yishuv. The international community refrained from intervention, barring hesitant expressions of verbal displeasure.

But, thereafter, the Western Great Powers (the Russians usually took Israel's side), acting both through the United Nations and often directly and independently, significantly cramped the IDF's style and curtailed its battlefield successes in a series of cease-fire and truce resolutions. Whereas the imposition of the First Truce, which started on 11 June, favored both sides—both needed a respite, though the resulting four weeks of quiet were better used by Israel to regroup and rearm—all the subsequent international interventions clearly and strongly favored the Arabs. Thus it was on 18 July, at the end of the Ten Days, when IDF troops were victorious in the Galilee and the Lydda-Ramla area, and even more tellingly in October and November, when IDF advances had brought the Egyptian forces in the south to the verge of defeat. The UN–Great Power interventions in December 1948 and early January 1949, after Israel had invaded the Sinai Peninsula, quite simply saved the Egyptian army from annihilation. The IDF had twice been on the verge of closing the trap, first at El ʿArish, and then at Rafah, when the United States and Britain ordered it to pull back—the British bluntly threatening direct military intervention—and Ben-Gurion complied. From July 1948 on, the IDF General Staff planned all its campaigns with an eye to a UN-imposed time-limit or intervention that might snatch victory from the jaws of victory and compelled the Israelis repeatedly to cheat and "steal" extra days of fighting to achieve or partially achieve objectives.

Henceforward, Israel received a well-earned reputation for bamboozling or hampering the functioning of UN observers. But this was largely a consequence of the inequitable and unfair rules of engagement: the Arabs could launch offensives with impunity, but international interventions always hampered and restrained Israel's counterattacks.

As in subsequent wars—in October 1973 and in June 1982—the successive UN cease-fire–standstill resolutions prevented a clear Israeli victory and saved the Arabs from ever greater humiliations. And it was Great Power and UN pressure and intercession that afforded the Egyptians and Syrians face-saving terms in the armistice agreements of 1949. Without these intercessions, it is likely that the talks both with Egypt and with Syria would have broken down and hostilities would have been renewed, ending in further Arab defeats and loss of territory. As it was, the agreements eventually reached assured the Arab states of the retention of some territory inside Palestine (the Gaza Strip) and of demilitarized strips in which neither side was sovereign.

Taken together, these events left Israel with a permanent resentment toward and suspicion of the United Nations, which was only reinforced down the decades by the emergence of the automatic Arab–Muslim–Third World–Communist block–voting majorities against Israel, whatever the merits of each problem brought before the General Assembly and, occasionally, the Security Council.

Like most wars involving built-up areas, the 1948 War resulted in the killing, and occasional massacre, of civilians. During the civil war half of the war, both sides paid little heed to the possible injury or death of civilians as battle raged in the mixed cities and rural landscape of Palestine, though Haganah operational orders frequently specifically cautioned against harming women and children. But the IZL and LHI seem to have indulged in little discrimination, and the Palestinian Arab militias often deliberately targeted civilians. Moreover, the disorganization of the two sides coupled with the continued presence and nominal rule of the Mandate government obviated the establishment by either side of regular POW camps. This meant that both sides generally refrained from taking prisoners. When the civil war gave way to the conventional war, as the Jewish militias—the Haganah, IZL, and LHI—changed into the IDF and as the Arab militias were replaced by more or less disciplined regular armies, the killing of civilians and prisoners of war almost stopped, except for the series of atrocities committed by IDF troops in Lydda in July and in the Galilee at the end of October and beginning of November 1948.

After the war, the Israelis tended to hail the "purity of arms" of its militiamen and soldiers and to contrast this with Arab barbarism, which on occasion expressed itself in the mutilation of captured Jewish corpses. This reinforced the Israelis' positive self-image and helped them "sell" the new state abroad; it also demonized the enemy. In truth, however, the Jews committed far more atrocities than the Arabs and killed far more civilians and POWs in deliberate acts of brutality in the course of 1948. This was probably due to the circumstance that the victorious Israelis captured some four hundred Arab villages and towns during April–November 1948, whereas the Palestinian Arabs and ALA failed to take any settlements and the Arab armies that invaded in mid-May overran fewer than a dozen Jewish settlements.

Arab rhetoric may have been more blood curdling and inciteful to atrocity than Jewish public rhetoric—but the war itself afforded the Arabs infinitely fewer opportunities to massacre their foes. Thus, in the course of the civil war the Palestinian Arabs, besides killing the odd prisoner of war, committed only two large massacres—involving forty workers in the Haifa oil refinery and about 150 surrendering or unarmed Haganah men in Kfar ʿEtzion (a massacre in which Jordanian Legionnaires participated—though other Legionnaires at the site prevented atrocities). Some commentators add a third "massacre," the destruction of the convoy of doctors and nurses to Mount Scopus in Jerusalem in mid-April 1948, but this was actually a battle, involving Haganah and Palestine Arab militiamen, though it included, or was followed by, the mass killing of the occupants of a Jewish bus, most of whom were unarmed medical personnel.

The Arab regular armies committed few atrocities and no large-scale massacres of POWs and civilians in the conventional war—even though they conquered the Jewish Quarter of the Old City of Jerusalem and a number of rural settlements, including ʿAtarot and Neve Yaʿakov near Jerusalem, and Nitzanim, Gezer, and Mishmar Hayarden elsewhere.

The Israelis' collective memory of fighters characterized by "purity of arms" is also undermined by the evidence of rapes committed in conquered towns and villages. About a dozen cases—in Jaffa, Acre, and so on—are reported in the available contemporary documentation and, given Arab diffidence about reporting such incidents and the (understandable) silence of the perpetrators, and IDFA censorship of many documents, more, and perhaps many more, cases probably occurred. Arabs appear to have committed few acts of rape. Again, this is explicable in terms of their general failure to conquer Jewish settlements. Altogether, the 1948 War was characterized, in relative terms, by an extremely low incidence of rape (as contrasted with, for example, the Soviet army's conquest of Prussia and eastern Germany in 1945 or the recent Balkan wars).

In the yearlong war, Yishuv troops probably murdered some eight hundred civilians and prisoners of war all told—most of them in several clusters of massacres in captured villages during April–May, July, and October–November 1948. The round of massacres, during Operation Hiram and its immediate aftermath in the Galilee and southern Lebanon, at the end of October and the first week of November 1948 is noteworthy in having occurred so late in the war, when the IDF was generally well disciplined and clearly victorious. This series of killings—at ʿEilabun, Jish, ʿArab al-Mawasi, Saliha, Majd al-Kurum, and so on—was apparently related to a general vengefulness and a desire by local commanders to precipitate a civilian exodus.

In general, from May 1948 onward, both Israel and the Arab states abided by the Geneva convention, took prisoners, and treated them reasonably well. Given that the first half of the war involved hostilities between militias based in a large number of interspersed civilian communities, the conquest of some two hundred villages and urban centers, and the later conquest of two hundred additional villages, 1948 is actually noteworthy for the relatively small number of civilian casualties both in the battles themselves and in the atrocities that accompanied them or followed (compare this, for example, to the casualty rates and atrocities in the Yugoslav wars of the 1990s or the Sudanese civil wars of the past fifty years).

In the 1948 war, the Yishuv suffered 5,700–5,800 dead[23]—one quarter of them civilians. This represented almost 1 percent of the Jewish community in Palestine, which stood at 628,000 at the end of November 1947 and 649,000 in May 1948.[24] Of the dead, more than five hundred were female (108 in uniform).[25] The Yishuv suffered about twelve thousand seriously wounded.

Palestinian losses, in civilians and armed irregulars, are unclear: they may have been slightly higher, or much higher, than the Israeli losses. In the 1950s, Haj Amin al-Husseini claimed that "about" twelve thousand Palestinians had died.[26] Egyptian losses, according to an official Egyptian announcement made in June 1950, amounted to some fourteen hundred dead and 3,731 "permanently invalided."[27] The Jordanian, Iraqi, and Syrian armies each suffered several hundred dead, and the Lebanese suffered several dozen killed.

The war resulted in the creation of some seven hundred thousand Arab refugees.[28] In part, this was a product of the expulsionist elements in the ideologies of both sides in the conflict. By 1948, many in the Zionist leadership accepted the idea and necessity of transfer, and this affected events during the war. But this gradual acceptance was in large part a response to the expulsionist ideology and violent praxis of al-Husseini and his followers during the previous two decades.

Both national movements entered the mid-1940s with an expulsionist element in their ideological baggage. Among the Zionists, it was a minor and secondary element, occasionally entertained and enunciated by key leaders, including Ben-Gurion and Chaim Weizmann. But it had not been part of the original Zionist ideology and was usually trotted out in response to expulsionist or terroristic violence by the Arabs. The fact that the Peel Commission in 1937 supported the transfer of Arabs out of the Jewish state-to-be without doubt consolidated the wide acceptance of the idea among the Zionist leaders.

Although, from Theodor Herzl onward, Zionist leaders and proponents had occasionally suggested transfer, only in the mid-1930s and in the early 1940s did Zionist leaders clearly advocate the idea—in response to the Arab Revolt, which killed hundreds of settlers and threatened to destroy the Yishuv, and Nazi anti-Semitism, which threatened to destroy German, and then European, Jewry. The Zionist leaders believed that a safe and relatively spacious haven was an existential necessity for Europe's hounded Jews, and that this haven could only be found in Palestine—but that to achieve safety and create the necessary space, some or all Palestinian Arabs, given their unremitting belligerence, would have to be transferred. Arab support for a Nazi victory and Haj Amin al-Husseini's employment by the Nazis in World War II Berlin also played a part in this thinking. Zionist expulsionist thinking was thus at least in part a response to expulsionist, or murderous, thinking and behavior by Arabs and European Christians.

Nonetheless, transfer or expulsion was never adopted by the Zionist movement or its main political groupings as official policy at any stage of the movement's evolution—not even in the 1948 War. No doubt this was due in part to Israelis' suspicion that the inclusion of support for transfer in their platforms would alienate Western support for Zionism and cause dissension in Zionist ranks. It was also the result of moral scruples.

During the 1948 War, which was universally viewed, from the Jewish side, as a war for survival, although there were expulsions and although an atmosphere of what would later be called ethnic cleansing prevailed during critical months, transfer never became a general or declared Zionist policy. Thus, by war's end, even though much of the country had been "cleansed" of Arabs, other parts of the country—notably central Galilee—were left with substantial Muslim Arab populations, and towns in the heart of the Jewish coastal strip, Haifa and Jaffa, were left with an Arab minority. These Arab communities have since prospered and burgeoned and now constitute about 20 percent of Israel's citizenry. At the same time, the Arabs who had fled or been driven out of the areas that became Israel were barred by Israeli government decision and policy from returning to their homes and lands.

By contrast, expulsionist thinking and, where it became possible, behavior, characterized the mainstream of the Palestinian national movement since its inception. "We will push the Zionists into the sea—or they will send us back into the desert," the Jaffa Muslim-Christian Association told the King-Crane Commission as early as 1919.[29]

For the Palestinians, from the start, the clash with the Zionists was a zero-sum game. The Palestinian national movement's leader during the 1920s, 1930s, and 1940s, Haj Amin al-Husseini, consistently rejected territorial compromise and espoused a solution to the Palestine problem that posited all of Palestine as an Arab state and allowed for a Jewish minority composed only of those who had lived in the country before 1914 (or, in a variant, 1917). Thus he marked out all Jews who had arrived in the country after World War I and their progeny for, at the very least, noncitizenship or expulsion—or worse. In Arabic, before Arab audiences, he was often explicit. With Westerners, he was usually evasive, but one cannot doubt his meaning. In January 1937, for example, in his testimony before the Peel Commission, al-Husseini was asked: "Does his eminence think that this country can assimilate and digest the 400,000 Jews now in the country?"

Al-Husseini: "No."

Question: "Some of them would have to be removed by a process kindly or painful as the case may be?"

Al-Husseini: "We must leave all this to the future."

On which the commissioners commented: "We are not questioning the sincerity or the humanity of the Mufti's intentions . . . but we cannot forget what recently happened, despite treaty provisions and explicit assurances, to the Assyrian [Christian] minority in Iraq; nor can we forget that the hatred of the Arab politician for the [Jewish] National Home has never been concealed and that it has now permeated the Arab population as a whole."[30]

Al-Husseini was to remain consistent on this point for the rest of his life. During the war, al-Husseini's rhetoric was considerably upgraded. In March

1948 he told an interviewer in a Jaffa daily *Al Sarih* that the Arabs did not intend merely to prevent partition but "would continue fighting until the Zionists were annihilated and the whole of Palestine became a purely Arab state."[31] In 1974, just before his death, he told interviewers: "There is no room for peaceful coexistence with our enemies. The only solution is the liquidation of the foreign conquest in Palestine within its natural frontiers and the establishment of a national Palestinian state on the basis of its Muslim and Christian inhabitants and its Jewish [inhabitants] who lived here before the British conquest in 1917 and their descendants."[32]

Haj Amin was nothing if not consistent. In 1938, Ben-Gurion met Musa Husseini in London. Musa Husseini, a relative and supporter of the mufti (he was executed in 1951 by the Jordanians for his part in the assassination of King ʿAbdullah), told Ben-Gurion that Haj Amin "insists on seven per cent [as the maximal percentage of Jews in the total population of Palestine], as it was at the end of the World War." In 1938 the Jews constituted 30 percent of the country's population. How Haj Amin intended to reduce the proportion from 30 to 7 percent Musa Husseini did not explain.[33] (It is not without relevance that this objective was replicated in the constitution of the Palestine Liberation Organization [PLO], the Palestine National Charter, formulated in 1964 and revised in 1968. Clause 6 states: "The Jews who had normally resided in Palestine before the beginning of the Zionist invasion will be considered Palestinians." This "beginning" is defined elsewhere as "1917" or the moment of promulgation of the Balfour Declaration [2 November 1917].)

Such sentiments translated into action in 1948. During the "civil war," when the opportunity arose, Palestinian militiamen who fought alongside the Arab Legion consistently expelled Jewish inhabitants and razed conquered sites, as happened in the ʿEtzion Bloc and the Jewish Quarter of Jerusalem's Old City. Subsequently, the Arab armies behaved in similar fashion. All the Jewish settlements conquered by the invading Jordanian, Syrian, and Egyptian armies—about a dozen in all, including Beit Haʿarava, Neve Yaʿakov, and ʿAtarot in the Jordanian sector; Masada and Shaʿar Hagolan in the Syrian sector; and Yad Mordechai, Nitzanim, and Kfar Darom in the Egyptian sector—were razed after their inhabitants had fled or been incarcerated or expelled.

These expulsions by the Arab regular armies stemmed quite naturally from the expulsionist mindset prevailing in the Arab states. The mindset characterized both the public and the ruling elites. All vilified the Yishuv and opposed the existence of a Jewish state on "their" (sacred Islamic) soil, and all sought its extirpation, albeit with varying degrees of bloody-mindedness. Shouts of "Idbah al Yahud" (slaughter the Jews) characterized equally street demonstrations in Jaffa, Cairo, Damascus, and Baghdad both before and during the war and were, in essence, echoed, usually in tamer language, by most Arab leaders. We do not have verbatim minutes of what these leaders said in closed inter-Arab gatherings. But their statements to Western diplomats, where caution was usually required, were candid enough. "It was possible that in the first phases of the Jewish-Arab conflict the Arabs might meet with initial reverses," King Farouk told the American ambassador to Egypt, S. Pinckney Tuck, just after the passage of the UN General Assembly partition resolution. "[But] in the long run the Arabs would soundly defeat the Jews and drive them out of Palestine."[34] A few weeks earlier, that other potentate, King Ibn Sa'ud of Saudi Arabia, had written to President Truman: "The Arabs have definitely decided to oppose [the] establishment of a Jewish state in any part of the Arab world. The dispute between the Arab and Jew will be violent and long-lasting. . . . Even if it is supposed that the Jews will succeed in gaining support for the establishment of a small state by their oppressive and tyrannous means and their money, such a state must perish in a short time. The Arab will isolate such a state from the world and will lay siege to it until it dies by famine. . . . Its end will be the same as that of [the] Crusader states."[35] The establishment of Israel, and the international endorsement that it enjoyed, enraged the Arab world; destruction and expulsion were to be its lot. Without doubt, Arab expulsionism fueled Zionist expulsionist thinking during the 1930s and 1940s.

As it turned out, it was Palestinian Arab society that was smashed, not the Yishuv. The war created the Palestinian refugee problem. Looking back, Israel's Foreign Minister Moshe Shertok said, "There are those who say that we uprooted Arabs from their places. But even they will not deny that the source of the problem was the war: had there been no war, the Arabs would not have abandoned their villages, and we would not have expelled them. Had the Arabs from the start accepted the decision of 29 November [1947], a completely different Jewish state would have arisen. . . . In essence the State of Israel would have arisen with a large Arab minority, which would have left its impress on the state, on its manner of governance, and on its economic life, and [this Arab minority] would have constituted an organic part of the state."[36]

Shertok, of course, was right: the refugee problem was created by the war—which the Arabs had launched (though the Arabs would argue, then and subsequently, that the Zionist influx was, since its beginning, an act of aggression and that the Arab launch of the 1947–1948 war was merely an act of self-defense). And it was that war that propelled most of those displaced out of their houses and into refugeedom. Most fled when their villages and towns came under Jewish attack or out of fear of future attack. They wished to move out of harm's way. At first, during December 1947–March 1948, it was the middle- and upper-class families who fled, abandoning the towns; later, from April on, after the Yishuv shifted to the offensive, it was the urban and rural masses who fled, in a sense emulating their betters. Most of the displaced likely expected to return to their homes within weeks or months, on the coattails of victorious Arab armies or on the back of a UN decision or Great Power intervention. Few expected that their refugeedom would last a lifetime or encompass their children and grandchildren. But it did.

The permanence of the refugee problem owed much to Israel's almost instant decision, taken in the summer of 1948, not to allow back those who had fled or been expelled. The Zionist national and local leaderships almost instantly understood that a refugee return would destabilize the new state, demographically and politically. And the army understood that a refugee return would introduce a militarily subversive fifth column. Again, it was Shertok who explained: "We are resolute not to allow anyone under any circumstances to return. . . . [At best] the return can only be partial and small; the solution [to the problem] lies in the resettlement of the refugees in other countries."[37]

But the Arab states refused to absorb or properly resettle the refugees in their midst. This, too, accounts for the perpetuation of the refugee problem. The Arab states regarded the repatriation of the refugees as an imperative of "justice" and, besides, understood that, in the absence of a return, maintaining the refugees as an embittered, impoverished community would serve their anti-Israeli political and military purposes. As a tool of propaganda, the existence of the refugee communities, many of them in dilapidated "camps," bit into Israel's humane image. And the refugees and their descendants provided a ready pool for recruitment of guerrillas and terrorists who could continuously sting the Jewish state. Besides, many refugees refused permanently to resettle in the host countries because it could be seen as, and could promote, an abandonment of the dream of a return. Hence, the Middle East is dotted with large concentrations of Palestinian refugees—so-called camps that, in reality, are suburban slums, on the peripheries of large Arab towns (Beirut, Damascus, Amman, Nablus, and so on)—living on international handouts this past half-century while continuously stoking the Israeli-Arab conflict, one intifada following hard on the heels of its predecessor.

The Palestinian Arabs, backed by the wider Arab and Muslim worlds, continue to endorse the refugees' right of return and demand its implementation. Many Arabs no doubt view the return as a means of undermining Israel's existence. The Arabs are united in seeing the refugees as a standing reminder of their collective humiliation at the hands of the Yishuv in 1948 and as a token of the "injustice" perpetrated on the Arab world by Israel's creation (with Western backing). Israel, for its part, has quite logically persisted ever since in resisting the demand for a return, arguing that it would lead instantly, or over time, to its demise. Without doubt, the refugees constitute the most intractable, and explosive, of the problems left by the events of 1948.

The war indirectly created a second, major refugee problem. Partly because of the clash of Jewish and Arab arms in Palestine, some five to six hundred thousand Jews who lived in the Arab world emigrated, were intimidated into flight, or were expelled from their native countries, most of them reaching Israel, with a minority resettling in France, Britain, and the other Western countries. The immediate propellants to flight were the popular Arab hostility, including pogroms, triggered by the war in Palestine and specific governmental measures, amounting to institutionalized discrimination against and oppression of the Jewish minority communities.

Already before the war, Iraq's prime minister had warned British diplomats that if the United Nations decided on a solution to the Palestine problem that was not "satisfactory" to the Arabs, "severe measures should [would?] be taken against all Jews in Arab countries."[38] A few weeks later, the head of the Egyptian delegation to the United Nations, Muhammad Hussein Heykal, announced that "the lives of 1,000,000 Jews in Moslem countries would be jeopardized by the establishment of a Jewish State."[39]

The outbreak of hostilities triggered wide-ranging anti-Jewish measures throughout the Arab world, with the pogroms in Aden—where seventy-six Jews were killed and seventy-eight wounded—and Aleppo—where ten synagogues, five schools, and 150 houses were burnt to the ground—only the most prominent. Anti-Semitic outbreaks were reported as far afield as Peshawar, in Pakistan; Meshed-Izet and Isfahan, in Iran; and Bahrain.[40] An atmosphere of intimidation and terror against Jews was generated by anti-Zionist and anti-Semitic propaganda in the generally state-controlled media. Prime Minister Mahmoud Nuqrashi of Egypt explained to the British ambassador: "All Jews were potential Zionists [and] . . . anyhow all Zionists were Communists."[41] From the start of the clashes in Palestine, the Jewish communities were coerced into making large financial "contributions" to the Arab forces.[42]

In Egypt, the start of the conventional war in mid-May 1948 was accompanied by the promulgation of martial law and the suspension of civil rights, the prevention of Jews from leaving the country, mass detentions (and occasional torture) without charge (the British Jewish Board of Deputies in early June 1948 alleged that "2,500" Jews had been arrested; the Egyptians admitted to about "600")[43] in internment camps,[44] and the confiscation of Jewish property. Bomb attacks in the Jewish Quarter of Cairo killed dozens.[45] The summer of 1948 was characterized by sporadic street attacks on Jews (and foreigners). The *National-Zeitung* of Basel reported that "at least 50" persons, "most of them Jews," were killed in a series of incidents in Egypt during the week of 18–25 July. The mob attacks and knifings, according to the newspaper, were at least partly orchestrated by the government in order to divert popular attention—and anger—away from Egypt's acceptance of the Second Truce. Cairo, the newspaper reported, "was entirely given over to the terror of the Arab mob . . . which roamed about the streets, howling and screaming ʿYahudi, Yahudi' (Jews). Every European-looking person was attacked. . . . The worst scenes passed off in the Jewish Quarter, where the mob moved from house to house . . . killing hundreds of Jews."[46] On 23 September a bomb exploded in the Jewish Quarter, killing twenty-nine people, "mostly Jews."[47]

In Iraq, following the May 1948 declaration of martial law, hundreds of Jews were arrested (the Iraqi government admitted to "276" Jews detained and "1,188" non-Jews),[48] and Jewish property was arbitrarily confiscated. Jewish students were banned from high schools and universities. Some fifteen hundred Jews were dismissed from government positions, the Iraqi Ministry of Health refused to renew the licenses of Jewish physicians or issue new ones, Jewish merchants' import and export licenses were canceled, and various economic sanctions were imposed on the Jewish community.[49] In January 1949, Prime Minister Nuri Saʾid threatened "that all Iraqi Jews would be expelled if the Israelis did not allow the Arab refugees to return to Palestine."[50] A new "wave of persecution" was unleashed against the 125,000-strong community in early October 1949, with about two thousand being packed off to jails and "concentration camps" and vast amounts of money being extorted in fines on various pretexts.[51] But the Iraqi government kept a tight leash on the "street."

Elsewhere in the Arab world, mobs were given their head. In April 1948, Arabs ransacked Jewish property and attacked Jews in Beirut,[52] and in June, a mob rampaged in British-administered Tripoli, Libya, killing thirteen.[53] That month, in Oujda and Djerada, in French-ruled Morocco, Arab mobs killed dozens of Jews, including some twenty women and children.[54]

Because of this atmosphere of intimidation and violence and oppressive governmental measures—though also because of the "pull" of Zionism (which before 1948 and the establishment of the State of Israel had had little purchase among the Jews of the Islamic world) and Zionist "missionary" efforts—the Jewish communities in the Arab world were propelled into emigration.

The first to leave were Yemen's Jews, the only Oriental Jewish community with a tradition of (religious) Zionism. (About sixteen thousand Yemeni Jews had emigrated to Palestine in the decades before 1948.) Between May 1949 and August 1950, some forty-three thousand of the forty-five-thousand-strong community packed their bags and trekked to Aden, from where they were airlifted, in Operation Magic Carpet, to Israel. In 1968 there were only two hundred Jews left in Yemen.

Iraq's Jews—a relatively prosperous and well-educated community—began leaving in 1948, even though emigration was illegal. By early 1950, thousands had crossed the border into Iran. In March 1950, the Iraqi government legalized emigration, though the departees had to forfeit their citizenship and property. Between May 1950 and August 1951, the Israeli authorities, assisted by international welfare organizations, airlifted the remaining eighty to ninety thousand Iraqi Jews to Israel. A small number of Iraqi Jews eventually settled in Britain and Brazil.

Four-fifths of Egypt's sixty-five thousand Jews were not Egyptian citizens (they held assorted European passports). About twenty-five thousand left in 1948–1950. The bulk of the remainder left under duress or were deported, with their property confiscated, in 1955–1957, immediately before and after the Sinai-Suez War. By 1970, only about a thousand remained. These, too, subsequently departed.

Most of Syria's fifteen thousand Jews left, illegally, in the wake of the Aleppo pogrom of December 1947 and the declaration of Israeli statehood in May 1948. Palestinian refugees were often installed in their former homes in Damascus and Aleppo. The remainder trickled out during the following decades, as Syria intermittently allowed emigration. All forfeited their property.

The bulk of Libya's forty thousand Jews left the country in 1949–1951, mostly for Israel. Most of Morocco's, Algeria's, and Tunisia's Jews left in the mid-1950s and the 1960s. Apparently, despite the Moroccan pogroms of June 1948, these communities felt relatively safe under French rule. In Morocco, which had the largest of the Maghrebi communities, the sultan, Muhammad V, also afforded the Jews protection. But with the onset of independence, almost all of Morocco's Jews moved to Israel; the elite immigrated to France. A pogrom in Mazagan (El Jadida), near Casablanca, in which eight Jews died and forty houses were torched in August 1955, acted as an important precipitant. Around sixty thousand—of the community's pre-1948 total of about three hundred thousand—left in 1955–1956. A second major wave followed hard on the heels of Muhammad V's death in 1961. Today Morocco's approximately four thousand Jews are the largest Jewish community in the Arab world.

The Arab governments and societies were generally glad to be rid of their

Jewish communities. At base, there was the traditional religious alienation, unease, and animosity. And against the backdrop of the Palestine war, there was vengefulness and genuine fear of the Jews' potential subversiveness; the Jews were identified with Zionism and Israel. As well, the Arab states derived massive economic benefit from the confiscations of property that accompanied the exodus, though the wealthier émigrés, from Baghdad and Egypt, managed to take out some of their assets. But the vast majority, most of them poorly educated or illiterate, lost everything or almost everything. They arrived in Israel penniless or almost penniless. They were immediately granted citizenship and accommodation. But Israel was poor, most of the immigrants knew no Hebrew, and many—especially from the Maghreb— were unsuited to the rigors and demands of life in postwar Israel. There was also a measure of discrimination against the new immigrants. The travails of absorption created a "Sephardi" problem and a cultural divide that wrenched Israeli society in the following decades.

The experience of discrimination and persecution in the Arab world, and the centuries of subjection and humiliation that preceded 1948, had left the emigrant Sephardi communities with a deep dislike, indeed hatred, of that world, which, in the internal Israeli political realm, translated into Arabophobia and hard-line, right-wing voting patterns, both among the first generation of émigrés and among their descendents. This, too, was an indirect by-product of the 1948 War.

Israel's leaders, already in 1948, by way of rebuffing Arab efforts to achieve repatriation of the Palestinian refugees, pointed out that what had taken place was a double exodus, or an unplanned "exchange of population," more or less of equal numbers, with a similar massive loss of property affecting both the Palestinian refugees and the Jewish refugees from Arab lands. These canceled each other out, went the argument, in both humanitarian and economic terms. The Israeli leaders usually added that the Palestinian refugees had brought their demise on themselves by initiating the war on their Jewish neighbors, which resulted in their dispossession and exile, whereas the Jews of the Arab lands had by and large done nothing to offend or aggress and had nonetheless been driven out. And one last difference: the Jewish refugee problem quickly disappeared as Israel absorbed them; the Palestinian refugee problem persisted (and persists), as the Arab states largely failed to absorb their refugees, leaving many of them stateless and languishing in refugee camps and living on international charity.

Economically, the war had done limited harm to Israel, in terms of manpower destroyed, houses and fields trashed, and production impeded. But this was largely offset by the massive influx of Jewish immigrants and the financial contributions sent by world, especially American, Jewry and by the grants and loans that soon began to arrive from Western governments. A giant demographic and agrarian revolution took place that, within five years, led to the doubling of the Jewish population and of the number of settlements, with all that this implied in terms of agricultural productivity and demographic expansion and dispersion. To some degree, the war had also been beneficial to Israel's fledgling industrial sector.

For the Arab combatants, the war had notched up only economic losses. Their in any case weak economies were further undermined by an increase in foreign debts. And all (save Iraq), to one degree or another, were forced to cope with Palestinian refugees—though by and large this failed to harm them economically as the advent of UNRWA and a steady flow of Western relief capital more than compensated for any losses they may initially have incurred. The major economic harm inflicted by the war on the Arab side was largely to the Palestinians, who lost much of their property, especially land and houses, to the victors.

The war formally ended with the signing of the armistice agreements. Each had included a preamble defining the accord as a step on the road to a comprehensive peace. But none of the agreements had any such immediate issue. During the 1950s and 1960s, with the humiliation of 1948 fresh on its mind, the Arab world was unwilling to make peace with the Jewish state that had arisen in its midst; indeed, the Arab world was not ready for peace. This was demonstrated by the fate of the series of bilateral contacts Israel held during the following years with Egyptian, Syrian, and Jordanian officials and leaders. Occasionally, the Egyptians hinted at the possibility of nonbelligerency or even "peace" in return for an Israeli cession of all or much of the Negev (something the Egyptians probably knew the Israelis would never agree to); Syria's president, Hosni Za'im, during summer 1949 spoke of peace in exchange for an Israeli cession of half the Sea of Galilee and all of its eastern shoreline, and half the Jordan river (again, something it is unlikely he believed Israel would or could concede). Israel's response to both—as well as to the demands that it accept the repatriation of the refugees (the Arabs usually said they numbered nine hundred thousand to a million persons) and withdraw to the 1947 partition borders—was a resounding "no."

The most serious and protracted negotiations were with Jordan's King ʿAbdullah, who appeared sincerely interested in peace (he was largely motivated by the fear that, in the absence of peace, Israel would gobble up the West Bank—which it eventually did, in 1967). But he, too, demanded territory and a substantial measure of refugee repatriation—and, in the end, proved unable to overcome the resistance to peace of his "street" and ministers. When presented with something less than full peace, a five-year nonbel-ligerency draft agreement, already initialed by his prime minister, he at the last minute balked and declined to sign.

It can be—and has been—argued that with all three countries, but espe-cially with Jordan, Israel could and should have been more forthcoming and that had it assented to the concessions demanded, peace could have been reached and concluded. I have my doubts. Would the ʿulema of Al-Azhar University have agreed? Would the "street" have acquiesced? Would ʿAbdul-lah's fellow leaders have resigned themselves to such a breaking of ranks? Given the atmosphere prevailing in the postwar Arab world, it seems unlikely that any leader could have signed and delivered real, lasting peace, whatever concessions Israel made. The antagonism toward a Jewish state, of any size, was deep and consensual; peace with Israel was seen as treasonous. And the only Arab leader who had seriously conducted peace negotiations was, in fact, murdered (King ʿAbdullah in 1951)—as, in fact, was the next Arab leader who dared (President Anwar Sadat of Egypt in 1981).

In addition, a question arises about the reasonableness, justice, and logic of the concessions Israel was being asked to make. After all, the Arab states had attacked Israel, collectively aiming at Israel's destruction or, at the least, truncation. They had failed. But in the process, they had caused grievous losses and destruction to the new state, which was minute by any standards, even with the additional territory won in the war (some two thousand square miles were then added to the six thousand square miles originally allocated for Jewish statehood in the UN partition resolution). And many Arab lead-ers continued during the following years to speak quite openly of a necessary "second round" and of uprooting the "Zionist entity." Was it reasonable to expect Israel to make major concessions to its would-be destroyers? Would any leader, anywhere, but especially in the semiarid Middle East, have been prepared to give up half of his country's major water resources (the Sea of Galilee and Jordan River) or a large part of its territory (the Negev) in ex-change for assurances of peace? Who would have guaranteed the Arabs' con-tinued adherence to their peaceful undertakings after they had swallowed the Israeli concessions?

So much for the bilateral tracks. But, simultaneously, the international community tried, in the wake of 1948, to inaugurate a multilateral negotia-tion: perhaps what each Arab leader was afraid to do alone he might be in-duced to pursue together with his peers? United Nations General Assembly Resolution 194 of December 1948 provided for the creation of the Palestine Conciliation Commission, which began operating, under American chair-manship, early the following year. The members shuttled between the Mid-dle East's capitals in search of the contours of a settlement.

But by April 1949, they had achieved nothing. They decided on a giant gamble: they convoked a full- scale peace conference at Lausanne, Switzerland. The Arabs refused to meet with the Israelis, and made any progress on the major issues—borders, recognition, Jerusalem—contingent on Tel Aviv's agreement to full-scale refugee repatriation. The Arabs also demanded that Israel accept the November 1947 partition borders as the basis for negotiation. Israel refused. A belated Israeli offer, in July, to take back one hundred thousand refugees (actually sixty-five thousand plus those who had already illegally or legally returned to Israeli territory) if the Arab states agreed to settle the rest on their territory, was rejected out of hand. Israel, for its part, turned down an American proposal that it take in about 250,000 refugees. Nothing happened, and in September the delegations went home. The next bout of serious Israeli-Arab peace-making occurred almost thirty years later, after Sadat's astonishing visit to Jerusalem in November 1977.

Negotiating peace with Israel was not the only thing that undermined the legitimacy of Arab leaders. The war itself, and its outcome, had done this as well. The war seriously damaged the ancien régimes of the Arab world. All tottered; some fell within a few years. The Lebanese foreign minister had predicted such consequences a fortnight before the pan-Arab invasion, as the British minister to Beirut reported: "I found His Excellency very depressed. . . . The state of affairs in Egypt and Iraq filled him with gloom. He felt that if the Arabs were defeated in Palestine the Governments of Egypt, Iraq and Syria would tumble like a house of cards, with repercussions which would be felt throughout the Arab world."[55]

He was pretty close. A string of assassinations were directly or indirectly linked to the war. Egyptian prime minister Nuqrashi was killed by Muslim Brotherhood gunmen on 28 December 1948 while his troops were still battling the IDF in eastern Sinai. Riad al-Sulh, the Lebanese prime minister, was murdered in Amman more than a year later; and, of course, King ʿAbdullah was assassinated in 1951.

But the war's repercussions went far deeper. In March 1949, shortly before Damascus entered into the armistice negotiations with Israel, the civilian regime was overthrown by a coup d'état engineered by the army's chief of staff, Hosni Zaʿim. Zaʿim himself was overthrown—and murdered—by fellow officers, in August, less than five months after taking power. As it turned out, these events inaugurated two decades of tumultuous military governments, one coup following another, until the accession to power of Hafiz al-Assad in 1970–1971.

And Egypt, too, fell into the hands of the colonels. King Farouk was overthrown by a junta of young officers, led by Colonel Gamal ʿAbdel Nasser, the veteran of the Faluja Pocket, in July 1952. General Neguib, his fellow veteran, was installed as the first president of the republic. Farouk and his coterie were vilified as the men who had lost, or betrayed, Palestine. The military dictatorship installed that summer for all intents and purposes continues to rule down to the present day (current President Hosni Mubarak, an air force general, inherited the mantle from his mentor, Colonel Anwar Sadat, who was a member of the original revolutionary junta).

The Iraqi monarchy was the last to tumble—though its demise, too, in front of television cameras, in July 1958, was, in part at least, an aftershock of 1948. There, the young colonels, who in effect ruled Baghdad until Saddam Hussein's ouster in 2003, murdered the last of the major Palestine war politicians, Nuri Saʿid.

Perhaps it is not accidental that the only 1948 regime to enjoy longevity, that of the Hashemites of Jordan, was also the only one that emerged from the war relatively victorious. It went on to weather the intake of hundreds of thousands of hostile, destitute Palestinians, King ʿAbdullah's assassination, years of border clashes with Israel, the war of 1967 and the loss of the West Bank, a brief, bloody civil war with the PLO ("Black September") in 1970, and a peace treaty with Israel. Today, the Hashemite regime flourishes, under ʿAbdullah's great-grandson, King ʿAbdullah II.

But 1948 has haunted, and still haunts, the Arab world on the deepest levels of collective identity, ego, and pride. The war was a humiliation from which that world has yet to recover—the antithesis of the glory days of Arab Islamic dominance of the Middle East and the eastern and southern Mediterranean basins. The sense of humiliation only deepened over the succeeding sixty years as Israel visibly grew and prospered while repeatedly beating the Arabs in new wars, as the Palestinian refugee camps burst at the seams while sinking in the mire of international charity and terrorism, and as the Arab world shuttled between culturally self-effacing Westernization and religious fundamentalism.

For almost a millennium, the Arab peoples were reared on tales of power and conquest. Ottoman subjugation ate away at the Arabs' self-image; even more destructive were the gradual encroachment and dominance of (infidel) Western powers, led by Britain and France. The 1948 War was the culminating affront, when a community of some 650,000 Jews—Jews, no less—crushed Palestinian Arab society and then defeated the armies of the surrounding states. The failure was almost complete. The Arab states had failed to "save" the Palestinians and failed to prevent Israel's emergence and acceptance into the comity of nations. And what little Palestine territory the Arabs had managed to retain fell under Israeli sway two decades later.

Viewed from the Israeli perspective, however, 1948 wasn't the irreversible triumph it at first appeared. True, the state had been established, Zionism's traditional chief goal, and its territory had increased; true, the Arab armies had been crushed to such an extent that they would not represent a mortal threat to the Jewish state for two decades.

But the dimensions of the success had given birth to reflexive Arab nonacceptance and powerful revanchist urges. The Jewish state had arisen at the heart of the Muslim Arab world—and that world could not abide it. Peace treaties may eventually have been signed by Egypt and Jordan; but the Arab world—the man in the street, the intellectual in his perch, the soldier in his dugout—refused to recognize or accept what had come to pass. It was a cosmic injustice. And there would be plenty of Arabs, by habit accustomed to think in the long term and egged on by the ever-aggrieved Palestinians, who would never acquiesce in the new Middle Eastern order. Whether 1948 was a passing fancy or has permanently etched the region remains to be seen.

Notes

CHAPTER I. STAKING CLAIMS

1. Vladimir (Ze'eve) Dubnow, Palestine, to Simon Dubnow, St. Petersburg, 20 October 1882, quoted in Shapira, *Land and Power,* 55.
2. Goldstein, *From Fighters to Soldiers,* 13.
3. Finlayson, *Shaftesbury,* 441; Garfinkle, "Origin, Meaning, Use and Abuse of a Phrase." Shaftesbury wrote that a "country without a nation" must be mated with a "nation without a country."
4. Eliezer Ben-Yehuda and Yehiel Michal Pines, Palestine, to Rashi Pin, Vilna, 18 October 1882, quoted in Be'eri, *Beginning of Arab-Israeli Conflict,* 38–39.
5. Ahad Ha'am, "Emet Me'eretz Yisrael," *Hamelitz,* 19–30 June 1891.
6. Gorny, *Zionism and the Arabs,* 27.
7. Mandel, *Arabs and Zionism,* 41; Be'eri, *Beginning of Arab-Israeli Conflict,* 82.
8. Yusuf Dia al-Khalidi to Zadok Kahn, 1 March 1899, quoted in Be'eri, *Beginning of Arab-Israeli Conflict,* 89–90; Mandel, *Arabs and Zionism,* 47–48.
9. Khalidi, ed., *From Haven to Conquest,* 91–93.
10. 'Azoury, *Le reveil de la nation arabe,* 6–7, v.
11. Teveth, *Ben-Gurion and Palestinian Arabs,* 15–16.
12. Teveth, *Ben-Gurion and Palestinian Arabs,* 13.
13. Morris, *Righteous Victims,* 57–58.
14. Mandel, *Arabs and Zionism,* 174, 175.
15. Morris, *Righteous Victims,* 75.
16. Antonius, *Arab Awakening,* 267.
17. Talmi, "The Christians in Jaffa," 2 May 1947, HA 105/193 bet.

18. Unsigned, "Arabs with a Tendency to Cooperation with the Jews," undated, HA 105/54.
19. Stein, *Land Question in Palestine*, 228–239, gives a partial list of specific sales, with both Husseinis and Nashashibis among the sellers.
20. Cohen, *Army of Shadows*.
21. Teveth, *Ben-Gurion and Palestinian Arabs*, 167–168.
22. Unsigned, "Legal Arab Immigrants to Eretz Yisrael," 17 July 1947, HA 105/215 bet.
23. Teveth, *Ben-Gurion and Palestinian Arabs*, 132.
24. Eliahu Elath, "Minutes of a Meeting between Representatives of the Jewish Agency for Palestine and the Secretariat of the Syrian National Bloc held at Damascus on the 9th of August, 1936," CZA S25-3267.
25. Metzer, *Divided Economy of Mandatory Palestine*, 239–242.
26. Eppel, *Palestine Conflict in Modern Iraq*, 31.
27. "Short Minutes of Meeting Held on Thursday, January 30th, 1941, at 77 Great Russell Street, London WC.1," unsigned, Chaim Weizmann Archive, 2271; Ivan Maiskii, "Meeting: I. M. Maiskii–Ch. Weizmann (London, 3 February 1941)," in *Documents on Israeli-Soviet Relations, 1941–1953*, 1:3–5.
28. Basil Newton to FO, 6 July 1939, PRO FO 371-23211, quoting Nuri Sa'id's speech the previous day before the Iraqi parliament ("Our aim is first of all that Zionism should be destroyed in Palestine"). One Foreign Office official minuted: "'The destruction of Zionism' is an unfortunate phrase." But Iraqi politicians often said different things to different audiences. A few years later, Sa'id was to speak in favor of partition and even the transfer of Arabs out of the area of the Jewish state-to-be (see illegible signature, "Note on Conversation with General Nuri Sa'id, the Iraqi Prime Minister and the Iraqi Minister of Foreign Affairs in Baghdad on 5th and 6th December 1944," 18 December 1944, PRO FO 921-149). As Kamil al-Jadirji, head of Iraq's National Democratic Party, put it in 1945: "In Iraq, everyone has two faces" (see Eppel, *Palestine Conflict in Modern Iraq*, 141).
29. Alec Kirkbride to Thomas Wikeley, Eastern Department, FO, 29 July 1946, PRO FO 816/85.
30. Kirkbride to FO, 23 August 1946 (nos. 1387, 1364), both in PRO FO 816/85.
31. Al-Sakakini, *"Such Am I, Oh World,"* diary entry for 27 July 1942, 212–213.
32. Cohen, *Army of Shadows*, 175 n.
33. Elpeleg, *In the Eyes of the Mufti*, 106.
34. Elpeleg, *In the Eyes of the Mufti*, 148–149.
35. Zweig, *Britain and Palestine*, 112.
36. Hurewitz, *Struggle for Palestine*, 116.
37. Cohen, *Palestine, Retreat from the Mandate*, 130.
38. Hurewitz, *Struggle for Palestine*, 158.
39. Hurewitz, *Struggle for Palestine*, 213.
40. Schoenbaum, *United States and State of Israel*, 32.
41. Schoenbaum, *United States and State of Israel*, 32.

42. Cohen, *Palestine and Great Powers,* 293.

43. Cohen, *Palestine and Great Powers,* 293, quoting a letter from Harry Truman to Eleanor Roosevelt, August 1947.

44. Hurewitz, *Struggle for Palestine,* 229.

45. Ronald Campbell to FO, 25 April 1946, PRO CO 537-1853.

46. Cohen, *Palestine to Israel,* 181.

47. Hurewitz, *Struggle for Palestine,* 189.

48. Khalaf, *Politics in Palestine,* 93–95; Hurewitz, *Struggle for Palestine,* 183–184.

49. Hurewitz, *Struggle for Palestine,* 186; Khalaf, *Politics in Palestine,* 87–89.

50. Porath, *In Search of Arab Unity,* 257–311.

51. Hurewitz, *Struggle for Palestine,* 192.

52. Hurewitz, *Struggle for Palestine,* 194.

53. Khalaf, *Politics in Palestine,* 96–98.

54. Khalaf, *Politics in Palestine,* 115–130.

55. Hurewitz, *Struggle for Palestine,* 232.

56. Zweig, *Britain and Palestine,* 173, n. 106.

57. Zweig, *Britain and Palestine,* 165, n. 68.

58. Levenberg, *Military Preparations of Arab Community in Palestine,* 145. Levenberg speaks of twenty-two thousand men and four thousand women; about ten thousand of these served in combat units. He puts the number of Palestinian Arabs who served with the British during World War II at twelve thousand.

59. Heller, *LEHI,* 1:125–130.

60. Niv, *Battles of the IZL,* 4:20–32, 32–36, 46–48, 50–57, 60–63; *STH,* 3, pt. 2:523–527.

61. Hurewitz, *Struggle for Palestine,* 200.

62. Niv, *Battles of the IZL,* 4:88–117; *STH,* 3, pt. 2:531–543.

63. Hurewitz, *Struggle for Palestine,* 225.

64. Hurewitz, *Struggle for Palestine,* 228.

65. Cohen, *Palestine to Israel,* 177.

66. Gilead, ed., *Book of the Palmah,* 1:629–640.

67. Zertal, *From Catastrophe to Power.*

68. British Military Administration, Tripolitania, "Report on the Anti-Jewish Riots, 4th to 8th November, 1945," undated, PRO FO 371-69374; unsigned, "Anti-Jewish Riots in Tripolitania," undated, CZA S25-5219.

69. "Editorial Note," *Political Documents of the Jewish Agency,* 1:201–202.

70. Hurewitz, *Struggle for Palestine,* 237–239.

71. Nachmani, *Great Power Discord in Palestine,* 111–113.

72. Nachmani, *Great Power Discord in Palestine,* 161.

73. Nachmani, *Great Power Discord in Palestine,* 167.

74. Crossman, *Palestine Mission,* 148.

75. Nachmani, *Great Power Discord in Palestine,* 178.

76. Nachmani, *Great Power Discord in Palestine,* 187.

77. "Notes on an Interview with Jamal Husseini by His Excellency the High Commissioner on 3rd May, 1946," undated, PRO CO 537-1756.

78. Stonehewer Bird, Baghdad, to FO, 9 May 1946, PRO CO 537-1756.

79. Freundlich, *From Destruction to Resurrection,* 42–49; Cohen, *Palestine and Great Powers,* 141–147.

80. Hurewitz, *Struggle for Palestine,* 256.

81. Abba Hillel Silver to David Ben-Gurion, 9 October 1946, *Political Documents of the Jewish Agency,* 2:675–680.

82. Cohen, *Palestine and Great Powers,* 166.

CHAPTER 2. THE UNITED NATIONS STEPS IN

1. Ernest Bevin to Douglas Busk, "Conversation with the Iraqi Foreign Minister," 23 December 1947, PRO FO 371-61893.

2. Bandman, *When Will Britain Withdraw from Jerusalem?* 12.

3. Cohen, *Palestine and Great Powers,* 223.

4. Freundlich, *From Destruction to Resurrection,* 62.

5. Hurewitz, *Struggle for Palestine,* 281–282.

6. Niv, *Battles of the IZL,* 5:161–163, 274–280.

7. Cohen, *Palestine and Great Powers,* 245.

8. Louis, *British Empire in the Middle East,* 475.

9. Cohen, *Palestine and Great Powers,* 245.

10. Sela, "Question of Palestine," 317–322; Ben-Dror, "UNSCOP," 20–21.

11. Unsigned, "Jewish Displaced Persons and Refugees May 1947," undated, CZA S25-5353.

12. Text of Andrei Gromyko's speech, *Documents on Israeli-Soviet Relations, 1941–1953,* 1:189–196.

13. Ben-Dror, "UNSCOP," 39–55.

14. Urquhart, *Bunche,* 140 (quoting Bunche to his wife, Ruth, 29 June 1947).

15. Ben-Dror, "UNSCOP," 41.

16. Emanuel Neumann, protocol of meeting of US Section, JAE, 26 September 1947, CZA Z5-59.

17. Ben-Dror, "UNSCOP," 73.

18. Freundlich, *From Destruction to Resurrection,* 104–108; Ben-Dror, "UNSCOP," 76.

19. Ben-Dror, "UNSCOP," 109.

20. Horowitz, *State in the Making,* 169; Ben-Dror, "UNSCOP," 109.

21. Freundlich, *From Destruction to Resurrection,* 109.

22. García Granados, *Birth of Israel,* 85–87; Horowitz, *State in the Making,* 171.

23. Ben-Dror, "UNSCOP," 115.

24. Ben-Dror, "UNSCOP," 137.

25. Ben-Dror, "UNSCOP," 139.

26. Ben-Dror, "UNSCOP," 142.

27. Ben-Dror, "UNSCOP," 145.

28. Ben-Dror, "UNSCOP," 173–175, 170–172.

29. Ben-Dror, "UNSCOP," 125–129; Cohen, *Palestine and Great Powers*, 242–250.

30. Levenberg, *Military Preparations of Arab Community in Palestine*, 90.

31. Halamish, *Exodus*, 58–60; Zertal, *From Catastrophe to Power*, 118–122; Freundlich, *From Destruction to Resurrection*, 110.

32. Halamish, *Exodus*, 75–77.

33. Halamish, *Exodus*, 84–96.

34. Halamish, *Exodus*, 134.

35. *New York Herald Tribune*, 19 July 1948. The spectacle was explicitly referred to in the UNSCOP Report.

36. Ben-Dror, "UNSCOP," 131.

37. Ben-Dror, "UNSCOP," 177–180.

38. Ben-Dror, "UNSCOP," 175–177.

39. Khalaf, *Politics in Palestine*, 157.

40. Christopher Pirie-Gordon to FO, 30 June 1947, PRO FO 371-61875.

41. Quoted in Ben-Dror, "UNSCOP," 201; Cohen, *Palestine and Great Powers*, 264–267.

42. Ignatius Mubarak, "Mubarak's Memorandum to UNSCOP," 13 October 1947, CZA S25-9026. Some leading Maronites, including Mubarak, regarded Lebanon's Christians as non-Arab descendants of the Phoenicians.

43. Ben-Dror, "UNSCOP," 211–213.

44. Nevo, *King Abdallah and Palestine*, 65; Ben-Dror, "UNSCOP," 215.

45. García Granados, *Birth of Israel*, 228–233; Ben-Dror, "UNSCOP," 233, 235; Freundlich, *From Destruction to Resurrection*, 111–112. Some researchers have cast doubt on the sincerity of the Zionist professions of the DPs, arguing that these were a product of intensive coaching, browbeating, and threats by Zionist officials (see, e.g., Grodzinski, *Good Human Material*). But it is clear that many of those interviewed by UNSCOP were chosen randomly on the spot by the members, not by Zionist prearrangement. All the UNSCOP members were convinced that they had heard what really was in the DPs' minds and hearts (Ben-Dror, "UNSCOP," 237–238).

46. García Granados, *Birth of Israel*, 233–246.

47. Ben-Dror, "UNSCOP," 254.

48. Khalaf, *Politics in Palestine*, 156–157.

49. Ben-Dror, "UNSCOP," 255–258; Horowitz, *State in the Making*, 208–209.

50. Horowitz, *State in the Making*, 179–223. The lobbyists used a variety of means. Horowitz tantalizingly hints at how he recruited "a young Australian girl" employed at the UN offices in Geneva to "reach" the Australian UNSCOP delegation (193–194).

51. Horowitz, *State in the Making*, 202–207; Ben-Dror, "UNSCOP," 260–262. Horowitz wrote: "[Crossman's] statement produced an unforgettable impression on the UNSCOP members" (207).

52. Gelber, *Jewish-Transjordanian Relations*, 224–225.

53. Ben-Dror, "UNSCOP," 287.

54. Horowitz, *State in the Making*, 223.

55. Unsigned, "Justice Sandstrom's Talk on Palestine," undated, PRO FO 371-61797.

56. Ben-Dror, "UNSCOP," contrary to common wisdom, asserts that most of the UNSCOP members were not constrained by their governments and decided independently how to vote.

57. The Jewish Agency thought the UNSCOP numbers faulty—and believed that the Jewish state would have altogether 513,000 Jews and 416,000 Arabs (Ben-Dror, "UNSCOP," 301, n. 41).

58. UNSCOP Report.

59. Ben-Dror, "UNSCOP," 356.

60. Ben-Dror, "UNSCOP," 309; Ben-Gurion to Paula Ben-Gurion, 2 September 1947, *Political Documents of the Jewish Agency*, 2:618–619.

61. Beirut to FO, 17 September 1947, PRO FO 371-61529.

62. Minute by Harold Beeley, 5 September 1947, PRO FO 371-61952.

63. Abba Eban, "Conversation with ʿAbdul Rahman ʿAzzam Pasha 15th September, 1947," 19 September 1947, CZA S25-2965.

64. Quoted in Landis, "Syria and the Palestine War," 186.

65. Ben-Dror, "UNSCOP," 310–312.

66. Cohen, "British Policy," 103; Ben-Dror, "UNSCOP," 315.

67. Louis, *British Empire in the Middle East*, 473–477; Cohen, *Palestine and Great Powers*, 274–276.

68. Freundlich, *From Destruction to Resurrection*, 147–148; Cohen, *Palestine and Great Powers*, 284. Subcommittee One was chartered to examine and translate into proposals for the General Assembly the majority recommendations; Subcommittee Two, to work on proposals conforming to the minority recommendations, meaning the establishment of a unitary state; and Subcommittee Three, to try to forge a compromise that would bridge between the two sets of recommendations.

69. Walter Eytan, New York, to Gershon Hirsch (Avner), Jerusalem, 26 October 1947, CZA S25-463.

70. Moshe Shertok at meeting of the US Section of the JA Executive, 17 September 1947, CZA Z5-59.

71. Eytan to Hirsch, 26 October 1947, CZA S25-463. He rated the Soviet delegation second—they "work like slaves."

72. Eytan, New York, to Zeev Sharef, Jerusalem, 22 October 1947, CZA S25-463.

73. "List of Handlers of the Delegates to the States at the UN," CZA S25-5471.

74. Eytan, New York, to Arye [Levavi?], 26 September 1947, CZA S25-463.

75. Eytan to Arye [Levavi?], 26 September 1947, CZA S25-463.

76. Eytan, New York, to Sharef, Jerusalem, 13 October 1947, CZA S25-463.

77. Protocol of meeting of JAE, 2 November 1947, CZA 45/1.

78. Louis, *British Empire in the Middle East*, 484.

79. Weizmann, *Trial and Error*, 458–459; Chaim Weizmann to Henry Morgenthau,

Jr., 20 November 1947, *Political Documents of the Jewish Agency*, 1:861–862; "Memorandum for the File by Mr. Robert M. McClintock," Washington, DC, 19 November 1947, *FRUS, 1947*, 5:1271–1272 and n. 2.

80. Alan Cunningham to Arthur Creech Jones, 14 November 1947, PRO FO 371-61795. The British apparently had a spy in the top ranks of the JA.

81. Summary of conversations in "bugged" Palestinian rooms and telephone conversations in New York, CZA S25 3569.

82. UK delegation to UN to FO, 25 November 1947, PRO FO 371-61890.

83. UK delegation to UN to FO, 26 November 1947, PRO FO 371-61890.

84. Abba Hillel Silver, protocol of meeting of US Section, JAE, 22 October 1947, CZA Z5-2374.

85. Isaiah ("Si") Kenen, public relations officer of the American Jewish Conference, protocol of meeting of US Section, JAE, 22 October 1947, CZA Z5-2374.

86. See "Editorial Note," *Political Documents of the Jewish Agency*, 2:742.

87. Cohen, *Palestine and Great Powers*, 297–298.

88. See Weizmann to Samuel Zemmuray, 20 October 1947, *Political Documents of the Jewish Agency*, 2:743.

89. British Legation, Guatemala, to Bevin, 26 November 1947, PRO FO 371-61892.

90. Hahn, *Caught in the Middle East*, 37.

91. García Granados, *Birth of Israel*, 269.

92. Sykes, *Wingate*, 104–205, 236–320, 360–546.

93. Berl Locker to I. J. Linton, 26 November 1947, ISA FM 2267/6; Lorna Wingate to the emperor, 27 November 1947, ISA FM 2266/41.

94. Freundlich, *From Destruction to Resurrection*, 194.

95. Linton to Jan Smuts, 27 November 1947, *Political Documents of the Jewish Agency*, 2:885–886, n. 1; Cohen, *Palestine and Great Powers*, 297.

96. Both Jawaharlal Nehru and Mohammed Ali Jinnah, the Muslim Indian leader, had written Arab League secretary ʿAzzam early on assuring him that "they regarded Palestine as an Arab country and would support the Arab cause" (Ronald Campbell, Cairo, to FO, 28 April 1947, PRO FO 371-61875).

97. Hayim Greenberg to Albert Einstein, 5 June 1947; Helen Dukas (Einstein's secretary) to Greenberg, 9 June 1947; and Greenberg to Dukas, 11 June 1947, all in ISA FM 92/34.

98. Einstein to Nehru, 13 June 1947, and Nehru to Einstein, 11 July 1947, both in ISA FM 92/34. The file contains a response to Nehru's letter—drafted for Einstein by another Zionist official, Eliahu Ben-Horin—but it is unclear whether Einstein sent it. In it he complained that the Indian representative "was the most outspoken enemy of Jewish-Zionist aspirations" in UNSCOP. The file contains no reply from the Indian prime minister (strengthening the supposition that the second letter to Nehru was never mailed).

99. "Meeting of Executive of the Jewish Agency for Palestine, American Section," 27 September 1947, CZA Z5-2366. See also "Chinese, Indian and American Delegations," 6 November 1947, ISA FM 92/34.

100. Weizmann to Nehru, 27 November 1947, ISA FM 92/34.
101. Silver, protocol of meeting of US Section, JAE, 26 October 1947, CZA Z5-2375.
102. V. K. Wellington Koo to Sumner Welles, undated but c. 27 November, CZA F39-589.
103. Summary of tapped Palestinian conversations in New York, undated but c. 22 November 1947, CZA S25-3569.
104. Michael Comay to Zvi Infeld, 29 October 1947, *Political Documents of the Jewish Agency,* 2:790.
105. "Note of Conversation between M. Ramadier, Prime Minister of France, and Mr. B. Locker, at Lyons, on August 16, 1947, at 8.30 p.m.," ISA FM 92/38.
106. Eliahu Epstein to members of JAE, 14 January 1948, CZA F39-579.
107. Moshe Sneh to Shertok, 21 October 1947, in *Political Documents of the Jewish Agency,* 2:744.
108. See, e.g., Maurice Fischer to Nahum Goldmann, 28 November 1947; and *Political Documents of the Jewish Agency,* 2:890, n. 3.
109. Ashley Clarke, Paris, to Bernard Burrows, FO, 9 December 1947, PRO FO 371-61892. Cohen, *Palestine and Great Powers,* 298, says that Niles mobilized Bernard Baruch, a major American financier, to threaten Alexandre Parodi with a cut-off of American aid.
110. Gideon Rafael to Eliahu (Elias) Sasson, 8 December 1947, CZA S25-500; Comay to Gering, 3 December 1947, ISA FM 2266/11.
111. Shertok, protocol of meeting of US Section, JAE, and non-Zionist representatives, 26 October 1947, CZA Z5-2375.
112. Unsigned, "Telephone Report by Mr. Epstein of Conversation of Dr. Weizmann and Himself with Sumner Welles, November 17, 1947," ISA FM 2270/8.
113. Linton, "Report on a Visit to Brussels, October 27th to 30th, 1947," 4 November 1947, CZA S25-5353.
114. George Rendel to FO, 26 November 1947, and FO to Rendel, 27 November 1947, both in PRO FO 371-61795.
115. Linton to JAE, 4 November 1947, CZA S25-5353.
116. Comay to Gering, 3 December 1947, ISA FM 2266/11.
117. "Cabinet Conclusions," 25 November 1947, PRO FO 371-61795; FO to UK Delegation UN, 26, 29 November 1947, PRO FO 371-61890.
118. See, e.g., Burrows to Orme Sargent, "Votes of Commonwealth Countries on Palestine," 24 November 1947, PRO FO 371-61890, for British uncertainty about the Dominions' votes.
119. Comay to JAE, 6 June 1947, ISA FM 2267/37.
120. Comay to Marcell Sigalla, 3 December 1947, ISA FM 2266/15.
121. Freundlich, *From Destruction to Resurrection,* 179.
122. See, e.g., Comay to Sigalla, 8 October 1947, *Political Documents of the Jewish Agency,* 2:712.
123. Morgenthau to Walter Nash, 22 November 1947; Morgenthau to Peter Fraser,

24 November 1947; and Fraser to Morgenthau, 24 November 1947, all in ISA FM 2267/37.

124. Eytan, New York, to Goldie (Golda) Myerson (Meir), Jerusalem, 3 October 1947, CZA S25-463.

125. Summary of tapped Palestinian conversations, New York, undated but c. 22 November 1947, CZA S25 3569.

126. Comay to Gering, 3 December 1947.

127. Silver at meeting of US Section, JAE, and Non-Zionist Representatives, 19 September 1947, CZA Z5-2364.

128. Rose Halprin at meeting of US Section, JAE, 17 September 1947, CZA Z5-59.

129. See, e.g., Moshe Toff's statement, "Minutes of Meeting American Section of the Executive of the Jewish Agency for Palestine," 5 October 1947, 7–8.

130. Shertok at meeting of US Section, JAE, 22 October 1947, CZA Z5-2374.

131. Shertok at meeting of US Section, JAE, 5 October 1947, CZA Z5-59.

132. Quoted in Cohen, *Palestine and Great Powers*, 295.

133. Emanuel Neuman, reporting on what a Venezuelan diplomat in New York had told him; meeting of US Section, JAE, 26 September 1947, CZA Z5-59.

134. Robert Nathan, economic adviser to the JA in Washington, DC, reporting on what John Hilldring, a member of the American UN delegation, had said to him; protocol of meeting of US Section, JAE, 8 October 1947, CZA Z5-2371.

135. Weizmann to Truman, 25 November 1947, ISA FM 2270/8; Weizmann to Truman, 25 November 1947, *Political Documents of the Jewish Agency*, 2:879–880.

136. Cohen, *Palestine and Great Powers*, 294.

137. Louis, *British Empire in the Middle East*, 485. See, e.g., Congressman Emanuel Celler, Washington, DC, to Jewish Agency official Eliahu Epstein, New York, 25 November 1947, ISA FM 2266/26, saying that he had "spoken to [Assistant Secretary of State Robert] Lovett, [Truman's secretary] Matthew Connelly and [chairman of the National Committee of the Democratic Party Howard] McGrath on the necessity of our delegates getting after [waverers] . . . like the pan-American countries, the Philippines and Siam. . . . McGrath and Matt Connelly are putting pressure on the White House and the State Department."

138. Truman, *Memoirs*, 2:158.

139. Comay to Gering, 3 December 1947.

140. Cohen, *Palestine and Great Powers*, 296.

141. Cohen, *Palestine and Great Powers*, 296–297. Somewhat prematurely, the British UN delegation on 24 November was reporting an "American attempt to stampede the Assembly" (UK delegation to UN to FO, 24 November 1947, PRO FO 371-61795).

142. Fifteen senators (Owen Brewster, Styles Bridges, et al.) to ambassador of Honduras, Washington, DC, etc., 27 November 1947, and thirteen senators (Harley Kilgore, Raymond Baldwin, et al.) to ambassador of Honduras, Washington, DC, etc., 28 November 1947, both in CZA F39-589.

143. UK delegation to UN to FO, 27 November 1947, PRO FO 371-61890.

144. See, e.g., "Shertok's Plan . . . ," *Beirut al-Masa,* 29 December 1947, (trans. into Hebrew) in HA 105/37.

145. Summary of tapped Palestinian conversations in New York, 26 November 1947, CZA S25-3569.

146. Chief secretary, Palestine Government, to British legation, Damascus, 15 August 1947, PRO FO 371-61877.

147. Unsigned but by a Jewish Agency official, "Threats of Arab Holy War on the Eve of the UN Decision," 15 October 1947, CZA S25-5353.

148. Shertok, reporting what "a certain Arab"—probably ʿOmar Dajani—who had talked to Saudi Prince Ibn Saʿud, had told him, at meeting of US Section, JAE, 1 October 1947, CZA Z5-2369.

149. This is alluded to in the al-Qawuqji interview quoted in chief secretary, Palestine Government, to British legation, Damascus, 15 August 1947, PRO FO 371-61877.

150. Shertok, protocol of meeting of US Section and Labor Committee, JAE, 30 September 1947, CZA Z5-2367.

151. American Zionist Emergency Council, "Memorandum: Is There Any Substance to Arab Threats of a 'Break with the West'?" 26 September 1947, CZA F39-74.

152. J. L[inton], "Short Note on a Talk over Lunch with Mr. Trafford Smith, Monday, November 24th, 1947," 24 November 1947, CZA S25-7567; Freundlich, *From Destruction to Resurrection,* 197.

153. T[uvia] A[razi] to E[lias] S[asson], 7 December 1948, CZA S25-9026.

154. Epstein to members of JAE, 29 November 1947, *Political Documents of the Jewish Agency,* 2:894–896.

155. Comay to Gering, 3 December 1947.

156. Rafael to Sasson, 8 December 1947; Comay to Gering, 3 December 1947.

157. Cohen, *Palestine and Great Powers,* 298–299.

158. The thirty-three "ayes" were: Australia, Belgium, Bolivia, Brazil, Canada, Costa Rica, Czechoslovakia, Denmark, Dominican Republic, Ecuador, France, Guatemala, Haiti, Iceland, Liberia, Luxemburg, Netherlands, New Zealand, Nicaragua, Norway, Panama, Paraguay, Peru, Philippines, Poland, South Africa, Soviet Union, Sweden, Ukraine, the United States, Uruguay, Venezuela, and White Russia. Voting "nay" were Afghanistan, Cuba, Egypt, Greece, India, Iran, Iraq, Lebanon, Pakistan, Saudi Arabia, Syria, Turkey, and Yemen. Argentina, Chile, China, Colombia, El Salvador, Ethiopia, Honduras, Mexico, the United Kingdom, and Yugoslavia abstained.

159. García Granados, *Birth of Israel,* 268.

160. UK delegation to UN to FO, 29 November 1947 (no. 3566), PRO FO 371-61890.

161. Khalidi, *Before Their Diaspora,* 305.

162. Yolande Harmer, untitled memorandum of conversation with ʿAbd al-Hadi, 12 December 1947, CZA S25-4015a. ʿAbd al-Hadi's description of the shareout is

not accurate. More than half of the territory earmarked for Jewish statehood, the Negev, was desert, whereas the bulk of the Arab territory—central Galilee, Samaria, and Judea—was fertile, if hilly and rocky.

163. Khalidi, *Before Their Diaspora*, 305–306.

164. Unsigned, "Partition in Palestine and the Declaration of a Jihad," undated, PRO FO 371-61580.

165. [NAME TK] Roberts, "Anglo-American Conversations," 18 December 1947, PRO FO 371-61583.

166. Freundlich, *From Destruction to Resurrection*, 199.

167. Cohen, *Palestine and Great Powers*, 292. But Cohen added, "The Jews themselves tended to overestimate the depth of Western remorse, or conscience" (293).

168. Avraham Stern to president of Italy, 5 December 1947, CZA S25-9669. Titus was the roman general, later emperor, who defeated the Jewish rebellion of 66–73 CE and destroyed Jerusalem and Jewish sovereignty. The arch, built to honor his triumph, depicts Jews being hauled to Rome as slaves.

169. Segev, ed., *Behind the Screen*, 38.

170. Segev, ed., *Behind the Screen*, 42; Mayer, "Egypt's 1948 Invasion of Palestine," 21.

171. Sela, "Palestinian Arabs in the 1948 War," 133.

172. Shertok, protocol of meeting of US Section, JAE, 13 October 1947, CZA Z5-2372.

173. See Doran, *Pan-Arabism before Nasser*, 94–127, for a discussion of the functioning of the blocs.

174. Segev, ed., *Behind the Screen*, 49–50.

175. Tripp, "Iraq and the 1948 War," 131.

176. Segev, ed., *Behind the Screen*, 49–52.

177. Pirie-Gordon, Amman, to FO, 24 September 1947, PRO FO 371-61529; Segev, ed., *Behind the Screen*, 50. This provision was to prove crucial in facilitating the mass exodus that resulted in the creation of the Palestinian refugee problem. The Arab states' expectation of a massive flight of inhabitants from Palestine was based on the experience of 1936–1939, when tens of thousands of Palestinians fled to Lebanon, Syria, and Transjordan during the Arab Revolt. The League's Political Committee reaffirmed this provision at its meeting in Damascus on 11–15 May 1948, adding the proviso that able-bodied males, however, "would not be accepted by the Arab states" and that those of them who had already reached Arab states "would be sent back to Palestine" (*Behind the Screen*, 62).

178. Campbell to Jerusalem, 25 May 1946, PRO CO 537-1756.

179. Busk, Baghdad, to FO, 31 December 1947, PRO FO 371-68364.

180. Segev, ed., *Behind the Screen*, 66–68.

181. Segev, ed., *Behind the Screen*, 54.

182. Cohen, *Palestine and Great Powers*, 319–320.

183. Doran, *Pan-Arabism before Nasser*, 118–119.

184. Gelber, *Independence versus Nakba*, 33–34; Segev, ed., *Behind the Screen*, 55–56.

185. Sela, "Palestinian Arabs in the 1948 War," 149.

186. Gelber, *Independence versus Nakba,* 33.

187. Pappé, *Making of Arab-Israeli Conflict,* 72; Sela, "Palestinian Arabs in the 1948 War," 149–150.

188. Kimche and Kimche, *Both Sides of the Hill,* 60; Tripp, "Iraq and the 1948 War," 130–133.

189. Doran, *Pan-Arabism before Nasser,* 113.

190. Busk, Baghdad, to FO, 12 September 1947, quoting what he was told by the Iraqi prime minister.

191. Unsigned, "Memorandum on the Situation of the Jews in Iraq," undated but c. October 1949, with attached letter Victor Bernstein to Hector McNeil, 28 October 1949, PRO FO 371-75183.

192. Campbell to FO, 2, 3 December 1947, PRO FO 371-62994. For Beirut, see Houstoun Boswall to FO, 3, 12 December 1947, PRO FO 371-61743.

193. Campbell to FO, 4 December 1947, PRO FO 371-62994.

194. Campbell to FO, 5 December 1947, PRO FO 371-62994.

195. C. A. F. Dundas to FO, 1 December 1947, PRO FO 371-62184.

196. Dundas to Bevin, 3 December 1947, PRO FO 371-62184.

197. British Legation, Damascus, to Burrows, 2 December 1947, and Dundas to FO, 2 December 1947, both in PRO FO 371-62184.

198. "Translation of a Leading Article in '*Manar*' by Sheikh Mustafa Seba'i (the leader of the Muslim Brotherhood)—No. 323 of 3.12.47," PRO FO 371-62184.

199. E. Tuvia, "The Disaster of the Jews of Aden," 13 December 1947, CZA F39-76.

200. Elie Eliachar to Herbert Samuel, 31 January 1948, PRO FO 371-68366.

201. Unsigned, "What Happened in Aleppo on 30.11.47," undated, CZA S25-5288, which refers to dead and injured. Dundas, Damascus, to FO, 2 December 1947, PRO FO 371-62184, says there were "no casualties."

202. Eliachar to Samuel, 31 January 1948.

203. Dundas to FO, 2 December 1947, PRO FO 371-62184; Hahn, *Caught in the Middle East,* 41.

204. Campbell to FO, 2, 6 December 1947, PRO FO 371-62994.

205. Segev, ed., *Behind the Screen,* 71–72.

206. Busk, Baghdad, to FO, 14 December 1947, PRO FO 371-61583.

207. BMEO, Cairo, to FO, 11 December 1947, PRO FO 371-61580.

208. Campbell to FO, 8 December 1947, PRO FO 371-61580. The Syrian leaders told British diplomats similar things (see Dundas to FO, 5 December 1947 [no. 544], PRO FO 371-61580).

209. Mattar, *Mufti of Jerusalem,* 125–126.

210. Segev, ed., *Behind the Screen,* 55–56; Campbell to FO, 18 December 1947, PRO FO 371-61893.

211. F.A. and U.N. Department to Canada, etc., 10 January 1948, repeating telegram of 20 December 1947, PRO FO 371-61893.

212. G.J.C.C. Jenkins, "Conference of Arab Prime Ministers—December 1947," 30 December 1947, PRO FO 371-68365.

213. Burrows, untitled minute, 23 December 1947, PRO FO 371-61893.

214. Bandman, "Crystallization," 2:611. In fact, the quantities of equipment and ve-hicles shipped out of Palestine by 30 June 1948, the date of the actual comple-tion of the military withdrawal, were even greater (see "Crystallization," 2:637).

215. Louis, *British Empire in the Middle East*, 467.

216. Bandman, "Crystallization," 2:591.

217. Chiefs of staff committee, "Palestine—Implications of Withdrawal," 27 Octo-ber 1947, PRO FO 371-61796.

218. "Cabinet Meeting, 4th December 1947," PRO CAB 128/10; foreign and colo-nial secretaries, "Palestine," 3 December 1947, PRO CAB 129/22.

219. FO to UK delegation to UN, 5 December 1947, PRO FO 371-61890.

220. Eytan to Shertok, 4 March 1948, ISA FM 125/16.

221. Eytan, "Minutes of an Interview with the United Nations Secretariat Friday, March 5th, 1948," ISA FM 125/16.

CHAPTER 3. THE FIRST STAGE OF THE CIVIL WAR, NOVEMBER 1947–MARCH 1948

1. Milstein, *History of the War of Independence*, 2:62.

2. Milstein, *History of the War of Independence*, 2:22, 24–25.

3. Collins and Lapierre, *Jerusalem*, 40–41.

4. Entry for 30 December 1947, Yosef Nahmani Diary, Hashomer Archive.

5. Collins and Lapierre, *Jerusalem*, 43.

6. Tiroshi–Avshalom, "The Attack on the Buses near Petah Tikva on 30.11," 3 De-cember 1947, IDFA 481/49//62.

7. Ibrahim to Palmah GS, "Report on Patrol in Jaffa on 6–7.12.47," 7 December 1947, HA 73/98; HIS, "HIS Information," 30 November 1948, IDFA 900/52//58.

8. Tiroshi, "The Murder of 5 Shubaki Members near Ra'anana," 20 November 1947, HA 105/358.

9. Ada Ushpiz, "Yaldei Ha'ekdahim shel Halehi," *Haaretz*, 5 May 1995.

10. Jerusalem Haganah, "To the Members in the Bases," 3 December 1947, CZA S25-9210; E. L., "Tuviel, 6.12.47," 7 December 1947, CZA S25-4015 aleph.

11. Milstein, History of the *War of Independence*, 2:34–39.

12. Hapoel Ha'aravi, "Conversation with Hikmat al-Taji al-Faruqi," 2 February 1948, CZA S25-3569.

13. Bandman, *When Will Britain Withdraw from Jerusalem?* 93, n. 178, quoting chief of staff for commander-in-chief Middle East, 11 November 1947.

14. FO to UK delegation to UN, 5 December 1947, PRO FO 371-61890.

15. "Off-the-Record Background Press Conference with Sir Alan Cunningham," Jerusalem, 30 December 1947, CZA S25-9215.

16. Bandman, "Crystallization," 2:633.

17. David Ben-Gurion, protocol of meeting of JAE, 16 November 1947, CZA 45/1.

18. For a list of Arabs arrested and disarmed and Jews arrested and disarmed, see

Alan Cunningham to secretary of state for colonies, 24 December 1947, PRO FO 3721-61798.

19. Unsigned, "Initial Report on the Killing of the 4," 13 February 1948, CZA S25-4049; Jewish Agency, "Memorandum on British Policy in Palestine since the Adoption of the General Assembly's Palestine Resolution with Particular Reference to Security," 21 February 1948, CZA F39-580, 15.

20. Moshe Shertok to Karel Lisicky, 2 March 1948, CZA S25-5354.

21. Untitled minute, 22 December 1947, PRO FO 371-61583.

22. Indeed, one historian (Cohen, *Palestine and Great Powers,* 307) maintains that the Yishuv had a 1.5-to-1 edge over the Palestinians in this category.

23. Arab Department, HIS, "The Reaction of the Arab Public to the Internal Arab Terrorism (Summary for the Period 1.11.46–20.4.47)," 16 May 1947, HA 105/102. Among the prominent assassinations during this period are: Fawzi Darwish Husseini, who was killed by Husseini gunmen on 23 November 1946; George Anton, killed on 7 February 1947; and Farid Fakhr al-Din, killed on 24 March 1947.

24. Unsigned, "The Arab Institutions in Jerusalem Today: Organization and Leadership," 28 January 1948, IDFA 500/48//60.

25. Mordechai Abir, "The Local Arab Factor in the War of Independence," 1957/58, IDFA 1046/70//185; unsigned, "The Arab Institutions in Jerusalem Today: Organization and Leadership," 28 January 1948, IDFA 500/48//60.

26. Abba Hillel Silver, protocol of meeting of US Section, JAE, 11 March 1948, CZA Z5-2381.

27. Meir, *My Life,* 220–223.

28. G.J.C.C. Jenkins, "Conference of Arab Prime Ministers—December 1947," 30 December 1947, PRO FO 371-68365.

29. "Extract from: Monthly Political Intelligence Report Tripolitania," May 1948; E. C. S. Reid to I. W. Bell, 15 June 1948; and C. in C. MELF to War Office, 29 June 1948, all in PRO FO 371-69426A.

30. "*Al-Musawar,* 26.3.48 (translation)," 4 April 1948, CZA S25-8996.

31. Levenberg, *Military Preparations of Arab Community in Palestine,* 176–177.

32. Silver, protocol of meeting of US Section, JAE, 11 March 1948.

33. There are numerous references to British volunteers, often identified by name, in Haganah intelligence reports. One intercepted Arab letter, from Yusra Salah, Nablus, to Aida Oudi, Ramallah, from 14 April 1948 (CZA S25-9209), stated: "What surprises me is the British volunteers in the Arab army. Nablus is full of them. One of the nurses told me that a few of them are lying wounded in the hospital. . . . One day in the street I saw a group of these Britons. They looked cute in the *hatta* and *aakal* they were wearing. Why do you think they chose to serve in the Arab army? Was it because of hatred of the Jews? We also have among us some German soldiers in addition to the Yugoslavs." An intercepted letter from a British policeman, Gregory Kimston, serving in Jenin, to the British vice consul in Damascus, Peter Leslie, dated 13 April 1948, speaks of a group of British deserters in Arab ranks. "They receive PL40 per month with full board, free beer, and two packs of cigarettes a day" (CZA S25-9209).

34. Unsigned, "Muslim Fascists from Yugoslavia among the Arab Gangs in the Country," 13 February 1948, and "Proposals for Action Concerning the Europeans with the Gangs and Arab Armies," 11 June 1948, both in CZA S25-3991.

35. 01101 to HIS-AD, 5 January 1948, HA 105/37, names some of the Germans "serving in Haj Amin al-Husseini's HQ" in Nablus ("Adolf Schwabe," "Albert Grossman," "Rudolf Hoffman," etc.).

36. Milton M. Rubenfeld to JA, 8 December 1947, CZA S25-8172.

37. Markovizky, "Foreign Volunteers in the War of Independence," 1:539–550. Markovizky, *Fighting Ember*, 173–174.

38. Milstein, *History of the War of Independence*, 1:311.

39. *STH*, 3, pt. 2:1322.

40. Milstein, *History of the War of Independence*, 1:362.

41. Messer, *Hagana's Operations Plans*, 109–124.

42. Levenberg, *Military Preparations of Arab Community in Palestine*, 127, 134.

43. Unsigned (possibly Political Department, JA), "Report on the 'Najjada,'" undated (probably from 1946), CZA S25-9066.

44. Porath, *Palestinian Arab National Movement*, 76; Levenberg, *Military Preparations of Arab Community in Palestine*, 137.

45. Unsigned (but probably Political Department, JA), "Futuwwa," 30 October 1946, CZA S25-9066.

46. Levenberg, *Military Preparations of Arab Community in Palestine*, 210.

47. Shimoni (?) to Eliahu Sasson, 20 January 1948, CZA S25-4015 aleph.

48. See, e.g., unsigned, "Meeting with Arab Mukhtars," 18 January 1948, IDFA 2644/49//352. See also Morris, *Birth of Palestinian Problem Revisited*, 96–97; and Cohen, *Army of Shadows*, 232–234.

49. Cohen, *Army of Shadows*, 263–267. Quotation from Anderson, *Imagined Communities*, 7.

50. Josh Palmon, "Interrogation of a Prisoner Captured in the Battle of Yehiam on 21.1.48," HA 105/215 aleph.

51. Gershon Gilead, "The ALA," undated but from the mid-1950s, IDFA 922/75//648; Sela, "ALA in Galilee," 1:207–267.

52. Ilan, *Origin of Arab-Israeli Arms Race*, 56–57.

53. Sela, "ALA in Galilee," 237–238.

54. Nazzal, *Palestinian Exodus from Galilee*, 45, 50, 56, 65–66 ff.

55. Gelber, "Druze and Jews," 229–252.

56. Nazzal, *Palestinian Exodus from Galilee*, 11.

57. Ehud to Carmeli Brigade, "Report on Operation against Arms Convoy and Arab commanders on 17.3.1948," 19 March 1948, IDFA 5942/49//10.

58. A. L., "Arab League Military Committee," 2 April 1948, CZA S25-8996; Levenberg, *Military Preparations of Arab Community in Palestine*, 198.

59. Mordechai Rosenberg (Kidron) to Golda Myerson, 5 November 1947, CZA S25-9215.

60. A. L., "A Conversation with Zaʿafar Dajani, chairman of the Jaffa Chamber of Commerce," 26 November 1947, CZA S25-3300.

61. Pirim, "The Feeling among Palestine's Arabs," 29 October 1947, CZA S25-3300.

62. HGS-Operations, "Summary of the Situation of the [Haganah] Organization, Enemy Forces—in Light of the Recent Disturbances," 19 December 1947, IDFA 481/49//23.

63. Haganah spokesman, "A Trip across the Country," 2 February 1948, CZA S25-7719.

64. HIS, "The Atmosphere and Happenings among the Arab Christians," 9 February 1948, IDFA 500/48//60.

65. HIS, "Attacks on Christians," undated but from February or March 1948, HA 105/195.

66. Yavne to HIS-AD, 11 April 1948, HA 105/257.

67. HIS-AD to Hillel, 30 November 1947, HA 73/98.

68. Page of Haganah logbook covering 2 December 1947, HA 73/98; HIS-AD to Danin and Yisrael Galili, 1 December 1947, HA 73/98.

69. HIS, "HIS Information Circular," 9 December 1947, HA 105/61.

70. See S. P. Emory to bishop of Jerusalem, 13 December 1947, SAMECA, J&EM LXXI/2.

71. For more, see Morris, *Birth of Palestinian Refugee Problem Revisited*, 65–162.

72. Na'im, "Details from a Talk with Dr. Dajani," 24 December 1947, HA 105/215 aleph.

73. British Military HQ, Palestine, "Fortnightly Intelligence Newsletter," 30 January 1948, PRO WO-275-64.

74. "The Fifth Meeting [of the Haifa NC]," 9 December 1947, in Goren, *Fall of Arab Haifa*, 256–257.

75. The text of the communiqué is reproduced in Goren, *Fall of Arab Haifa*, 263–264.

76. Gelber, *Palestine, 1948*, 77; Hashmonai, "Doings among the Arabs," 12 January 1948, IDFA 500/48//60.

77. Tulkarm NC, communiqué, 27 February 1948, HA 105/102.

78. Husseini to Tiberias NC, undated but from March 1948, HA 105/257; Yavne to HIS-AD, 18 March 1948, reporting on a British censor's report on a letter from Husseini to the Jerusalem NC of 8 March. See also Yavne, report, 21 March 1948, and Gershon Avner to HIS-AD, 19 March 1948, both in HA 105/257.

79. HIS-AD, "The Migratory Movement . . . ," 30 June 1948, HHA-ACP 10.95.13 (1).

80. Campbell to Jerusalem, 25 May 1946, PRO CO 537-1756.

81. Pirie-Gordon to FO, 24 September 1947, PRO FO 371-61529; Segev, ed., *Behind the Screen*, 50.

82. Unsigned, "Summary of Intelligence for 4.12.47, 13:00–19:00 Hours," CZA S25-9210.

83. HIS, "Summary of Hiram Information," 10 February 1948, IDFA 7249/49//152.

84. HIS, "HIS Information," 28 March 1948, IDFA 900/52//58.

85. "Report of 'Shahar' [the Palmah's Arab Platoon] Patrol in Haifa," 10 April 1948, HA 105/257.

86. Hashmonai to general distribution, "State of Readiness for Tuesday and Wednesday, 23–24.12.47," IDFA 500/48//60.

87. JA, "In the Arab Public," 2 March 1948, HA 105/100.

88. Committee for Economic Defense, "Information on the Arab Economy, Bulletin No. 1," 11 April 1948, HA 105/146.

89. "Zarhi Says," 9 December 1947, IDFA 481/49//62.

90. Committee for Economic Defense, "Information on the Arab Economy, Bulletin No. 11," 11 May 1948, HA 105/146.

91. Untitled memorandum, possibly by HIS, undated but probably from mid- or late May 1948, HA 105/119.

92. Jenkins, "Conference of Arab Prime Ministers—December 1947," 30 December 1947.

93. Unsigned (possibly Reuven Zaslani), untitled memorandum, 11 December 1947, CZA S25-4046; unsigned, "Protocol of Meeting on Arab Affairs from 9.3.48," IDFA 8275/49//126.

94. Ben-Pazi, "Citrus Harvest."

95. HIS, "Information Circular," 24 November 1947, IDFA 900/52//58.

96. Unsigned, "Aryeh," 11 December 1947, CZA S25-4011.

97. Unsigned, untitled report, HIS, 31 December 1947, HA 105/123.

98. Cunningham to colonial secretary, 3 January 1948, PRO FO 816/115.

99. See, e.g., re Haifa, Haddad to Adina, 24 January 1948, CZA S25-4015 aleph.

100. Ben-Gurion, *War Diary,* entry for 19 January 1948, 163.

101. Haifa NC, "Communique No. 7," 22 February 1948, HA 105/54 aleph.

102. JA Political Department/Arab Division, "In the Arab Camp," 21 December 1947, CZA S25-9051; high commissioner to secretary of state, "Weekly Intelligence Appreciation," 3 January 1948, PRO FO 816/115.

103. HIS-AD to Hillel, 4 December 1947, HA 73/98.

104. For example, Ephraim Ben-Haim, of Kibbutz Kiryat Anavim: "It had not yet occurred to anybody to see those disturbances as a real war" (*Kiryat Anavim,* 86).

105. Ben-Gurion, protocol of meeting, JAE, 6 January 1948, CZA.

106. Gelber, *Emergence of Jewish Army,* 214, quoting Reuven Zaslani, Shiloah, to Shertok, 11 December 1947.

107. Galili, protocol of meeting, Defense Committee, 13 November 1947, CZA S25-9343.

108. Ben-Gurion, protocol of meeting, Defense Committee, 4 December 1947, CZA S25-9344.

109. Cunningham to colonial secretary, 9 December 1947, PRO FO 371-61797.

110. Hillel, "Meeting of [Haganah] N[ational] C[ommand] 10/12," IDFA 481/49//64.

111. Hillel to Sasha (Yigal Allon), "Operational Order 5.1.48," 5 January 1948, IDFA 922/75//1206.

112. Galili, protocol of meeting, Defense Committee, 11 December 1947, CZA S25-9344.

113. Jerusalem Information Bureau to members of Haganah, Jerusalem, 10 December 1947, CZA S25-9210.

114. Yigael Yadin to Alexandroni Battalion, "Document [i.e., Order] for Retaliatory Strike A," 9 December 1947, IDFA 922/75//949.

115. Arik, "The Sharon Battalion's Operation," 12 December 1947, IDFA 922/75//949.

116. Ben-Gurion to Eli'ezer Kaplan, 14 December 1947, CZA S25-1700.

117. Yadin to brigade OCs, etc., "Instructions on Planning Initiated Operations," 18 January 1948, IDFA 1196/52//1.

118. Alexandroni OC to battalions, 19 December 1947, IDFA 2687/49//35.

119. See, e.g., Hashmonai, "Relations with the Neighboring Villages," 24 December 1947, IDFA 500/48//60.

120. Haganah, "To the Arabs of Palestine," 29 December 1947, CZA S25-9051.

121. Yirmiyahu to battalions, etc., 3 February 1948, IDFA 922/75//1224.

122. Galili to brigade OCs, 24 March 1948, IDFA 922/75//1219. Similar thinking informed a memorandum by two senior JA Political Department officials submitted a few days before (see Haim Berman and Sasson, "Proposals," 13 March 1948, CZA S25-9383). The memorandum also proposed, despite the three-month-long Palestinian Arab assault on the Yishuv, the establishment of a Palestinian Arab state that would coexist, according to UN 1947 partition plan borders, alongside Israel.

123. "Summary of the Meeting of the Arab Affairs Advisers in Dora Camp, 31.3.48," IDFA 4663/49//125.

124. "Summary of the Meeting of the Arab Affairs Advisers in Dora Camp 6.4.48," IDFA 4663/49//125.

125. Haganah HQ, "To Our Members, Daily Information Bulletin No. 10," 18 December 1947, HA 105/61.

126. Transcript of broadcast on 7 December 1948, HA 105/358.

127. Lapidot, *Flames of Revolt*, 285; Milstein, *History of the War of Independence*, 1:52.

128. Milstein, *History of the War of Independence*, 2:50–51.

129. Cunningham to colonial secretary, 5 January 1948, PRO FO 371-68500.

130. Milstein, *History of the War of Independence*, 3:85–88.

131. Shertok, protocol of meeting, US Section, JAE, 26 September 1947, CZA Z5-59.

132. See, e.g., unsigned, "A Meeting with Nahariya Council on 14.10.47," CZA S25-210.

133. Galili, protocol of meeting, Defense Committee, 10 February 1948, CZA S25-9346.

134. Milstein, *History of the War of Independence*, 2:66–75.

135. Unsigned, "Reliable Information from 10.2.48," IDFA 500/48//60; Milstein, *History of the War of Independence*, 3:203.

136. Investigating Committee, "Report of the Yishuv's Investigating Committee

into the Disaster That Occurred in the Haifa Oil Refinery on Tuesday . . . (30.12.47)," 25 January 1948, CZA S25-4037.

137. 01101 to HIS-AD, 1 January 1948, HA 105/23.

138. Palmah logbook of operations, entry for 5 January 1948, IDFA 661/69//36; 01011 to HIS-AD, 6 January 1948, HA 105/32 aleph; 00001 to HIS-AD, "The Attacks on Balad ash Sheikh and Hawassa," 9 January 1948, HA 105/32 aleph; Milstein, *History of the War of Independence*, 2:93–97.

139. Yaakov Riftin and Ben-Gurion, protocol of meeting of Defense Committee, 1 January 1948, CZA S25-9345.

140. Milstein, *History of the War of Independence*, 2:142–144.

141. Pinhas to Ali, "Report on Khisas Operation," 22 December 1947, IDFA 922/75//1224; Cunningham to colonial secretary, 20 December 1947, PRO FO 371-61796; Moshe Dayan to Ya'akov Dori, 30 December 1947, IDFA 481/49//23; Morris, *Birth of Palestinian Refugee Problem Revisited*, 79.

142. Ezra Danin to Sasson, 23 December 1947, CZA S25-4057; Yosef Sapir, protocol of meeting of Defense Committee, 25 December 1947, CZA S25-9344.

143. Gelber, *Palestine, 1948*, 62.

144. Milstein, *History of the War of Independence*, 2:261–269.

145. Karmi, *In Search of Fatima*, 90.

146. Unsigned, "Following Is a Summary of Information on Hotel Semiramis, a Regional Arab Base for Security in Katamon," 8 January 1948, CZA S25-4013.

147. Protocol of meeting of JAE, 11 January 1948, CZA.

148. Cunningham to colonial secretary, 7 January 1948, PRO FO 816/115; Ben-Gurion, protocol of meeting of JAE, 6 January 1948, CZA; Ben-Gurion to Cunningham, 8 January 1948, CZA S25-4013.

149. HIS-AD, "Summary of the Influence of the Jewish Reprisals on the Arabs," 11 May 1948, HA 105/31.

150. Unsigned, "Report on the Ben Shemen Incident," undated, CZA S25-4148.

151. Milstein, *History of the War of Independence*, 3:43.

152. Levenberg, *Military Preparations of Arab Community in Palestine*, 192–193.

153. HIS, "Information from Tubas," 27 January 1948, HA 105/215 aleph.

154. Cunningham to colonial secretary, 4 February 1948, PRO FO 371-68367.

155. UK Delegation to the UN to FO, 9 February 1948, PRO FO 371-68366.

156. Milstein, *History of the War of Independence*, 3:46–53.

157. Palmah HQ, "Daily Report," 16 February 1948, IDFA 922/75//1066; Shertok, meeting of US Section, JAE, 11 March 1948, CZA Z5-2381.

158. Milstein, *History of the War of Independence*, 3:72.

159. Baruch to Golani, "Report on the Attack on Tirat-Tzvi on 16.2.48," 4 March 1948, IDFA 1196/52//1; Milstein, *History of the War of Independence*, 3:66–80; Ben-Gurion, *War Diary*, entry for 17 February 1948, 250–251; al-Qawuqji, "Memoirs, 1948," pt. 1:27–58.

160. Uzi, untitled memorandum, 19 January 1948, IDFA 922/75//283; Milstein, *History of the War of Independence*, 3:325.

161. Milstein, *History of the War of Independence,* 3:1–40.
162. Tall, *Memoirs,* 18.
163. Collins and Lapierre, *Jerusalem,* 173–175.
164. Milstein, *History of the War of Independence,* 3:106–107.
165. Ben-Gurion, protocol of meeting of Defense Committee, 24 February 1948, CZA S25-9346.
166. HIS, "Explosion in Ben-Yehuda Street (Tentative Summary)," undated, CZA S25-4151; Committee of Investigation of the Ben-Yehuda Street Bombing, "Session 5," 2 March 1948, CZA S25-10391; Ben-Gurion, protocol of meeting of Defense Committee, 24 February 1948, CZA S25-9346; Milstein, *History of the War of Independence,* 3:109–113.
167. Leo Kohn to William Macatee, 16 March 1948, and Macatee to Kohn, 18 March 1948, both in CZA S25-4151; Milstein, *History of the War of Independence,* 3:113–118.
168. See, e.g., al-Qawuqji, "Memoirs, 1948," pt. 1:31–34.
169. Milstein, *History of the War of Independence,* 4:108–116.
170. Milstein, *History of the War of Independence,* 4:121–59; Kohn, "Note for the Record," 28 March 1948, and unsigned, untitled memorandum, 28 March 1948, both in CZA S25-4147.
171. Milstein, *History of the War of Independence,* 4:80–107.
172. Milstein, *History of the War of Independence,* 4:161.
173. Milstein, *History of the War of Independence,* 4:160–180.
174. Levy, *Jerusalem in the War of Independence,* 137.
175. Cunningham to colonial secretary, "Weekly Intelligence Appreciation," 3 April 1948, PRO FO 371-68503.
176. JA Statistical Department, "Summary of Casualties in the Disturbances during the Months of December 1947–January–March 1948," May 1948, CZA S25-3986. The Arabs had suffered a similar number of dead (see "Summary of Events on 9/4/48," PRO CO 537-3857—"967" Arabs killed by "8/9.4.48").

CHAPTER 4. THE SECOND STAGE OF THE CIVIL WAR, APRIL–MID-MAY 1948

1. Alan Cunningham, "Weekly Intelligence Appreciation," 3 April 1948, PRO FO 371-68503.
2. Harry Truman to Henry Morgenthau, Jr., 2 December 1948, ISA 2267/30.
3. I. J. Linton to Golda Myerson, 22 December 1947, CZA S25-1700.
4. Baron Inverchapel to FO (no. 43), 5 January 1948, PRO FO 371-68402.
5. Inverchapel to FO (no. 44), 5 January 1948, PRO FO 371-68402.
6. Lord Samuel to Clement Attlee, 15 March 1948, and attached "Proposals for Palestine," PRO FO 371-68503.
7. Abba Hillel Silver, protocol of meeting of JAE, 25 January 1948, CZA 45/2.
8. State Department to president, undated but sent to Truman on 21 February

1948, and Truman to George C. Marshall, 22 February 1948, *FRUS, 1948*, 5:645, 637–640.

9. Warren Austin at Security Council meeting, 24 February 1948, *FRUS, 1948*, 5:651–654.

10. Eliahu Epstein, "Luncheon with the Editorial Board of *The New York Times* on March 4, 1948," 5 March 1948, CZA F39-580.

11. Policy planning staff, "Review of Current Trends U.S. Foreign Policy," 24 February 1948, *FRUS, 1948*, 5:655–657.

12. Marshall to Austin, 16 March 1948, *FRUS, 1948*, 5:728–729.

13. Robert M. McClintock, "Memorandum of Telephone Conversation," 17 March 1948, *FRUS, 1948*, 5:729–731.

14. McClintock to director of the Executive Secretariat, 17 March 1948, *FRUS, 1948*, 5:731–732.

15. Austin to Marshall, 17 March 1948, *FRUS, 1948*, 5:736–737.

16. M. Truman, *Truman*, 388; Weizmann, *Trial and Error*, 472. Truman himself was vague about what had happened (Truman, *Memoirs*, 2:161).

17. *FRUS, 1948*, 5:742–744.

18. ISA, *Documents, December 1947–May 1948*, "A. H. Silver: Address before the Security Council (19 March 1948)," 476.

19. M. Truman, *Truman*, 388–389, quoting from Truman's "calendar."

20. "Editorial Note," and Carlisle Humelsine, "Memorandum . . . ," 22 March 1948, both in *FRUS, 1948*, 5:744–746, 749–750.

21. *FRUS, 1948*, 5:750, n. 3.

22. Quoted in Gelber, *Independence versus Nakba*, 113.

23. Yitzhak Ben-Zvi at meeting of JAE, 10 April 1948, CZA.

24. Gelber, *Independence versus Nakba*, 112, quoting Levy ("Yavne") report of 31 March 1948. Ben-Gurion, *War Diary*, entry for 20 April 1948, 359, apparently citing David Shaltiel, was more explicit: "In our public morale is low, many shirkers, unwillingness to fight. The element [i.e., composition] in Jerusalem is 20% normal [people], 20% privileged ([the] university and others), 60% strange (provincials, Middle Ages [i.e., ultra-orthodox] and such)."

25. Michael Comay to Golda Myerson, Bernard Joseph, and Leo Kohn, 1 April 1948, ISA, *Documents, December 1947–May 1948*, 546–547.

26. Ben-Gurion, *War Diary*, entry for 31 March 1948, 330–331.

27. Ben-Gurion, *War Diary*, entry for 31 March 1948, 330; Milstein, *History of the War of Independence*, 4:244.

28. Bandman, *When Will Britain Withdraw from Jerusalem?* 48. Troop numbers were down to 10,730 by 1 May.

29. Pierson[CK] Dixon, Prague, to FO, 1 April 1948, and John Beith, "Arms Traffic to Palestine by Air from Czechoslovakia," 7 April 1948, both in PRO FO 371-68635; Milstein, *History of the War of Independence*, 4:249–250.

30. Milstein, *History of the War of Independence*, 4:251–256.

31. Ilan, *Origin of Arab-Israeli Arms Race*, 174.

32. David Ben-Gurion to Moshe Shertok, 16 April 1948, ISA, *Documents, December 1947–May 1948*, 647.

33. Zamiri, "Guidelines for Planning Regional Battles for the Month of February," 26 January 1948, IDFA 959/49//202.

34. Shiloni to Yisrael Galili, 4 January 1948, HA 80/105/1.

35. HGS/Operations, "Tochnit Dalet," 10 March 1948, IDFA 922/75//949.

36. See, e.g., HGS/Operations, "Tochnit Dalet," "Alexandroni [Brigade]," 10 March 1948, IDFA 922/75//949.

37. Khalidi, "Plan Dalet"; Pappé, *Making of Arab-Israeli Conflict*, 89–96.

38. HGS/Operations, "Tochnit Dalet," 10 March 1948.

39. "Nahshon" Corps HQ to Battalions A, B, C, etc., [?] April 1948, IDFA 922/75//1233.

40. Unsigned, "The Conquest of the Qastal, 3.4.48," undated, IDFA 661/69//45.

41. Gershon Avner to HIS-AD, 13 April 1948, HA 105/31. A later HIS report stated that "four German captains and two Englishmen" were among the dead (Avner to HIS-AD, 13 April 1948, HA 105/92 aleph).

42. Tenth Battalion to "Nahshon," etc., "Report on Operation "Yatom," [?] April 1948, IDFA 661/69//45; "Naʿim (Naaman)" to HIS-AD, "The Demolition of the Orphans House," 7 April 1948, HA 105/31; Ayalon, *Givʿati Brigade in the War of Establishment*, 392–422; Milstein, *History of the War of Independence*, 4:263–264.

43. Milstein, *History of the War of Independence*, 4:280.

44. Milstein, *History of the War of Independence*, 4:306–312.

45. Milstein, *History of the War of Independence*, 4:322.

46. Milstein, *History of the War of Independence*, 4:315.

47. Al-Sakakini, "*Such Am I, Oh World,*" entry for 9 April 1948, 235.

48. Milstein, *History of the War of Independence*, 4:327.

49. Unsigned, "The Re-Conquest of the Qastal," 9 April 1948, IDFA 922/75//1233.

50. Unsigned, "Report on the Reinforcement of the Qastal," 7 [sic] April 1948 (should be 9 April 1948), IDFA 661/69//45.

51. "The Meeting with the Heads of Branches, 4.4.48," IDFA 481/49//18. A similar instruction reached Yadin from Galili (Galili to Yigael Yadin, 5 (?) April 1948, IDFA 661/69//45), though it called for "harassing" the villages into flight.

52. Morris, *Birth of Palestinian Refugee Problem Revisited*, 91, 97.

53. Yavne to HIS-AD, 12 April 1948, IDFA 5254/49//372.

54. Yavne to HIS, 13 April 1948, IDFA 5254/49//372.

55. Eliʿezer to Tzadik, etc., "Report on the Conquest of Deir Yassin," 10 April 1948, IDFA 500/48//56.

56. Yavne to HIS-AD, 12 April 1948; Yizhar Beʾer, "The Hidden Villages," *Kol Haʿir*, Jerusalem, 25 November 1988.

57. Unsigned, "Announcement of the Haganah on the Deir Yassin Affair," 12 April 1948, HA 105/31; JA to King ʿAbdullah, 12 April 1948, ISA, *Documents, December 1947–May 1948*, 625–626.

58. Head of the Royal Diwan, Amman, to JA, 12 April 1948, CZA S25-9038.

59. Even Cunningham fell prey to the exaggerations. On 17 April he cabled Arthur Creech Jones: "Women and children were stripped, lined up, photographed and then slaughtered by automatic fire and the survivors have told of even more incredible bestialities" ("Weekly Intelligence Appreciation," PRO CO 537-3869). The British, apparently, were ready to believe anything about the IZL and LHI.

60. Hazem Nusseibeh, a Palestinian official, later explained the exaggerations thus: "We weren't sure that the Arab armies for all their talk were really going to come. We thought to shock the population of the Arab countries to stir pressures against their governments" ("Interview with [Hazem Nusseibeh], May 1968," Larry Collins Papers, Georgetown University Library).

61. Alec Kirkbride to Ernest Bevin (no. 244), 23 April 1948, conveying the text of ʿAbdullah to Cunningham, 23 April 1948, PRO FO 816/117.

62. IZL, "Announcement on the Deir Yassin Affair," undated but c. 12 April 1948, IDFA 5254/49/372.

63. Text of Kol Zion Halohemet broadcast, 14 April 1948, JI, IZL, kaf-4, 8/13.

64. Begin, *Revolt*, 164.

65. See, e.g., Hiram to Jeremiah, 15 April 1948, IDFA 5942/49//23; and Yavne to HIS-AD, 15 April 1948, HA 105/257.

66. Entry for 1 May 1948, Ben-Gurion, *War Diary*, 2:378.

67. British Army HQ Palestine, "Fortnightly Intelligence Newsletter, 21 April 1948," PRO WO 275–64.

68. Aharon Cohen, "In Face of the Arab Evacuation," 20 May 1948, HHA-ACP 10.95.11 (8); statement by Yaʿakov Hazan, protocol of meeting of Mapam Political Committee, 26 May 1948, HHA 66.90 (1).

69. HIS-AD, "The Migratory Movement," 30 June 1948, HHA-ACP 10.95.13 (1). For fuller treatments of Deir Yassin, see Morris, *Birth of Palestinian Refugee Problem Revisited*, 237–240; Morris, "Historiography of Deir Yassin"; Milstein, *History of the War of Independence*, 4:343–396.

70. Leo Kohn to General MacMillan, 16 April 1948, ISA, *Documents, December 1947–May 1948*, 649.

71. Ben-Gurion, protocol of meeting of JAE, 21 April 1948, CZA 45/2.

72. Ben-Gurion, *War Diary*, entry for 20 April 1948, 359–360.

73. Collins and Lapierre, *Jerusalem*, 283–291.

74. Ben-Gurion to Nahshon OC, 13 April 1948, IDFA 661/69//45.

75. See, e.g., Nahshon HQ to Battalion 1, 15 April 1948, concerning the conquest of al-Qubeib and Beit Jiz, and Nahshon HQ to Battalion 2, 15 April 1948, regarding the conquest of Beit Suriq, both in IDFA 236/53/1; and Palmah HQ to HGS, 18 April 1948, IDFA 196/71//83 ("to cause a wandering of refugees").

76. General staff to Yevussi, etc., "Document," 19 April 1948, IDFA 661/69//45.

77. Harel Corps HQ to Battalions 1, 2, etc., "Operational Order," 22 April 1948, IDFA 922/75//1233.

78. Palmah HQ to General Staff, "Daily Report," 23 April 1948, IDFA 922/75//1066.

79. Palmah HQ to General Staff, "Daily Report," 25 April 1948, IDFA 922/75//1066; Levy, *Jerusalem in the War of Independence*, 212–213; Gilead, ed., *Book of the Palmah*, 2:245, 914; Ben-Gurion, *War Diary*, entry for 25 April 1948, 268–269.

80. Levy, *Jerusalem in the War of Independence*, 222.

81. Morris, *Birth of Palestinian Refugee Problem Revisited*, 121–123.

82. Ben-Gurion, *War Diary*, entry for 25 April 1948, 369; Tal, *War in Palestine*, 118.

83. Gilead, ed., *Book of the Palmah*, 2:247.

84. Levy, *Jerusalem in the War of Independence*, 218.

85. Among those who fled, bullets whizzing past, were the educator and diarist Khalil al-Sakakini and his family. They eventually ended up in Cairo (Sakakini, *Jerusalem and I*, 121–122).

86. Levy, *Jerusalem in the War of Independence*, 220.

87. Levy, *Jerusalem in the War of Independence*, 169–180.

88. Al-Qawuqji, "Memoirs, 1948," pt. 1:37.

89. Levenberg, *Military Preparations of Arab Community in Palestine*, 207.

90. Tzuri to HIS-AD, "The Battle of Mishmar Ha'emek," 8 May 1948, HA 105/127; al-Qawuqji, "Memoirs, 1948," pt. 1:39.

91. *Mishmar Ha'emek at War*, 13–14.

92. Cunningham to secretary of state, 10 April 1948, PRO CO 537-3869.

93. *Mishmar Ha'emek at War*, 42–43.

94. Golani to Galili, 8 April 1948, 21:30 hrs., IDFA 128/51//50.

95. Tzuri to HIS-AD, "The Battle of Mishmar Ha'emek," 8 May 1948.

96. Protocol of meeting of Mapai Center, 24 July 1948, LPA 23 aleph/48. Already on 5 April 1948, Yadin had instructed the Golani Brigade to expel the inhabitants of Daliyat al-Ruha and Abu Shusha, neighboring Mishmar Ha'emek (Yadin to Golani, IDFA 922/75//1025).

97. Reports in *Al-Ahram* (Cairo), 16 April 1948, and *Al-Masri*, 18 April 1948, both quoted in "In the Arab Press," c. 19 April 1948, CZA S25-8996.

98. Major C. de B. de Lisle, M.I.3, "Present Situation in Palestine," 22 April 1948, PRO FO 371-68504.

99. OC B Company to OC Hittin Battalion, undated, IDFA 922/75//648.

100. Dror, *Life and Times of Sadeh*, 356.

101. Kirkbride to FO, 16 April 1948, PRO FO 371-68852.

102. P. M. Broadmead, Damascus, to FO, 21 April 1948, PRO FO 371-68370.

103. Ben-Gurion, *War Diary*, entry for 18 April 1948, 356.

104. Golani to HGS, Yadin, etc., 12 April 1948, IDFA 128/51//50.

105. "Logbook of the Battle," entry for 15 April 1948, IDFA 1058/52//1.

106. Tiroshi, Eytan, to HIS-AD, 20 April 1948, HA 105/31. "We now have the opportunity to cleanse the whole Carmel and Hills of Ephraim areas of their Arab inhabitants," commented the HIS officer.

107. Tzuri, 19 April 1948, HA 105/31.

108. Eliezer Bauer to Galili, Moshe Mann, Baruch Rabinov, and Ya'akov Riftin, 14 April 1948, Eliezer Bauer Papers, Kibbutz Hazore'a Archive.

109. For fuller descriptions of the battle, see Orren, "Rebuffing of ALA at Mishmar Ha'emek"; al-Qawuqji, "Memoirs, 1948"; and *Mishmar Ha'mek at War.*

110. HIS, "In the Arab Press," c. 19 April 1948, CZA S25-8996.

111. Unsigned, "Report on the Battle in the Ramat Yohanan Bloc," undated, IDFA 7353/49//46.

112. Shakib Wahab to ALA HQ, [?] (possibly 15) April 1948, HA 105/127 aleph.

113. Eshel, *Carmeli Brigade,* 122.

114. *STH,* 3, pt. 2:1567.

115. Wahab to ALA HQ, 17 April 1948, HA 105/127 aleph.

116. Eshel, *Carmeli Brigade,* 108–124.

117. Wahab to ALA HQ, 17 April 1948. A somewhat different translation of the (Arabic) letter is in Eshel, *Carmeli Brigade,* 123–124.

118. Segal to all branches, "Summary of Information in the Area from Friday 16.4.48 14:00 hrs. until Sunday 18.4.48 08:00 hrs.," IDFA 7353/49//46.

119. Wahab to ALA HQ, 2 May 1948, HA 105/127 aleph.

120. Wahab to ALA HQ, undated but c. 5 May 1948, HA 105/127 aleph.

121. Gelber, "Druze and Jews," 235.

122. Segal to all branches, "Summary of Information in the Area from Friday 16.4.48 14:00 hrs. until Sunday 18.4.48 08:00 hrs.," undated, IDFA 7353/49//46.

123. Unsigned, "Report on the Battle in the Ramat Yohanan Bloc," undated, IDFA 7353/49//46.

124. Morris, *1948 and After,* 171–176.

125. Tzuri, Chava, to HIS-AD, 21 April 1948, HA 105/257.

126. Morris, *Birth of Palestinian Refugee Problem Revisited,* 183.

127. Tzuri, Chava, to HIS-AD, "Miscellaneous Information about the Evacuation of Tiberias," 21 April 1948, HA 105/257; Av, *Struggle for Tiberias,* 199–207.

128. Twelfth Battalion/Intelligence to Golani Brigade/Intelligence, [?] April 1948, IDFA 128/51//18. The Haganah attributed the decision mainly to "demoralization," economic conditions, the prior flight of local leaders, the events at Nasir al-Din, and the Haganah's military successes. Palestinian leaders later—falsely—charged variously that the Jews and/or the British had "expelled" the population (colonial secretary, New York, to Cunningham, 24 April 1948, SAMECA CP III/4/23; E. N. Koussa, letter to the editor, *Palestine Post,* 6 February 1949). A (highly imaginative) description of the fall of Arab Tiberias is to be found in *Falastin,* 4 September 1955 (an abridged translation is in IDFA 922/75//695).

129. Entries for 21, 22 April 1948, Yosef Nahmani Diary, Hashomer Archive.

130. Morris, *Birth of Palestinian Refugee Problem Revisited,* 183–185; unsigned, "The Fall of Tiberias," *Falastin,* 4 September 1955, IDFA 922/75//695.

131. Protocol of meeting of Defense Committee, 18 April 1948, CZA S25-9348.

132. Gen. Hugh Stockwell, "Report," 24 April 1948, SAMECA CP V/4/102.

133. Carmel, *Northern Battles,* 86.

134. Stockwell, "Report," 24 April 1948, put the numbers at "400 trained Jews, backed by an indeterminate number of reserves" and "some 2,000 Arabs." Haj

Nimr al-Khatib later claimed that the Arab militias in the town had "415" rifles, "15" Sten submachine guns, and a handful of machineguns and 2-inch and 60-mm mortars (see translation of al-Khatib, "Following the Naqba," 13, IDFA 922/75//932).

135. Eshel, *Carmeli Brigade,* 138.

136. Carmel, *Northern Battles,* 102.

137. Max to Bar-Kochva, "Report on the Operation in Arab Halissa, 22–24 April 1948," undated, IDFA 7353/49//46.

138. Tactical HQ, 1st Battalion Coldstream Guards, "Battalion Sitrep. No 16," 22 April 1948, PRO WO 261-297.

139. Protocol of meeting of Mistaaravim [i.e., Palmah scouts/spies], quoting from a report by "Havakuk," written c. 23 April 1948, HA 25/12.

140. Segev, ed., *In Enemy Eyes,* 23–24.

141. Cunningham to secretary of state, "Weekly Intelligence Appreciation," 1 May 1948, PRO FO 371-68503.

142. Stockwell, "Report," 24 April 1948.

143. Stockwell, "Report," 24 April 1948.

144. Stockwell, "Report," 24 April 1948.

145. Houstoun Boswall, Beirut, to FO, 22 April 1948, 13:32 hrs.; Broadmead, Damascus, to FO, 22 April 1948, 11:58hrs.; and Campbell, Cairo, to FO, 22 April 1948, 21:07 hrs., all in PRO CO 537-3901.

146. Harry Beilin, "Operation Haifa," 25 April 1948, CZA S25-10584.

147. Stockwell, "Report," 24 April 1948, "Annexure II."

148. Carmel, *Northern Battles,* 107; Sasson to Shertok, New York, 23 April 1948, ISA, *Documents, December 1947–May 1948,* 670.

149. Tamir Goren, "Haifa," 189, basing himself on the transcripts of interviews in the early 1970s with two HIS officers, Ephraim Alro'i and Aharon Kremer, argues that orders had reached the local notables by telephone from someone in Beirut to evacuate the city. But the evidence is of dubious value: the two "witnesses" were unable to say who had given the wiretapped orders to whom, and in any case, their testimony was elicited or volunteered some twenty-five years after the event. See also Goren, *Haifa,* 217–223.

150. Hiram to HIS-AD, 28 May 1948, HA 105/252.

151. Stockwell, "Report," 24 April 1948; Cyril Marriott to Bevin, 26 April 1948, PRO FO 371-68505; Beilin, "Operation Haifa," 25 April 1948.

152. Solomon to Political Department, Israel Foreign Ministry, 1 April 1949, ISA FM 2401/11.

153. Beilin, "Operation Haifa," 25 April 1948; Carmel, *Northern Battles,* 107. But neither Stockwell nor Cyril Marriott, the British consul-to-be, mention Levy's appeal.

154. Carmel, *Northern Battles,* 107.

155. For reports on these orders, see Hiram to HIS-AD, 28 April 1948 ("The AHC's Order to the Arabs of Haifa"), HA 105/257; Aubrey Lippincott to secretary of state, 26 April 1948, USNA, Haifa Consulate, Classified Records 1948, 800–Po-

litical Affairs; and Cunningham to Secretary of State, 25 April 1948, SAMECA CP III/4/52. For the "treachery" charge, see, e.g., "Summary of Carmeli Brigade Information No. 1, from 1.5 to 5.5," 5 May 1948, IDFA 273/52//5.

156. Haganah Haifa District OC, "Announcement No. 2 by Commander of the Haganah," 22 April 1948, HA 105/92.

157. Morris, *Birth of Palestinian Refugee Problem Revisited*, 200–201.

158. Haifa Workers Council, "Announcement by Haifa Workers Council," 28 April 1948, IDFA 481/49//62.

159. Lippincott to secretary of state, 29 April 1948, USNA, Haifa Consulate, Classified Records 1948, 800–Political Affairs; *Times* (London), 26 April 1948; high commissioner to secretary of state, 25 April 1948, SAMECA CP III/4/52.

160. Beilin, "Operation Haifa," 25 April 1948.

161. JA Political Department, Arab Division, "In the Arab Public," 28 June 1948, IDFA 260/51//4.

162. Avner to HID-AD, "On Events in Jaffa from the Attack on Her. A General Survey," 6 May 1948, HA 105/92 aleph.

163. Cunningham to secretary of state, 26 April 1948, SAMECA CP III/4/71; Sir Henry Gurney, "Palestine," 84, SAMECA.

164. Gelber, *Budding Fleur-de-Lis,* 187.

165. Bandman, "British Military Intervention," 284.

166. Kiryati/Intelligence, "Daily Summary from 18:00, 30 [April] to 18:00 [1 May]," HA 105/94.

167. Menachem Begin, "The Conquest of Jaffa," undated but from May or June 1948, JI, IZL, kaf-4, 8/1.

168. Avner to HIS-AD, "Events in Jaffa since the [Start of the Attack on It]. General Survey," 6 May 1948, HA 105/92 aleph.

169. Cunningham to secretary of state, 3 May 1948, SAMECA CP III/5/43.

170. Lazar, *Conquest of Jaffa,* 124, 126.

171. Unsigned, "Summary of the Interrogation of the Manshiya POWs from 28 April 1948," JI, IZL, kaf-8, 8/8; "Miscellaneous (Events in Jaffa, from Prisoner Interrogations by 'Ham')," 28 April 1948, IDFA 8275/49//136.

172. Alexandroni Brigade to Yadin, "Summary of Operation Hametz," 3 May 1948, IDFA 922/75//949.

173. Quoted in Gabbay, *Political Study of the Arab-Jewish Conflict,* 90.

174. Avner to HIS-AD, "Events in Jaffa 18:45, 7.5.48–10:00, 8.5.48," IDFA 8275/49//162.

175. Bandman, "British Military Intervention," 282–283.

176. Gurney, "Palestine," 28 April 1948, SAMECA.

177. "Fortnightly Intelligence Newsletter No. 67 Issued by HQ British Troops Palestine," 6 May 1948, PRO WO 275-64, quotes an Iraqi cabinet minister as saying that Britain "has purposely engineered Jewish domination in Haifa as an integral part of its programme for Palestine."

178. War Office to parliamentary secretary of the prime minister, etc., "Extract from Middle East Special Situation Report 29 April 1948," PRO CO 537-3875.

179. Montgomery, *Memoirs*, 473–474.
180. "Note of a Meeting Held at 10 Downing Street at 5:15 p.m. on Friday 7th May 1948," 7 May 1948, PRO CAB 127-341.
181. "Note of a Meeting Held at 10 Downing Street at 5:15 p.m. on Friday 7th May 1948," 7 May 1948; Montgomery, *Memoirs*, 474; minutes attached to PRO FO 371-68544 E5102/4/31G.
182. Bandman, "British Military Intervention," 298.
183. W. A. C. Mathieson, minute, 4 May 1948, PRO CO 537-3870.
184. Bandman, "British Military Intervention," 302–304.
185. Bandman, *When Will Britain Withdraw from Jerusalem?* 76.
186. Bandman, "British Military Intervention," 304–309.
187. Mathieson, minute, 4 May 1948.
188. Bandman, "British Military Intervention," 283.
189. Bandman, "British Military Intervention," 283–284; Montgomery, *Memoirs*, 474; *STH*, 3, pt. 2:1552; Haganah Logbook, 27 April 1948, IDFA 922/75//949. In the last document, a British brigadier is quoted as telling an HIS officer that the British would protect Jaffa for "about three weeks," after which Jaffa would be "no longer the brigadier's concern."
190. Bandman, "British Military Intervention," 285–286, n. 27. The British lost one tank commander killed.
191. Gurney to Ben-Gurion, 29 April 1948, CZA S25-4011. The Jewish response (Kohn to Gurney, 29 April 1948, ISA, *Documents, December 1947–May 1948*, 703–705), asserted that the British had done nothing for five months to prevent Arab attacks on Jews.
192. Hamilton, *Monty: Final Years*, 696–697.
193. Bandman, "British Military Intervention," 292–294; Ben-Gurion, *War Diary*, entry for 30 May 1948, 377.
194. HGS/Operations to Alexandroni, etc., "Orders for Operation Hametz," 26 April 1948, IDFA 6647/49//15; Operation Hametz HQ to Giv'ati, etc., 27 April 1948, IDFA 67/51//677.
195. Alexandroni to brigades, etc., 8 May 1948, IDFA 2323/49//6.
196. Tiroshi to HIS-AD, "Initial Interrogation of 13 Arab Prisoners Captured after the Conquest of Kheiriya and Sakiyya," 2 May 1948, HA 105/54 aleph.
197. Ben-Gurion, *War Diary*, entry for 30 April 1948, 377.
198. For example, Sergei to battalions, "Instructions on Behavior with Prisoners of War," 11 March 1948, IDFA 6809/49//8, and 01203 to HIS-AD, 26 December 1947, IDFA 481/49//62, on the execution of two Jewish scouts in Jaffa.
199. Klein, "Arab Prisoners of War."
200. Unsigned, "Latest Reports from the Front," 28 April 1948, HA 48/3.
201. Kiryati-Dafna to fronts, 30 April 1948, IDFA 8275/49//130.
202. Kiryati-Dafna to fronts, "Events in Jaffa, Survey, Night of 3–4.5.48," IDFA 8275/49//; and Kiryati/Intelligence, "Daily Summary, from 18:00, 30 [April] to 18:00, 1 [May]," HA 105/94.
203. Segev, ed., *In Enemy Eyes*, 34.

204. Unsigned, "Events in Jaffa," 12:30, 4 May 1948, IDFA 8275/49//162; Cunningham to secretary of state, 5 May 1948, SAMECA CP III/5/92; Gurney, "Palestine," 94, SAMECA.

205. Ben-Gurion, *War Diary,* entry for 18 May 1948, 438.

206. "Protocol of Meeting between the Commander of the Haganah in Tel Aviv and His Aides and Representatives of the Inhabitants of Jaffa, in Tel Aviv, on 12 May 1948," and "Second Meeting between the Haganah OC in Tel Aviv and Representatives of the Jaffa Emergency Committee in Tel Aviv on 13 May 1948, at 10:45 hrs.," both in IDFA 321/48//97.

207. Texts of "Agreement" and "Instructions . . . ," both in HA 55/31.

208. Unsigned, "Report on an Effort to Prevent Theft in Manshiya," 20 May 1948, IDFA 8275/49//136.

209. Gefen to minister of police and minority affairs, 25 May 1948, ISA MAM 306/77.

210. Military governor's office, Jaffa, "Summary, 15.5.48," IDFA 321/48//97; Emergency Committee to representative of commander Tel Aviv District, 22 May 1948, and Emergency Committee to representative of the International Red Cross Organization, Tel Aviv, 21 May 1948, both in ISA FM 2564/9.

211. Nicola Saba, Jaffa Emergency Committee, "Note," 27 May 1948; Dr. M. Mishalany, Dr. G. Ayoub, and Dr. H. Pharaon, "Report on the Bodies That Were Found Dead [sic] on Jabalieh Area on 25.5.48 and Examined by Us on 27.5.48"; and "Second Memorandum Submitted by the Emergency Committee of Jaffa Protesting against the Irregular Activities of the Jewish Forces in Jaffa Area," 28 May 1948, all in ISA FM 2406/2. Some of the bodies had identity cards issued by the Haganah after 15 May 1948; all had been shot.

212. "Statement by Mr. B. Shitrit," meeting of People's Administration, 3 May 1948, ISA, *People's Administration,* 32.

213. "A Call from His Majesty King Abdullah to the Arab People of Palestine on Behalf of the Arab League," as carried in *Al-Nasr,* Amman, 5 May 1948, USNA, US Consulate General, Jerusalem, Classified Records 1948, 800–Political Affairs.

214. Weitz, *Diary and Letters,* entry for 26 April 1948, 3:273.

215. Unsigned, undated HIS report, HA 105/217; Alexandroni, "Bulletin No. 1," 7 May 1948, IDFA 2323/49//5.

216. Texts of broadcasts by Kol Hamagen Ha'ivri (Haganah Radio), Jerusalem, 5, 6 May 1948, CZA S25-8918; "Information about the Arabs of Palestine (According to Arab Radio Transmissions, 6–7 May 1948)," CZA S25-9045; "Daily Monitoring Report No. 28," 6 May 1948, DBGA.

217. Aharon Cohen, "In Face of the Arab Evacuation," summer 1948, HHA-ACP 10.95.11 (8); "HIS Information," 13 May 1948, KMA-PA 100/MemVavDalet/35–158; "Information about the Arabs of Palestine (from Arab Broadcasts, 10–11 May)" and "Information about the Arabs of Palestine (from Arab Broadcasts, 14–15 May)," both in CZA S25-9045.

218. Yigal Allon to Yadin and Galili, 22 April 1948, KMA-PA 170-44. In the copy of

this document in IDFA 957/51//25, the passage relating to Beisan is censored out—though Allon's recommendation "to harass Arab Safad to speed up the evacuation" was left intact.

219. HGS to Allon, etc., 25 April 1948, IDFA 67/51//677.

220. Palmah HQ to HGS, "Daily Report," 22 April 1948, IDFA 922/75//1066; Gilead, ed., *Book of the Palmah*, 2:219–222.

221. Palmah HQ to HGS, "Daily Report," 4 May 1948, IDFA 922/75//1066; Yiftah to HGS, 5 May 1948, IDFA 128/51//50.

222. *Beineinu*, no. 13, 9 May 1948, KMA 2-20/aleph.

223. Tzuri, Cochba, to HIS, "A Letter Sent by the Priest Boniface . . . ," 4 June 1948, HA 105/92.

224. Palmah HQ to HGS, "Daily Report," 2 May 1948, IDFA 922/75//1044.

225. Shertok to Alexandre Parodi, 5 May 1948, ISA, *Documents, December 1947–May 1948*, 738.

226. Tzuri, Dori, to HIS-AD, "Events in Safad after Its Conquest," 1 June 1948, HA 105/222.

227. Abbasi, "Safad in the War of Independence," 129.

228. Abbasi, "Safad in the War of Independence," 131.

229. Abbasi, "Safad in the War of Independence," 131.

230. Abbasi, "Safad in the War of Independence," 133.

231. Ben-Yehuda, *Through the Ropes*, 243; Abbasi, "Safad in the War of Independence," 135–136.

232. Elad Peled, "The Conquest of Safad," HA 2/222; Yiftah to HGS, 19:15 hrs., 21:00 hrs., 2 May 1948, both in IDFA 128/51//50.

233. Yiftah to HGS, 6 May 1948, IDFA 128/51//50; Palmah HQ to HGS, "Daily Report," 7 May 1948, IDFA 922/75//1066.

234. Golani HQ, "Weekly Summary," 7 May 1948, IDFA 1196/52//1.

235. Sari al-Fnaish to Adib Shishakli, 5 May 1948, quoted in Abbasi, "Safad in the War of Independence," 138.

236. Gilead, ed., *Book of the Palmah*, 2:283–284.

237. Abbasi, "Safad in the War of Independence," 139.

238. Abbasi, "Safad in the War of Independence," 142.

239. Yiftah HQ to Palmah HQ, HGS, etc., "Report on Operation," 10 May 1948, IDFA 922/75//1066.

240. Yiftah HQ to Palmah HQ, HGS, etc., "Report on Operation," 10 May 1948.

241. Abbasi, "Safad in the War of Independence," 144.

242. Tzuri to HIS-AD, "Events in Safad after Its Conquest," 1 June 1948, HA 105/222.

243. Yiftah to Golani and Yiftah to Palmah HQ, etc., 10 May 1948, both in IDFA 128/51//50; Tzuri, Dori, to HIS-AD, 2 July 1948, HA 105/127 aleph.

244. Elad Peled, "The Conquest of Safad," HA 222/2.

245. Tzuri, Dori, to HIS-AD, "Events in Safad after Its Conquest," 1 June 1948, HA 105/222; Ben-Gurion, *War Diary*, entry for 7 June 1948, 494; Moshe Carmel to IDF/GS, 14 August 1948, IDFA 260/51//4.

246. See Oded to Golani, 20 April 1948, regarding the evacuation of women and children from Dawwara and ʿAbisiya, and Yiftah to HGS, 2 May 1948, 21:00 hrs., regarding the evacuation of women and children in the area around Rosh Pina, both in IDFA 128/51//50; see Palmah HQ to HGS, "Daily Report," 8 May 1948, IDFA 922/75//1066, regarding orders to the village of Hunin to evacuate.

247. Gilead, ed., *Book of the Palmah,* 2:286; Yiftah to Palmah HQ and Golani, 14 May 1948, 17:30 hrs., IDFA 128/51//50; Palmah HQ to HGS, "Daily Report," 15 May 1948, IDFA 922/75//1066.

248. Flyer, and Tzuri, Drori, to HIS-AD, 16 May 1948, HA 105/54 aleph.

249. Dori to Tzuri, etc., 25 May 1948, IDFA 922/75//1082.

250. For example, Daniel, Battalion 11/"D" Company, to Eleventh Battalion HQ, "Report on Zawiya Operation, 19 May 1948," IDFA 128/51//32.

251. Palmah HQ to HGS, "Daily Report," 23 May 1948, IDFA 922/75//1066.

252. Yiftah HQ, "Daily Report," 22 May 1948, IDFA 922/75//1082.

253. Dori to Tzuri, etc., 25 May 1948, IDFA 922/75//1082.

254. Palmah HQ to HGS, "Daily Report," 24 May 1948, IDFA 922/75//1066.

255. Golani/Barak, "Report on Operation in Samakh," IDFA 128/51//33.

256. Tzuri to HIS-AD, "Information about Samakh upon Its Depopulation," 10 May 1948, IDFA 1196/52//1.

257. Weitz diary, entry for 4 May 1948, CZA A246-13, 2373.

258. Tzuri to HIS-AD, "The Battle for Beit Shean," 14 May 1948, HA 105/92 bet.

259. Unsigned, "Events on 12.5.48," undated, HA 105/94 aleph.

260. Jura to Utz, 19 May 1948, HA 105/92 bet.

261. Morris, *Birth of Palestinian Refugee Problem Revisited,* 227-228.

262. ʿEtzioni, ed., *Tree and Sword,* 146.

263. ʿEtzioni, ed., *Tree and Sword,* 146.

264. Yadin to People's Administration, 12 May 1948 (first session), ISA, *People's Administration,* 66.

265. See, e.g., Golani to battalion OCs, 13 May 1948, IDFA 9322/75//1082.

266. Morris, *Birth of Palestinian Refugee Problem Revisited,* 254-255.

267. Givʿati HQ, "Operation 'Barak'—General Instructions," [?] May 1948, and Givʿati HQ to Battalions 51, 52, etc., 10 May 1948, both in IDFA 7011/49//5.

268. Ayalon, *Givʿati Brigade in the War of Establishment,* 532.

269. Doron, Elitzur, to HIS-AD, "Batani Sharqi," 13 May 1948, HA 105/92 aleph. See also Ayalon, *Givʿati Brigade in the War of Establishment,* 527-552.

270. Morris, *Birth of Palestinian Refugee Problem Revisited,* 257.

271. Fifty-first Battalion HQ to C Company, "Operational Order 'Medina,'" 17 May 1948, IDFA 170/51//49.

272. Ayalon, *Givʿati Brigade in the War of Establishment,* 541, 552.

273. Morris, *Birth of Palestinian Refugee Problem Revisited,* 258.

274. Broadmead to Kirkbride, 5 May 1948, PRO FO 816/119.

275. Jerusalem Brigade/Operations/Eldad, to Moriah, Metzuda, etc., "Annex No. 3 to Operational Order 'Kilshon,'" 10 May 1948, IDFA 500/48//33.

276. Yosef Schnurman, "Report on the Receipt of Security Zones B and C," 17 May 1948, CZA S25-10526.

277. Walter Eytan, "American Consul's Representations on Looting in Jerusalem," apparently 4 June 1948, CZA S25-5035. See also Senator David Warner to David Shaltiel, 3 June 1948, and attached Senator Warner, "Conquered Areas," undated, both in CZA S25-9186.

278. Ben-Gurion, *War Diary*, entry for 11 May 1948, 409.

279. Alexandroni Intelligence Officer, "The Attack on Arab Kafr Saba on 13.5," undated, IDFA 2323/49//6; Rivlin and Sinai, eds., *Alexandroni Brigade*, 194–207.

280. Katz, "Arab Departure." See also Pappé, "Tantura Case"; and "Tantura Massacre," a compilation of oral testimonies. See Rivlin and Sinai, eds., *Alexandroni Brigade*, 220–230.

281. Morris, "Tantura Massacre Affair"; Morris, *Birth of Palestinian Refugee Problem Revisited*, 247–248, 299–301, n. 671. In the available archival records on *mivtza namal* (Operation Harbor), only one piece of evidence refers to killings after the battle: it describes the execution of a handful of captured snipers (entry for 23 May 1948, Tulik Makovsky Diary, Kibbutz Nahsholim Archive). Otherwise, there is no mention of a massacre. An Arab broadcast from 21 June, as reported by Israeli monitors, stated that "an Arab woman who fled from Tantura relates that the Jews raped women in addition to [committing] acts of robbery, theft and arson" ("Jerusalem 16:00 [21 June 1948]," HA 105/92 aleph; "Palestine in Arab Broadcasts 21–22.6.48," HA 105/88). There is no mention of a massacre.

282. Yadin, protocol of meeting, 12 May 1948, ISA, *People's Administration* (early session), 64.

283. "Operation 'Ehud,'" undated, IDFA 7353/49//46. An early version of the order (Carmeli/Operations, [?] April 1948, IDFA 5942/49//53) described the objectives as breaking through to the isolated kibbutzim and to resupply them "for three months," "to attack the villages: Kabri, al-Nahar, Bassa, al-Zib; to destroy the gangs; the menfolk; to destroy property."

284. "Hiram" to HIS-AD, undated but either 13 or 14 May 1948, HA 105/127.

285. Carmeli to General Staff/Operations, etc., "Operation Ben-Ami," 15 May 1948, IDFA 2687/49//35.

286. "A Letter Written on 26.4.48 from Acre by a Father to His Son Munir Effendi Nur, an Inspector in Police HQ in Nablus," undated, HA 105/252.

287. "Hiram," untitled intelligence report, 7 May 1948, HA 105/237.

288. "Hiram" to HIS-AD, 11 May 1948, HA 105/54.

289. "Hiram," untitled intelligence report, 11 May 1948, HA 105/237.

290. IDF History Branch, "The Arab Salvation Army—31.12.47–23.9.55," 71, IDFA 1046/70//182; "Hiram" to HIS-AD, "The Town of Acre after Its Conquest on 17.5," 21 May 1948, HA 105/92 bet.

291. Carmel to the notables of Acre, 17 May 1948, IDFA 922/75//1025.

292. Carmeli to High Command, 19 May 1948, and appended untitled instrument of surrender, signed by "OC Haganah Acre Sector" and Albert Rock, Ahmed Effendi ʿAbdu, Sheikh Musa Effendi al-Tabari, etc., 18 May 1948, both in IDFA 922/75//1022.

293. "Hiram" to HIS-AD, "The Town of Acre after Its Conquest on 17.5," 21 May 1948, HA 105/92 bet.

294. Carmel to Haganah General Staff, 18 May 1948, IDFA 922/75//1022.

295. "Hiram" to HIS-AD, 30 May 1948, HA 105/252.

296. [?] to prime minister of Israel, 2 December 1948, and General Eitan Avissar, president of IDF Supreme Court, 20 December 1948, both in IDFA 121/50//165.

297. Tzuri, Carmeli, to Eitan, Tzidoni, etc., 19 May 1948, IDFA 6680/49//5.

298. Rivlin and Sinai, eds., *Alexandroni Brigade*, 173.

299. Nazzal, *Palestinian Exodus from Galilee*, 62.

300. See Morris, *Birth of Palestinian Refugee Problem Revisited*, 254, 515–516. For a misleading account, see Eshel, *Carmeli Brigade*, 173.

301. Unsigned, ʿEin-Gev, "[Testimony] Taken from Ezra Klopfeny, 9.10.48," IDFA 1235/52//1. See also Carmon, ed., ʿEin-Gev, 35.

302. Unsigned, ʿEin-Gev, "[Testimony] Taken 4.7.48, from Zili Diter, OC 'Persian' Sector," IDFA 1235/52//1; Carmon, ed., ʿEin-Gev, 34, 71; Yitah, MAM, to military governor, Western Galilee, 26 October 1948, and Hassan Zickrallah to OC Acre, 20 October 1948, both in IDFA 922/52//564.

303. Segev, ed., *In Enemy Eyes*, 80–82.

304. Unsigned but HIS, "The Situation in the Area of Kfar ʿEtzion," 2 November 1947, HA 105/54.

305. Unsigned but HIS, "Details and Echoes of the Attack on Kfar ʿEtzion on 14.1.48," 20 January 1948, IDFA 500/48//60; Knohl, ed., *Battle of ʿEtzion Bloc*, 113–131, 150–151.

306. Knohl, ed., *Battle of ʿEtzion Bloc*, 137–149.

307. Orren, "Contribution of Settlements," 206.

308. Major Yitzhak Yaʿakobson, History Branch, IDF, "The ʿEtzion Bloc in the War of Independence," undated but from mid-1950s, IDFA 922/75//283, 89.

309. Yaʿakobson, "ʿEtzion Bloc," 91–92.

310. Yaʿakobson, "ʿEtzion Bloc," 96.

311. Yaʿakobson, "ʿEtzion Bloc," 102.

312. Tall, *Memoirs*, 39.

313. Glubb, *Soldier*, 78.

314. Gelber, *Independence versus Nakba*, 129.

315. Knohl, ed., *Battle of ʿEtzion Bloc*, 434.

316. Knohl, ed., *Battle of ʿEtzion Bloc*, 448.

317. J. L. Fishman to chief secretary, 12 May 1948, CZA S25-5.

318. Knohl, ed., *Battle of ʿEtzion Bloc*, 477; Yaʿakobson, "ʿEtzion Bloc," 128–129.

319. Glubb, *Soldier*, 78.

320. Knohl, ed., *Battle of ʿEtzion Bloc,* 535, quoting unnamed local Arabs.

321. Yaʿakobson, "ʿEtzion Bloc," 130; Tall, *Memoirs,* 42; Kirkbride to FO, 14 May 1948, PRO CO 537-3904; Glubb, *Soldier,* 78. Abu Nowar, *Jordanian-Israeli War,* 61, goes one better and blames the duplicitous Jews for the massacre, which he doesn't explicitly admit occurred, by writing: "The Haganah raised some white flags, but as soon as the [Arab] assault troops came within range, they resumed firing at the advancing troops." The Arab troops then assaulted the kibbutz and took it in "fierce fighting."

322. Knohl, ed., *ʿEtzion Bloc,* 478–479.

323. Knohl, ed., *ʿEtzion Bloc,* 483. Yaʿakobson, "ʿEtzion Bloc," 144, attributed the massacre to "the Arab mentality."

324. Yaʿakobson, "ʿEtzion Bloc," 132.

325. Ben-Gurion, protocol of Cabinet meeting, 23 May 1948, ISA.

326. Cunningham, "Weekly Intelligence Appreciation," 17 April 1948, PRO FO 371-68503.

327. "District Commissioner's Report on Galilee District for 15–31 March," 6 April 1948, CZA S25-5634.

328. Dorothy Adelson to Shertok, (?) April 1948, CZA S25-5471.

329. Abba Eban to John Ross, 12 April 1948, and attached "Appendix," ISA, *Documents, December 1947–May 1948,* 608–621.

330. Quoted in I. J. Linton, New York, to S. Brodetsky, London, 2 May 1948, ISA, *Documents, December 1947–May 1948,* 714–718.

331. Shertok at meeting of People's Administration, 12 May 1948 (first session), ISA, *People's Administration* 47.

332. "The Palestine Situation (Summary of Conclusions Reached by Representatives of CIA, State, War, and Navy in Conference 5 May 1948)," USNA CIA-RDP67-00059A000200200011-5.

333. For drafts of the truce proposals and Shertok to Ben-Gurion, 28 April 1948, see ISA, *Documents, December 1947–May 1948,* 821–832, 692–693, respectively.

334. The five successive versions of the proposals are in ISA, *Documents, December 1947–May 1948,* 821–832.

335. "Second Provisional Draft," 29 April 1948, ISA, *Documents, December 1947–May 1948,* 828–830.

336. See, e.g., Shertok to Marshall, 29 April 1948, ISA, *Documents, December 1947–May 1948,* 695–696.

337. JA, New York, to JA, Palestine, 7 May 1948, and Shertok to Ben-Gurion, 4 May 1948, ISA, *Documents, December 1947–May 1948,* 746–747, 726–727, n. 2.

338. Ben-Gurion, protocol of meeting, JAE, 16 April 1948, CZA; ISA, *Documents, December 1947–May 1948,* 727, n. 3; and Ben-Gurion to Shertok, 4 May 1948, *Documents, December 1947–May 1948,* 729.

339. "Meeting: M. Shertok, E. Epstein–G. Marshall, R. Lovett, D. Rusk (Washington, 8 May 1948)," ISA, *Documents, December 1947–May 1948,* 757–769.

340. Lippman, "View from 1947," 23–26.

341. Lourie, New York, to Shertok, Palestine, 11 May 1948, ISA, *Documents, December 1947–May 1948*, 776–777.

342. Epstein to Ben-Gurion, 11 May 1948, ISA, *Documents, December 1947–May 1948*, 777.

343. Yadin, protocol of meeting of People's Administration, 12 May 1948, ISA, *People's Administration*, 63–64, 66, 67. Ben Gurion (57) commented that the attack on the bloc could be considered the start of the pan-Arab invasion.

344. Ben-Gurion, protocol of meeting of People's Administration, 12 May 1948, ISA, *People's Administration*, 75–76.

345. Ben-Gurion, protocol of meeting of People's Administration, 12 May 1948, ISA, *People's Administration*, 73.

346. Sharef, *Three Days*, 123.

347. Ben-Gurion, protocol of meeting of People's Administration, 12 May 1948 (evening session), ISA, *People's Administration*, 113.

348. Naor, "Big Wednesday."

349. Sharef, *Three Days*, 281.

350. Sharef, *Three Days*, 285.

351. Sharef, *Three Days*, 288.

352. "Editorial Note," *FRUS*, 5:993.

353. Chaim Weizmann to Truman, 13 May 1948, ISA, *Documents, December 1947–May 1948*, 988–989.

354. Ben-Gurion, *War Diary*, entry for 14 May 1948, 416.

CHAPTER 5. THE PAN-ARAB INVASION, 15 MAY–11 JUNE 1948

Epigraph. Abba Eban, "Conversation with ʿAbdul Rahman ʿAzzam Pasha, 15th September 1947," 19 September 1947, CZA S25-9020.

1. Ismail Safwat, "Second Report," 27 November 1947, in Segev, ed., *Behind the Screen*, 71–72.

2. For the effect of Deir Yassin on the Syrians, see Troop, Damascus, to secretary of state, 3 May 1948, USNA, 800 Syria/3-548.

3. Gelber, *Independence versus Nakba*, 208.

4. Robert Memminger, Damascus, to secretary of state, 9 May 1948, USNA, 800 Syria/9-548.

5. Unsigned, "Memorandum by the Arab Section of the Jewish Agency's Political Department," 1 March 1948, ISA, *Documents, December 1947–May 1948*, 400.

6. Dean Rusk, Baghdad, to FO, 1 December 1947, PRO FO 371-61580.

7. Alan Cunningham to secretary of state, 28 December 1947, PRO FO 371-61583.

8. Alec Kirkbride to FO, 2 May 1948, PRO CO 537-3901.

9. For example, Jaffa mayor Yusuf Haikal's statement in Baghdad in late April, reported in unsigned, "The Military Operations in Palestine According to the Arab Press," 26 April 1948, CZA S25-8996.

10. Gelber, *Independence versus Nakba,* 191.

11. Kirkbride, Amman, to FO, 21 December 1947, PRO FO 371-61583.

12. Ronald Campbell to FO, 27 April 1948, PRO FO 371-68370.

13. Gerges, "Egypt and the 1948 War," 154.

14. Landis, "Syria and the Palestine War," 191.

15. P. M. Broadmead to FO, 3 May 1948, PRO FO 371-68371.

16. Eppel, *Palestine Conflict in Modern Iraq,* 158–189.

17. Campbell to FO, 1 May 1948 (no. 536), PRO FO 371-68371. In another cable, Ambassador Campbell commented: "Ulema's pronouncement is likely to excite irresponsible and fanatical elements who have been clamouring for more action by Arab Governments. . . . [The Egyptian Government] may feel unable to resist for long an intense and sustained popular clamour for urging [i.e., urgent] intervention" (Campbell to FO, 1 May 1948 [no. 533], PRO FO 371-68371).

18. Campbell to Ernest Bevin, 17 April 1948, PRO FO 371-68370.

19. Campbell to FO, 19 May 1948, PRO FO 371-68506.

20. Ilan, *Origin of Arab-Israeli Arms Race,* 26–29, 35–37, 51–52.

21. Gerges, "Egypt and the 1948 War," 155.

22. Nasser, "Memoirs," 10.

23. Collins and Lapierre, *Jerusalem,* 302.

24. Pappé, *Making of Arab-Israeli Conflict,* 109.

25. Kimche and Kimche, *Both Sides of the Hill,* 153.

26. Gerges, "Egypt and the 1948 War," 155.

27. Kimche and Kimche, *Both Sides of the Hill,* 154.

28. Sadat, *Revolt on the Nile,* 106.

29. Kimche and Kimche, *Both Sides of the Hill,* 154.

30. Campbell to FO, 2 May 1946, PRO CO 537-1756.

31. Collins and Lapierre, *Jerusalem,* 338.

32. Doran, *Pan-Arabism before Nasser,* 128–131.

33. Campbell to FO, 17 May 1948, PRO FO 371-68373. A similar lone voice of reason was heard also in the Syrian parliament, where Farzat Mamlouk, on 27 April, spoke of Syrian unpreparedness and impending disaster (see Landis, "Syria and the Palestine War," 191–192).

34. Golda Meir, protocols of meeting of People's Administration, 12 May 1948, ISA, *People's Administration,* 43.

35. Pappé, *Making of Arab-Israeli Conflict,* 112.

36. Campbell to Bevin, 17 April 1948.

37. Segev, ed., *In Enemy Eyes,* 83.

38. Neguib, *Egypt's Destiny,* 20.

39. Sadat, *Revolt on the Nile,* 152, 108.

40. Glubb, *Soldier,* 93.

41. BMEO, Cairo, to British legation, Amman, 29 April 1948, PRO FO 816/118.

42. Shlaim, *Collusion across the Jordan,* 227–228.

43. HIS-AD, "In the Arab Public," 5 May 1948, IDFA 1196/52//1.

44. Collins and Lapierre, *Jerusalem,* 408.

45. Campbell to FO, 15 May 1948, PRO FO 371-68372.

46. Unsigned but either HIS-AD or Israel Foreign Ministry, "Bulletin of Arab [Radio] Broadcasts," 17 May 1948, HA 105/90.

47. Glubb, *Soldier,* 93, claims that there was no plan: "There had been no joint planning of any kind. The Israelis subsequently claimed knowledge of an Arab master plan, combining the strategy of all the Arab armies. No such plan existed, nor had any attempt been made to prepare one." See also Abu Nowar, *Jordanian-Israeli War,* 153.

48. Collins and Lapierre, *Jerusalem,* 157.

49. Trefor Evans, Beirut, to FO, 12 October 1947, PRO FO 371-61530, conveying the thinking of Jordanian prime minister Samir Rifaʿi.

50. Segev, ed., *Behind the Screen,* 148–149.

51. Gerges, "Egypt and the 1948 War," 159.

52. Segev, ed., *Behind the Screen,* 27.

53. Unsigned, "The Arab Plan of Attack after the 15th of May," 5 May 1948, IDFA 49/5942//53; Yerubaʿal, General Staff Division/3, to "Amitai" (Ben-Gurion), Yadin, etc., 9 May 1948, IDFA922/75//595.

54. Segev, ed., *Behind the Screen,* 27; Shlaim, *Collusion across the Jordan,* 199. Kimche and Kimche, *Both Sides of the Hill,* 150, offer a variant of the plan.

55. Glubb, *Soldier,* 85.

56. Shlaim, *Collusion across the Jordan,* 226.

57. Glubb, *Soldier,* 85.

58. Maʿayan, "Losing the North," 1:273.

59. Shlaim, *Collusion across the Jordan,* 199–201. The Lebanese, Syrian, and Iraqi elements of the plan were telegraphically conveyed in Kirkbride to Bevin, 14 May 1948, PRO FO 816/120.

60. Tripp, "Iraq and the 1948 War," 137. So long as Iraq's archives remain closed, the point must remain moot.

61. Eliahu Sasson, untitled memoranda, 12, 19 August 1946, CZA S25-9036. For ʿAbdullah's and Ben-Gurion's support of such a partition scheme even before the Sasson-ʿAbdullah meetings, see, respectively, Kirkbride to Thomas Wikeley, FO, 29 July 1946, PRO FO 816/85; and Gelber, *Jewish-Transjordanian Relations,* 205.

62. Kirkbride to FO, 23 August 1946 (nos. 1364, 1387), PRO FO 816/85.

63. Ezra Danin, "Conversation with ʿAbdullah 17.11.47," undated, CZA S25-4004; Golda Meir, protocol of meeting of People's Administration, 12 May 1948, ISA, *People's Administration,* 40.

64. Pirie-Gordon to Peter Garran, FO, 27 August 1947, PRO FO 816/88.

65. Unsigned, "Off-the-Record Talks in Transjordan of Two British Correspondents," 21 October 1947, CZA S25-9038.

66. Kirkbride to Bevin, 29 October 1947, PRO FO 816/89.

67. Packard, "Trans-Jordan—A Possible Forecast of Events in Palestine," 5 March 1948, PRO FO 371-68369.

68. Kirkbride to FO, 12 January 1948, PRO FO 371-68365.

69. Jordan Legation to UK, "Notes Concerning the Jewish Claim to the Negev," 17 November 1948, PRO FO 371-68643.

70. Bevin to Kirkbride, "Conversation with the Jordan Prime Minister," 9 November 1948, PRO FO 371-68366.

71. Bevin to Kirkbride, "Conversation with the Jordan Prime Minister"; 9 February FO to Kirkbride, 10 February 1948, PRO FO 371-68818.

72. Glubb, *Soldier,* 62–66.

73. Abul Huda, London, to Rais al-Diwan (head of the king's bureau), Amman, 8 February 1948, PRO FO 816/12.

74. Kirkbride to FO, 25 April 1948, PRO FO 371-68370.

75. Meir, protocol of meeting of People's Administration, 12 May 1948 (first session), ISA, *People's Administration,* 40–44.

76. "Meeting of the Arab Section of the Political Department of the Jewish Agency (13 May 1948)," ISA, *Documents, December 1947–May 1948,* 789–791.

77. Meir, protocol of meeting of People's Administration, 12 May 1948, 40–44; Shertok to Nahum Goldmann, 13 May 1948, ISA, *Documents, December 1947– May 1948,* 791; Tall, *Memoirs,* 48–50; Shlaim, *Collusion across the Jordan,* 205–214.

78. "S.R." (Shlomo Rabinowitz [Shamir]), "Report," 3 May 1948, ISA FM 2513/2.

79. Glubb, *Soldier,* 152.

80. Collins and Lapierre, *Jerusalem,* 365.

81. Doran, *Pan-Arabism before Nasser,* 134, quoting from Hashimi's memoirs.

82. Kimche and Kimche, *Both Sides of the Hill,* 165. Shlaim, *Collusion across the Jordan,* 226, argues that Egypt's last-minute decision to participate in the invasion was in large measure dictated by Farouk's desire to frustrate ʿAbdullah's suspected intention of taking over a large chunk of Palestine.

83. Al-Qawuqji, "Memoirs, 1948," pt. 2:3–33; Shlaim, *Collusion across the Jordan,* 203.

84. For example, J. B. Pruen, "Conversation with Major ʿAbdullah Tell [Tall], Military Governor of Arab Jerusalem . . . and Dr. Mousa Husseini on 24th May, 1948," 24 May 1948, PRO FO 371-68641: "All reference to the Arab Higher Committee gave the impression that it is regarded [by Tall and Husseini] as being non existent [sic]. Members of the Arab National Committee in Jerusalem are subordinated to Major Tell."

85. Shlaim, "Rise and Fall of the All-Palestine Government in Gaza"; Elpeleg, *In the Eyes of the Mufti,* 80–81.

86. Ben-Gurion, *As Israel Fights,* 68–69, giving the text of Ben-Gurion's speech at the Mapai Council, 7 February 1948.

87. Shertok, protocol of Cabinet meeting, 16 June 1948, ISA.

88. Ben-Gurion, protocol of meeting of JAE, 16 April 1948, CZA.

89. Ben-Gurion, *In the Battle,* 135–137.

90. Ostfeld, *An Army Is Born,* 1:15.

91. Gelber, *Emergence of Jewish Army,* 132–140.

92. Gelber, *Emergence of Jewish Army,* 146, 153, 159.

93. Pa'il, *Emergence of Zahal*, 372–373; Gelber, *Emergence of Jewish Army*, 212–214.

94. Gelber, *Emergence of Jewish Army*, 219–220.

95. Gelber, *Emergence of Jewish Army*, 225–226.

96. Cohen, History of Israeli *Air Force*, 1:325–366; Ilan, *Origin of Arab-Israeli Arms Race*, 89–104.

97. Ilan, *Origin of Arab-Israeli Arms Race*, 189.

98. Evans, Beirut, to FO, 10 October 1947, PRO FO 371-61530.

99. Evans, Beirut, to FO, 12 October 1947, PRO FO 371-61530.

100. Sherok speech at Security Council, 15 April 1948, ISA, *Documents, December 1947–May 1948*, 638.

101. Abu Nowar, *Jordanian-Israeli War*, 80–82.

102. "In the Arab Camp," 3 May 1948, CZA S25-9046.

103. "Information about the Arabs of Palestine (According to Arab Broadcasts, 7–9 May)," CZA S25-9045.

104. Ben-Gurion, *War Diary*, entry for 7 May 1948, 397.

105. Unsigned, "The Arab Attack Plan after the 15th of May," 5 May 1948, IDFA 49/5942//53. The plan also called for Jordanian and Saudi troops to "destroy" the 'Etzion Bloc. It does not mention Iraqi participation. A variant, which included the Iraqis, was penned by the head of the Intelligence Department of HGS, Major Ezra Omer ("Yeruba'al"), on 9 May (Operations/3 to Ben-Gurion, Yadin, etc., IDFA 922/75//595).

106. Unsigned, "Meeting of the Arab Section of the Political Department of the Jewish Agency (13 May 1948)," undated, CZA S25-5634. See also Haim Berman and Leo Kohn to Reuven Zaslani, 12 May 1948, CZA S25-9390.

107. Ben-Gurion, *War Diary*, entry for 2 May 1948, 1016.

108. Gelber, *Emergence of Jewish Army*, 243.

109. Ilan, *Origin of Arab-Israeli Arms Race*, 64, 69.

110. Ilan, *Origin of Arab-Israeli Arms Race*, 67; Kimche and Kimche, *Both Sides of the Hill*, 161.

111. Gelber, *Budding Fleur-de-Lis*, 1:416–436, says that the Yishuv knew almost nothing about the Arab armies until midway through the conventional war.

112. Pappé, *Making of Arab-Israeli Conflict*, 109.

113. Ben-Gurion, *Restored State of Israel*, 1:71.

114. Glubb, *Soldier*, 95; Pappé, *Making of Arab-Israeli Conflict*, 109–110, 122. Of the Arab governments, only Hashemite Jordon's felt secure enough to commit almost its whole army to the war.

115. The best up-to-date estimates are in Agin, "Balance of Forces"; Ben-Arieh, "Beginning of Historiography of the War of Independence"; and Ilan, "Few against the Many," all in Kadish and Kedar, eds., *The Few against the Many?*

Ilan, *Origin of Arab-Israeli Arms Race*, 67, speaks of "27,500" Arab troops in Palestine at the end of May; Glubb, *Soldier*, 94, speaks of "21,500" on 15 May; and Kimche and Kimche, *Both Sides of the Hill*, 162, speaks of "23,000" or "24,000" on 15 May. Glubb and the Kimches leave out the Palestinian militiamen, Muslim Brothers, and ALA troops inside Palestine in mid-May. Khalidi, ed., *From Haven to Conquest,* 867–871, offers a total, on 15 May, of "13,876" for the invaders. But he fails to mention that the invaders, whatever their real number, were all combat troops and that they were supported by large numbers of rear-echelon troops and by thousands of irregulars.

116. Glubb, *Soldier,* 92, spoke of "4,500." IDF intelligence (Dan Ram, "The Transjordan Army—the Legion," undated, IDFA 863/50//363) spoke of "4,000–4,500" invading Legionnaires.

117. The number of irregulars is impossible to calculate. But there were probably some 3,000 ALA and 1,000 Muslim Brotherhood troops in Palestine on 14 May, as well as thousands of Palestinian militiamen (most of them in the West Bank and Jerusalem. Those in and around Jerusalem participated in the fighting).

118. Galili, Yadin, and Wallach, eds., *Carta's Atlas . . . Haganah,* 114.

119. Galili, Yadin, and Wallach, eds., *Carta's Atlas . . . Haganah,* 114.

120. Ilan, *Origin of Arab-Israeli Arms Race,* 61. By comparison, 20–44-year-old males constituted 14 percent of the population of Arab Palestine. Had the United States conscripted 13 percent of its population in World War II, it would have had 21 million under arms.

121. Ben-Gurion, *War Diary,* entries for 19 October 1948, 5 January 1949, 754, 1018.

122. British embassy, Jedda, to Bernard Burrows, 18 August 1948, PRO FO 371-68788, speaks of 1,200 "regular" Saudi troops as well as irregulars.

123. Ilan, *Origin of Arab-Israeli Arms Race,* 67. Glubb, *Soldier,* 195, says that on 1 October the Arab armies engaged in Palestine fielded "55,700" troops ("15,000" Egyptians, "15,000" Iraqis, "10,000" Jordanians, "8,000" Syrians, "2,000" Lebanese, and "700" Saudis; he adds to this "5,000" irregulars). The Israelis, he said, had at this time "120,000" troops.

124. Ilan, *Origin of Arab-Israeli Arms Race,* 1.

125. Ilan, *Origin of Arab-Israeli Arms Race,* 5.

126. Houstoun Boswall to FO, 30 July 1948 (retransmitted to Amman on 31 July), PRO FO 816/127.

127. Ilan, *Origin of Arab-Israeli Arms Race,* 62; Greenberg, "Financing the War of Independence," 63–78.

128. Ilan, *Origin of Arab-Israeli Arms Race,* 104.

129. Morris, *Road to Jerusalem,* 261–262, nn. 296, 298, for discussion of numbers and sources. Some tribal auxiliaries were already in Palestine in early May, serving in the ALA independently (e.g., in Bab al-Wad-Latrun) or alongside local militiamen (in Safad and Jerusalem).

130. Ilan, *Origin of Arab-Israeli Arms Race,* 45; Morris, *Road to Jerusalem,* 122.

131. Glubb, *Soldier,* 92, 94.

132. The exact number of Legion companies left behind and the mechanics of the British connivance in this are unclear. It appears that between two and six companies and several independent platoons were left behind. See Morris, *Road to Jerusalem,* 268, n. 375.

133. Ilan, *Origin of Arab-Israeli Arms Race,* 47.

134. Bandman, "Arab Legion"; Tall, *Memoirs*, 65–67.

135. Morris, *Road to Jerusalem*, 172, 181.

136. Ilan, *Origin of Arab-Israeli Arms Race*, 49. In a "parade of generosity," the Egyptians in July gave the Legion four hundred shells from those confiscated from the "Rameses" (Pirie-Gordon to Burrows, 25 July 1948, PRO FO 816/127)—but the Legion was then expending five hundred shells a day.

137. Ilan, *Origin of Arab-Israeli Arms Race*, 48–49.

138. Morris, *Road to Jerusalem*, 183–184.

139. Abu Nowar, *Jordanian-Israeli War*, 86–87.

140. Kirkbride, *From the Wings*, 28. Other sources say the crossing began just before dawn, 15 May.

141. Glubb, *Soldier*, 99.

142. Segev, ed., *In Enemy Eyes*, 144–145.

143. Abu Nowar, *Jordanian-Israeli War*, 86.

144. Shlaim, *Collusion across the Jordan*, 239.

145. Levy, *Jerusalem in the War of Independence*, 225–235; Yanait, Avrahami, and ʿEtzion, eds., *Haganah in Jerusalem*, 220–272.

146. Ben-Gurion, protocol of Cabinet meeting, 16 May 1948, ISA.

147. Morris, *Road to Jerusalem*, 155–156.

148. Dov Steiger, "Arab Legion," 74, IDFA 1046/70//178.

149. Glubb, *Soldier*, 108–109. See also Kirkbride to Bevin (no. 331), 15 May 1948, PRO FO 816/120.

150. HIS, "Arab [Affairs] Information Bulletin from 18.5.48," IDFA 500/48//55.

151. Glubb, *Soldier*, 118, reproducing the text; Sela, "Transjordan, Israel and 1948 War," 651.

152. Abu Nowar, *Jordanian-Israeli War*, 93–94.

153. Glubb, *Soldier*, 110.

154. Steiger, "Arab Legion," 73, 75, IDFA 1046/70//178.

155. Kirkbride to FO, 19 May 1948, PRO FO 371-68829.

156. Sela, "Transjordan, Israel and 1948 War," 647.

157. Apparently on the direct command of ʿAbdullah, bypassing Glubb (see Abu Nowar, *Jordanian-Israeli War*, 95–96).

158. Glubb, *Soldier*, 111, 113.

159. ʿAbdullah had already spoken explicitly on 20 April of sending Glubb "to conquer Jerusalem" and hinted as much both before and after (see Morris, *Road to Jerusalem*, 153–155).

160. Letter, apparently published in *Al-Nisr*, 17 May 1948, PRO FO 816/120; HIS, "HIS Information, Daily Summary," 27 May 1948, IDFA 900/52//58; Nevo, *King Abdallah and Palestine*, 137.

161. Glubb, *Soldier*, 107.

162. Lapidot, *Flames of Revolt*, 376–377.

163. Arieli, ed., *Youth Battalion (Gadna)*, 93–97; Levy, *Jerusalem in the War of Independence*, 244–247; Avizohar, *Battle for Jerusalem*, 164–168; Abu Nowar, *Jordanian-Israeli War*, 113–117.

164. Levy, *Jerusalem in the War of Independence*, 247.

165. Mrs. Campbell, diary entry for 20 May 1948 (by "Mrs. MacInnes"), PRO FO 371-68511.

166. Arieli, ed., Youth Battalion (*Gadna*), 116–118; Levy, *Jerusalem in the War of Independence*, 247–248.

167. Kirkbride to Bevin, 21 May 1948, PRO FO 816/120.

168. Ben-Gurion, protocol of Cabinet meeting, 19 May 1948, ISA: "The Legion has apparently begun its move and it has three aims: the Old City, the whole of the city, and its environs."

169. Gruenbaum, protocol of Cabinet meeting, 20 June 1948, ISA.

170. See Ben-Gurion and Interior Minister Yitzhak Greenbaum, protocol of Cabinet meeting, 23 May 1948, ISA. Ironically, Whitehall simultaneously was warning ʿAbdullah against attacking West Jerusalem (FO to Kirkbride, 19 May 1948, PRO FO 371-68853: "A full-scale Arab Legion attack in Jerusalem is exactly the kind of situation which would produce the greatest possible difficulty for us in our relations with Transjordan").

171. Ben-Gurion, protocol of Cabinet meeting, 30 May 1948, ISA.

172. Shertok to Chaim Weizmann, 23 May 1948, ISA, *DFPI*, 1:66. But some Jordanians believed that the Legion's ultimate objective was to conquer West Jerusalem (see J. B. Pruen, "Conversation with Major ʿAbdullah Tell," 24 May 148, PRO FO 371-68641).

173. Jerusalem Brigade and District OC, 21 May 1948, IDFA 661/69//45.

174. [?] to Shiloah, 7 June 1948, CZA S25-5035.

175. Levy, *Jerusalem in the War of Independence*, 256–259; Abu Nowar, *Jordanian-Israeli War*, 175–177; Segev, ed., *In Enemy Eyes*, 87–89.

176. Glubb, *Soldier*, 116.

177. Mrs. Campbell, diary entry for 23 May 1948, PRO FO 371-8511.

178. Collins and Lapierre, *Jerusalem*, 474.

179. Arieli, ed., Youth Battalion (*Gadna*), 113–122.

180. Abu Nowar, *Jordanian-Israeli War*, 120–126; Glubb, *Soldier*, 115–125; Levy, *Jerusalem in the War of Independence*, 250–251; Avizohar, *Battle for Jerusalem*, 169–172; Collins and Lapierre, *Jerusalem*, 473–476. The figure for Legion casualties varies: Glubb speaks of about a hundred, Abu Nowar of "300."

181. Glubb, *Soldier*, 126.

182. Richard Beaumont to Bevin, 30 May 1948, PRO FO 371-68510.

183. Avizohar, *Battle for Jerusalem*, 132–135.

184. Palmah HQ to HGS, "Daily Report," 19 May 1948, IDFA 922/75//1066; Ehrnvald, *Siege within Siege*, 208–210.

185. Yosef Mizrahi's statement, as recorded by Z. Maimon, "The Battle in the Old City," 3 June 1948, CZA S25-7723.

186. Levy, *Jerusalem in the War of Independence*, 45–57.

187. Ben-Gurion, *Restored State of Israel*, 1:130.

188. David Balfour to Beaumont, 17 June 1948, PRO FO 371-68508.

189. Ehrnvald, *Siege within Siege*, 230.

190. Levy, *Jerusalem in the War of Independence,* 53–57, 70–71. See also Narkis, *Soldier of Jerusalem,* 96–97, for the events of 18–19 May.

191. See Ehrnvald, *Siege within Siege,* 229–241, for the surrender. The original document was lost.

192. Levy, *Jerusalem in the War of Independence,* 29–30.

193. Yosef Mizrahi's statement, as recorded by Z. Maimon, "The Battle in the Old City," 3 June 1948, CZA S25-7723. See also Beaumont to FO, 31 May 1948, PRO FO 371-68509.

194. Levy, *Jerusalem in the War of Independence,* 66–71; Tall, *Memoirs,* 103–112.

195. Beaumont to Bevin, 30 May 1948, PRO FO 371-68510.

196. Even before the pan-Arab invasion, Harel Brigade HQ had concluded that "the Latrun Junction is turning into the decisive spot in this battle [for Jerusalem]" (see Harel HQ to Palmah HQ, "Report on the Brigade's Activities No. 33," 13–14 May 1948, IDFA 661/69//45)—but this appreciation was not shared by HGS until a week later.

197. Glubb, *Soldier,* 110. See also Royle, *Glubb Pasha,* 363; Itzchaki, *Latrun,* 153–155; and Shlaim, *Collusion across the Jordan,* 244.

198. Steiger, "Arab Legion," 109, IDFA 1046/70//178.

199. Ben-Gurion, *War Diary,* entry for 22 May 1948, 450.

200. Itzchaki, *Latrun,* 180–184.

201. Levy, *Jerusalem in the War of Independence,* 266.

202. Gelber, *Budding Fleur-de-Lis,* 455; Itzchaki, *Latrun,* 185–186.

203. Itzchaki, *Latrun,* 195–196.

204. Itzchaki, *Latrun,* 202.

205. Itzchaki, *Latrun,* 212–213, quoting Mordechai Ya'akobovich.

206. Rivlin and Sinai, eds., *Alexandroni Brigade,* 231–259.

207. Segev, ed., *In Enemy Eyes,* 176.

208. Sharon, *Warrior,* 57.

209. Sharon, *Warrior,* 56.

210. Itzchaki, *Latrun,* 226–227; Shapira, "Historiography and Memory." During the following decades, Ben-Gurion's political rivals, from left and right, and Arab chroniclers, enormously exaggerated the Israeli losses at Latrun, each for his own reasons: Mahmoud al-Ghussan speaks of "800" Israeli dead (Segev, ed., *In Enemy Eyes,* 176); Glubb, *Soldier,* 132, speaks of "six hundred dead Jews." Itzchaki and Shapira, who checked the rosters, write of seventy-two to seventy-four dead and dismiss the charge that most or many of the dead were immigrants just off the boats and with no military training.

211. Abu Nowar, *Jordanian-Israeli War,* 142.

212. Ben-Gurion, protocol of Cabinet meeting, 26 May 1948, ISA.

213. Seventh Brigade HQ/Intelligence, "Intelligence Survey," 4 June 1948, IDFA 922/75//1018.

214. Levy, *Jerusalem in the War of Independence,* 263–275, gives a good overview of the battle.

215. Itzchaki, *Latrun,* 233.

216. Itzchaki, *Latrun*, 253.

217. Gelber, *Emergence of Jewish Army*, 456.

218. Itzchaki, *Latrun*, 258–260.

219. Collins and Lapierre, *Jerusalem*, 509–514; Itzchaki, *Latrun*, 252–268; Segev, ed., *In Enemy Eyes*, 183–189; Shamir, "Latrun Battles."

220. Levy, *Jerusalem in the War of Independence*, 282.

221. Segev, ed., *In Enemy Eyes*, 183–189.

222. Quoted in Itzchaki, *Latrun*, 263.

223. Segev, ed., *In Enemy Eyes*, 188, and Abu Nowar, *Jordanian-Israeli War*, 145, say that two Legionnaires were killed and seven wounded.

224. Levy, *Jerusalem in the War of Independence*, 295–302; Itzchaki, *Latrun*, 292–320.

225. Levy, *Jerusalem in the War of Independence*, 301.

226. Segev, ed., *In Enemy Eyes*, 199. Ben-Gurion, unusually, gave the Cabinet detailed explanations of what had gone wrong in each of the Latrun battles (protocols of Cabinet meetings, 26 May, 20 June 1948, ISA).

227. Abu Nowar, *Jordanian-Israeli War*, 147–150.

228. *Gezer's Day*, 37; Ayalon, *Giv'ati Brigade in Face of the Egyptian Invader*, 199–206. Abu Shusha, a neighboring Arab village, had been captured a month before and atrocities had been reported.

229. *Gezer's Day*, 35–68.

230. Abu Nowar, *Jordanian-Israeli War*, 147–150; Levy *in the War of Independence, Jerusalem*, 302–303; Itzchaki, *Latrun*, 327–332.

231. Levy, *Jerusalem in the War of Independence*, 285–294; Itzchaki, *Latrun*, 269–282.

232. As Kirkbride emphasized, "The Arab Legion is the only Arab army which has not (repeat not) entered the Jewish State" (Kirkbride to FO, 20 May 1948, PRO FO 371-68506).

233. Unsigned, untitled report, 24 June 1948, HA 105/127 aleph.

234. Ilan, *Origin of Arab-Israeli Arms Race*, 234–235.

235. Ilan, *Origin of Arab-Israeli Arms Race*, 42.

236. Unsigned, "Report on Monitoring of Arab Radio Stations for 15.5.48," HA 105/90.

237. Campbell to Bevin, 4 June 1948, PRO FO 371-68527.

238. Major Lord Douglas Gordon, War Office, to D.M.H. Riches, FO, 22 October 1947, and Riches to Gordon, 11 November 1947, both in PRO FO 371-63077.

239. This paragraph and the preceding paragraph are based on Ilan, *Origin of Arab-Israeli Arms Race*, 35–41. Israeli intelligence at this time offered far higher estimates of Egyptian strength ("seven" infantry brigades, "200 to 250 aircraft," etc.) though noted that the infantry units were substantially under-strength and much of the equipment was in disrepair (see HIS, Research Section, "The Arab Armies," 25 May 1948, CZA S25-8009).

240. Ilan, *Origin of Arab-Israeli Arms Race*, 40.

241. Nasser, "Memoirs," 5–6, n. 4 (by Walid Khalidi, ed.).

242. Segev, ed., *In Enemy Eyes*, 76–77, 79–81.

243. Segev, ed., *In Enemy Eyes*, 85–86; Tal, *War in Palestine*, 176–177.

244. Kirkbride to FO, 24 May 1948, PRO FO 371-68373.

245. Nasser, "Memoirs," 12.

246. Cohen, *History of Israeli Air Force*, 1:127–129.

247. Cohen, *History of Israeli Air Force*, 1:132–134.

248. Cohen, *History of Israeli Air Force*, 1:135–142. The British warned Egypt to stop bombing civilians (see FO to Campbell, 19 May 1948, PRO 371-68373).

249. Cohen, *History of Israeli Air Force*, 1:142–146; Campbell to Ahmed Muhammad Khashaba, 23 May 1948, PRO FO 371-69223. The Egyptians killed four British soldiers and seriously wounded five, and they destroyed three British aircraft and damaged eight. Already on 15 May the Egyptians had mistakenly attacked a British-manned airfield—at al-Bureij, near Gaza, killing one and wounding eight.

250. Ben-Gurion, *War Diary*, entry for 16 May 1948, 430.

251. Nasser, "Memoirs," 10.

252. Nasser, "Memoirs," 10.

253. Nasser, "Memoirs," 10.

254. Haim (Jerry) to Sergei (Bibi), "Summary Report on the Egyptian Army Attack on Nirim on 15, 16, 17.5.48," 25 May 1948, IDF 922/75//1223; *Negev Brigade*, 66–70; and Nasser, "Memoirs," 10.

255. Givʿati, *Path of Desert and Fire*, 54.

256. Segev, ed., *In Enemy Eyes*, 76–82.

257. IDF History Department, *War of Establishment*, 219.

258. Ayalon, *Givʿati Brigade in Face of the Egyptian Invader*, 40.

259. Gilead, ed., *Book of the Palmah*, 2:476.

260. Ben-Gurion, protocol of Cabinet meeting, 19 May 1948, ISA.

261. Nasser, "Memoirs," 12.

262. Gilead, ed., *Book of the Palmah*, 2:476.

263. Givʿati, *Path of Desert and Fire*, 5; *Negev Brigade*, 75–79.

264. Gilead, ed., Book of the *Palmah*, 2:476.

265. Turgan, "Yad Mordechai," 196–197.

266. Givʿati, *Path of Desert and Fire*, 64.

267. Doron (Elitzur) to HIS-AD, 28 May 1948, HA 105/92 aleph; Cohen, *History of Israeli Air Force*, 1:243–246.

268. Ben-Gurion, protocol of Cabinet meeting, 30 May 1948, ISA.

269. Egyptian Foreign Ministry to British ambassador, Cairo, "Note," 27 May 1948, and Campbell to FO, 26 May 1948, both in PRO FO 371-68508. Cohen (*Under Cover*, 232–233), argues that their mission was to collect intelligence; although they had initially been ordered to poison wells, the order was rescinded before they crossed the lines.

270. Gelber, *Budding Fleur-de-Lis*, 2:573. It is possible that, weeks earlier, Haganah

agents had poisoned waterworks near Acre, where an outbreak of typhus was recorded by British and Arab officials (Morris, *Birth of Palestinian Refugee Problem Revisited*, 230).

271. Beith and Evans, minutes, 23 June 1948, PRO FO 371-68509.

272. Kirkbride to FO, 24 May 1948, PRO FO 371-68373.

273. Ben-Gurion, protocol of Cabinet meeting, 30 May 1948, ISA. See also Nasser, "Memoirs," 14.

274. Ben-Gurion, protocol of Cabinet meeting, 14 June 1948, ISA.

275. Ilan, *Origin of Arab-Israeli Arms Race*, 158, 162. Ten Messerschmitt Avia S-199s, the Czech version of the German fighter, were purchased in Prague by Haganah agents on 23 April. They were disassembled and, beginning on 21 May, shuttled in parts in an American Skymaster cargo plane to Israel, where Czech technicians hastily assembled them. By 29 May, four were ready for action. By the end of August, another fifteen had been added to what remained of the original ten. They constituted the backbone of the IAF. In general, and in contrast with the Spitfires, which arrived later, they performed poorly.

276. Cohen, *History of Israeli Air Force*, 1:251.

277. Weizman, *On Eagles' Wings*, 67.

278. Ben-Gurion, protocol of Cabinet meeting, 30 May 1948, ISA.

279. Cohen, *History of Israeli Air Force*, 1:253.

280. Cohen, *History of Israeli Air Force*, 1:254-255.

281. Ayalon, *Giv'ati Brigade in Face of the Egyptian Invader*, 113-114.

282. Giv'ati/Intelligence, "Report on Operation 'Yitzhak'—2-3.6.48," 4 June 1948, IDFA922/75//949.

283. Ayalon, *Giv'ati Brigade in Face of the Egyptian Invader*, 140-141.

284. Cohen, *History of Israeli Air Force*, 1:280-82.

285. Segev, ed., *In Enemy Eyes*, 85.

286. Gerges, "Egypt and the 1948 War," 161.

287. Nasser, "Memoirs," 13.

288. Ben-Gurion, *War Diary*, entry for 22 May 1948, 449.

289. Ayalon, *Giv'ati Brigade in Face of the Egyptian Invader*, 71-77; Giv'ati, *Path of Desert and Fire*, 101-103.

290. Kirkbride to FO, 7 June 1948, PRO FO 371-68510.

291. Ayalon, *Giv'ati Brigade in Face of the Egyptian Invader*, 151-165; Dror, *Nitzanim*, 98-115.

292. Ayalon, *Giv'ati Brigade in Face of the Egyptian Invader*, 161.

293. Dror, *Nitzanim*, 18.

294. Dror, *Nitzanim*, 153-166.

295. This paragraph and the preceding one are based on Ilan, *Origin of Arab-Israeli Arms Race*, 28-33.

296. Sela, "Question of Palestine," 553.

297. Henry Mack to FO, 30 April 1948, PRO FO 371-68371.

298. Mack to FO, 29 April 1948 (no. 460), PRO FO 371-68371.

299. Mack to FO, 29 April 1948 (no. 463), PRO FO 371-68371.

300. Lorch, *Edge of the Sword,* 167–168.

301. Agin, "Battle to Contain the Invasion," 125.

302. Agin, "Battle to Contain the Invasion," 175.

303. ʿEtzioni, ed., *Tree and Sword,* 178–185; Abu Nowar, *Jordanian-Israeli War,* 168–170.

304. Tripp, "Iraq and the 1948 War," 137.

305. Glubb, *Soldier,* 130.

306. Ilan, *Origin of Arab-Israeli Arms Race,* 33–35.

307. Ilan, *Origin of Arab-Israeli Arms Race,* 227.

308. Ilan, *Origin of Arab-Israeli Arms Race,* 35.

309. Gad to Oded (though Alex), 29 May 1948, and OC Area 2, "Attack on Geulim," undated, both in IDFA 2506/49//75.

310. Cohen, *History of Israeli Air Force,* 1:255–257, 260–261.

311. Tal, *War in Palestine,* 232.

312. Eshel, *Carmeli Brigade,* 191.

313. Elpeleg, *In the Eyes of the Mufti,* 142.

314. Eshel, *Carmeli Brigade,* 194–195.

315. Pinhas Ofer, "The Battle of Jenin," July 1959, IDFA 1045/70//22.

316. Eshel, *Carmeli Brigade,* 201.

317. Eshel, *Carmeli Brigade,* 187–203; ʿEtzioni, ed., *Tree and Sword,* 198–219.

318. Al-Nafuri, "Syrian Army," 30–32. Ilan, *Origin of Arab-Israeli Arms Race,* 236, writes of "15,000" in "the autumn."

319. Al-Nafuri, "Syrian Army," 31.

320. Al-Nafuri, "Syrian Army," 31; Agin, "Balance of Forces" (expanded, unpublished version), n. 25. Ilan, *Origin of Arab-Israeli Arms Race,* 67, writes of "6,000" Syrian troops on the Palestine front at end of May 1948.

321. Ilan, *Origin of Arab-Israeli Arms Race,* 51–53.

322. Aharon Gilead quoted in Agin, "Battle to Contain the Invasion," 126.

323. Al-Nafuri, "Syrian Army," 30.

324. Kirkbride to FO, 12 February 1948, PRO FO 371-68367.

325. Broadmead to FO, 18 May 1948, PRO FO 371-68373.

326. ʿEin-Gev, 35–44.

327. Agin, "Battle to Contain the Invasion," 124.

328. Ben-Gurion, protocol of Cabinet meeting, 16 May 1948, ISA.

329. Agin, "Battle to Contain the Invasion," 134.

330. Agin, "Battle to Contain the Invasion," 149–150.

331. Al-Nafuri, "Syrian Army," 31.

332. Agin, "Battle to Contain the Invasion," 160.

333. Gelber, *Budding Fleur-de-Lis,* 400.

334. Ben-Gurion, *War Diary,* entry for 18 May 1948, 438; Ben-Gurion, protocol of Cabinet meeting, 19 May 1948, ISA.

335. Ben-Gurion, protocol of Cabinet meeting, 19, 23 May 1948, ISA; Agin, "Battle to Contain the Invasion," 172–174, 181, 184.

336. Ben-Zion Katz and Yehoshuʿa Ben-Arieh, "Testimony Taken from Murdi

(Mordechai Malhi) about His Activities in the Golani Brigade Especially in the Battles of the Jordan Valley during the War of Independence," undated, IDFA 922/75//943; Palmah HQ to Haganah GS, "Daily Report (Addition)," 19 May 1948, IDFA 922/75//1066.

337. Hadari, "War of Independence in the North," 140.

338. Palmah HQ to Heganah General Staff, "Daily Report (Addition)," 19 May 1948, IDFA 922/75//1066.

339. Alex Pereg and Ya'akov Klein to high command, 19 May 1948, quoted in Agin, "Battle to Contain the Invasion," 185.

340. Yigael Yadin to Golani, 19 May 1948, quoted in Agin, "Battle to Contain the Invasion," 188.

341. Agin, "Battle to Contain the Invasion," 188.

342. Agin, "Battle to Contain the Invasion," 190.

343. Agin, "Battle to Contain the Invasion," 205.

344. Agin, "Battle to Contain the Invasion," 195–203. Apparently only one tank was actually destroyed (it stands today on the lawn in the center of Degania Aleph). During the following decades Degania's members relentlessly debated who had actually destroyed it, and with what weapon. The Syrians were later to claim that their pullback had been prompted by a direct order from King 'Abdullah (Agin, "Battle to Contain the Invasion," 234)—but this is nonsense.

345. Al-Nafuri, "Syrian Army," 31.

346. Golani to Yadin, 21 May 1948, IDFA 922/75//1175.

347. Gelber, *Budding Fleur-de-Lis,* 446.

348. Katz and Ben-Arieh, "Testimony"; 'Etzioni, ed., *Tree and Sword,* 162–177.

349. Al-Nafuri, "Syrian Army," 31.

350. Gelber, *Budding Fleur-de-Lis,* 400–401.

351. HIS, "HIS Information, Daily Summary," 6 June 1948, HA 105/94.

352. Sela, "ALA in Galilee," 1:229, argues that the offensive was part of a grand Syrian-Lebanese-ALA design and an attempt by the Syrians to "return to the original Arab invasion plan, which aimed at gaining control of the Galilee, dismembering the State of Israel . . . and threatening Haifa." This is highly speculative, with no moorings in documentation, common sense, or fact.

353. Tzuri, Dori, to HIS-AD, "Report on the Attack on Mishmar Hayarden 10.6.48–11.6.48," 14 June 19438, HA 105/127 aleph.

354. Al-Nafuri, "Syrian Army," 32.

355. Ehrlich, *Lebanon Tangle,* 182.

356. Ilan, *Origin of Arab-Israeli Arms Race,* 54–55.

357. Gelber, *Budding Fleur-de-Lis,* 444.

358. Gelber, *Budding Fleur-de-Lis,* 397.

359. Tzuri to HIS-AD, 24 May 1948, HA 105–126.

360. Ma'ayan, "To Lose the North: The Arab States and the Galilee in the 1948 War," 1:275; Erlich, *Lebanon Tangle,* 175–182.

361. Ma'ayan, "Losing the North," 1:276.

362. Sela, "ALA in Galilee," 1:225–226.

363. Ehrlich, *Lebanon Tangle*, 195–197. The Yiftah Brigade and, in its wake, Israeli historiography wrongly believed that the Palmahniks had fought the "invading Lebanese Army" at Malikiya (see, e.g., Lorch, *Edge of the Sword*, 155–156).

364. Sela, "ALA in Galilee," 1:226.

365. Yiftah Brigade to Palmah HQ, 15 May 1948, 18:30 hrs., IDFA 922/75//1066; Gilead, ed., *Book of the Palmah*, 2:455–464; *Yiftah in a Storm*, 143–149.

366. Tzuri to HIS-AD, 21 May 1948, HA 105/128.

367. HIS, "HIS-AD Information," 16 June 1948, HA 105/126.

368. Gilead, ed., *Book of the Palmah*, 2:461; *Yiftah in a Storm*, 98–99.

369. Gilead, ed., *Book of the Palmah*, 2:293–296; *Yiftah in a Stor,* 150–151.

370. Ehrlich, *Lebanon Tangle*, 198–200; Ma'ayan, "Losing the North," 1:279–281.

371. General Staff/Operations, Southern Front, to Giv'ati, Sergei [Sarig], etc., 9 June 1948, IDFA 957/51//16.

372. Ayalon, *Giv'ati Brigade in Face of the Egyptian Invader,* 183–198.

373. Cohen, *History of Israeli Air Force,* 1:258.

374. Ben-Gurion, *War Diary,* entry for 24 May 1948, 453–454.

375. Kirkbride to FO, 1 June 1948, PRO FO 371-68374.

376. Ben-Gurion, protocol of Cabinet meeting, 2 June 1948, ISA; Ben-Gurion, *War Diary,* entry for 2 June 1948, 478, n. 5; Cohen, *History of Israeli Air Force,* 1: 266–271.

377. Cohen, *History of Israeli Air Force,* 1:305–307. A planned bombing of Cairo that morning was canceled for technical reasons.

378. Tal, *Naval Operations in Israel's War of Independence,* 61–62, 88, 96–97.

379. Tal, *Naval Operations in Israel's War of Independence,* 88–95; Cohen, *History of Israeli Air Force,* 1:282–285.

380. Moshe Carmel, protocol of "[General] Staff Meeting after [Start of] First Truce," undated, IDFA 121/50//172.

CHAPTER 6. THE FIRST TRUCE, 11 JUNE–8 JULY 1948, AND THE INTERNATIONAL COMMUNITY AND THE WAR

1. Ilan, *Bernadotte in Palestine,* 61.

2. Ilan, *Bernadotte in Palestine,* 61–62.

3. Ilan, *Bernadotte in Palestine,* 63.

4. Henry Mack to FO, 22 May 1948, PRO FO 371-68373.

5. Ilan, *Bernadotte in Palestine,* 73.

6. Houstoun Boswall to FO, 28 May 1948, PRO FO 371-68374.

7. Yigael Yadin to "managers," 10 June 10948, 19:45 hrs., IDFA 2687/49//35.

8. David Ben-Gurion, protocol of Cabinet meeting, 6 June 1948, ISA.

9. Ilan, *Bernadotte in Palestine,* 80.

10. Ilan, *Bernadotte in Palestine,* 87.

11. Abba Eban to Trygve Lie, 1 June 1948, ISA, *DFPI,* 1:108–109.

12. Boswall to FO, 30 July 1948, PRO FO 816/127, quoting 'Azzam.

13. Ilan, *Bernadotte in Palestine,* 93.

14. Moshe Shertok to Abba Eban, 7 June 1948, ISA, *DFPI*, I, 132.

15. Ben-Gurion, protocol of Cabinet meeting, 14 June 1948, ISA.

16. HIS, "HIS Information, Daily Precis," 11 June 1948, HA 105/94.

17. Beaumont to Bernard Burrows, 18 July 1948, PRO FO 371-68375.

18. Nasser, "Memoirs," 17–19.

19. Ilan, *Origin of Arab-Israeli Arms Race,* 185, 195.

20. Ilan, *Origin of Arab-Israeli Arms Race,* 206–207.

21. Ilan, *Origin of Arab-Israeli Arms Race,* 116, 177–178, 194.

22. Ben-Gurion, protocol of Cabinet meeting, 14 June 1948.

23. Morris, *Birth of Palestinian Refugee Problem Revisited,* 372.

24. Nasser, "Memoirs," 22, n. 26.

25. Ilan, *Bernadotte in Palestine,* 125.

26. Shertok to Nahum Goldmann, 15 June 1948, ISA, *DFPI,* 1:163.

27. Ilan, *Bernadotee in Palestine,* 147, quoting "Report of the UN Mediator for Palestine to the Security Council," July 1948.

28. Ilan, *Bernadotte in Palestine,* 135.

29. Ilan, *Bernadotte in Palestine,* 137.

30. Ilan, *Bernadotte in Palestine,* 172.

31. See, e.g., Burrows, untitled minute, 9 February 1948 , PRO FO 371-68368; and Ilan, *Bernadotte in Palestine,* 69, quoting Bevin memorandum, "Mediation in Palestine," 26 May 1948.

32. "TRL," untitled memorandum on meeting with Neguib Armenazi, 23 June 1948, PRO FO 371-68374.

33. Tzuri to Yirmiyahu, 28 June 1948, IDFA 128/51//84.

34. Unsigned but Middle East Department, Israel Foreign Ministry, "Palestine in Arab Broadcasts, 3–4.7.48," undated, CZA S25-9047.

35. Alec Kirkbride to Bevin (no. 546), 9 July 1948, PRO FO 816/125.

36. Glubb, *Soldier,* 150.

37. Campbell to FO, 7 July 1948, PRO FO 371-68375.

CHAPTER 7. THE "TEN DAYS" AND AFTER

1. David Ben-Gurion, protocol of Cabinet meeting, 11 July 1948, ISA.

2. Kimche and Kimche, *Both Sides of the Hill,* 213. Ben-Gurion often "fell ill" during crises.

3. See Shapira, *Army Controversy, 1948;* and Gelber, *Why Was the Palmah Disbanded?*

4. Ayalon, *Giv'ati Brigade in Face of the Egyptian Invader,* 226–228; Giv'ati, "An-Far Operations," 7 July 1948, IDFA 7011/49//1.

5. Giv'ati HQ, "An-Far Operations," 7 July 1948, IDFA 7011/49//1. Regarding refugee encampments, the battalions were ordered to "destroy, kill, and expel."

6. Nasser, "Memoirs," 17–20.

7. Nasser, "Memoirs," 19.

8. Ayalon, *Giv'ati Brigade in Face of the Egyptian Invader,* 219–222.

9. Unsigned, "Appreciation of Probable Intention on Southern Front after Cease Fire," undated but c. 7 July 1948, IDFA704/49//5.

10. Ronald Campbell to FO, 10 July 1948, PRO FO 371-68375.

11. Ayalon, *Givʿati Brigade in Face of the Egyptian Invader*, 233–242.

12. Nasser, "Memoirs," 22–23.

13. Nasser, "Memoirs," 27.

14. Nasser, "Memoirs," 28–29.

15. Campbell to FO, 10 July 1948.

16. Givʿati HQ, "Combat Page Early 14.7.48," IDFA 6127/49//118.

17. Ayalon, *Givʿati Brigade in Face of the Egyptian Invader*, 290.

18. Ayalon, *Givʿati Brigade in Face of the Egyptian Invader*, 278–292.

19. Neguib, *Egypt's Destiny*, 22–23.

20. Ilan, *Bernadotte in Palestine*, 159.

21. Givʿati Brigade logbook, 16 July 1948, unsigned, IDFA 922/75//1226.

22. Ayalon, *Givʿati Brigade in Face of the Egyptian Invader*, 293–340; Givʿati, *Path of Desert and Fire*, 178–184.

23. Givʿati, *Path of Desert and Fire*, 173–178.

24. Ayalon, *Givʿati Brigade in Face of the Egyptian Invader*, 341–349.

25. Avneri, *Fields of Philistia*, 171.

26. Gerges, "Egypt and the 1948 War," 162–163.

27. Carmel, "Operation[s] 'Brosh' and 'Dekel,'" 6 July 1948, IDFA 4858/49//495.

28. Tzuri to Golani, "Nazareth," 8 July 1948, 7429/49//138.

29. Eshel, *Carmeli Brigade*, 206–207.

30. Gelber, "Druze and Jews," 236; Parsons, "Druze and Birth of Israel," 63–64.

31. Seventh Brigade Tactical HQ, "Operation 'Dekel,'" 8 July 1948, IDFA 1137/49//84.

32. Hiram to IDF-IS, "The Investigation [of the fall of Nazareth?] by . . . from Tulkarm," 3 August 1948, IDFA 7249/49//138.

33. Tzuri, Leshem, to HIS-AD, 26 June 1948, IDFA 7249/49//138. The HIS was dismantled during June-July, and its component parts became the core of the "IDF Intelligence Service" (*sherut hamodiʿin shel tzahal*) (IDF-IS), the "General Security Service" (*sherut habitahon haklali*, or *shin bet*) (GSS), and the "Political Department" of the Foreign Ministry, the forerunner of Israel's foreign intelligence service, later renamed the Institute for Intelligence and Special Duties (*hamossad lemodiʿin vetafkidim meyuhadim*) or, simply, the "Mossad."

34. Tzuri, Leshem, to HIS-AD, 26 June, 7, 11 July 1948, IDFA 7249/49//138.

35. Tzuri, Shaʿanan, to HIS-AD, 11 July 1948, IDFA 7149/49//138.

36. Elisha Sultz, "Report on the Activities of the Military Governor in Nazareth . . . for 17.7–17.10.48," undated, IDFA 121/50//223.

37. Unsigned, "Copy," undated, memorandum, IDFA 5205/49//1; Nahum Golan, OC Golani Brigade, to OC Northern Front, "Probe of Facts Relating to Nazareth and Surrounding Villages," 4 September 1948, IDFA 260/51//54.

38. Untitled report, Golani/Intelligence, 15 July 1948, IDFA 7249/49//138.

39. ʿEtzioni, ed., *Tree and Sword*, 23.

40. Ben-Gurion to Yigael Yadin, 15 July 1948, IDFA 922/75//1025.

41. Carmel, "Order of the Day for 16.7.48," IDFA 2384/50//1.

42. Tzuri, Leshem, to HIS-AD, "The Conquest of Nazareth," 19 July 1948, HA 105/92 bet.

43. Hiram to IDF-IS, 25 July 1948, IDFA 7249/49//138.

44. Twelfth Battalion to Golani HQ, 16 July 1948, 19:00 hrs., IDFA 128/51//50.

45. Hiram to IDF-IS, "The Investigation by . . . from Tulkarm," 3 August 1948, IDFA 7249/49//138 (the name of the Arab author of the report was deleted by IDFA censors).

46. Eshel, *Carmeli Brigade,* 218–221.

47. Tzuri, Leshem, to HIS-AD, "The Conquest of Nazareth," 19 July 1948.

48. Seventh Brigade HQ/Intelligence, to General Staff/Operations, "Report on the Conquest of Nazareth," 17 July 1948, IDFA 82/54//260.

49. "The Conditions of Surrender," unsigned, Nazareth, 16 July 1948, IDFA 2315/50//15.

50. Tzuri, Leshem, to HIS-AD, "The Conquest of Nazareth," 19 July 1948.

51. Tzuri, Yosef, to IDF-IS, 31 August 1948, IDFA 7349/49//138.

52. Ben-Gurion, *War Diary,* entry for 18 July 1948, 599.

53. Peretz Kidron, "Truth Whereby Nations Live," 86–87.

54. Seventh Brigade Combat HQ to General Staff, 17 July 1948, 14:30 hrs., IDFA 922/75//1025.

55. Yirmiyahu to Golani, 17 July 1948, 18:30 hrs., IDFA 1281/51//50.

56. Northern Front HQ to Golani HQ, 22 July 1948, IDFA 5205/49//1.

57. Tzuri, Leshem, to HIS-AD, 21 July 1948, and Tzuri, Shaltiel, to IDF-IS, 29 July 1948, both in IDFA 7249/49//138.

58. IDF General Staff, logbook of incoming cables, entry for 18 July 1948, IDFA 922/75//1176; Northern Front HQ to General Staff/Operations/Intelligence, etc., "Report for 18/7/48 08:00 hrs.," IDFA 7249/49//170.

59. Sela, "ALA in Galilee," 1:234.

60. Israeli intelligence subsequently reported that 12 ALA officers had died at Sejera (see Tzuri, Shaltiel, to IDF-IS, 29 July 1948, IDFA 7249/49//138); Sela, "ALA in Galilee," 1:235.

61. ʿEtzioni, ed., *Tree and Sword,* 254–277.

62. Combat HQ Seventh Brigade, Intelligence, to General Staff/Operations, "Report on Activities in Western Galilee," 19 July 1948, IDFA 1094/49//77.

63. Tzuri, Paltiel, to IDF-IS, "Doings in the North of the Country," 29 July 1948, HA 105/92 bet.

64. ʿAbd al-Qadir al-Dib, Nimr Qassam, etc., "Surrender Instrument of the Village of ʿEin Mahal," 18 July 1948, IDFA 2315/50//15.

65. Ben-Zion Ken and Yehoshua Ben-Arieh, "Testimony Taken from Reuven Ron, a Company OC in Golani [Brigade's] 12th Battalion in the War of Independence. His Activities in the Battalion during the War Up until [the Brigade's] 'Descent to the Negev,'" 23 March 1957, IDFA 922/75//943.

66. See, e.g., Golani Intelligence Officer, "Summary from Noon 17.7.48 until 24:00 hours," undated, IDFA 128/51//84.

67. Intelligence Officer Tzidoni Battalion, "Report on the Operations of the Tzidoni Battalion from 10.7.48 until 27.7.48," undated, IDFA 5492/49//3.

68. Northern Front HQ to Oded, Golani, etc., "Operation[s] 'Brosh' and 'Dekel,'" 6 July 1948, IDFA 4858/49//495.

69. The exact size of the Syrian force in the bridgehead and immediately to its rear, on the east bank of the Jordan, is unclear. Al-Nafuri, "Syrian Army," 32, speaks of "three battalions of infantry, one of armor, altogether 1,500 troops," whereas Tal, *War in Palestine,* 340, writes of "two brigades," consisting of "seven or eight battalions."

70. Northern Front HQ to General Staff/Operations/Intelligence, etc., "Report for 18/7/48 08:00 hrs.," IDFA 7249/49//170.

71. Eshel, *Carmeli Brigade,* 227–248.

72. Ben-Gurion, protocol of Cabinet meeting, 14 June 1948, ISA: "The Arab Legion is an army that inspires respect among all our boys. It knows the craft of war."

73. Ben-Gurion, *War Diary,* entry for 30 May 1948, 468.

74. Ben-Gurion, protocol of Cabinet meeting, 16 June 1948, ISA.

75. Ben-Gurion, *War Diary,* entries for 11, 24 May, 4 June 1948, 410, 453, 485.

76. Alexandroni, "Bulletin No. 55," 7 July 1948, IDFA 2323/49//6; Orren, *Operation "Danni,"* 41–42.

77. IDF GS/Operations, Southern Front, to Kiryati, etc., 26 June 1948, IDFA 922/75//1237.

78. Glubb, *Soldier,* 142–143; Pirie-Gordon to B. A. B. Burrows, 25 July 1948, PRO FO 371-68822.

79. Kadish, Sela, and Golan, *Occupation of Lydda,* 24, write of "1,000" armed locals in Lydda alone, surely an exaggeration.

80. Glubb, *Soldier,* 157–159; Orren, *Operation "Danni,"* 42.

81. Ben-Gurion, protocol of Cabinet meeting, 6 October 1948, ISA (an interjection in the middle of a statement by Yitzhak Gruenbaum). Gruenbaum interpreted the ease with which the towns were captured as proof that "Abdullah refused to fight."

82. Alec Kirkbride to secretary of state (no. 548), 10 July 1948, PRO FO 816/125.

83. Ben-Gurion, protocol of Cabinet meeting, 14 July 1948, ISA.

84. Dayan, *Story,* 71.

85. Kadish, Sela, and Golan, *Occupation of Lydda,* 143–144. The raid was honestly described by Natan Alterman, Israel's leading poet, in the poem "'Al zot" (On this), published in the socialist daily *Davar* in November 1948.

86. Ben-Gurion, protocol of Cabinet meeting, 14 July 1948, said Dayan's "chutzpah" raid "astounded" the town.

87. Third Battalion Intelligence Officer, "Report on the 11th of July—Operation in Lydda" and "Report on the 12th of the Month," 14 July 1948, IDFA 922/75//1237.

88. Arshid Marshud, OC First Regiment, "The Recollections of Arshid Marshud, of the 1st Regiment, on the 1st Regiment's Battles in Palestine," 9 December 1948, IDFA 922/75//693.

89. Third Battalion Intelligence, "Comprehensive Report on the Activities of the 3rd Battalion from Friday 9.7 until Sunday 18.7," 18 July 1948, IDFA 922/75//1237; and "Miki" Operation HQ/Intelligence, "Operation 'Dani' (Concluding Report)," 15 August 1948, IDFA 922/75//1237.

90. See Morris, *Birth of Palestinian Refugee Problem Revisited*, 429; and Ben-Gurion, protocol of Cabinet meeting, 16 June 1948, in which a relevant paragraph has been blanked out by government censors.

91. "Yitzhak R," Dani HQ, to Yiftah HQ, 10 July 1948, 16:00 hrs., and Operation Dani HQ to IDF GS, 10 July 1948, both in IDFA 922/75//1234.

92. "Yitzhak R" to Yiftah and Eighth Brigade, 12 July 1948, 13:30 hrs., IDFA 922/75//1234. The order exists in a number of variants, including one in which Yiftah is instructed "to differentiate between [persons of different] ages" (IDFA 922/75//1237).

93. See Kiryati HQ to Zvi Aurbach, 13 July 1948, 14:50 hrs., HA 80/774/12.

94. Alexander Tzur, "The Conditions of Surrender of the Town of Ramla," 12 July 1948, IDFA 2315/50//60.

95. Kiryati HQ to OC Ramla Garrison, 13 July 1948, 19:15 hrs., HA 80/774/12.

96. Morris, *Birth of Palestinian Refugee Problem Revisited*, 432.

97. Intelligence officer to OC Forty-third Battalion, 13 July 1948, IDFA 922/75//1237.

98. Gilead, ed., *Book of the Palmah*, 2:718.

99. Morris, *Birth of Palestinian Refugee Problem Revisited*, 433.

100. Glubb, *Soldier*, 162.

101. Untitled, undated, printed report, signed "Yigal," KMA-PA 142–51.

102. Meir Ya'ari, 12 December 1948, protocol of meeting of Kibbutz Artzi Council, 10–12 December 1948, HHA 5.20.5 (4).

103. Page from untitled intelligence logbook (possibly Giv'ati Brigade HQ), entry for 15 July 1948, IDFA 922/75//1226; (sigint intercept) "SVC" to "Damascus," possibly 15 July 1948, HA 105/92 bet.

104. Steiger, "Arab Legion," 206.

105. Abu Nowar, *Jordanian-Israeli War*, 206–207.

106. IDF Intelligence Service/Arab Department, "From Listening to the Legion Wavelength," 21 July 1948, ISA FM 2569/13; Consul general, Jerusalem, to FO, 25 July 1948, PRO FO 816/139.

107. Morris, *Road to Jerusalem*, 176.

108. Pirie-Gordon to Burrows, 25 July 1948; Hiram to IDF Intelligence Service/Arab Department, "A Visit to Amman, Irbid, Nablus," 17 July 1948, ISA FM 2569/13. Tall, *Memoirs*, 194–196, says simply that Glubb "handed over" the two towns to the IDF on British instructions.

109. "Report by Informers Who Have Returned from a Journey through Nazareth–

Irbid–Zarqa–Amman–Jericho–Nablus–Nazareth," 15 September 1948, ISA FM 2569/13.

110. Kirkbride, *From the Wings*, 48.

111. Glubb, *Soldier*, 163–164.

112. Pirie-Gordon to Ernest Bevin (no. 570), 14 July 1948, PRO FO 816/126; Campbell, Cairo, to Kirkbride, 16 July 1948, PRO FO 816/126; Shlaim, *Collusion across the Jordan*, 269.

113. Kirkbride to Bevin, 6 August 1948, PRO FO 816/127.

114. Kirkbride to Bevin, 29 July 1948, PRO FO 816/127.

115. Kirkbride to Bevin, 6 August 1948, PRO FO 816/127.

116. Glubb, *Soldier*, 179.

117. Pirie-Gordon to Burrows, 25 July 1948; Glubb, *Soldier*, 165–166.

118. Pirie-Gordon to Bevin (no. 570), 14 July 1948; Pirie-Gordon, "Major General Glubb's Relations with the Trans-Jordan Government," 15 July 1948, quoted in Norton, "Last Pasha," 358.

119. Kirkbride to Bevin, 6 August 1948, PRO FO 816/127.

120. Ben-Gurion, protocol of Cabinet meeting of 14 July 1948. For a fuller treatment of the events of Lydda-Ramla on 11–13 July, see Morris, *Birth of Palestinian Refugee Problem Revisited*, 424–435; and Morris, "Operation Dani and Palestinian Exodus."

121. See, e.g., Y. Gvirtz to Minorities Minister, 21 July 1948, Minority Affairs Ministry, 297/5 gimel, and Military Governor of Ramla-Lydda, "Monthly Report on the Activities of the Military Governor of Ramla-Lydda and on the General Situation in the Area," [?] October 1948, IDFA 1860/50//30.

122. Rivlin and Sinai, eds., *Alexandroni Brigade*, 290–299; unsigned, "Investigation of the Disaster at Qula," undated, and Shaul Rosenberg, OC A Company, Thirty-second Battalion, to OC Thirty-second Battalion 15 August 1948, both in IDFA 922/75//949.

123. Battalion 32, Alexandroni Brigade, to brigade intelligence officer, 19 July 1948, IDFA 922/75//949.

124. Ben-Gurion, *War Diary*, entry for 11 July 1948, 582.

125. Tal, *War in Palestine*, 324.

126. Orren, *Operation "Danni,"* 207.

127. Amit Goodes, "The Battle of Khirbet Kureikur," in Shiran, ed., *Jews and Arabs*, 319–341; Orren, *Operation "Danni,"* 196–203; "Recollections of Arshid Marshud," IDFA 922/75//693 (who speaks of "300" Israeli dead).

128. Levy, *Jerusalem in the War of Independence*, 313–319; Lapidot, *Flames of Revolt*, 414–425. Lapidot, an IZL veteran, (mistakenly) argues that the operation was deliberately torpedoed by Ben-Gurion because he did not want to conquer the Old City.

129. Dani HQ to Harel, Yiftah, Eighth and Kiryati brigades, 19 July 1948, IDFA 922/75//1235.

130. See, e.g., Kiryati/Operations to Dani HQ, 21 July 1948, IDFA 922/75//1235.

131. Pirie-Gordon to secretary of state, 18 July 1948 (no. 585), PRO FO 816/126; Pirie-Gordon to Burrows, 25 July 1948, PRO FO 816/127.

132. *Haaretz,* 16 July 1948; Cohen, *History of Israeli Air Force,* 1:644–649.

133. Ben-Gurion, protocol of Cabinet meeting, 16 July 1948, ISA.

134. Cohen, *History of Israeli Air Force,* 1:647.

135. Ben-Gurion, *War Diary,* entry for 12 August 1948, 646.

136. Lachish, "Bombing," 44–57.

137. Cohen, *History of Israeli Air Force,* 1:649–652.

138. Cohen, *History of Israeli Air Force,* 1:665.

139. P. M. Broadmead to Burrows, 19 July 1948, PRO FO 371-68813; Cohen, *Air Force,* 1:667.

140. Cohen, *History of Israeli Air Force,* 1:667–668.

141. The Beirut daily *Al-Hayat,* quoted in Houstoun Boswall to FO, 21 July 1948, PRO FO 371-68494.

142. Stabler to SecState, 25 July 1948, *FRUS,* 5:1237–1238; Pirie-Gordon to Burrows, 25 July 1948, PRO FO 816/127, citing the Iraqis' recognition of their weakness.

143. Houstoun Boswall to chargé, Amman, 26 July 1948 (reproducing Boswall to FO, 24 July 1948), PRO FO 816/127. Boswall wrote: "It is difficult to assess the Prime Minister's real attitude. He has twice given us the impression that he would urge moderation at the Arab League meetings, and has twice acted in the opposite sense." The duplicity of the Arab leaders never ceased to surprise their British interlocutors.

144. Boswall to FO, 21 July 1948, PRO FO 371-68494; Ilan, *Bernadotte in Palestine,* 149.

145. Kirkbride to Bevin, 6 August 1948, PRO FO 816/127.

146. Pirie-Gordon to FO, 27 July 1948, PRO FO 816/127.

147. Ben-Gurion, *War Diary,* entry for 12 August 1948, 646.

148. Gerges, "Egypt and the 1948 War," *War,* 163.

149. FO to British Embassy, Washington, DC, 8 August 1948, PRO FO 371-68379.

150. Tal, *War in Palestine,* 345.

151. Ben-Gurion, protocol of Cabinet meeting, 14 July 1948, ISA.

152. "Bentz," "Operational Order for Operation 'Shoter,'" 24 July 1948, IDFA 352/53//28.

153. Cohen, *History of Israeli Air Force,* 1:673–682.

154. Morris, *Birth of Palestinian Refugee Problem Revisited,* 438–441.

155. Yadin, protocol of Cabinet meeting, 8 September 1948, ISA.

156. Yadin, protocol of Cabinet meeting, 8 September 1948.

157. Ilan, *Bernadotte in Palestine,* 159.

158. Ilan, *Bernadotte in Palestine,* 161.

159. Unsigned, "Summary of the Meeting of the Advisers on Arab Affairs in Camp Dora 31.3.48," and unsigned, "Summary of the Meeting of the Arab Affairs Advisers at Dora Camp 6.4.48," both in IDFA 4663/49//125.

160. Myerson, protocol of meeting of JAE, 6 May 1948, CZA 45/2.

161. Morris, *Birth of Palestinian Refugee Problem Revisited,* 311 and 321.

162. Protocol of meeting in Haifa, 6 June 1948, ISA MAM 303/41.

163. Morris, *Birth of Palestinian Refugee Problem Revisited*, 316.

164. OC IDF Intelligence Department, 16 June 1948, ISA FM 2426/9.

165. Moshe Shertok, "[Talk] with Yosef Weitz," 28 May 1948, ISA FM 2564/20.

166. Weitz, Danin, Sasson, "Retroactive . . . ," undated but from early June 1948, ISA FM 2564/19.

167. Morris, "Weitz and Transfer Committees," 533–535.

168. Ben-Gurion, *War Diary,* entry for 1 June 1948, 477.

169. Oded/Operations to battalions, 13 June 1948, IDFA 6309/49//2.

170. Ben-Gurion, Shertok, Cisling, protocol of Cabinet meeting, 16 June 1948, ISA.

171. See, e.g., OC Golani Brigade, Nahum, Golan, to Shimon, Binyamin, and Levi, 16 June 1948, IDFA 1096/49//51, and Yitzhak Rabin, Dani HQ, to Harel, Yiftah, Kiryati, and Eighth Brigades, 19 July 1948, KMA-PA 141-419.

172. Protocol of Cabinet meeting of 28 July 1948, ISA.

173. Foreign minister to Cabinet members, "Instructions to the Israeli Delegation to the UN General Assembly," 10 September 1948, appended to protocol of Cabinet meeting of 12 September 1948, ISA. See also Yaʿakov Shimoni to Eliahu Sasson, 16 September 1948, ISA FM 3749/1.

174. OC Fifty-first Battalion to C Company, etc., 20 July 1948, IDFA 922/75//899.

175. Fifty-first Battalion/Intelligence to Givʿati HQ/Intelligence, 19 July 1948, IDFA 1041/49//12.

176. Givʿati Brigade, untitled logbook page, entries for 21–25 July 1948, IDFA 922/75//899. The entry for 21 July, dealing with the fate of the three detainees, was blacked out by IDFA censors.

177. Intelligence officer, Fifty-third Battalion, to Givʿati HQ/Intelligence, 24 July 1948, IDFA 1041/49//12.

178. Givʿati Brigade logbook, entries for 6, 13 August 1948, IDFA 922/75//899.

179. OC Givʿati to Fifty-fifth Battalion, etc., 24 August 1948, IDFA 7011/49//5.

180. Fifty-fifth Battalion/Intelligence officer, to Givʿati/Operations, "Report on Operation 'Nikayon,'" 29 August 1948, IDFA 922/75//899.

181. OC First Company to Jezreel Battalion, 5 August 21948, IDFA 128/51//32.

182. Golani Brigade/Intelligence, "Daily Summary 25–26.8," IDFA 1096/49//64.

183. Third Battalion/Intelligence to Yiftah HQ/Intelligence, 27 September 1948, IDFA 922/75//1227.

184. Jezreel Battalion to Golani/Intelligence, 8 August 1948, IDFA 128/51//32.

185. Fifty-second Battalion to Givʿati/Intelligence, 25 August 1948, IDFA 1041/49//12.

186. Golani ?, to Golani and Carmeli HQs, 9 April 1948, IDFA 128/51//50.

187. Palmah HQ to HGS, "Daily Report," 10 April 1948, IDFA 922/75//1066.

188. Palmah HQ to HGS, "Daily Report," 12 April 1948, IDFA 922/75//1214.

189. Palmah HQ to HGS, "Daily Report," 15 April 1948, IDFA 922/75//1066.

190. Nahshon Corps HQ to battalion HQs "A," "B," and "C," etc., 4 (?) April 1948, IDFA 922/75//1233.

191. Unsigned, "Report on the Conquest of Qaluniya," 9 April 1948, IDFA 922/75//1233.

192. Levine, *Jerusalem,* entry for 12 April 1948, 67.

193. Palmah HQ to HGS, "Daily Report," 16 April 1948, IDFA 922/75//1214.

194. Nahshon Corps HQ to Second Battalion, etc., 15 April 1948, IDFA 236/53//1.

195. Nahshon Corps HQ to Fifty-second Battalion, Giv'ati, 15 April 1948, IDFA 236/53//1.

196. Nahshon HQ to First Battalion, 15 April 1948, IDFA 236/53//1.

197. Cisling, statement in Cabinet, 16 June 1948, KMA-AZP 9/9/3.

198. Gvirtz to Shitrit, 23 June 1948, and Gvirtz, "Report for the Month of June," undated, but from early July 1948, both in ISA AM gimel/19/aleph.

199. Gordon to *Davar* editorial board, 14 December 1948, IDFA 1292/51//68.

200. Eli'ezer Kaplan, protocol of meeting of Ministerial Committee for Abandoned Property (which he chaired), 5 November 1948, ISA FM 2401/21 aleph.

201. Morris, *Birth of Palestinian Refugee Problem Revisited,* 361.

202. Kibbutz Neve-Yam to Agricultural Center, 3 August 1948, LA 235 IV, 2251.

203. Weitz, *Diary and Letters,* entry for 20 May 1948, 3:288.

204. Morris, *Birth of Palestinian Refugee Problem Revisited,* 366–367.

205. Weitz, "To Settle New Lands," 1949, ISA AM 29/7.

206. Weitz, Harzfeld, and Horin, "Proposal for New Settlements by the Agricultural Settlements Committee of the National Institutions . . . ," 28 July 1948, KMA-ACP 8/4 aleph; Weitz, protocol of meeting of JNF directorate, 16 August 1948, CZA KKL 10.

207. Ra'anan Weitz, secretary of the Jewish Agency Settlement Department (and son of Yosef Weitz), memorandum submitted to Ministerial Committee for Abandoned Property, 30 November 1948, KMA-ACP 4, aleph/8.

208. Weitz, *Diary and Letters,* entries for 3, 10 December, 3:360, 364.

209. Weitz, *Diary and Letters,* entries for 18, 19 December 1948, 3:366, 369.

210. Ben-Gurion, *War Diary,* entry for 31 January 1948, 197.

211. Morris, *Birth of Palestinian Refugee Problem Revisited,* 384–385.

212. Morris, *Birth of Palestinian Refugee Problem Revisited,* 384–393.

213. Chapman Andrews, Cairo, to FO, 16 August 1948, PRO FO 371-68677.

214. Kirkbride to FO, 18 August 1948, PRO FO 371-68677.

215. James McDonald to secretary of state, 17 October 1948, USNA 501, BB Palestine/10–1748.

216. Stanton Griffis, Cairo, to secretary of state, 6 October 1948, USNA 501, BB Palestine/10–648.

217. Ben-Gurion, protocol of Cabinet meeting, 1 August 1948, ISA.

218. Eliahu Epstein to Shertok, 20 August 1948, *DFPI,* 1:540.

219. Ben-Gurion, protocol of Cabinet meeting, 21 September 1948, ISA.

220. Yadin, protocol of Cabinet meeting, 8 September 1948, ISA.

221. Ben-Gurion, *War Diary,* entry for 9 September 1948, 679.

222. Douglas, London, to secretary of state, 27 August 1948, and Douglas to secretary of state, 3 September 1948, both in *FRUS, 1948,* 5, pt. 2:1354–1357, 1373–1375.

223. Ilan, *Bernadotte in Palestine*, 186–189.

224. Ilan, *Bernadotte in Palestine*, 190.

225. Ilan, *Bernadotte in Palestine*, 196–199.

226. Acting secretary of state (Lovett) to certain diplomatic and consular office (conveying Marshall's statement), 21 September 1948, *FRUS, 1948*, 5, pt. 2:1415–16; Ilan, *Bernadotte in Palestine*, 226.

227. Trefor Evans to FO, 21 September 1948, PRO FO 371-68376.

228. Harold Beeley to Burrows, 11 November 1948, PRO FO 371-68643.

229. Ilan, *Bernadotte in Palestine*, 224.

230. Gerges, "Egypt and the 1948 War," 164.

231. Cohen-Shani, *Paris Operation*, 73–95.

232. Sasson to Foreign Ministry, 23 September 1948, ISA, *DFPI*, 1:632–634.

233. "Appendix 1," 22 September 1948, ISA, *DFPI*, 1:34–636.

234. Shertok to Walter Eytan, Tel Aviv, 5 October 1948, ISA, *DFPI*, 2:21–22. It is not clear from the available documents whether the Egyptians were insisting on the whole of the Negev (plus the southern Coastal Strip) or only the northwestern strip of the Negev earmarked in the UN partition resolution for Palestinian sovereignty. Doran, *Pan-Arabism before Nasser*, 181–182, thinks the former.

235. "Appendix II," "Appendix III," ISA, *DFPI*, 2:25–25–27.

236. "Appendix IV," ISA, *DFPI*, 2:28–29. See also Doran, *Pan-Arabism before Nasser*, 181–184, for these negotiations.

237. Ben-Gurion, protocol of Cabinet meeting, 6 October 1948, ISA.

238. Gelber, *Independence versus Nakba*, 312.

239. Foreign minister to minority affairs minister, 8 August 1948, ISA FM 2570/10. See also Haim Berman and Sasson, "Proposals," 13 March 1948, CZA S25-9383.

240. Gelber, *Independence versus Nakba*, 312.

241. One incident, in which four persons were shot dead in an Arab ambush on 22 September, is described in a radio message from Bunche to the chief of staff of the UN observer mission from 30 September 1948, intercepted by IDF intelligence (see Ta to "Daat," undated, HA 105/119).

242. Protocol of Cabinet meeting, 26 September 1948, ISA.

243. Ben-Gurion, protocol of Cabinet meeting, 6 October 1948.

244. Ben-Gurion, *War Diary*, entry for 6 October 1948, 735.

245. Protocol of Cabinet meeting, 6 October 1948, ISA.

246. Ben-Gurion, protocol of Cabinet meeting, 10 October 1948, ISA.

247. "Meeting of the IDF General Staff, Defense Ministry . . . 6.10.48," IDFA 121/50//172.

CHAPTER 8. OPERATIONS YOAV AND HIRAM

1. Ben-Gurion, protocol of Cabinet meeting, 26 September 1948, ISA.

2. Rabin, *Memoirs*, 37: "We were ready and eager for action."

3. Fifth Brigade to Battalions 51, etc., "Operational Order Operation 'Yoav,'" 11

October 1948, IDFA 922/75//899; Ayalon, *Giv'ati Brigade in Face of the Egyptian Invader*, 425–426.

4. Tal, "Military Decision in the Shadow of Political Struggle," 1:450–456.

5. "The Battle for the Negev, a Stenogram of the Lecture by General Yigal Allon, OC Southern Front, on 1.11.48 to the Cultural Officers," IDFA 2289/50//80.

6. Gelber, *Budding Fleur-de-Lis*, 2:706–707.

7. Ayalon, *Giv'ati Brigade in Face of the Egyptian Invader*, 416–417; Ilan, *Origin of Arab-Israeli Arms Race*, 256.

8. Ilan, *Origin of Arab-Israeli Arms Race*, 257–258. In the corruption charge sheet drawn up against senior Egyptian officers after the war, it stated that, in one significant purchase, 42 percent of the ammunition was spoiled and "more dangerous to the user than the enemy."

9. Ben-Gurion, *War Diary*, 6 October 1948, 736.

10. Ben-Gurion, *War Diary*, 7 October 1948, 736–737; Ben-Gurion, protocol of Cabinet meeting, 5 September 1948, ISA.

11. Gelber, *Budding Fleur-de-Lis*, 2:732.

12. Ben-Gurion, protocol of Cabinet meeting, 5 September 1948, ISA.

13. Cohen, *History of Israeli Air Force*, 3:35.

14. Rabin, *Memoirs*, 37.

15. Cohen, *History of Israeli Air Force*, 3:36.

16. Cohen, *History of Israeli Air Force*, 3:35–36.

17. Cohen, *History of Israeli Air Force*, 3:37–42.

18. Cohen, *History of Israeli Air Force*, 3:46.

19. Cohen, *History of Israeli Air Force*, 3:45.

20. Ilan, *Origin of Arab-Israeli Arms Race*, 232.

21. Ayalon, *Giv'ati Brigade in Face of the Egyptian Invader*, 431–436.

22. Giv'ati, *Path of Desert and Fire*, 210–212.

23. Ayalon, *Giv'ati Brigade in Face of the Egyptian Invader*, 443.

24. Ayalon, *Giv'ati Brigade in Face of the Egyptian Invader*, 455.

25. Ben-Gurion, *War Diary*, entry for 18 October 1948, 753.

26. Ben-Gurion, *War Diary*, entry for 19 October 1948, 754.

27. *Yiftah in a Storm*, 213.

28. Ayalon, *Giv'ati Brigade in Face of the Egyptian Invader*, 505–524.

29. Giv'ati, *Path of Desert and Fire*, 216.

30. Alec Kirkbride to secretary of state, 21 October 1948, PRO FO 816/131.

31. Ben-Gurion, *War Diary*, entry for 20 October 1948, 756–757; Ben-Gurion, protocol of Cabinet meeting, 21 October 1948, ISA.

32. Ben-Gurion, protocol of Cabinet meeting, 21 October 1948.

33. "Editorial Note," DFPI, 2:72.

34. Ben-Gurion, protocol of Cabinet meeting, 20 October 1948, ISA. But Ben-Gurion objected: "The first truce favored us . . . We were on the verge of complete exhaustion."

35. Ben-Gurion, protocol of Cabinet meeting, 21 October 1948.

36. Gruenbaum, protocol of Cabinet meeting, 20 October 1948, ISA.

37. "The Battle for the Negev, a Stenogram . . . ," IDFA 2289/50//80.

38. Ben-Gurion, protocol of Cabinet meeting, 26 October 1948, ISA.

39. Ben-Gurion, protocol of Cabinet meeting, 20 October 1948.

40. Ben-Gurion, protocol of Cabinet meeting, 21 October 1948.

41. Guri, *Breaking*, 72–73.

42. Givʿati, *Path of Desert and Fire*, 228; and Michael Cohen, "Teddy Eytan, 'the French Commando' and Battalion 75 in the War of Independence," in Shiran, ed., *Jews and Arabs in Protracted Struggle*, 124–125.

43. Morris, *Birth of Palestinian Refugee Problem Revisited*, 467.

44. Eldar, *Flotilla 13*, 142–152; Tal, *Naval Operations in Israel's War of Independence*, 161–169.

45. Harel Fifth Battalion/Intelligence, "Summary of the Battalion's Battles in the Deiraban-Beit Jimal Sector," 1 November 1948, IDFA 922/75//1233.

46. *Friends Speak about Jimmy*.

47. Intelligence Officer/Jerusalem Area, "The Conquest of Deiraban, Deir al-Hawa and Beit Jimal," 21 October 1948, IDFA 6308/49//141.

48. Ben-Gurion, protocol of Cabinet meeting, 26 October 1948; Ben-Gurion, *War Diary*, entry for 22 October 1948, 760–761; Gilead, ed., *Book of the Palmah*, 2:424.

49. Kirkbride to secretary of state, 21 October 18948, PRO 816/131.

50. Glubb to Goldie, 16 October 1948, quoted in Shlaim, *Collusion across the Jordan*, 329.

51. Abu Nowar, *Jordanian-Israeli War*, 242; Glubb, *Soldier*, 200.

52. Gelber, *Budding Fleur-de-Lis*, 750–751.

53. Eliahu Elath to Walter Eytan, 21 October 1948, *DFPI*, 2:83.

54. Gerges, "Egypt and the 1948 War," 165.

55. Gelber, *Independence versus Nakba*, 32; Segev, ed., *Behind the Screen*, 168–169.

56. Kirkbride to secretary of state, 21 October 1948, PRO FO 816/131.

57. IDF General Staff Logbook, entry for 28 October 1948, IDFA 922/75//1176.

58. IDF General Staff Logbook, entry for 30 October 1948, IDFA 922/75//1176.

59. "5th Brigade War Logbook, for the Month of October," entries from 22, 23, 24, 25 October 1948, IDFA 922/75//900.

60. Yigael Yadin to Southern Front, "Guideline for Operation 'Peten,'" 27 October 1948, IDFA 6127/49//93.

61. Vered, *Fighters for the Freedom of Israel*, 3:170–174; Glubb, *Soldier*, 204–209.

62. Glubb, *Soldier*, 209.

63. Vered, *Fighters for the Freedom of Israel*, 3:178–179.

64. Fifth Brigade/Intelligence, "Summary of Operations 30–31.10.48," 1 November 1948, IDFA 922/75//900.

65. Ben-Gurion, *War Diary*, entry for 30 October 1948, 786.

66. OC Southern Front to brigades, districts, etc., 27 October 1948, IDFA 1046/70//434.

67. Vered, *Fighters for the Freedom of Israel*, 3:184.

68. Vered, *Fighters for the Freedom of Israel*, 3:184–185.

69. Kaplan to Peri, 8 November 1948, KMA-ACP 6/6/4.

70. Morris, *Birth of Palestinian Refugee Problem Revisited,* 469–471.

71. Morris, *Birth of Palestinian Refugee Problem Revisited,* 471–472.

72. Shin Mem 3/Rehovot Base, to Shin Mem 3/HQ, "Report on the Situation in Ashdod," 8 November 1948, IDFA 922/75//1017.

73. Shin Mem 3/Rehovot Base, to Operations Officer, Southern Command, etc., "Report on the Entry into Majdal," 7 November 1948, IDFA 922/75//1017.

74. Morris, *Birth of Palestinian Refugee Problem Revisited,* 471–472. In 1950 the military authorities transferred the Arab inhabitants to Gaza, with a small number moving to Ramle, in Israel (see Morris, *1948 and After,* 323–347).

75. Fifth Brigade/Intelligence, "Summary of Operations 3–4.11.48 [sic]," 5 November 1948, IDFA 715/49//16.

76. P. M. Broadmead to FO, 12 November 1948, PRO FO 371-68386, reporting on what Syrian President al-Quwwatli had told a fellow British diplomat. The Syrian believed—or at least argued—that the Jews were being steadily supplied with armaments by the Russians and "the whole of Palestine would [soon] become a Russian-controlled base."

77. Kirkbride to FO, 3 November 1948, PRO FO 371-68643.

78. Ayalon, *Givʿati Brigade in Face of the Egyptian Invader,* 576–583.

79. Ayalon, *Givʿati Brigade in Face of the Egyptian Invader,* 589–590.

80. Cohen, *By Light and in Darkness,* 206–211.

81. Coastal Plain District HQ to Battalion 151, etc., "Operational Order No. 40," 25 November 1948, IDFA 6308/49//141.

82. Coastal Plain District HQ to Southern Front/Operations, 30 November 1948, IDFA 1978/50//1; Southern Front/Operations to General Staff Division, 2 December 1948, IDFA 922/75//1025.

83. Ben-Gurion, protocol of Cabinet meeting, 31 October 1948, ISA.

84. Ben-Gurion, protocol of Cabinet meeting, 20 October 1948.

85. Shertok, protocol of Cabinet meeting, 4 November 1948, ISA.

86. Shlaim, *Collusion across the Jordan,* 347.

87. List of points, protocol of Cabinet meeting, 4 November 1948, ISA.

88. "Excerpts from M. Shertok's Report to the Provisional Government of Israel (Tel Aviv, 26 October 1948)," in *Documents on Israeli-Soviet Relations, 1941–1953,* 390. Vyshinskii, according to Shertok, had said that this "was not a problem."

89. Carmel, *Northern Battles,* 255.

90. Luria, "Hiram," 15–19.

91. Erlich, *Lebanon,* 210.

92. Ben-Gurion, protocol of Cabinet meeting, 26 September 1948 (the passage was censored by ISA officials).

93. Northern Front to Brigades, Districts, etc., "Operational Order 'Snir,' 'Hiram,' 'Yehoshafat,'" 4 September 1948, IDFA 2289/50//277. See also Yitzhak Modaʿi, "Operation Hiram," 15–51, IDFA 922/75//189.

94. "Meeting of the General Staff of the Israel Defense Forces, Defense Ministry . . . 6.10.48," IDFA 172/50//121.

95. Gelber, *Independence versus Nakba*, 328.

96. Ben-Gurion, *War Diary*, entry for 22 October 1948, 761.

97. Eshel, *Carmeli*, 251–273.

98. Hughes, "Armed Forces," 36.

99. Maʿayan, "The North," 1:290–291.

100. Hughes, "Armed Forces," 35.

101. Shertok, protocol of Cabinet meeting, 26 September 1948, ISA.

102. Carmel, *Northern Battles*, 262.

103. Ben-Gurion, *War Diary*, entry for 16 October 1948, 749.

104. Ben-Gurion, *War Diary*, entry for 24 October 1948, 770.

105. "A" [Northern] Front to brigades, districts, etc, "Operational Order 'Hiram,'" 26 October 1948, IDFA 854/52//321.

106. Haifa District HQ, "Operational Order No. 2, 'Hiram,'" 16 September 1948, IDFA 240/54//2. The words following "evicting the inhabitants of the conquered villages" have been deleted by IDFA censors in the copy made available to researchers. They may refer to the prospective final destination of the evictees—Lebanon.

107. HQ Israel Air Force/Office of chief of staff of Air Intelligence to CoS, Operations, etc., 1 November 1948 and unsigned, "Summary of Assessments of Results of Air Force Bombings in Operation 'Hiram' for the Liberation of the Galilee," 29 February 1949, both in IDFA 600137/51//941.

108. Emmanuel Sharon, "Operation Hiram—79th Battalion," undated, IDFA 1046/70//6.

109. Seventy-ninth Battalion/Intelligence Officer to Seventh Brigade HQ, etc., "Report on Operation 'Hiram Bet,'" 1 November 1948, IDFA 2289/50//277; Sharon, "Operation Hiram—79th Battalion."

110. Sharon, "Operation Hiram—79th Battalion."

111. Yitzhak Pundak, OC Ninth Brigade, "Report on Operation 'Hiram,'" undated, IDFA 715/49//9; Carmel, *Northern Battles*, 270–271.

112. Intelligence Officer Northern Front to Intelligence Service Shin Mem 1, etc., 30 October 1948, IDFA 7249/49//138; Cohen, *History of Israeli Air Force*, 3:95–96.

113. Intelligence Officer, Seventy-first Battalion, to OC Seventy-first Battalion, etc., "Report on the Battalion's Operations in Operations 'Hiram' and 'Atzmon' during 27.10.48–1.11.48," 8 November 1948, IDFA 1094/49//77.

114. Two reports by Hemed (Science Corps) Bet to Hemed Staff, 11 November 1948, IDFA 121/50//223.

115. Lt. Col. Binyamin Ben-David (Dunkelman), "Statement by OC 7th Brigade with the Liberation of the Galilee," 30 October 1948, IDFA 957/51//16.

116. Gershon Gilad, Northern Front Intelligence Officer, "Intelligence Report on Operation 'Hiram' (28/10–31/10)," 21 November 1948, IDFA 715/49//15.

117. Erlich, *Lebanon*, 211–214; entry for 6 November 1948, Yosef Nahmani Diary, Hashomer Archive.

118. Gilad, "Intelligence Report on Operation 'Hiram' (28/10–31/10)."

119. Northern Front to brigades, etc., 7:30 hrs., 31 October 18948, IDFA 715/49//3.

120. Erlich, *Lebanon*, 214–215.

121. Ben-Gurion, protocol of Cabinet meeting, 31 October 1948. Perhaps Ben-Gurion was afraid that informing them might raise the question of who had authorized the crossing of the international frontier and why the Cabinet had not been consulted.

122. "Khirbet Lahis," *Ha'olam Hazeh*, 1 March 1978; Erlich, *Lebanon*, 214, 623, n. 180.

123. Morris, *Birth of Palestinian Refugee Problem Revisited*, 479–482.

124. Morris, *Birth of Palestinian Refugee Problem Revisited*, 486–489.

125. Ben-Gurion, protocol of Cabinet meeting, 31 October 1948. But Intelligence Service 1, "Daily Intelligence Report," 11 November 1948, IDFA 5942/49//72, states that "more than 50,000 new refugees reached Lebanon after the liberation of the Galilee."

126. Shimoni to Eytan, "On Problems of Policy in the Galilee and on the Northern Border and on the Link between the Foreign Ministry and the Army Staff," 18 November 1948, ISA FM 186/17.

127. Shimoni to Eliahu Sasson, Paris, 12 November 1948, ISA FM 2570/11.

128. Ezra Danin to Sasson, Paris, 24 October 1948, ISA FM 2570/11.

129. Ben-Gurion, *War Diary*, entry for 31 October 1948, 788.

130. Carmel to brigades and districts, 10:00 hrs., 31 October 1948, IDFA 715/49//3.

131. Northern Front to Second and Ninth Brigades, 09:30 hrs., 10 November 1948, IDFA 4858/49//495.

132. Northern Front to Second and Ninth brigades, 09:30 hrs., 10 November 1948.

133. Eleventh Battalion Intelligence to Ninth Brigade/Intelligence, "Report on Daily Activity 3/11," 3 November 1948, IDFA 1012/49//71.

134. Intelligence Officer Fourteenth Battalion to OC Fourteenth Battalion, "Report on a Patrol," 4 November 1948, IDFA 128/51//71.

135. Ninety-first Battalion to Ninth Brigade Operations, etc., "Report on Activities No. 056," 12 November 1948, IDFA 1012/49//75.

136. Ben-Gurion, *War Diary*, entry for 6 November 1948, 800.

137. Yehoshua Eshel to Northern Front, [?] November 1948, IDFA 756/61//128; Kaplan, Cisling, etc., protocol of Cabinet meeting, 18 November 1948, ISA.

138. Ben-Gurion, protocol of Cabinet meeting, 9 January 1949, ISA.

139. Ma'ayan, "The North," 1:292.

140. Sela, "ALA in Galilee," 1:248.

141. Ben-Gurion, protocol of Cabinet meeting, 31 October 1948; "Ami (Assaf)" to Intelligence Service 1, 16 November 1948, IDFA 7249/49//138.

142. Ben-Gurion, protocol of Cabinet meeting, 31 October 1948.

143. Shertok to Eytan (for Ben-Gurion), 11 November 1948, ISA, DFPI, 2:164–165.

144. Ninth Brigade/Operations to military governor, Acre, etc., "The Organisation of the Government in the Conquered Area. General Instructions," 16 November 1948, IDFA 128/51//34.

145. Northern Front to military governor, Western Galilee, etc., 18 November 1948, IDFA 260/51//54.

CHAPTER 9. OPERATION HOREV, DECEMBER 1948–JANUARY 1949

1. Hard on the heels of Operation Hiram, David Ben-Gurion proposed to Yigael Yadin the conquest of parts or all of the West Bank (Ben-Gurion, *War Diary*, entry for 31 October 1948, 790).

2. Ben-Gurion, *War Diary*, entry for 10 November 1948, 808.

3. Moshe Shertok to Goldie Myerson (Meir), 5 November 1948, and Chaim Weizmann to Truman, 5 November 1948, both in ISA, *DFPI*, 2:141–143, 143–146.

4. Truman to Weizmann, 29 November 1948, ISA, DFPI, 2:247.

5. "Meeting of the Israeli Delegation to the United Nations General Assembly (Paris, 17 November 1948)," ISA, *DFPI*, 2:190.

6. Walter Eytan to Ralph Bunche, 6 December 1948, ISA, *DFPI*, 2:271.

7. Doran, *Pan-Arabism before Nasser*, 189.

8. Glubb, *Soldier*, 214–216; Abu Nowar, *Jordanian-Israeli War*, 247–348.

9. Shertok to Eytan, 30 November 1948, ISA, *DFPI*, 2:248.

10. Paul Mohn to Ben-Gurion, 9 December 1948, ISA, *DFPI*, 2:278.

11. Ben-Gurion, protocol of Cabinet meeting, 8 December 1948, ISA.

12. Ben-Gurion, *War Diary*, entry for 27 November 1948, 853.

13. Ben-Gurion and Bentov, protocol of Cabinet meeting, 15 December 1948, ISA. ISA censors have blacked out part of Bentov's statement-question; presumably the missing passage dealt with the possible expulsion of the inhabitants.

14. The text in the ISA cabinet protocol actually says the opposite—but it would appear that a "no" was mistakenly dropped from the transcript.

15. Protocol of Cabinet meeting, 19 December 1948, ISA.

16. Ben-Gurion, *War Diary*, entry for 19 December 1948, ISA. One of the Russians, Second Secretary Nikolai Sergeev, advised Ben-Gurion "to cleanse [i.e., destroy] the Arab armies one after the other."

17. Ben-Gurion, *War Diary*, entry for 17 November 1948, 831–832.

18. "Meeting: D. Ben-Gurion–P.I. Ershov (Tel Aviv, 27 December 1948)," in *Documents on Israeli-Soviet Relations, 1941–1953*, 423.

19. "Meeting: D. Ben-Gurion–P.I. Ershov (Tel Aviv, 27 December 1948)," 422.

20. Gelber, *Independence versus Nakba*, 331.

21. I. J. Linton, "Meeting: I. J. Linton–H. McNeil (London, 30 December 1948)," 4 January 1949, ISA, DFPI, 2:343.

22. "D" [Southern] Front HQ/Operations to 1, 3, 8, 10, 12 brigades, etc., "Operational Order Horev," undated, IDFA 922/75//561.

23. Segev, ed., *In Enemy Eyes*, 105.

24. Neguib, *Egypt's Destiny*, 25–27.

25. Segev, ed., *In Enemy Eyes*, 106.

26. ʿEtzioni, ed., *Tree and Sword*, 345.

27. ʿEtzioni, ed., *Tree and Sword*, 337–344.

28. ʿEtzioni, ed., *Tree and Sword*, 337–349.

29. Givʿati, *Path* of Desert and Fire, 252; Ben-Gurion, *War Diary*, entry for 24 December 1948, 900.

30. Givʿati, *Path* of Desert and Fire, 255–257.

31. Vered, *Fighters for the Freedom of Israel*, 331–359.

32. *Negev Brigade*, 212.

33. Segev, ed., *In Enemy Eyes*, 116.

34. *Negev Brigade*, 212.

35. Segev, ed., *In Enemy Eyes*, 118.

36. Ben-Gurion, *War Diary*, entries for 27–29 December 1948; Vered, *Fighters for the Freedom of Israel*, 3:368–370.

37. Ben-Gurion, protocol of Cabinet meeting, 29 December 1948, ISA.

38. Quoted in Vered, *Fighters for the Freedom of Israel*, 3:369.

39. Quoted in Vered, *Fighters for the Freedom of Israel*, 3:372.

40. Ben-Gurion, protocol of Cabinet meeting, 29 December 1948.

41. Rabin, *Memoirs*, 38.

42. Vered, *Fighters for the Freedom of Israel*, 3:374. The sight of endless abandoned shoes in the sands of Sinai was to characterize the Israeli victories in the selfsame battlefields in 1956 and 1967.

43. Vered, *Fighters for the Freedom of Israel*, 3:376.

44. Vered, *Fighters for the Freedom of Israel*, 3:378; Rabin, *Memoirs*, 40.

45. Cohen, *By Light and in Darkness*, 238.

46. Rabin, *Memoirs*, 40.

47. Ben-Gurion, *War Diary*, entry for 30 December 1948, 913.

48. Ben-Gurion, protocol of Cabinet meeting, 2 January 1949, ISA.

49. D. Ginsburg, Washington, DC, to Shertok, 3 January 1949, ISA, DFPI, 2:339.

50. Ronald Campbell to FO, 11:01, 29 December 1948, "Most Immediate," PRO FO 371-69289.

51. Campbell to FO, 17:11, 29 December 1948, PRO FO 371-69289.

52. *New York Times*, 28 December 1948.

53. Campbell to FO, (no time) 29 December 1948 (no. 1805), and 19:38, 29 December 1948 (no. 1897), both in PRO FO 371-69289.

54. Beirut to FO, 31 December 1948, PRO FO 371-69289.

55. FO to Cairo, 19:00, 30 December 1948, PRO FO 371-69289.

56. FO to Washington, DC, 14:25, 29 December 1948, PRO FO 371-69289.

57. Tal, *War in Palestine*, 450, quoting FO to Washington, DC, 30 December 1948, PRO FO 371-68692. There was an irony here: British activation of the treaty was contingent on an Egyptian request. And Egypt had refrained from requesting such activation because its major foreign policy objective since the end of World War II was the complete withdrawal of Britain's troops and bases from Egyptian

soil; this remained true through 1948. Publicly requesting British military intervention would have been humiliating.

58. Oliver Franks to FO, 20:32, 29 December 1948, PRO FO 371-69289.

59. Uriel Heyd, Washington, DC, to Shertok, 30 December 1948, ISA, DFPI, 2:319.

60. McDonald to Shertok, "Statement Made by the Special Representative of the United States to the Foreign Minister of Israel, December 31st 1948," ISA, DFPI 2:331–332.

61. McDonald, *Mission in Israel*, 117–118.

62. McDonald, *Mission in Israel*, 120–121; Ben-Gurion, *War Diary*, entry for 31 December 1948, 916–918.

63. Ben-Gurion, *War Diary*, entry for 31 December 1948, 918.

64. McDonald, *Mission in Israel*, 124.

65. See, e.g., FO to British Embassy, Cairo, 4 June 1948, PRO FO 371-68372.

66. Shertok to McDonald, 3 January, and Weizmann to Truman, 3 January 1949, ISA, DFPI, 3:335–337, 337–338.

67. Gelber, *Independence versus Nakba*, 338.

68. Eighth Brigade HQ, "Report on Operation Horev ('Ayin')," 21 February 1949, IDFA 922/75//561.

69. Shertok, protocol of Cabinet meeting, 9 January 1949, ISA.

70. Ben-Gurion, *War Diary*, entry for 6 January 1949, 931.

71. Elath to Shertok, 6 January 1949, ISA, DFPI, 2:347.

72. Dori to Yigal Allon, 11 January 1949, IDFA 1046/70//434.

73. Vered, *Fighters for the Freedom of Israel*, 3:416.

74. Allon to defense minister, 7 January 1948, IDFA 1046/70//434.

75. Cohen, *History of Israeli Air Force*, 3:551–569; and "Aircraft Loss, Middle East (Inquiry's Findings)," PRO FO 371-75247.

76. Ben-Gurion, *War Diary*, entry for 7 December 1948, 934.

77. Asia, *Conflict*, 78.

78. See Cabinet minutes, 17 January 1949, PRO CAB/6359. The force in ʿAqaba, designed to safeguard the town and Glubb's supply route from Brirtain's Canal-side bases, was reinforced in March by a company of tanks and naval commandos (see Gelber, *Independence versus Nakba*, 341).

79. "A. Eban to the President of the Security Council (Lake Success)," 11 January 1949, ISA, DFPI, 2:355–358.

80. McDonald, *Mission in Israel*, 126. See also Ben-Gurion, *War Diary*, entry for 16 January 1949, 952.

81. Ben-Gurion, *War Diary*, entry for 16 January 1949, 951–952.

82. IDF General Staff/Operations, "Basic Proposal for Operation Yefet," 16.1.49, and "B" Front Staff, "Operational Order 'Yefet,'" 19 January 1949, both in IDFA 854/52//236; Cohen-Shani, *From Battlefield to Negotiating Table*, 83–108.

83. Ben-Gurion, *War Diary*, entry for 19 January 1949, 959.

84. Ben-Gurion, protocol of Cabinet meeting, 29 December 1948, ISA.

85. Third Brigade, "Summary of Operation 'Hisul,'" 26 February 1949, IDFA 922/75//949.

86. Third Brigade, "Summary of Operation 'Hisul,'" 26 February 1949.
87. Gelber, *Independence versus Nakba,* 334.
88. Kirkbride to FO, 29 December 1948, PRO FO 371-68644.

CHAPTER 10. THE ARMISTICE AGREEMENTS, JANUARY–JULY 1949

1. Ben-Gurion, protocol of Cabinet meeting, 19 December 1948, ISA.
2. Walter Eytan to Moshe Shertok, 16 January 1949, ISA, *DFPI,* 3:27.
3. Eliahu Sasson to Shertok, 11 February 1949, ISA, *DFPI,* 3:235.
4. See, e.g., Yigal Allon to Yitzhak Rabin, 15 February 1949, IDFA 1046/70//434 ("I fear for the fate of the ʿAuja sector"). See also Cohen-Shani, *From Battlefield to Negotiating Table,* 109–137.
5. Eytan to Shertok, 13 January 1949, Israel, ISA, *DFPI,* 3:19.
6. Ralph Bunche, "Provisional Truce Demarcation Lines in the Negev Communication and Memorandum of 13 November 1948," Israel, ISA, *DFPI,* 3:682–684.
7. Sasson to Shertok, 11 February 1949, Israel, ISA, *DFPI,* 3:235.
8. Abba Eban to Eytan, 3 March 1949, Israel, ISA, *DFPI,* 3:275–278.
9. "Israeli-Egyptian General Armistice Agreement (24 February 1949)," Israel, ISA, *DFPI,* 3:688–704.
10. See Morris, *Israel's Border Wars.*
11. Rosenne to Sasson, 13 March 1949, Israel, ISA, *DFPI,* 3:311.
12. Makleff to Dori, 14 January 1949, Israel, ISA, *DFPI,* 3:281–283; Yadin, Cabinet meeting of 16 January 1949, ISA.
13. Ben-Gurion, protocol of Cabinet meetings of 10, 20 March 1949, ISA.
14. "Israeli-Lebanese General Armistice Agreement (23 March 1949)," Israel, ISA, *DFPI,* 3:705–711.
15. Ben-Gurion, protocol of Cabinet meeting, 20 March 1949.
16. Southern Front/Operations to First, Third, Twelfth brigades, etc., "Operational Order 'Uvda,'" 1 March 1949, IDFA 6308/49//146. The order included an instruction to "expel" all Negev bedouin who had not sworn loyalty to Israel.
17. Ben-Gurion to Louis Brandeis, "The Land Problem with Special Regard to Negev and Akaba," 4 June 1935, BGA, Memoranda.
18. Southern Front HQ/Operations, "Operational Order 'Lot,'" 20 November 1948, IDFA 922/75//1076.
19. Ben-Gurion, protocol of Cabinet meeting, 19 January 1949, ISA.
20. Moshe Sharett, protocol of Cabinet meeting, 21 June 1949, ISA.
21. Sharett, protocol of Cabinet meeting, 2 March 1949, ISA; Ben-Gurion, protocol of Cabinet meeting, 10 March 1949.
22. Some American diplomats agreed (see Burdett, Jerusalem, to secretary of state, 10 March 1949, USNA, 501.BB Palestine/3-1049).
23. Ben-Gurion and Sharett, protocol of Cabinet meeting, 10 March 1949, ISA; Glubb, *Soldier,* 229–32; Shlaim, *Collusion across the Jordan,* 401–406.
24. "Meeting: I. J. Linton–M. Wright (London, 9 March 1949)," Israel, ISA, *DFPI,* 2:482–483.

25. "Israel-Jordan General Cease-fire Agreement," 11 March 1949, Israel, ISA, *DFPI*, 3:382–383.
26. Sharett, protocol of Cabinet meeting, 10 March 1949, ISA.
27. Ben-Gurion, *War Diary*, entry for 11 March 1949, 974.
28. See Morris, *Birth of Palestinian Refugee Problem Revisited*, 519–520.
29. Ben-Gurion, protocol of Cabinet meeting of 20 March 1949.
30. Stabler, Amman, to secretary of state, 23 March 1949, USNA, 501.BB Palestine/ 3–2349.
31. Shlaim, *Collusion across the Jordan*, 386–433.
32. Front "A" to brigades, etc., "Operational Order Shin-Taf-Shin," 16 March 1949, IDFA 922/75//1076.
33. Cohen-Shani, *From Battlefield to Negotiating Table*, 147–161.
34. Morris, *Israel's Border Wars*, 10–13.
35. Allon to Ben-Gurion, 27 March 1949, IDFA 1046/70//434.
36. Ben-Gurion, protocol of Cabinet meeting, 27 March 1949, ISA. Ben-Gurion said: "There is not one inch of land from which we are withdrawing. On the contrary, everywhere we are moving into their territory."
37. Text in ISA, *DFPI*, 3:712–722.
38. Selo in "Meeting of the Delegations of Israel and Syria (10 May 1949)," ISA, *DFPI*, 3:557.
39. Rosenne to Eytan, 15 May 1949, ISA, *DFPI*, 3:566–568.
40. Reuven Shiloah to Bunche, 12 May 1949, ISA, *DFPI*, 3:562.
41. Rosenne to Robinson, New York, and Sasson, Paris, 6 April 1949, ISA, *DFPI*, 3:520.
42. Front "A" to OC Seventh Brigade, "Operational Order 'Oren,'" 16 June 1949, IDFA 2289/50//286; Cohen-Shani, *From Battlefield to Negotiating Table*, 163–188.
43. Ben-Gurion, protocol of Cabinet meeting, 18 May 1949, ISA.
44. Rosenne to Ben-Gurion and Sharett, 18 May 1949, ISA, *DFPI*, 3:581–583.
45. Shiloah to Bunche, 12 May 1949, ISA, *DFPI*, 3:563.
46. Paul Mohn to Sharett, 8 June 1949, ISA, *DFPI*, 3:599–600.
47. "Israeli-Syrian General Armistice Agreement (20 July 1949)," ISA, *DFPI*, 3:723–734.

CHAPTER 11. SOME CONCLUSIONS

1. Richard Beaumont to Bernard Burrows, 18 July 1948, PRO FO 371-68375.
2. Protocol of meeting of JAE, 7 July 1938, BGA.
3. Goldmann, *Jewish Paradox*, 99.
4. See Morris, *Righteous Victims*, 8–13.
5. El-Awaisi, *Muslim Brothers*, 8.
6. Thomas Wikeley, Jedda, to FO, 29 August 1943, PRO CO 733/443/18.
7. Ibn Saʿud to Franklin D. Roosevelt, 30 April 1943, PRO CO 733/443/18.
8. "Poster of 'the Shabab Saidna Muhammad' (Cairo)," 2 November 1947, CZA S25-9034.

9. "Off-the-Record Talks in Transjordan of Two British Correspondents," unsigned, Amman, 21 October 1947, CZA S25-9038. The idea that the Jews were responsible for the two world wars was, and remains, pervasive in the Arab world (see, e.g., the fundamentalist Hamas Movement's "Charter," from August 1988).

10. Alec Kirkbride to Ernest Bevin, 13 February 1948, PRO FO 816/116; Kirkbride to Bevin (no. 244), 23 April 1948, PRO FO 816/117.

11. El-Awaisi, *Muslim Brothers,* 9–10.

12. El-Awaisi, *Muslim Brothers,* 14.

13. *Al-Difaʿa,* 8 April 1948, 2.

14. El-Awaisi, *Muslim Brothers,* 15. Al-Banna extolled such martyrdom in the service of jihad as "the art of death" and vilified the Muslims' "love of life" (see Mitchell, *Society,* 207).

15. El-Awaisi, *Muslim Brothers,* 15.

16. Nadia Lourie, "Interview with Mrs. Mogannam [Mughannam]," 10 January 1948, CZA S25-9005.

17. Kirkbride to Bevin (no. 270), 1 May 1948, PRO FO 816/118.

18. Ronald Campbell to FO, 13 December 1948, PRO FO 371-68644.

19. The phrase—"to drive the Jews in Palestine into the sea"—was reportedly used, for example, by ʿIzzedin Shawa, a representative of the AHC in London, in a conversation with an American diplomat (see Gallman, London, to secretary of state, 21 January 1948, USNA, box 5, Jerusalem Consulate General, Classified Records 1948, 800–Palestine). In his memoirs, Kirkbride quoted Arab League secretary-general ʿAzzam saying to him, just before the invasion: "We will sweep them into the sea" (Kirkbride, *From the Wings,* 24).

20. Sam Souki, UP, quoting al-Qawuqji speaking to his troops, undated but from February or March 1948, CZA S25-8996.

21. Jordanian prime minister Abul Huda said as much to Kirkbride (see Kirkbride to Bevin, 15 May 1948, PRO FO 816/120).

22. A shallow, inadequate explanation of the Arab states' defeat, based solely on (often poor) secondary sources, is found in Pollack, *War,* 15–27, 149–155, 269–284, 448–457.

23. Sivan, *1948,* 20.

24. Sivan, *1948,* 21.

25. Sivan, *1948,* 36, 39.

26. Elpeleg, *In the Eyes of the Mufti,* 29.

27. *Jerusalem Post,* 15 June 1950, 3.

28. The word *refugees* is inaccurate as regards two-thirds of this number because they were displaced from their homes in areas that became the State of Israel and came to rest in other parts of Palestine (the West Bank and Gaza Strip)—and refugees are usually defined as people displaced from their countries. (About a third came to rest in Lebanon, Syria, and Transjordan.) Still less accurate is the definition of the descendants of the bulk of those displaced—their children, grandchildren, and great-grandchildren—as refugees, because they themselves were never displaced and, in any case, live in areas of Palestine. Nonetheless, the United Nations

applied the term to all those displaced from their homes in the course of the war—and to their descendants, wherever they now reside. The United Nations now has about four million Palestinian "refugees" on its rolls (the Palestinians claim that the true number is five million).

29. Wasserstein, *Palestine*, 41.

30. *Peel Commission Report*, 141. The reference was to the massacre of more than three hundred Assyrian (Nestorian) Christians by Iraqi troops at Sumayyil in northern Iraq on 11 August 1933. The massacre occurred despite government assurances of protection.

31. Reported in unsigned, untitled Zionist memorandum, 10 March 1948, CZA S25-7733. The memorandum also quoted an interview, in *Al-Ahram*, 9 March 1948, in which al-Qawuqji stated that his objectives in Palestine were "the defeat of partition and the annihilation of the Zionists."

32. Quoted in Shemesh, "Crisis," pt. 2:342.

33. Ben-Gurion, *My Meetings with Arab Leaders*, 197. The two met on 23 February 1938.

34. Tuck to secretary of state, 3 December 1947, *FRUS, 1947,* 5:1295–1296.

35. Ibn Saʿud to Truman, 26 October 1947, *FRUS, 1947,* 5:1212–1213.

36. Moshe Shertok, meeting of Cabinet, 9 February 1949, ISA.

37. Shertok, meeting of Cabinet, 6 February 1949, ISA.

38. Douglas Busk to FO, 12 September 1947, PRO FO 371-61529.

39. JA, "Memorandum on the Situation of the Jews in Iraq," undated but accompanied by a letter from Victor Bernstein to Hector McNeil, 28 October 1949, PRO FO 371-75183.

40. "Memorandum Submitted to the U.N. Economic and Social Council, by the World Jewish Congress," 19 January 1948, PRO FO 371-68366.

41. Campbell to Bevin, 14 June 1948, PRO FO 371-69259.

42. "Memorandum Submitted to the U.N. Economic and Social Council by the World Jewish Congress," 19 January 1948; Elie Eliachar to Herbert Samuel, 31 January 1948, PRO FO 371-68366.

43. Campbell to FO, 26 June 1948, PRO FO 371-69259.

44. A description of a visit to two of these camps by the acting British consul general in Cairo—"the general atmosphere was free and easy"—is appended to Campbell to Bevin, 23 July 1948, PRO FO 371-69259.

45. Unsigned, "Anglo-Jewish Association, Egyptian Crisis," 13 July 1948, PRO FO 371-69259.

46. Translation into English of "Days of Terror," 10, 13 August 1948, *National-Zeitung,* Basel, PRO FO 371-69260. The "hundreds" was probably an exaggeration.

47. Chapman Andrews to FO, 23 September 1948, PRO FO 371-69260.

48. Government of Iraq, Ministry of Foreign Affairs, untitled memorandum, received by US embassy, Baghdad, 18 November 1949, PRO FO 371-75183.

49. JA, "Memorandum on the Situation of the Jews of Iraq," undated but accompanied by letter from 29 October 1949, PRO FO 371-75183.

50. Henry Mack, Baghdad, to Bevin, 3 March 1949, PRO FO 371-75182.

51. Robert Marcus, World Jewish Congress, to Trygve Lie, United Nations, 8 November 1949, PRO FO 371-75183; World Jewish Congress, "Memorandum on the Treatment of the Jewish Population in Iraq . . . ," 22 October 1949, PRO FO 371-75183.

52. Houstoun Boswall to FO, 24 April 1948, PRO FO 371-68493.

53. British Military Administration, Tripolitania, "Arab-Jewish Disturbances Tripoli, 12th/13th June, 1948," 21 June 1948, and D. Mowshowitch, Jewish Board of Deputies, London, to R. D. J. Scott-Fox, FO, 17 June 1948, both in PRO FO 371-69422.

54. British consulate general, Rabat, to J. W. Blanch, FO, 15 June 1948, FO 371-73022.

55. Boswall to FO, 2 May 1948, PRO FO 371-68371; unsigned, "Anglo-Jewish Association, the Jews in Moslem Countries, Extracts from a Report Given by a Member of the A.J.A., Who Recently Visited the Countries of the Middle East," 2 September 1948, PRO FO 371-68377.

Bibliography

PRIMARY SOURCES

Central Zionist Archives (CZA), Jerusalem
Chaim Weizmann Archive, Rehovot
David Ben-Gurion Archive (BGA), Sdeh Boqer
Haganah Archive (HA), Tel Aviv
Hashomer Archive, Kfar Giladi
    Yosef Nahmani Diary
Hashomer Hatzair Archive (HHA), Giv'at Haviva
    Aharon Cohen Papers (ACP)
Israel State Archive (ISA), Jerusalem
Jabotinsky Institute (JI), Tel Aviv
Kibbutz Hazore'a Archive, Kibbutz Hazore'a
    Eliezer Bauer Papers
Kibbutz Meuhad Archive (KMA), Efal
    Aharon Cisling Papers (ACP)
Kibbutz Nahsholim Archive, Kibbutz Nahsholim
    Tulik Makovsky Diary
Labor Archive (LA), Tel Aviv
Public Record Office (PRO), London
SAMECA: St. Antony's College Middle East Centre Archive (SAMECA), Oxford
    Henry Gurney, "Palestine Postscript"
    Alan Cunningham Papers (CP)
    Jerusalem and East Mission Papers
    John Glubb Papers

United States National Archive (USNA), College Park, Maryland
United Nations Archive (UNA), New York City

PUBLISHED DOCUMENTS

Ben-Gurion, David. [Hebrew.] *War Diary, 1948–1949*. Ed. Gershon Rivlin and El-
hannan Orren. Tel Aviv: Society for the Dissemination of Ben-Gurion's Her-
itage/Defense Ministry Press, 1982.
———. [Hebrew.] *In the Battle*. Vol. 5. Tel Aviv: ʿAm ʿOved, 1957.
ISA. [Hebrew.] *The People's Administration: Protocols, 18 April–13 May 1948*.
Jerusalem, 1978.
ISA. *Documents on the Foreign Policy of Israel (DFPI)*. Vols. 1–4 (May 1948–De-
cember 1949). Jerusalem, 1981–1986.
ISA and World Zionist Organization. *Political and Diplomatic Documents, Decem-
ber 1947–May 1948*.
ISA/World Zionist Organization/Russian Federal Archives. *Documents on Israeli-
Soviet Relations, 1941–1953*. 2 vols. London: Frank Cass, 2000.
ISA/World Zionist Organization/Tel Aviv University. *Political Documents of the
Jewish Agency*. Vol. 1: May 1945–December 1946. Vol. 2, January–November
1947. Jerusalem: Hasifriya Hatziyonit, 1996, 1998.
USNA. *Foreign Relations of the United States, 1947* and *1948*.

NEWSPAPERS

Al-Ahram
Al-Difaʿa
Davar
Falastin
Haaretz
Kol Haʿir
New York Times
Palestine Post
The Times (London)

Secondary Works

Abbasi, Mustafa. [Hebrew.] "Safad in the War of Independence: A Fresh Look."
Cathedra 107 (2003).
Abu Nowar, Maʿan. *The Jordanian-Israeli War, 1948–1951*. Reading, UK: Ithaca
Press, 2002.
Agin, Assaf. [Hebrew.] "The Balance of Forces in the 1948 War." *Maʿarachot* 390
(July 2003).
———. "The Battle to Contain the Invasion in the Jordan Valley—May 1948."
M.A. thesis, Haifa University, 2001.

Anderson, Benedict. *Imagined Communities: Reflections on the Origin and Spread of Nationalism.* 2nd ed. London: Verso, 1991.

Antonius, George. *The Arab Awakening: The Story of the Arab National Movement.* New York: Capricorn Books, 1965.

Arieli, Yehoshuʿa, ed. [Hebrew.] *The Youth Battalion (Gadʾna) in Jerusalem during the War of Independence, 1948.* Israel: Defense Ministry Press, 2003.

Asia, Ilan. [Hebrew.] *The Core of the Conflict: The Struggle for the Negev, 1947–1956.* Jerusalem: Yad Izhak Ben-Zvi Press/Ben-Gurion Research Center/Ben-Gurion University Press, 1994.

Av, Nahum. [Hebrew.] *The Struggle for Tiberias.* Tel Aviv: Defense Ministry Press, 1991.

Avizohar, Meir [Hebrew.] *The Battle for Jerusalem, 1948.* Lydda: Moriah Battalion Veterans Association, 2002.

Avneri, Uri. [Hebrew.] *In the Fields of Philistia 1948.* Tel Aviv: Twersky, 1949.

Ayalon, Avraham. [Hebrew.] *The Givʿati Brigade in Face of the Egyptian Invader.* Israel: Maʿarachot/IDF Press, 1963.

———. [Hebrew.] *The Givʿati Brigade in the War of Establishment.* Tel Aviv: Maʿarachot, 1959.

ʿAzoury, Negib. *Le reveil de la nation arabe dans l'Asie turque.* Paris: Plon, 1905.

Bandman, Yona. [Hebrew.] "The Arab Legion before the War of Independence." *Maʿarachot* 294–295 (July 1984): 36–45.

———. [Hebrew.] "The British Military Intervention against the IZL Attack on Manshiya." *ʿIyunim Betkumat Yisrael* 2 (1992).

———. [Hebrew.] "The Crystallization of the British Plan to Evacuate Palestine." In Alon Kadish, ed., *Israel's War of Independence, 1948–1949.* 2 vols., 2:589–660. Tel Aviv: Defense Ministry Press, 2004.

———. [Hebrew.] *When Will Britain Withdraw from Jerusalem?* Israel: Defense Ministry Press/Galili Center for Defense Studies, 2004.

Beʾeri, Eliezer. [Hebrew.] *The Beginning of the Israeli-Arab Conflict.* Haifa: Sifriyat Poʿalim/Haifa University Press, 1985.

Begin, Menachem. *The Revolt.* London: W. H. Allen, n.d.

Ben-Ari, Uri. [Hebrew.] *Follow Me.* Tel Aviv: Maʿariv Books, 1994.

Ben-Arieh, Yehoshuʿa. [Hebrew.] "The Beginning of the Historiography of the War of Independence and the State of Knowledge about the Balance of Forces." In Alon Kadish and Binyamin Zeev Kedar, eds., *The Few against the Many? Studies in the Balance of Forces in the Battles of Judah the Maccabee and in the War of Independence,* 141–167. Jerusalem: Magnes, 2006.

Ben-Dror, Elad. [Hebrew.] "UNSCOP: The Beginning of the United Nations Involvement in the Arab-Israeli Conflict." Ph.D. thesis, Bar-Ilan University, 2002.

Ben-Gurion, David. [Hebrew.] *As Israel Fights.* Tel Aviv: Mapai, 1952.

———. [Hebrew.] *My Meetings with Arab Leaders.* Tel Aviv: ʿAm ʿOved/Keren Hanegev, 1975.

———. [Hebrew.] *The Restored State of Israel.* Tel Aviv: ʿAm ʿOved, 1969.

Ben-Pazi, Shmaryahu. "The Citrus Harvest and Its Influence on the Development of the Communal War in the Land of Israel, 1947–1948." In Mordechai Bar-On and Meir Hazan, eds., *A People at War,* 155–187. Jerusalem: Yad Yitzhak Ben-Zvi/Institute for the Study of Zionism and Israel–Tel Aviv University/Galili Association for the Study of the Defense Force, 2006.

Ben-Yehuda, Netiva. [Hebrew.] *Through the Ropes.* Jerusalem: Domino Press, 1985.

Carmel, Moshe. [Hebrew.] *Northern Battles.* Tel Aviv: Maʿarachot/Kibbutz Meuhad Press, 1949.

Carmon, David, ed. [Hebrew.] ʿ*Ein-Gev in the War.* Tel Aviv: Maʿarachot, 1950.

Cohen, Avi. [Hebrew.] *The History of the Israeli Air Force in the War of Independence.* 3 vols. Tel Aviv: Defense Ministry Press, 2004.

Cohen, Gamliel. [Hebrew.] *Under Cover: The Untold Story of the Palmah's Undercover Arab Unit.* Israel: Galili Center for Defense Studies/Defense Ministry Press, 2002.

Cohen, Gavriel. "British Policy on the Eve of the War of Independence." In Jehuda Wallach, ed., *We Were as Dreamers,* 13–177. Tel Aviv: Masada, 1985.

Cohen, Hillel. *Army of Shadows.* Berkeley: University of California Press, 2007.

———. [Hebrew.] *An Army of Shadows.* Jerusalem: ʿIvrit, 2004.

———. [Hebrew.] *The Present Absentees: The Palestinian Refugees in Israel since 1948.* Jerusalem: Institute for Israeli Arab Studies, 2000.

Cohen, Michael J. *Palestine and the Great Powers, 1945–1948.* Princeton, NJ: Princeton University Press, 1982.

———. *Palestine, Retreat from the Mandate: The Making of British Policy, 1945.* London: Elek, 1978.

———. *Palestine to Israel: From Mandate to Independence.* London: Frank Cass, 1988.

Cohen, Mulla. [Hebrew.] *To Give and to Receive: Personal Memoirs.* Tel Aviv: Kibbutz Meuhad Press, 2000.

Cohen, Yeruham. [Hebrew.] *By Light and in Darkness.* Tel Aviv: ʿAmikam, 1969.

Cohen-Shani, Shmuel. [Hebrew.] *Paris Operation.* Ramot: Tel Aviv University Press, 1994.

———. [Hebrew.] *From the Battlefield to the Negotiating Table: The End of the 1948 War.* Tel Aviv: Defense Ministry Press, 2002.

Collins, Larry, and Dominique Lapierre. *O Jerusalem!* London: History Book Club, 1972.

Crossman, Richard. *Palestine Mission: A Personal Record.* New York: Harper and Brothers, 1947.

Crum, Bartley C. *Behind the Silken Curtain: A Personal Account of Anglo-American Diplomacy in Palestine and the Middle East.* New York: Simon and Schuster, 1947.

Dayan, Moshe. [Hebrew.] *Story of My Life.* Tel Aviv: Yediʿot Aharonot/Dvir/Idanim, 1976.

Days of Gesher. [Hebrew.] Tel Aviv: Kibbutz Gesher Press, n.d.

Doran, Michael. *Pan-Arabism before Nasser: Egyptian Power Politics and the Palestine Question.* New York: Oxford University Press, 1999.

Dror, Tzvika. [Hebrew.] *The Life and Times of Yitzhak Sadeh.* Tel Aviv: Kibbutz Meuhad Press, 1996.

————. [Hebrew.] *Nitzanim: A Settlement Built Twice.* Tel Aviv: Kibbutz Meuhad Press/Defense Ministry Press, 1990.

Ehrnvald, Moshe. [Hebrew.] *Siege within Siege: The Jewish Quarter in the Old City of Jerusalem during the War of Independence.* N.p.: Ben-Gurion Research Institute/Galili Center for Defense Studies/Defense Ministry Press/Haganah Archive, 2004.

El-Awaisi, ʿAbd al-Fattah. *The Muslim Brothers and the Palestine Question, 1928–1947.* London: I. B. Tauris, 1998.

Eldar, Mike. [Hebrew.] *Flotilla 13.* Tel Aviv: Maʿariv Books, 1993.

Elpeleg, Zvi. [Hebrew.] *Grand Mufti.* Tel Aviv: Defense Ministry Press, 1989.

Elpeleg, Zvi, ed. [Hebrew.] *In the Eyes of the Mufti: The Essays of Haj Amin Translated and Annotated.* Israel: Moshe Dayan Center, Tel Aviv University/Kibbutz Meuhad Press, 1995.

Eppel, Michael. *The Palestine Conflict in the History of Modern Iraq: The Dynamics of Involvement, 1928–1948.* London: Frank Cass, 1994.

Erlich, Reuven. [Hebrew.] *The Lebanon Tangle.* Tel Aviv: Defense Ministry Press, 2000.

Eshel, Tzadok. [Hebrew.] *The Carmeli Brigade in the War of Establishment.* Tel Aviv: Maʿarachot/Defense Ministry Press, 1973.

————. [Hebrew.] *Haganah Battles in Haifa.* Tel Aviv: Haifa Haganah Members Association/Defense Ministry Press, 1978.

ʿEtzioni, Binyamin, ed. [Hebrew.] *Tree and Sword.* Tel Aviv: Maʿarachot, n.d.

Finlayson, Geoffrey B. A. M. *The Seventh Earl of Shaftesbury, 1801–1885.* London: Eyre Methuen, 1981.

The Fort at the Entrance to the Kinneret: ʿEin-Gev in the War. [Hebrew.] Israel: Maʿarachot/IDF Press, 1950.

Freundlich, Yehoshua. [Hebrew.] *From Destruction to Resurrection.* Israel: Universities Press, 1994.

Friends Speak about Jimmy. [Hebrew.] Tel Aviv: Kibbutz Meuhad Press, 1952.

Furlonge, Geoffrey. *Palestine Is My Country: The Story of Musa Alami.* New York: Praeger, 1969.

Gabbay, Rony. *A Political Study of the Arab-Jewish Conflict: The Arab Refugee Problem, a Case Study.* Geneva: E. Droz, 1959.

Galili, Yisrael, Yigael Yadin, and Jehuda Wallach, eds. [Hebrew.] *Carta's Historical Atlas of the "Haganah."* Jerusalem: Carta, 1991.

García Granados, Jorge. *The Birth of Israel: The Drama as I Saw It.* New York: A. A. Knopf, 1948.

Garfinkle, Adam. "On the Origin, Meaning, Use and Abuse of a Phrase." *Middle Eastern Studies* 27, no. 4 (1991): 539–550.

Gelber, Yoav. [Hebrew.] *A Budding Fleur-de-Lis: Israeli Intelligence Services during the War of Independence, 1948–1949.* 2 vols. N.p.: Defense Ministry Press, 2000.

———. "Druze and Jews in the War of 1948." *Middle Eastern Studies* 31, no. 2 (1995): 229–252.

———. [Hebrew.] *The Emergence of a Jewish Army: The Veterans of the British Army in the IDF.* Jerusalem: Yad Yizhak Ben-Zvi Institute, 1986.

———. [Hebrew.] *Independence versus Nakba.* Or Yehuda: Dvir, 2004.

———. *Jewish-Transjordanian Relations, 1921–48.* London: Frank Cass, 1997.

———. *Palestine, 1948: War, Escape, and the Emergence of the Palestinian Refugee Problem.* Brighton: Sussex Academic Press, 2001.

———. [Hebrew.] *Why Was the Palmah Disbanded?* Jerusalem: Schocken Books, 1986.

Gerges, Fawaz. "Egypt and the 1948 War: Internal Conflict and Regional Ambition." In Eugene L. Rogan and Avi Shlaim, eds., *The War for Palestine: Rewriting the History of 1948,* 151–177. Cambridge: Cambridge University Press, 2001.

Gezer's Day: The Kibbutz during the War of Independence, December 1947–June 1949. [Hebrew.] Tel Aviv: Kibbutz Hadassah-Gezer Press, 1950.

Gilead, Zerubavel, ed. [Hebrew.] *The Book of the Palmah.* 2 vols. Tel Aviv: Organization of Palmah Members/Kibbutz Meuhad Press, 1956.

Giv'ati, Moshe. [Hebrew.] *In the Path of Desert and Fire: The History of the Ninth Armor Battalion, 1948–1984.* Tel Aviv: Ma'arachot IDF Press/Defense Ministry Press, 1994.

Glubb, John. *A Soldier with the Arabs.* London: Hodder and Stoughton, 1957.

Golan, Arnon. [Hebrew.] *Wartime Spatial Changes: Former Arab Territories within the State of Israel, 1948–1950.* N.p.: Ben-Gurion Research Center/Ben-Gurion University Press, 2001.

Goldmann, Nahum. *The Jewish Paradox.* Trans. Steve Cox. London: Weidenfeld and Nicolson, 1978.

Goldstein, Yaacov. *From Fighters to Soldiers: How the Israeli Defense Forces Began.* Brighton, UK: Sussex Academic Press, 1998.

Goren, Tamir. [Hebrew.] *The Fall of Arab Haifa in 1948.* Tel Aviv: Ben-Gurion University Press/Defense Ministry Press, 2006.

———. [Hebrew.] "Why did the Arab Inhabitants of Haifa Leave? An Examination of a Controversial Question." *Cathedra* 80 (June 1996): 175–208.

Gorny, Yosef. *Zionism and the Arabs, 1882–1948: A Study in Ideology.* Oxford: Clarendon Press, 1987.

Greenberg, Yitzhak. "Financing the War of Independence." *Studies in Zionism* 9, no. 1 (1988): 63–78.

Grodzinski, Yosef. [Hebrew.] *Good Human Material: Jews Opposite Zionists, 1945–1951.* Jerusalem: Hed Artzi, 1998.

Guri, Haim. [Hebrew.] *Until the Breaking of Day.* Tel Aviv: Kibbutz Meuhad Press, 2000.

Hadari, Dani. [Hebrew.] "The War of Independence in the North." In Alon

Kadish, ed., *Israel's War of Independence, 1948–1949*. 2 vols., 1:119–169. Tel Aviv: Defense Ministry Press, 2004.

Hahn, Peter. *Caught in the Middle East: U.S. Policy toward the Arab-Israeli Conflict, 1945–1961*. Chapel Hill: University of North Carolina Press, 2004.

Halamish, Aviva. [Hebrew.] *Exodus: The Real Story*. Tel Aviv: ʿAm ʿOved, 1990.

Hamilton, Nigel. *Monty: Final Years of the Field Marshall, 1944–1976*. London: Hamish Hamilton, 1986.

Harari, Dani, ed. [Hebrew.] *Homat Magen: Eighty Years to the Haganah*. Israel: Defense Ministry Press/Haganah Archive/Galili Association for Defense Studies, 2002.

Harpaz, Yoav. [Hebrew.] *Through Fire: Palmah Fifth Battalion in the War of Independence*. Israel: Maʿarachot/Kibbutz Dalia, 2001.

Heller, Joseph. [Hebrew.] *LEHI: Ideology and Politics, 1940–1949*. Jerusalem: Zalman Shazar Center/Keter, 1989.

Hitchens, Christopher, and Edward W. Said, eds. *Blaming the Victims: Spurious Scholarship and the Palestinian Question*. London: Verso, 1988.

Horowitz, David. *State in the Making*. Trans. Julian Melzer. New York: Knopf, 1953.

Hurewitz, J. C. *The Struggle for Palestine*. New York: Schocken Books, 1976.

Hughes, Matthew. "Lebanon's Armed Forces in the Arab-Israeli War, 1948–1949." *Journal of Palestine Studies* 34, no. 2 (2005): 24–41.

Ilan, Amitzur. *Bernadotte in Palestine: A Study in Modern Humanitarian Knight Errantry*. New York: St. Martin's Press, New York, 1989.

———. [Hebrew.] "The Few against the Many, the Weak against the Strong: The Case of the War of Independence." In Alon Kadish and Binyamin Zeev Kedar, eds., *The Few against the Many? Studies in the Balance of Forces in the Battles of Judah the Maccabee and in the War of Independence*, 49–63. Jerusalem: Magnes, 2006.

———. *The Origin of the Arab-Israeli Arms Race: Arms, Embargo, Military Power, and Decision in the 1948 Palestine War*. New York: New York University Press, 1996.

In a Storm: The War at the Gates of Degania, May 1948. [Hebrew.] Degania Aleph: Kibbutz Degania Aleph Press, 1949.

Israel Defense Forces History Branch. [Hebrew.] *History of the War of Independence*. Israel: Maʿarachot/IDF Press, 1959.

Itzchaki, Arieh. [Hebrew.] *Latrun: The Battle on the Road to Jerusalem*. Jerusalem: Cana, 1982.

Joseph, Dov. *The Faithful City: The Siege of Jerusalem, 1948*. New York: Simon and Schuster, 1960.

Kadish, Alon, ed. [Hebrew.] *Israel's War of Independence, 1948–1949*. 2 vols. Tel Aviv: Defense Ministry Press, 2004.

Kadish, Alon, and Binyamin Zeev Kedar, eds. [Hebrew.] *The Few against the Many? Studies in the Balance of Forces in the Battles of Judah the Maccabee and in the War of Independence*. Jerusalem: Magnes, 2006.

Kadish, Alon, Avraham Sela, and Arnon Golan. [Hebrew.] *The Occupation of Lydda, July 1948*. Israel: Defense Ministry Press, 2000.

Karmi, Ghada. *In Search of Fatima: A Palestinian Story*. London: Verso, 2002.

Katz, Teddy [Hebrew.] "The Arab Departure from the Villages at the Foot of the Southern Carmel in 1948." M.A. thesis, Haifa University, 1998.

Khalaf, Issa. *Politics in Palestine: Arab Factionalism and Social Disintegration, 1939–1948*. Albany: SUNY Press, 1991.

Khalidi, Walid. *All That Remains*. Washington, DC: Institute for Palestine Studies, 1992.

———. *Before Their Diaspora: A Photographic History of the Palestinians, 1876–1948*. Washington, DC: Institute for Palestine Studies, 1991.

———. "Plan Dalet: Master Plan for the Conquest of Palestine." *Journal of Palestine Studies* 18, no. 1 (1988): 4–33.

Khalidi, Walid, ed. *From Haven to Conquest: Readings in Zionism and the Palestine Problem until 1948*. Washington, DC: Institute for Palestine Studies, 1987.

Kidron, Peretz. "Truth Whereby Nations Live." In Christopher Hitchens and Edward W. Said, eds., *Blaming the Victims: Spurious Scholarship and the Palestinian Question*, 85–96. London: Verso, 1988.

Kimche, Jon, and David Kimche. *Both Sides of the Hill: Britain and the Palestine War*. London: Secker and Warburg, 1960.

Kirkbride, Alec. *A Crackle of Thorns: Experiences in the Middle East*. London: John Murray, 1956.

———. *From the Wings: Amman Memoirs, 1947–1951*. London: Frank Cass, 1976.

Klein, Aharon. [Hebrew.] "The Arab Prisoners of War in the War of Independence." In Kadish, ed., *The War of Independence, 1948–1949*, 1:567–586.

Knohl, Dov. *Siege in the Hills of Hebron: The Battle of the ʿEtzion Bloc*. New York: Thomas Yoseloff, 1958.

Knohl, Dov, ed. [Hebrew.] *The Battle of the ʿEtzion Bloc*. Israel: Youth and Hehalutz Department, World Zionist Organisation, 1957.

Korn, David. [Hebrew.] *The Western Galilee in the War of Independence*. Tel Aviv: Yad Tabenkin/Defense Ministry Press, 1988.

Lachish, Zeev. [Hebrew.] "The Bombing of the Arab Capitals in the War of Independence." *Maʿarachot* 324 (1992): 44–57.

Landis, Joshua. "Syria and the Palestine War: Fighting King Abdullah's 'Greater Syria Plan.'" In Eugene L. Rogan and Avi Shlaim, eds., *The War for Palestine: Rewriting the History of 1948*, 178–205. Cambridge: Cambridge University Press, 2001.

Lapidot, Yehuda. [Hebrew.] *Upon Thy Walls*. Tel Aviv: Defense Ministry Press, 1992.

———. [Hebrew.] *The Flames of Revolt*. Tel Aviv: Defense Ministry Press, 1996.

Lazar (Litai), Haim. [Hebrew.] *The Conquest of Jaffa*. Israel: Shelah Press, n.d.

Levenberg, Haim. *The Military Preparations of the Arab Community in Palestine, 1945–1948*. London: Frank Cass, 1993.

Levin, Harry. *Jerusalem Embattled*. London: Gollancz, 1950.

Levy, Itzhak. [Hebrew.] *Jerusalem in the War of Independence.* Tel Aviv: Ma'ara-chot/Defense Ministry Press, 1986.

Lippman, Thomas W. "The View from 1947: The CIA and the Partition of Palestine." *Middle East Journal* 61, no. 1 (2007): 17–28.

Lorch, Netanel. *The Edge of the Sword: Israel's War of Independence, 1947–1949.* New York: Putnam's, 1961.

Louis, William Roger. *The British Empire in the Middle East, 1945–1951: Arab Nationalism, the United States, and Postwar Imperialism.* Oxford: Clarendon Press, 1984.

Luria, Gavriel. [Hebrew.] "The Planning of Operation Hiram." *Ma'arachot* 145 (July 1962): 15–19.

Ma'ayan, Guy. [Hebrew.] "Losing the North: The Arab States and the Galilee in the War of 1948." In Alon Kadish, ed., *Israel's War of Independence, 1948–1949.* 2 vols., 1:269–306. Tel Aviv: Defense Ministry Press, 2004.

Mandel, Neville J. *The Arabs and Zionism before World War I.* Berkeley: University of California Press, 1976.

Maoz, Moshe, and B. Z. Kedar, eds. [Hebrew.] *The Palestinian National Movement.* Tel Aviv: Defense Ministry Press, 1996.

Markovizky, Jacob. [Hebrew.] *Fighting Ember: Gahal Forces in the War of Independence.* Israel: Defense Ministry Press/Galili Center for Defense Studies, 1995.

———. [Hebrew.] "The Foreign Volunteers in the War of Independence." In Alon Kadish, ed., *Israel's War of Independence, 1948–1949.* 2 vols., 1:539–550. Tel Aviv: Defense Ministry Press, 2004.

Mattar, Philip. *The Mufti of Jerusalem: Al-Hajj Amin al-Husayni and the Palestinian National Movement.* New York: Columbia University Press, 1988.

Mayer, Thomas. "Egypt's 1948 Invasion of Palestine." *Middle Eastern Studies* 22, no. 1 (1986): 20–36.

McDonald, James G. *My Mission in Israel, 1948–51.* London: Gollancz, 1951.

Meir, Golda. *My Life.* London: Futura, 1976.

Messer, Oded. [Hebrew.] *Hagana's Operations Plans, 1937–1948.* Israel: Galili Center for Defense Studies/Tag, 1996.

Metzer, Jacob, *The Divided Economy of Mandatory Palestine.* Cambridge: Cambridge University Press, 1998.

Milstein, Uri. *History of the War of Independence.* Trans. Alan Sacks. 4 vols. Lanham, MD: University Press of America, 1996–1998.

Mishmar Ha'emek in the War. [Hebrew.] Tel Aviv: Sifriyat Po'alim, 1950.

Mitchell, Richard P. *The Society of Muslim Brothers.* New York: Oxford University Press, 1993.

Montgomery of Alamein, Viscount. *The Memoirs of Field Marshall the Viscount Montgomery of Alamein.* London: Collins, 1958.

Morris, Benny. *The Birth of the Palestinian Refugee Problem Revisited.* Cambridge: Cambridge University Press, 2004.

———. "The Historiography of Deir Yassin." *Journal of Israeli History* 24, no. 1 (2005): 76–104.

———. *Israel's Border Wars, 1949–1956: Arab Infiltration, Israeli Retaliation, and the Countdown to the Suez War*. Oxford: Clarendon Press, 1997.

———. *1948 and After: Israel and the Palestinians*. Rev. and expanded ed. Oxford: Clarendon Press, 1994.

———. "Operation Dani and the Palestinian Exodus from Lydda and Ramle in 1948." *Middle East Journal* 40, no. 1 (1986): 82–109.

———. *The Road to Jerusalem: Glubb Pasha, Palestine and the Jews*. London: I. B. Tauris, 2002.

———. *Righteous Victims: A History of the Zionist-Arab Conflict, 1881–2001*. New York: Vintage, 2001.

———. "The Tantura Massacre Affair." *Jerusalem Report*, 4 February 2004.

———. "Yosef Weitz and the Transfer Committees, 1948–1949." *Middle Eastern Studies* 22, no. 4 (1986): 522–561.

Nachmani, Amikam. *Great Power Discord in Palestine: The Anglo-American Committee of Inquiry into the Problems of European Jewry and Palestine, 1945–1946*. London: Routledge, 1987.

Nafuri, Amin al-. [Hebrew.] "The Syrian Army in the 1948 War." *Ma'arachot* 279–280 (May 1981): 30–32.

Naor, Mordechai. [Hebrew.] "Big Wednesday." *Haaretz*, 1 May 2006.

Narkis, Uzi. [Hebrew.] *Soldier of Jerusalem*. Israel: Defense Ministry Press, 1991.

Nasser, Gamal Abdel. "Nasser's Memoirs of the First Palestine War." *Journal of Palestine Studies* 2, no. 2 (1973): 3–32.

Nazzal, Nafez. *The Palestinian Exodus from Galilee, 1948*. Beirut: Institute for Palestine Studies, 1978.

The Negev Brigade in the War. [Hebrew.] Tel Aviv: Ma'arachot, n.d.

Neguib, Mohammed. *Egypt's Destiny: A Personal Statement*. London: Gollancz, 1955.

Nevo, Joseph. *King Abdallah and Palestine: A Territorial Ambition*. London: Macmillan, 1996.

Nicosia, Francis R. *The Third Reich and the Palestine Question*. 2nd ed. New Brunswick, NJ: Transaction, 2000.

Niv, David. [Hebrew.] *Battles of the IZL*. 6 vols. Tel Aviv: Klausner Institute, 1980.

Norton, Maureen Heaney. "The Last Pasha: Sir John Glubb and the British Empire in the Middle East, 1920–1949." Ph.D. diss., Johns Hopkins University, 1997.

On the Road: Kiryat Anavim in the War. [Hebrew.] Jerusalem: Kiryat Anavim Press, 1949.

Orren, Elhannan. [Hebrew.] "The Contribution of the Settlements in the War of Independence." In Varda Pilovsky [Hebrew], *The Passage from the Yishuv to the State*. Haifa: Haifa University Press, 1990.

———. [Hebrew.] *Operation "Danni": July 1948*. Tel Aviv: Ma'arachot IDF Press / Defense Ministry Press, 1976.

———. [Hebrew.] "The Rebuffing of the ALA at Mishmar Ha'emek." *Ma'arachot* 294–295 (1984): 84–90.

Orren, Elhannan, and Meir Avizohar, eds. [Hebrew.] *Operation ʿUvda*. Israel: Ben-Gurion Research Institute/Sdeh Boqer College, 2002.

Ostfeld, Zahava. [Hebrew.] *An Army Is Born*. 2 vols. Tel Aviv: Defense Ministry Press, 1994.

Paʿil, Meir. [Hebrew.] *The Emergence of Zahal (I.D.F.)*. Tel Aviv: Zmora, Bitan, Modan, 1979.

Pappé, Ilan. *The Making of the Arab-Israeli Conflict, 1947–1951*. London: I. B. Tauris, 1992.

———. "The Tantura Case in Israel: The Katz Research and Trial." *Journal of Palestine Studies* 30, no. 3 (2001): 19–39.

Parsons, Laila. "The Druze and the Birth of Israel." In Eugene L. Rogan and Avi Shlaim, eds., *The War for Palestine: Rewriting the History of 1948*, 60–78. Cambridge: Cambridge University Press, 2001.

Pollack, Kenneth. *Arabs at War: Military Effectiveness, 1948–1991*. Lincoln: University of Nebraska Press, 2002.

Porat, Dina. [Hebrew.] *Beyond the Reaches of Our Souls (Hamlet, I, iv, 55–6): The Life and Times of Abba Kovner*. Tel Aviv: ʿAm ʿOved, 2000.

Porath, Yehoshua. *In Search of Arab Unity, 1930–1945*. London: Frank Cass, 1986.

———. *The Palestinian Arab National Movement: From Riots to Rebellion, 1929–1939*. London: Frank Cass, 1977.

Qawuqji, Fauzi al-. "Memoirs, 1948." Parts 1 and 2. *Journal of Palestine Studies* 1, no. 4 (1972): 27–58; 2, no. 1 (1973): 3–33.

Rabin, Yitzhak. *The Rabin Memoirs*. Expanded ed. Berkeley: University of California Press, 1996.

Rivlin, Gershon, ed. [Hebrew.] *Days of Rama*. Tel Aviv: Maʿarachot/IDF Press, 1964.

Rivlin, Gershon, and Zvi Sinai. [Hebrew.] *The Alexandroni Brigade in the War of Establishment*. Israel: Maʿarachot, 1964.

Rogan, Eugene L., and Avi Shlaim, eds. *The War for Palestine: Rewriting the History of 1948*. Cambridge: Cambridge University Press, 2001.

Royle, Trevor. *Glubb Pasha*. London: Abacus, 1992.

Sadat, Anwar. *Revolt on the Nile*. New York: John Day, 1957.

Sakakini, Hala. *Jerusalem and I: A Personal Record*. Amman, Jordan: Economic Press, 1990.

Sakakini, Khalil al-. [Hebrew.] *"Such Am I, Oh World": Diaries of Khalil al-Sakakini*. Jerusalem: Keter, 1990.

Schoenbaum, David. *The United States and the State of Israel*. New York: Oxford University Press, 1993.

Segev, Shmuel, ed. [Hebrew.] *Behind the Screen*. Tel Aviv: Maʿarachot, 1954.

———. [Hebrew.] *In Enemy Eyes*. Tel Aviv: Maʿarachot, 1954.

Sela, Avraham. [Hebrew.] "The ALA in the Galilee in the 1948 War." In Alon Kadish, ed., *Israel's War of Independence, 1948–1949*. 2 vols., 1:207–267. Tel Aviv: Defense Ministry Press, 2004.

———. [Hebrew.] "Palestinian Arabs in the 1948 War." In Moshe Maoz and B. Z. Kedar, eds., *The Palestinian National Movement*, 115–203. Tel Aviv: Defense Ministry Press, 1996.

———. [Hebrew.] "The Question of Palestine in the Inter-Arab System from the Foundation of the Arab League until the Invasion of Palestine by the Arab Armies, 1945–1948." Ph.D. thesis, Hebrew University, 1986.

———. "Transjordan, Israel and the 1948 War: Myth, Historiography and Reality." *Middle Eastern Studies* 28, no. 4 (1992): 623–688.

Shamir, Shlomo. [Hebrew.] "The Latrun Battles: Three Comments and an Assessment." *Ma'arachot* 304 (June 1986): 2–6.

Shapira, Anita. [Hebrew.] *The Army Controversy, 1948*. Tel Aviv: Kibbutz Meuhad Press, 1985.

———. [Hebrew.] "Historiography and Memory: The Case of Latrun, 1948." In Shapira, *New Jews, Old Jews*, 46–85. Tel Aviv: 'Am 'Oved, 1997.

———. *Land and Power.* New York: Oxford University Press, 1992.

Sharef, Zeev. *Three Days.* Trans. Julian Louis Meltzer. Garden City, NY: Doubleday, 1962.

Sharon, Ariel, with Daviod Chanoff. *Warrior: An Autobiography.* New York: Simon and Schuster, 1989.

Shemesh, Moshe. [Hebrew.] "The Crisis in Palestinian Leadership." Parts 1 and 2. *Iyunim Betkumat Yisrael* 14 (2004): 285–335; 15 (2005): 301–348.

Shiran, Assnat, ed. [Hebrew.] *Jews and Arabs in a Protracted Struggle.* Israel: Defense Ministry Press/Galili Center for Defense Studies, 2006.

Shlaim, Avi. *Collusion across the Jordan: King Abdullah, the Zionist Movement, and the Partition of Palestine.* New York: Columbia University Press, 1988.

———. "The Rise and Fall of the All-Palestine Government in Gaza." *Journal of Palestine Studies* 20, no. 1 (1990): 37–53.

Sivan, Emmanuel. [Hebrew.] *The 1948 Generation: Myth, Profile, and Memory.* Tel Aviv: Ma'arachot, 1991.

Slutzky, Yehuda, ed. [Hebrew.] *History of the Haganah* (STH). 3 vols. in 8. Tel Aviv: 'Am 'Oved/Ma'arachot, 1954–1964.

Stein, Kenneth W. *The Land Question in Palestine, 1917–1939.* Chapel Hill: University of North Carolina Press, 1984.

Sykes, Christopher. *Orde Wingate.* London: Collins, 1959.

Tal, David. "Military Decision in the Shadow of Political Struggle: The Israeli-Egyptian War, 1948–1949." In Kadish, ed., *War*, 450–456.

———. *War in Palestine, 1948: Strategy and Diplomacy.* London: Routledge, 2004.

Tal, Eliezer. [Hebrew.] *Naval Operations in Israel's War of Independence.* Israel: Ma'arachot/IDF Press, 1964.

Tall, Abdullah. [Hebrew.] *Memoirs of Abdullah Tall.* Tel Aviv: Ma'arachot/IDF Press, 1964.

"The Tantura Massacre, 22–23 May 1948." *Journal of Palestine Studies* 30, no. 3 (2001): 5–18.

Teveth, Shabtai. *Ben-Gurion and the Palestinian Arabs: From Peace to War.* New York: Oxford University Press, 1985.

Tripp, Charles. "Iraq and the 1948 War: Mirror of Iraq's Disorder." In Eugene L. Rogan and Avi Shlaim, eds., *The War for Palestine: Rewriting the History of 1948,* 125–150. Cambridge: Cambridge University Press, 2001.

Truman, Harry S. *Memoirs.* 2 vols. Garden City, NY: Doubleday, 1955–1956.

Truman, Margaret. *Harry S. Truman.* New York: William Morrow, 1973.

Turgan, Saguy. [Hebrew.] "Yad Mordechai." In Dani Harari, ed., *Homat Magen: Eighty Years to the Haganah,* 185–204. Jerusalem: Defense Ministry Press/Haganah Archive/Galili Association for Defense Studies, 2002.

United Nations. Official Records of the Second Session. Supplement no. 11. United Nations Special Committee on Palestine [UNSCOP]. *Report to the General Assembly.* Vols. 1–4. 1948.

Urquhart, Brian. *Ralph Bunche: An American Life.* New York: W. W. Norton, 1998.

Vered, Avraham. [Hebrew.] *Fighters for the Freedom of Israel in the War of Independence.* 3 vols. Tel Aviv: Yair Press, 1998.

Wallach, Jehuda, ed. [Hebrew.] *We Were as Dreamers.* Tel Aviv: Masada, 1985.

Wallach, Jehuda, and Moshe Lissak, eds. [Hebrew.] *Carta's Atlas of Israel: The First Years, 1948–1961.* Jerusalem: Carta, 1978.

Wasserstein, Bernard. *The British in Palestine: The Mandatory Government and the Arab-Jewish Conflict, 1917–1929.* London: Royal Historical Society, 1978.

Weizman, Ezer. *On Eagles' Wings:* The Personal Story of the Leading Commander of the Israeli Air Force. London: Weidenfeld and Nicolson, 1976.

Weizmann, Chaim. *Trial and Error: The Autobiography of Chaim Weizmann.* New York: Harper and Brothers, 1949.

Weitz, Yosef. [Hebrew.] *My Diary and Letters to the Sons.* 5 vols. Ramat-Gan: Masada, 1965.

Yanait, Rachel, Yitzhak Avrahami, and Yerah ʿEtzion, eds. [Hebrew.] *The Haganah in Jerusalem.* Jerusalem: Organization of Haganah Members in Jerusalem, 1976.

Yiftah in a Storm: The Story of the Palmah-Yiftah Brigade. [Hebrew.] Bat-Yam: Association of Palmah-Yiftah Brigade Veterans, n.d.

Zertal, Idit. *From Catastrophe to Power: Holocaust Survivors and the Emergence of Israel.* Berkeley: University of California Press, 1998.

Zweig, Ronald. *Britain and Palestine during the Second World War.* London: Boydell Press for the Royal Historical Society, 1986.

Index

507